AZ

GREAT BRITAIN ROAD ATLAS

Journey Route Planning maps

Southern Britain........II-III

Northern Britain........IV-V

Mileage Chart..........2

Airport plans

Access maps to principal Airports in Great Britain 216

Great Britain Road map section

Key to map pages inside front cover

Reference..................3

Road Maps..............4-173

Over 32,000 Index References

A

Abbas Combe. *Som* 4C **22**
Abberley. *Worc* 4B **60**
Abberley Common. *Worc* 4B **60**
Abberton. *Essx* 4D **54**
Abberton. *Worc* 5D **61**
Abberwick. *Nmbd* 3F **121**
Abbess Roding. *Essx* 4F **53**

Including cities, towns, villages, hamlets and locations..............217-269

Detailed Main Route maps

London.................174-181

Birmingham..........182-183

Manchester..............184

Index to Places of Interest

J

Jackfield Tile Mus. (TF8 7ND) . . . .
Jane Austen's House Mus. (GU34 1SD) . . . . .
Jarlshof Prehistoric & Norse Settlement
(ZE3 9JN) . . . .
Jedburgh Abbey (TD8 6JQ) . . . .
Jervaulx Abbey (HG4 4PH) . . . .
JM Barrie's Birthplace (DD8 4BX) . . . .

Full postcodes to easily locate over 1,700 selected places of interest on your SatNav....270-273

City and Town centre maps

Plans of 80 principal cities and towns in Great Britain

Reference...............185-186

Cities and Towns.....187-214

Motorway Junctions

M25
Junction **5**
Clockwise: No exit to M26 Eastbound
Anti-clockwise: No access from M26 Westbound

Details of motorway junctions with limited interchange........274-275

Sea Port & Channel Tunnel plans

Principal Sea Ports in Great Britain................215

Folkestone and Calais Terminals..................276

Safety Camera Information

Details of Safety Camera symbols used on the maps, and the responsible use of camera information ....inside back cover

EDITION 25 2018

Copyright © Geographers' A-Z Map Company Ltd.

A-Z AZ AtoZ
registered trade marks of
Geographers' A-Z Map Company Ltd

www./az.co.uk

Contains Ordnance Survey data © Crown copyright and database right 2017

Safety Camera & Fuel Station Databases copyright 2017, © PocketGPSWorld.com.
PocketGPSWorld.com's CamerAlert is a self-contained speed and red light camera warning system for SatNavs and Android or Apple iOS smartphones/tablets.
Visit www.cameralert.com to download.

Base Relief by Geo-Innovations, ©, www.geoinnovations.co.uk

The Shopmobility logo is a registered symbol of The National Federation of Shopmobility.

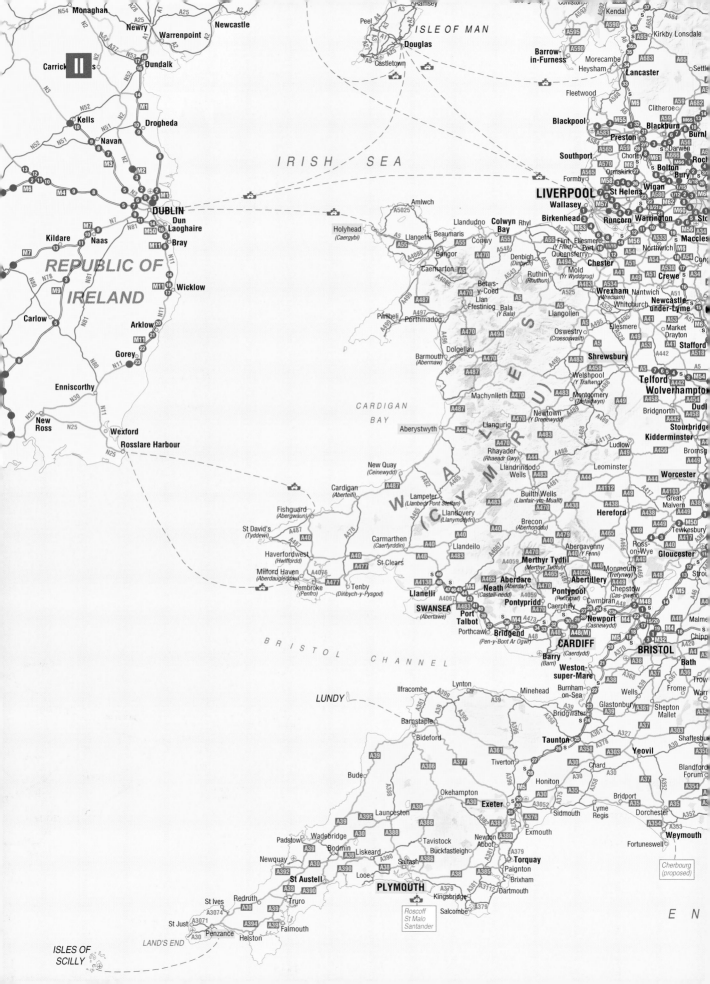

REFERENCE

MOTORWAY WITH NUMBER	M4 s — Service Area
MOTORWAY (Under Construction / Proposed)	
MOTORWAY JUNCTIONS	5 — 7 Limited
PRIMARY ROUTE	A5
A ROAD	A272
NATIONAL BOUNDARY	
TOWNS SHOWN IN THE MILEAGE CHART	**NORWICH**

SCALE

0 — 10 — 20 — 30 Miles

0 — 10 — 20 — 30 — 40 Kilometres

NORTH SEA

THE WASH

STRAIT OF DOVER

Channel Tunnel

ENGLISH CHANNEL

FRANCE

Rotterdam Zeebrugge

Hook of Holland

Dieppe

Bilbao
Caen
Cherbourg
Guernsey
Jersey
Le Havre
St Malo
Santander

Cherbourg
Guernsey
Jersey
St Malo

ISLE OF WIGHT

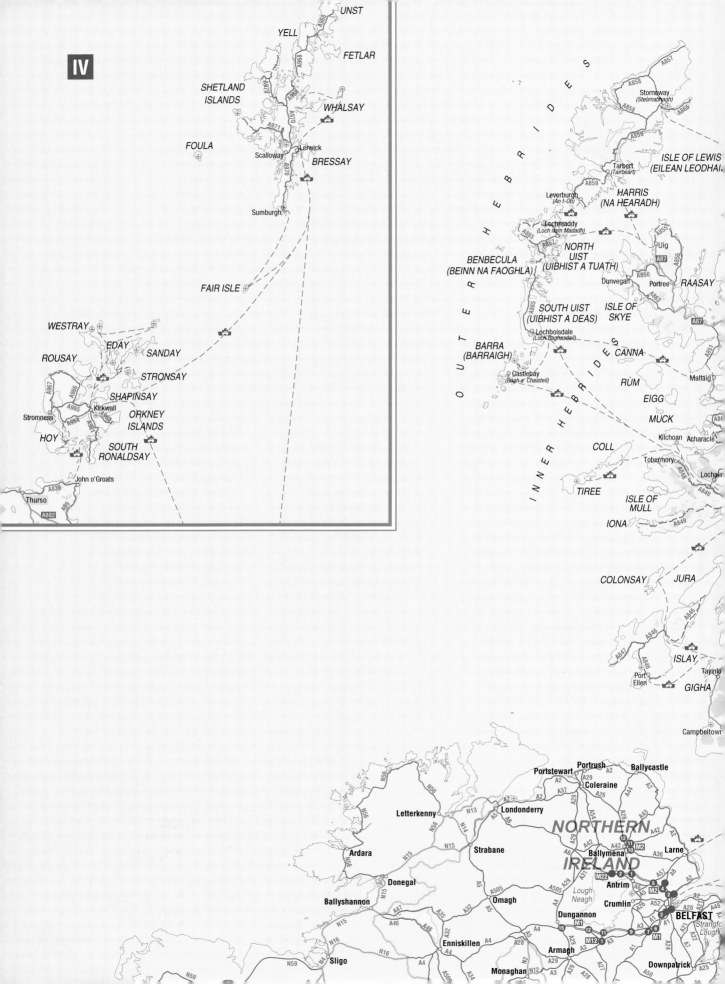

IV

UNST
YELL
FETLAR

SHETLAND
ISLANDS
WHALSAY

FOULA
Scalloway
Lerwick
BRESSAY

Sumburgh

FAIR ISLE

WESTRAY
ROUSAY
EDAY
SANDAY
STRONSAY
SHAPINSAY
Stromness
Kirkwall
ORKNEY
ISLANDS
HOY
SOUTH
RONALDSAY

John o'Groats
Thurso

OUTER HEBRIDES

Stornoway
(Steòrnabhagh)

ISLE OF LEWIS
(EILEAN LEODHAIS)

Tarbert
(Tairbeart)

Leverburgh
(An t-Ob)
HARRIS
(NA HEARADH)

Lochmaddy
(Loch nam Madadh)
Uig

BENBECULA
(BEINN NA FAOGHLA)
NORTH
UIST
(UIBHIST A TUATH)

Dunvegan
Portree
RAASAY

SOUTH UIST
(UIBHIST A DEAS)
ISLE OF
SKYE

Lochboisdale
(Loch Baghasdail)

BARRA
(BARRAIGH)
CANNA

Castlebay
(Bàgh a' Chaisteil)
RÙM
EIGG

MUCK
Kilchoan
Acharacle
Mallaig

COLL

INNER HEBRIDES

TIREE
ISLE OF
MULL
Tobermory
Lochalir

IONA

COLONSAY
JURA

ISLAY
Tayinlo

Port
Ellen
GIGHA

Campbeltown

NORTHERN
IRELAND

Portstewart
Portrush
Ballycastle
Coleraine

Letterkenny
Londonderry
Larne

Strabane
Ballymena
Antrim

Ardara
Crumlin
BELFAST

Donegal
Lough
Neagh

Ballyshannon
Omagh
Dungannon

Enniskillen
Armagh
Downpatrick

Sligo
Monaghan

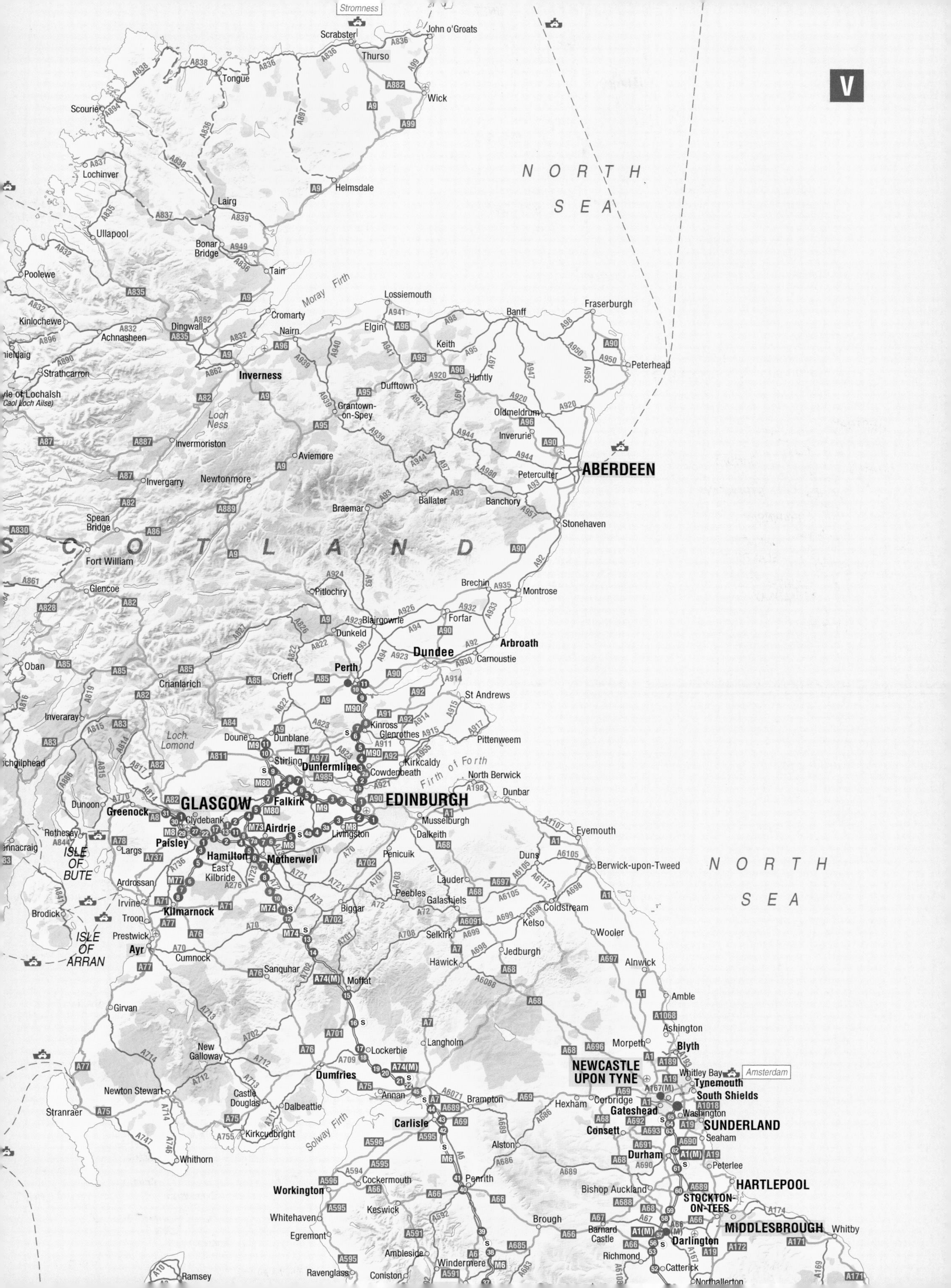

NORTH SEA

SCOTLAND

Stromness
Scrabster
Thurso
John o'Groats
Tongue
Wick
Scourie
Helmsdale
Lochinver
Lairg
Ullapool
Bonar Bridge
Tain
Poolewe
Cromarty
Lossiemouth
Banff
Fraserburgh
Kinlochewe
Dingwall
Nairn
Elgin
Keith
Achnasheen
Peterhead
Strathcarron
Inverness
Dufftown
Huntly
Kyle of Lochalsh
(Caol Loch Ailse)
Loch Ness
Grantown-on-Spey
Oldmeldrum
Inverurie
Invermoriston
Aviemore
Newtonmore
Peterculter
ABERDEEN
Invergarry
Spean Bridge
Braemar
Ballater
Banchory
Stonehaven
Fort William
Glencoe
Pitlochry
Brechin
Montrose
Blairgowrie
Forfar
Dunkeld
Dundee
Arbroath
Oban
Crianlarich
Crieff
Perth
Carnoustie
Inveraray
Doune
Dunblane
Kinross
Glenrothes
St Andrews
Pittenweem
Loch Lomond
Stirling
Dunfermline
Kirkcaldy
Cowdenbeath
North Berwick
Dunoon
GLASGOW
Falkirk
EDINBURGH
Dunbar
Greenock
Clydebank
Airdrie
Musselburgh
Eyemouth
Paisley
Livingston
Dalkeith
Duns
Berwick-upon-Tweed
Rothesay
Hamilton
Motherwell
Penicuik
Lauder
ISLE OF BUTE
Largs
East Kilbride
Peebles
Galashiels
Coldstream
Wooler
Ardrossan
Biggar
Selkirk
Kelso
Irvine
Troon
Kilmarnock
Jedburgh
Alnwick
Prestwick
Ayr
Cumnock
Hawick
Brodick
ISLE OF ARRAN
Sanquhar
Moffat
Amble
Girvan
New Galloway
Ashington
Morpeth
Blyth
Newton Stewart
Lockerbie
Langholm
NEWCASTLE UPON TYNE
Whitley Bay
Tynemouth
Amsterdam
Dumfries
Annan
Brampton
Hexham
Corbridge
South Shields
Stranraer
Castle Douglas
Dalbeattie
Carlisle
Gateshead
Washington
SUNDERLAND
Kirkcudbright
Consett
Seaham
Whithorn
Alston
Durham
Peterlee
Solway Firth
Cockermouth
Penrith
Bishop Auckland
HARTLEPOOL
Workington
Keswick
Brough
STOCKTON-ON-TEES
Whitehaven
Barnard Castle
MIDDLESBROUGH
Whitby
Egremont
Ambleside
Richmond
Darlington
Ravenglass
Coniston
Windermere
Catterick
Ramsey
Northallerton

Moray Firth
Firth of Forth
Loch Fyne
NORTH SEA

This chart shows the distance in miles and journey time between two cities or towns in Great Britain. Each route has been calculated using a combination of motorways, primary routes and other major roads. This is normally the quickest, though not always the shortest route.

Average journey times are calculated whilst driving at the maximum speed limit. These times are approximate and do not include traffic congestion or convenience breaks.

To find the distance and journey time between two cities or towns, follow a horizontal line and vertical column until they meet each other.

For example, the 285 mile journey from London to Penzance is approximately 4 hours and 59 minutes.

Britain

Journey times

The chart shows distances in miles (lower-left portion) and journey times in hours:minutes (upper-right portion) between the following locations:

Aberdeen, Aberystwyth, Ayr, Birmingham, Bradford, Brighton, Bristol, Cambridge, Cardiff, Carlisle, Coventry, Derby, Doncaster, Dover, Edinburgh, Exeter, Fort William, Glasgow, Gloucester, Harwich, Holyhead, Inverness, Ipswich, Kendal, Kingston upon Hull, Leeds, Leicester, Lincoln, Liverpool, Manchester, Middlesbrough, Newcastle upon Tyne, Norwich, Nottingham, Oxford, Penzance, Perth, Plymouth, Portsmouth, Reading, Salisbury, Sheffield, Shrewsbury, Southampton, Southend-on-Sea, Stoke-on-Trent, Swansea, Thurso, Worcester, York, London.

Distance in miles

Motorway
Autoroute
Autobahn
M1

Motorway Under Construction
Autoroute en construction
Autobahn im Bau

Motorway Proposed
Autoroute prévue
Geplante Autobahn

Motorway Junctions with Numbers
Unlimited Interchange   4
Limited Interchange   5
5

Autoroute échangeur numéroté
Echangeur complet
Echangeur partiel

Autobahnanschlußstelle mit Nummer
Unbeschränkter Fahrtrichtungswechsel
Beschränkter Fahrtrichtungswechsel

Motorway Service Area (with fuel station)
with access from one carriageway only   S / S

Aire de services d'autoroute (avec station service)
accessible d'un seul côté
Rastplatz oder Raststätte (mit tankstelle)
Einbahn

Major Road Service Area (with fuel station) with 24 hour facilities

Primary Route   S   Class A Road   S

Aire de services sur route prioritaire (avec station service) Ouverte 24h sur 24
Route à grande circulation   Route de type A
Raststätte (mit tankstelle) Durchgehend geöffnet
Hauptverkehrsstraße   A- Straße

Major Road Junctions   Detailed   4
    Détaillé
Jonctions grands routiers   Ausführlich
Hauptverkehrsstraße Kreuzungen

    Other   Autre   Andere

Truckstop (selection of)
Sélection d'aire pour poids lourds
Auswahl von Fernfahrerrastplatz
T

Primary Route
Route à grande circulation
Hauptverkehrsstraße
A41

Primary Route Junction with Number
Echangeur numéroté
Hauptverkehrsstraßenkreuzung mit Nummer
5

Primary Route Destination
Route prioritaire, direction
Hauptverkehrsstraße Richtung
DOVER

Dual Carriageways (A & B roads)
Route à double chaussées séparées (route A & B)
Zweispurige Schnellstraße (A- und B- Straßen)

Class A Road
Route de type A
A-Straße
A129

Class B Road
Route de type B
B-Straße
B177

Narrow Major Road (passing places)
Route prioritaire étroite (possibilité de dépassement)
Schmale Hauptverkehrsstaße (mit Überholmöglichkeit)

Major Roads Under Construction
Route prioritaire en construction
Hauptverkehrsstraße im Bau

Major Roads Proposed
Route prioritaire prévue
Geplante Hauptverkehrsstraße

Safety Cameras with Speed Limits
Single Camera   30
Multiple Cameras located along road   50
Single & Multiple Variable Speed Cameras   V   V

Radars de contrôle de vitesse
Radar simple
Radars multiples situés le long de la route
Radars simples et multiples de contrôle de vitesse variable

Sicherheitskameras mit Tempolimit
Einzelne Kamera
Mehrere Kameras entlang der Straße
Einzelne und mehrere Kameras für variables Tempolimit

Fuel Station
Station service
Tankstelle

Gradient 1:7 (14%) **& steeper**
(descent in direction of arrow)   »»
Pente égale ou supérieure à 14% (dans le sens de la descente)
14% Steigung und steiler (in Pfeilrichtung)

Toll
Barrière de péage
Gebührenpflichtig
Toll

Dart Charge
www.gov.uk/pay-dartford-crossing-charge
C

Park & Ride
Parking avec Service Navette
Parken und Reisen
P+R

Mileage between markers
Distence en miles entre les flèches   8
Strecke zwischen Markierungen in Meilen

Airport
Aéroport
Flughafen

Airfield
Terrain d'aviation
Flugplatz

Heliport
Héliport
Hubschrauberlandeplatz
H

Ferry
(vehicular, sea)   Bac   Fähre
(vehicular, river)   (véhicules, mer)   (auto, meer)
(foot only)   (véhicules, rivière)   (auto, fluß)
   (piétons)   (nur für Personen)

Railway and Station
Voie ferrée et gare
Eisenbahnlinie und Bahnhof

Level Crossing and Tunnel
Passage à niveau et tunnel
Bahnübergang und Tunnel

River or Canal
Rivière ou canal
Fluß oder Kanal

County or Unitary Authority Boundary
Limite de comté ou de division administrative
Grafschafts- oder Verwaltungsbezirksgrenze

National Boundary
Frontière nationale
Landesgrenze

Built-up Area
Agglomération
Geschloßene Ortschaft

Town, Village or Hamlet
Ville, Village ou hameau
Stadt, Dorf oder Weiler

Wooded Area
Zone boisée
Waldgebiet

Spot Height in Feet
Altitude (en pieds)   · 813
Höhe in Fuß

Relief above 400' (122m)
Relief par estompage au-dessus de 400' (122m)
Reliefschattierung über 400' (122m)

National Grid Reference (kilometres)
Coordonnées géographiques nationales (Kilomètres)   ¹00
Nationale geographische Koordinaten (Kilometer)

Page Continuation
Suite à la page indiquée
Seitenfortsetzung
48

Area covered by Main Route map
Repartition des cartes des principaux axes routiers   MAIN ROUTE 180
Von Karten mit Hauptverkehrsstrecken

Area covered by Town Plan
Ville ayant un plan à la page indiquée   PAGE 194
Von Karten mit Stadtplänen erfaßter Bereich

Abbey, Church, Friary, Priory   †
Abbaye, église, monastère, prieuré
Abtei, Kirche, Mönchskloster, Kloster

Animal Collection
Ménagerie
Tiersammlung

Aquarium
Aquarium
Aquarium

Arboretum, Botanical Garden
Jardin Botanique
Botanischer Garten

Aviary, Bird Garden
Volière
Voliere

Battle Site and Date   1066
Champ de bataille et date
Schlachtfeld und Datum

Blue Flag Beach
Plage Pavillon Bleu
Blaue Flagge Strand

Bridge
Pont
Brücke

Castle (open to public)
Château (ouvert au public)
Schloß / Burg (für die Öffentlichkeit zugänglich)

Castle with Garden (open to public)
Château avec parc (ouvert au public)
Schloß mit Garten (für die Öffentlichkeit zugänglich)

Cathedral   ✝
Cathédrale
Kathedrale

Cidermaker
Cidrerie (fabrication)
Apfelwein Hersteller

Country Park
Parc régional
Landschaftspark

Distillery
Distillerie
Brennerei

Farm Park, Open Farm
Park Animalier
Bauernhof Park

Fortress, Hill Fort
Château Fort
Festung

Garden (open to public)
Jardin (ouvert au public)
Garten (für die Öffentlichkeit zugänglich)

Golf Course
Terrain de golf
Golfplatz

Historic Building (open to public)
Monument historique (ouvert au public)
Historisches Gebäude (für die Öffentlichkeit zugänglich)

Historic Building with Garden (open to public)
Monument historique avec jardin (ouvert au public)
Historisches Gebäude mit Garten (für die Öffentlichkeit zugänglich)

Horse Racecourse
Hippodrome
Pferderennbahn

Industrial Monument
Monument Industrielle
Industriedenkmal

Leisure Park, Leisure Pool
Parc d'Attraction, Loisirs Piscine
Freizeitpark, Freizeit pool

Lighthouse
Phare
Leuchtturm

Mine, Cave
Mine, Grotte
Bergwerk, Höhle

Monument
Monument
Denkmal

Motor Racing Circuit
Circuit Automobile
Automobilrennbahn

Museum, Art Gallery
Musée
Museum, Galerie

National Park
Parc national
Nationalpark

National Trust Property
National Trust Property
National Trust- Eigentum

Nature Reserve or Bird Sanctuary
Réserve naturelle botanique ou ornithologique
Natur- oder Vogelschutzgebiet

Nature Trail or Forest Walk
Chemin forestier, piste verte
Naturpfad oder Waldweg

Picnic Site
Lieu pour pique-nique
Picknickplatz

Place of Interest   Craft Centre •
Site, curiosité
Sehenswürdigkeit

Prehistoric Monument
Monument Préhistorique
Prähistorisches Denkmal

Railway, Steam or Narrow Gauge
Chemin de fer, à vapeur ou à voie étroite
Eisenbahn, Dampf- oder Schmalspurbahn

Roman Remains
Vestiges Romains
Römischen Ruinen

Theme Park
Centre de loisirs
Vergnügungspark

Tourist Information Centre
Office de Tourisme
Touristeninformationen

Viewpoint   (360 degrees)   (180 degrees)
Vue panoramique   (360 degrés)   (180 degrés)
Aussichtspunkt   (360 Grade)   (180 Grade)

Vineyard
Vignoble
Weinberg

Visitor Information Centre   V
Centre d'information touristique
Besucherzentrum

Wildlife Park
Réserve de faune
Wildpark

Windmill
Moulin à vent
Windmühle

Zoo or Safari Park
Parc ou réserve zoologique
Zoo oder Safari-Park

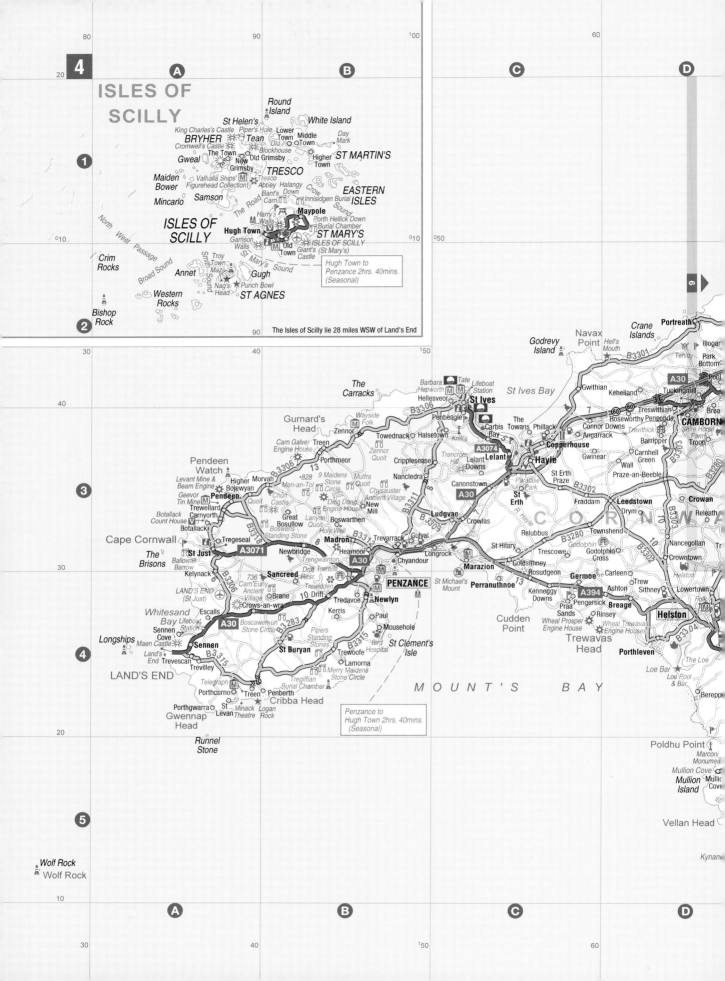

4

ISLES OF SCILLY

Round Island

St Helen's
White Island

King Charles's Castle   Piper's Hole   Lower
BRYHER   Tean   Town   Middle
Cromwell's Castle   Old   Town   Day
The Town   Blockhouse   Higher   Mark
Gweal   New   Old Grimsby   Town   **ST MARTIN'S**
Grimsby   **TRESCO**
Maiden   Valhalla Ships'   Tresco
Bower   Figurehead Collection   Abbey   Halangy
Samson   Bant's   Down   Crow   **EASTERN**
Mincarlo   Carn   Innisidgen Burial   Sound   **ISLES**
The Road   Chamber
Harry's   **Maypole**
Walls   Porth Hellick Down
Hugh Town   Burial Chamber
Garrison   Old   **ST MARY'S**
Walls   Town   **ISLES OF SCILLY**
Giant's   (St Mary's)
Troy   Castle
ISLES OF   Town
SCILLY   Maze
Crim   Nag's   Punch Bowl
Rocks   Annet   Head   **ST AGNES**
Gugh

Hugh Town to
Penzance 2hrs. 40mins.
(Seasonal)

North West Passage
Broad Sound   Smith Sound
Western   St Mary's Sound
Rocks

Bishop
Rock

The Isles of Scilly lie 28 miles WSW of Land's End

Godrevy   Navax   Crane   **Portreath**
Island   Point   Hell's   Islands   Illogar
Mouth   Park
The Carracks   Tehloy   Bottom
Barbara   Tate   Lifeboat   St Ives Bay   Gwithian   Kehelland   **A30**   Pool
Hepworth   Station   **CAMBORN**
The   Hellesveor   **St Ives**   Treswithian
Carracks   Penbeagle   The Towans   Phillack   Connor Downs   Roseworthy   Penponds   Brea
Wayside   Carbis   Trevithick   Troon
Gurnard's   Folk   Bay   **Copperhouse**   Angarrack   Shire Horse
Head   Zennor   Towednack   Halsetown   **A3074**   **Hayle**   Barripper   Farm
Cripplesease   Lelant   St Erth   Carnhell   Wall
Carn Galver   Treen   Trencrom   Downs   Praze   Green   Praze-an-Beeble
Engine House   Porthmeor   Zennor   Hill   **Lelant**   Paradise
Pendeen   Quoit   Nancledra   Park   **CORNWA**
Watch   828   9 Maidens   Mulfra   Canonstown   St   Fraddam   Leedstown   **Crowan**
Levant Mine &   Higher   Morvah   Men-an-Tol   Stone   Quoit   Erth   Reteath
Beam Engine   Bojewyan   Circle   **A30**   Drym
Geevor   Chûn   Ding Dong   New   Relubbus   Townshend   Nancegollan
Tin Mine   **Pendeen**   Castle   Engine House   Mill   **Ludgvan**   Crowlas   B3280   Godolphin   Crowntown
Trewellard   Great   Lanyon   Boswarthen   R. Hayle   Trescowe   Godolphin   Helston
Carnyorth   Bosullow   Quoit   Holy Well   St Hilary   Cross
Botallack   Boswens   **Madron**   Trevarrack   Gulval   Goldsithney   Rosudgeon   Germoe
Count House   Standing Stone   Heamoor   Longrock   **Marazion**   A394   Carleen
Botallack   Tregeseal   8   Newbridge   Trengwainton   Chyandour   **PENZANCE**   Kenneggy   Ashton   Trew
Cape Cornwall   **A3071**   Trereife   **A30**   St Michael's   Downs   Pengersick   Sithney   Lowertown
The   **St Just**   Sancreed   Drift   Mount   Praa   Rinsey   **Breage**
Brisons   Ballowall   Crows-an-wra   Trewidden   **Newlyn**   Perranuthnoe   Sands   Wheal Prosper   **Helston**
Barrow   736   Drift   13   Engine House
Kelynack   Carn Euny Ancient   Kerris   **Cudden**   Wheal Trewavas   **Porthleven**
Village   Brane   Paul   **Point**   Engine Houses
Whitesand   Escalls   10   Mousehole   **Trewavas**   Loe Bar
Bay   Boscawen-un   **Head**   Loe Pool
Sennen   Stone Circle   Pipers   Bird   Loe Bar
Cove   **A30**   Standing   St Clement's   & Bar
Longships   Maen Castle   Stones   Hospital   Isle   Bereppa
Land's   **Sennen**   Kerris   M O U N T ' S   B A Y
End   Trevescan   **St Buryan**   Trewoofe   Lamorna
LAND'S END   B3315   Trevilley   Tregiffian   Merry Maidens
Burial Chamber   Stone Circle
Telegraph   **Cribba Head**
Porthcurno   Treen
Porthgwarra   St   Penberth   *Penzance to*   Poldhu Point
Gwennap   Levan   Minack   Logan   *Hugh Town 2hrs. 40mins.*   Marconi
Head   Theatre   Rock   *(Seasonal)*   Monumen
Mullion Cove
Runnel   Mullion   Mullic
Stone   Island   Cove

Wolf Rock   Vellan Head
Wolf Rock

Kynan

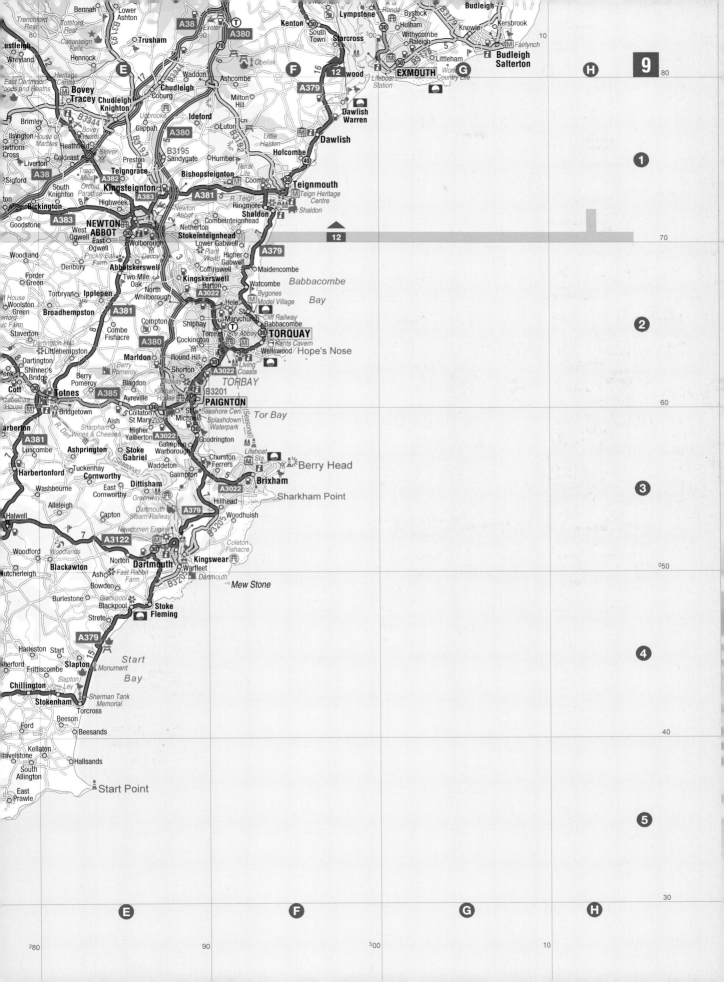

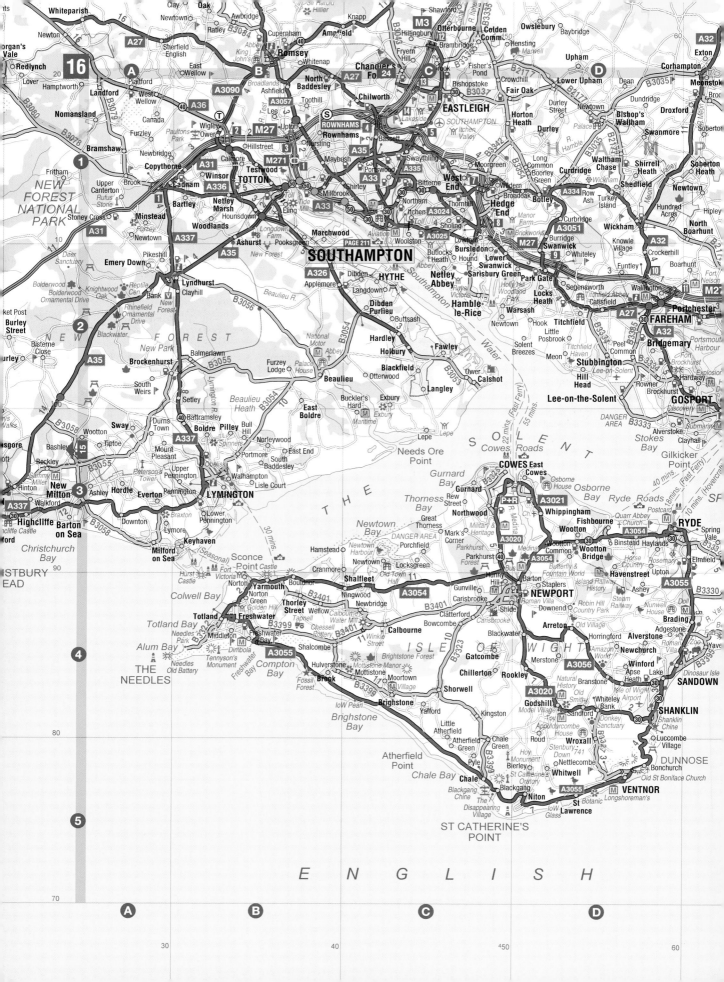

60

B R I S T O L

150

North West
Point

LUNDY

Lundy Marine
Conservation Zone

Lundy to:
Bideford 2hrs. (Seasonal)
Ilfracombe 2hrs. (Seasonal)

Rat Island

South West
Point

40

30

BARNSTAPLE

OR

BIDEFORD BAY

HARTLAND POINT   Windbury
Point

Titchberry

Hartland
Abbey   Chenstow
Lavender   Clovelly
Court   **Clovelly**

Hartland   Hartland
Quay   Stoke   **Hartland**   B3248   Velly   Clovelly
Donkeys

Docton
Mill   Natcott   Higher Clovelly   Buck's   Buck's
Cross   Mills

Milford   Philham   24   710   Milky Way
Adventure Park   **A39**

Elmscott   Edistone   Welsford   **Woolfardisworthy**
or Woolsery

South   Alminstone   Parkham
Hole   Cross   Ash

20   **10**
Knaps   Ashmansworthy
Longpeak   Welcombe   771   R. *Torridge*

Mead   East
Woolley   Meddon   West   Putford
Gooseham   Woolley   Putford

Eastcott   East   Dinworthy   Gnome Reserve &   Colsco
Morwenstow   Shop   Youlstone   Wild Flower Garden
Higher Sharpnose   Hawker's   West
Point   Hut   Youlstone   **Bradworthy**

Woodford   Upper
Lower Sharpnose   Tamar   **Sutcombe**
Point   **CORNWALL**   Lakes

Tamar   Lower   R.   Venngre
Kilkhampton   **A39**   Alfardisworthy   Waldon
Coombe   Thurdon   Tamar Lake   Soldon
Stibb   Cross

10   **A**   **B**   **10**   **C**   B3254   Dexbeer   **D**   **A388**

Poughill   Hersham   Dunsdon   Holsworthy
Flexbury   Bush   Farm   Beacon
Stratton   Grimscott   Lana   Chilsworthy
Castle Heritage   1643
Centre   **Stratton**   Launcells   Pancrasweek

Bude   **Bude**

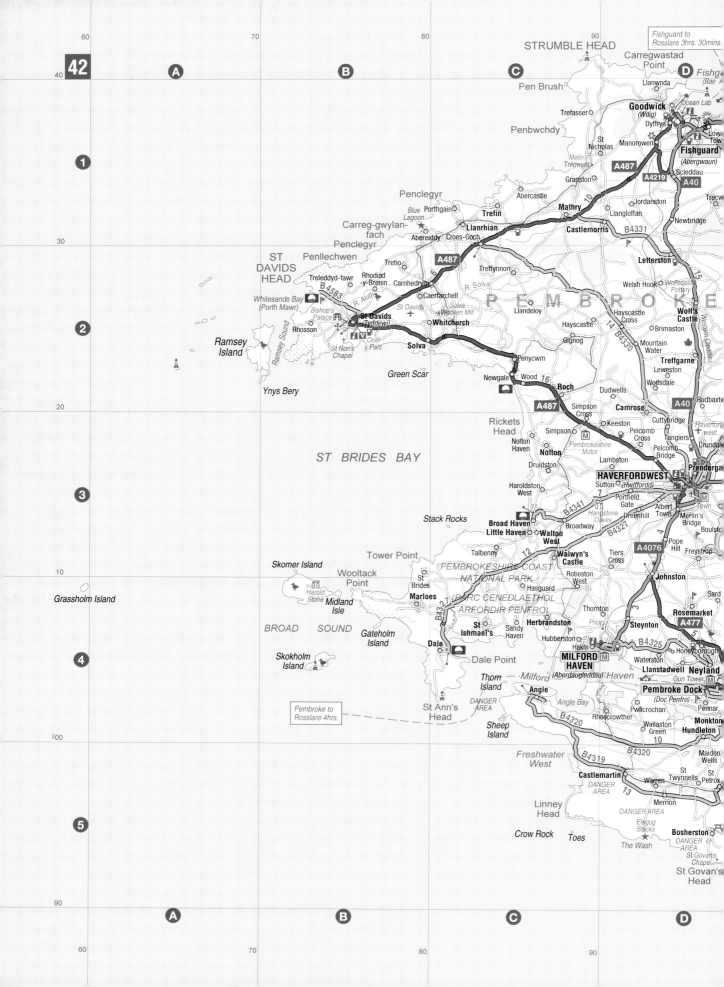

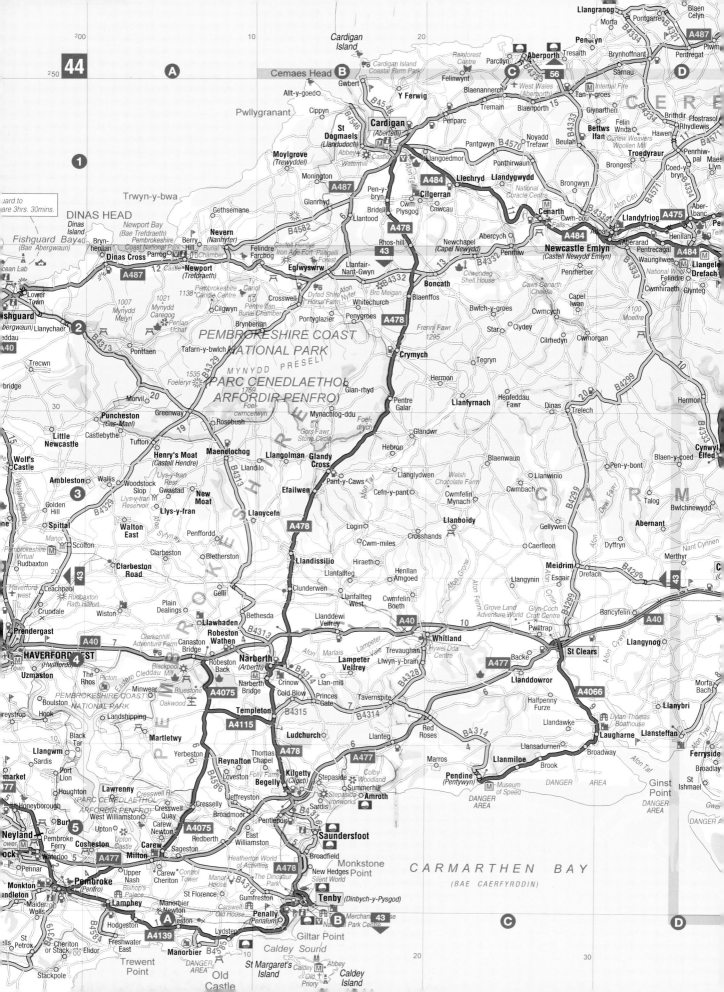

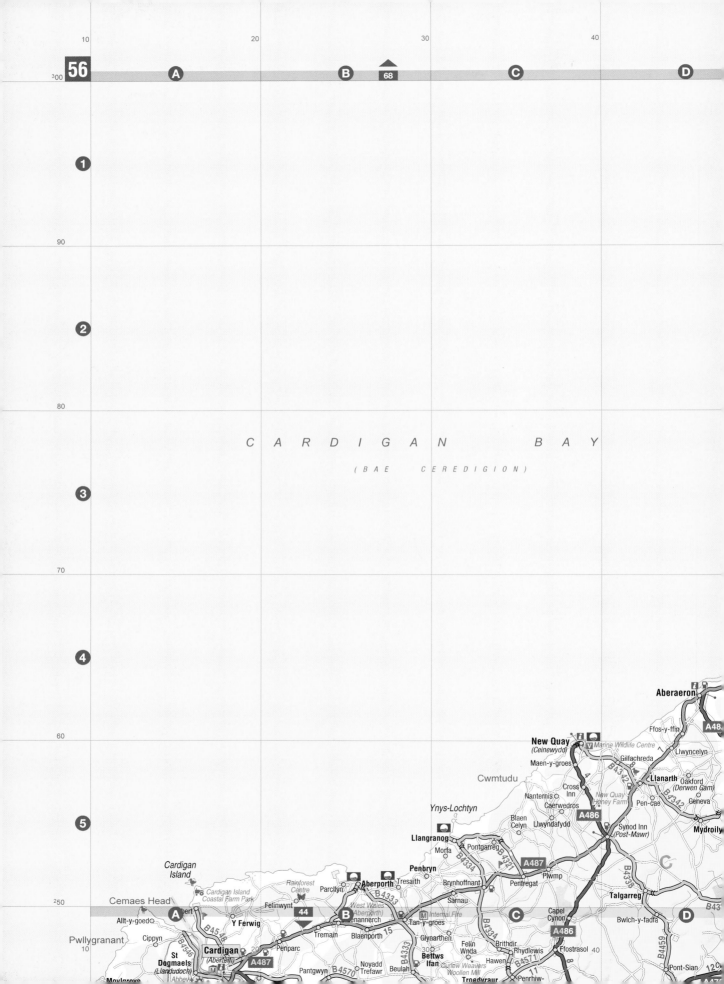

CARDIGAN BAY

(BAE CEREDIGION)

Aberaeron

Ffos-y-ffin   A48,

New Quay   i   A48
(Ceinewydd)   v Marine Wildlife Centre
Maen-y-groes   Llwyncelyn
Gilfachreda

Cwmtudu   Cross   Llanarth   Oakford
Inn   New Quay   (Derwen Gam)
Nanternis   Honey Farm   Pen-cae   Geneva
Caerwedros
Ynys-Lochtyn   Blaen   A486
Celyn   Llwyndafydd   Synod Inn   Mydroily
Llangranog   (Post-Mawr)
Morfa   Pontgarreg   B4321
Penbryn   B4334   A487   Plwmp
Brynhoffnant   Pentregat   B4338
Aberporth   Tresaith   Talgarreg
Rainforest   Parcllyn   Sarnau   B4334   Capel
Centre   West Wales   A486   Cynon   Bwlch-y-fadfa   D
Cemaes Head   (Aberporth)   Internal Fire   C
Allt-y-goed   Felinwynt   Penannerch   Tan-y-groes   B4459
Pwllgranant   Y Ferwig   Tremain   Blaenporth   Glynarthen   Brithdir   A486   Pont-Sian
Cippyn   Penparc   Felin   Rhydlewis   Ffostrasol
St   Cardigan   Noyadd   Beulah   Bettws   Wnda   Curlew Weavers
Dogmaels   (Aberteifi)   Trefawr   Ifan   Hawen   Woollen Mil   Penrhiw-
Moylgrove   Abbey   Pantgwyn   B4570   Troedyraur

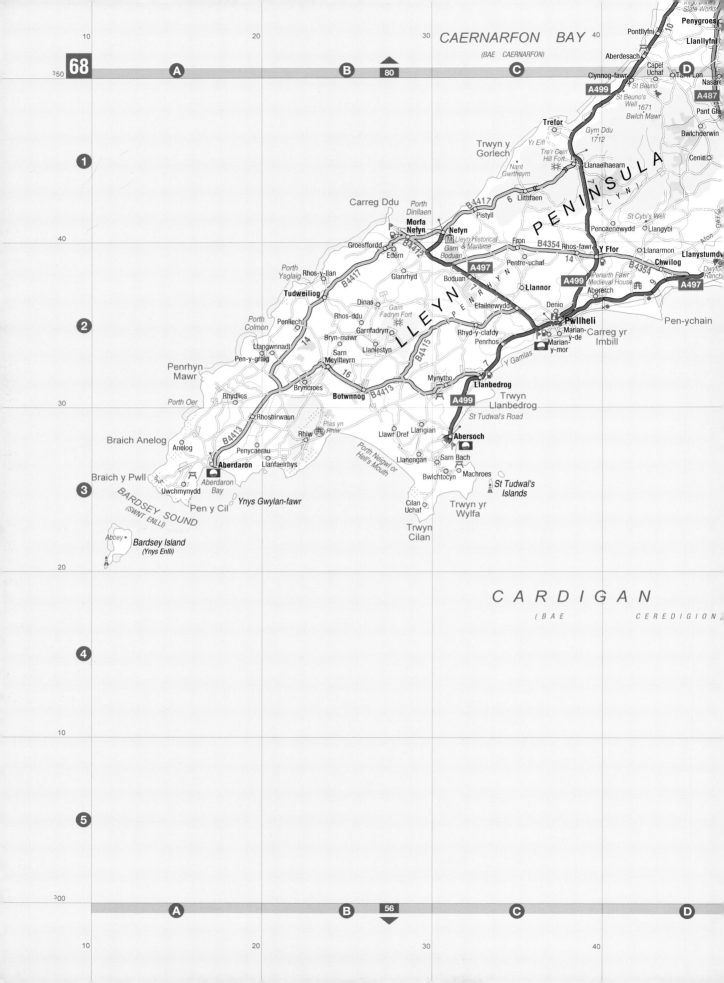

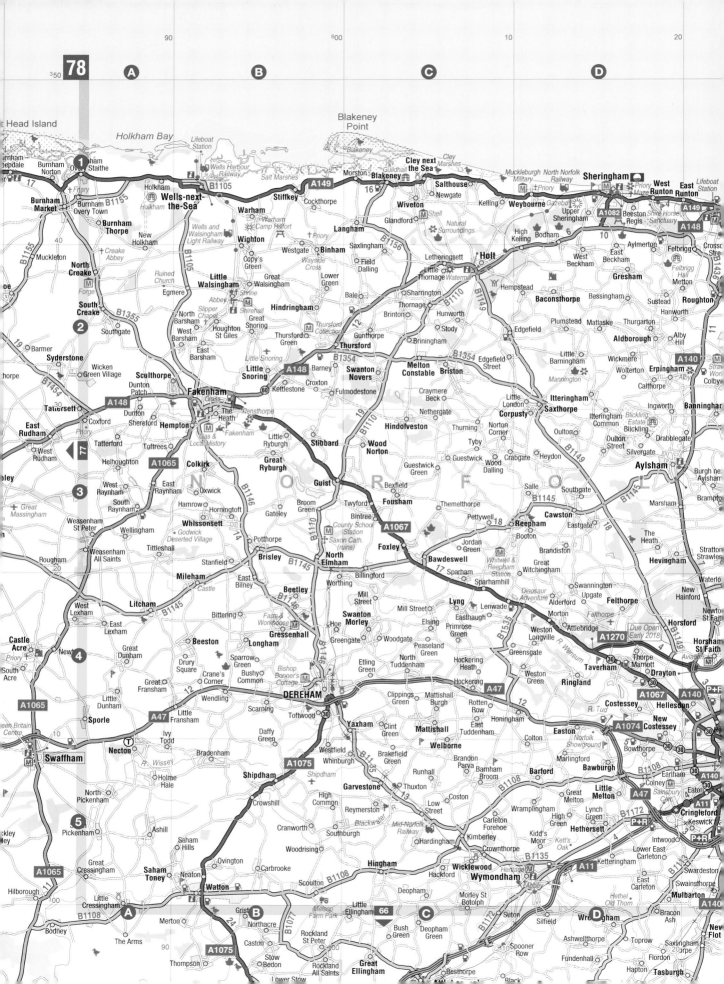

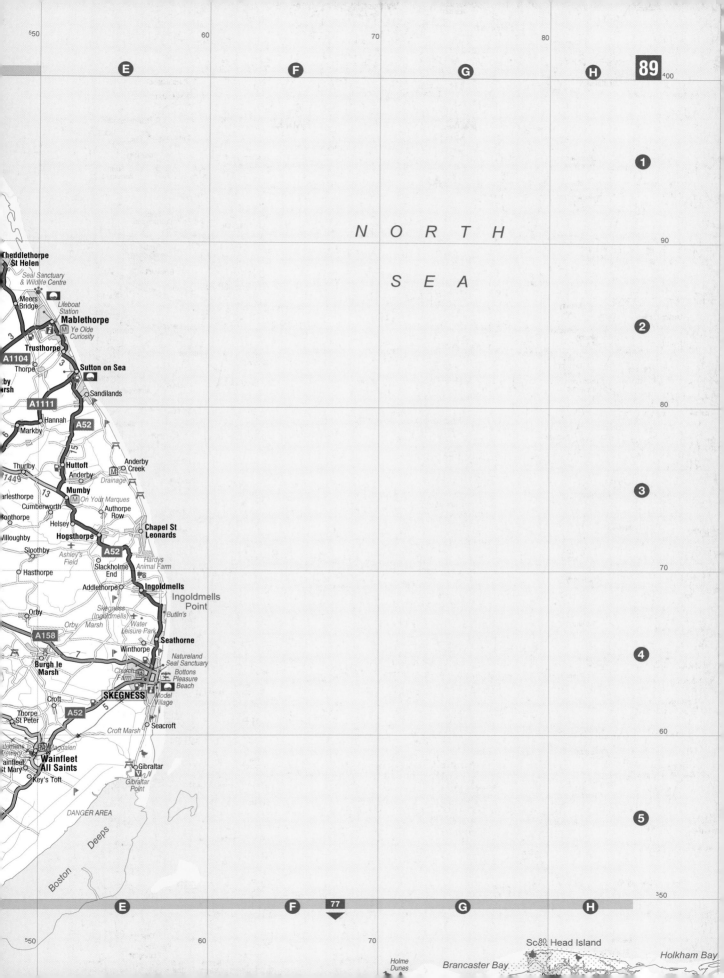

N O R T H

S E A

Cheddlethorpe
St Helen
*Seal Sanctuary
& Wildlife Centre*
Meers
Bridge
*Lifeboat
Station*
Mablethorpe
M *Ye Olde
Curiosity*
Trusthorpe
A1104
Thorpe
Sutton on Sea
*by
arsh*
Sandilands
A1111
Hannah
Markby
A52
Thurlby
15
Huttoft
Anderby
Creek
Anderby
M
Drainage
1449
Mumby
13
M *On Your Marques*
arlesthorpe
Cumberworth
Authorpe
Row
onthorpe
Helsey
**Chapel St
Leonards**
illoughby
Hogsthorpe
Sloothby
A52
*Ashley's
Field*
*Hardys
Animal Farm*
Hasthorpe
Slackholme
End
Addlethorpe
Ingoldmells
Ingoldmells
Point
Orby
*Skegness
(Ingoldmells)*
Butlin's
Orby Marsh
*Water
Leisure Park*
A158
Seathorne
7
Winthorpe
*Natureland
Seal Sanctuary*
**Burgh le
Marsh**
*Church
Farm*
*Bottons
Pleasure
Beach*
i
SKEGNESS
*Model
Village*
Croft
A52
5
Thorpe
St Peter
Seacroft
Croft Marsh
60
M *Magdalen*
*atemans
rewen*
**Wainfleet
All Saints**
*ainfleet
t Mary*
Gibraltar
V
Key's Toft
*Gibraltar
Point*

DANGER AREA

Deeps

Boston

Sc Head Island

*Holme
Dunes* *Brancaster Bay* *Holkham Bay*

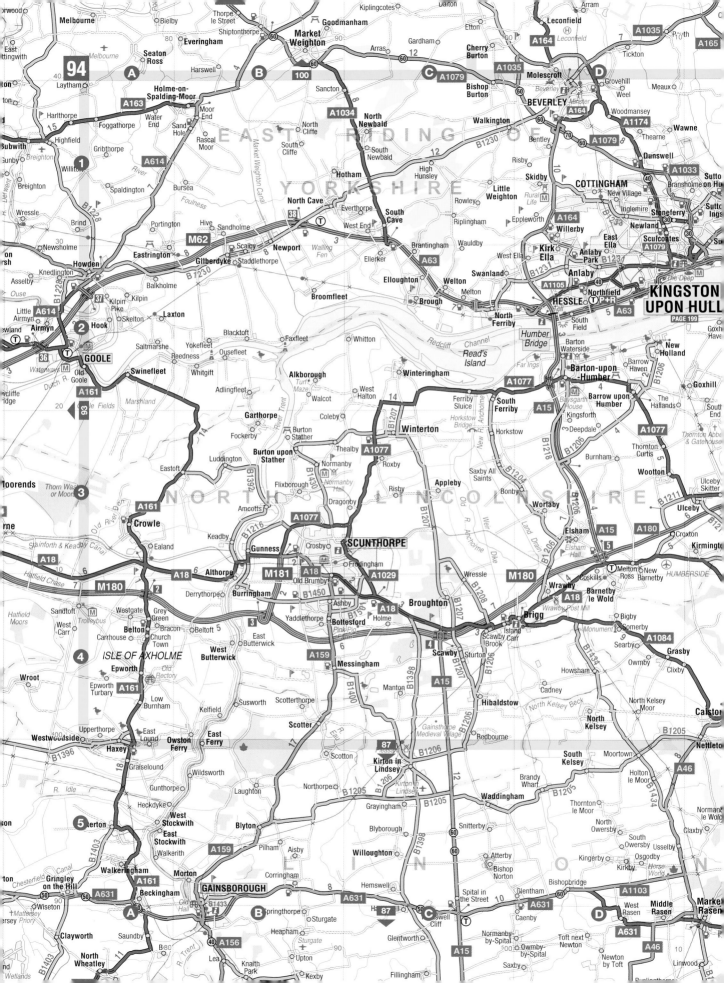

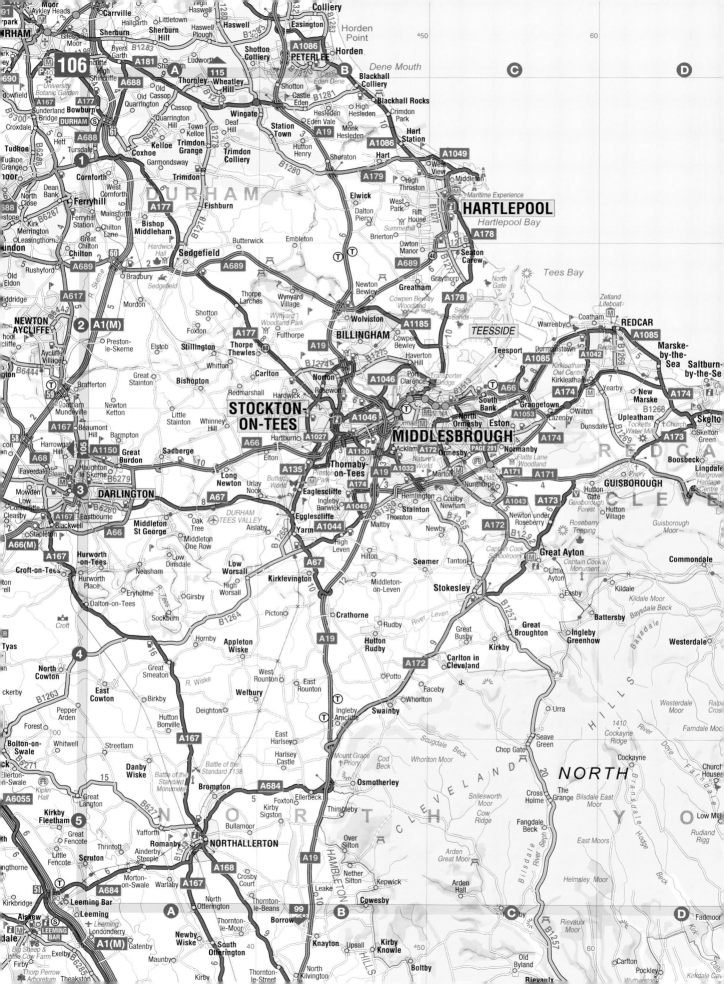

70   80   90   5 00   40

1

N O R T H

S E A

30

2

20

Brotton   Skinningrove
Boulby Cliffs
Carlin How   Loftus   *Ironstone Mining*   *Cowbar*   *Lifeboat Station*   Captain Cook & Staithes Heritage
Cleveland
North Skelton   A174   Staithes
Kilton Thorpe   Easington   Dalehouse   Port Mulgrave
Liverton Mines   Hinderwell   *Runswick Bay*
Stanghow   Liverton   Roxby   Borrowby   Runswick   Kettleness   Goldsborough
Moorsholm   Newton Mulgrave   Ellerby
B 1266
A171   Scaling Dam   Scaling   Mickleby   West Barnby   East Barnby   14   A174   Lythe   Sandsend   East Row
Moorsholm Moor   B1366   21   *Scaling Dam Reservoir*   Raithwaite   *Dracula Experience*
Roxby High Moor   Ugthorpe   Dunsley   **WHITBY**
Danby Low Moor   *Lealholm Moor*   Newholm   Castle Park   *Captain Cook Memorial*
3
10

Danby Beacon 981   Stonegate   Hutton Mulgrave   Ruswarp   *Saltwick Bay*
Danby   *Moors Centre*   Houlsyke   A171   Aislaby   Briggswath   Golden Grove   Long Lease   *Ness Point or North Cheek*
Castleton   Ainthorpe   Lealholm   B1410   Iburndale   Stainsacre   High Hawsker
Duck Bridge   Sleights   Ugglebarnby   Sneaton   Low Hawsker
Danby Botton   *Victoria Science*   Egton   A169   Sneatonthorpe   Raw   **Robin Hood's Bay**
Botton   Street   Glaisdale   Egton Bridge   Lease Rigg   Grosmont   *The Hermitage*   Fylingthorpe   *Old Coastguard Station*
Glaisdale Rigg   Key Green   Esk Valley   *Falling Foss (Waterfall)*   *Robin Hood's Bay & Fylingdales*   Boggle Hole
4

NORTH YORK MOORS
Loose Howe   Green End   *Thomason Foss Waterfall*   *Coastal Centre*   *Old Peak or South Cheek*
Rosedale Moor   Beck Hole   *Peak Alum Works*   Ravenscar
Pike Hill Moor   *Mallyan Spout*   Goathland
NATIONAL PARK
Blakey Ridge   *Nelly Ayre Foss Waterfall*   *Fylingdales Moor*
5 00

YORK   **MOORS**   *Wheeldale Moor*   *Wheeldale Roman Road*   *959 Lilla Cross*   *Burn Howe Rigg*   20   Staintondale
Low Bell End   *North Yorkshire Moors Railway*   *Goathland Moor*   Crowdon   *Staintondale Shire Horse Farm*
Thorgill   Rosedale Abbey   *Newton Dale Spring*   Saltergate   **LANGDALE FOREST**   *Harwood Dale Forest*   Cloughton Newlands
Rosedale Chimney Ironworks   Toll   *Mauley Cross*   *Malo Cross*   *Blakey Topping*   *Harwood Dale*   Cloughton
Spaunton Moor   Hartoft End   Stape   *Skelton Tower*   *Hole of Horcum*   Burniston
Gillamoor   Lastingham   *Cawthorne Camps*   Levisham   *Bridestones*   Bickley   Toll   Broxa   Silpho   Suffield   A171   A165   Scalby Mills   *Sea Life*
Hutton-le-Hole   Spaunton   100   Newton-on-Rawcliffe   Lockton   *Langdale End*   Hackness   Scalby   *North Bay Railway*
A169   *Wykeham Forest*   101   H
Kirkbymoorside   Appleton-le-Moors   *Cropton Brewery*   Cawthorne   Cropton   Low Dalby   *Dalby Forest Drive*   Everley   Barrowcliff   *Art Gallery*
Keldholme   Sinnington   Wrelton   Aislaby   *North Yorkshire Moors Railway*   *Dalby Forest*   *North Moor*   *Forge Valley Woods*   East Ayton   A170   Falsgrave   **SCARBOROUGH**
Kirkby   *Beck Isle*   *Wykeham*   P+R   P+R

River Seven   *Stain Dale*   *Trouts Dale*   *Newton Dale*

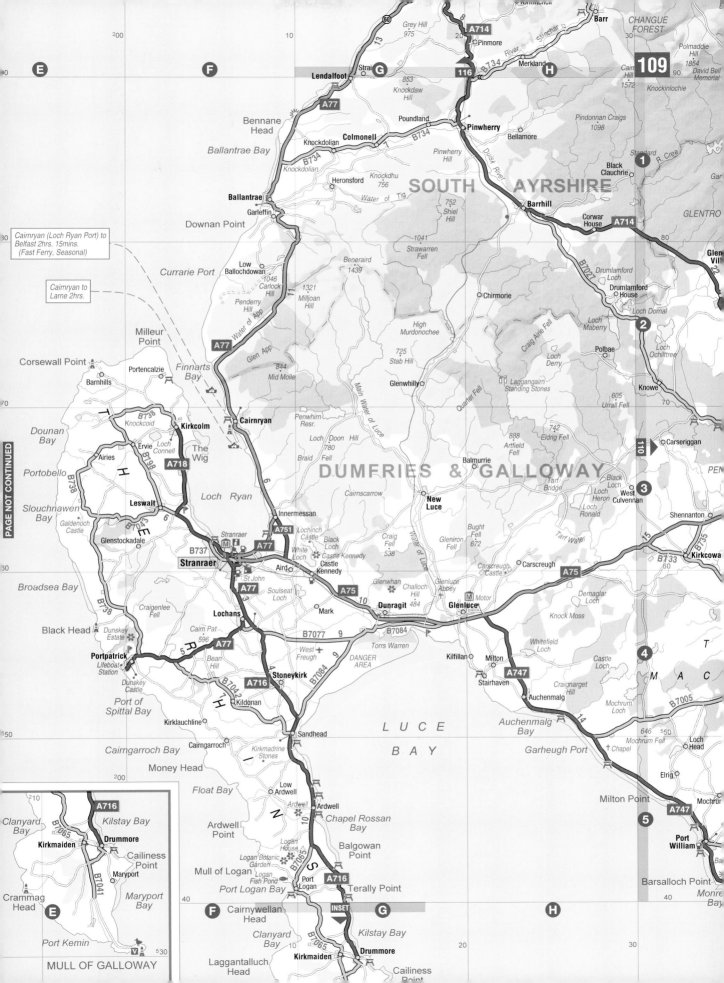

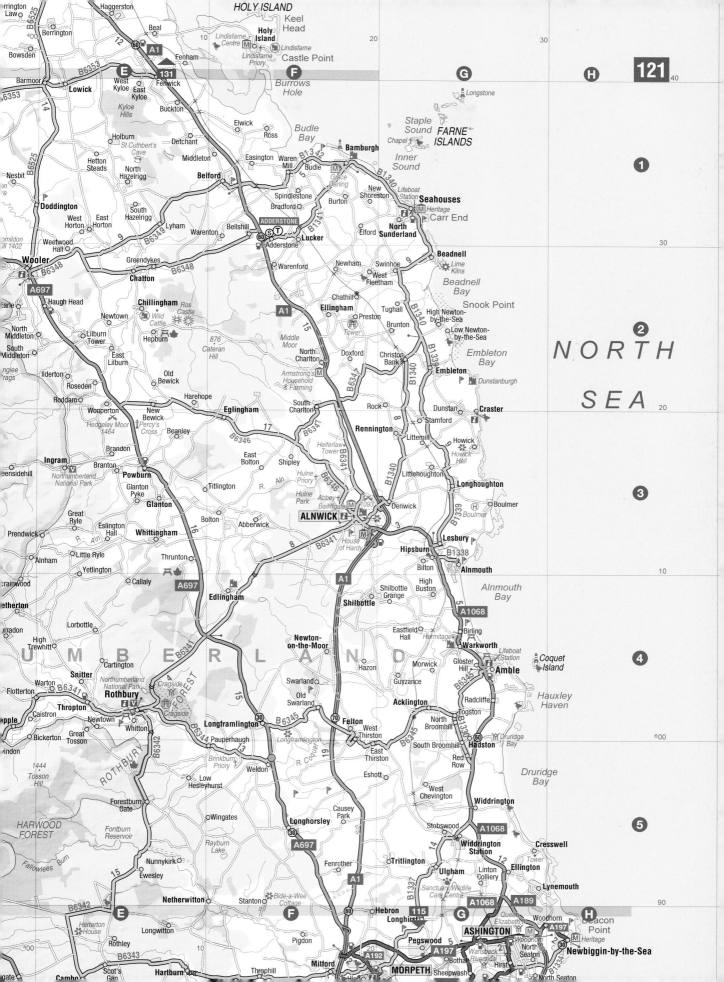

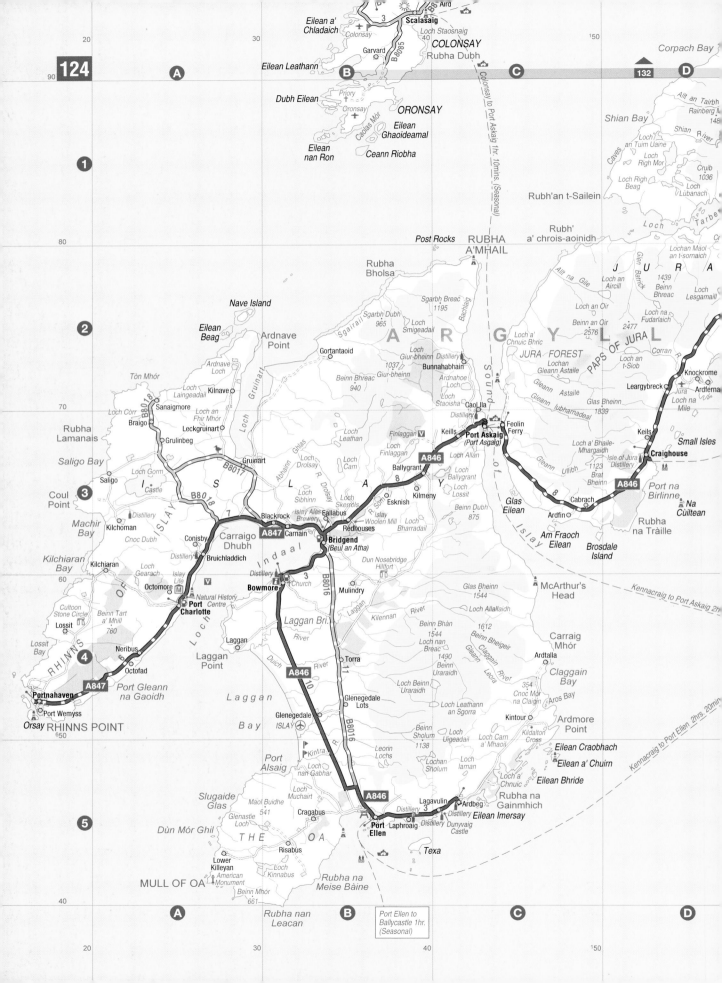

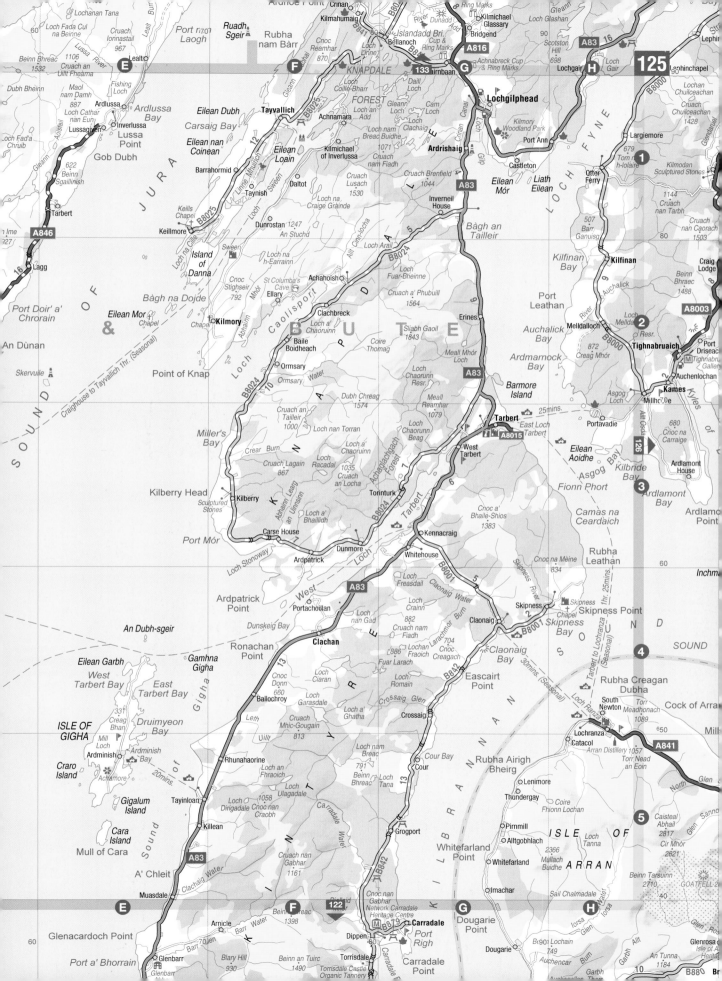

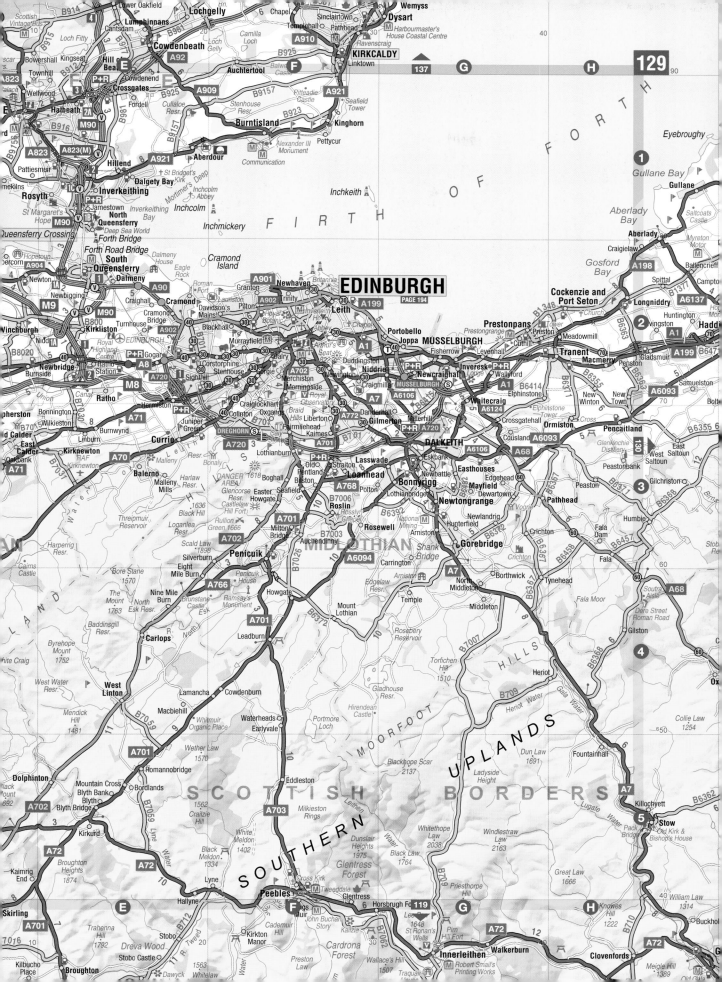

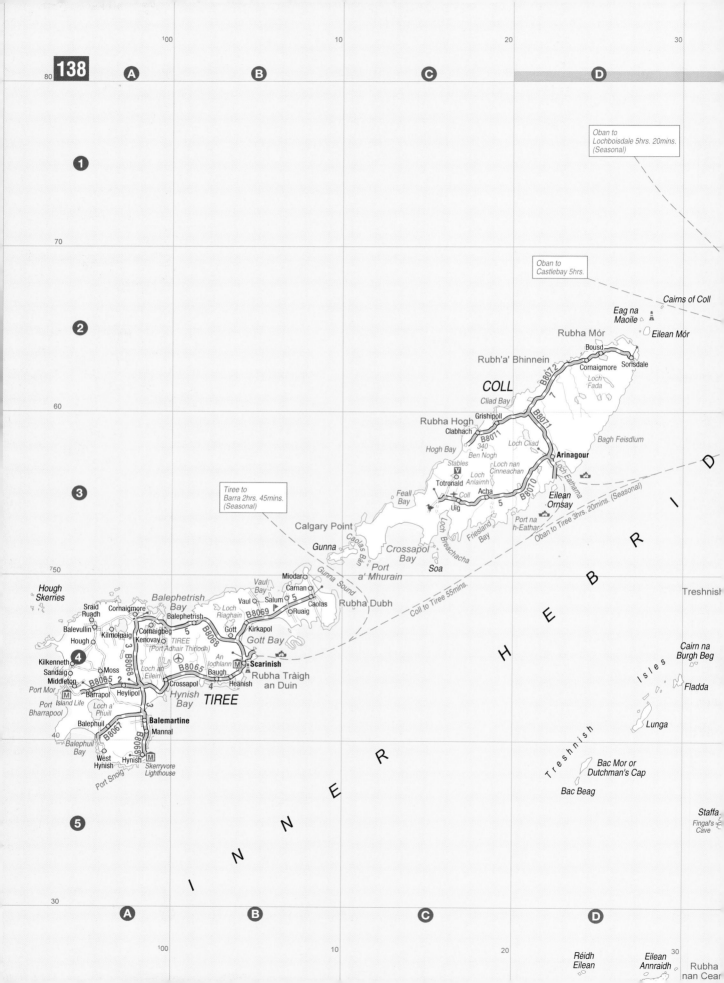

A · B · C · D

80

70

60

750

40

30

100 · 10 · 20 · 30

COLL

TIREE

Oban to Lochboisdale 5hrs. 20mins. (Seasonal)

Oban to Castlebay 5hrs.

Cairns of Coll

Eag na Maoile

Rubha Mór

Eilean Mór

Bousd

Cornaigmore

Sorisdale

Rubh'a' Bhinnein

Loch Fada

B8072

7

B8071

Cliad Bay

Grishipoll

Bagh Feisdlum

Rubha Hogh

Clabhach

B8011

Loch Cliad

Hogh Bay

340

Ben Nogh

Loch nan Cinneachan

Arinagour

Stables

V

Loch Anlaimh

Totronald

Feall Bay

Coll

Acha

5

B8010

Loch Eatharna

Eilean Ornsay

Uig

Port na h-Eathar

Oban to Tiree 3hrs. 20mins. (Seasonal)

Tiree to Barra 2hrs. 45mins. (Seasonal)

Calgary Point

Gunna

Caolas Bay

Crossapol Bay

Soa

Port a' Mhurain

Loch Breachacha

Friesland Bay

Rubha Dubh

Gunna Sound

Coll to Tiree 55mins.

Miodar

Carnan

Vaul Bay

Salum

Caolas

5

Vaul

Loch Riaghain

Ruaig

B8069

Gott

Kirkapol

H E B R I D

Treshnish

Hough Skerries

Sraid Ruadh

Balephetrish Bay

Cornaigmore

Balephetrish

Cornaigbeg

Kenovay

TIREE (Port Adhair Thiriodh)

Gott Bay

Balevullin

Kilmoluaig

Hough

An Iodhlann

Cairn na Burgh Beg

Isles

Kilkenneth

Loch an Eilein

M

Scarinish

B8065

Fladda

Sandaig

Moss

B8068

3

Baugh

Rubha Tràigh an Duin

Middleton

B8065

2

Crossapol

4

Heanish

Lunga

Port Mor

M

Barrapol

Heylipol

Island Life

Port Bharrapool

Loch a' Phuill

Hynish Bay

TIREE

Treshnish

Bac Mor or Dutchman's Cap

Balephuil

B8067

Mannal

Balemartine

Bac Beag

Balephuil Bay

B8068

West Hynish

Hynish

M

Skerryvore Lighthouse

Staffa
Fingal's Cave

Port Snoig

I N N E R

100 · 10 · 20 · 30

Réidh Eilean

Eilean Annraidh

Rubha nan Cear

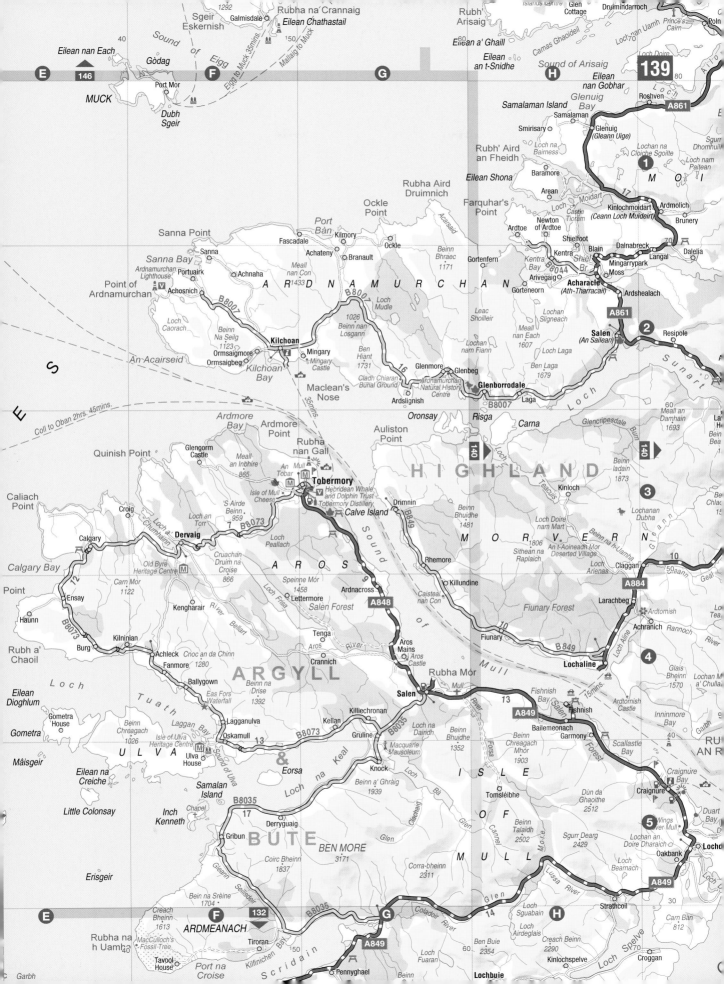

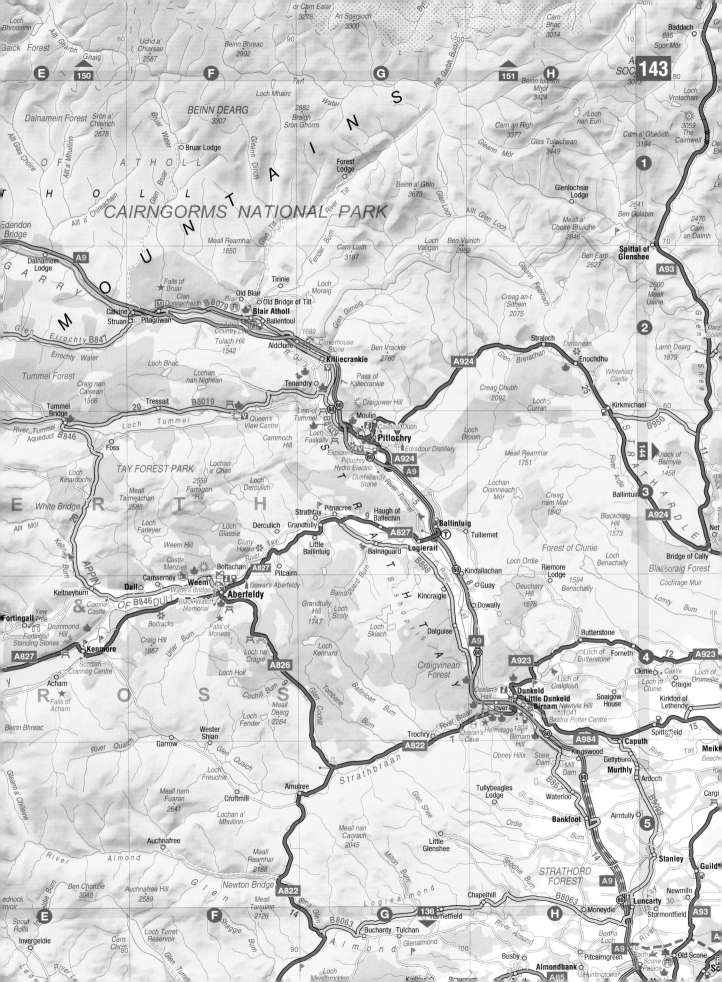

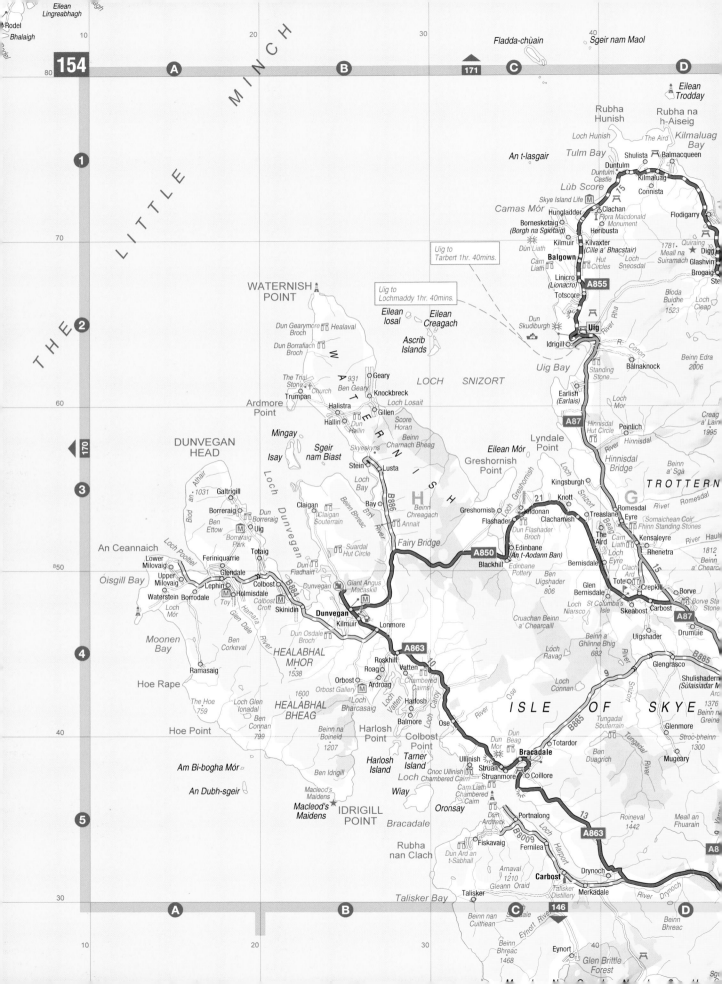

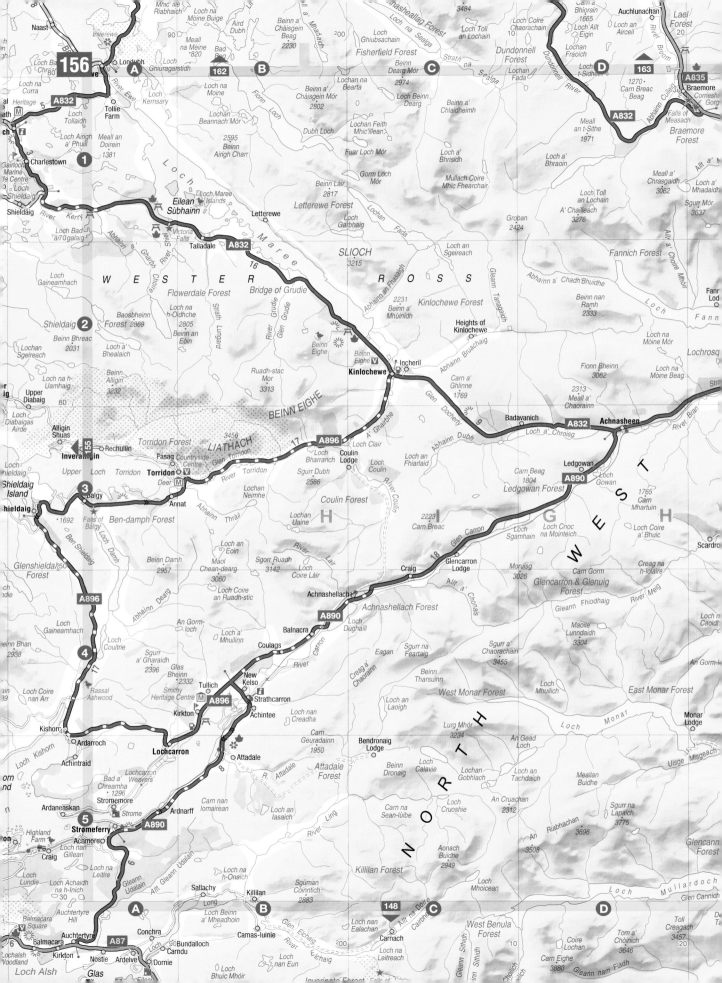

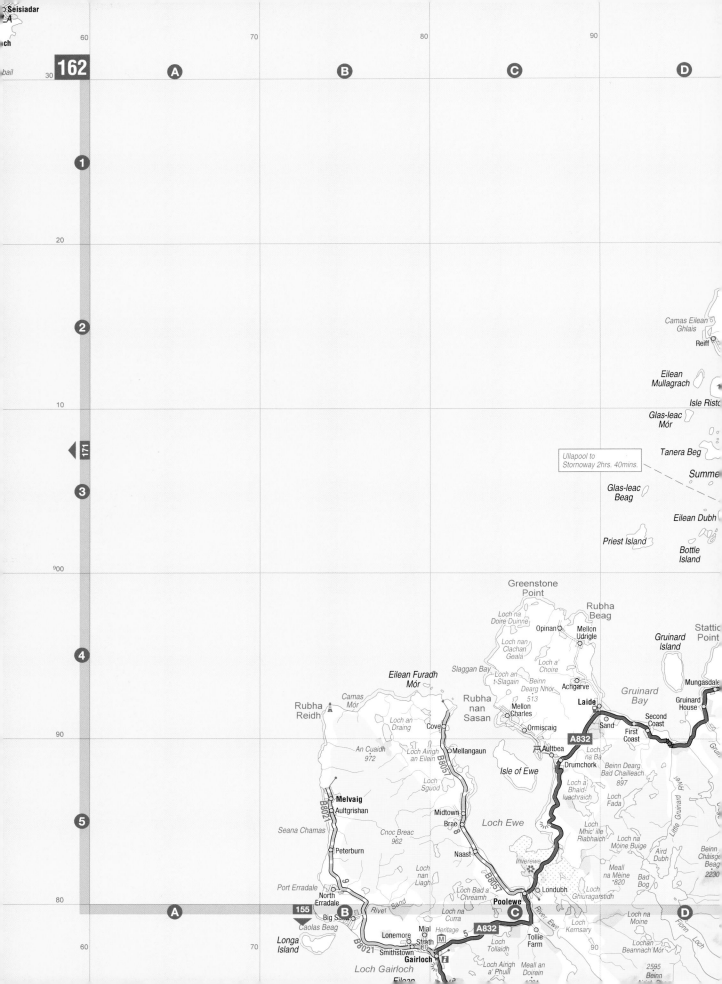

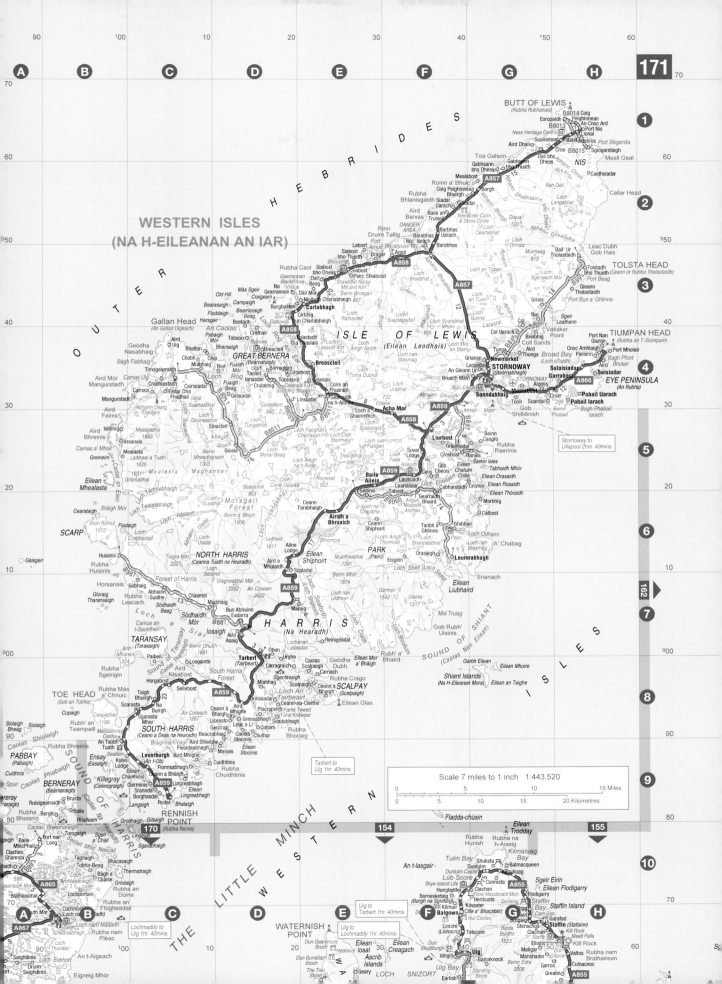

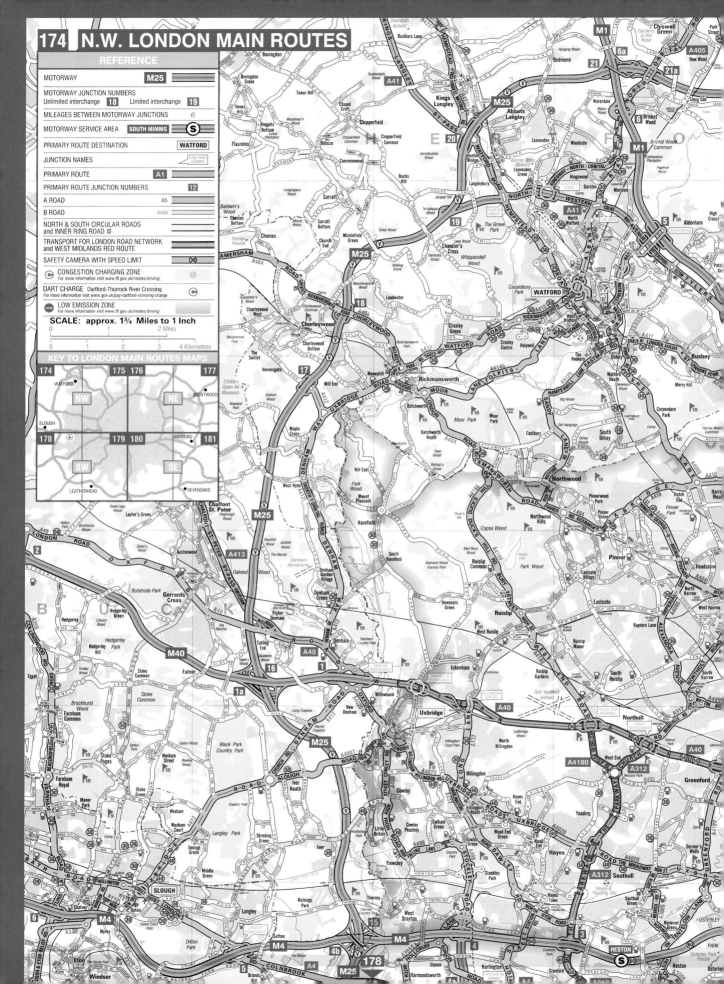

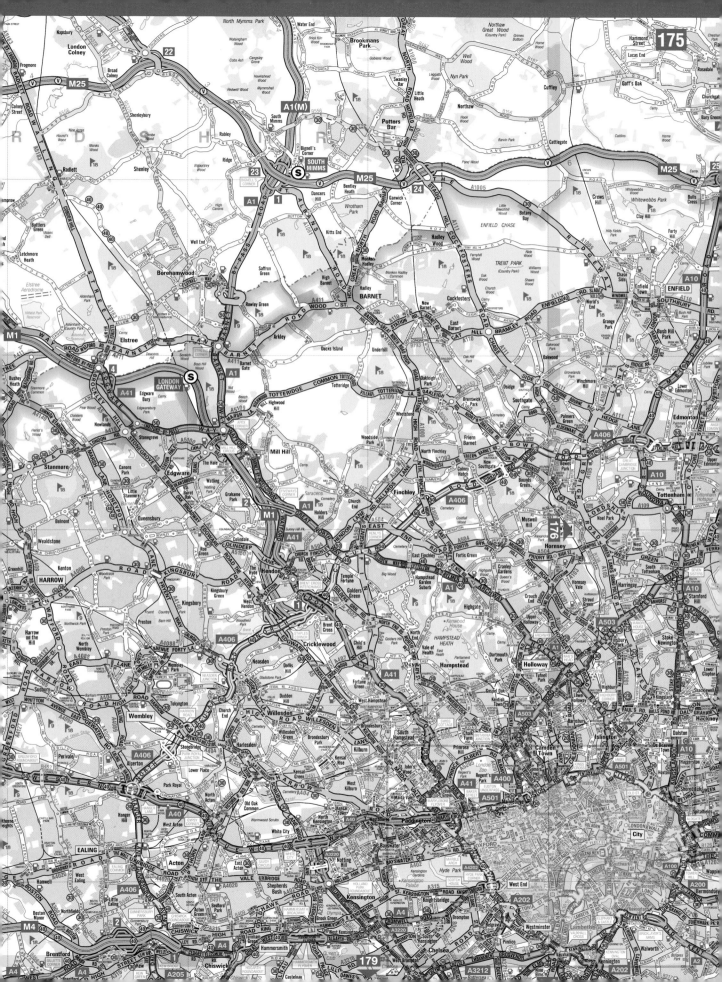

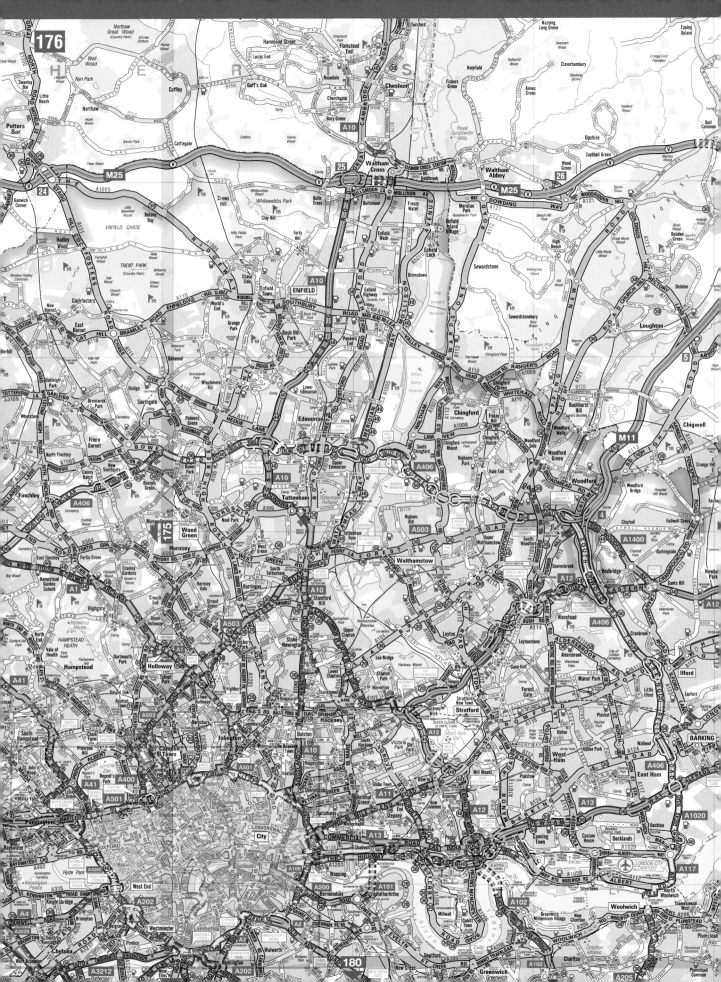

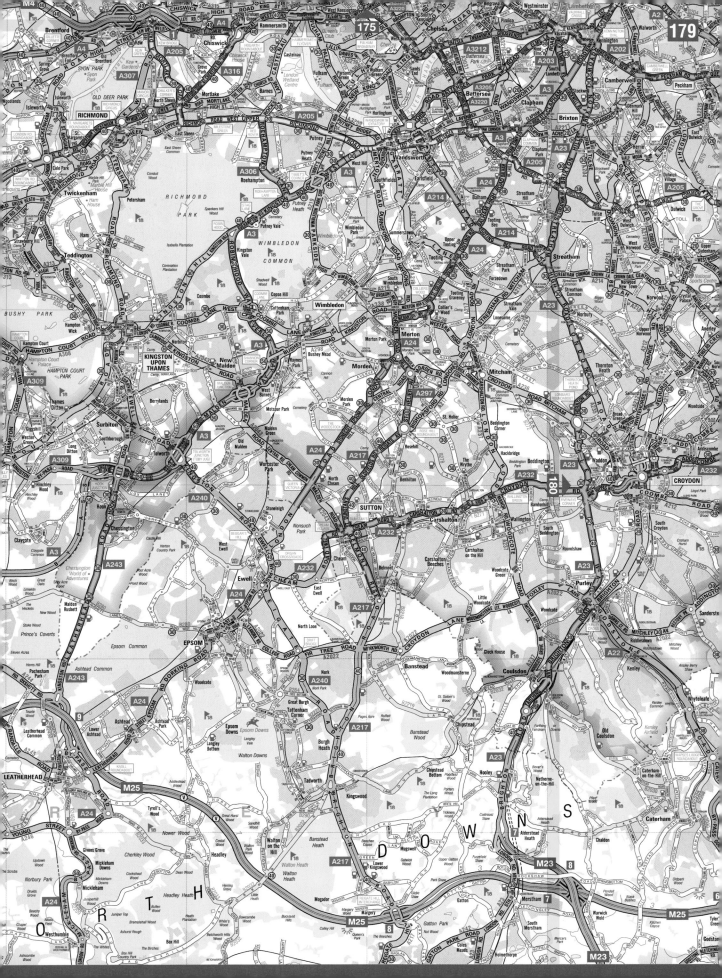

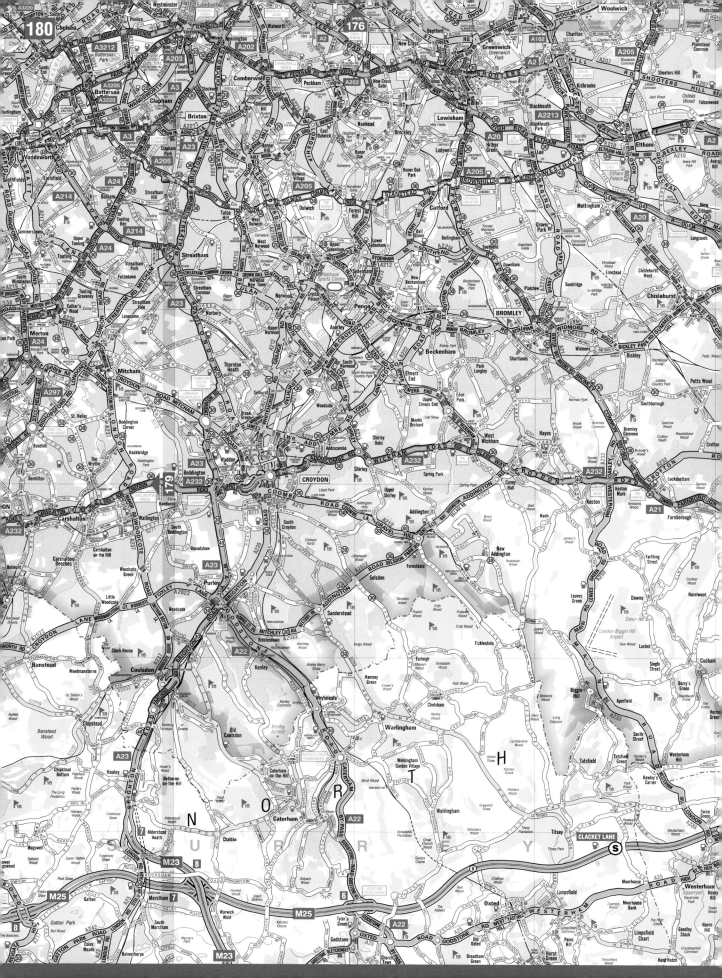

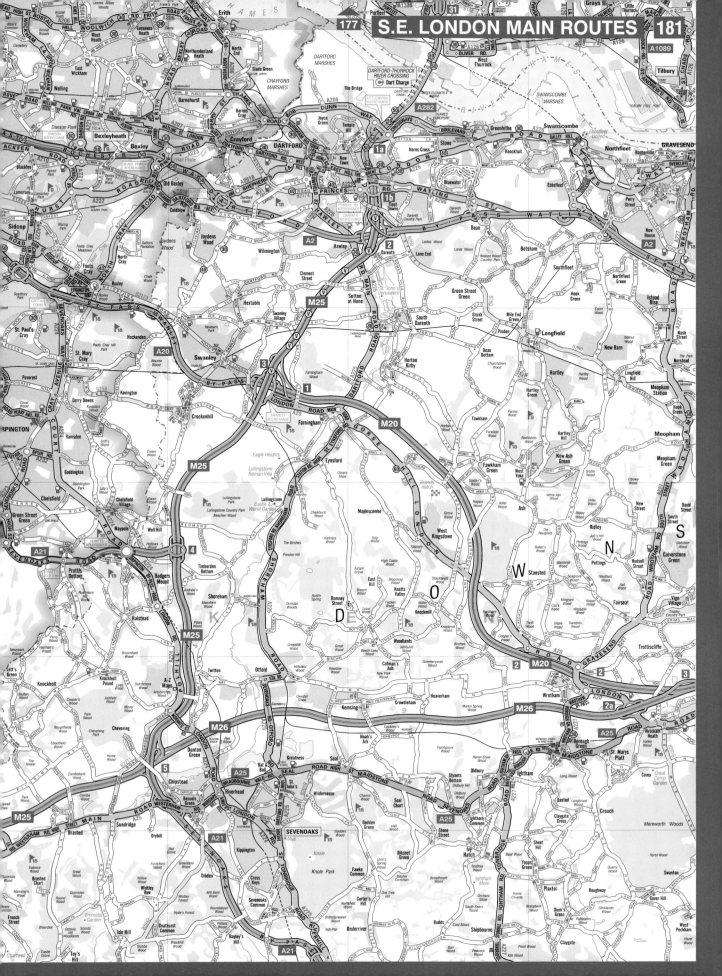

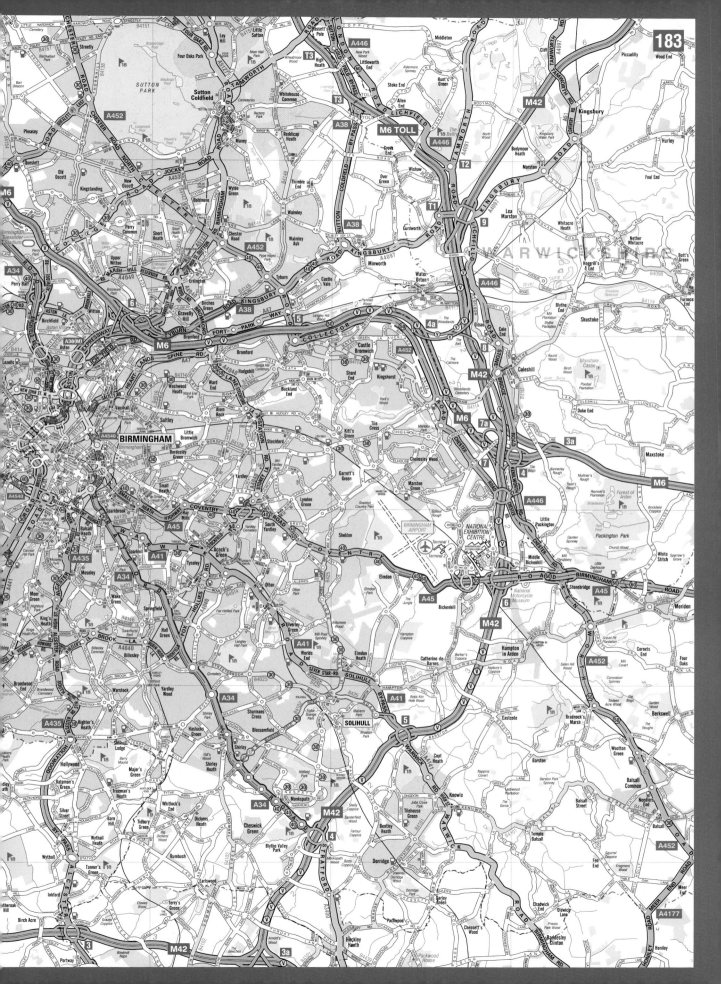

Town Plans

Aberdeen	187
Aberystwyth	187
Ayr	187
Bath	187
Bedford	188
Birmingham	188
Blackpool	188
Bournemouth	190
Bradford	190
Brighton & Hove	189
Bristol	189
Caernarfon	190
Cambridge	191
Canterbury	190
Cardiff (Caerdydd)	191
Carlisle	192
Cheltenham	192
Chester	192
Coventry	192
Derby	193
Dover	193
Dumfries	193
Dundee	194
Durham	194
Eastbourne	195
Edinburgh	194
Exeter	195
Folkestone	195
Glasgow	196
Gloucester	196
Great Yarmouth	196
Guildford	197
Harrogate	197
Hereford	197
Inverness	198
Ipswich	198
Kilmarnock	198
Kingston upon Hull	199
Leeds	199
Leicester	200
Lincoln	198
Liverpool	200
London	202-203
Luton	201
Manchester	201
Medway Towns	204
Middlesbrough	201
Milton Keynes	204
Newcastle upon Tyne	205
Newport (Casnewydd)	205
Northampton	206
Norwich	205
Nottingham	206
Oban	206
Oxford	207
Paisley	207
Perth	207
Peterborough	208
Plymouth	208
Portsmouth	209
Preston	208
Reading	209
St Andrews	209
Salisbury	210
Sheffield	210
Shrewsbury	210
Southampton	211
Stirling	211
Stoke-on-Trent	211
Stratford-upon-Avon	212
Sunderland	212
Swansea (Abertawe)	212
Swindon	212
Taunton	213
Winchester	213
Windsor	213
Wolverhampton	213
Worcester	214
Wrexham (Wrecsam)	214
York	214

Port Plans

Harwich	215
Kingston upon Hull	215
Newcastle upon Tyne	215
Newhaven	215
Pembroke Dock (Doc Penfro)	215
Poole	215
Portsmouth	215
Weymouth	215

Airport Plans

Birmingham	216
East Midlands	216
Glasgow	216
London Gatwick	216
London Heathrow	216
London Luton	216
London Stansted	216
Manchester	216

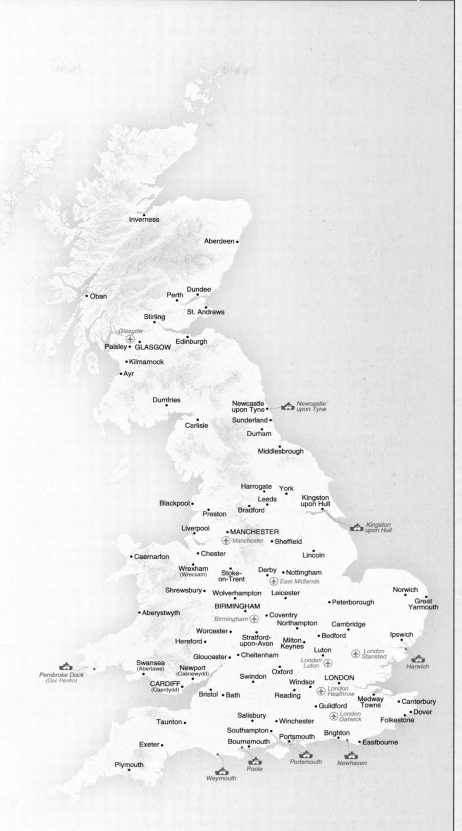

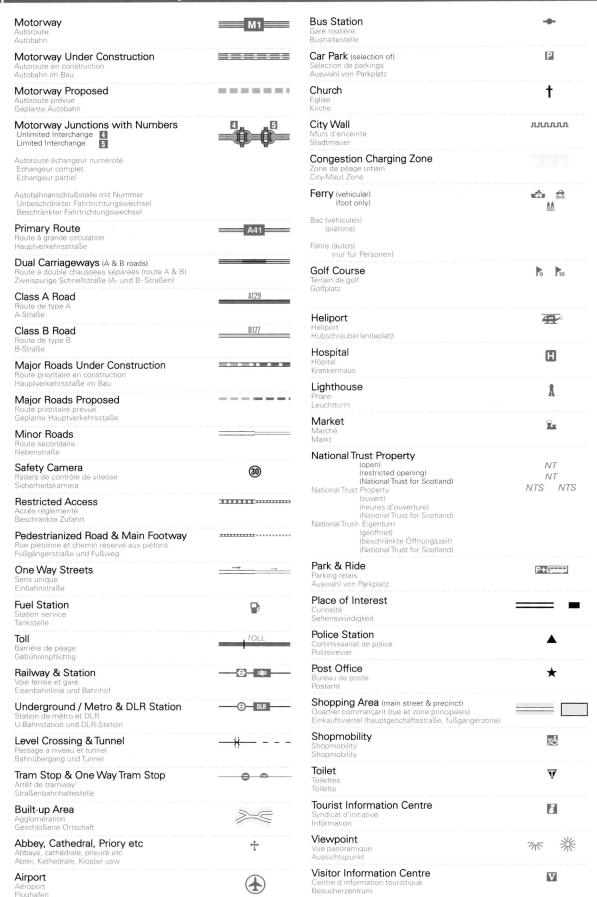

Motorway Autoroute Autobahn	**M1**
Motorway Under Construction Autoroute en construction Autobahn im Bau	
Motorway Proposed Autoroute prévue Geplante Autobahn	
Motorway Junctions with Numbers Unlimited Interchange **4** Limited Interchange **5** Autoroute échangeur numéroté Echangeur complet Echangeur partiel Autobahnanschlußstelle mit Nummer Unbeschränkter Fahrtrichtungswechsel Beschränkter Fahrtrichtungswechsel	**4** **5**
Primary Route Route à grande circulation Hauptverkehrsstraße	**A41**
Dual Carriageways (A & B roads) Route à double chaussées séparées (route A & B) Zweispurige Schnellstraße (A- und B- Straßen)	
Class A Road Route de type A A-Straße	A129
Class B Road Route de type B B-Straße	B177
Major Roads Under Construction Route prioritaire en construction Hauptverkehrsstraße im Bau	
Major Roads Proposed Route prioritaire prévue Geplante Hauptverkehrsstraße	
Minor Roads Route secondaire Nebenstraße	
Safety Camera Radars de contrôle de vitesse Sicherheitskamera	(30)
Restricted Access Accès règlementé Beschränkte Zufahrt	
Pedestrianized Road & Main Footway Rue piétonne et chemin réservé aux piétons Fußgängerstraße und Fußweg	
One Way Streets Sens unique Einbahnstraße	
Fuel Station Station service Tankstelle	
Toll Barrière de péage Gebührenpflichtig	TOLL
Railway & Station Voie ferrée et gare Eisenbahnlinie und Bahnhof	
Underground / Metro & DLR Station Station de métro et DLR U-Bahnstation und DLR-Station	DLR
Level Crossing & Tunnel Passage à niveau et tunnel Bahnübergang und Tunnel	
Tram Stop & One Way Tram Stop Arrêt de tramway Straßenbahnhaltestelle	
Built-up Area Agglomération Geschloßene Ortschaft	
Abbey, Cathedral, Priory etc Abbaye, cathédrale, prieuré etc Abtei, Kathedrale, Kloster usw	†
Airport Aéroport Flughafen	✈

Bus Station Gare routière Bushaltestelle	
Car Park (selection of) Sélection de parkings Auswahl von Parkplatz	**P**
Church Eglise Kirche	†
City Wall Murs d'enceinte Stadtmauer	
Congestion Charging Zone Zone de péage urbain City-Maut Zone	
Ferry (vehicular) (foot only) Bac (véhicules) (piétons) Fähre (autos) (nur für Personen)	
Golf Course Terrain de golf Golfplatz	
Heliport Héliport Hubschrauberlandeplatz	
Hospital Hôpital Krankenhaus	**H**
Lighthouse Phare Leuchtturm	
Market Marché Markt	
National Trust Property (open) (restricted opening) (National Trust for Scotland) National Trust Property (ouvert) (heures d'ouverture) (National Trust for Scotland) National Trust- Eigentum (geöffnet) (beschränkte Öffnungszeit) (National Trust for Scotland)	NT NT NTS NTS
Park & Ride Parking relais Auswahl von Parkplatz	P+
Place of Interest Curiosité Sehenswürdigkeit	■
Police Station Commissariat de police Polizeirevier	▲
Post Office Bureau de poste Postamt	★
Shopping Area (main street & precinct) Quartier commerçant (rue et zone principales) Einkaufsviertel (hauptgeschäftsstraße, fußgängerzone)	
Shopmobility Shopmobility Shopmobility	
Toilet Toilettes Toilette	▽
Tourist Information Centre Syndicat d'initiative Information	**i**
Viewpoint Vue panoramique Aussichtspunkt	
Visitor Information Centre Centre d'information touristique Besucherzentrum	**V**

Please note: symbols have been enlarged for clarity

ABERDEEN

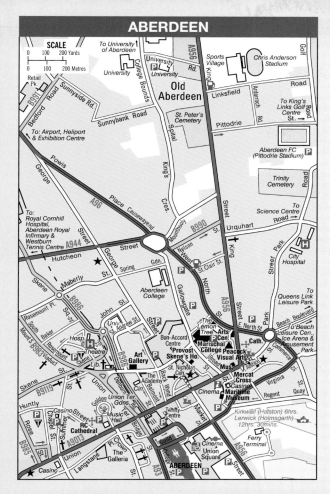

ABERYSTWYTH

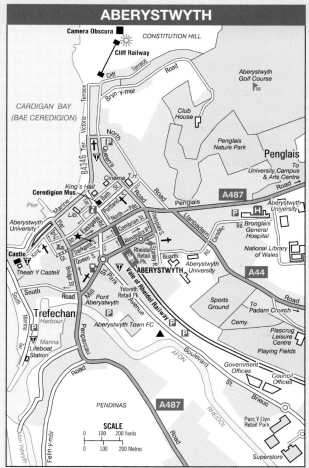

AYR

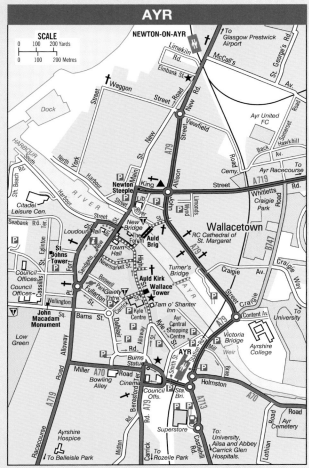

BATH

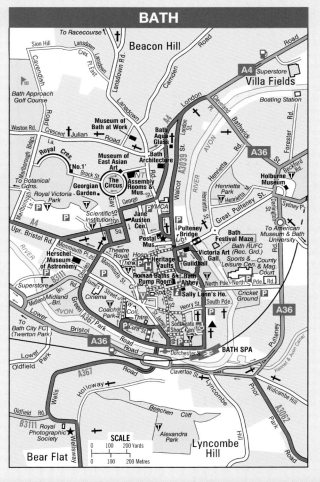

BEDFORD

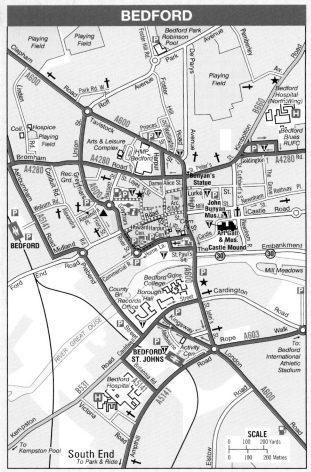

BLACKPOOL

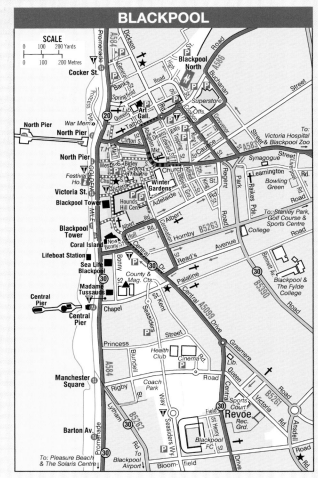

BIRMINGHAM (CITY CENTRE)

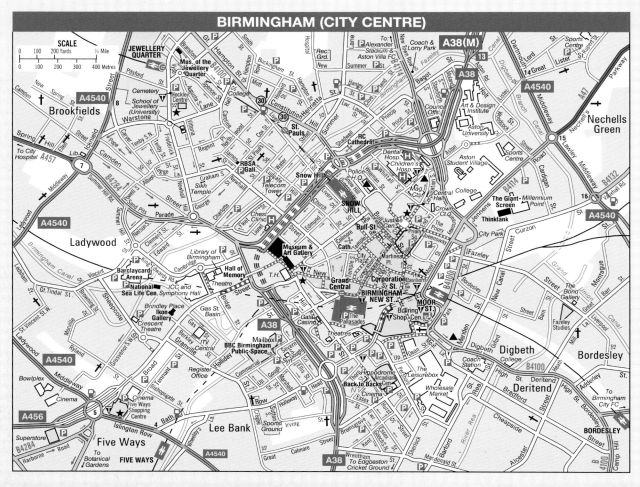

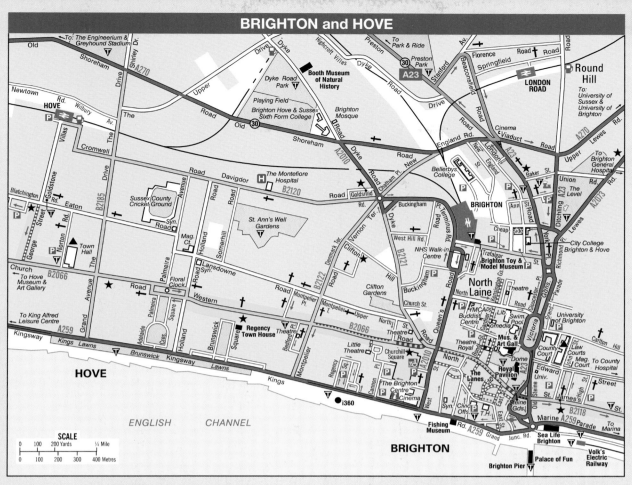

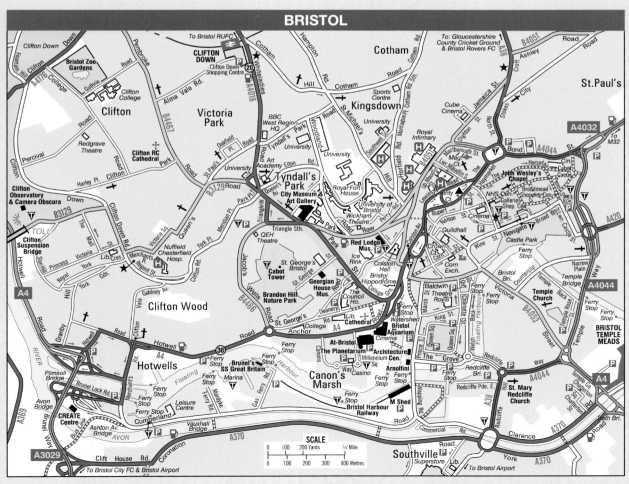

BOURNEMOUTH

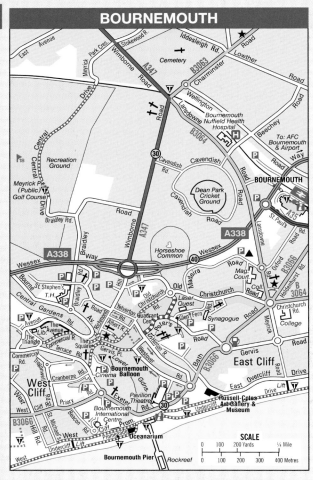

SCALE
0   100   200 Yards   ¼ Mile
0   100   200   300   400 Metres

BRADFORD

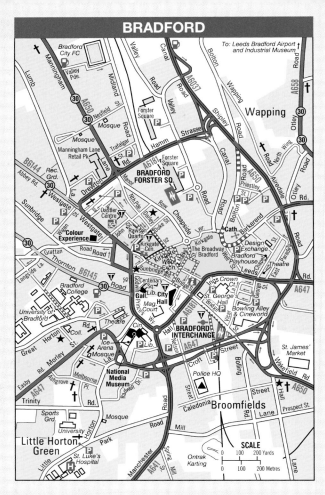

SCALE
0   100   200 Yards
0   100   200 Metres

CAERNARFON

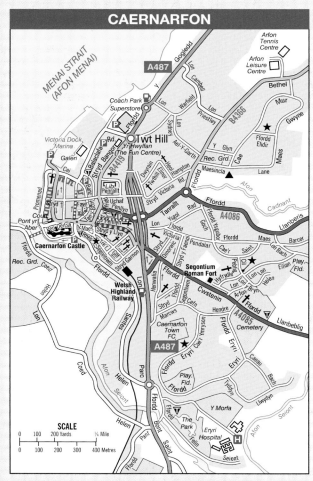

SCALE
0   100   200 Yards   ¼ Mile
0   100   200   300   400 Metres

CANTERBURY

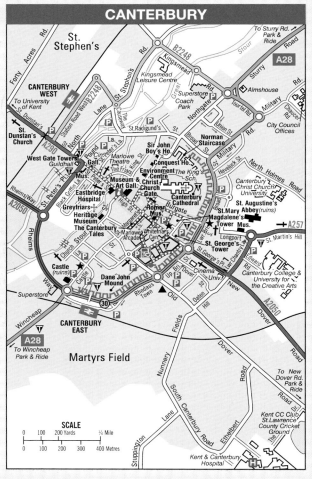

SCALE
0   100   200 Yards   ¼ Mile
0   100   200   300   400 Metres

CAMBRIDGE

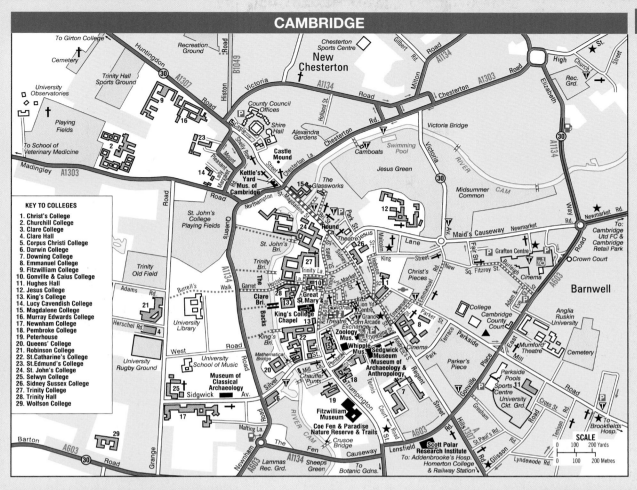

KEY TO COLLEGES

1. Christ's College
2. Churchill College
3. Clare College
4. Clare Hall
5. Corpus Christi College
6. Darwin College
7. Downing College
8. Emmanuel College
9. Fitzwilliam College
10. Gonville & Caius College
11. Hughes Hall
12. Jesus College
13. King's College
14. Lucy Cavendish College
15. Magdalene College
16. Murray Edwards College
17. Newnham College
18. Pembroke College
19. Peterhouse
20. Queens' College
21. Robinson College
22. St.Catharine's College
23. St.Edmund's College
24. St. John's College
25. Selwyn College
26. Sidney Sussex College
27. Trinity College
28. Trinity Hall
29. Wolfson College

CARDIFF (CAERDYDD)

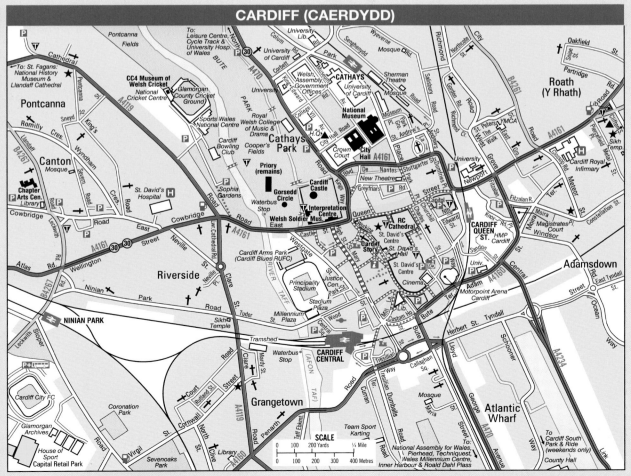

CARLISLE

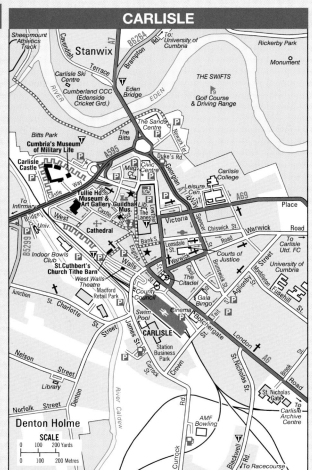

CHELTENHAM

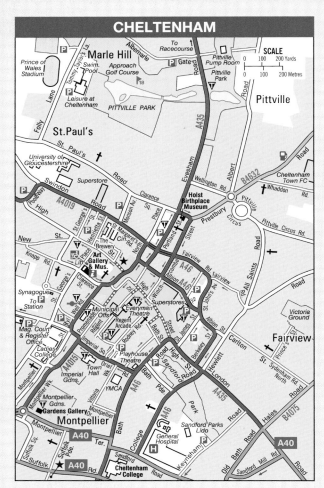

CHESTER

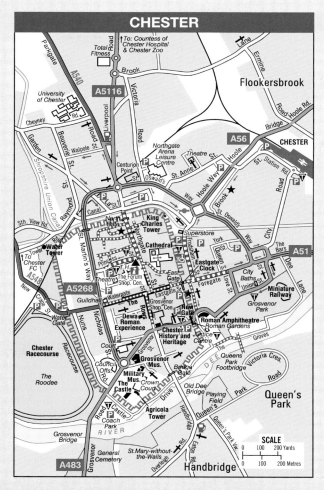

COVENTRY

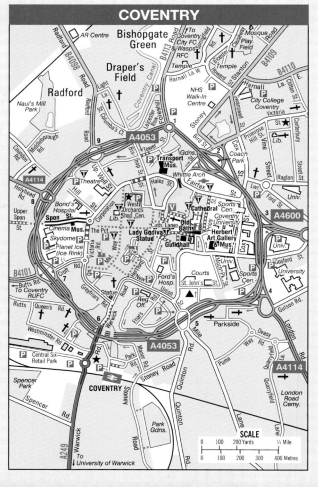

DERBY

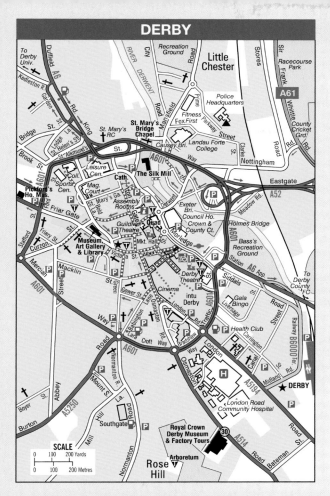

DUMFRIES

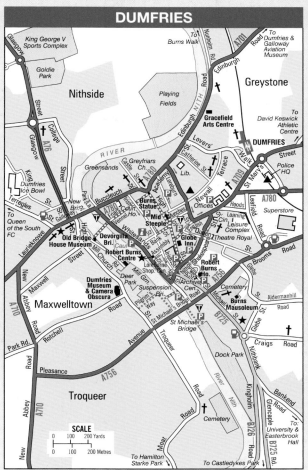

DOVER

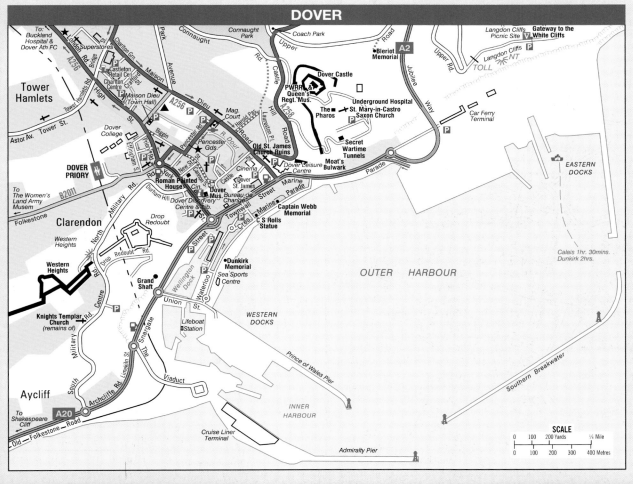

DUNDEE

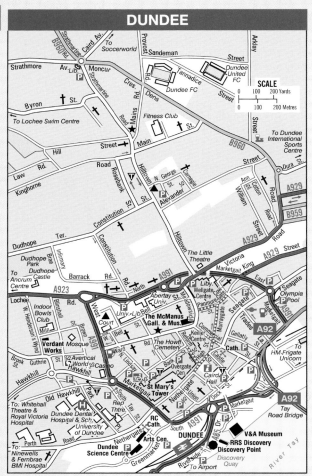

DURHAM

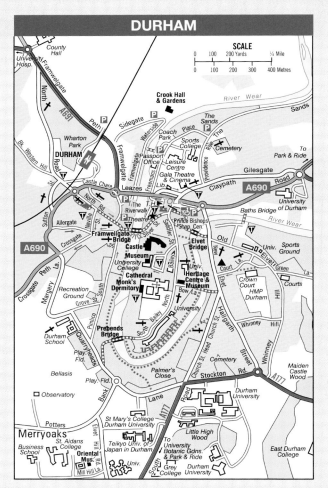

EDINBURGH

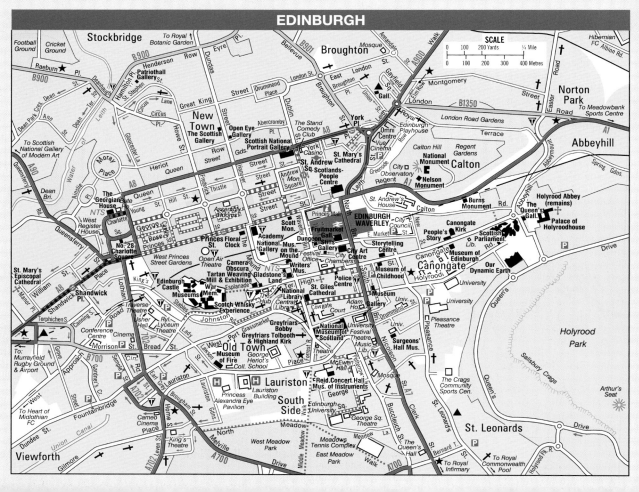

EXETER

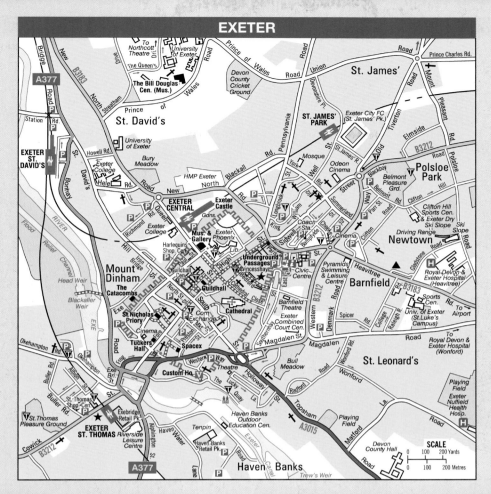

EASTBOURNE

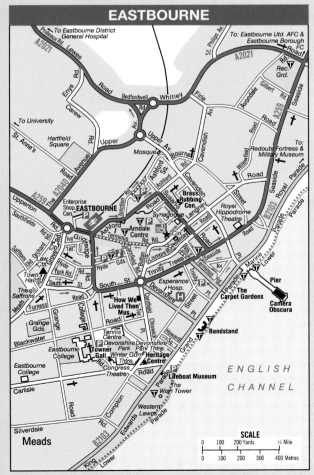

FOLKESTONE

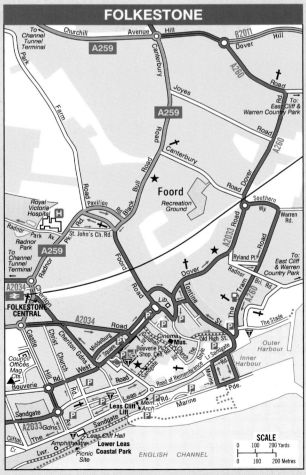

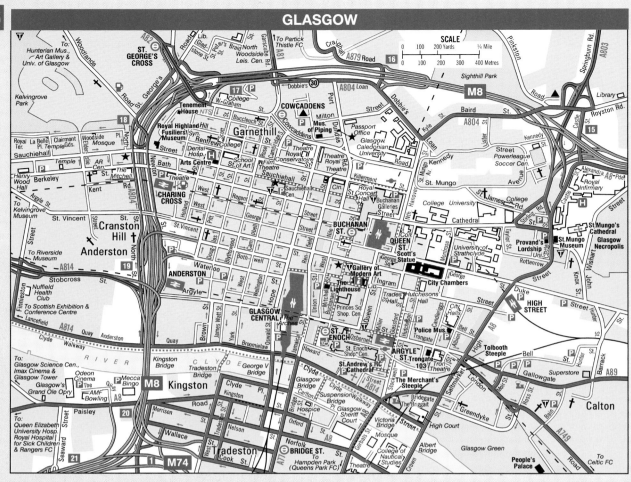

GLOUCESTER

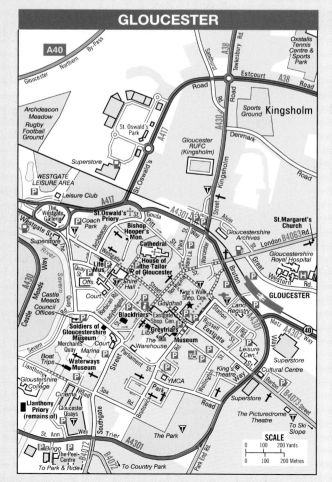

GREAT YARMOUTH

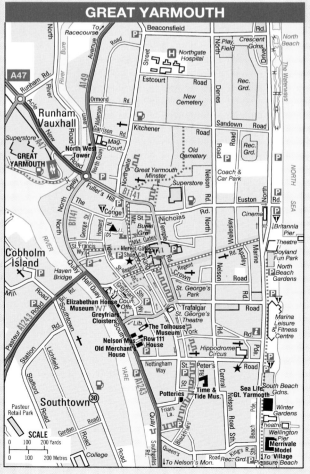

GUILDFORD

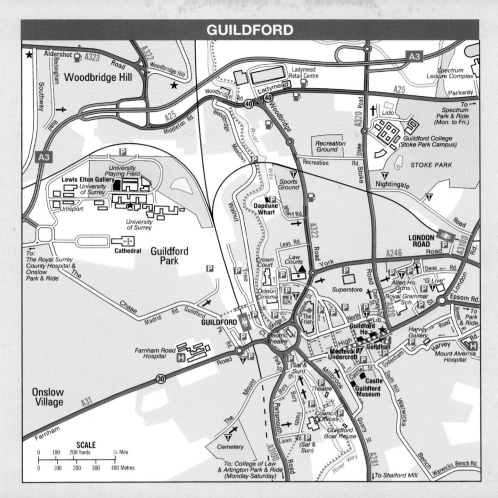

HARROGATE

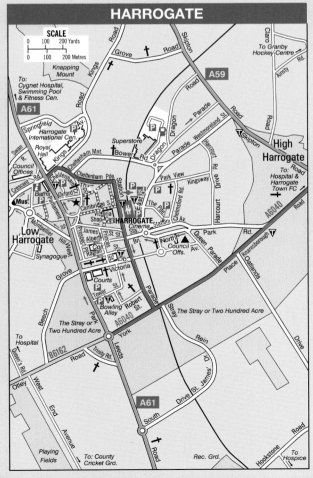

HEREFORD

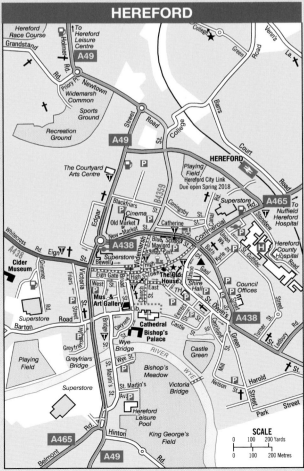

INVERNESS

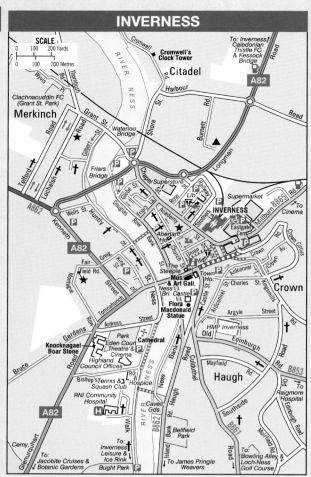

IPSWICH

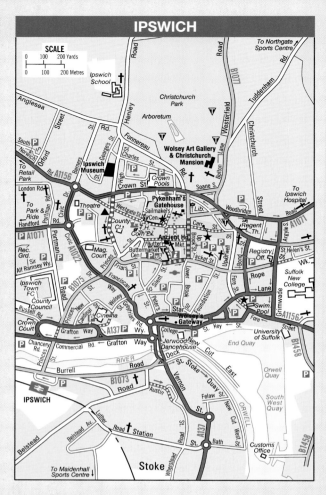

KILMARNOCK

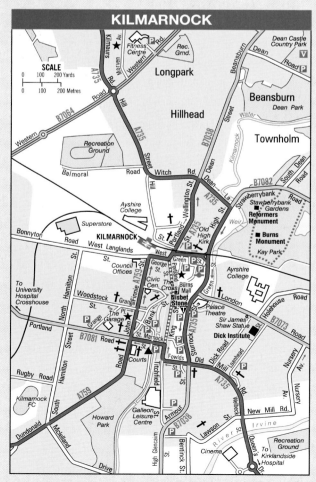

LINCOLN

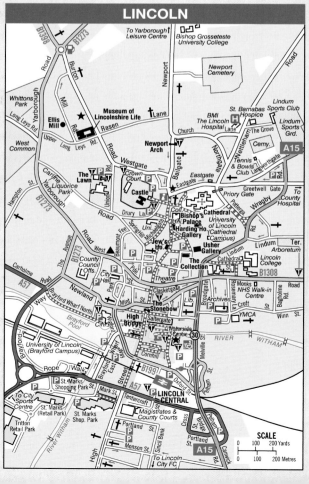

KINGSTON upon HULL

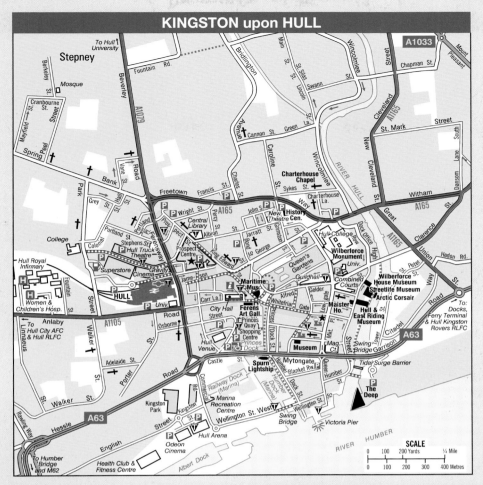

LEEDS

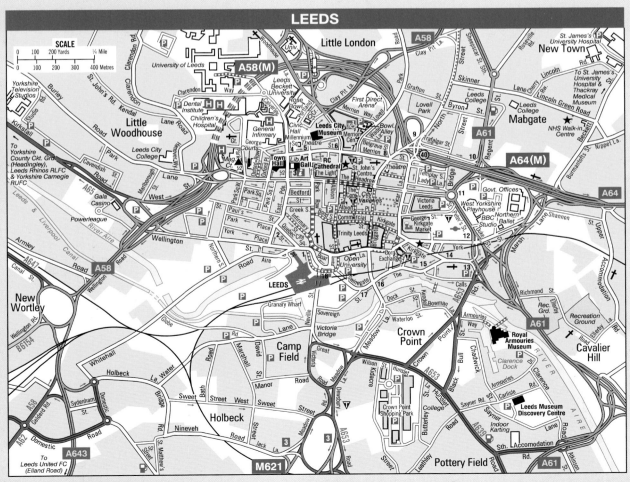

LEICESTER

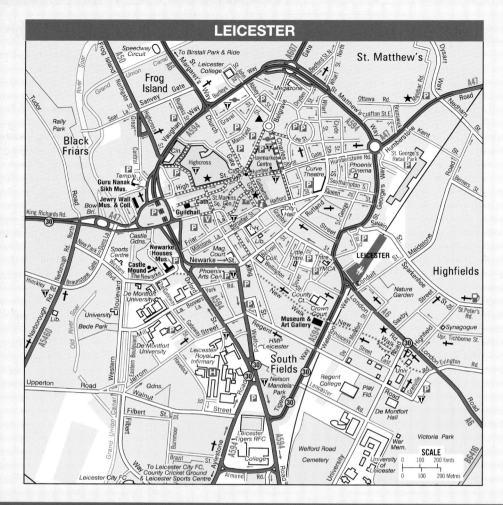

LIVERPOOL

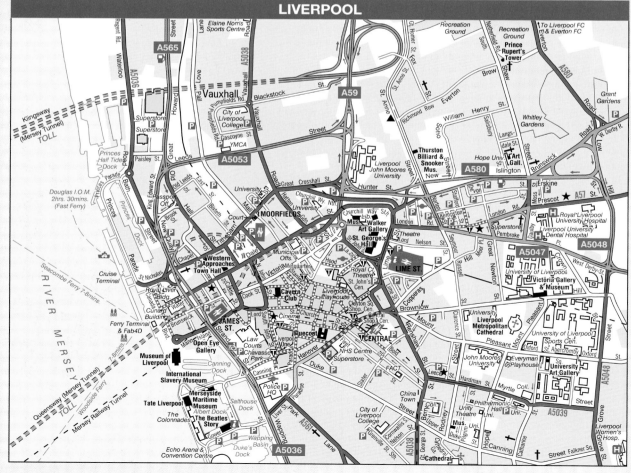

LUTON

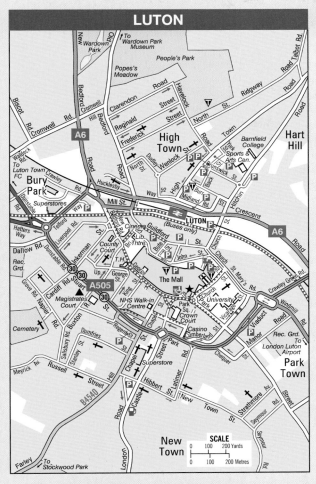

MIDDLESBROUGH

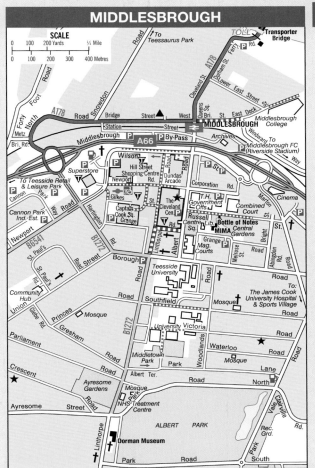

MANCHESTER (CITY CENTRE)

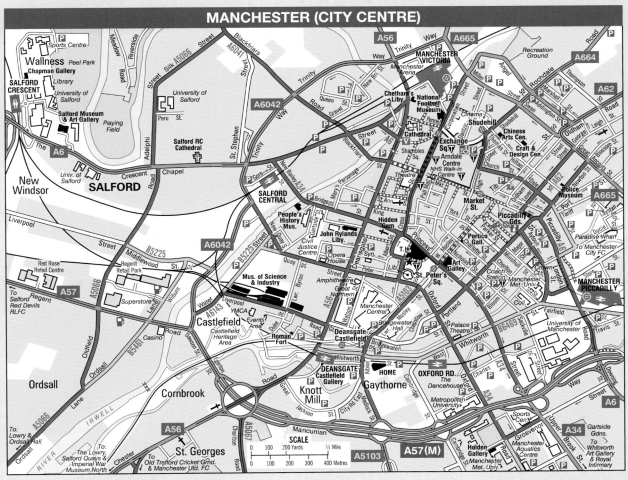

St. John's Wood • Maida Vale • Warwick Avenue • Paddington • Westbourne Green • Royal Oak • Bayswater • Queensway • Lancaster Gate

REGENT'S PARK • Regent's Park • London Zoo • Snowdon Aviary • The Hub • Queen Mary's Gardens • Regent's University London • Royal Academy of Music • Mornington Crescent • Somers Town • Euston • Euston Square • Warren St. • Great Portland St. • Goodge St.

Marylebone • Baker St. • Madame Tussaud's • Sherlock Holmes Museum • Wallace Collection • Oxford Circus • Bond St. • Soho • West End • Tottenham Court Rd. • Marble Arch • Speakers' Corner

HYDE PARK • The Serpentine • 7/7 Memorial • Hyde Park Corner • Apsley Ho. • Mayfair • Piccadilly Circus • Green Park • St. James's • St. James's Palace • Clarence House • Lancaster House • Queen Victoria Memorial • Buckingham Palace • The Queen's Gallery • The Royal Mews • St. James's Park

KENSINGTON GARDENS • Round Pond • Kensington Palace • Serpentine Gallery • Serpentine Sackler Gallery • Diana, Princess of Wales Memorial Fountain • Albert Memorial • Royal Albert Hall • Royal College of Art • Royal College of Music • Imperial College • Science Museum • Natural History Museum • Victoria & Albert Museum • Brompton Oratory • High St. Kensington • Gloucester Road • South Kensington • Knightsbridge • Harrods • Belgravia • Sloane Square • Victoria • Westminster AC Cathedral • Pimlico

Chelsea • West Brompton • Royal Hospital Chelsea • National Army Museum • Chilianwalla Memorial • Chelsea Physic Garden • Carlyle's House • Saatchi Gallery • Royal Brompton Hospital • Chelsea and Westminster Hospital

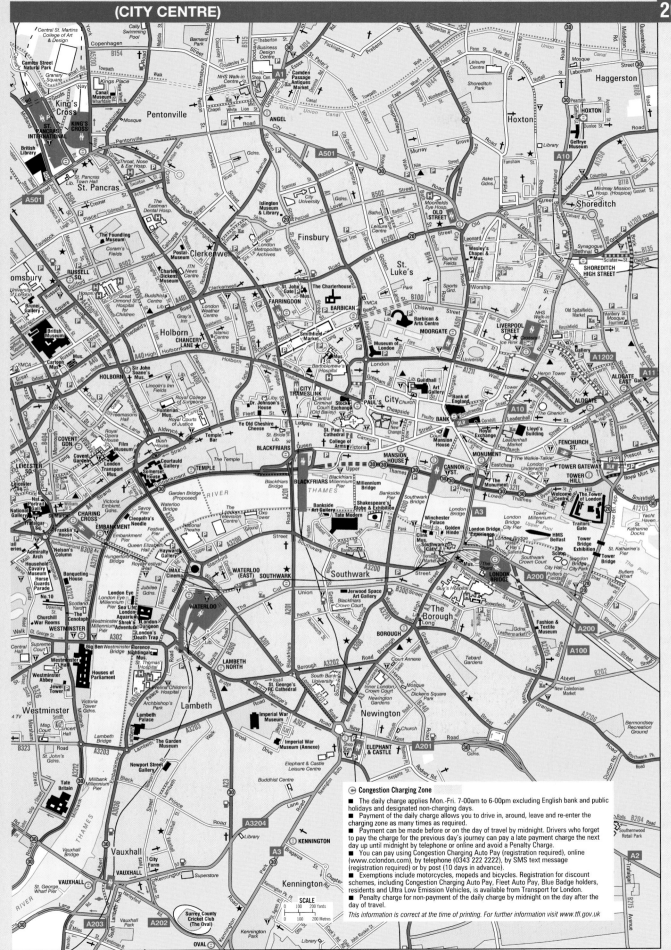

MEDWAY TOWNS

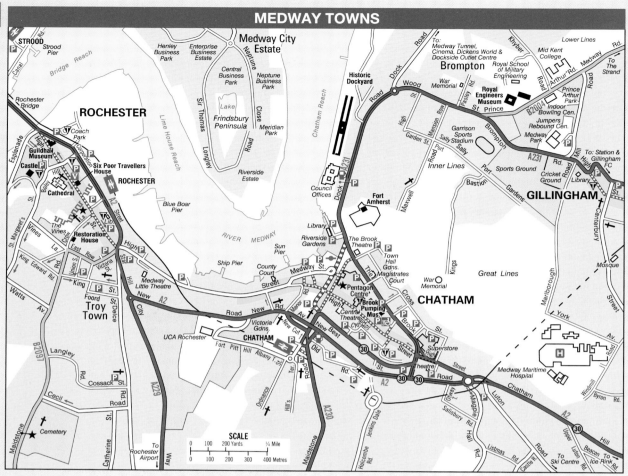

MILTON KEYNES

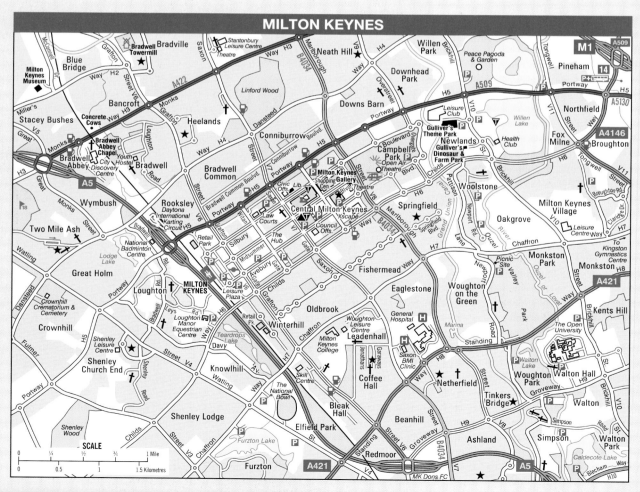

NORWICH

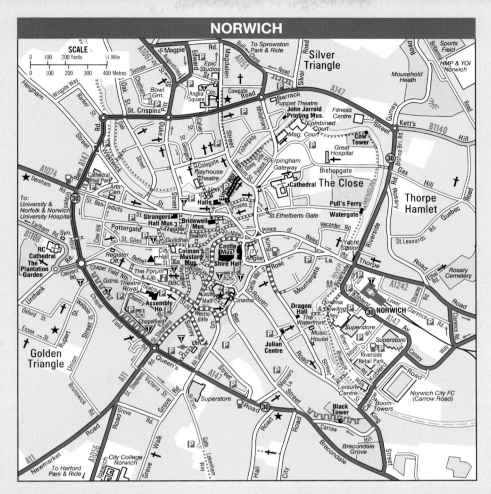

NEWCASTLE UPON TYNE

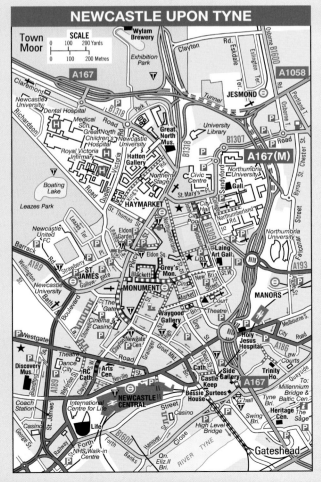

NEWPORT (CASNEWYDD)

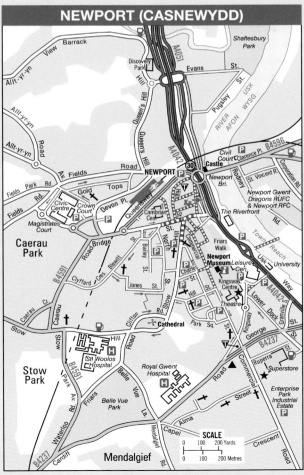

NOTTINGHAM

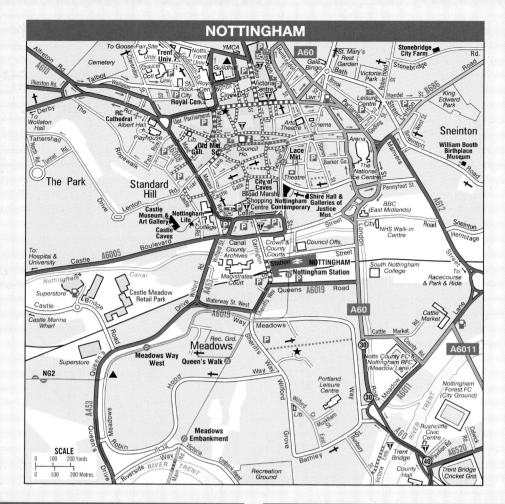

NORTHAMPTON

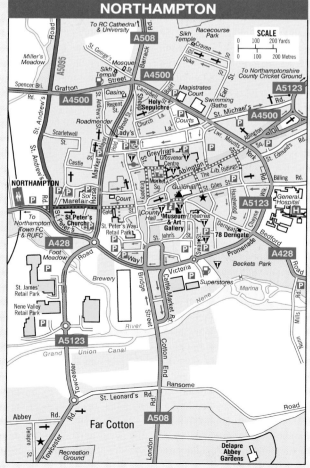

OBAN

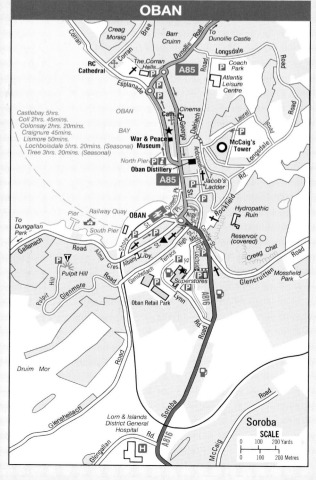

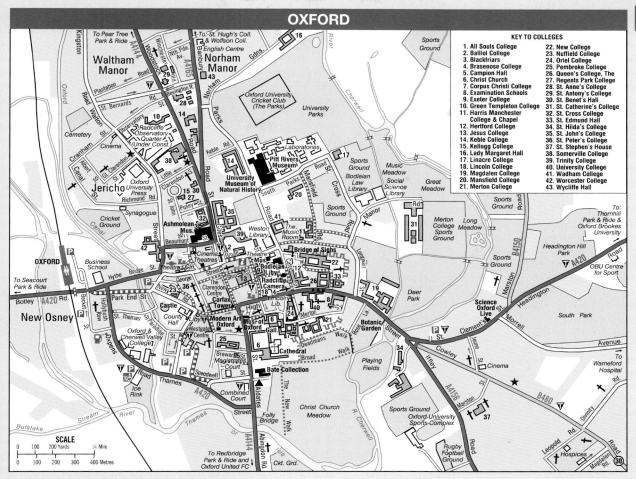

KEY TO COLLEGES

1. All Souls College
2. Balliol College
3. Blackfriars
4. Brasenose College
5. Campion Hall
6. Christ Church
7. Corpus Christi College
8. Examination Schools
9. Exeter College
10. Green Templeton College
11. Harris Manchester College & Chapel
12. Hertford College
13. Jesus College
14. Keble College
15. Kellogg College
16. Lady Margaret Hall
17. Linacre College
18. Lincoln College
19. Magdalen College
20. Mansfield College
21. Merton College
22. New College
23. Nuffield College
24. Oriel College
25. Pembroke College
26. Queen's College, The
27. Regents Park College
28. St. Anne's College
29. St. Antony's College
30. St. Benet's Hall
31. St. Catherine's College
32. St. Cross College
33. St. Edmund Hall
34. St. Hilda's College
35. St. John's College
36. St. Peter's College
37. St. Stephen's House
38. Somerville College
39. Trinity College
40. University College
41. Wadham College
42. Worcester College
43. Wycliffe Hall

PAISLEY

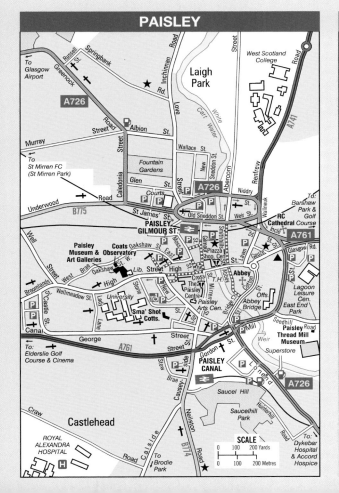

PERTH

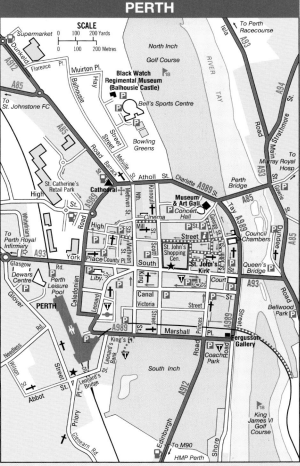

PLYMOUTH

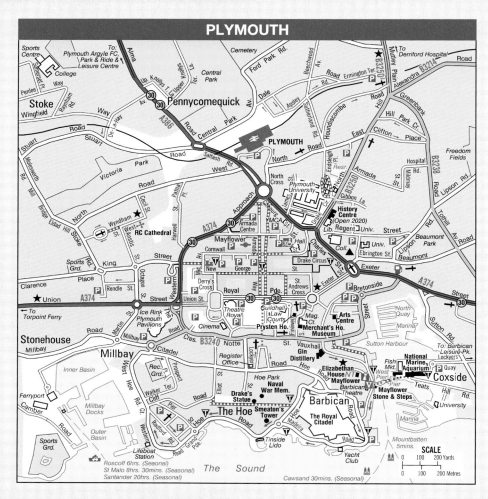

PETERBOROUGH

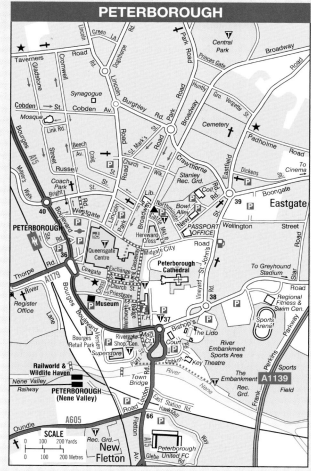

PRESTON

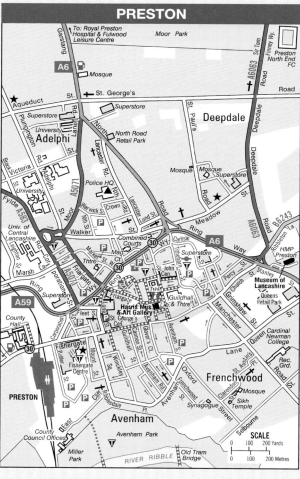

PORTSMOUTH

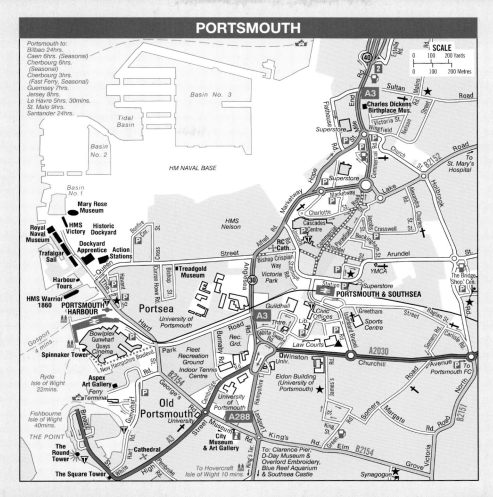

READING

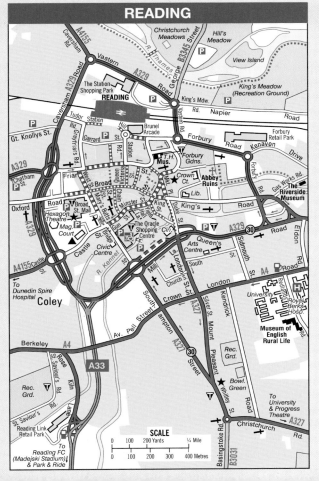

ST ANDREWS

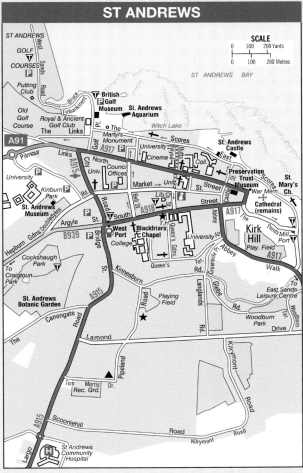

SALISBURY

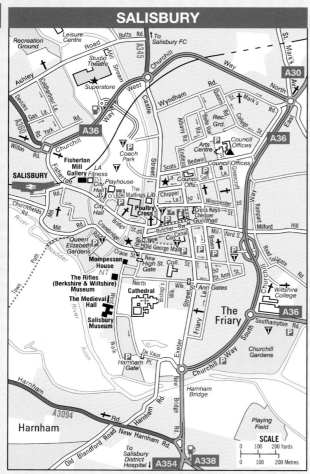

SHREWSBURY

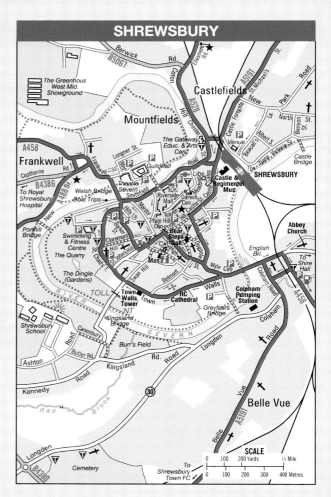

SHEFFIELD

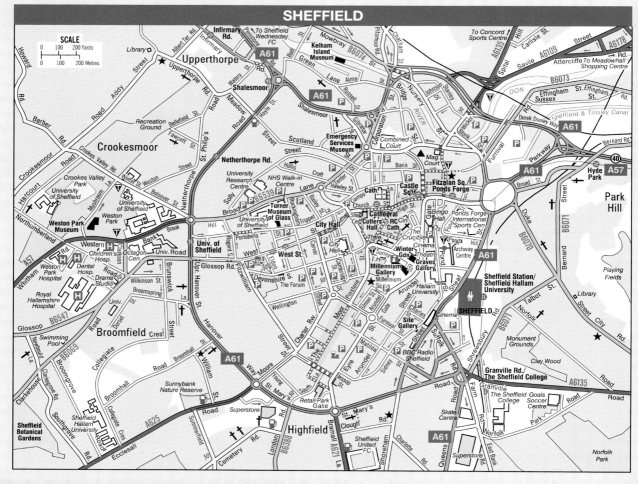

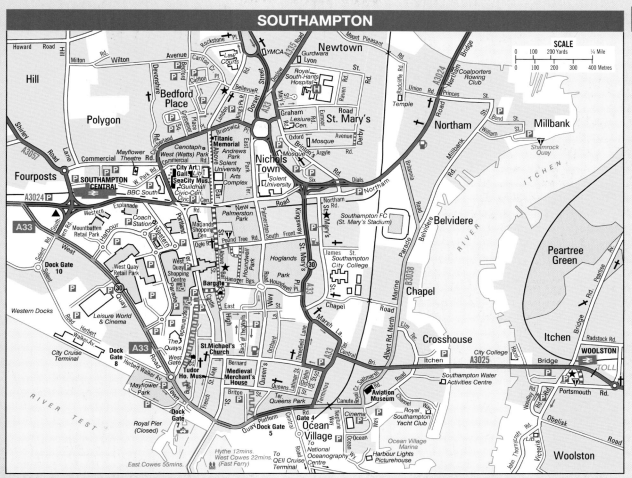

STIRLING

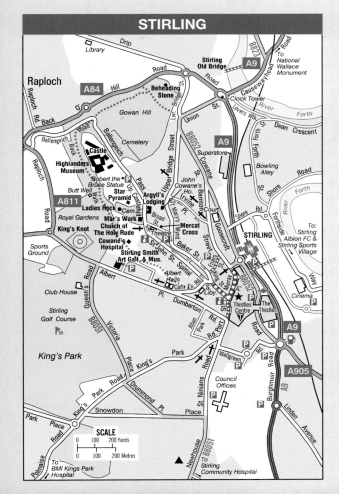

STOKE-ON-TRENT

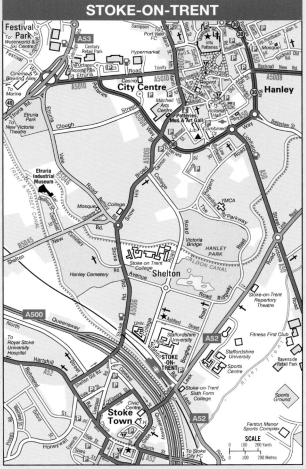

STRATFORD upon AVON

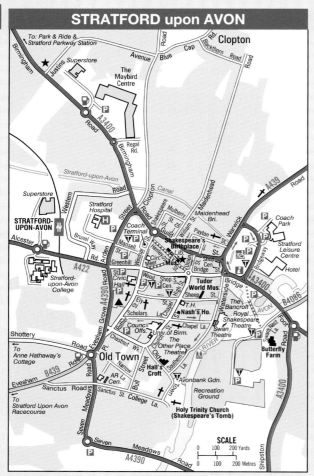

SUNDERLAND

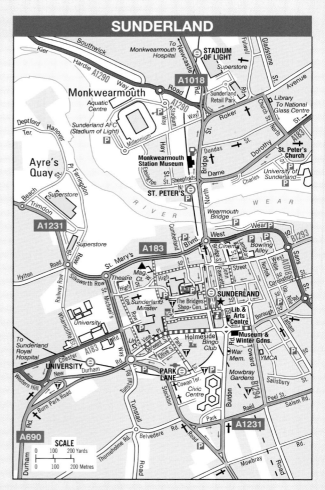

SWANSEA (ABERTAWE)

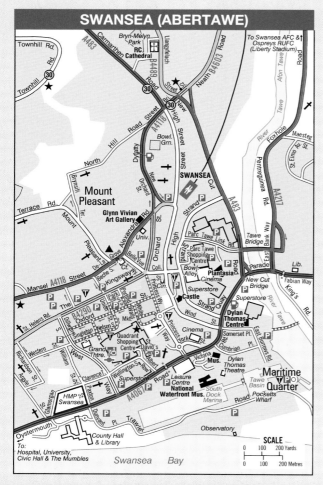

SWINDON

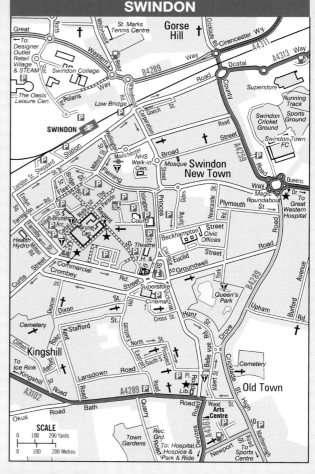

TAUNTON

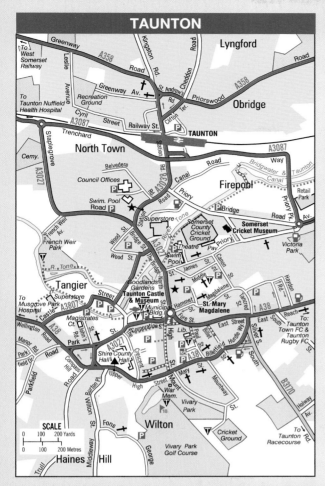

WINCHESTER

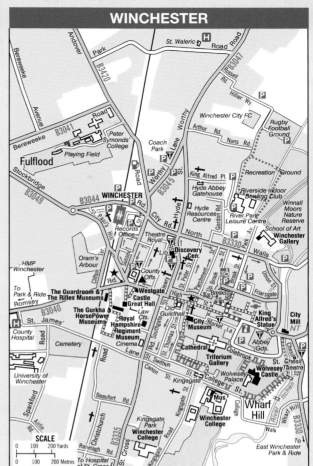

WINDSOR

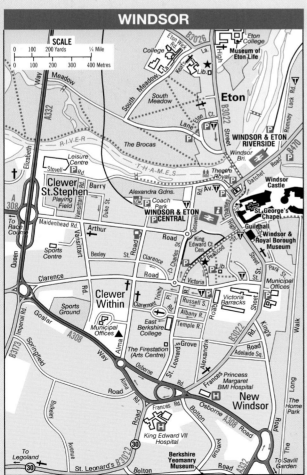

WOLVERHAMPTON

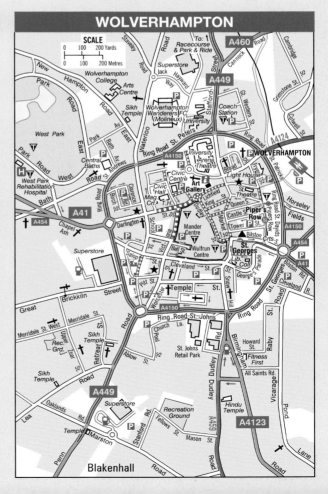

WORCESTER

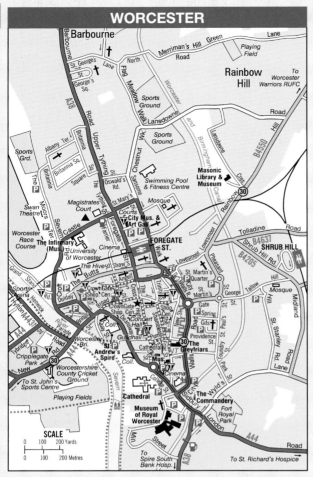

WREXHAM (WRECSAM)

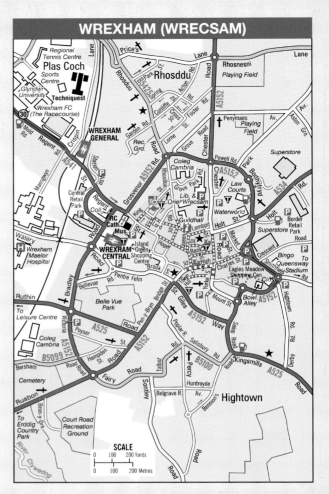

YORK

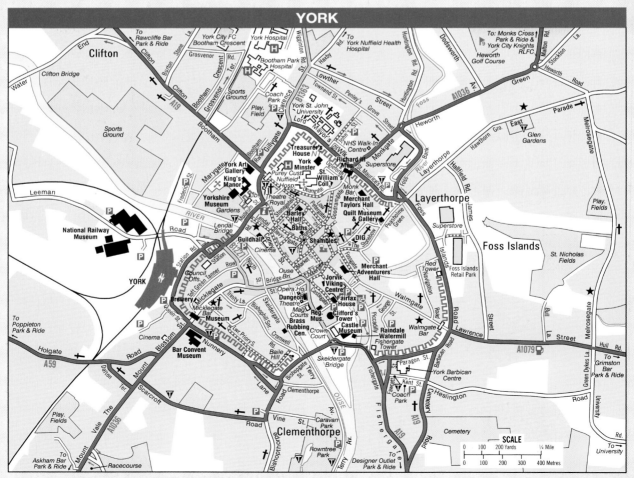

HARWICH

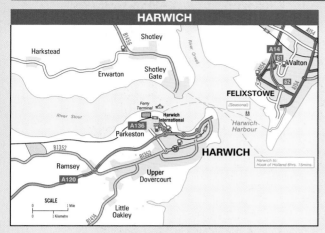

KINGSTON UPON HULL

NEWCASTLE UPON TYNE

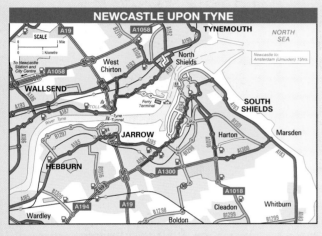

NEWHAVEN

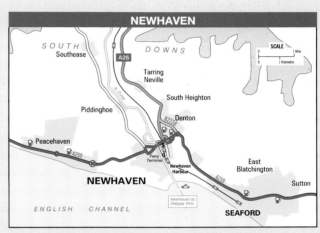

PEMBROKE DOCK (DOC PENFRO)

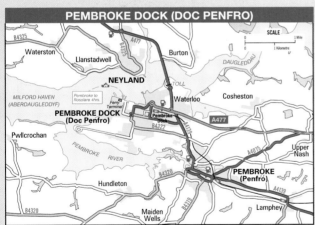

POOLE

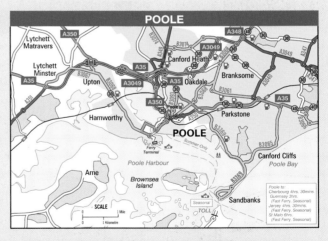

PORTSMOUTH

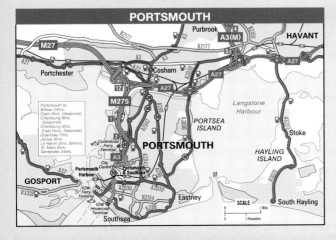

WEYMOUTH

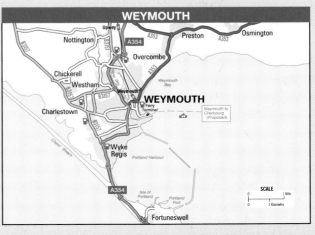

BIRMINGHAM

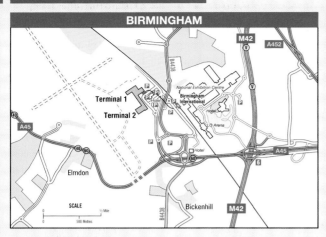

EAST MIDLANDS

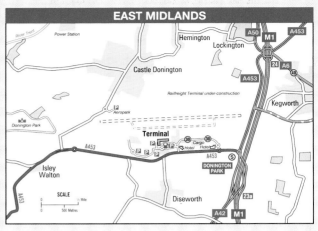

GLASGOW

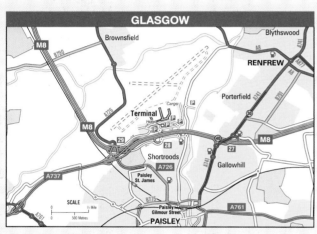

LONDON GATWICK

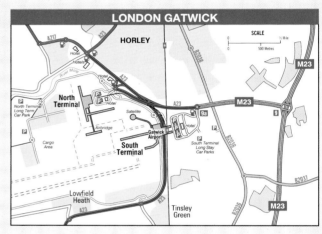

LONDON HEATHROW

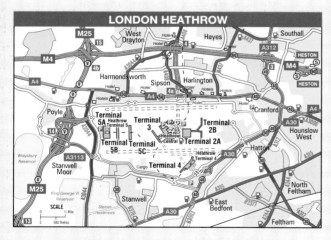

LONDON LUTON

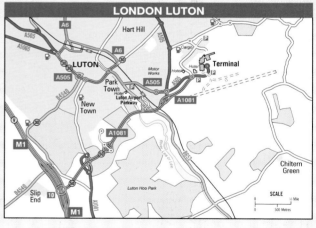

LONDON STANSTED

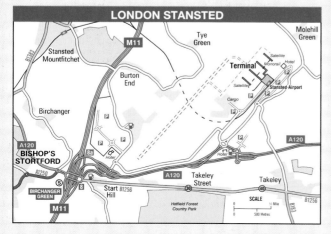

MANCHESTER

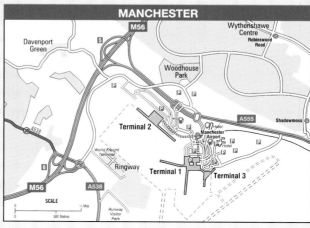

INDEX TO CITIES, TOWNS, VILLAGES, HAMLETS, LOCATIONS, AIRPORTS & PORTS

(1) A strict alphabetical order is used e.g. An Dùnan follows Andreas but precedes Andwell.

(2) The map reference given refers to the actual map square in which the town spot or built-up area is located and not to the place name.

(3) Major towns and destinations are shown in bold, i.e. **Aberdeen.** *Aber* **187** (3G **153**)
Page references for Town Plan entries are shown first.

(4) Where two or more places of the same name occur in the same County or Unitary Authority, the nearest large town is also given; e.g. Achiemore. High nr. Durness . . .2D **166** indicates that Achiemore is located in square 2D on page **166** and is situated near Durness in the Unitary Authority of Highland.

(5) Only one reference is given although due to page overlaps the place may appear on more than one page.

COUNTIES and UNITARY AUTHORITIES with the abbreviations used in this index

Aberdeen : *Aber*
Aberdeenshire : *Abers*
Angus : *Ang*
Argyll & Bute : *Arg*
Bath & N E Somerset : *Bath*
Bedford : *Bed*
Blackburn with Darwen : *Bkbn*
Blackpool : *Bkpl*
Blaenau Gwent : *Blae*
Bournemouth : *Bour*
Bracknell Forest : *Brac*
Bridgend : *B'end*
Brighton & Hove : *Brig*
Bristol : *Bris*
Buckinghamshire : *Buck*
Caerphilly : *Cphy*
Cambridgeshire : *Cambs*
Cardiff : *Card*
Carmarthenshire : *Carm*
Central Bedfordshire : *C Beds*
Ceredigion : *Cdgn*
Cheshire East : *Ches E*
Cheshire West & Chester : *Ches W*
Clackmannanshire : *Clac*
Conwy : *Cnwy*
Cornwall : *Corn*
Cumbria : *Cumb*
Darlington : *Darl*
Denbighshire : *Den*

Derby : *Derb*
Derbyshire : *Derbs*
Devon : *Devn*
Dorset : *Dors*
Dumfries & Galloway : *Dum*
Dundee : *D'dee*
Durham : *Dur*
East Ayrshire : *E Ayr*
East Dunbartonshire : *E Dun*
East Lothian : *E Lot*
East Renfrewshire : *E Ren*
East Riding of Yorkshire : *E Yor*
East Sussex : *E Sus*
Edinburgh : *Edin*
Essex : *Essx*
Falkirk : *Falk*
Fife : *Fife*
Flintshire : *Flin*
Glasgow : *Glas*
Gloucestershire : *Glos*
Greater London : *G Lon*
Greater Manchester : *G Man*
Gwynedd : *Gwyn*
Halton : *Hal*
Hampshire : *Hants*
Hartlepool : *Hart*
Herefordshire : *Here*
Hertfordshire : *Herts*
Highland : *High*

Inverclyde : *Inv*
Isle of Anglesey : *IOA*
Isle of Man : *IOM*
Isle of Wight : *IOW*
Isles of Scilly : *IOS*
Kent : *Kent*
Kingston upon Hull : *Hull*
Lancashire : *Lanc*
Leicester : *Leic*
Leicestershire : *Leics*
Lincolnshire : *Linc*
Luton : *Lutn*
Medway : *Medw*
Merseyside : *Mers*
Merthyr Tydfil : *Mer T*
Middlesbrough : *Midd*
Midlothian : *Midl*
Milton Keynes : *Mil*
Monmouthshire : *Mon*
Moray : *Mor*
Neath Port Talbot : *Neat*
Newport : *Newp*
Norfolk : *Norf*
Northamptonshire : *Nptn*
North Ayrshire : *N Ayr*
North East Lincolnshire : *NE Lin*
North Lanarkshire : *N Lan*
North Lincolnshire : *N Lin*
North Somerset : *N Som*

Northumberland : *Nmbd*
North Yorkshire : *N Yor*
Nottingham : *Nott*
Nottinghamshire : *Notts*
Orkney : *Orkn*
Oxfordshire : *Oxon*
Pembrokeshire : *Pemb*
Perth & Kinross : *Per*
Peterborough : *Pet*
Plymouth : *Plym*
Poole : *Pool*
Portsmouth : *Port*
Powys : *Powy*
Reading : *Read*
Redcar & Cleveland : *Red C*
Renfrewshire : *Ren*
Rhondda Cynon Taff : *Rhon*
Rutland : *Rut*
Scottish Borders : *Bord*
Shetland : *Shet*
Shropshire : *Shrp*
Slough : *Slo*
Somerset : *Som*
Southampton : *Sotn*
South Ayrshire : *S Ayr*
Southend-on-Sea : *S'end*
South Gloucestershire : *S Glo*
South Lanarkshire : *S Lan*
South Yorkshire : *S Yor*

Staffordshire : *Staf*
Stirling : *Stir*
Stockton-on-Tees : *Stoc T*
Stoke-on-Trent : *Stoke*
Suffolk : *Suff*
Surrey : *Surr*
Swansea : *Swan*
Swindon : *Swin*
Telford & Wrekin : *Telf*
Thurrock : *Thur*
Torbay : *Torb*
Torfaen : *Torf*
Tyne & Wear : *Tyne*
Vale of Glamorgan, The : *V Glam*
Warrington : *Warr*
Warwickshire : *Warw*
West Berkshire : *W Ber*
West Dunbartonshire : *W Dun*
Western Isles : *W Isl*
West Lothian : *W Lot*
West Midlands : *W Mid*
West Sussex : *W Sus*
West Yorkshire : *W Yor*
Wiltshire : *Wilts*
Windsor & Maidenhead : *Wind*
Wokingham : *Wok*
Worcestershire : *Worc*
Wrexham : *Wrex*
York : *York*

INDEX

A

Abbas Combe. Som 4C 22
Abberley. Worc 4B 60
Abberley Common. Worc 4B 60
Abberton. Essx 4D 54
Abberton. Worc 5D 61
Abberwick. Nmbd 3F 121
Abbess Roding. Essx 4F 53
Abbey. Devn 1E 13
Abbey-cwm-hir. Powy 3C 58
Abbeydale. S Yor 2H 85
Abbeydale Park. S Yor 2H 85
Abbey Dore. Here 2G 47
Abbey Gate. Devn 3F 13
Abbey Hulton. Stoke 1D 72
Abbey St Bathans. Bord 3D 130
Abbeystead. Lanc 4E 97
Abbeytown. Cumb 4C 112
Abbey Village. Lanc 2E 91
Abbey Wood. G Lon 3F 39
Abbots Bickington. Devn 1D 11
Abbots Bromley. Staf 3E 73
Abbotsbury. Dors 4A 14
Abbotsham. Devn 4E 19
Abbotskerswell. Devn 2E 9
Abbots Langley. Herts 5A 52
Abbots Leigh. N Som 4A 34
Abbotsley. Cambs 5B 64
Abbots Morton. Worc 5E 61
Abbots Ripton. Cambs 3B 64
Abbot's Salford. Warw 5E 61
Abbotstone. Hants 3D 24
Abbots Worthy. Hants 3C 24
Abbotts Ann. Hants 2B 24
Abcott. Shrp 3F 59
Abdon. Shrp 2H 59
Abenhall. Glos 4B 48
Aber. Cdgn 1E 45
Aberaeron. Cdgn 4D 56
Aberafan. Neat 3G 31
Aberaman. Rhon 5D 46
Aberangell. Gwyn 4H 69
Aberarad. Carm 1H 43
Aberarder. High 1A 150
Aberargie. Per 2D 136
Aberarth. Cdgn 4D 57
Aberavon. Neat 3G 31
Aber-banc. Cdgn 1D 44
Aberbargoed. Cphy 2E 33
Aberbechan. Powy 1D 58
Aberbeeg. Blae 5F 47
Aberbowlan. Carm 2G 45
Aberbran. Powy 3C 46
Abercanaid. Mer T 5D 46
Abercarn. Cphy 2F 33
Abercastle. Pemb 1C 42
Abercegir. Powy 5H 69
Aberchalder. High 3F 149
Aberchirder. Abers 3D 160
Aberchwiler. Den 4C 82
Abercorn. W Lot 2D 129
Abercraf. Powy 4B 46
Abercregan. Neat 2B 32
Abercrombie. Fife 3H 137
Abercwmboi. Rhon 2D 32
Abercych. Pemb 1C 44
Abercynon. Rhon 2D 32
Aber-Cywarch. Gwyn 4A 70
Aberdalgie. Per 1C 136
Aberdar. Rhon 5C 46
Aberdare. Rhon 5C 46
Aberdaron. Gwyn 3A 68
Aberdaugleddau. Pemb 4D 42
Aberdeen. Aber **187** (3G **153**)
Aberdeen International Airport.
Aber 2F **153**

Aberdesach. Gwyn 5D 80
Aberdour. Fife 1E 129
Aberdovey. Gwyn 1F 57
Aberdulais. Neat 5A 46
Aberdyfi. Gwyn 1F 57
Aberedw. Powy 1D 46
Abereiddy. Pemb 1B 42
Abererch. Gwyn 2C 68
Aberfan. Mer T 5D 46
Aberfeldy. Per 4F 143
Aberffraw. IOA 4C 80
Aberffrwd. Cdgn 3F 57
Aberford. W Yor 1E 93
Aberfoyle. Stir 3E 135
Abergarw. B'end 3C 32
Abergarwed. Neat 5B 46
Abergavenny. Mon 4G 47
Abergele. Cnwy 3B 82
Aber-Giâr. Carm 1F 45
Abergorlech. Carm 2F 45
Abergwaun. Pemb 1D 42
Abergwesyn. Powy 5A 58
Abergwili. Carm 3E 45
Abergwynfi. Neat 2B 32
Abergwyngregyn. Gwyn 3F 81
Abergwynolwyn. Gwyn 5F 69
Aberhafesp. Powy 1C 58
Aberhonddu. Powy 3D 46
Aberhosan. Powy 1H 57
Aberkenfig. B'end 3B 32
Aberlady. E Lot 1A 130
Aberlemno. Ang 3E 145
Aberllefenni. Gwyn 5G 69
Abermaw. Gwyn 4F 69
Abermeurig. Cdgn 5E 57
Aber-miwl. Powy 1D 58
Abermule. Powy 1D 58
Abernant. Carm 2H 43
Abernant. Rhon 5D 46
Abernethy. Per 2D 136
Abernyte. Per 5B 144
Aber-oer. Wrex 1E 71
Aberpennar. Rhon 2D 32
Aberporth. Cdgn 5B 56
Aberriw. Powy 5D 70
Abersoch. Gwyn 3C 68
Abersychan. Torf 5F 47
Abertawe. Swan **212** (3F **31**)
Aberteifi. Cdgn 1B 44
Aberthin. V Glam 4D 32
Abertillery. Blae 5F 47
Abertridwr. Cphy 3E 32
Abertridwr. Powy 4C 70
Abertyleri. Blae 5F 47
Abertysswg. Cphy 5E 47
Aberuthven. Per 2B 136
Aber Village. Powy 3E 46
Aberwheeler. Den 4C 82
Aberyscir. Powy 3C 46
Aberystwyth. Cdgn **187** (2E **57**)
Abhainn Suidhe. W Isl 7C 171
Abingdon-on-Thames. Oxon 2C 36
Abinger Common. Surr 1C 26
Abinger Hammer. Surr 1B 26
Abington. S Lan 2B 118
Abington Pigotts. Cambs 1D 52
Ab Kettleby. Leics 3E 74
Ab Lench. Worc 5E 61
Ablington. Glos 5G 49
Ablington. Wilts 2G 23
Abney. Derbs 3F 85
Aboyne. Abers 4C 152
Abram. G Man 4E 90
Abriachan. High 5H 157
Abridge. Essx 1F 39
Abronhill. N Lan 2A 128
Abson. S Glo 4C 34
Abthorpe. Nptn 1E 51

Abune-the-Hill. Orkn 5B 172
Aby. Linc 3D 88
Acairseid. W Isl 8C 170
Acaster Malbis. York 5H 99
Acaster Selby. N Yor 5H 99
Accott. Devn 3G 19
Accrington. Lanc 2F 91
Acha. Arg 3C 138
Achachork. High 4D 155
Achadh a' Chuirn. High 1E 147
Achahoish. Arg 2F 125
Achaleven. Arg 5D 140
Achallader. Arg 4H 141
Acha Mor. W Isl 5F 171
Achanalt. High 2E 157
Achandunie. High 1A 158
Ach' an Todhair. High 1E 141
Achany. High 3C 164
Achaphubuil. High 1E 141
Acharacle. High 2A 140
Acharn. Ang 1B 144
Acharn. Per 4E 143
Acharole. High 3E 169
Achateny. High 2G 139
Achavanich. High 4D 169
Achdalieu. High 1E 141
Achduart. High 3E 163
Achentoul. High 5A 168
Achfary. High 5C 166
Achfrish. High 2C 164
Achgarve. High 4C 162
Achiemore. High
  nr. Durness 2D 166
  nr. Thurso 3A 168
A' Chill. High 3A 146
Achiltibuie. High 3E 163
Achina. High 2H 167
Achinahuagh. High 2F 167
Achindarroch. High 3E 141
Achinduich. High 3C 164
Achinduin. Arg 5C 140
Achininver. High 2F 167
Achintee. High 4B 156
Achintraid. High 5H 155
Achleck. Arg 4F 139
Achlorachan. High 3F 157
Achluachrach. High 5E 149
Achlyness. High 3C 166
Achmelvich. High 1E 163
Achmony. High 5H 157
Achmore. High
  nr. Stromeferry 5A 156
  nr. Ullapool 4E 163
Achnacarnin. High 1E 163
Achnacarry. High 5D 148
Achnaclerach. High 2G 157
Achnacloich. High 3D 147
Achnaconeran. High 2G 149
Achnacroish. Arg 4C 140
Achnafalnich. Arg 1B 134
Achnagarron. High 1A 158
Achnagoul. Arg 3H 133
Achnaha. High 2F 139
Achnahanat. High 4C 164
Achnahannet. High 1D 151
Achnairn. High 2C 164
Achnamara. Arg 1F 125
Achnanellan. High 5C 148
Achnasheen. High 3D 156
Achnashellach. High 4C 156
Achosnich. High 2F 139
Achow. High 5E 169
Achranich. High 4B 140
Achreamie. High 2C 168
Achriabhach. High 2F 141
Achriesgill. High 3C 166
Achrimsdale. High 3G 165

Achscrabster. High 2C 168
Achtoty. High 2G 167
Achurch. Nptn 2H 63
Achuvoldrach. High 3F 167
Achvaich. High 4E 164
Achvoan. High 3E 165
Ackenthwaite. Cumb 1E 97
Ackergill. High 3F 169
Ackergillshore. High 3F 169
Acklam. Midd 3B 106
Acklam. N Yor 3B 100
Ackleton. Shrp 1B 60
Acklington. Nmbd 4G 121
Ackton. W Yor 2E 93
Ackworth Moor Top. W Yor 3E 93
Acle. Norf 4G 79
Acocks Green. W Mid 2F 61
Acol. Kent 4H 41
Acomb. Nmbd 3C 114
Acomb. York 4H 99
Aconbury. Here 2A 48
Acre. G Man 4H 91
Acre. Lanc 2F 91
Acrefair. Wrex 1E 71
Acrise. Kent 1F 29
Acton. Ches E 5A 84
Acton. Dors 5E 15
Acton. G Lon 2C 38
Acton. Shrp 2F 59
Acton. Staf 1C 72
Acton. Suff 1B 54
Acton. Worc 4C 60
Acton. Wrex 5F 83
Acton Beauchamp. Here 5A 60
Acton Bridge. Ches W 3H 83
Acton Burnell. Shrp 5H 71
Acton Green. Here 5A 60
Acton Pigott. Shrp 5H 71
Acton Round. Shrp 1A 60
Acton Scott. Shrp 2G 59
Acton Trussell. Staf 4D 72
Acton Turville. S Glo 3D 34
Adabroc. W Isl 1H 171
Adam's Hill. Worc 3D 60
Adbaston. Staf 3B 72
Adber. Dors 4B 22
Adderbury. Oxon 2C 50
Adderley. Shrp 2A 72
Adderstone. Nmbd 1F 121
Addiewell. W Lot 3C 128
Addingham. W Yor 5C 98
Addington. Buck 3F 51
Addington. G Lon 4E 39
Addington. Kent 5A 40
Addinston. Bord 4B 130
Addiscombe. G Lon 4E 39
Addlestone. Surr 4B 38
Addlethorpe. Linc 4E 89
Adeney. Telf 4B 72
Adfa. Powy 5C 70
Adforton. Here 3G 59
Adgestone. IOW 4D 16
Adisham. Kent 5G 41
Adlestrop. Glos 3H 49
Adlingfleet. E Yor 2B 94
Adlington. Ches E 2D 84
Adlington. Lanc 3E 90
Admaston. Staf 3E 73
Admaston. Telf 4A 72
Admington. Warw 1H 49
Adpar. Cdgn 1D 44
Adsborough. Som 4F 21
Adstock. Buck 2F 51
Adstone. Nptn 5C 62
Adversane. W Sus 3B 26
Advie. High 5F 159
Adwalton. W Yor 2C 92
Adwell. Oxon 2E 37

Adwick le Street. S Yor 4F 93
Adwick upon Dearne.
  S Yor 4E 93
Adziel. Abers 3G 161
Ae. Dum 1A 112
Affleck. Abers 1F 153
Affpuddle. Dors 3D 14
Affric Lodge. High 1D 148
Afon-wen. Flin 3D 82
Agglethorpe. N Yor 1C 98
Aglionby. Cumb 4F 113
Aigburth. Mers 2F 83
Aiginis. W Isl 4G 171
Aike. E Yor 5E 101
Aikers. Orkn 8D 172
Aiketgate. Cumb 5F 113
Aikhead. Cumb 5D 112
Aikton. Cumb 4D 112
Ailey. Here 1G 47
Ailsworth. Pet 1A 64
Ainderby Quernhow. N Yor 1F 99
Ainderby Steeple. N Yor 5A 106
Aingers Green. Essx 3E 54
Ainsdale. Mers 3B 90
Ainsdale-on-Sea. Mers 3B 90
Ainstable. Cumb 5G 113
Ainsworth. G Man 3F 91
Ainthorpe. N Yor 4E 107
Aintree. Mers 1F 83
Aird. Arg 3E 133
Aird. Dum 3F 109
Aird. High
  nr. Port Henderson 1G 155
  nr. Tarskavaig 3D 147
Aird, The. High 3D 154
Aird. W Isl
  on Benbecula 3C 170
  on Isle of Lewis 4H 171
Àird a Bhasair. High 3E 147
Aird a Mhachair. W Isl 4C 170
Aird a Mhulaidh. W Isl 6D 171
Aird Asaig. W Isl 7D 171
Aird Dhail. W Isl 1G 171
Airdens. High 4D 164
Airdeny. Arg 1G 133
Aird Mhidhinis. W Isl 8C 170
Aird Mhighe. W Isl
  nr. Ceann a Bhaigh 8D 171
  nr. Fionnsabhagh 9C 171
Aird Mhor. W Isl
  on Barra 8C 170
  on South Uist 4D 170
Airdrie. N Lan 3A 128
Aird Shleibhe. W Isl 9D 171
Aird Thunga. W Isl 4G 171
Aird Uig. W Isl 4C 171
Airedale. W Yor 2E 93
Airidh a Bhruaich. W Isl 6E 171
Airies. Dum 3E 109
Airmyn. E Yor 2H 93
Airntully. Per 5H 143
Airor. High 3F 147
Airth. Falk 1C 128
Airton. N Yor 4B 98
Aisby. Linc
  nr. Gainsborough 1F 87
  nr. Grantham 2H 75
Aisgernis. W Isl 6C 170
Aish. Devn
  nr. Buckfastleigh 2C 8
  nr. Totnes 3E 9
Aisholt. Som 3E 21
Aiskew. N Yor 1E 99
Aislaby. N Yor
  nr. Pickering 1B 100
  nr. Whitby 4F 107
Aislaby. Stoc T 3B 106
Aisthorpe. Linc 2G 87

Aith. *Shet*
  on Fetlar 3H 173
  on Mainland 6E 173
Aithsetter. *Shet* 8F 173
Akeld. *Nmbd* 2D 120
Akeley. *Buck* 2F 51
Akenham. *Suff* 1E 55
Albaston. *Corn* 5E 11
Alberbury. *Shrp* 4F 71
Albert Town. *Pemb* 3D 42
Albert Village. *Leics* 4H 73
Albourne. *W Sus* 4D 26
Albrighton. *Shrp*
  nr. Shrewsbury 4G 71
  nr. Telford 5C 72
Alburgh. *Norf* 2E 67
Albury. *Herts* 3E 53
Albury. *Surr* 1B 26
Albyfield. *Cumb* 4G 113
Alby Hill. *Norf* 2D 78
Alcaig. *High* 3H 157
Alcaston. *Shrp* 2G 59
Alcester. *Warw* 5E 61
Alciston. *E Sus* 5G 27
Alcombe. *Som* 2C 20
Alconbury. *Cambs* 3A 64
Alconbury Weston. *Cambs* 3A 64
Aldborough. *Norf* 2D 78
Aldborough. *N Yor* 3G 99
Aldbourne. *Wilts* 4A 36
Aldbrough. *E Yor* 1F 95
Aldbrough St John. *N Yor* 3F 105
Aldbury. *Herts* 4H 51
Aldcliffe. *Lanc* 3D 96
Aldclune. *Per* 2G 143
Aldeburgh. *Suff* 5G 67
Aldeby. *Norf* 1G 67
Aldenham. *Herts* 1C 38
Alderbury. *Wilts* 4G 23
Aldercar. *Derbs* 1B 74
Alderford. *Norf* 4D 78
Alderholt. *Dors* 1G 15
Alderley. *Glos* 2C 34
Alderley Edge. *Ches E* 3C 84
Aldermaston. *W Ber* 5D 36
Aldermaston Soke. *Hants* 5E 36
Aldermaston Wharf. *W Ber* 5E 36
Alderminster. *Warw* 1H 49
Alder Moor. *Staf* 3G 73
Aldersey Green. *Ches W* 5G 83
Aldershot. *Hants* 1G 25
Alderton. *Glos* 2F 49
Alderton. *Nptn* 1F 51
Alderton. *Shrp* 3G 71
Alderton. *Suff* 1G 55
Alderton. *Wilts* 3D 34
Alderton Fields. *Glos* 2F 49
Alderwasley. *Derbs* 5H 85
Aldfield. *N Yor* 3E 99
Aldford. *Ches W* 5G 83
Aldgate. *Rut* 5G 75
Aldham. *Essx* 3C 54
Aldham. *Suff* 1D 54
Aldingbourne. *W Sus* 5A 26
Aldingham. *Cumb* 2B 96
Aldington. *Kent* 2E 29
Aldington. *Worc* 1F 49
Aldington Frith. *Kent* 2E 29
Aldochlay. *Arg* 4C 134
Aldon. *Shrp* 3G 59
Aldoth. *Cumb* 5C 112
Aldreth. *Cambs* 3D 64
Aldridge. *W Mid* 5E 73
Aldringham. *Suff* 4G 67
Aldsworth. *Glos* 4G 49
Aldsworth. *W Sus* 2F 17
Aldwark. *Derbs* 5G 85
Aldwark. *N Yor* 3G 99
Aldwick. *W Sus* 3H 17
Aldwincle. *Nptn* 2H 63
Aldworth. *W Ber* 4D 36
Alexandria. *W Dun* 1E 127
Aley. *Som* 3E 21
Aley Green. *C Beds* 4A 52
Alfardisworthy. *Devn* 1C 10
Alfington. *Devn* 3E 12
Alfold. *Surr* 2B 26
Alfold Bars. *W Sus* 2B 26
Alfold Crossways. *Surr* 2B 26
Alford. *Abers* 2C 152
Alford. *Linc* 3D 88
Alford. *Som* 3B 22
Alfreton. *Derbs* 5B 86
Alfrick. *Worc* 5B 60
Alfrick Pound. *Worc* 5B 60
Alfriston. *E Sus* 5G 27
Algarkirk. *Linc* 2B 76
Alhampton. *Som* 3B 22
Aline Lodge. *W Isl* 6D 171
Alkborough. *N Lin* 2B 94
Alkerton. *Oxon* 1B 50
Alkham. *Kent* 1G 29
Alkington. *Shrp* 2H 71
Alkmonton. *Derbs* 2F 73
Alladale Lodge. *High* 5B 164
Allaleigh. *Devn* 3E 9
Allanbank. *N Lan* 4B 128
Allanton. *N Lan* 4B 128
Allanton. *Bord* 4E 131
Allaston. *Glos* 5B 48
Allbrook. *Hants* 4C 24
All Cannings. *Wilts* 5F 35
Allendale Town. *Nmbd* 4B 114
Allenheads. *Nmbd* 5B 114
Allensford. *Dur* 5D 115
Allen's Green. *Herts* 4E 53
Allensmore. *Here* 2H 47
Allenton. *Derb* 2A 74
Aller. *Som* 4H 21
Allerby. *Cumb* 1B 102

Allercombe. *Devn* 3D 12
Allerford. *Som* 2C 20
Allerston. *N Yor* 1C 100
Allerthorpe. *E Yor* 5B 100
Allerton. *Mers* 2G 83
Allerton. *W Yor* 1B 92
Allerton Bywater. *W Yor* 2E 93
Allerton Mauleverer. *N Yor* 4G 99
Allesley. *W Mid* 2G 61
Allestree. *Derb* 1A 74
Allet. *Corn* 4B 6
Allexton. *Leics* 5F 75
Allgreave. *Ches E* 4D 84
Allhallows. *Medw* 3C 40
Allhallows-on-Sea. *Medw* 3C 40
Alligin Shuas. *High* 3H 155
Allimore Green. *Staf* 4C 72
Allington. *Kent* 5B 40
Allington. *Linc* 1F 75
Allington. *Wilts*
  nr. Amesbury 3H 23
  nr. Devizes 5F 35
Allithwaite. *Cumb* 2C 96
Alloa. *Clac* 4A 136
Allonby. *Cumb* 5B 112
Allostock. *Ches W* 3B 84
Alloway. *S Ayr* 3C 116
Allowenshay. *Som* 1G 13
All Saints South Elmham.
  Suff 2F 67
Allscott. *Shrp* 1B 60
Allscott. *Telf* 4A 72
All Stretton. *Shrp* 1G 59
Allt. *Carm* 5F 45
Alltami. *Flin* 4E 83
Alltgobhlach. *N Ayr* 5G 125
Alltmawr. *Powy* 1D 46
Alltnacaillich. *High* 4E 167
Allt na h' Airbhe. *High* 4F 163
Alltour. *High* 5E 148
Alltsigh. *High* 2G 149
Alltwalis. *Carm* 2E 45
Alltwen. *Neat* 5H 45
Alltyblacca. *Cdgn* 1F 45
Allt-y-goed. *Pemb* 1B 44
Almeley. *Here* 5F 59
Almeley Wooton. *Here* 5F 59
Almer. *Dors* 3E 15
Almholme. *S Yor* 4F 93
Almington. *Staf* 2B 72
Alminstone Cross. *Devn* 4D 18
Almodington. *W Sus* 3G 17
Almondbank. *Per* 1C 136
Almondbury. *W Yor* 3B 92
Almondsbury. *S Glo* 3B 34
Alne. *N Yor* 3G 99
Alness. *High* 2A 158
Alnessferry. *High* 2A 158
Alnham. *Nmbd* 3D 121
Alnmouth. *Nmbd* 3G 121
Alnwick. *Nmbd* 3F 121
Alphamstone. *Essx* 2B 54
Alpheton. *Suff* 5A 66
Alphington. *Devn* 3C 12
Alpington. *Norf* 5E 79
Alport. *Derbs* 4G 85
Alport. *Powy* 1E 59
Alpraham. *Ches E* 5H 83
Alresford. *Essx* 3D 54
Alrewas. *Staf* 4F 73
Alsager. *Ches E* 5B 84
Alsagers Bank. *Staf* 1C 72
Alsop en le Dale. *Derbs* 5F 85
Alston. *Cumb* 5A 114
Alston. *Devn* 2G 13
Alstone. *Glos* 2E 49
Alstone. *Som* 2G 21
Alstonefield. *Staf* 5F 85
Alston Sutton. *Som* 1H 21
Alswear. *Devn* 4H 19
Altandhu. *High* 2D 163
Altanduin. *High* 1F 165
Altarnun. *Corn* 4C 10
Altass. *High* 3B 164
Alterwall. *High* 2E 169
Altgaltraig. *Arg* 2B 126
Altham. *Lanc* 1F 91
Althorne. *Essx* 1D 40
Althorpe. *N Lin* 4B 94
Altnabreac. *High* 4C 168
Altnacealgach. *High* 2G 163
Altnafeadh. *High* 3G 141
Altnaharra. *High* 5F 167
Altofts. *W Yor* 2D 93
Alton. *Derbs* 4A 86
Alton. *Hants* 3F 25
Alton. *Staf* 1E 73
Alton Barnes. *Wilts* 5G 35
Altonhill. *E Ayr* 1D 116
Alton Pancras. *Dors* 2C 14
Alton Priors. *Wilts* 5G 35
Altrincham. *G Man* 2B 84
Altrua. *High* 4E 149
Alva. *Clac* 4A 136
Alvanley. *Ches W* 3G 83
Alvaston. *Derb* 2A 74
Alvechurch. *Worc* 3E 61
Alvecote. *Warw* 5G 73
Alvediston. *Wilts* 4E 23
Alveley. *Shrp* 2B 60
Alverdiscott. *Devn* 4F 19
Alverstoke. *Hants* 3D 16
Alverstone. *IOW* 4D 16
Alverthorpe. *W Yor* 2D 92
Alverton. *Notts* 1E 75
Alves. *Mor* 2F 159
Alvescot. *Oxon* 5A 50
Alveston. *S Glo* 3B 34
Alveston. *Warw* 5G 61
Alvie. *High* 3C 150
Alvingham. *Linc* 1C 88

Alvington. *Glos* 5B 48
Alwalton. *Cambs* 1A 64
Alweston. *Dors* 1B 14
Alwington. *Devn* 4E 19
Alwinton. *Nmbd* 4D 120
Alwoodley. *W Yor* 5E 99
Alyth. *Per* 4B 144
Amatnatua. *High* 4B 164
Am Baile. *W Isl* 7C 170
Ambaston. *Derbs* 2B 74
Ambergate. *Derbs* 5H 85
Amber Hill. *Linc* 1B 76
Amberley. *Glos* 5D 48
Amberley. *W Sus* 4B 26
Amble. *Nmbd* 4G 121
Amblecote. *W Mid* 2C 60
Ambler Thorn. *W Yor* 2A 92
Ambleside. *Cumb* 4E 103
Ambleston. *Pemb* 2E 43
Ambrosden. *Oxon* 4E 50
Amcotts. *N Lin* 3B 94
Amersham. *Buck* 1A 38
Amerton. *Staf* 3D 73
Amesbury. *Wilts* 2G 23
Amisfield. *Dum* 1B 112
Amlwch. *IOA* 1D 80
Amlwch Port. *IOA* 1D 80
Ammanford. *Carm* 4G 45
Amotherby. *N Yor* 2B 100
Ampfield. *Hants* 4B 24
Ampleforth. *N Yor* 2H 99
Ampleforth College. *N Yor* 2H 99
Ampney Crucis. *Glos* 5F 49
Ampney St Mary. *Glos* 5F 49
Ampney St Peter. *Glos* 5F 49
Amport. *Hants* 2A 24
Ampthill. *C Beds* 2A 52
Ampton. *Suff* 3A 66
Amroth. *Pemb* 4F 43
Amulree. *Per* 5G 143
Amwell. *Herts* 4B 52
Anaheilt. *High* 2C 140
An Aird. *High* 3D 147
An Camus Darach. *High* 4E 147
Ancaster. *Linc* 1G 75
Anchor. *Shrp* 2D 58
Anchorsholme. *Lanc* 5C 96
Anchor Street. *Norf* 3F 79
An Cnoc. *W Isl* 4G 171
An Cnoc Ard. *W Isl* 1H 171
An Coroghon. *High* 3A 146
Ancroft. *Nmbd* 5G 131
Ancrum. *Bord* 2A 120
Ancton. *W Sus* 5A 26
Anderby. *Linc* 3E 89
Anderby Creek. *Linc* 3E 89
Anderson. *Dors* 3D 15
Anderton. *Ches W* 3A 84
Andertons Mill. *Lanc* 3D 90
Andover. *Hants* 2B 24
Andover Down. *Hants* 2B 24
Andoversford. *Glos* 4F 49
Andreas. *IOM* 2D 108
An Dùnan. *High* 1D 147
Andwell. *Hants* 1E 25
Anelog. *Gwyn* 3A 68
Anfield. *Mers* 1F 83
Angarrack. *Corn* 3C 4
Angelbank. *Shrp* 3H 59
Angersleigh. *Som* 1E 13
Angerton. *Cumb* 4D 112
Angle. *Pemb* 4C 42
An Gleann Ur. *W Isl* 4G 171
Angmering. *W Sus* 5B 26
Angmering-on-Sea. *W Sus* 5B 26
Angram. *N Yor*
  nr. Keld 5B 104
  nr. York 5H 99
Anick. *Nmbd* 3C 114
Ankerbold. *Derbs* 4A 86
Ankerville. *High* 1C 158
Anlaby. *E Yor* 2D 94
Anlaby Park. *Hull* 2D 94
An Leth Meadhanach. *W Isl* 7C 170
Anmer. *Norf* 3G 77
Anmore. *Hants* 1E 17
Annan. *Dum* 3D 112
Annaside. *Cumb* 1A 96
Annat. *Arg* 1H 133
Annat. *High* 3A 156
Annathill. *N Lan* 2A 128
Anna Valley. *Hants* 2B 24
Annbank. *S Ayr* 2D 116
Annesley. *Notts* 5C 86
Annesley Woodhouse. *Notts* 5C 86
Annfield Plain. *Dur* 4E 115
Annscroft. *Shrp* 5G 71
Ansdell. *Lanc* 2B 90
Ansford. *Som* 3B 22
Ansley. *Warw* 1G 61
Anslow. *Staf* 3G 73
Anslow Gate. *Staf* 3F 73
Ansteadbrook. *Surr* 2A 26
Anstey. *Herts* 2E 53
Anstey. *Leics* 5C 74
Anston. *S Lan* 5D 128
Anstruther Easter. *Fife* 3H 137
Anstruther Wester. *Fife* 3H 137
Ansty. *Warw* 2A 62
Ansty. *W Sus* 3D 27
Ansty. *Wilts* 4E 23
An Taobh Tuath. *W Isl* 1E 170
An t-Aodann Ban. *High* 3C 154
An t Ath Leathann. *High* 1E 147
An Teanga. *High* 3E 147
Anthill Common. *Hants* 1E 17
Anthorn. *Cumb* 4C 112
Antingham. *Norf* 2E 79
An t-Ob. *W Isl* 9C 171
Anton's Gowt. *Linc* 1B 76

Antony. *Corn* 3A 8
An t-Òrd. *High* 2E 147
Antrobus. *Ches W* 3A 84
Anvil Corner. *Devn* 2D 10
Anwick. *Linc* 5A 88
Anworth. *Dum* 4C 110
Apethorpe. *Nptn* 1H 63
Apeton. *Staf* 4C 72
Apley. *Linc* 3A 88
Apperknowle. *Derbs* 3A 86
Apperley. *Glos* 3D 48
Apperley Dene. *Nmbd* 4D 114
Appersett. *N Yor* 5B 104
Appin. *Arg* 4D 140
Appleby. *N Lin* 3C 94
Appleby-in-Westmorland.
  Cumb 2H 103
Appleby Magna. *Leics* 5H 73
Appleby Parva. *Leics* 5H 73
Applecross. *High* 4G 155
Appledore. *Devn*
  nr. Bideford 3E 19
  nr. Tiverton 1D 12
Appledore. *Kent* 3D 28
Appledore Heath. *Kent* 2D 28
Appleford. *Oxon* 2D 36
Applegarthtown. *Dum* 1C 112
Applemore. *Hants* 2B 16
Appleshaw. *Hants* 2B 24
Applethwaite. *Cumb* 2D 102
Appleton. *Hal* 2H 83
Appleton. *Oxon* 5C 50
Appleton-le-Moors. *N Yor* 1B 100
Appleton-le-Street. *N Yor* 2B 100
Appleton Roebuck. *N Yor* 5H 99
Appleton Thorn. *Warr* 2A 84
Appleton Wiske. *N Yor* 4A 106
Appletree. *Nptn* 1C 50
Appletreehall. *Bord* 3H 119
Appletreewick. *N Yor* 3C 98
Appley. *Som* 4D 20
Appley Bridge. *Lanc* 3D 90
Apse Heath. *IOW* 4D 16
Apsley End. *C Beds* 2B 52
Apuldram. *W Sus* 2G 17
Arabella. *High* 1C 158
Arasaig. *High* 5E 147
Arbeadie. *Abers* 4D 152
Arberth. *Pemb* 3F 43
Arbirlot. *Ang* 4F 145
Arborfield. *Wok* 5F 37
Arborfield Cross. *Wok* 5F 37
Arborfield Garrison. *Wok* 5F 37
Arbourthorne. *S Yor* 2A 86
Arbroath. *Ang* 4F 145
Arbuthnott. *Abers* 1H 145
Arcan. *High* 3H 157
Archargary. *High* 3H 167
Archdeacon Newton. *Darl* 3F 105
Archiestown. *Mor* 4G 159
Arclid. *Ches E* 4B 84
Arclid Green. *Ches E* 4B 84
Ardachu. *High* 3D 164
Ardalanish. *Arg* 2A 132
Ardaneaskan. *High* 5H 155
Ardarroch. *High* 5H 155
Ardbeg. *Arg*
  nr. Dunoon 1C 126
  on Islay 5C 124
  on Isle of Bute 3B 126
Ardcharnich. *High* 5F 163
Ardchiavaig. *Arg* 2A 132
Ardchonnell. *Arg* 2G 133
Ardchrishnish. *Arg* 1B 132
Ardchronie. *High* 5D 164
Ardchullarie. *Stir* 2E 135
Ardchyle. *Stir* 1E 135
Arddleen. *Powy* 4E 71
Arddlîn. *Powy* 4E 71
Ardechive. *High* 4D 148
Ardeley. *Herts* 3D 52
Ardelve. *High* 1A 148
Arden. *Arg* 1E 127
Ardendrain. *High* 5H 157
Arden Hall. *N Yor* 5C 106
Ardens Grafton. *Warw* 5F 61
Ardentinny. *Arg* 1C 126
Ardeonaig. *Stir* 5D 142
Ardersier. *High* 3B 158
Ardessie. *High* 5E 163
Ardfern. *Arg* 2D 124
Ardfernal. *Arg* 2D 124
Ardfin. *Arg* 3C 124
Ardgartan. *Arg* 3B 134
Ardgay. *High* 4D 164
Ardgour. *High* 2E 141
Ardheslaig. *High* 3G 155
Ardindrean. *High* 5F 163
Ardingly. *W Sus* 3E 27
Ardington. *Oxon* 3C 36
Ardlamont House. *Arg* 3A 126
Ardleigh. *Essx* 3D 54
Ardler. *Per* 4B 144
Ardley. *Oxon* 3D 50
Ardlui. *Arg* 2C 134
Ardlussa. *Arg* 1E 125
Ardmair. *High* 4F 163
Ardmay. *Arg* 3B 134
Ardminish. *Arg* 5E 125
Ardmolich. *High* 1B 140
Ardmore. *High*
  nr. Kinlochbervie 3C 166
  nr. Tain 5E 164
Ardnacross. *Arg* 4G 139
Ardnadam. *Arg* 1C 126
Ardnagrask. *High* 4H 157
Ardnamurach. *High* 4G 147
Ardnarff. *High* 5A 156
Ardnastang. *High* 2C 140

Ardoch. *Per* 5H 143
Ardochy House. *High* 3E 148
Ardpatrick. *Arg* 3F 125
Ardrishaig. *Arg* 1G 125
Ardroag. *High* 4B 154
Ardross. *High* 1A 158
Ardrossan. *N Ayr* 5D 126
Ardshealach. *High* 2A 140
Ardslignish. *High* 2G 139
Ardtalla. *Arg* 4C 124
Ardtalnaig. *Per* 5E 142
Ardtoe. *High* 1A 140
Arduaine. *Arg* 2E 133
Ardullie. *High* 2H 157
Ardvasar. *High* 3E 147
Ardvorlich. *Per* 1F 135
Ardwell. *Dum* 5G 109
Ardwell. *Mor* 5A 160
Arean. *High* 1A 140
Areley Common. *Worc* 3C 60
Areley Kings. *Worc* 3C 60
Arford. *Hants* 3G 25
Argoed. *Cphy* 2E 33
Argoed Mill. *Powy* 4B 58
Aridhglas. *Arg* 2B 132
Arinacrinachd. *High* 3G 155
Arinagour. *Arg* 3D 138
Arisaig. *High* 5E 147
Ariundle. *High* 2C 140
Arivegaig. *High* 2A 140
Arkendale. *N Yor* 3F 99
Arkesden. *Essx* 2E 53
Arkholme. *Lanc* 2E 97
Arkle Town. *N Yor* 4D 104
Arkley. *G Lon* 1D 38
Arksey. *S Yor* 4F 93
Arkwright Town. *Derbs* 3B 86
Arlecdon. *Cumb* 3B 102
Arlescote. *Warw* 1B 50
Arlesey. *C Beds* 2B 52
Arleston. *Telf* 4A 72
Arley. *Ches E* 2A 84
Arlingham. *Glos* 4C 48
Arlington. *Devn* 2G 19
Arlington. *E Sus* 5G 27
Arlington. *Glos* 5G 49
Arlington Beccott. *Devn* 2G 19
Armadail. *High* 3E 147
Armadale. *High*
  nr. Isleornsay 3E 147
  nr. Strathy 2H 167
Armadale. *W Lot* 3C 128
Armathwaite. *Cumb* 5G 113
Arminghall. *Norf* 5E 79
Armitage. *Staf* 4E 73
Armitage Bridge. *W Yor* 3B 92
Armley. *W Yor* 1C 92
Arms, The. *Norf* 1A 66
Armscote. *Warw* 1H 49
Armston. *Nptn* 2H 63
Armthorpe. *S Yor* 4G 93
Arncliffe. *N Yor* 2B 98
Arncliffe Cote. *N Yor* 2B 98
Arncroach. *Fife* 3H 137
Arne. *Dors* 4E 15
Arnesby. *Leics* 1D 62
Arnicle. *Arg* 2B 122
Arnisdale. *High* 2G 147
Arnish. *High* 4E 155
Arniston. *Midl* 3G 129
Arnol. *W Isl* 3F 171
Arnold. *E Yor* 5F 101
Arnold. *Notts* 1C 74
Arnprior. *Stir* 4F 135
Arnside. *Cumb* 2D 96
Aros Mains. *Arg* 4G 139
Arpafeelie. *High* 3A 158
Arrad Foot. *Cumb* 1C 96
Arram. *E Yor* 5E 101
Arras. *E Yor* 5D 100
Arrathorne. *N Yor* 5E 105
Arreton. *IOW* 4D 16
Arrington. *Cambs* 5C 64
Arrochar. *Arg* 3B 134
Arrow. *Warw* 5E 61
Arscaig. *High* 2C 164
Artafallie. *High* 4A 158
Arthington. *W Yor* 5E 99
Arthingworth. *Nptn* 2E 63
Arthog. *Gwyn* 4F 69
Arthrath. *Abers* 5G 161
Arthurstone. *Per* 4B 144
Artington. *Surr* 1A 26
Arundel. *W Sus* 5B 26
Asby. *Cumb* 2B 102
Ascog. *Arg* 3C 126
Ascot. *Wind* 4A 38
Ascott-under-Wychwood.
  Oxon 4B 50
Asenby. *N Yor* 2F 99
Asfordby. *Leics* 4E 74
Asfordby Hill. *Leics* 4E 74
Asgarby. *Linc*
  nr. Horncastle 4C 88
  nr. Sleaford 1A 76
Ash. *Devn* 4E 9
Ash. *Dors* 1D 14
Ash. *Kent*
  nr. Sandwich 5G 41
  nr. Swanley 4H 39
Ash. *Som* 4H 21
Ash. *Surr* 1G 25
Ashampstead. *W Ber* 4D 36
Ashbocking. *Suff* 5D 66
Ashbourne. *Derbs* 1F 73
Ashbrittle. *Som* 4D 20
Ashbrook. *Shrp* 1G 59
Ashburton. *Devn* 2D 8
Ashbury. *Devn* 3F 11
Ashbury. *Oxon* 3A 36

Ashby—Ballochgoy

Ashby. N Lin 4B 94
Ashby by Partney. Linc 4D 88
Ashby cum Fenby. NE Lin 4F 95
Ashby de la Launde. Linc 5H 87
Ashby-de-la-Zouch. Leics 4A 74
Ashby Folville. Leics 4E 74
Ashby Magna. Leics 1C 62
Ashby Parva. Leics 2C 62
Ashby Puerorum. Linc 3C 88
Ashby St Ledgars. Nptn 4C 62
Ashby St Mary. Norf 5F 79
Ashchurch. Glos 2E 49
Ashcombe. Devn 5C 12
Ashcott. Som 3H 21
Ashdon. Essx 1F 53
Ashe. Hants 2D 24
Asheldham. Essx 5C 54
Ashen. Essx 1H 53
Ashendon. Buck 4F 51
Ashey. IOW 4D 16
Ashfield. Hants 1B 16
Ashfield. Here 3A 48
Ashfield. Shrp 2H 59
Ashfield. Stir 3G 135
Ashfield. Suff 4E 66
Ashfield Green. Suff 3E 67
Ashfold Crossways. W Sus 3D 26
Ashford. Devn
nr. Barnstaple 3F 19
nr. Kingsbridge 4C 8
Ashford. Hants 1G 15
Ashford. Kent 1E 28
Ashford. Surr 3B 38
Ashford Bowdler. Shrp 3H 59
Ashford Carbonel. Shrp 3H 59
Ashford Hill. Hants 5D 36
Ashford in the Water. Derbs 4F 85
Ashgill. S Lan 5A 128
Ash Green. Warw 2H 61
Ashgrove. Mor 2G 159
Ashill. Devn 1D 12
Ashill. Norf 5A 78
Ashill. Som 1G 13
Ashingdon. Essx 1C 40
Ashington. Nmbd 1F 115
Ashington. W Sus 4C 26
Ashkirk. Bord 2G 119
Ashleworth. Glos 3D 48
Ashley. Cambs 4F 65
Ashley. Ches E 2B 84
Ashley. Dors 2G 15
Ashley. Glos 2E 35
Ashley. Hants
nr. New Milton 3A 16
nr. Winchester 3B 24
Ashley. Kent 1H 29
Ashley. Nptn 1E 63
Ashley. Staf 2B 72
Ashley. Wilts 5D 34
Ashley Green. Buck 5H 51
Ashley Heath. Dors 2G 15
Ashley Heath. Staf 2B 72
Ashley Moor. Here 4G 59
Ash Magna. Shrp 2H 71
Ashmanhaugh. Norf 3F 79
Ashmansworth. Hants 1C 24
Ashmansworthy. Devn 1D 10
Ashmead Green. Glos 2C 34
Ash Mill. Devn 4A 20
Ashmill. Devn 3D 11
Ashmore. Dors 1E 15
Ashmore Green. W Ber 5D 36
Ashorne. Warw 5H 61
Ashover. Derbs 4A 86
Ashow. Warw 3H 61
Ash Parva. Shrp 2H 71
Ashperton. Here 1B 48
Ashprington. Devn 3E 9
Ash Priors. Som 4E 21
Ashreigney. Devn 1G 11
Ash Street. Suff 1D 54
Ashtead. Surr 5C 38
Ash Thomas. Devn 1D 12
Ashton. Corn 4D 4
Ashton. Here 4H 59
Ashton. Inv 2D 126
Ashton. Nptn
nr. Oundle 2H 63
nr. Roade 1F 51
Ashton. Pet 5A 76
Ashton Common. Wilts 1D 23
Ashton Hayes. Ches W 4H 83
Ashton-in-Makerfield. G Man 1H 83
Ashton Keynes. Wilts 2F 35
Ashton under Hill. Worc 2E 49
Ashton-under-Lyne. G Man 1D 84
Ashton upon Mersey. G Man 1B 84
Ashurst. Hants 1B 16
Ashurst. Kent 2G 27
Ashurst. Lanc 4C 90
Ashurst. W Sus 4C 26
Ashurst Wood. W Sus 2F 27
Ash Vale. Surr 1G 25
Ashwater. Devn 3D 11
Ashwell. Herts 2C 52
Ashwell. Rut 4F 75
Ashwellthorpe. Norf 1D 66
Ashwick. Som 2B 22
Ashwicken. Norf 4G 77
Ashwood. Staf 2C 60
Askam in Furness. Cumb 2B 96
Askern. S Yor 3F 93
Askerswell. Dors 3A 14
Askett. Buck 5G 51
Askham. Cumb 2G 103
Askham. Notts 3E 87
Askham Bryan. York 5H 99
Askham Richard. York 5H 99
Askrigg. N Yor 5C 104
Askwith. N Yor 5D 98
Aslackby. Linc 2H 75
Aslacton. Norf 1D 66
Aslockton. Notts 1E 75
Aspatria. Cumb 5C 112
Aspenden. Herts 3D 52
Asperton. Linc 2B 76
Aspley Guise. C Beds 2H 51
Aspley Heath. C Beds 2H 51
Aspull. G Man 4E 90
Asselby. E Yor 2H 93
Assington. Suff 2C 54
Assington Green. Suff 5G 65
Astbury. Ches E 4C 84
Astcote. Nptn 5D 62
Asterby. Linc 3B 88
Asterley. Shrp 5F 71
Asterton. Shrp 1F 59
Asthall. Oxon 4A 50
Asthall Leigh. Oxon 4B 50
Astle. High 4E 165
Astley. G Man 4F 91
Astley. Shrp 4H 71
Astley. Warw 2H 61
Astley. Worc 4B 60
Astley Abbotts. Shrp 1B 60
Astley Bridge. G Man 3F 91
Astley Cross. Worc 4C 60
Aston. Ches E 1A 72
Aston. Ches W 3H 83
Aston. Derbs
nr. Hope 2F 85
nr. Sudbury 2F 73
Aston. Flin 4F 83
Aston. Here 4G 59
Aston. Herts 3C 52
Aston. Oxon 5B 50
Aston. Shrp
nr. Bridgnorth 1C 60
nr. Wem 3H 71
Aston. S Yor 2B 86
Aston. Staf 1B 72
Aston. Telf 5A 72
Aston. W Mid 1E 61
Aston. Wok 3F 37
Aston Abbotts. Buck 3G 51
Aston Botterell. Shrp 2A 60
Aston-by-Stone. Staf 2D 72
Aston Cantlow. Warw 5F 61
Aston Clinton. Buck 4G 51
Aston Crews. Here 3B 48
Aston Cross. Glos 2E 49
Aston End. Herts 3C 52
Aston Eyre. Shrp 1A 60
Aston Fields. Worc 4D 60
Aston Flamville. Leics 1B 62
Aston Ingham. Here 3B 48
Aston juxta Mondrum. Ches E 5A 84
Astonlane. Shrp 1A 60
Aston le Walls. Nptn 5B 62
Aston Magna. Glos 2G 49
Aston Munslow. Shrp 2H 59
Aston on Carrant. Glos 2E 49
Aston on Clun. Shrp 2F 59
Aston-on-Trent. Derbs 3B 74
Aston Pigott. Shrp 5F 71
Aston Rogers. Shrp 5F 71
Aston Rowant. Oxon 2F 37
Aston Sandford. Buck 5F 51
Aston Somerville. Worc 2F 49
Aston Subedge. Glos 1G 49
Aston Tirrold. Oxon 3D 36
Aston Upthorpe. Oxon 3D 36
Astrop. Nptn 2D 50
Astwick. C Beds 2C 52
Astwood. Mil 1H 51
Astwood Bank. Worc 4E 61
Aswarby. Linc 2H 75
Aswardby. Linc 3C 88
Atcham. Shrp 5H 71
Atch Lench. Worc 5E 61
Athelhampton. Dors 3C 14
Athelington. Suff 3E 66
Athelney. Som 4G 21
Athelstaneford. E Lot 2B 130
Atherfield Green. IOW 5C 16
Atherington. Devn 4F 19
Atherington. W Sus 5B 26
Athersley. S Yor 4D 92
Atherstone. Warw 1H 61
Atherstone on Stour. Warw 5G 61
Atherton. G Man 4E 91
Ath-Tharracail. High 2A 140
Atlow. Derbs 5G 85
Attadale. High 5B 156
Attenborough. Notts 2C 74
Atterby. Linc 1G 87
Atterley. Shrp 1A 60
Atterton. Leics 1A 62
Attleborough. Norf 1C 66
Attleborough. Warw 1A 62
Attlebridge. Norf 4D 78
Atwick. E Yor 4F 101
Atworth. Wilts 5D 34
Auberrow. Here 1H 47
Aubourn. Linc 4G 87
Aucharnie. Abers 4D 160
Auchattie. Abers 4D 152
Auchavan. Ang 2A 144
Auchbreck. Mor 1G 151
Auchenback. E Ren 4G 127
Auchenblae. Abers 1G 145
Auchenbrack. Dum 5G 117
Auchenbreck. Arg 1B 126
Auchencairn. Dum
nr. Dalbeattie 4E 111
nr. Dumfries 1A 112
Auchencarroch. W Dun 1F 127
Auchencrow. Bord 3E 131
Auchendennan. Arg 1E 127
Auchendinny. Midl 3F 129
Auchengray. S Lan 4C 128
Auchenhalrig. Mor 2A 160
Auchenheath. S Lan 5B 128
Auchenlochan. Arg 2A 126
Auchenmade. N Ayr 5E 127
Auchenmalg. Dum 4H 109
Auchentiber. N Ayr 5E 127
Auchenvennel. Arg 1D 126
Auchindrain. Arg 3H 133
Auchininna. Abers 4D 160
Auchinleck. Dum 2B 110
Auchinleck. E Ayr 2E 117
Auchinloch. N Lan 2H 127
Auchinstarry. N Lan 2A 128
Auchleven. Abers 1D 152
Auchlochan. S Lan 1H 117
Auchlunachan. High 5F 163
Auchmillan. E Ayr 2E 117
Auchmithie. Ang 4F 145
Auchmuirbridge. Fife 3E 136
Auchmull. Ang 1E 145
Auchnacree. Ang 2D 144
Auchnafree. Per 5F 143
Auchnagallin. High 5E 159
Auchnagatt. Abers 4G 161
Aucholzie. Abers 4H 151
Auchreddie. Abers 4F 161
Auchterarder. Per 2B 136
Auchteraw. High 3F 149
Auchterderran. Fife 4E 136
Auchterhouse. Ang 5C 144
Auchtermuchty. Fife 2E 137
Auchterneed. High 3G 157
Auchtertool. Fife 4E 136
Auchtertyre. High 1G 147
Auchtubh. Stir 1E 135
Auckengill. High 2F 169
Auckley. S Yor 4G 93
Audenshaw. G Man 1D 84
Audlem. Ches E 1A 72
Audley. Staf 5B 84
Audley End. Essx 2F 53
Audmore. Staf 3C 72
Auds. Abers 2D 160
Aughertree. Cumb 1D 102
Aughton. E Yor 1H 93
Aughton. Lanc
nr. Lancaster 3E 97
nr. Ormskirk 4B 90
Aughton. S Yor 2B 86
Aughton. Wilts 1H 23
Aughton Park. Lanc 4C 90
Auldearn. High 3D 158
Aulden. Here 5G 59
Auldgirth. Dum 1G 111
Auldhouse. S Lan 4H 127
Ault a' chruinn. High 1B 148
Aultbea. High 5C 162
Aultdearg. High 2E 157
Aultgrishan. High 5B 162
Aultguish Inn. High 1F 157
Ault Hucknall. Derbs 4B 86
Aultibea. High 1H 165
Aultiphurst. High 2A 168
Aultivullin. High 2A 168
Aultmore. Mor 3B 160
Aultnamain Inn. High 5D 164
Aunby. Linc 4H 75
Aunsby. Linc 2H 75
Aust. S Glo 3A 34
Austerfield. S Yor 1D 86
Austin Fen. Linc 1C 88
Austrey. Warw 5G 73
Austwick. N Yor 3G 97
Authorpe. Linc 2D 88
Authorpe Row. Linc 3E 89
Avebury. Wilts 5G 35
Avebury Trusloe. Wilts 5F 35
Aveley. Thur 2G 39
Avening. Glos 2D 35
Averham. Notts 5E 87
Aveton Gifford. Devn 4C 8
Avielochan. High 2D 150
Aviemore. High 2C 150
Avington. Hants 3D 24
Avoch. High 3B 158
Avon. Hants 3G 15
Avonbridge. Falk 2C 128
Avon Dassett. Warw 5B 62
Avonmouth. Bris 4A 34
Avonwick. Devn 3D 8
Awbridge. Hants 4B 24
Awliscombe. Devn 2E 13
Awre. Glos 5C 48
Awsworth. Notts 1B 74
Axbridge. Som 1H 21
Axford. Hants 2E 24
Axford. Wilts 5H 35
Axminster. Devn 3G 13
Axmouth. Devn 3F 13
Aycliffe Village. Dur 2F 105
Aydon. Nmbd 3D 114
Aykley Heads. Dur 5F 115
Aylburton. Glos 5B 48
Aylburton Common. Glos 5B 48
Ayle. Nmbd 5A 114
Aylesbeare. Devn 3D 12
Aylesbury. Buck 4G 51
Aylesby. NE Lin 4F 95
Aylescott. Devn 1G 11
Aylesford. Kent 5B 40
Aylesham. Kent 5G 41
Aylestone. Leic 5C 74
Aylmerton. Norf 2D 78
Aylsham. Norf 3D 78
Aylton. Here 2B 48
Aylworth. Glos 3G 49
Aymestrey. Here 4G 59
Aynho. Nptn 2D 50
Ayot Green. Herts 4C 52
Ayot St Lawrence. Herts 4B 52
Ayot St Peter. Herts 4C 52
Ayr. S Ayr 187 (2C 116)
Ayres of Selivoe. Shet 7D 173
Ayreville. Torb 2E 9
Aysgarth. N Yor 1C 98
Ayshford. Devn 1D 12
Ayside. Cumb 1C 96
Ayston. Rut 5F 75
Ayton. Bord 3F 131
Aywick. Shet 3G 173
Azerley. N Yor 2E 99

B

Babbacombe. Torb 2F 9
Babbinswood. Shrp 2F 71
Babbs Green. Herts 4D 53
Babcary. Som 4A 22
Babel. Carm 2B 46
Babell. Flin 3D 82
Babingley. Norf 3F 77
Bablock Hythe. Oxon 5C 50
Babraham. Cambs 5E 65
Babworth. Notts 2D 86
Bac. W Isl 3G 171
Bachau. IOA 2D 80
Bacheldre. Powy 1E 59
Bachymbyd Fawr. Den 4C 82
Backaland. Orkn 4E 172
Backaskaill. Orkn 2D 172
Backbarrow. Cumb 1C 96
Backe. Carm 3G 43
Backfolds. Abers 3H 161
Backford. Ches W 3G 83
Backhill. Abers 5E 161
Backhill of Clackriach.
Abers 4G 161
Backies. High 3F 165
Backmuir of New Gilston.
Fife 3G 137
Back of Keppoch. High 5E 147
Back Street. Suff 5G 65
Backwell. N Som 5H 33
Backworth. Tyne 2G 115
Bacon End. Essx 4G 53
Baconsthorpe. Norf 2D 78
Bacton. Here 2G 47
Bacton. Norf 2F 79
Bacton. Suff 4C 66
Bacton Green. Norf 2F 79
Bacup. Lanc 2G 91
Badachonacher. High 1A 158
Badachro. High 1G 155
Badanloch Lodge. High 5H 167
Badavanich. High 3D 156
Badbury. Swin 3G 35
Badby. Nptn 5C 62
Badcall. High 3C 166
Badcaul. High 4E 163
Baddeley Green. Stoke 5D 84
Baddesley Clinton. W Mid 3G 61
Baddesley Ensor. Warw 1G 61
Baddidarach. High 1E 163
Baddoch. Abers 5F 151
Badenscallie. High 3E 163
Badenscoth. Abers 5E 160
Badentarbat. High 2E 163
Badgall. Corn 4C 10
Badgers Mount. Kent 4F 39
Badgeworth. Glos 4E 49
Badgworth. Som 1G 21
Badicaul. High 1F 147
Badingham. Suff 4F 67
Badlesmere. Kent 5E 40
Badlipster. High 4E 169
Badluarach. High 4D 163
Badminton. S Glo 3D 34
Badnaban. High 1E 163
Badnabay. High 4C 166
Badnagie. High 5D 168
Badnellan. High 3F 165
Badninish. High 4E 165
Badrallach. High 4E 163
Badsey. Worc 1F 49
Badshot Lea. Surr 2G 25
Badsworth. W Yor 3E 93
Badwell Ash. Suff 4B 66
Bae Cinmel. Cnwy 2B 82
Bae Colwyn. Cnwy 3A 82
Bae Penrhyn. Cnwy 2H 81
Bagby. N Yor 1G 99
Bag Enderby. Linc 3C 88
Bagendon. Glos 5F 49
Bagginswood. Shrp 2A 60
Bàgh a Chàise. W Isl 1E 170
Bàgh a' Chaisteil. W Isl 9B 170
Bagham. Kent 5E 41
Baghasdal. W Isl 7C 170
Bagh Mor. W Isl 3D 170
Bagh Shiarabhagh. W Isl 8C 170
Bagillt. Flin 3E 82
Baginton. Warw 3H 61
Baglan. Neat 2A 32
Bagley. Shrp 3G 71
Bagley. Som 2H 21
Bagnall. Staf 5D 84
Bagnor. W Ber 5C 36
Bagshot. Surr 4A 38
Bagshot. Wilts 5B 36
Bagstone. S Glo 3B 34
Bagthorpe. Norf 2G 77
Bagthorpe. Notts 5B 86
Bagworth. Leics 5B 74
Bagwy Llydiart. Here 3H 47
Baildon. W Yor 1B 92
Baildon Green. W Yor 1B 92
Baile. W Isl 1E 170
Baile Ailein. W Isl 5E 171
Baile an Truiseil. W Isl 2F 171
Baile Boidheach. Arg 2F 125
Baile Glas. W Isl 3D 170
Bailemeonach. Arg 4A 140
Baile Mhanaich. W Isl 3C 170
Baile Mhartainn. W Isl 1C 170
Baile MhicPhail. W Isl 1D 170
Baile Mór. Arg 2A 132
Baile Mor. W Isl 2C 170
Baile nan Cailleach. W Isl 3C 170
Baile Raghaill. W Isl 2C 170
Bailey Green. Hants 4E 25
Baileyhead. Cumb 1G 113
Bailiesward. Abers 5B 160
Bail' Iochdrach. W Isl 3D 170
Baillieston. Glas 3H 127
Bailrigg. Lanc 4D 97
Bail Uachdraich. W Isl 2D 170
Bail' Ur Tholastaidh. W Isl 3H 171
Bainbridge. N Yor 5C 104
Bainsford. Falk 1B 128
Bainshole. Abers 5D 160
Bainton. E Yor 4D 100
Bainton. Oxon 3D 50
Bainton. Pet 5H 75
Baintown. Fife 3F 137
Baker Street. Thur 2H 39
Bakewell. Derbs 4G 85
Bala. Gwyn 2B 70
Y Bala. Gwyn 2B 70
Balachuirn. High 4E 155
Balbeg. High
nr. Cannich 5G 157
nr. Loch Ness 1G 149
Balbeggie. Per 1D 136
Balblair. High
nr. Bonar Bridge 4C 164
nr. Invergordon 2B 158
nr. Inverness 4H 157
Balby. S Yor 4F 93
Balcathie. Ang 5F 145
Balchladich. High 1E 163
Balchraggan. High 4H 157
Balchrick. High 3B 166
Balcombe. W Sus 2E 27
Balcombe Lane. W Sus 2E 27
Balcurvie. Fife 3F 137
Baldersby. N Yor 2F 99
Baldersby St James. N Yor 2F 99
Balderstone. Lanc 1E 91
Balderton. Ches W 4F 83
Balderton. Notts 5F 87
Baldinnie. Fife 2G 137
Baldock. Herts 2C 52
Baldrine. IOM 3D 108
Baldslow. E Sus 4C 28
Baldwin. IOM 3C 108
Baldwinholme. Cumb 4E 113
Baldwin's Gate. Staf 2B 72
Bale. Norf 2C 78
Balearn. Abers 3H 161
Balemartine. Arg 4A 138
Balephetrish. Arg 4B 138
Balephuil. Arg 4A 138
Balerno. Edin 3E 129
Balevullin. Arg 4A 138
Balfield. Ang 2E 145
Balfour. Orkn 6D 172
Balfron. Stir 1G 127
Balgaveny. Abers 4D 160
Balgonar. Fife 4C 136
Balgowan. High 4A 150
Balgown. High 2C 154
Balgrochan. E Dun 2H 127
Balgy. High 3H 155
Balhalgardy. Abers 1E 153
Baliasta. Shet 1H 173
Baligill. High 2A 168
Balintore. Ang 3B 144
Balintore. High 1C 158
Balintraid. High 1B 158
Balk. N Yor 1G 99
Balkeerie. Ang 4C 144
Balkholme. E Yor 2A 94
Ball. Shrp 3F 71
Ballabeg. IOM 4B 108
Ballacannell. IOM 3D 108
Ballacarnane Beg. IOM 3C 108
Ballachulish. High 3E 141
Ballagyr. IOM 3B 108
Ballajora. IOM 2D 108
Ballaleigh. IOM 3C 108
Ballamodha. IOM 4B 108
Ballantrae. S Ayr 1F 109
Ballards Gore. Essx 1D 40
Ballasalla. IOM
nr. Castletown 4B 108
nr. Kirk Michael 2C 108
Ballater. Abers 4A 152
Ballaugh. IOM 2C 108
Ballencrieff. E Lot 2A 130
Ballencrieff Toll. W Lot 2C 128
Ballentoul. Per 2F 143
Ball Hill. Hants 5C 36
Ballidon. Derbs 5G 85
Balliemore. Arg
nr. Dunoon 1B 126
nr. Oban 1F 133
Ballieward. High 5E 159
Ballig. IOM 3B 108
Ballimore. Stir 2E 135
Ballingdon. Suff 1B 54
Ballinger Common. Buck 5H 51
Ballingham. Here 2A 48
Ballingry. Fife 4D 136
Ballinluig. Per 3G 143
Ballintuim. Per 3A 144
Balliveolan. Arg 4C 140
Balloan. High 3C 164
Balloch. High 4B 158
Balloch. N Lan 2A 128
Balloch. Per 2H 135
Balloch. W Dun 1E 127
Ballochan. Abers 4C 152
Ballochgoy. Arg 3B 126

Ballochmyle—Bellerby

Ballochmyle. E Ayr 2E 117
Ballochroy. Arg 4F 125
Balls Cross. W Sus 3A 26
Ball's Green. E Sus 2F 27
Ballygown. Arg 4F 139
Ballygrant. Arg 3B 124
Ballymichael. N Ayr 2D 122
Balmacara. High 1G 147
Balmaclellan. Dum 2D 110
Balmacqueen. High 1D 154
Balmaha. Stir 4D 134
Balmalcolm. Fife 3F 137
Balmalloch. N Lan 2A 128
Balmeanach. High 5E 155
Balmedie. Abers 2G 153
Balmerino. Fife 1F 137
Balmerlawn. Hants 2B 16
Balmore. E Dun 2H 127
Balmore. High 4B 154
Balmullo. Fife 1G 137
Balmurrie. Dum 3H 109
Balnaboth. Ang 2C 144
Balnabruaich. High 1B 158
Balnabruich. High 5D 168
Balnacoil. High 2F 165
Balnacra. High 4B 156
Balnacroft. Abers 4G 151
Balnageith. Mor 3E 159
Balnaglaic. High 5G 157
Balnagrantach. High 5G 157
Balnaguard. Per 3G 143
Balnahard. Arg 4B 132
Balnain. High 5G 157
Balnakeil. High 2D 166
Balnaknock. High 2D 154
Balnamoon. Abers 3G 161
Balnamoon. Ang 2E 145
Balnapaling. High 2B 158
Balornock. Glas 3H 127
Balquhidder. Stir 1E 135
Balsall. W Mid 3G 61
Balsall Common. W Mid 3G 61
Balscote. Oxon 1B 50
Balsham. Cambs 5E 65
Balstonia. Thur 2A 40
Baltasound. Shet 1H 173
Balterley. Staf 5B 84
Baltersan. Dum 3B 110
Balthangie. Abers 3F 161
Baltonsborough. Som 3A 22
Balvaird. High 3H 157
Balvaird. Per 2D 136
Balvenie. Mor 4H 159
Balvicar. Arg 2E 133
Balvraid. High 2G 147
Balvraid Lodge. High 5C 158
Bamber Bridge. Lanc 2D 90
Bamber's Green. Essx 3F 53
Bamburgh. Nmbd 1F 121
Bamford. Derbs 2G 85
Bamfurlong. G Man 4D 90
Bampton. Cumb 3G 103
Bampton. Devn 4C 20
Bampton. Oxon 5B 50
Bampton Grange. Cumb 3G 103
Banavie. High 1F 141
Banbury. Oxon 1C 50
Bancffosfelen. Carm 4E 45
Banchory. Abers 4D 152
Banchory-Devenick. Abers 3G 153
Bancycapel. Carm 4E 45
Bancyfelin. Carm 3H 43
Banc-y-ffordd. Carm 2E 45
Banff. Abers 2D 160
Bangor. Gwyn 3E 81
Bangor-is-y-coed. Wrex 1F 71
Bangors. Corn 3C 10
Bangor's Green. Lanc 4B 90
Banham. Norf 2C 66
Bank, The. Ches E 5C 84
Bank. Hants 2A 16
Bank, The. Shrp 1A 60
Bankend. Dum 3B 112
Bankfoot. Per 5H 143
Bankglen. E Ayr 3F 117
Bankhead. Aber 2F 153
Bankhead. Abers 3D 152
Bankhead. S Lan 5B 128
Bankland. Som 4G 21
Bank Newton. N Yor 4B 98
Banknock. Falk 2A 128
Banks. Cumb 3G 113
Banks. Lanc 2B 90
Bankshill. Dum 1C 112
Bank Street. Worc 4A 60
Bank Top. Lanc 4D 90
Banners Gate. W Mid 1E 61
Banningham. Norf 3E 78
Banniskirk. High 3D 168
Bannister Green. Essx 3G 53
Bannockburn. Stir 4H 135
Banstead. Surr 5D 38
Bantham. Devn 4C 8
Banton. N Lan 2A 128
Banwell. N Som 1G 21
Banyard's Green. Suff 3F 67
Bapchild. Kent 4D 40
Bapton. Wilts 3E 23
Barabhas. W Isl 2F 171
Barabhas Iarach. W Isl 3F 171
Baramore. High 1A 140
Barassie. S Ayr 1C 116
Baravullin. Arg 4D 140
Barbaraville. High 1B 158
Barber Booth. Derbs 2F 85
Barber Green. Cumb 1C 96
Barbhas Uarach. W Isl 2F 171
Barbieston. S Ayr 3D 116
Barbon. Cumb 1F 97
Barbourne. Worc 5C 60
Barbridge. Ches E 5A 84
Barbrook. Devn 2H 19
Barby. Nptn 3C 62
Barby Nortoft. Nptn 3C 62
Barcaldine. Arg 4D 140
Barcheston. Warw 2A 50
Barclose. Cumb 3F 113
Barcombe. E Sus 4F 27
Barcombe Cross. E Sus 4F 27
Barden. N Yor 5E 105
Barden Scale. N Yor 4C 98
Bardfield End Green. Essx 2G 53
Bardfield Saling. Essx 3G 53
Bardister. Shet 4E 173
Bardnabeinne. High 4E 164
Bardney. Linc 4A 88
Bardon. Leics 4B 74
Bardon Mill. Nmbd 3A 114
Bardowie. E Dun 2G 127
Bardrainney. Inv 2E 127
Bardsea. Cumb 2C 96
Bardsey. W Yor 5F 99
Bardsley. G Man 4H 91
Bardwell. Suff 3B 66
Bare. Lanc 3D 96
Barelees. Nmbd 1C 120
Barewood. Here 5F 59
Barford. Hants 3G 25
Barford. Norf 5D 78
Barford. Warw 4G 61
Barford St John. Oxon 2C 50
Barford St Martin. Wilts 3F 23
Barford St Michael. Oxon 2C 50
Barfrestone. Kent 5G 41
Bargeddie. N Lan 3H 127
Bargod. Cphy 2E 33
Bargoed. Cphy 2E 33
Bargrennan. Dum 2A 110
Barham. Cambs 3A 64
Barham. Kent 5G 41
Barham. Suff 5D 66
Barharrow. Dum 4D 110
Bar Hill. Cambs 4C 64
Barholm. Linc 4H 75
Barkby. Leics 5D 74
Barkestone-le-Vale. Leics 2E 75
Barkham. Wok 5F 37
Barking. G Lon 2F 39
Barking. Suff 5C 66
Barkingside. G Lon 2F 39
Barking Tye. Suff 5C 66
Barkisland. W Yor 3A 92
Barkston. Linc 1G 75
Barkston Ash. N Yor 1E 93
Barkway. Herts 2D 53
Barlanark. Glas 3H 127
Barlaston. Staf 2C 72
Barlavington. W Sus 4A 26
Barlborough. Derbs 3B 86
Barlby. N Yor 1G 93
Barlestone. Leics 5B 74
Barley. Herts 2D 53
Barley. Lanc 5H 97
Barley Mow. Tyne 4F 115
Barleythorpe. Rut 5F 75
Barling. Essx 2D 40
Barlings. Linc 3H 87
Barlow. Derbs 3H 85
Barlow. N Yor 2G 93
Barlow. Tyne 3E 115
Barmby Moor. E Yor 5B 100
Barmby on the Marsh. E Yor 2G 93
Barmer. Norf 2H 77
Barming. Kent 5B 40
Barming Heath. Kent 5B 40
Barmoor. Nmbd 1E 121
Barmouth. Gwyn 4F 69
Barmpton. Darl 3A 106
Barmston. E Yor 4F 101
Barmulloch. Glas 3H 127
Barnack. Pet 5H 75
Barnacle. Warw 2A 62
Barnard Castle. Dur 3D 104
Barnard Gate. Oxon 4C 50
Barnardiston. Suff 1H 53
Barnbarroch. Dum 4F 111
Barnburgh. S Yor 4E 93
Barnby. Suff 2G 67
Barnby Dun. S Yor 4G 93
Barnby in the Willows. Notts 5F 87
Barnby Moor. Notts 2D 86
Barnes. G Lon 3D 38
Barnes Street. Kent 1H 27
Barnet. G Lon 1D 38
Barnetby le Wold. N Lin 4D 94
Barney. Norf 2B 78
Barnham. Suff 3A 66
Barnham. W Sus 5A 26
Barnham Broom. Norf 5C 78
Barnhead. Ang 3F 145
Barnhill. D'dee 5D 145
Barnhill. Mor 3F 159
Barnhill. Per 1D 136
Barnhills. Dum 2E 109
Barningham. Dur 3D 105
Barningham. Suff 3B 66
Barnoldby le Beck. NE Lin 4F 95
Barnoldswick. Lanc 5A 98
Barns Green. W Sus 3C 26
Barnsley. Glos 5F 49
Barnsley. Shrp 1B 60
Barnsley. S Yor 4D 92
Barnstaple. Devn 3F 19
Barnston. Essx 4G 53
Barnston. Mers 2E 83
Barnstone. Notts 2E 75
Barnt Green. Worc 3E 61
Barnton. Ches W 3A 84
Barnwell. Cambs 5D 64
Barnwell. Nptn 2H 63
Barnwood. Glos 4D 48
Barons Cross. Here 5G 59
Barony, The. Orkn 5B 172
Barr. Dum 4G 117
Barr. S Ayr 5B 116
Barra Airport. W Isl 8B 170
Barrachan. Dum 5A 110
Barraglom. W Isl 4D 171
Barrahormid. Arg 1F 125
Barrapol. Arg 4A 138
Barrasford. Nmbd 2C 114
Barravullin. Arg 3F 133
Barregarrow. IOM 3C 108
Barrhead. E Ren 4G 127
Barrhill. S Ayr 1H 109
Barri. V Glam 5E 32
Barrington. Cambs 1D 53
Barrington. Som 1G 13
Barripper. Corn 3D 4
Barrmill. N Ayr 4E 127
Barrock. High 1E 169
Barrow. Lanc 1F 91
Barrow. Rut 4F 75
Barrow. Shrp 5A 72
Barrow. Som 3C 22
Barrow. Suff 4G 65
Barroway Drove. Norf 5E 77
Barrow Bridge. G Man 3E 91
Barrowburn. Nmbd 3C 120
Barrowby. Linc 2F 75
Barrowcliff. N Yor 1E 101
Barrow Common. N Som 5A 34
Barrowden. Rut 5G 75
Barrowford. Lanc 1G 91
Barrow Gurney. N Som 5A 34
Barrow Haven. N Lin 2D 94
Barrow Hill. Derbs 3B 86
Barrow-in-Furness. Cumb 3B 96
Barrow Nook. Lanc 4C 90
Barrows Green. Cumb 1E 97
Barrow's Green. Hal 2H 83
Barrow Street. Wilts 3D 22
Barrow upon Humber. N Lin 2D 94
Barrow upon Soar. Leics 4C 74
Barrow upon Trent. Derbs 3A 74
Barry. Ang 5E 145
Barry. V Glam 5E 32
Barry Island. V Glam 5E 32
Barsby. Leics 4D 74
Barsham. Suff 2F 67
Barston. W Mid 3G 61
Bartestree. Here 1A 48
Barthol Chapel. Abers 5F 161
Bartholomew Green. Essx 3H 53
Barthomley. Ches E 5B 84
Bartley. Hants 1B 16
Bartley Green. W Mid 2E 61
Bartlow. Cambs 1F 53
Barton. Cambs 5D 64
Barton. Ches W 5G 83
Barton. Cumb 2F 103
Barton. Glos 3G 49
Barton. IOW 4D 16
Barton. Lanc
nr. Ormskirk 4B 90
nr. Preston 1D 90
Barton. N Som 1G 21
Barton. N Yor 4F 105
Barton. Oxon 5D 50
Barton. Torb 2F 9
Barton. Warw 5F 61
Barton Bendish. Norf 5G 77
Barton Gate. Staf 4F 73
Barton Green. Staf 4F 73
Barton Hartsthorn. Buck 2E 51
Barton Hill. N Yor 3B 100
Barton in Fabis. Notts 2C 74
Barton in the Beans. Leics 5A 74
Barton-le-Clay. C Beds 2A 52
Barton-le-Street. N Yor 2B 100
Barton-le-Willows. N Yor 3B 100
Barton Mills. Suff 3G 65
Barton on Sea. Hants 3H 15
Barton-on-the-Heath. Warw 2A 50
Barton St David. Som 3A 22
Barton Seagrave. Nptn 3F 63
Barton Stacey. Hants 2C 24
Barton Town. Devn 2G 19
Barton Turf. Norf 3F 79
Barton-Under-Needwood. Staf 4F 73
Barton-upon-Humber. N Lin 2D 94
Barton Waterside. N Lin 2D 94
Barugh Green. S Yor 4D 92
Barway. Cambs 3E 65
Barwell. Leics 1B 62
Barwick. Herts 4D 53
Barwick. Som 1A 14
Barwick in Elmet. W Yor 1D 93
Baschurch. Shrp 3G 71
Bascote. Warw 4B 62
Basford Green. Staf 5D 85
Bashall Eaves. Lanc 5F 97
Bashall Town. Lanc 5G 97
Bashley. Hants 3H 15
Basildon. Essx 2B 40
Basingstoke. Hants 1E 25
Baslow. Derbs 3G 85
Bason Bridge. Som 2G 21
Bassaleg. Newp 3F 33
Bassendean. Bord 5C 130
Bassenthwaite. Cumb 1D 102
Bassett. Sotn 1C 16
Bassingbourn. Cambs 1D 52
Bassingfield. Notts 2D 74
Bassingham. Linc 4G 87
Bassingthorpe. Linc 3G 75
Bassus Green. Herts 3D 52
Basta. Shet 2G 173
Baston. Linc 4A 76
Bastonford. Worc 5C 60
Bastwick. Norf 4G 79
Batchley. Worc 4E 61
Batchworth. Herts 1B 38
Batcombe. Dors 2B 14
Batcombe. Som 3B 22
Bate Heath. Ches E 3A 84
Bath. Bath 187 (5C 34)
Bathampton. Bath 5C 34
Bathealton. Som 4D 20
Batheaston. Bath 5C 34
Bathford. Bath 5C 34
Bathgate. W Lot 3C 128
Bathley. Notts 5E 87
Bathpool. Corn 5C 10
Bathpool. Som 4F 21
Bathville. W Lot 3C 128
Bathway. Som 1A 22
Batley. W Yor 2C 92
Batsford. Glos 2G 49
Batson. Devn 5D 8
Battersby. N Yor 4C 106
Battersea. G Lon 3D 39
Battisborough Cross. Devn 4C 8
Battisford. Suff 5C 66
Battisford Tye. Suff 5C 66
Battle. E Sus 4B 28
Battle. Powy 2D 46
Battleborough. Som 1G 21
Battledown. Glos 3E 49
Battlefield. Shrp 4H 71
Battlesbridge. Essx 1B 40
Battlesden. C Beds 3H 51
Battlesea Green. Suff 3E 66
Battleton. Som 4C 20
Battram. Leics 5B 74
Battramsley. Hants 3B 16
Batt's Corner. Surr 2G 25
Bauds of Cullen. Mor 2B 160
Baugh. Arg 4B 138
Baughton. Worc 1D 49
Baughurst. Hants 5D 36
Baulking. Oxon 2B 36
Baumber. Linc 3B 88
Baunton. Glos 5F 49
Baverstock. Wilts 3F 23
Bawburgh. Norf 5D 78
Bawdeswell. Norf 3C 78
Bawdrip. Som 3G 21
Bawdsey. Suff 1G 55
Bawsey. Norf 4F 77
Bawtry. S Yor 1D 86
Baxenden. Lanc 2F 91
Baxterley. Warw 1G 61
Baxter's Green. Suff 5G 65
Bay. High 3B 154
Baybridge. Hants 4D 24
Baybridge. Nmbd 4C 114
Baycliff. Cumb 2B 96
Baydon. Wilts 4A 36
Bayford. Herts 5D 52
Bayford. Som 4C 22
Bayles. Cumb 5A 114
Baylham. Suff 5D 66
Baynard's Green. Oxon 3D 50
Bayston Hill. Shrp 5G 71
Baythorne End. Essx 1H 53
Baythorpe. Linc 1B 76
Bayton. Worc 3A 60
Bayton Common. Worc 3B 60
Bayworth. Oxon 5D 50
Beach. S Glo 4C 34
Beachampton. Buck 2F 51
Beachamwell. Norf 5G 77
Beachley. Glos 2A 34
Beacon. Devn 2E 13
Beacon End. Essx 3C 54
Beacon Hill. Surr 3G 25
Beacon's Bottom. Buck 2F 37
Beaconsfield. Buck 1A 38
Beacrabhaic. W Isl 8D 171
Beadlam. N Yor 1A 100
Beadnell. Nmbd 2G 121
Beaford. Devn 1F 11
Beal. Nmbd 5G 131
Beal. N Yor 2F 93
Bealsmill. Corn 5D 10
Beam Hill. Staf 3G 73
Beamhurst. Staf 2E 73
Beaminster. Dors 2H 13
Beamish. Dur 4F 115
Beamond End. Buck 1A 38
Beamsley. N Yor 4C 98
Bean. Kent 3G 39
Beanacre. Wilts 5E 35
Beanley. Nmbd 3E 121
Beaquoy. Orkn 5C 172
Beardwood. Bkbn 2E 91
Beare Green. Surr 1C 26
Bearley. Warw 4F 61
Bearpark. Dur 5F 115
Bearsbridge. Nmbd 4A 114
Bearsden. E Dun 2G 127
Bearsted. Kent 5B 40
Bearstone. Shrp 2B 72
Bearwood. Pool 3F 15
Bearwood. W Mid 2E 61
Beattock. Dum 4C 118
Beauchamp Roding. Essx 4F 53
Beauchief. S Yor 2H 85
Beaufort. Blae 4E 47
Beaulieu. Hants 2B 16
Beauly. High 4H 157
Beaumaris. IOA 3F 81
Beaumont. Cumb 4E 113
Beaumont. Essx 3E 55
Beaumont Hill. Darl 3F 105
Beaumont Leys. Leic 5C 74
Beausale. Warw 3G 61
Beauvale. Notts 1B 74
Beauworth. Hants 4D 24
Beaworthy. Devn 3E 11
Beazley End. Essx 3H 53
Bebington. Mers 2F 83
Bebside. Nmbd 1F 115
Beccles. Suff 2G 67
Becconsall. Lanc 2C 90
Beckbury. Shrp 5B 72
Beckenham. G Lon 4E 39
Beckermet. Cumb 4B 102
Beckett End. Norf 1G 65
Beck Foot. Cumb 5H 103
Beckfoot. Cumb
nr. Broughton in Furness 1A 96
nr. Seascale 4C 102
nr. Silloth 5B 112
Beckford. Worc 2E 49
Beckhampton. Wilts 5F 35
Beck Hole. N Yor 4F 107
Beckingham. Linc 5F 87
Beckingham. Notts 1E 87
Beckington. Som 1D 22
Beckley. E Sus 3C 28
Beckley. Hants 3H 15
Beckley. Oxon 4D 50
Beck Row. Suff 3F 65
Beck Side. Cumb
nr. Cartmel 1C 96
nr. Ulverston 1B 96
Beckside. Cumb 1F 97
Beckton. G Lon 2F 39
Beckwithshaw. N Yor 4E 99
Becontree. G Lon 2F 39
Bedale. N Yor 1E 99
Bedburn. Dur 1E 105
Bedchester. Dors 1D 14
Beddau. Rhon 3D 32
Beddgelert. Gwyn 1E 69
Beddingham. E Sus 5F 27
Beddington. G Lon 4E 39
Bedfield. Suff 4E 66
Bedford. Bed 188 (1A 52)
Bedford. G Man 1A 84
Bedham. W Sus 3B 26
Bedhampton. Hants 2F 17
Bedingfield. Suff 4D 66
Bedingham Green. Norf 1E 67
Bedlam. N Yor 3E 99
Bedlar's Green. Essx 3F 53
Bedlington. Nmbd 1F 115
Bedlinog. Mer T 5D 46
Bedminster. Bris 4A 34
Bedmond. Herts 5A 52
Bednall. Staf 4D 72
Bedrule. Bord 3A 120
Bedstone. Shrp 3F 59
Bedwas. Cphy 3E 33
Bedwellty. Cphy 5E 47
Bedworth. Warw 2A 62
Beeby. Leics 5D 74
Beech. Hants 3E 25
Beech. Staf 2C 72
Beechcliffe. W Yor 5C 98
Beech Hill. W Ber 5E 37
Beechingstoke. Wilts 1F 23
Beedon. W Ber 4C 36
Beeford. E Yor 4F 101
Beeley. Derbs 4G 85
Beelsby. NE Lin 4F 95
Beenham. W Ber 5D 36
Beeny. Corn 3B 10
Beer. Devn 4F 13
Beer. Som 3H 21
Beercrocombe. Som 4G 21
Beer Hackett. Dors 1B 14
Beesands. Devn 4E 9
Beesby. Linc 2D 88
Beeson. Devn 4E 9
Beeston. C Beds 1B 52
Beeston. Ches W 5H 83
Beeston. Norf 4B 78
Beeston. Notts 2C 74
Beeston. W Yor 1C 92
Beeston Regis. Norf 1D 78
Beeswing. Dum 3F 111
Beetham. Cumb 2D 97
Beetham. Som 1F 13
Beetley. Norf 4B 78
Beffcote. Staf 4C 72
Began. Card 3F 33
Begbroke. Oxon 4C 50
Begdale. Cambs 5D 76
Begelly. Pemb 4F 43
Beggar Hill. Essx 5G 53
Beggar's Bush. Powy 4E 59
Beggearn Huish. Som 3D 20
Beguildy. Powy 3D 58
Beighton. Norf 5F 79
Beighton. S Yor 2B 86
Beighton Hill. Derbs 5G 85
Beinn Casgro. W Isl 5G 171
Beith. N Ayr 4E 127
Bekesbourne. Kent 5F 41
Belaugh. Norf 4E 79
Belbroughton. Worc 3D 60
Belchalwell. Dors 2C 14
Belchalwell Street. Dors 2C 14
Belchamp Otten. Essx 1B 54
Belchamp St Paul. Essx 1A 54
Belchamp Walter. Essx 1B 54
Belchford. Linc 3B 88
Belfatton. Abers 3H 161
Belford. Nmbd 1F 121
Belgrano. Cnwy 3B 82
Belhaven. E Lot 2C 130
Belhelvie. Abers 2G 153
Belhinnie. Abers 1B 152
Bellabeg. Abers 2A 152
Belladrum. High 4H 157
Bellamore. S Ayr 1H 109
Bellanoch. Arg 4F 133
Bell Busk. N Yor 4B 98
Belleau. Linc 3D 88
Belleheiglash. Mor 5F 159
Bell End. Worc 3D 60
Bellerby. N Yor 5E 105

Bellerby Camp—Blackwall Tunnel

Bellerby Camp. *N Yor* 5D 105
Bellever. *Devn* 5G 11
Belle Vue. *Cumb* 1C 102
Belle Vue. *Shrp* 4G 71
Bellfield. *S Lan* 1H 117
Belliehill. *Ang* 2E 145
Bellingdon. *Buck* 5H 51
Bellingham. *Nmbd* 1B 114
Bellmount. *Norf* 3E 77
Bellochantuy. *Arg* 2A 122
Bellsbank. *E Ayr* 4D 117
Bell's Cross. *Suff* 5D 66
Bellshill. *N Lan* 4A 128
Bellshill. *Nmbd* 1F 121
Bellside. *N Lan* 4B 128
Bellspool. *Bord* 1D 118
Bellsquarry. *W Lot* 3D 128
Bells Yew Green. *E Sus* 2H 27
Belmaduthy. *High* 3A 158
Belmesthorpe. *Rut* 4H 75
Belmont. *Bkbn* 3E 91
Belmont. *Shet* 1G 173
Belmont. *S Ayr* 2C 116
Belnacraig. *Abers* 2A 152
Belnie. *Linc* 2B 76
Belowda. *Corn* 2D 6
Belper. *Derbs* 1A 74
Belper Lane End. *Derbs* 1H 73
Belph. *Derbs* 3C 86
Belsay. *Nmbd* 2E 115
Belsford. *Devn* 3D 8
Belsize. *Herts* 5A 52
Belstead. *Suff* 1E 55
Belston. *S Ayr* 2C 116
Belstone. *Devn* 3G 11
Belstone Corner. *Devn* 3G 11
Belthorn. *Lanc* 2F 91
Beltinge. *Kent* 4F 41
Beltoft. *N Lin* 4B 94
Belton. *Leics* 3B 74
Belton. *Linc* 2G 75
Belton. *Norf* 5G 79
Belton. *N Lin* 4A 94
Belton-in-Rutland. *Rut* 5F 75
Beltring. *Kent* 1A 28
Belts of Collonach. *Abers* 4D 152
Belvedere. *G Lon* 3F 39
Belvoir. *Leics* 2F 75
Bembridge. *IOW* 4E 17
Bemersyde. *Bord* 1H 119
Bemerton. *Wilts* 3G 23
Bempton. *E Yor* 2F 101
Benacre. *Suff* 2H 67
Ben Alder Lodge. *High* 1C 142
Ben Armine Lodge. *High* 2E 164
Benbecula Airport. *W Isl* 3C 170
Benbuie. *Dum* 5G 117
Benchill. *G Man* 2C 84
Benderloch. *Arg* 5D 140
Bendish. *Herts* 3B 52
Bendronaig Lodge. *High* 5C 156
Benenden. *Kent* 2C 28
Benfieldside. *Dur* 4D 115
Bengate. *Norf* 3F 79
Bengeworth. *Worc* 1F 49
Benhall Green. *Suff* 4F 67
Benholm. *Abers* 2H 145
Beningbrough. *N Yor* 4H 99
Benington. *Herts* 3C 52
Benington. *Linc* 1C 76
Benington Sea End. *Linc* 1D 76
Benllech. *IOA* 2E 81
Benmore Lodge. *High* 2H 163
Bennacott. *Corn* 3C 10
Bennah. *Devn* 4B 12
Bennecarrigan. *N Ayr* 3D 122
Bennethead. *Cumb* 2F 103
Benniworth. *Linc* 2B 88
Benover. *Kent* 1B 28
Benson. *Oxon* 2E 36
Benston. *Shet* 6F 173
Benstonhall. *Orkn* 4E 172
Bent. *Abers* 1F 145
Benthall. *Shrp* 5A 72
Bentham. *Glos* 4E 49
Bentlawnt. *Shrp* 5F 71
Bentley. *E Yor* 1D 94
Bentley. *Hants* 2F 25
Bentley. *S Yor* 4F 93
Bentley. *Suff* 2E 54
Bentley. *Warw* 1G 61
Bentley. *W Mid* 1D 61
Bentley Heath. *Herts* 1D 38
Bentley Heath. *W Mid* 3F 61
Bentpath. *Dum* 5F 119
Bents. *W Lot* 3C 128
Bentworth. *Hants* 2E 25
Benvie. *D'dee* 5C 144
Benville. *Dors* 2A 14
Benwell. *Tyne* 3F 115
Benwick. *Cambs* 1C 64
Beoley. *Worc* 4E 61
Beoraidbeg. *High* 4E 147
Bepton. *W Sus* 1G 17
Berden. *Essx* 3E 53
Bere Alston. *Devn* 2A 8
Bere Ferrers. *Devn* 2A 8
Berepper. *Corn* 4D 4
Bere Regis. *Dors* 3D 14
Bergh Apton. *Norf* 5F 79
Berinsfield. *Oxon* 2D 36
Berkeley. *Glos* 2B 34
Berkhamsted. *Herts* 5H 51
Berkley. *Som* 2D 22
Berkswell. *W Mid* 3G 61
Bermondsey. *G Lon* 3E 39
Bernera. *High* 1G 147
Bernice. *Arg* 4A 134
Bernisdale. *High* 3D 154
Berrick Salome. *Oxon* 2E 36
Berriedale. *High* 1H 165
Berrier. *Cumb* 2E 103
Berriew. *Powy* 5D 70
Berrington. *Nmbd* 5G 131
Berrington. *Shrp* 5H 71
Berrington. *Worc* 4H 59
Berrington Green. *Worc* 4H 59
Berrington Law. *Nmbd* 5F 131
Berrow. *Som* 1G 21
Berrow Green. *Worc* 5B 60
Berry Cross. *Devn* 1E 11
Berry Down Cross. *Devn* 2F 19
Berry Hill. *Glos* 4A 48
Berry Hill. *Pemb* 1A 44
Berryhillock. *Mor* 2C 160
Berrynarbor. *Devn* 2F 19
Berry Pomeroy. *Devn* 2E 9
Berryscaur. *Dum* 5D 118
Berry's Green. *G Lon* 5F 39
Bersham. *Wrex* 1F 71
Berthengam. *Flin* 3D 82
Berwick. *E Sus* 5G 27
Berwick Bassett. *Wilts* 4G 35
Berwick Hill. *Nmbd* 2E 115
Berwick St James. *Wilts* 3F 23
Berwick St John. *Wilts* 4E 23
Berwick St Leonard. *Wilts* 3E 23
Berwick-upon-Tweed. *Nmbd* 4F 131
Berwyn. *Den* 1D 70
Bescaby. *Leics* 3F 75
Bescar. *Lanc* 3B 90
Besford. *Worc* 1E 49
Bessacarr. *S Yor* 4G 93
Bessels Leigh. *Oxon* 5C 50
Bessingby. *E Yor* 3F 101
Bessingham. *Norf* 2D 78
Best Beech Hill. *E Sus* 2H 27
Besthorpe. *Norf* 1C 66
Besthorpe. *Notts* 4F 87
Bestwood Village. *Notts* 1C 74
Beswick. *E Yor* 5E 101
Betchworth. *Surr* 5D 38
Bethania. *Cdgn* 4E 57
Bethania. *Gwyn*
nr. Blaenau Ffestiniog 1G 69
nr. Caernarfon 5F 81
Bethel. *Gwyn*
nr. Bala 2B 70
nr. Caernarfon 4E 81
Bethel. *IOA* 3C 80
Bethersden. *Kent* 1D 28
Bethesda. *Gwyn* 4F 81
Bethesda. *Pemb* 3E 43
Bethlehem. *Carm* 3G 45
Bethnal Green. *G Lon* 2E 39
Betley. *Staf* 1B 72
Betsham. *Kent* 3H 39
Betteshanger. *Kent* 5H 41
Bettiscombe. *Dors* 3H 13
Bettisfield. *Wrex* 2G 71
Betton. *Shrp* 2A 72
Betton Strange. *Shrp* 5H 71
Bettws. *B'end* 3C 32
Bettws. *Newp* 2F 33
Bettws Bledrws. *Cdgn* 5E 57
Bettws Cedewain. *Powy* 1D 58
Bettws Gwerfil Goch. *Den* 1C 70
Bettws Ifan. *Cdgn* 1D 44
Bettws Newydd. *Mon* 5G 47
Bettyhill. *High* 2H 167
Betws. *Carm* 4G 45
Betws Garmon. *Gwyn* 5E 81
Betws-y-Coed. *Cnwy* 5G 81
Betws-yn-Rhos. *Cnwy* 3B 82
Beulah. *Cdgn* 1C 44
Beulah. *Powy* 5B 58
Beul an Atha. *Arg* 3B 124
Bevendean. *Brig* 5E 27
Bevercotes. *Notts* 3E 86
Beverley. *E Yor* 1D 94
Beverston. *Glos* 2D 34
Bevington. *Glos* 2B 34
Bewaldeth. *Cumb* 1D 102
Bewcastle. *Cumb* 2G 113
Bewdley. *Worc* 3B 60
Bewerley. *N Yor* 3D 98
Bewholme. *E Yor* 4F 101
Bexfield. *Norf* 3C 78
Bexhill. *E Sus* 5B 28
Bexley. *G Lon* 3F 39
Bexleyheath. *G Lon* 3F 39
Bexleyhill. *W Sus* 3A 26
Bexwell. *Norf* 5F 77
Beyton. *Suff* 4B 66
Bhalton. *W Isl* 4C 171
Bhatarsaigh. *W Isl* 9B 170
Bibbington. *Derbs* 3E 85
Bibury. *Glos* 5G 49
Bicester. *Oxon* 3D 50
Bickenhall. *Som* 1F 13
Bickenhill. *W Mid* 2F 61
Bicker. *Linc* 2B 76
Bicker Bar. *Linc* 2B 76
Bicker Gauntlet. *Linc* 2B 76
Bickershaw. *G Man* 4E 91
Bickerstaffe. *Lanc* 4C 90
Bickerton. *Ches E* 5H 83
Bickerton. *Nmbd* 4D 121
Bickerton. *N Yor* 4G 99
Bickford. *Staf* 4C 72
Bickington. *Devn*
nr. Barnstaple 3F 19
nr. Newton Abbot 5A 12
Bickleigh. *Devn*
nr. Plymouth 2B 8
nr. Tiverton 2C 12
Bickleton. *Devn* 3F 19
Bickley. *N Yor* 5G 107
Bickley Moss. *Ches W* 1H 71
Bickmarsh. *Worc* 1G 49
Bicknacre. *Essx* 5A 54
Bicknoller. *Som* 3E 20
Bicknor. *Kent* 5C 40
Bickton. *Hants* 1G 15
Bicton. *Here* 4G 59
Bicton. *Shrp*
nr. Bishop's Castle 2E 59
nr. Shrewsbury 4G 71
Bicton Heath. *Shrp* 4G 71
Bidborough. *Kent* 1G 27
Biddenden. *Kent* 2C 28
Biddenden Green. *Kent* 1C 28
Biddenham. *Bed* 5H 63
Biddestone. *Wilts* 4D 34
Biddisham. *Som* 1G 21
Biddlesden. *Buck* 1E 51
Biddlestone. *Nmbd* 4D 120
Biddulph. *Staf* 5C 84
Biddulph Moor. *Staf* 5D 84
Bideford. *Devn* 4E 19
Bidford-on-Avon. *Warw* 5E 61
Bidlake. *Devn* 4F 11
Bidston. *Mers* 2E 83
Bielby. *E Yor* 5B 100
Bieldside. *Aber* 3F 153
Bierley. *IOW* 5D 16
Bierley. *W Yor* 1B 92
Bierton. *Buck* 4G 51
Bigbury. *Devn* 4C 8
Bigbury-on-Sea. *Devn* 4C 8
Bigby. *Linc* 4D 94
Biggar. *Cumb* 3A 96
Biggar. *S Lan* 1C 118
Biggin. *Derbs*
nr. Hartington 5F 85
nr. Hulland 1G 73
Biggin. *N Yor* 1F 93
Biggings. *Shet* 5C 173
Biggin Hill. *G Lon* 5F 39
Biggleswade. *C Beds* 1B 52
Bighouse. *High* 2A 168
Bighton. *Hants* 3E 24
Biglands. *Cumb* 4D 112
Bignall End. *Staf* 5C 84
Bignor. *W Sus* 4A 26
Bigrigg. *Cumb* 3B 102
Big Sand. *High* 1G 155
Bigton. *Shet* 9E 173
Bilberry. *Corn* 3E 6
Bilborough. *Nott* 1C 74
Bilbrook. *Som* 2D 20
Bilbrook. *Staf* 5C 72
Bilbrough. *N Yor* 5H 99
Bilbster. *High* 3E 169
Bilby. *Notts* 2D 86
Bildershaw. *Dur* 2F 105
Bildeston. *Suff* 1C 54
Billericay. *Essx* 1A 40
Billesdon. *Leics* 5E 74
Billesley. *Warw* 5F 61
Billingborough. *Linc* 2A 76
Billinge. *Mers* 4D 90
Billingford. *Norf*
nr. Dereham 3C 78
nr. Diss 3D 66
Billingham. *Stoc T* 2B 106
Billinghay. *Linc* 5A 88
Billingley. *S Yor* 4E 93
Billingshurst. *W Sus* 3B 26
Billingsley. *Shrp* 2B 60
Billington. *C Beds* 3H 51
Billington. *Lanc* 1F 91
Billington. *Staf* 3C 72
Billockby. *Norf* 4G 79
Billy Row. *Dur* 1E 105
Bilsborrow. *Lanc* 5E 97
Bilsby. *Linc* 3D 88
Bilsham. *W Sus* 5A 26
Bilsington. *Kent* 2E 29
Bilson Green. *Glos* 4B 48
Bilsthorpe. *Notts* 4D 86
Bilston. *Midl* 3F 129
Bilston. *W Mid* 1D 60
Bilstone. *Leics* 5A 74
Bilting. *Kent* 1E 29
Bilton. *E Yor* 1E 95
Bilton. *Nmbd* 3G 121
Bilton. *N Yor* 4F 99
Bilton. *Warw* 3B 62
Bilton in Ainsty. *N Yor* 5G 99
Bimbister. *Orkn* 6C 172
Binbrook. *Linc* 1B 88
Binchester. *Dur* 1F 105
Bincombe. *Dors* 4B 14
Bindal. *High* 5G 165
Binegar. *Som* 2B 22
Bines Green. *W Sus* 4C 26
Binfield. *Brac* 4G 37
Binfield Heath. *Oxon* 4F 37
Bingfield. *Nmbd* 2C 114
Bingham. *Notts* 2E 74
Bingham's Melcombe. *Dors* 2C 14
Bingley. *W Yor* 1B 92
Bings Heath. *Shrp* 4H 71
Binham. *Norf* 2B 78
Binley. *Hants* 1C 24
Binley. *W Mid* 3A 62
Binnegar. *Dors* 4D 15
Binniehill. *Falk* 2B 128
Binsoe. *N Yor* 2E 99
Binstead. *IOW* 3D 16
Binsted. *Hants* 2F 25
Binsted. *W Sus* 5A 26
Binton. *Warw* 5F 61
Bintree. *Norf* 3C 78
Binweston. *Shrp* 5F 71
Birch. *Essx* 4C 54
Birch. *G Man* 4G 91
Birchall. *Staf* 5D 85
Bircham Newton. *Norf* 2G 77
Bircham Tofts. *Norf* 2G 77
Birchanger. *Essx* 3F 53
Birchburn. *N Ayr* 3D 122
Birch Cross. *Staf* 2F 73
Bircher. *Here* 4G 59
Birch Green. *Essx* 4C 54
Birchgrove. *Card* 3E 33
Birchgrove. *Swan* 3G 31
Birch Heath. *Ches W* 4H 83
Birch Hill. *Ches W* 3H 83
Birchill. *Devn* 2G 13
Birchington. *Kent* 4G 41
Birchley Heath. *Warw* 1G 61
Birchmoor. *Warw* 5G 73
Birchmoor Green. *C Beds* 2H 51
Birchover. *Derbs* 4G 85
Birch Vale. *Derbs* 2E 85
Birchview. *Mor* 5F 159
Birchwood. *Linc* 4G 87
Birchwood. *Som* 1F 13
Birchwood. *Warr* 1A 84
Bircotes. *Notts* 1D 86
Birdbrook. *Essx* 1H 53
Birdham. *W Sus* 2G 17
Birdholme. *Derbs* 4A 86
Birdingbury. *Warw* 4B 62
Birdlip. *Glos* 4E 49
Birdsall. *N Yor* 3C 100
Birds Edge. *W Yor* 4C 92
Birds Green. *Essx* 5F 53
Birdsgreen. *Shrp* 2B 60
Birdsmoorgate. *Dors* 2G 13
Birdston. *E Dun* 2H 127
Birdwell. *S Yor* 4D 92
Birdwood. *Glos* 4C 48
Birgham. *Bord* 1B 120
Birichen. *High* 4E 165
Birkby. *Cumb* 1B 102
Birkby. *N Yor* 4A 106
Birkdale. *Mers* 3B 90
Birkenhead. *Mers* 2F 83
Birkenhills. *Abers* 4E 161
Birkenshaw. *N Lan* 3H 127
Birkenshaw. *W Yor* 2C 92
Birkhall. *Abers* 4H 151
Birkhill. *Ang* 5C 144
Birkholme. *Linc* 3G 75
Birkin. *N Yor* 2F 93
Birley. *Here* 5G 59
Birling. *Kent* 4A 40
Birling. *Nmbd* 4G 121
Birling Gap. *E Sus* 5G 27
Birlingham. *Worc* 1E 49
Birmingham. *W Mid* 188 (2E 61)
Birmingham Airport. *W Mid* 216 (2F 61)
Birnam. *Per* 4H 143
Birse. *Abers* 4C 152
Birsemore. *Abers* 4C 152
Birstall. *Leics* 5C 74
Birstall. *W Yor* 2C 92
Birstall Smithies. *W Yor* 2C 92
Birstwith. *N Yor* 4E 99
Birthorpe. *Linc* 2A 76
Birtle. *G Man* 3G 91
Birtley. *Here* 4F 59
Birtley. *Nmbd* 2B 114
Birtley. *Tyne* 4F 115
Birtsmorton. *Worc* 2D 48
Birts Street. *Worc* 2C 48
Bisbrooke. *Rut* 1F 63
Bisham. *Wind* 3G 37
Bishampton. *Worc* 5D 61
Bish Mill. *Devn* 4H 19
Bishop Auckland. *Dur* 2F 105
Bishopbridge. *Linc* 1H 87
Bishopbriggs. *E Dun* 2H 127
Bishop Burton. *E Yor* 1C 94
Bishopdown. *Wilts* 3G 23
Bishop Middleham. *Dur* 1A 106
Bishopmill. *Mor* 2G 159
Bishop Monkton. *N Yor* 3F 99
Bishop Norton. *Linc* 1G 87
Bishopsbourne. *Kent* 5F 41
Bishops Cannings. *Wilts* 5F 35
Bishop's Castle. *Shrp* 2F 59
Bishop's Caundle. *Dors* 1B 14
Bishop's Cleeve. *Glos* 3E 49
Bishop's Down. *Dors* 1B 14
Bishop's Frome. *Here* 1B 48
Bishop's Green. *Essx* 4G 53
Bishop's Green. *Hants* 5D 36
Bishop's Hull. *Som* 4F 21
Bishop's Itchington. *Warw* 5A 62
Bishops Lydeard. *Som* 4E 21
Bishop's Norton. *Glos* 3D 48
Bishop's Nympton. *Devn* 4A 20
Bishop's Offley. *Staf* 3B 72
Bishop's Stortford. *Herts* 3E 53
Bishop's Sutton. *Hants* 3E 24
Bishop's Tachbrook. *Warw* 4H 61
Bishop's Tawton. *Devn* 3F 19
Bishopsteignton. *Devn* 5C 12
Bishopstoke. *Hants* 1C 16
Bishopston. *Swan* 4E 31
Bishopstone. *Buck* 4G 51
Bishopstone. *E Sus* 5F 27
Bishopstone. *Here* 1H 47
Bishopstone. *Swin* 3H 35
Bishopstone. *Wilts* 4F 23
Bishopstrow. *Wilts* 2D 23
Bishop Sutton. *Bath* 1A 22
Bishop's Waltham. *Hants* 1D 16
Bishopswood. *Som* 1F 13
Bishops Wood. *Staf* 5C 72
Bishopsworth. *Bris* 5A 34
Bishop Thornton. *N Yor* 3E 99
Bishopthorpe. *York* 5H 99
Bishopton. *Darl* 2A 106
Bishopton. *Dum* 5B 110
Bishopton. *N Yor* 2E 99
Bishopton. *Ren* 2F 127
Bishopton. *Warw* 5F 61
Bishop Wilton. *E Yor* 4B 100
Bishton. *Newp* 3G 33
Bishton. *Staf* 3E 73
Bisley. *Glos* 5E 49
Bisley. *Surr* 5A 38
Bispham. *Bkpl* 5C 96
Bispham Green. *Lanc* 3C 90
Bissoe. *Corn* 4B 6
Bisterne. *Hants* 2G 15
Bisterne Close. *Hants* 2H 15
Bitchfield. *Linc* 3G 75
Bittadon. *Devn* 2F 19
Bittaford. *Devn* 3C 8
Bittering. *Norf* 4B 78
Bitterley. *Shrp* 3H 59
Bitterne. *Sotn* 1C 16
Bitteswell. *Leics* 2C 62
Bitton. *S Glo* 5B 34
Bix. *Oxon* 3F 37
Bixter. *Shet* 6E 173
Blaby. *Leics* 1C 62
Blackawton. *Devn* 3E 9
Black Bank. *Cambs* 2E 65
Black Barn. *Linc* 3D 76
Blackborough. *Devn* 2D 12
Blackborough. *Norf* 4F 77
Blackborough End. *Norf* 4F 77
Black Bourton. *Oxon* 5A 50
Blackboys. *E Sus* 3G 27
Blackbrook. *Derbs* 1H 73
Blackbrook. *Mers* 1H 83
Blackbrook. *Staf* 2B 72
Blackbrook. *Surr* 1C 26
Blackburn. *Abers* 2F 153
Blackburn. *Bkbn* 2E 91
Blackburn. *W Lot* 3C 128
Black Callerton. *Tyne* 3E 115
Black Carr. *Norf* 1C 66
Black Clauchrie. *S Ayr* 1H 109
Black Corries. *High* 3G 141
Black Crofts. *Arg* 5D 140
Black Cross. *Corn* 2D 6
Blackden Heath. *Ches E* 3B 84
Blackditch. *Oxon* 5C 50
Blackdog. *Abers* 2G 153
Black Dog. *Devn* 2B 12
Blackdown. *Dors* 2G 13
Blackdyke. *Cumb* 4C 112
Blacker Hill. *S Yor* 4D 92
Blackfen. *G Lon* 3F 39
Blackfield. *Hants* 2C 16
Blackford. *Cumb* 3E 113
Blackford. *Per* 3A 136
Blackford. *Shrp* 2H 59
Blackford. *Som*
nr. Burnham-on-Sea 2H 21
nr. Wincanton 4B 22
Blackfordby. *Leics* 4H 73
Blackgang. *IOW* 5C 16
Blackhall. *Edin* 2F 129
Blackhall. *Ren* 3F 127
Blackhall Colliery. *Dur* 1B 106
Blackhall Mill. *Tyne* 4E 115
Blackhall Rocks. *Dur* 1B 106
Blackham. *E Sus* 2F 27
Blackheath. *Essx* 3D 54
Blackheath. *G Lon* 3E 39
Blackheath. *Suff* 3G 67
Blackheath. *Surr* 1B 26
Blackheath. *W Mid* 2D 61
Black Heddon. *Nmbd* 2D 115
Blackhill. *Abers* 4H 161
Blackhill. *High* 3C 154
Black Hill. *Warw* 5G 61
Blackhills. *Abers* 2G 161
Blackhills. *High* 3D 158
Blackjack. *Linc* 2B 76
Blackland. *Wilts* 5F 35
Black Lane. *G Man* 4F 91
Blackleach. *Lanc* 1C 90
Blackley. *G Man* 4G 91
Blackley. *W Yor* 3B 92
Blacklunans. *Per* 2A 144
Blackmill. *B'end* 3C 32
Blackmoor. *G Man* 4E 91
Blackmoor. *Hants* 3F 25
Blackmoor Gate. *Devn* 2G 19
Blackmore. *Essx* 5G 53
Blackmore End. *Essx* 2H 53
Blackmore End. *Herts* 4B 52
Black Mount. *Arg* 4G 141
Blackness. *Falk* 2D 128
Blacknest. *Hants* 2F 25
Blackney. *Dors* 3H 13
Blacknoll. *Dors* 4D 14
Black Notley. *Essx* 3A 54
Blacko. *Lanc* 5A 98
Black Pill. *Swan* 3F 31
Blackpool. *Bkpl* 188 (1B 90)
Blackpool. *Devn* 4E 9
Blackpool Airport. *Lanc* 1B 90
Blackpool Corner. *Dors* 3G 13
Blackpool Gate. *Cumb* 2G 113
Blackridge. *W Lot* 3B 128
Blackrock. *Arg* 3B 124
Blackrock. *Mon* 4F 47
Blackrod. *G Man* 3E 90
Blackshaw. *Dum* 3B 112
Blackshaw Head. *W Yor* 2H 91
Blackshaw Moor. *Staf* 5E 85
Blacksmith's Green. *Suff* 4D 66
Blacksnape. *Bkbn* 2F 91
Blackstone. *W Sus* 4D 26
Black Street. *Suff* 2H 67
Black Tar. *Pemb* 4D 43
Blackthorn. *Oxon* 4E 50
Blackthorpe. *Suff* 4B 66
Blacktoft. *E Yor* 2B 94
Blacktop. *Aber* 3F 153
Black Torrington. *Devn* 2E 11
Blacktown. *Newp* 3F 33
Blackwall Tunnel. *G Lon* 2E 39

Blackwater. *Corn* 4B 6
Blackwater. *Hants* 1G 25
Blackwater. *IOW* 4D 16
Blackwater. *Som* 1F 13
Blackwaterfoot. *N Ayr* 3C 122
Blackwell. *Darl* 3F 105
Blackwell. *Derbs*
  nr. Alfreton 5B 86
  nr. Buxton 3F 85
Blackwell. *Som* 4D 20
Blackwell. *Warw* 1H 49
Blackwell. *Worc* 3D 61
Blackwood. *Cphy* 2E 33
Blackwood. *Dum* 1G 111
Blackwood. *S Lan* 5A 128
Blackwood Hill. *Staf* 5D 84
Blacon. *Ches W* 4F 83
Bladnoch. *Dum* 4B 110
Bladon. *Oxon* 4C 50
Blaenannerch. *Cdgn* 1C 44
Blaenau Dolwyddelan. *Cnwy* . . .5F 81
Blaenau Ffestiniog. *Gwyn* 1G 69
Blaenavon. *Torf* 5F 47
Blaenawey. *Mon* 4F 47
Blaen Celyn. *Cdgn* 5C 56
Blaen Clydach. *Rhon* 2C 32
Blaencwm. *Rhon* 2C 32
Blaendulais. *Neat* 5B 46
Blaenffos. *Pemb* 1F 43
Blaengarw. *B'end* 2C 32
Blaen-geuffordd. *Cdgn* 2F 57
Blaengwrach. *Neat* 5B 46
Blaengwynfi. *Neat* 2B 32
Blaenllechau. *Rhon* 2C 32
Blaenpennal. *Cdgn* 4F 57
Blaenplwyf. *Cdgn* 3E 57
Blaenporth. *Cdgn* 1C 44
Blaenrhondda. *Rhon* 5C 46
Blaenwaun. *Carm* 2G 43
Blaen-y-coed. *Carm* 2H 43
Blagdon. *N Som* 1A 22
Blagdon. *Torb* 2E 9
Blagdon Hill. *Som* 1F 13
Blagill. *Cumb* 5A 114
Blaguegate. *Lanc* 4C 90
Blaich. *High* 1E 141
Blain. *High* 2A 140
Blaina. *Blae* 5F 47
Blair Atholl. *Per* 2F 143
Blair Drummond. *Stir* 4G 135
Blairgowrie. *Per* 4A 144
Blairhall. *Fife* 1D 128
Blairingone. *Per* 4B 136
Blairlogie. *Stir* 4H 135
Blairmore. *Abers* 5B 160
Blairmore. *Arg* 1C 126
Blairmore. *High* 3B 166
Blairquhanan. *W Dun* 1F 127
Blaisdon. *Glos* 4C 48
Blakebrook. *Worc* 3C 60
Blakedown. *Worc* 3C 60
Blake End. *Essx* 3H 53
Blakemere. *Here* 1G 47
Blakeney. *Glos* 5B 48
Blakeney. *Norf* 1C 78
Blakenhall. *Ches E* 1B 72
Blakeshall. *Worc* 2C 60
Blakesley. *Nptn* 5D 62
Blanchland. *Nmbd* 4C 114
Blandford Camp. *Dors* 2E 15
Blandford Forum. *Dors* 2D 15
Blandford St Mary. *Dors* 2D 15
Bland Hill. *N Yor* 4E 98
Blandy. *High* 2G 167
Blanefield. *Stir* 2G 127
Blankney. *Linc* 4H 87
Blantyre. *S Lan* 4H 127
Blarmachfoldach. *High* 2E 141
Blarnalearoch. *High* 4F 163
Blashford. *Hants* 2G 15
Blaston. *Leics* 1F 63
Blatchbridge. *Som* 2C 22
Blathaisbhal. *W Isl* 1D 170
Blatherwycke. *Nptn* 1G 63
Blawith. *Cumb* 1B 96
Blaxhall. *Suff* 5F 67
Blaxton. *S Yor* 4G 93
Blaydon. *Tyne* 3E 115
Bleadney. *Som* 2H 21
Bleadon. *N Som* 1G 21
Blean. *Kent* 4F 41
Bleasby. *Linc* 2A 88
Bleasby. *Notts* 1E 74
Bleasby Moor. *Linc* 2A 88
Blebocraigs. *Fife* 2G 137
Bleddfa. *Powy* 4E 58
Bledington. *Glos* 3H 49
Bledlow. *Buck* 5F 51
Bledlow Ridge. *Buck* 2F 37
Blencarn. *Cumb* 1H 103
Blencogo. *Cumb* 5C 112
Blendworth. *Hants* 1F 17
Blennerhasset. *Cumb* 5C 112
Bletchingdon. *Oxon* 4D 50
Bletchingley. *Surr* 5E 39
Bletchley. *Mil* 2G 51
Bletchley. *Shrp* 2A 72
Bletherston. *Pemb* 2E 43
Bletsoe. *Bed* 5H 63
Blewbury. *Oxon* 3D 36
Blickling. *Norf* 3D 78
Blidworth. *Notts* 5C 86
Blindburn. *Nmbd* 3C 120
Blindcrake. *Cumb* 1C 102
Blindley Heath. *Surr* 1E 27
Blindmoor. *Som* 1F 13
Blisland. *Corn* 5B 10
Blissford. *Hants* 1G 15
Bliss Gate. *Worc* 3B 60
Blists Hill. *Telf* 5A 72
Blisworth. *Nptn* 5E 63

Blithbury. *Staf* 3E 73
Blitterlees. *Cumb* 4C 112
Blockley. *Glos* 2G 49
Blofield. *Norf* 5F 79
Blofield Heath. *Norf* 4F 79
Blo' Norton. *Norf* 3C 66
Bloomfield. *Bord* 2H 119
Blore. *Staf* 1F 73
Blount's Green. *Staf* 2E 73
Bloxham. *Oxon* 2C 50
Bloxholm. *Linc* 5H 87
Bloxwich. *W Mid* 5D 73
Bloxworth. *Dors* 3D 15
Blubberhouses. *N Yor* 4D 98
Blue Anchor. *Som* 2D 20
Blue Anchor. *Swan* 3E 31
Blue Bell Hill. *Kent* 4B 40
Blue Row. *Essx* 4D 54
Bluetown. *Kent* 5D 40
Blundeston. *Suff* 1H 67
Blunham. *C Beds* 5A 64
Blunsdon St Andrew. *Swin* . . .3G 35
Bluntington. *Worc* 3C 60
Bluntisham. *Cambs* 3C 64
Blunts. *Corn* 2H 7
Blurton. *Stoke* 1C 72
Blyborough. *Linc* 1G 87
Blyford. *Suff* 3G 67
Blymhill. *Staf* 4C 72
Blymhill Lawns. *Staf* 4C 72
Blyth. *Nmbd* 1G 115
Blyth. *Notts* 2D 86
Blyth. *Bord* 5E 129
Blyth Bank. *Bord* 5E 129
Blyth Bridge. *Bord* 5E 129
Blythburgh. *Suff* 3G 67
Blythe, The. *Staf* 3E 73
Blythe Bridge. *Staf* 1D 72
Blythe Marsh. *Staf* 1D 72
Blyton. *Linc* 1F 87
Boarhills. *Fife* 2H 137
Boarhunt. *Hants* 2E 16
Boarshead. *E Sus* 2G 27
Boar's Head. *G Man* 4D 90
Boars Hill. *Oxon* 5C 50
Boarstall. *Buck* 4E 51
Boasley Cross. *Devn* 3F 11
Boath. *High* 1H 157
Boat of Garten. *High* 2D 150
Bobbing. *Kent* 4C 40
Bobbington. *Staf* 1C 60
Bobbingworth. *Essx* 5F 53
Bocaddon. *Corn* 3F 7
Bocking. *Essx* 3A 54
Bocking Churchstreet. *Essx* . . .3A 54
Boddam. *Abers* 4H 161
Boddam. *Shet* 10E 173
Boddington. *Glos* 3D 49
Bodedern. *IOA* 2C 80
Bodelwyddan. *Den* 3C 82
Bodenham. *Here* 5H 59
Bodenham. *Wilts* 4G 23
Bodewryd. *IOA* 1C 80
Bodfari. *Den* 3C 82
Bodffordd. *IOA* 3D 80
Bodham. *Norf* 1D 78
Bodiam. *E Sus* 3B 28
Bodicote. *Oxon* 2C 50
Bodieve. *Corn* 1D 6
Bodinnick. *Corn* 3F 7
Bodle Street Green. *E Sus* 4A 28
Bodmin. *Corn* 2E 7
Bodnant. *Cnwy* 3H 81
Bodney. *Norf* 1H 65
Bodorgan. *IOA* 4C 80
Bodrane. *Corn* 2G 7
Bodsham. *Kent* 1F 29
Boduan. *Gwyn* 2C 68
Bodymoor Heath. *Warw* 1F 61
Bog, The. *Shrp* 1F 59
Bogallan. *High* 3A 158
Bogbrae Croft. *Abers* 5H 161
Bogend. *S Ayr* 1C 116
Boghall. *Midl* 3F 129
Boghall. *W Lot* 3C 128
Boghead. *S Lan* 5A 128
Bogindollo. *Ang* 3D 144
Bogmoor. *Mor* 2A 160
Bogniebrae. *Abers* 4C 160
Bognor Regis. *W Sus* 3H 17
Bograxie. *Abers* 2E 152
Bogside. *N Lan* 4B 128
Bogton. *Abers* 3D 160
Bogue. *Dum* 1D 110
Bohenie. *High* 5E 149
Bohortha. *Corn* 5C 6
Boirseam. *W Isl* 9C 171
Bokiddick. *Corn* 2E 7
Bolam. *Dur* 2E 105
Bolam. *Nmbd* 1D 115
Bolberry. *Devn* 5C 8
Bold Heath. *Mers* 2H 83
Boldon. *Tyne* 3G 115
Boldon Colliery. *Tyne* 3G 115
Boldre. *Hants* 3B 16
Boldron. *Dur* 3D 104
Bole. *Notts* 2E 87
Bolehall. *Staf* 5G 73
Bolehill. *Derbs* 5G 85
Bolenowe. *Corn* 5A 6
Boleside. *Bord* 1G 119
Bolham. *Devn* 1C 12
Bolham Water. *Devn* 1E 13
Bolingey. *Corn* 3B 6
Bollington. *Ches E* 3D 84
Bolney. *W Sus* 3D 26
Bolnhurst. *Bed* 5H 63
Bolshan. *Ang* 3F 145
Bolsover. *Derbs* 3B 86
Bolsterstone. *S Yor* 1G 85
Bolstone. *Here* 2A 48

Boltachan. *Per* 3F 143
Boltby. *N Yor* 1G 99
Bolton. *Cumb* 2H 103
Bolton. *E Lot* 2B 130
Bolton. *E Yor* 4B 100
Bolton. *G Man* 4F 91
Bolton. *Nmbd* 3F 121
Bolton Abbey. *N Yor* 4C 98
Bolton-by-Bowland. *Lanc* 5G 97
Boltonfellend. *Cumb* 3F 113
Boltongate. *Cumb* 5D 112
Bolton Green. *Lanc* 3D 90
Bolton-le-Sands. *Lanc* 3D 97
Bolton Low Houses. *Cumb* . . .5D 112
Bolton New Houses. *Cumb* . . .5D 112
Bolton-on-Swale. *N Yor* 5F 105
Bolton Percy. *N Yor* 5H 99
Bolton Town End. *Lanc* 3D 97
Bolton upon Dearne. *S Yor* . . .4E 93
Bolton Wood Lane. *Cumb* 5D 112
Bolventor. *Corn* 5B 10
Bomarsund. *Nmbd* 1F 115
Bomere Heath. *Shrp* 4G 71
Bonar Bridge. *High* 4D 164
Bonawe. *Arg* 5E 141
Bonby. *N Lin* 3D 94
Boncath. *Pemb* 1G 43
Bonchester Bridge. *Bord* 3H 119
Bonchurch. *IOW* 5D 16
Bond End. *Staf* 4F 73
Bondleigh. *Devn* 2G 11
Bonds. *Lanc* 5D 97
Bonehill. *Devn* 5H 11
Bonehill. *Staf* 5F 73
Bo'ness. *Falk* 1C 128
Boney Hay. *Staf* 4E 73
Bonham. *Wilts* 3C 22
Bonhill. *W Dun* 2E 127
Boningale. *Shrp* 5C 72
Bonjedward. *Bord* 2A 120
Bonkle. *N Lan* 4B 128
Bonnington. *Ang* 5E 145
Bonnington. *Edin* 3E 129
Bonnington. *Kent* 2E 29
Bonnybank. *Fife* 3F 137
Bonnybridge. *Falk* 1B 128
Bonnykelly. *Abers* 3F 161
Bonnyton. *Ang* 5C 144
Bonnytown. *Fife* 2H 137
Bonsall. *Derbs* 5G 85
Bont. *Mon* 4G 47
Bontddu. *Gwyn* 4F 69
Bont Dolgadfan. *Powy* 5A 70
Y Bont-Faen. *V Glam* 4C 32
Bontgoch. *Cdgn* 2F 57
Bonthorpe. *Linc* 3D 89
Bontnewydd. *Cdgn* 4F 57
Bontnewydd. *Cnwy* 3C 82
Bont Newydd. *Gwyn* 1G 69
Bontnewydd. *Gwyn* 4D 81
Bontuchel. *Den* 5C 82
Bonvilston. *V Glam* 4D 32
Bon-y-maen. *Swan* 3F 31
Booker. *Buck* 2G 37
Booley. *Shrp* 3H 71
Boorley Green. *Hants* 1D 16
Boosbeck. *Red C* 3D 106
Boot. *Cumb* 4C 102
Booth. *W Yor* 2A 92
Boothby Graffoe. *Linc* 5G 87
Boothby Pagnell. *Linc* 2G 75
Booth Green. *Ches E* 2D 84
Booth of Toft. *Shet* 4F 173
Boothstown. *G Man* 4F 91
Boothville. *Nptn* 4E 63
Bootle. *Cumb* 1A 96
Bootle. *Mers* 1F 83
Booton. *Norf* 3D 78
Booze. *N Yor* 4D 104
Boquhan. *Stir* 1G 127
Boraston. *Shrp* 3A 60
Borden. *Kent* 4C 40
Borden. *W Sus* 4G 25
Bordlands. *Bord* 5E 129
Bordley. *N Yor* 3B 98
Bordon. *Hants* 3F 25
Boreham. *Essx* 5A 54
Boreham. *Wilts* 2D 23
Boreham Street. *E Sus* 4A 28
Borehamwood. *Herts* 1C 38
Boreland. *Dum* 5D 118
Boreston. *Devn* 3D 8
Borestone Brae. *Stir* 4G 135
Boreton. *Shrp* 5H 71
Borgh. *W Isl*
  on Barra 8B 170
  on Benbecula 3C 170
  on Berneray 1E 170
  on Isle of Lewis 2G 171
Borghasdal. *W Isl* 9C 171
Borghastan. *W Isl* 3D 171
Borgh na Sgiotaig. *High* 1C 154
Borgie. *High* 3H 167
Borgue. *Dum* 5D 110
Borgue. *High* 1H 165
Borley. *Essx* 1B 54
Borley Green. *Essx* 1B 54
Borley Green. *Suff* 4B 66
Borlum. *High* 1H 149
Bornais. *W Isl* 6C 170
Bornesketaig. *High* 1C 154
Boroughbridge. *N Yor* 3F 99
Borough Green. *Kent* 5H 39
Borreraig. *High* 3A 154
Borrobol Lodge. *High* 1F 165
Borrodale. *High* 4A 154
Borrowash. *Derbs* 2B 74
Borrowby. *N Yor*
  nr. Northallerton 1G 99
  nr. Whitby 3E 107

Borrowston. *High* 4F 169
Borrowstonehill. *Orkn* 7D 172
Borrowstoun. *Falk* 1C 128
Borth. *Cdgn* 2F 57
Borthwick. *Midl* 4G 129
Borth-y-Gest. *Gwyn* 2E 69
Borve. *High* 4D 154
Borwick. *Lanc* 2E 97
Bosbury. *Here* 1B 48
Boscastle. *Corn* 3A 10
Boscombe. *Bour* 3G 15
Boscombe. *Wilts* 3H 23
Boscoppa. *Corn* 3E 7
Bosham. *W Sus* 2G 17
Bosherston. *Pemb* 5D 42
Bosley. *Ches E* 4D 84
Bossall. *N Yor* 3B 100
Bossiney. *Corn* 4A 10
Bossingham. *Kent* 1F 29
Bossington. *Som* 2B 20
Bostadh. *W Isl* 3D 171
Bostock Green. *Ches W* 4A 84
Boston. *Linc* 1C 76
Boston Spa. *W Yor* 5G 99
Boswarthen. *Corn* 3B 4
Boswinger. *Corn* 4D 6
Botallack. *Corn* 3A 4
Botany Bay. *G Lon* 1D 39
Botcheston. *Leics* 5B 74
Botesdale. *Suff* 3C 66
Bothal. *Nmbd* 1F 115
Bothampstead. *W Ber* 4D 36
Bothamsall. *Notts* 3D 86
Bothel. *Cumb* 1C 102
Bothenhampton. *Dors* 3H 13
Bothwell. *S Lan* 4A 128
Botley. *Buck* 5H 51
Botley. *Hants* 1D 16
Botley. *Oxon* 5C 50
Botloe's Green. *Glos* 3B 48
Botolph Claydon. *Buck* 3F 51
Botolphs. *W Sus* 5C 26
Bottacks. *High* 2G 157
Bottesford. *Leics* 2F 75
Bottesford. *N Lin* 4B 94
Bottisham. *Cambs* 4E 65
Bottlesford. *Wilts* 1G 23
Bottomcraig. *Fife* 1F 137
Bottom o' th' Moor. *G Man* . . .3E 91
Botton. *N Yor* 4D 107
Botton Head. *Lanc* 3F 97
Bottreaux Mill. *Devn* 4B 20
Botus Fleming. *Corn* 2A 8
Botwnnog. *Gwyn* 2B 68
Bough Beech. *Kent* 1F 27
Boughrood. *Powy* 2E 47
Boughspring. *Glos* 2A 34
Boughton. *Norf* 5F 77
Boughton. *Nptn* 4E 63
Boughton. *Notts* 4D 86
Boughton Aluph. *Kent* 1E 29
Boughton Green. *Kent* 5B 40
Boughton Lees. *Kent* 1E 28
Boughton Malherbe. *Kent* 1C 28
Boughton Monchelsea. *Kent* . . .5B 40
Boughton under Blean. *Kent* . . .5E 41
Boulby. *Red C* 3E 107
Bouldon. *IOW* 4B 16
Bouldon. *Shrp* 2H 59
Boulmer. *Nmbd* 3G 121
Boulston. *Pemb* 3D 42
Boultham. *Linc* 4G 87
Boulton. *Derb* 2A 74
Boundary. *Staf* 1D 73
Bounds. *Here* 2B 48
Bourn. *Cambs* 5C 64
Bournbrook. *W Mid* 2E 61
Bourne. *Linc* 3H 75
Bourne, The. *Surr* 2G 25
Bourne End. *Bed* 4H 63
Bourne End. *Buck* 3G 37
Bourne End. *C Beds* 1H 51
Bournemouth. *Bour* 190 (3F 15)
Bournemouth Airport. *Dors* . . .3G 15
Bournes Green. *Glos* 5E 49
Bournes Green. *S'end* 2D 40
Bournheath. *Worc* 3D 60
Bournmoor. *Dur* 4G 115
Bournville. *W Mid* 2E 61
Bourton. *Dors* 3C 22
Bourton. *N Som* 5G 33
Bourton. *Oxon* 3H 35
Bourton. *Shrp* 1H 59
Bourton. *Wilts* 5F 35
Bourton on Dunsmore.
  Warw 3B 62
Bourton-on-the-Hill. *Glos* 2G 49
Bourton-on-the-Water. *Glos* . . .3G 49
Bousd. *Arg* 2D 138
Bousta. *Shet* 6D 173
Boustead Hill. *Cumb* 4D 112
Bouth. *Cumb* 1C 96
Bouthwaite. *N Yor* 2D 98
Boveney. *Buck* 3A 38
Boveridge. *Dors* 1F 15
Boverton. *V Glam* 5C 32
Bovey Tracey. *Devn* 5B 12
Bovingdon. *Herts* 5A 52
Bovingdon Green. *Buck* 3G 37
Bovinger. *Essx* 5F 53
Bovington Camp. *Dors* 4D 14
Bow. *Devn* 2H 11
Bowbank. *Dur* 2C 104
Bow Brickhill. *Mil* 2H 51
Bowbridge. *Glos* 5D 48
Bowburn. *Dur* 1A 106
Bowcombe. *IOW* 4C 16
Bowd. *Devn* 4E 12
Bowden. *Devn* 4E 9

Bowden. *Bord* 1H 119
Bowden Hill. *Wilts* 5E 35
Bowdens. *Som* 4H 21
Bowderdale. *Cumb* 4H 103
Bowdon. *G Man* 2B 84
Bower. *Nmbd* 1A 144
Bowerchalke. *Wilts* 4F 23
Bowerhill. *Wilts* 5E 35
Bower Hinton. *Som* 1H 13
Bowermadden. *High* 2E 169
Bowers. *Staf* 2C 72
Bowers Gifford. *Essx* 2B 40
Bowershall. *Fife* 4C 136
Bowertower. *High* 2E 169
Bowes. *Dur* 3C 104
Bowgreave. *Lanc* 5D 97
Bowhousebog. *N Lan* 4B 128
Bowithick. *Corn* 4B 10
Bowland Bridge. *Cumb* 1D 96
Bowlees. *Dur* 2C 104
Bowley. *Here* 5H 59
Bowlhead Green. *Surr* 2A 26
Bowling. *W Dun* 2F 127
Bowling. *W Yor* 1B 92
Bowling Bank. *Wrex* 1F 71
Bowling Green. *Worc* 5C 60
Bowlish. *Som* 2B 22
Bowmanstead. *Cumb* 5E 102
Bowmore. *Arg* 4B 124
Bowness-on-Solway. *Cumb* . . .3D 112
Bowness-on-Windermere.
  Cumb 5F 103
Bow of Fife. *Fife* 2F 137
Bowriefauld. *Ang* 4E 145
Bowscale. *Cumb* 1E 103
Bowsden. *Nmbd* 5F 131
Bowside Lodge. *High* 2A 168
Bowston. *Cumb* 5F 103
Bowthorpe. *Norf* 5D 78
Box. *Glos* 5D 48
Box. *Wilts* 5D 34
Boxbush. *Glos* 3B 48
Box End. *Bed* 1A 52
Boxford. *Suff* 1C 54
Boxford. *W Ber* 4C 36
Boxgrove. *W Sus* 5A 26
Box Hill. *Wilts* 5D 34
Boxley. *Kent* 5B 40
Boxmoor. *Herts* 5A 52
Box's Shop. *Corn* 2C 10
Boxted. *Essx* 2C 54
Boxted. *Suff* 5H 65
Boxted Cross. *Essx* 2D 54
Boxworth. *Cambs* 4C 64
Boxworth End. *Cambs* 4C 64
Boyden End. *Suff* 5G 65
Boyden Gate. *Kent* 4G 41
Boylestone. *Derbs* 2F 73
Boylestonfield. *Derbs* 2F 73
Boyndie. *Abers* 2D 160
Boynton. *E Yor* 3F 101
Boys Hill. *Dors* 1B 14
Boythorpe. *Derbs* 4A 86
Boyton. *Corn* 3D 10
Boyton. *Suff* 1G 55
Boyton. *Wilts* 3E 23
Boyton Cross. *Essx* 5G 53
Boyton End. *Essx* 2G 53
Boyton End. *Suff* 1H 53
Bozeat. *Nptn* 5G 63
Braaid. *IOM* 4C 108
Braal Castle. *High* 3D 168
Brabling Green. *Suff* 4E 67
Brabourne. *Kent* 1F 29
Brabourne Lees. *Kent* 1E 29
Brabster. *High* 2F 169
Bracadale. *High* 5C 154
Bracara. *High* 4F 147
Braceborough. *Linc* 4H 75
Bracebridge. *Linc* 4G 87
Bracebridge Heath. *Linc* 4G 87
Braceby. *Linc* 2H 75
Bracewell. *Lanc* 5A 98
Brackenber. *Cumb* 3A 104
Brackenfield. *Derbs* 5A 86
Brackenlands. *Cumb* 5D 112
Brackenthwaite. *Cumb* 5D 112
Brackenthwaite. *N Yor* 4E 99
Brackla. *B'end* 4C 32
Bracklesham. *W Sus* 3G 17
Brackletter. *High* 5D 148
Brackley. *Nptn* 2D 50
Brackley Hatch. *Nptn* 1E 51
Brackloch. *High* 1F 163
Bracknell. *Brac* 5G 37
Braco. *Per* 3H 135
Bracobrae. *Mor* 3C 160
Bracon. *N Lin* 4A 94
Bracon Ash. *Norf* 1D 66
Bradbourne. *Derbs* 5G 85
Bradda. *IOM* 4A 108
Bradden. *Nptn* 1E 51
Bradenham. *Buck* 2G 37
Bradenham. *Norf* 5B 78
Bradenstoke. *Wilts* 4F 35
Bradfield. *Essx* 2E 55
Bradfield. *Norf* 2E 79
Bradfield. *W Ber* 4E 36
Bradfield Combust. *Suff* 5A 66
Bradfield Green. *Ches E* 5A 84
Bradfield Heath. *Essx* 3E 55
Bradfield St Clare. *Suff* 5B 66
Bradfield St George. *Suff* 4B 66
Bradford. *Derbs* 4G 85
Bradford. *Devn* 2E 11
Bradford. *Nmbd* 1F 121
Bradford. *W Yor* 190 (1B 92)
Bradford Abbas. *Dors* 1A 14

Bradford Barton. *Devn* 1B 12
Bradford Leigh. *Wilts* 5D 34
Bradford-on-Avon. *Wilts* . . .5D 34
Bradford-on-Tone. *Som* . . .4E 21
Bradford Peverell. *Dors* . . .3B 14
Bradford. *Devn* 3F 19
Brading. *IOW* 4E 16
Bradley. *Ches W* 3H 83
Bradley. *Derbs* 1G 73
Bradley. *Glos* 2C 34
Bradley. *Hants* 2E 25
Bradley. *NE Lin* 4F 95
Bradley. *N Yor* 1C 98
Bradley. *Staf* 4C 72
Bradley. *W Mid* 1D 60
Bradley. *W Yor* 2B 92
Bradley. *Wrex* 5F 83
Bradley Cross. *Som* 1H 21
Bradley Green. *Ches W* . . .1H 71
Bradley Green. *Som* 3F 21
Bradley Green. *Warw* 5G 73
Bradley Green. *Worc* 4D 61
Bradley in the Moors. *Staf* . . .1E 73
Bradley Mount. *Ches E* . . .3D 84
Bradley Stoke. *S Glo* 3B 34
Bradlow. *Here* 2C 48
Bradmore. *Notts* 2C 74
Bradmore. *W Mid* 1C 60
Bradninch. *Devn* 2D 12
Bradnop. *Staf* 5E 85
Bradpole. *Dors* 3H 13
Bradshaw. *G Man* 3F 91
Bradstone. *Devn* 4D 11
Bradwall Green. *Ches E* . . .4B 84
Bradway. *S Yor* 2H 85
Bradwell. *Derbs* 2F 85
Bradwell. *Essx* 3B 54
Bradwell. *Mil* 2G 51
Bradwell. *Norf* 5H 79
Bradwell-on-Sea. *Essx* . . .5D 54
Bradwell Waterside. *Essx* . . .5C 54
Bradworthy. *Devn* 1D 10
Brae. *High* 5C 162
Brae. *Shet* 5E 173
Braeantra. *High* 1H 157
Braefield. *High* 5G 157
Braefindon. *High* 3A 158
Braegrum. *Per* 1C 136
Braehead. *Ang* 3F 145
Braehead. *Dum* 4B 110
Braehead. *Mor* 4G 159
Braehead. *Orkn* 3D 172
Braehead. *S Lan*
  nr. Coalburn 1H 117
  nr. Forth 4C 128
Braehoulland. *Shet* 4D 173
Braemar. *Abers* 4F 151
Braemore. *High*
  nr. Dunbeath 5C 168
  nr. Ullapool 1D 156
Brae of Achnahaird. *High* . .2E 163
Brae Roy Lodge. *High* . . .4F 149
Braeside. *Abers* 5G 161
Braeside. *Inv* 2D 126
Braes of Coul. *Ang* 3B 144
Braeswick. *Orkn* 4F 172
Braetongue. *High* 3F 167
Braeval. *Stir* 3E 135
Braevallich. *Arg* 3G 133
Braewick. *Shet* 6E 173
Brafferton. *Darl* 2F 105
Brafferton. *N Yor* 2G 99
Brafield-on-the-Green. *Nptn* . .5F 63
Bragar. *W Isl* 3E 171
Bragbury End. *Herts* 3C 52
Bragleenbeg. *Arg* 1G 133
Braichmelyn. *Gwyn* 4F 81
Braides. *Lanc* 4D 96
Braidwood. *S Lan* 5B 128
Braigo. *Arg* 3A 124
Brailsford. *Derbs* 1G 73
Braintree. *Essx* 3A 54
Braiseworth. *Suff* 3D 66
Braishfield. *Hants* 4B 24
Braithwaite. *Cumb* 2D 102
Braithwaite. *S Yor* 3G 93
Braithwaite. *W Yor* 5C 98
Braithwell. *S Yor* 1C 86
Brakefield Green. *Norf* . . .5C 78
Bramber. *W Sus* 4C 26
Brambridge. *Hants* 4C 24
Bramcote. *Notts* 2C 74
Bramcote. *Warw* 2B 62
Bramdean. *Hants* 4E 24
Bramerton. *Norf* 5E 79
Bramfield. *Herts* 4C 52
Bramfield. *Suff* 3F 67
Bramford. *Suff* 1E 54
Bramhall. *G Man* 2C 84
Bramham. *W Yor* 5G 99
Bramhope. *W Yor* 5E 99
Bramley. *Hants* 1E 25
Bramley. *S Yor* 1B 86
Bramley. *Surr* 1B 26
Bramley. *W Yor* 1C 92
Bramley Green. *Hants* . . .1E 25
Bramley Head. *N Yor* . . .4D 98
Bramley Vale. *Derbs* 4B 86
Bramling. *Kent* 5G 41
Brampford Speke. *Devn* . . .3C 12
Brampton. *Cambs* 3B 64
Brampton. *Cumb*
  nr. Appleby-in-Westmorland
    . . . .2H 103
  nr. Carlisle 3G 113
Brampton. *Linc* 3F 87
Brampton. *Norf* 3E 78
Brampton. *S Yor* 4E 93
Brampton. *Suff* 2G 67
Brampton Abbotts. *Here* . . .3B 48
Brampton Ash. *Nptn* 2E 63

Brampton Bryan. *Here* 3F 59
Brampton en le Morthen. *S Yor* . .2B 86
Bramshall. *Staf* 2E 73
Bramshaw. *Hants* 1A 16
Bramshill. *Hants* 5F 37
Bramshott. *Hants* 3G 25
Branault. *High* 2G 139
Brancaster. *Norf* 1G 77
Brancaster Staithe. *Norf* . . .1G 77
Brancepeth. *Dur* 1F 105
Branch End. *Nmbd* 3D 114
Branchill. *Mor* 3E 159
Brand End. *Linc* 1C 76
Branderburgh. *Mor* 1G 159
Brandesburton. *E Yor* . . .5F 101
Brandeston. *Suff* 4E 67
Brand Green. *Glos* 3C 48
Brandhill. *Shrp* 3G 59
Brandis Corner. *Devn* . . .2E 11
Brandish Street. *Som* . . .2C 20
Brandiston. *Norf* 3D 78
Brandon. *Dur* 1F 105
Brandon. *Linc* 1G 75
Brandon. *Nmbd* 3E 121
Brandon. *Suff* 2G 65
Brandon. *Warw* 3B 62
Brandon Bank. *Cambs* . . .2F 65
Brandon Creek. *Norf* 1F 65
Brandon Parva. *Norf* 5C 78
Brandsby. *N Yor* 2H 99
Brandy Wharf. *Linc* 1H 87
Brane. *Corn* 4B 4
Bran End. *Essx* 3G 53
Branksome. *Pool* 3F 15
Bransbury. *Hants* 2C 24
Bransby. *Linc* 3F 87
Branscombe. *Devn* 4E 13
Bransford. *Worc* 5B 60
Bransgore. *Hants* 3G 15
Bransholme. *Hull* 1E 94
Branshay. *Shrp* 3A 60
Branston. *Leics* 3F 75
Branston. *Linc* 4H 87
Branston. *Staf* 3G 73
Branston Booths. *Linc* . . .4H 87
Branstone. *IOW* 4D 16
Bransty. *Cumb* 3A 102
Brant Broughton. *Linc* . . .5G 87
Brantham. *Suff* 2E 54
Branthwaite. *Cumb*
  nr. Caldbeck 1D 102
  nr. Workington 2B 102
Brantingham. *E Yor* 2C 94
Branton. *Nmbd* 3E 121
Branton. *S Yor* 4G 93
Branton Green. *N Yor* . . .3G 99
Branxholme. *Bord* 3G 119
Branxton. *Nmbd* 1C 120
Brassington. *Derbs* 5G 85
Brasted. *Kent* 5F 39
Brasted Chart. *Kent* 5F 39
Bratch, The. *Staf* 1C 60
Brathens. *Abers* 4D 152
Bratoft. *Linc* 4D 88
Brattleby. *Linc* 2G 87
Bratton. *Som* 2C 20
Bratton. *Telf* 4A 72
Bratton. *Wilts* 1E 23
Bratton Clovelly. *Devn* . . .3E 11
Bratton Fleming. *Devn* . . .3G 19
Bratton Seymour. *Som* . . .4B 22
Braughing. *Herts* 3D 53
Braulen Lodge. *High* . . .5E 157
Braunston. *Nptn* 4C 62
Braunstone Town. *Leics* . . .5C 74
Braunston-in-Rutland. *Rut* . .5F 75
Braunton. *Devn* 3E 19
Brawby. *N Yor* 2B 100
Brawl. *High* 2A 168
Brawlbin. *High* 3C 168
Bray. *Wind* 3A 38
Braybrooke. *Nptn* 2E 63
Brayford. *Devn* 3G 19
Bray Shop. *Corn* 5D 10
Braystones. *Cumb* 4B 102
Brayton. *N Yor* 1G 93
Bray Wick. *Wind* 4G 37
Brazacott. *Corn* 3C 10
Brea. *Corn* 4A 6
Breach. *W Sus* 2F 17
Breachwood Green. *Herts* . .3B 52
Breacleit. *W Isl* 4D 171
Breaden Heath. *Shrp* . . .2G 71
Breadsall. *Derbs* 1A 74
Breadstone. *Glos* 5C 48
Breage. *Corn* 4D 4
Breakachy. *High* 4G 157
Breakish. *High* 1E 147
Bream. *Glos* 5B 48
Breamore. *Hants* 1G 15
Bream's Meend. *Glos* . . .5B 48
Brean. *Som* 1F 21
Breanais. *W Isl* 5B 171
Brearton. *N Yor* 3F 99
Breascleit. *W Isl* 4E 171
Breaston. *Derbs* 2B 74
Brecais Ard. *High* 1E 147
Brecais Iosal. *High* 1E 147
Brechfa. *Carm* 2F 45
Brechin. *Ang* 3F 145
Breckles. *Norf* 1B 66
Brecon. *Powy* 3D 46
Bredbury. *G Man* 1D 84
Brede. *E Sus* 4C 28
Bredenbury. *Here* 5A 60
Bredfield. *Suff* 5E 67
Bredgar. *Kent* 4C 40
Bredhurst. *Kent* 4B 40
Bredicot. *Worc* 5D 60
Bredon. *Worc* 2E 49
Bredon's Norton. *Worc* . . .2E 49

Bredwardine. *Here* 1G 47
Breedon on the Hill. *Leics* . .3B 74
Breibhig. *W Isl*
  on Barra 9B 170
  on Isle of Lewis 4G 171
Breich. *W Lot* 3C 128
Breightmet. *G Man* 4F 91
Breighton. *E Yor* 1H 93
Breinton. *Here* 2H 47
Breinton Common. *Here* . . .2H 47
Breiwick. *Shet* 7F 173
Brelston Green. *Here* . . .3A 48
Bremhill. *Wilts* 4E 35
Brenachie. *High* 1B 158
Brenchley. *Kent* 1A 28
Brendon. *Devn* 2A 20
Brent Cross. *G Lon* 2D 38
Brent Eleigh. *Suff* 1C 54
Brentford. *G Lon* 3C 38
Brentingby. *Leics* 4E 75
Brent Knoll. *Som* 1G 21
Brent Pelham. *Herts* 2E 53
Brentwood. *Essx* 1G 39
Brenzett. *Kent* 3E 28
Brereton. *Staf* 4E 73
Brereton Cross. *Staf* 4E 73
Brereton Green. *Ches E* . . .4B 84
Brereton Heath. *Ches E* . . .4C 84
Bressingham. *Norf* 2C 66
Bretby. *Derbs* 3G 73
Bretford. *Warw* 3B 62
Bretforton. *Worc* 1F 49
Bretherdale Head. *Cumb* . .4G 103
Bretherton. *Lanc* 2C 90
Brettabister. *Shet* 6F 173
Brettenham. *Norf* 2B 66
Brettenham. *Suff* 5B 66
Bretton. *Flin* 4F 83
Bretton. *Pet* 5A 76
Brewlands Bridge. *Ang* . . .2A 144
Brewood. *Staf* 5C 72
Briantspuddle. *Dors* 3D 14
Bricket Wood. *Herts* 5B 52
Brickhampton. *Worc* 1E 49
Bride. *IOM* 1D 108
Bridekirk. *Cumb* 1C 102
Bridell. *Pemb* 1B 44
Bridestowe. *Devn* 4F 11
Brideswell. *Abers* 5C 160
Bridford. *Devn* 4B 12
Bridge. *Corn* 4A 6
Bridge. *Kent* 5F 41
Bridge. *Som* 2G 13
Bridge End. *Bed* 5H 63
Bridge End. *Cumb*
  nr. Broughton in Furness . .5D 102
  nr. Dalston 5E 113
Bridge End. *Linc* 2A 76
Bridge End. *Shet* 8E 173
Bridgefoot. *Ang* 5C 144
Bridgefoot. *Cumb* 2B 102
Bridge Green. *Essx* 2E 53
Bridgehampton. *Som* . . .4A 22
Bridge Hewick. *N Yor* . . .2F 99
Bridgehill. *Dur* 4D 115
Bridgemary. *Hants* 2D 16
Bridgemere. *Ches E* 1B 72
Bridgemont. *Derbs* 2E 85
Bridgend. *Abers*
  nr. Huntly 5C 160
  nr. Peterhead 5H 161
Bridgend. *Ang*
  nr. Brechin 2E 145
  nr. Kirriemuir 4C 144
Bridgend. *Arg*
  nr. Lochgilphead 4F 133
  on Islay 3B 124
Bridgend. *B'end* 3C 32
Bridgend. *Cumb* 3E 103
Bridgend. *Devn* 4B 8
Bridgend. *Fife* 2F 137
Bridgend. *High* 3F 157
Bridgend. *Mor* 5A 160
Bridgend. *Per* 1D 136
Bridgend. *W Lot* 2D 128
Bridgend of Lintrathen.
  Ang 3B 144
Bridgeness. *Falk* 1D 128
Bridge of Alford. *Abers* . . .2C 152
Bridge of Allan. *Stir* 4G 135
Bridge of Avon. *Mor* 5F 159
Bridge of Awe. *Arg* 1H 133
Bridge of Balgie. *Per* 4C 142
Bridge of Brown. *High* . . .1F 151
Bridge of Cally. *Per* 3A 144
Bridge of Canny. *Abers* . . .4D 152
Bridge of Dee. *Dum* 3E 111
Bridge of Don. *Aber* 2G 153
Bridge of Dun. *Ang* 3F 145
Bridge of Dye. *Abers* 5D 152
Bridge of Earn. *Per* 2D 136
Bridge of Ericht. *Per* 3C 142
Bridge of Feugh. *Abers* . . .4E 152
Bridge of Gairn. *Abers* . . .4A 152
Bridge of Gaur. *Per* 3C 142
Bridge of Muchalls. *Abers* . .4F 153
Bridge of Oich. *High* 3F 149
Bridge of Orchy. *Arg* 5H 141
Bridge of Walls. *Shet* 6D 173
Bridge of Weir. *Ren* 3E 127
Bridge Reeve. *Devn* 1G 11
Bridgerule. *Devn* 2C 10
Bridge Sollers. *Here* 1H 47
Bridge Street. *Suff* 1B 54
Bridgetown. *Devn* 2E 9
Bridgetown. *Som* 3C 20
Bridge Town. *Warw* 5G 61
Bridge Trafford. *Ches W* . . .3G 83
Bridgeyate. *S Glo* 4B 34
Bridgham. *Norf* 2B 66
Bridgnorth. *Shrp* 1B 60

Bridgtown. *Staf* 5D 73
Bridgwater. *Som* 3G 21
Bridlington. *E Yor* 3F 101
Bridport. *Dors* 3H 13
Bridstow. *Here* 3A 48
Brierfield. *Lanc* 1G 91
Brierley. *Glos* 4B 48
Brierley. *Here* 5G 59
Brierley. *S Yor* 3E 93
Brierley Hill. *W Mid* 2D 60
Brierton. *Hart* 1B 106
Briestfield. *W Yor* 3C 92
Brigg. *N Lin* 4D 94
Briggate. *Norf* 3F 79
Briggswath. *N Yor* 4F 107
Brigham. *Cumb* 1B 102
Brigham. *E Yor* 4E 101
Brighouse. *W Yor* 2B 92
Brighstone. *IOW* 4C 16
Brightgate. *Derbs* 5G 85
Brighthampton. *Oxon* . . .5B 50
Brightholmlee. *S Yor* 1G 85
Brightley. *Devn* 3G 11
Brightling. *E Sus* 3A 28
Brightlingsea. *Essx* 4D 54
Brighton. *Brig* 189 (5E 27)
Brighton. *Corn* 3D 6
Brighton Hill. *Hants* 2E 24
Brightons. *Falk* 2C 128
Brightwalton. *W Ber* 4C 36
Brightwalton Green. *W Ber* . .4C 36
Brightwell. *Suff* 1F 55
Brightwell Baldwin. *Oxon* . .2E 37
Brightwell-cum-Sotwell.
  Oxon 2D 36
Brigmerston. *Wilts* 2G 23
Brignall. *Dur* 3D 104
Brig o' Turk. *Stir* 3E 135
Brigsley. *NE Lin* 4F 95
Brigsteer. *Cumb* 1D 97
Brigstock. *Nptn* 2G 63
Brill. *Buck* 4E 51
Brill. *Corn* 4E 5
Brilley. *Here* 1F 47
Brimaston. *Pemb* 2D 42
Brimfield. *Here* 4H 59
Brimington. *Derbs* 3B 86
Brimley. *Devn* 5B 12
Brimpsfield. *Glos* 4E 49
Brimpton. *W Ber* 5D 36
Brims. *Orkn* 9B 172
Brimscombe. *Glos* 5D 48
Brimstage. *Mers* 2F 83
Brincliffe. *S Yor* 2H 85
Brind. *E Yor* 1H 93
Brindister. *Shet*
  nr. West Burrafirth . . .6D 173
  nr. West Lerwick 8F 173
Brindle. *Lanc* 2D 90
Brindley. *Ches E* 5H 83
Brindley Ford. *Stoke* 5C 84
Brineton. *Staf* 4C 72
Bringhurst. *Leics* 1F 63
Bringsty Common. *Here* . . .5A 60
Brington. *Cambs* 3H 63
Brinian. *Orkn* 5D 172
Briningham. *Norf* 2C 78
Brinkhill. *Linc* 3C 88
Brinkley. *Cambs* 5F 65
Brinklow. *Warw* 3B 62
Brinkworth. *Wilts* 3F 35
Brinscall. *Lanc* 2E 91
Brinscombe. *Som* 1H 21
Brinsley. *Notts* 1B 74
Brinsworth. *S Yor* 2B 86
Brinton. *Norf* 2C 78
Brisco. *Cumb* 4F 113
Brisley. *Norf* 3B 78
Brislington. *Bris* 4B 34
Brissenden Green. *Kent* . . .2D 28
Bristol. *Bris* 189 (4A 34)
Bristol Airport. *N Som* . . .5A 34
Briston. *Norf* 2C 78
Britannia. *Lanc* 2G 91
Britford. *Wilts* 4G 23
Brithdir. *Cphy* 5E 47
Brithdir. *Cdgn* 1D 44
Brithdir. *Gwyn* 4G 69
Briton Ferry. *Neat* 3G 31
Britwell Salome. *Oxon* . . .2E 37
Brixham. *Torb* 3F 9
Brixton. *Devn* 3B 8
Brixton. *G Lon* 3E 39
Brixton Deverill. *Wilts* . . .3D 22
Brixworth. *Nptn* 3E 63
Brize Norton. *Oxon* 5B 50
Broad, The. *Here* 4G 59
Broad Alley. *Worc* 4C 60
Broad Blunsdon. *Swin* . . .2G 35
Broadbottom. *G Man* . . .1D 85
Broadbridge. *W Sus* 2G 17
Broadbridge Heath. *W Sus* . .2C 26
Broad Campden. *Glos* . . .2G 49
Broad Chalke. *Wilts* 4F 23
Broadclyst. *Devn* 3C 12
Broadfield. *Inv* 2E 127
Broadfield. *Pemb* 4F 43
Broadfield. *W Sus* 2D 26
Broadford. *High* 1E 147
Broadford Bridge. *W Sus* . .3B 26
Broadgate. *Cumb* 1A 96
Broad Green. *Cambs* . . .5F 65
Broad Green. *C Beds* . . .1H 51
Broad Green. *Worc*
  nr. Bromsgrove 3D 61
  nr. Worcester 5B 60
Broadhaven. *High* 3F 169
Broad Haven. *Pemb* 3C 42
Broadheath. *G Man* 2B 84
Broad Heath. *Staf* 3C 72
Broadheath. *Worc* 4A 60

Broadheath Common. *Worc* . .5C 60
Broadhembury. *Devn* 2E 12
Broadhempston. *Devn* . . .2E 9
Broad Hill. *Cambs* 3E 65
Broad Hinton. *Wilts* 4G 35
Broadholme. *Derbs* 1A 74
Broadholme. *Linc* 3F 87
Broadlay. *Carm* 5D 44
Broad Laying. *Hants* 5C 36
Broadley. *Lanc* 3G 91
Broadley. *Mor* 2A 160
Broadley Common. *Essx* . . .5E 53
Broad Marston. *Worc* . . .1G 49
Broadmayne. *Dors* 4C 14
Broadmere. *Hants* 2E 24
Broadmoor. *Pemb* 4E 43
Broad Oak. *Carm* 3F 45
Broad Oak. *Cumb* 5C 102
Broad Oak. *Dors* 3D 12
Broad Oak. *Dors* 1C 14
Broadoak. *Dors* 3H 13
Broad Oak. *E Sus*
  nr. Hastings 4C 28
  nr. Heathfield 3H 27
Broadoak. *Glos* 4B 48
Broadoak. *Hants* 1D 16
Broad Oak. *Here* 3H 47
Broad Oak. *Kent* 4F 41
Broadrashes. *Mor* 3B 160
Broadsea. *Abers* 2G 161
Broad's Green. *Essx* 4G 53
Broadshard. *Som* 1H 13
Broadstairs. *Kent* 4H 41
Broadstone. *Pool* 3F 15
Broadstone. *Shrp* 2H 59
Broad Street. *E Sus* 4C 28
Broad Street. *Kent*
  nr. Ashford 1F 29
  nr. Maidstone 5C 40
Broad Street Green. *Essx* . .5B 54
Broad Town. *Wilts* 4F 35
Broadwas. *Worc* 5B 60
Broadwath. *Cumb* 4F 113
Broadway. *Carm*
  nr. Kidwelly 5D 45
  nr. Laugharne 4G 43
Broadway. *Pemb* 3C 42
Broadway. *Som* 1G 13
Broadway. *Suff* 3F 67
Broadway. *Worc* 2F 49
Broadwell. *Glos*
  nr. Cinderford 4A 48
  nr. Stow-on-the-Wold . .3H 49
Broadwell. *Oxon* 5A 50
Broadwell. *Warw* 4B 62
Broadwell House. *Nmbd* . . .4C 114
Broadwey. *Dors* 4B 14
Broadwindsor. *Dors* 2H 13
Broadwoodkelly. *Devn* . . .2G 11
Broadwoodwidger. *Devn* . .4E 11
Broallan. *High* 4G 157
Brobury. *Here* 1G 47
Brochel. *High* 4E 155
Brockamin. *Worc* 5B 60
Brockbridge. *Hants* 1E 16
Brockdish. *Norf* 3E 66
Brockencote. *Worc* 3C 60
Brockenhurst. *Hants* 2A 16
Brocketsbrae. *S Lan* 1H 117
Brockford Street. *Suff* . . .4D 66
Brockhall. *Nptn* 4D 62
Brockham. *Surr* 1C 26
Brockhampton. *Glos*
  nr. Bishop's Cleeve . . .3E 49
  nr. Sevenhampton . . .3F 49
Brockhampton. *Here* 2A 48
Brockhill. *Bord* 2F 119
Brockholes. *W Yor* 3B 92
Brockhurst. *Hants* 2D 16
Brocklesby. *Linc* 3E 95
Brockley. *N Som* 5H 33
Brockley Corner. *Suff* . . .3H 65
Brockley Green. *Suff*
  nr. Bury St Edmunds . . .1H 53
  nr. Haverhill 5H 65
Brockleymoor. *Cumb* 1F 103
Brockmoor. *W Mid* 2D 60
Brockton. *Shrp*
  nr. Bishop's Castle . . .2F 59
  nr. Madeley 5B 72
  nr. Much Wenlock . . .1H 59
  nr. Pontesbury 5F 71
Brockton. *Staf* 2C 72
Brockton. *Telf* 4B 72
Brockweir. *Glos* 5A 48
Brockworth. *Glos* 4D 49
Brocton. *Staf* 4D 72
Brodick. *N Ayr* 2E 123
Brodie. *Mor* 3D 159
Brodiesord. *Abers* 3C 160
Brodsworth. *S Yor* 4F 93
Brogaig. *High* 2D 154
Brogborough. *C Beds* . . .2H 51
Brokenborough. *Wilts* . . .3E 35
Broken Cross. *Ches E* . . .3C 84
Bromborough. *Mers* 2F 83
Bromdon. *Shrp* 2A 60
Brome. *Suff* 3D 66
Brome Street. *Suff* 3D 66
Bromeswell. *Suff* 5F 67
Bromfield. *Cumb* 5C 112
Bromfield. *Shrp* 3G 59
Bromford. *W Mid* 1F 61
Bromham. *Bed* 5H 63
Bromham. *Wilts* 5E 35
Bromley. *G Lon* 4F 39
Bromley. *Herts* 3E 53
Bromley. *Shrp* 1B 60
Bromley Cross. *G Man* . . .3F 91
Bromley Green. *Kent* 2D 28
Bromley Wood. *Staf* 3F 73

Brompton—Burton Pedwardine

Brompton. *Medw* 4B **40**
Brompton. *N Yor*
nr. Northallerton 5A **106**
nr. Scarborough 1D **100**
Brompton. *Shrp* 5H **71**
Brompton-on-Swale. *N Yor* 5F **105**
Brompton Ralph. *Som* 3D **20**
Brompton Regis. *Som* 3C **20**
Bromsash. *Here* 3B **48**
Bromsberrow. *Glos* 2C **48**
Bromsberrow Heath. *Glos* 2C **48**
Bromsgrove. *Worc* 3D **60**
Bromstead Heath. *Staf* 4B **72**
Bromyard. *Here* 5A **60**
Bromyard Downs. *Here* 5A **60**
Bronaber. *Gwyn* 2G **69**
Broncroft. *Shrp* 2H **59**
Brongest. *Cdgn* 1D **44**
Brongwyn. *Cdgn* 1C **44**
Bronington. *Wrex* 2G **71**
Bronllys. *Powy* 2E **47**
Bronnant. *Cdgn* 4F **57**
Bronwydd Arms. *Carm* 3E **45**
Bronydd. *Powy* 1F **47**
Bronygarth. *Shrp* 2E **71**
Brook. *Carm* 4G **43**
Brook. *Hants*
nr. Cadnam 1A **16**
nr. Romsey 4B **24**
Brook. *IOW* 4B **16**
Brook. *Kent* 1E **29**
Brook. *Surr*
nr. Guildford 1B **26**
nr. Haslemere 2A **26**
Brooke. *Norf* 1E **67**
Brooke. *Rut* 5F **75**
Brookenby. *Linc* 1B **88**
Brookend. *Glos* 5B **48**
Brook End. *Worc* 1D **48**
Brookfield. *Lanc* 1D **90**
Brookfield. *Ren* 3F **127**
Brookhouse. *Lanc* 3E **97**
Brookhouse. *S Yor* 2C **86**
Brookhouse Green.
Ches E 4C **84**
Brookhouses. *Staf* 1D **73**
Brookhurst. *Mers* 2F **83**
Brookland. *Kent* 3D **28**
Brooklands. *G Man* 1B **84**
Brooklands. *Shrp* 1H **71**
Brookmans Park. *Herts* 5C **52**
Brooks. *Powy* 1D **58**
Brooksby. *Leics* 4D **74**
Brooks Green. *W Sus* 3C **26**
Brook Street. *Essx* 1G **39**
Brook Street. *Kent* 2D **28**
Brook Street. *W Sus* 3E **27**
Brookthorpe. *Glos* 4D **48**
Brookville. *Norf* 1G **65**
Brookwood. *Surr* 5A **38**
Broom. *C Beds* 1B **52**
Broom. *Fife* 3F **137**
Broom. *Warw* 5E **61**
Broome. *Norf* 1F **67**
Broome. *Shrp*
nr. Cardington 1H **59**
nr. Craven Arms 2G **59**
Broome. *Worc* 3D **60**
Broomedge. *Warr* 2B **84**
Broomend. *Abers* 2E **153**
Broomer's Corner. *W Sus* 3C **26**
Broomfield. *Abers* 5G **161**
Broomfield. *Essx* 4H **53**
Broomfield. *Kent*
nr. Herne Bay 4F **41**
nr. Maidstone 5C **40**
Broomfield. *Som* 3F **21**
Broomfleet. *E Yor* 2B **94**
Broom Green. *Norf* 3B **78**
Broomhall. *Ches E* 1A **72**
Broomhall. *Wind* 4A **38**
Broomhaugh. *Nmbd* 3D **114**
Broom Hill. *Dors* 2F **15**
Broomhill. *High*
nr. Grantown-on-Spey 1D **151**
nr. Invergordon 1B **158**
Broomhill. *Norf* 5F **77**
Broomhill. *S Yor* 4E **93**
Broom Hill. *Worc* 3D **60**
Broomhillbank. *Dum* 5D **118**
Broomholm. *Norf* 2F **79**
Broomlands. *Dum* 4C **118**
Broomley. *Nmbd* 3D **114**
Broom of Moy. *Mor* 3E **159**
Broompark. *Dur* 5F **115**
Broom's Green. *Glos* 2C **48**
Brora. *High* 3G **165**
Broseley. *Shrp* 5A **72**
Brotherhouse Bar. *Linc* 4B **76**
Brotheridge Green. *Worc* 1D **48**
Brotherlee. *Dur* 1C **104**
Brothertoft. *Linc* 1B **76**
Brotherton. *N Yor* 2E **93**
Brotton. *Red C* 3D **107**
Broubster. *High* 2C **168**
Brough. *Cumb* 3A **104**
Brough. *Derbs* 2F **85**
Brough. *E Yor* 2C **94**
Brough. *High* 1E **169**
Brough. *Notts* 5F **87**
Brough. *Orkn*
nr. Finstown 6C **172**
nr. St Margaret's Hope 9D **172**
Brough. *Shet*
nr. Benston 6F **173**
nr. Booth of Toft 4F **173**
on Bressay 7G **173**
on Whalsay 5G **173**
Broughall. *Shrp* 1H **71**
Brougham. *Cumb* 2G **103**
Brough Lodge. *Shet* 2G **173**
Brough Sowerby. *Cumb* 3A **104**
Broughton. *Cambs* 3B **64**
Broughton. *Flin* 4F **83**
Broughton. *Hants* 3B **24**
Broughton. *Lanc* 1D **90**
Broughton. *Mil* 2G **51**
Broughton. *Nptn* 3F **63**
Broughton. *N Lin* 4C **94**
Broughton. *N Yor*
nr. Malton 2B **100**
nr. Skipton 4B **98**
Broughton. *Orkn* 3D **172**
Broughton. *Oxon* 2C **50**
Broughton. *Bord* 1D **118**
Broughton. *Staf* 2B **72**
Broughton. *V Glam* 4C **32**
Broughton Astley. *Leics* 1C **62**
Broughton Beck. *Cumb* 1B **96**
Broughton Cross. *Cumb* 1B **102**
Broughton Gifford. *Wilts* 5D **35**
Broughton Green. *Worc* 4D **60**
Broughton Hackett. *Worc* 5D **60**
Broughton in Furness.
Cumb 1B **96**
Broughton Mills. *Cumb* 5D **102**
Broughton Moor. *Cumb* 1B **102**
Broughton Park. *G Man* 4G **91**
Broughton Poggs. *Oxon* 5H **49**
Broughtown. *Orkn* 3F **172**
Broughty Ferry. *D'dee* 5D **144**
Browland. *Shet* 6D **173**
Brownbread Street. *E Sus* 4A **28**
Brown Candover. *Hants* 3D **24**
Brown Edge. *Lanc* 3B **90**
Brown Edge. *Staf* 5D **84**
Brownhill. *Bkbn* 1E **91**
Brownhill. *Shrp* 3G **71**
Brownhills. *Shrp* 2A **72**
Brownhills. *W Mid* 5E **73**
Brown Knowl. *Ches W* 5G **83**
Brownlow. *Ches E* 4C **84**
Brownlow Heath. *Ches E* 4C **84**
Brown's Green. *W Mid* 1E **61**
Brownshill. *Glos* 5D **49**
Brownston. *Devn* 3C **8**
Brownstone. *Devn* 2A **12**
Browston Green. *Norf* 5G **79**
Broxa. *N Yor* 5G **107**
Broxbourne. *Herts* 5D **52**
Broxburn. *E Lot* 2C **130**
Broxburn. *W Lot* 2D **128**
Broxholme. *Linc* 3G **87**
Broxted. *Essx* 3F **53**
Broxton. *Ches W* 5G **83**
Broxwood. *Here* 5F **59**
Broyle Side. *E Sus* 4F **27**
Brù. *W Isl* 3F **171**
Bruach Mairi. *W Isl* 4G **171**
Bruairnis. *W Isl* 8C **170**
Bruan. *High* 5F **169**
Bruar Lodge. *Per* 1F **143**
Brucehill. *W Dun* 2E **127**
Brucklay. *Abers* 3G **161**
Bruera. *Ches W* 4G **83**
Bruern Abbey. *Oxon* 3A **50**
Bruichladdich. *Arg* 3A **124**
Bruisyard. *Suff* 4F **67**
Bruisyard Street. *Suff* 4F **67**
Brund. *Staf* 4F **85**
Brundall. *Norf* 5F **79**
Brundish. *Norf* 1F **67**
Brundish. *Suff* 4E **67**
Brundish Street. *Suff* 3E **67**
Brunery. *High* 1B **140**
Brunswick Village. *Tyne* 2F **115**
Brunthwaite. *W Yor* 5C **98**
Bruntingthorpe. *Leics* 1D **62**
Brunton. *Fife* 1F **137**
Brunton. *Nmbd* 2G **121**
Brunton. *Wilts* 1H **23**
Brushford. *Devn* 2G **11**
Brushford. *Som* 4C **20**
Brusta. *W Isl* 1E **170**
Bruton. *Som* 3B **22**
Bryanston. *Dors* 2D **14**
Bryant's Bottom. *Buck* 2G **37**
Brydekirk. *Dum* 2C **112**
Brymbo. *Cnwy* 3H **81**
Brymbo. *Wrex* 5E **83**
Brympton D'Evercy. *Som* 1A **14**
Bryn. *Carm* 5F **45**
Bryn. *G Man* 4D **90**
Bryn. *Neat* 2B **32**
Bryn. *Shrp* 2E **59**
Brynamman. *Carm* 4H **45**
Brynberian. *Pemb* 1F **43**
Brynbryddan. *Neat* 2A **32**
Bryncae. *Rhon* 3C **32**
Bryncethin. *B'end* 3C **32**
Bryncir. *Gwyn* 1D **69**
Bryncoch. *Neat* 3G **31**
Bryncroes. *Gwyn* 2B **68**
Bryncrug. *Gwyn* 5F **69**
Bryn Du. *IOA* 3C **80**
Bryn Eden. *Gwyn* 3G **69**
Bryneglwys. *Den* 1D **70**
Bryn Eglwys. *Gwyn* 4F **81**
Brynford. *Flin* 3D **82**
Bryn Gates. *G Man* 4D **90**
Bryn Golau. *Rhon* 3D **32**
Bryngwran. *IOA* 3C **80**
Bryngwyn. *Mon* 5G **47**
Bryngwyn. *Powy* 1E **47**
Bryn-henllan. *Pemb* 1E **43**
Brynhoffnant. *Cdgn* 5C **56**
Bryn-llwyn. *Den* 2C **82**
Brynllywarch. *Powy* 2D **58**
Brynmawr. *Blae* 4E **47**
Bryn-mawr. *Gwyn* 2B **68**
Brynmenyn. *B'end* 3C **32**
Brynmill. *Swan* 3F **31**
Brynna. *Rhon* 3C **32**
Brynrefail. *Gwyn* 4E **81**
Brynrefail. *IOA* 2D **81**
Brynsadler. *Rhon* 3D **32**
Bryn-Saith Marchog. *Den* 5C **82**
Brynsiencyn. *IOA* 4D **81**
Brynteg. *IOA* 2D **81**
Brynteg. *Wrex* 5F **83**
Brynygwenyn. *Mon* 4G **47**
Bryn-y-maen. *Cnwy* 3H **81**
Buaile nam Bodach. *W Isl* 8C **170**
Bualintur. *High* 1C **146**
Bubbenhall. *Warw* 3A **62**
Bubwith. *E Yor* 1H **93**
Buccleuch. *Bord* 3F **119**
Buchanan Smithy. *Stir* 1F **127**
Buchanhaven. *Abers* 4H **161**
Buchanty. *Per* 1B **136**
Buchany. *Stir* 3G **135**
Buchley. *E Dun* 2G **127**
Buchlyvie. *Stir* 4E **135**
Buckabank. *Cumb* 5E **113**
Buckden. *Cambs* 4A **64**
Buckden. *N Yor* 2B **98**
Buckenham. *Norf* 5F **79**
Buckerell. *Devn* 2E **12**
Buckfast. *Devn* 2D **8**
Buckfastleigh. *Devn* 2D **8**
Buckhaven. *Fife* 4F **137**
Buckholm. *Bord* 1G **119**
Buckholt. *Here* 4A **48**
Buckhorn Weston. *Dors* 4C **22**
Buckhurst Hill. *Essx* 1F **39**
Buckie. *Mor* 2B **160**
Buckingham. *Buck* 2E **51**
Buckland. *Buck* 4G **51**
Buckland. *Glos* 2F **49**
Buckland. *Here* 5H **59**
Buckland. *Herts* 2D **52**
Buckland. *Kent* 1H **29**
Buckland. *Oxon* 2B **36**
Buckland. *Surr* 5D **38**
Buckland Brewer. *Devn* 4E **19**
Buckland Common. *Buck* 5H **51**
Buckland Dinham. *Som* 1C **22**
Buckland Filleigh. *Devn* 2E **11**
Buckland in the Moor. *Devn* 5H **11**
Buckland Monachorum.
Devn 2A **8**
Buckland Newton. *Dors* 2B **14**
Buckland Ripers. *Dors* 4B **14**
Buckland St Mary. *Som* 1F **13**
Buckland-tout-Saints. *Devn* 4D **8**
Bucklebury. *W Ber* 4D **36**
Bucklegate. *Linc* 2C **76**
Buckleigh. *Devn* 4E **19**
Buckler's Hard. *Hants* 3C **16**
Bucklesham. *Suff* 1F **55**
Buckley. *Flin* 4E **83**
Buckley Green. *Warw* 4F **61**
Buckley Hill. *Mers* 1F **83**
Bucklow Hill. *Ches E* 2B **84**
Buckminster. *Leics* 3F **75**
Bucknall. *Linc* 4A **88**
Bucknall. *Stoke* 1D **72**
Bucknell. *Oxon* 3D **50**
Bucknell. *Shrp* 3F **59**
Buckpool. *Mor* 2B **160**
Bucksburn. *Aber* 3F **153**
Buck's Cross. *Devn* 4D **18**
Bucks Green. *W Sus* 2B **26**
Buckshaw Village. *Lanc* 2D **90**
Bucks Hill. *Herts* 5A **52**
Bucks Horn Oak. *Hants* 2G **25**
Buck's Mills. *Devn* 4D **18**
Buckton. *E Yor* 2F **101**
Buckton. *Here* 3F **59**
Buckton. *Nmbd* 1E **121**
Buckton Vale. *G Man* 4H **91**
Buckworth. *Cambs* 3A **64**
Budby. *Notts* 4D **86**
Bude. *Corn* 2C **10**
Budge's Shop. *Corn* 3H **7**
Budlake. *Devn* 2C **12**
Budle. *Nmbd* 1F **121**
Budleigh Salterton. *Devn* 4D **12**
Budock Water. *Corn* 5B **6**
Buerton. *Ches E* 1A **72**
Buffler's Holt. *Buck* 2E **51**
Bugbrooke. *Nptn* 5D **62**
Buglawton. *Ches E* 4C **84**
Bugle. *Corn* 3E **6**
Bugthorpe. *E Yor* 4B **100**
Buildwas. *Shrp* 5A **72**
Builth Road. *Powy* 5C **58**
Builth Wells. *Powy* 5C **58**
Bulbourne. *Herts* 4H **51**
Bulby. *Linc* 3H **75**
Bulcote. *Notts* 1D **74**
Buldoo. *High* 2B **168**
Bulford. *Wilts* 2G **23**
Bulford Camp. *Wilts* 2G **23**
Bulkeley. *Ches E* 5H **83**
Bulkington. *Warw* 2A **62**
Bulkington. *Wilts* 1E **23**
Bulkworthy. *Devn* 1D **11**
Bullamoor. *N Yor* 5A **106**
Bull Bay. *IOA* 1D **80**
Bullbridge. *Derbs* 5A **86**
Bullgill. *Cumb* 1B **102**
Bull Hill. *Hants* 3B **16**
Bullinghope. *Here* 2A **48**
Bull's Green. *Herts* 4C **52**
Bullwood. *Arg* 2C **126**
Bulmer. *Essx* 1B **54**
Bulmer. *N Yor* 3A **100**
Bulmer Tye. *Essx* 2B **54**
Bulphan. *Thur* 2H **39**
Bulverhythe. *E Sus* 5B **28**
Bulwark. *Abers* 4G **161**
Bulwell. *Nott* 1C **74**
Bulwick. *Nptn* 1G **63**
Bumble's Green. *Essx* 5E **53**
Bun Abhainn Eadarra. *W Isl* 7D **171**
Bunacaimb. *High* 5E **147**
Bun a' Mhuillinn. *W Isl* 7C **170**
Bunarkaig. *High* 5D **148**
Bunbury. *Ches E* 5H **83**
Bunchrew. *High* 4A **158**
Bundalloch. *High* 1A **148**
Buness. *Shet* 1H **173**
Bunessan. *Arg* 1A **132**
Bungay. *Suff* 2F **67**
Bunkegivie. *High* 2H **149**
Bunker's Hill. *Cambs* 5D **76**
Bunkers Hill. *Linc* 5B **88**
Bunker's Hill. *Suff* 5H **79**
Bunloit. *High* 1H **149**
Bunnahabhain. *Arg* 2C **124**
Bunny. *Notts* 3C **74**
Bunoich. *High* 3F **149**
Bunree. *High* 2E **141**
Bunroy. *High* 5E **149**
Buntait. *High* 5G **157**
Buntingford. *Herts* 3D **52**
Bunting's Green. *Essx* 2B **54**
Bunwell. *Norf* 1D **66**
Burbage. *Derbs* 3E **85**
Burbage. *Leics* 1B **62**
Burbage. *Wilts* 5H **35**
Burcher. *Here* 4F **59**
Burchett's Green. *Wind* 3G **37**
Burcombe. *Wilts* 3F **23**
Burcot. *Oxon* 2D **36**
Burcot. *Worc* 3D **61**
Burcote. *Shrp* 1B **60**
Burcott. *Buck* 3G **51**
Burcott. *Som* 2A **22**
Burdale. *N Yor* 3C **100**
Burdrop. *Oxon* 2B **50**
Bures. *Suff* 2C **54**
Burf, The. *Worc* 4C **60**
Burford. *Oxon* 4A **50**
Burford. *Shrp* 4H **59**
Burg. *Arg* 4E **139**
Burgate Great Green. *Suff* 3C **66**
Burgate Little Green. *Suff* 3C **66**
Burgess Hill. *W Sus* 4E **27**
Burgh. *Suff* 5E **67**
Burgh by Sands. *Cumb* 4E **113**
Burgh Castle. *Norf* 5G **79**
Burghclere. *Hants* 5C **36**
Burghead. *Mor* 2F **159**
Burghfield. *W Ber* 5E **37**
Burghfield Common.
W Ber 5E **37**
Burghfield Hill. *W Ber* 5E **37**
Burgh Heath. *Surr* 5D **38**
Burghill. *Here* 1H **47**
Burgh le Marsh. *Linc* 4E **89**
Burgh Muir. *Abers* 2E **153**
Burgh next Aylsham. *Norf* 3E **78**
Burgh on Bain. *Linc* 2B **88**
Burgh St Margaret. *Norf* 4G **79**
Burgh St Peter. *Norf* 1G **67**
Burghwallis. *S Yor* 3F **93**
Burham. *Kent* 4B **40**
Buriton. *Hants* 4F **25**
Burland. *Ches E* 5A **84**
Burland. *Shet* 8E **173**
Burlawn. *Corn* 2D **6**
Burleigh. *Glos* 5D **48**
Burleigh. *Wind* 4G **37**
Burlescombe. *Devn* 1D **12**
Burleston. *Dors* 3C **14**
Burlestone. *Devn* 4E **9**
Burley. *Hants* 2H **15**
Burley. *Rut* 4F **75**
Burley. *W Yor* 1C **92**
Burleydam. *Ches E* 1A **72**
Burley Gate. *Here* 1A **48**
Burley in Wharfedale. *W Yor* 5D **98**
Burley Street. *Hants* 2H **15**
Burley Woodhead. *W Yor* 5D **98**
Burlingjobb. *Powy* 5E **59**
Burlington. *Shrp* 4B **72**
Burlton. *Shrp* 3G **71**
Burmantofts. *W Yor* 1D **92**
Burmarsh. *Kent* 2F **29**
Burmington. *Warw* 2A **50**
Burn. *N Yor* 2F **93**
Burnage. *G Man* 1C **84**
Burnaston. *Derbs* 2G **73**
Burnbanks. *Cumb* 3G **103**
Burnby. *E Yor* 5C **100**
Burncross. *S Yor* 1H **85**
Burneside. *Cumb* 5G **103**
Burness. *Orkn* 3F **172**
Burneston. *N Yor* 1F **99**
Burnett. *Bath* 5B **34**
Burnfoot. *E Ayr* 4D **116**
Burnfoot. *Per* 3B **136**
Burnfoot. *Bord*
nr. Hawick 3H **119**
nr. Roberton 3G **119**
Burngreave. *S Yor* 2A **86**
Burnham. *Buck* 2A **38**
Burnham. *N Lin* 3D **94**
Burnham Deepdale. *Norf* 1H **77**
Burnham Green. *Herts* 4C **52**
Burnham Market. *Norf* 1H **77**
Burnham Norton. *Norf* 1H **77**
Burnham-on-Crouch. *Essx* 1D **40**
Burnham-on-Sea. *Som* 2G **21**
Burnham Overy Staithe.
Norf 1H **77**
Burnham Overy Town.
Norf 1H **77**
Burnham Thorpe. *Norf* 1A **78**
Burnhaven. *Abers* 4H **161**
Burnhead. *Dum* 5A **118**
Burnhervie. *Abers* 2E **153**
Burnhill Green. *Staf* 5B **72**
Burnhope. *Dur* 5E **115**
Burnhouse. *N Ayr* 4E **127**
Burniston. *N Yor* 5H **107**
Burnlee. *W Yor* 4B **92**
Burnley. *Lanc* 1G **91**
Burnmouth. *Bord* 3F **131**
Burn Naze. *Lanc* 5C **96**
Burn of Cambus. *Stir* 3G **135**
Burnopfield. *Dur* 4E **115**
Burnsall. *N Yor* 3C **98**
Burnside. *Ang* 3E **145**
Burnside. *E Ayr* 3E **117**
Burnside. *Per* 3D **136**
Burnside. *Shet* 4D **173**
Burnside. *S Lan* 4H **127**
Burnside. *W Lot*
nr. Broxburn 2D **129**
nr. Winchburgh 2D **128**
Burntcommon. *Surr* 5B **38**
Burntheath. *Derbs* 2G **73**
Burnt Heath. *Essx* 3D **54**
Burnt Hill. *W Ber* 4D **36**
Burnt Houses. *Dur* 2E **105**
Burntisland. *Fife* 1F **129**
Burnt Oak. *G Lon* 1D **38**
Burnton. *E Ayr* 4D **117**
Burntstalk. *Norf* 2G **77**
Burntwood. *Staf* 5E **73**
Burntwood Green. *Staf* 5E **73**
Burnt Yates. *N Yor* 3E **99**
Burnwynd. *Edin* 3E **129**
Burpham. *Surr* 5B **38**
Burpham. *W Sus* 5B **26**
Burradon. *Nmbd* 4D **121**
Burradon. *Tyne* 2F **115**
Burrafirth. *Shet* 1H **173**
Burragarth. *Shet* 1G **173**
Burras. *Corn* 5A **6**
Burraton. *Corn* 3A **8**
Burravoe. *Shet*
nr. North Roe 3E **173**
on Mainland 5E **173**
on Yell 4G **173**
Burray Village. *Orkn* 8D **172**
Burrells. *Cumb* 3H **103**
Burrelton. *Per* 5A **144**
Burridge. *Hants* 1D **16**
Burridge. *Som* 2G **13**
Burrigill. *High* 5E **169**
Burrill. *N Yor* 1E **99**
Burringham. *N Lin* 4B **94**
Burrington. *Devn* 1G **11**
Burrington. *Here* 3G **59**
Burrington. *N Som* 1H **21**
Burrough End. *Cambs* 5F **65**
Burrough Green. *Cambs* 5F **65**
Burrough on the Hill.
Leics 4E **75**
Burroughston. *Orkn* 5E **172**
Burrow. *Devn* 4D **12**
Burrow. *Som* 2C **20**
Burrowbridge. *Som* 4G **21**
Burrowhill. *Surr* 4A **38**
Burry. *Swan* 3D **30**
Burry Green. *Swan* 3D **30**
Burry Port. *Carm* 5E **45**
Burscough. *Lanc* 3C **90**
Burscough Bridge. *Lanc* 3C **90**
Bursea. *E Yor* 1B **94**
Burshill. *E Yor* 5E **101**
Bursledon. *Hants* 2C **16**
Burslem. *Stoke* 1C **72**
Burstall. *Suff* 1D **54**
Burstock. *Dors* 2H **13**
Burston. *Devn* 2H **11**
Burston. *Norf* 2D **66**
Burston. *Staf* 2D **72**
Burstow. *Surr* 1E **27**
Burstwick. *E Yor* 2F **95**
Burtersett. *N Yor* 1A **98**
Burtholme. *Cumb* 3G **113**
Burthorpe. *Suff* 4G **65**
Burthwaite. *Cumb* 5F **113**
Burtle. *Som* 2H **21**
Burtoft. *Linc* 2B **76**
Burton. *Ches W*
nr. Kelsall 4H **83**
nr. Neston 3F **83**
Burton. *Dors*
nr. Christchurch 3G **15**
nr. Dorchester 3B **14**
Burton. *Nmbd* 1F **121**
Burton. *Pemb* 4D **43**
Burton. *Som* 2E **21**
Burton. *Wilts*
nr. Chippenham 4D **34**
nr. Warminster 3D **22**
Burton. *Wrex* 5F **83**
Burton Agnes. *E Yor* 3F **101**
Burton Bradstock. *Dors* 4H **13**
Burton-by-Lincoln. *Linc* 3G **87**
Burton Coggles. *Linc* 3G **75**
Burton Constable. *E Yor* 1E **95**
Burton Corner. *Linc* 1C **76**
Burton End. *Cambs* 1G **53**
Burton End. *Essx* 3F **53**
Burton Fleming. *E Yor* 2E **101**
Burton Green. *Warw* 3G **61**
Burton Green. *Wrex* 5F **83**
Burton Hastings. *Warw* 2B **62**
Burton-in-Kendal. *Cumb* 2E **97**
Burton in Lonsdale. *N Yor* 2F **97**
Burton Joyce. *Notts* 1D **74**
Burton Latimer. *Nptn* 3G **63**
Burton Lazars. *Leics* 4E **75**
Burton Leonard. *N Yor* 3F **99**
Burton on the Wolds.
Leics 3C **74**
Burton Overy. *Leics* 1D **62**
Burton Pedwardine. *Linc* 1A **76**

Burton Pidsea. *E Yor* 1F **95**
Burton Salmon. *N Yor* 2E **93**
Burton's Green. *Essx* 3B **54**
Burton Stather. *N Lin* 3B **94**
Burton upon Stather. *N Lin* 3B **94**
Burton upon Trent. *Staf* 3G **73**
Burton Wolds. *Leics* 3D **74**
Burtonwood. *Warr* 1H **83**
Burwardsley. *Ches W* 5H **83**
Burwarton. *Shrp* 2A **60**
Burwash. *E Sus* 3A **28**
Burwash Common. *E Sus* 3H **27**
Burwash Weald. *E Sus* 3A **28**
Burwell. *Cambs* 4E **65**
Burwell. *Linc* 3C **88**
Burwen. *IOA* 1D **80**
Burwick. *Orkn* 9D **172**
Bury. *Cambs* 2B **64**
Bury. *G Man* 3G **91**
Bury. *Som* 4C **20**
Bury. *W Sus* 4B **26**
Burybank. *Staf* 2C **72**
Bury End. *Worc* 2F **49**
Bury Green. *Herts* 3E **53**
Bury St Edmunds. *Suff* 4H **65**
Burythorpe. *N Yor* 3B **100**
Busbridge. *Surr* 1A **26**
Busby. *E Ren* 4G **127**
Busby. *Per* 1C **136**
Buscot. *Oxon* 2H **35**
Bush. *Corn* 2C **10**
Bush Bank. *Here* 5G **59**
Bushbury. *W Mid* 5D **72**
Bushby. *Leics* 5D **74**
Bushey. *Dors* 4E **15**
Bushey. *Herts* 1C **38**
Bushey Heath. *Herts* 1C **38**
Bush Green. *Norf*
   nr. Attleborough 1C **66**
   nr. Harleston 2E **66**
Bush Green. *Suff* 5B **66**
Bushley. *Worc* 2D **49**
Bushley Green. *Worc* 2D **48**
Bushmead. *Bed* 4A **64**
Bushmoor. *Shrp* 2G **59**
Bushton. *Wilts* 4F **35**
Busk. *Cumb* 5H **113**
Buslingthorpe. *Linc* 2H **87**
Bussage. *Glos* 5D **49**
Bussex. *Som* 3G **21**
Busta. *Shet* 5E **173**
Butcher's Cross. *E Sus* 3G **27**
Butcombe. *N Som* 5A **34**
Bute Town. *Cphy* 5E **46**
Butleigh. *Som* 3A **22**
Butleigh Wootton. *Som* 3A **22**
Butlers Marston. *Warw* 1B **50**
Butley. *Suff* 5F **67**
Butley High Corner. *Suff* 1G **55**
Butlocks Heath. *Hants* 2C **16**
Butterburn. *Cumb* 2H **113**
Buttercrambe. *N Yor* 4B **100**
Butterknowle. *Dur* 2E **105**
Butterleigh. *Devn* 2C **12**
Buttermere. *Cumb* 3C **102**
Buttermere. *Wilts* 5B **36**
Buttershaw. *W Yor* 2B **92**
Butterstone. *Per* 4H **143**
Butterton. *Staf*
   nr. Leek 5E **85**
   nr. Stoke-on-Trent 1C **72**
Butterwick. *Dur* 2A **106**
Butterwick. *Linc* 1C **76**
Butterwick. *N Yor*
   nr. Malton 2B **100**
   nr. Weaverthorpe 2D **101**
Butteryhaugh. *Nmbd* 5A **120**
Butt Green. *Ches E* 5A **84**
Buttington. *Powy* 5E **71**
Buttonbridge. *Shrp* 3B **60**
Buttonoak. *Shrp* 3B **60**
Buttsash. *Hants* 2C **16**
Butt's Green. *Essx* 5A **54**
Butt Yeats. *Lanc* 3E **97**
Buxhall. *Suff* 5C **66**
Buxted. *E Sus* 3F **27**
Buxton. *Derbs* 3E **85**
Buxton. *Norf* 3E **79**
Buxworth. *Derbs* 2E **85**
Bwcle. *Flin* 4E **83**
Bwlch. *Powy* 3E **47**
Bwlchderwin. *Gwyn* 1D **68**
Bwlchgwyn. *Wrex* 5E **83**
Bwlch-Llan. *Cdgn* 5E **57**
Bwlchnewydd. *Carm* 3D **44**
Bwlch-y-cibau. *Powy* 4D **70**
Bwlchtocyn. *Gwyn* 3C **68**
Bwlchyddar. *Powy* 3D **70**
Bwlch-y-fadfa. *Cdgn* 1E **45**
Bwlch-y-ffridd. *Powy* 1C **58**
Bwlch y Garreg. *Powy* 1C **58**
Bwlch-y-groes. *Pemb* 1G **43**
Bwlch-y-sarnau. *Powy* 3C **58**
Bybrook. *Kent* 1E **28**
Byermoor. *Tyne* 4E **115**
Byers Garth. *Dur* 5G **115**
Byers Green. *Dur* 1F **105**
Byfield. *Nptn* 5C **62**
Byfleet. *Surr* 4B **38**
Byford. *Here* 1G **47**
Bygrave. *Herts* 2C **52**
Byker. *Tyne* 3F **115**
Byland Abbey. *N Yor* 2H **99**
Bylchau. *Cnwy* 4B **82**
Byley. *Ches W* 4B **84**
Bynea. *Carm* 3E **31**
Byram. *N Yor* 2E **93**
Byrness. *Nmbd* 4B **120**
Bystock. *Devn* 4D **12**
Bythorn. *Cambs* 3H **63**

Byton. *Here* 4F **59**
Bywell. *Nmbd* 3D **114**
Byworth. *W Sus* 3A **26**

C

Cabharstadh. *W Isl* 6F **171**
Cabourne. *Linc* 4E **95**
Cabrach. *Arg* 3C **124**
Cabrach. *Mor* 1A **152**
Cabus. *Lanc* 5D **97**
Cadbury. *Devn* 2C **12**
Cadder. *E Dun* 2H **127**
Caddington. *C Beds* 4A **52**
Caddonfoot. *Bord* 1G **119**
Cadeby. *Leics* 5B **74**
Cadeby. *S Yor* 4F **93**
Cadeleigh. *Devn* 2C **12**
Cade Street. *E Sus* 3H **27**
Cadgwith. *Corn* 5E **5**
Cadham. *Fife* 3E **137**
Cadishead. *G Man* 1B **84**
Cadle. *Swan* 3F **31**
Cadley. *Lanc* 1D **90**
Cadley. *Wilts*
   nr. Ludgershall 1H **23**
   nr. Marlborough 5H **35**
Cadmore End. *Buck* 2F **37**
Cadnam. *Hants* 1A **16**
Cadney. *N Lin* 4D **94**
Cadole. *Flin* 4E **82**
Cadoxton-juxta-Neath. *Neat* 2A **32**
Cadwell. *Herts* 2B **52**
Cadwst. *Den* 2C **70**
Caeathro. *Gwyn* 4E **81**
Caehopkin. *Powy* 4B **46**
Caenby. *Linc* 2H **87**
Caerau. *B'end* 2B **32**
Caerau. *Card* 4E **33**
Cae'r-bont. *Powy* 4B **46**
Cae'r-bryn. *Carm* 4F **45**
Caerdeon. *Gwyn* 4F **69**
Caerdydd. *Card* 191 (4E **33**)
Caerfarchell. *Pemb* 2B **42**
Caerfilli. *Cphy* 3E **33**
Caerfyrddin. *Carm* 4E **45**
Caergeiliog. *IOA* 3C **80**
Caergwrle. *Flin* 5F **83**
Caergybi. *IOA* 2B **80**
Caerlaverock. *Per* 2A **136**
Caerleon. *Newp* 2G **33**
Caerllan. *Carm* 2G **43**
Caerllion. *Newp* 2G **33**
Caernarfon. *Gwyn* 190 (4D **81**)
Caerphilly. *Cphy* 3E **33**
Caersws. *Powy* 1C **58**
Caerwedros. *Cdgn* 5C **56**
Caerwent. *Mon* 2H **33**
Caerwys. *Flin* 3D **82**
Caim. *IOA* 2F **81**
Caio. *Carm* 2G **45**
Cairinis. *W Isl* 2D **170**
Cairisiadar. *W Isl* 4C **171**
Cairminis. *W Isl* 9C **171**
Cairnbaan. *Arg* 4F **133**
Cairnbulg. *Abers* 2H **161**
Cairncross. *Ang* 1D **145**
Cairndow. *Arg* 2A **134**
Cairness. *Abers* 2H **161**
Cairneyhill. *Fife* 1D **128**
Cairngarroch. *Dum* 5F **109**
Cairnhill. *Abers* 5D **160**
Cairnie. *Abers* 4B **160**
Cairnorrie. *Abers* 4F **161**
Cairnryan. *Dum* 3F **109**
Cairston. *Orkn* 6B **172**
Caister-on-Sea. *Norf* 4H **79**
Caistor. *Linc* 4E **94**
Caistor St Edmund. *Norf* 5E **79**
Caistron. *Nmbd* 4D **121**
Cakebole. *Worc* 3C **60**
Calais Street. *Suff* 1C **54**
Calanais. *W Isl* 4E **171**
Calbost. *W Isl* 6G **171**
Calbourne. *IOW* 4C **16**
Calceby. *Linc* 3C **88**
Calcot. *Glos* 4F **49**
Calcot Row. *W Ber* 4E **37**
Calcott. *Kent* 4F **41**
Calcott. *Shrp* 4G **71**
Caldback. *Shet* 1H **173**
Caldbeck. *Cumb* 1E **102**
Caldbergh. *N Yor* 1C **98**
Caldecote. *Cambs*
   nr. Cambridge 5C **64**
   nr. Peterborough 2A **64**
Caldecote. *Herts* 2C **52**
Caldecote. *Nptn* 5D **62**
Caldecote. *Warw* 1A **62**
Caldecott. *Nptn* 4G **63**
Caldecott. *Oxon* 2C **36**
Caldecott. *Rut* 1F **63**
Calderbank. *N Lan* 3A **128**
Calder Bridge. *Cumb* 4B **102**
Caldercruix. *N Lan* 3B **128**
Calder Grove. *W Yor* 3D **92**
Calder Mains. *High* 3C **168**
Caldermill. *S Lan* 5H **127**
Calder Vale. *Lanc* 5E **97**
Calderwood. *S Lan* 4H **127**
Caldicot. *Mon* 3H **33**
Caldwell. *Derbs* 4G **73**
Caldwell. *N Yor* 3E **105**
Caldy. *Mers* 2E **83**
Calebrack. *Cumb* 1E **103**
Calf Heath. *Staf* 5D **72**
Calford Green. *Suff* 1G **53**
Calfsound. *Orkn* 4E **172**
Calgary. *Arg* 3E **139**

Califer. *Mor* 3E **159**
California. *Cambs* 2E **65**
California. *Falk* 2C **128**
California. *Norf* 4H **79**
California. *Suff* 1E **55**
Calke. *Derbs* 3A **74**
Callakille. *High* 3F **155**
Callaly. *Nmbd* 4E **121**
Callander. *Stir* 3F **135**
Callaughton. *Shrp* 1A **60**
Callendoun. *Arg* 1E **127**
Callestick. *Corn* 3B **6**
Calligarry. *High* 3E **147**
Callington. *Corn* 2H **7**
Callingwood. *Staf* 3F **73**
Callow. *Here* 2H **47**
Callow. *S Yor* 4G **93**
Callowell. *Glos* 5D **48**
Callow End. *Worc* 1D **48**
Callow Hill. *Wilts* 3F **35**
Callow Hill. *Worc*
   nr. Bewdley 3B **60**
   nr. Redditch 4E **61**
Calmore. *Hants* 1B **16**
Calmsden. *Glos* 5F **49**
Calne. *Wilts* 4E **35**
Calow. *Derbs* 3B **86**
Calshot. *Hants* 2C **16**
Calstock. *Corn* 2A **8**
Calstone Wellington. *Wilts* 5F **35**
Calthorpe. *Norf* 2D **78**
Calthorpe Street. *Norf* 3G **79**
Calthwaite. *Cumb* 5F **113**
Calton. *N Yor* 4B **98**
Calton. *Staf* 5F **85**
Calveley. *Ches E* 5H **83**
Calver. *Derbs* 3G **85**
Calverhall. *Shrp* 2A **72**
Calverleigh. *Devn* 1C **12**
Calverley. *W Yor* 1C **92**
Calvert. *Buck* 3E **51**
Calverton. *Mil* 2F **51**
Calverton. *Notts* 1D **74**
Calvine. *Per* 2F **143**
Calvo. *Cumb* 4C **112**
Cam. *Glos* 2C **34**
Camaghael. *High* 1F **141**
Camas-luinie. *High* 1B **148**
Camasnacroise. *High* 3D **140**
Camastianavaig. *High* 5E **155**
Camasunary. *High* 2D **146**
Camault Muir. *High* 4H **157**
Camb. *Shet* 2G **173**
Camber. *E Sus* 4D **28**
Camberley. *Surr* 5G **37**
Camberwell. *G Lon* 3E **39**
Camblesforth. *N Yor* 2G **93**
Cambo. *Nmbd* 1D **114**
Cambois. *Nmbd* 1G **115**
Camborne. *Corn* 5A **6**
Cambourne. *Cambs* 5C **64**
Cambridge. *Cambs* 191 (5D **64**)
Cambridge. *Glos* 5C **48**
Cambrose. *Corn* 4A **6**
Cambus. *Clac* 4A **136**
Cambusbarron. *Stir* 4G **135**
Cambuskenneth. *Stir* 4H **135**
Cambuslang. *S Lan* 3H **127**
Cambusnethan. *N Lan* 4B **128**
Cambus o' May. *Abers* 4B **152**
Camden Town. *G Lon* 2D **39**
Cameley. *Bath* 1B **22**
Camelford. *Corn* 4B **10**
Camelon. *Falk* 1B **128**
Camelsdale. *W Sus* 3G **25**
Camer's Green. *Worc* 2C **48**
Camerton. *Bath* 1B **22**
Camerton. *Cumb* 1B **102**
Camerton. *E Yor* 2F **95**
Camghouran. *Per* 3C **142**
Cammachmore. *Abers* 4G **153**
Cammeringham. *Linc* 2G **87**
Camore. *High* 4E **165**
Camp, The. *Glos* 5E **49**
Campbelton. *N Ayr* 4C **126**
Campbeltown. *Arg* 3B **122**
Campbeltown Airport. *Arg* 3A **122**
Cample. *Dum* 5A **118**
Campmuir. *Per* 5B **144**
Campsall. *S Yor* 3F **93**
Campsea Ashe. *Suff* 5F **67**
Camps End. *Cambs* 1G **53**
Campton. *C Beds* 2B **52**
Camptoun. *E Lot* 2B **130**
Camptown. *Bord* 3A **120**
Camrose. *Pemb* 2D **42**
Camserney. *Per* 4F **143**
Camster. *High* 4E **169**
Camus Croise. *High* 2E **147**
Camuscross. *High* 2E **147**
Camusdarach. *High* 4E **147**
Camusnagaul. *High*
   nr. Fort William 1E **141**
   nr. Little Loch Broom 5E **163**
Camusteel. *High* 4G **155**
Camusterrach. *High* 4G **155**
Camusvrachan. *Per* 4D **142**
Canada. *Hants* 1A **16**
Canada. *E Sus* 4B **28**
Canaston Bridge. *Pemb* 3E **43**
Candlesby. *Linc* 4D **88**
Candle Street. *Suff* 3C **66**
Candy Mill. *S Lan* 5D **128**
Cane End. *Oxon* 4E **37**
Canewdon. *Essx* 1D **40**
Canford Cliffs. *Pool* 4F **15**
Canford Heath. *Pool* 3F **15**
Canford Magna. *Pool* 3F **15**
Cangate. *Norf* 4F **79**
Canham's Green. *Suff* 4C **66**
Canholes. *Derbs* 3E **85**
Canisbay. *High* 1F **169**

Canley. *W Mid* 3H **61**
Cann. *Dors* 4D **22**
Cann Common. *Dors* 4D **23**
Cannich. *High* 5F **157**
Cannington. *Som* 3F **21**
Cannock. *Staf* 4D **73**
Cannock Wood. *Staf* 4E **73**
Canonbie. *Dum* 2E **113**
Canon Bridge. *Here* 1H **47**
Canon Frome. *Here* 1B **48**
Canon Pyon. *Here* 1H **47**
Canons Ashby. *Nptn* 5C **62**
Canonstown. *Corn* 3C **4**
Canterbury. *Kent* 190 (5F **41**)
Cantley. *Norf* 5F **79**
Cantley. *S Yor* 4G **93**
Cantlop. *Shrp* 5H **71**
Canton. *Card* 4E **33**
Cantray. *High* 4B **158**
Cantraybruich. *High* 4B **158**
Cantraywood. *High* 4B **158**
Cantsdam. *Fife* 4D **136**
Cantsfield. *Lanc* 2F **97**
Canvey Island. *Essx* 2B **40**
Canwick. *Linc* 4G **87**
Canworthy Water. *Corn* 3C **10**
Caol. *High* 1F **141**
Caolas. *Arg* 4B **138**
Caolas. *W Isl* 9B **170**
Caolas Liubharsaigh. *W Isl* 4D **170**
Caolas Scalpaigh. *W Isl* 8E **171**
Caolas Stocinis. *W Isl* 8D **171**
Caol Ila. *Arg* 2C **124**
Caol Loch Ailse. *High* 1F **147**
Caol Reatha. *High* 1F **147**
Capel. *Kent* 1H **27**
Capel. *Surr* 1C **26**
Capel Bangor. *Cdgn* 2F **57**
Capel Betws Lleucu. *Cdgn* 5F **57**
Capel Coch. *IOA* 2D **80**
Capel Curig. *Cnwy* 5G **81**
Capel Cynon. *Cdgn* 1D **45**
Capel Dewi. *Carm* 3E **45**
Capel Dewi. *Cdgn*
   nr. Aberystwyth 2F **57**
   nr. Llandysul 1E **45**
Capel Garmon. *Cnwy* 5H **81**
Capel Green. *Suff* 1G **55**
Capel Gwyn. *IOA* 3C **80**
Capel Gwynfe. *Carm* 3H **45**
Capel Hendre. *Carm* 4F **45**
Capel Isaac. *Carm* 3F **45**
Capel Iwan. *Carm* 1G **43**
Capel-le-Ferne. *Kent* 2G **29**
Capel Llanilltern. *Card* 4D **32**
Capel Mawr. *IOA* 3D **80**
Capel Newydd. *Pemb* 1G **43**
Capel St Andrew. *Suff* 1G **55**
Capel St Mary. *Suff* 2D **54**
Capel Seion. *Carm* 4F **45**
Capel Seion. *Cdgn* 3F **57**
Capel Uchaf. *Gwyn* 1D **68**
Capel-y-ffin. *Powy* 2F **47**
Capenhurst. *Ches W* 3F **83**
Capernwray. *Lanc* 2E **97**
Capheaton. *Nmbd* 1D **114**
Cappercleuch. *Bord* 2E **119**
Capplegill. *Dum* 4D **118**
Capton. *Devn* 3E **9**
Capton. *Som* 3D **20**
Caputh. *Per* 5H **143**
Caradon Town. *Corn* 5C **10**
Carbis Bay. *Corn* 3C **4**
Carbost. *High*
   nr. Loch Harport 5C **154**
   nr. Portree 4D **154**
Carbrook. *S Yor* 2A **86**
Carbrooke. *Norf* 5B **78**
Carburton. *Notts* 3D **86**
Carcluie. *S Ayr* 3C **116**
Car Colston. *Notts* 1E **74**
Carcroft. *S Yor* 4F **93**
Cardenden. *Fife* 4E **136**
Cardeston. *Shrp* 4F **71**
Cardewlees. *Cumb* 4E **113**
Cardiff. *Card* 191 (4E **33**)
Cardiff Airport. *V Glam* 5D **32**
Cardigan. *Cdgn* 1B **44**
Cardinal's Green. *Cambs* 1G **53**
Cardington. *Bed* 1A **52**
Cardington. *Shrp* 1H **59**
Cardinham. *Corn* 2F **7**
Cardno. *Abers* 2G **161**
Cardow. *Mor* 4F **159**
Cardross. *Arg* 2E **127**
Cardurnock. *Cumb* 4C **112**
Careby. *Linc* 4H **75**
Careston. *Ang* 2E **145**
Carew. *Pemb* 4E **43**
Carew Cheriton. *Pemb* 4E **43**
Carew Newton. *Pemb* 4E **43**
Carey. *Here* 2A **48**
Carfin. *N Lan* 4A **128**
Carfrae. *Bord* 4B **130**
Cargate Green. *Norf* 4F **79**
Cargenbridge. *Dum* 2G **111**
Cargill. *Per* 5A **144**
Cargo. *Cumb* 4E **113**
Cargreen. *Corn* 2A **8**
Carham. *Nmbd* 1C **120**
Carhampton. *Som* 2D **20**
Carharrack. *Corn* 4B **6**
Carie. *Per*
   nr. Loch Rannah 3D **142**
   nr. Loch Tay 5D **142**
Carisbrooke. *IOW* 4C **16**
Cark. *Cumb* 2C **96**
Carkeel. *Corn* 2A **8**
Carlabhagh. *W Isl* 3E **171**
Carland Cross. *Corn* 3C **6**
Carlbury. *Darl* 3F **105**

Carlby. *Linc* 4H **75**
Carlecotes. *S Yor* 4B **92**
Carleen. *Corn* 4D **4**
Carlesmoor. *N Yor* 2D **98**
Carleton. *Cumb*
   nr. Carlisle 4F **113**
   nr. Egremont 4B **102**
   nr. Penrith 2G **103**
Carleton. *Lanc* 5C **96**
Carleton. *N Yor* 5B **98**
Carleton. *W Yor* 2E **93**
Carleton Forehoe. *Norf* 5C **78**
Carleton Rode. *Norf* 1D **66**
Carleton St Peter. *Norf* 5F **79**
Carlidnack. *Corn* 4E **5**
Carlin How. *Red C* 3E **107**
Carlisle. *Cumb* 192 (4F **113**)
Carloonan. *Arg* 2H **133**
Carlops. *Bord* 4E **129**
Carlton. *Bed* 5G **63**
Carlton. *Cambs* 5F **65**
Carlton. *Leics* 5A **74**
Carlton. *N Yor*
   nr. Helmsley 1A **100**
   nr. Middleham 1C **98**
   nr. Selby 2G **93**
Carlton. *Notts* 1D **74**
Carlton. *S Yor* 3D **92**
Carlton. *Stoc T* 2A **106**
Carlton. *Suff* 4F **67**
Carlton. *W Yor* 2D **92**
Carlton Colville. *Suff* 1H **67**
Carlton Curlieu. *Leics* 1D **62**
Carlton Husthwaite. *N Yor* 2G **99**
Carlton in Cleveland. *N Yor* 4C **106**
Carlton in Lindrick. *Notts* 2C **86**
Carlton-le-Moorland. *Linc* 5G **87**
Carlton Miniott. *N Yor* 1F **99**
Carlton-on-Trent. *Notts* 4F **87**
Carlton Scroop. *Linc* 1G **75**
Carluke. *S Lan* 4B **128**
Carlyon Bay. *Corn* 3E **7**
Carmarthen. *Carm* 4E **45**
Carmel. *Carm* 4F **45**
Carmel. *Flin* 3D **82**
Carmel. *Gwyn* 5D **81**
Carmel. *IOA* 2C **80**
Carmichael. *S Lan* 1B **118**
Carmunnock. *Glas* 4H **127**
Carmyle. *Glas* 3H **127**
Carmyllie. *Ang* 4E **145**
Carnaby. *E Yor* 3F **101**
Carnach. *High*
   nr. Lochcarron 1C **148**
   nr. Ullapool 4E **163**
Carnach. *Mor* 4E **159**
Carnach. *W Isl* 8E **171**
Carnachy. *High* 3H **167**
Carnain. *Arg* 3B **124**
Carnais. *W Isl* 4C **171**
Carnan. *Arg* 4B **138**
Carnan. *W Isl* 4C **170**
Carnbee. *Fife* 3H **137**
Carnbo. *Per* 3C **136**
Carn Brea Village. *Corn* 4A **6**
Candu. *High* 1A **148**
Carne. *Corn* 5D **6**
Carnell. *S Ayr* 1D **116**
Carnforth. *Lanc* 2E **97**
Carn-gorm. *High* 1B **148**
Carnhedryn. *Pemb* 2C **42**
Carnhell Green. *Corn* 3D **4**
Carnie. *Abers* 3F **153**
Carnkie. *Corn*
   nr. Falmouth 5B **6**
   nr. Redruth 5A **6**
Carnkief. *Corn* 3B **6**
Carno. *Powy* 1B **58**
Carnock. *Fife* 1D **128**
Carnon Downs. *Corn* 4B **6**
Carnoustie. *Ang* 5E **145**
Carntyne. *Glas* 3H **127**
Carnwath. *S Lan* 5C **128**
Carnyorth. *Corn* 3A **4**
Carol Green. *W Mid* 3G **61**
Carpalla. *Corn* 3D **6**
Carperby. *N Yor* 1C **98**
Carradale. *Arg* 2C **122**
Carragraich. *W Isl* 8D **171**
Carrbridge. *High* 1D **150**
Carr Cross. *Lanc* 3B **90**
Carreglefn. *IOA* 2C **80**
Carrhouse. *N Lin* 4A **94**
Carrick Castle. *Arg* 4A **134**
Carrick Ho. *Orkn* 4E **172**
Carriden. *Falk* 1D **128**
Carrington. *G Man* 1B **84**
Carrington. *Linc* 5C **88**
Carrington. *Midl* 3G **129**
Carrog. *Cnwy* 1G **69**
Carrog. *Den* 1D **70**
Carron. *Falk* 1B **128**
Carron. *Mor* 4G **159**
Carronbridge. *Dum* 5A **118**
Carronshore. *Falk* 1B **128**
Carrow Hill. *Mon* 2H **33**
Carr Shield. *Nmbd* 5B **114**
Carrutherstown. *Dum* 2C **112**
Carr Vale. *Derbs* 4B **86**
Carrville. *Dur* 5G **115**
Carsaig. *Arg* 1C **132**
Carscreugh. *Dum* 3H **109**
Carsegowan. *Dum* 4B **110**
Carse House. *Arg* 3F **125**
Carseriggan. *Dum* 3A **110**
Carsethorn. *Dum* 4A **112**
Carshalton. *G Lon* 4D **39**
Carsington. *Derbs* 5G **85**
Carskiey. *Arg* 5A **122**
Carsluith. *Dum* 4B **110**

Carsphairn—Child's Ercall

Carsphairn. Dum 5E 117
Carstairs. S Lan 5C 128
Carstairs Junction. S Lan 5C 128
Cartbridge. Surr 5B 38
Carterhaugh. Ang 4D 144
Carter's Clay. Hants 4B 24
Carterton. Oxon 5A 50
Carterway Heads. Nmbd 4D 114
Carthew. Corn 3E 6
Carthorpe. N Yor 1F 99
Cartington. Nmbd 4E 121
Cartland. S Lan 5B 128
Cartmel. Cumb 2C 96
Cartmel Fell. Cumb 1D 96
Cartworth. W Yor 4B 92
Carwath. Cumb 5E 112
Carway. Carm 5E 45
Carwinley. Cumb 2F 113
Cascob. Powy 4E 59
Cas-gwent. Mon 2A 34
Cash Feus. Fife 3E 136
Cashlie. Per 4B 142
Cashmoor. Dors 1E 15
Cas-Mael. Pemb 2E 43
Casnewydd. Newp 205 (3G 33)
Cassington. Oxon 4C 50
Cassop. Dur 1A 106
Castell. Cnwy 4G 81
Castell. Den 4D 82
Castell Hendre. Pemb 2E 43
Castell-Nedd. Neat 2A 32
Castell Newydd Emlyn. Carm 1D 44
Castell-y-bwch. Torf 2F 33
Casterton. Cumb 2F 97
Castle. Som 2A 22
Castle Acre. Norf 4H 77
Castle Ashby. Nptn 5F 63
Castlebay. W Isl 9B 170
Castle Bolton. N Yor 5D 104
Castle Bromwich. W Mid 2F 61
Castle Bytham. Linc 4G 75
Castlebythe. Pemb 2E 43
Castle Caereinion. Powy 5D 70
Castle Camps. Cambs 1G 53
Castle Carrock. Cumb 4G 113
Castlecary. N Lan 2A 128
Castle Cary. Som 3B 22
Castle Combe. Wilts 4D 34
Castlecraig. High 2C 158
Castle Donington. Leics 3B 74
Castle Douglas. Dum 3E 111
Castle Eaton. Swin 2G 35
Castle Eden. Dur 1B 106
Castleford. W Yor 2E 93
Castle Frome. Here 1B 48
Castle Green. Surr 4A 38
Castle Green. Warw 3G 61
Castle Gresley. Derbs 4G 73
Castle Heaton. Nmbd 5F 131
Castle Hedingham. Essx 2A 54
Castle Hill. Kent 1A 28
Castlehill. Per 5B 144
Castlehill. S Lan 4B 128
Castle Hill. Suff 1E 55
Castlehill. W Dun 2E 127
Castle Kennedy. Dum 4G 109
Castle Lachlan. Arg 4H 133
Castlemartin. Pemb 5D 42
Castlemilk. Glas 4H 127
Castlemorris. Pemb 1D 42
Castlemorton. Worc 2C 48
Castle O'er. Dum 5E 119
Castle Park. N Yor 3F 107
Castlerigg. Cumb 2D 102
Castle Rising. Norf 3F 77
Castleside. Dur 5D 115
Castlethorpe. Mil 1F 51
Castleton. Abers 4F 151
Castleton. Arg 1G 125
Castleton. Derbs 2F 85
Castleton. G Man 3G 91
Castleton. Mor 1F 151
Castleton. Newp 3F 33
Castleton. N Yor 4D 107
Castleton. Per 2B 136
Castletown. Cumb 1G 103
Castletown. Dors 5B 14
Castletown. High 2D 169
Castletown. IOM 5B 108
Castletown. Tyne 4G 115
Castley. N Yor 5E 99
Caston. Norf 1B 66
Castor. Pet 1A 64
Caswell. Swan 4E 31
Catacol. N Ayr 5H 125
Catbrook. Mon 5A 48
Catchems End. Worc 3B 60
Catchgate. Dur 4E 115
Catcleugh. Nmbd 4B 120
Catcliffe. S Yor 2B 86
Catcott. Som 3G 21
Caterham. Surr 5E 39
Catfield. Norf 3F 79
Catfield Common. Norf 3F 79
Catfirth. Shet 6F 173
Catford. G Lon 3E 39
Catforth. Lanc 1C 90
Cathcart. Glas 3G 127
Cathedine. Powy 3E 47
Catherine-de-Barnes. W Mid 2F 61
Catherington. Hants 1E 17
Catherston Leweston. Dors 3G 13
Catherton. Shrp 3A 60
Catisfield. Hants 2D 16
Catlodge. High 4A 150
Catlowdy. Cumb 2F 113
Catmore. W Ber 3C 36
Caton. Devn 5A 12
Caton. Lanc 3E 97
Catrine. E Ayr 2E 117
Cat's Ash. Newp 2G 33
Catsfield. E Sus 4B 28
Catsgore. Som 4A 22
Catshill. Worc 3D 60
Cattal. N Yor 4G 99
Cattawade. Suff 2E 54
Catterall. Lanc 5E 97
Catterick. N Yor 5F 105
Catterick Bridge. N Yor 5F 105
Catterick Garrison. N Yor 5E 105
Catterlen. Cumb 1F 103
Catterline. Abers 1H 145
Catterton. N Yor 5H 99
Catteshall. Surr 1A 26
Catthorpe. Leics 3C 62
Cattistock. Dors 3A 14
Catton. Nmbd 4B 114
Catton. N Yor 2F 99
Catwick. E Yor 5F 101
Catworth. Cambs 3H 63
Caudle Green. Glos 4E 49
Caulcott. Oxon 3D 50
Cauldhame. Stir 4F 135
Cauldmill. Bord 3H 119
Cauldon. Staf 1E 73
Cauldon Lowe. Staf 1E 73
Cauldwells. Abers 3E 161
Caulkerbush. Dum 4G 111
Caulside. Dum 1F 113
Caunsall. Worc 2C 60
Caunton. Notts 4E 87
Causewayend. S Lan 1C 118
Causewayhead. Stir 4H 135
Causey Park. Nmbd 5F 121
Caute. Devn 1E 11
Cautley. Cumb 5H 103
Cavendish. Suff 1B 54
Cavendish Bridge. Leics 3B 74
Cavenham. Suff 3G 65
Caversfield. Oxon 3D 50
Caversham. Read 4F 37
Caversham Heights. Read 4F 37
Caverswall. Staf 1D 72
Cawdor. High 3C 158
Cawkwell. Linc 2B 88
Cawood. N Yor 1F 93
Cawsand. Corn 3A 8
Cawston. Norf 3D 78
Cawston. Warw 3B 62
Cawthorne. N Yor 1B 100
Cawthorne. S Yor 4C 92
Cawthorpe. Linc 3H 75
Cawton. N Yor 2A 100
Caxton. Cambs 5C 64
Caynham. Shrp 3H 59
Caythorpe. Linc 1G 75
Caythorpe. Notts 1D 74
Cayton. N Yor 1E 101
Ceallan. W Isl 3D 170
Ceann a Bhaigh. W Isl
on North Uist 2C 170
on Scalpay 8E 171
on South Harris 8D 171
Ceann a Bhàigh. W Isl 9C 171
Ceannacroc Lodge. High 2E 149
Ceann a Deas Loch Baghasdail. W Isl 7C 170
Ceann an Leothaid. High 5E 147
Ceann a Tuath Loch Baghasdail. W Isl 6C 170
Ceann Loch Ailleart. High 5F 147
Ceann Loch Muideirt. High 1B 140
Ceann-na-Cleithe. W Isl 8D 171
Ceann Shìphoirt. W Isl 6E 171
Ceann Tarabhaigh. W Isl 6E 171
Cearsiadar. W Isl 5F 171
Ceathramh Meadhanach. W Isl 1D 170
Cefn Berain. Cnwy 4B 82
Cefn-brith. Cnwy 5B 82
Cefn-bryn-brain. Carm 4H 45
Cefn Bychan. Cphy 2F 33
Cefn-bychan. Flin 4D 82
Cefncaeau. Carm 3E 31
Cefn Canol. Powy 2E 71
Cefn Coch. Powy 5C 70
Cefn-coch. Powy 3D 70
Cefn-coed-y-cymmer. Mer T 5D 46
Cefn Cribwr. B'end 3B 32
Cefn-ddwysarn. Gwyn 2B 70
Cefn Einion. Shrp 2E 59
Cefneithin. Carm 4F 45
Cefn Glas. B'end 3B 32
Cefngorwydd. Powy 1C 46
Cefn Llwyd. Cdgn 2F 57
Cefn-mawr. Wrex 1E 71
Cefn-y-bedd. Flin 5F 83
Cefn-y-coed. Powy 1D 58
Cefn-y-pant. Carm 2F 43
Cegidfa. Powy 4E 70
Ceinewydd. Cdgn 5C 56
Cellan. Cdgn 1G 45
Cellardyke. Fife 3H 137
Cellarhead. Staf 1D 72
Cemaes. IOA 1C 80
Cemmaes. Powy 5H 69
Cemmaes Road. Powy 5H 69
Cenarth. Cdgn 1C 44
Cenin. Gwyn 1D 68
Ceos. W Isl 5F 171
Ceres. Fife 2G 137
Ceri. Powy 2D 58
Cerist. Powy 2B 58
Cerne Abbas. Dors 2B 14
Cerney Wick. Glos 2F 35
Cerrigceinwen. IOA 3D 80
Cerrigydrudion. Cnwy 1B 70
Cess. Norf 4G 79
Cessford. Bord 2B 120
Ceunant. Gwyn 4E 81
Chaceley. Glos 2D 48
Chacewater. Corn 4B 6
Chackmore. Buck 2E 51
Chacombe. Nptn 1C 50
Chadderton. G Man 4H 91
Chaddesden. Derb 2A 74
Chaddesden Common. Derb 2A 74
Chaddesley Corbett. Worc 3C 60
Chaddlehanger. Devn 5E 11
Chaddleworth. W Ber 4C 36
Chadlington. Oxon 3B 50
Chadshunt. Warw 5H 61
Chadstone. Nptn 5F 63
Chad Valley. W Mid 2E 61
Chadwell. Leics 3E 75
Chadwell. Shrp 4B 72
Chadwell Heath. G Lon 2F 39
Chadwell St Mary. Thur 3H 39
Chadwick End. W Mid 3G 61
Chadwick Green. Mers 1H 83
Chaffcombe. Som 1G 13
Chafford Hundred. Thur 3H 39
Chagford. Devn 4H 11
Chailey. E Sus 4E 27
Chainbridge. Cambs 5D 76
Chain Bridge. Linc 1C 76
Chainhurst. Kent 1B 28
Chalbury. Dors 2F 15
Chalbury Common. Dors 2F 15
Chaldon. Surr 5E 39
Chaldon Herring. Dors 4C 14
Chale. IOW 5C 16
Chale Green. IOW 5C 16
Chalfont Common. Buck 1B 38
Chalfont St Giles. Buck 1A 38
Chalfont St Peter. Buck 2B 38
Chalford. Glos 5D 49
Chalgrove. Oxon 2E 37
Chalk. Kent 3A 40
Chalk End. Essx 4G 53
Chalk Hill. Glos 3G 49
Challaborough. Devn 4C 8
Challacombe. Devn 2G 19
Challister. Shet 5G 173
Challoch. Dum 3A 110
Challock. Kent 5E 40
Chalton. C Beds
nr. Bedford 5A 64
nr. Luton 3A 52
Chalton. Hants 1F 17
Chalvington. E Sus 5G 27
Champany. Falk 2D 128
Chance Inn. Fife 2F 137
Chancery. Cdgn 3E 57
Chandler's Cross. Herts 1B 38
Chandler's Cross. Worc 2C 48
Chandler's Ford. Hants 4C 24
Chanlockfoot. Dum 4G 117
Channel's End. Bed 5A 64
Channel Tunnel. Kent 2F 29
Channerwick. Shet 9F 173
Chantry. Som 2C 22
Chantry. Suff 1E 55
Chapel. Cumb 1D 102
Chapel. Fife 4E 137
Chapel Allerton. Som 1H 21
Chapel Allerton. W Yor 1C 92
Chapel Amble. Corn 1D 6
Chapel Brampton. Nptn 4E 63
Chapelbridge. Cambs 1B 64
Chapel Chorlton. Staf 2C 72
Chapel Cleeve. Som 2D 20
Chapel End. C Beds 1A 52
Chapel-en-le-Frith. Derbs 2E 85
Chapelfield. Abers 2G 145
Chapelgate. Linc 3D 76
Chapel Green. Warw
nr. Coventry 2G 61
nr. Southam 4B 62
Chapel Haddlesey. N Yor 2F 93
Chapelhall. N Lan 3A 128
Chapel Hill. Abers 5H 161
Chapel Hill. Linc 5B 88
Chapel Hill. Mon 5A 48
Chapelhill. Per
nr. Glencarse 1E 136
nr. Harrietfield 5H 143
Chapelknowe. Dum 2E 112
Chapel Lawn. Shrp 3F 59
Chapel le Dale. N Yor 2G 97
Chapel Milton. Derbs 2E 85
Chapel of Garioch. Abers 1E 152
Chapel Row. W Ber 5D 36
Chapels. Cumb 1B 96
Chapel St Leonards. Linc 3E 89
Chapel Stile. Cumb 4E 102
Chapelthorpe. W Yor 3D 92
Chapelton. Ang 4F 145
Chapelton. Devn 4F 19
Chapelton. High
nr. Grantown-on-Spey 2D 150
nr. Inverness 3H 157
Chapelton. S Lan 5H 127
Chapeltown. Bkbn 3F 91
Chapel Town. Corn 3C 6
Chapeltown. Mor 1G 151
Chapeltown. S Yor 1A 86
Chapmanslade. Wilts 2D 22
Chapmans Well. Devn 3D 10
Chapmore End. Herts 4D 52
Chappel. Essx 3B 54
Chard. Som 2G 13
Chard Junction. Dors 2G 13
Chardstock. Devn 2G 13
Charfield. S Glo 2C 34
Charing. Kent 1D 28
Charing Heath. Kent 1D 28
Charing Hill. Kent 5D 40
Charingworth. Glos 2H 49
Charlbury. Oxon 4B 50
Charlcombe. Bath 5C 34
Charlcutt. Wilts 4E 35
Charlecote. Warw 5G 61
Charles. Devn 3G 19
Charlesfield. Dum 3C 112
Charleshill. Surr 2G 25
Charleston. Ang 4C 144
Charleston. Ren 3F 127
Charlestown. Aber 3G 153
Charlestown. Abers 2H 161
Charlestown. Corn 3E 7
Charlestown. Dors 5B 14
Charlestown. Fife 1D 128
Charlestown. G Man 4G 91
Charlestown. High
nr. Gairloch 1H 155
nr. Inverness 4A 158
Charlestown. W Yor 2H 91
Charlestown of Aberlour. Mor 4G 159
Charles Tye. Suff 5C 66
Charlesworth. Derbs 1E 85
Charlton. G Lon 3F 39
Charlton. Hants 2B 24
Charlton. Herts 3B 52
Charlton. Nptn 2D 50
Charlton. Nmbd 1B 114
Charlton. Oxon 3C 36
Charlton. Som
nr. Radstock 1B 22
nr. Shepton Mallet 2B 22
nr. Taunton 4F 21
Charlton. Telf 4H 71
Charlton. W Sus 1G 17
Charlton. Wilts
nr. Malmesbury 3E 35
nr. Pewsey 1G 23
nr. Shaftesbury 4E 23
Charlton. Worc
nr. Evesham 1F 49
nr. Stourport-on-Severn 3C 60
Charlton Abbots. Glos 3F 49
Charlton Adam. Som 4A 22
Charlton All Saints. Wilts 4G 23
Charlton Down. Dors 3B 14
Charlton Horethorne. Som 4B 22
Charlton Kings. Glos 3E 49
Charlton Mackrell. Som 4A 22
Charlton Marshall. Dors 2E 15
Charlton Musgrove. Som 4C 22
Charlton-on-Otmoor. Oxon 4D 50
Charlton on the Hill. Dors 2D 15
Charlwood. Hants 3E 25
Charlwood. Surr 1D 26
Charlynch. Som 3F 21
Charminster. Dors 3B 14
Charmouth. Dors 3G 13
Charndon. Buck 3E 51
Charney Bassett. Oxon 2B 36
Charnock Green. Lanc 3D 90
Charnock Richard. Lanc 3D 90
Charsfield. Suff 5E 67
Chart, The. Kent 5F 39
Chart Corner. Kent 5B 40
Charter Alley. Hants 1D 24
Charterhouse. Som 1H 21
Charterville Allotments. Oxon 4B 50
Chartham. Kent 5F 41
Chartham Hatch. Kent 5F 41
Chartridge. Buck 5H 51
Chart Sutton. Kent 5B 40
Charvil. Wok 4F 37
Charwelton. Nptn 5C 62
Chase Terrace. Staf 5E 73
Chasetown. Staf 5E 73
Chastleton. Oxon 3H 49
Chasty. Devn 2D 10
Chatburn. Lanc 5G 97
Chatcull. Staf 2B 72
Chatham. Medw 204 (4B 40)
Chatham Green. Essx 4H 53
Chathill. Nmbd 2F 121
Chatley. Worc 4C 60
Chattenden. Medw 3B 40
Chatteris. Cambs 2C 64
Chattisham. Suff 1D 54
Chatton. Nmbd 2E 121
Chatwall. Shrp 1H 59
Chaulden. Herts 5A 52
Chaul End. C Beds 3A 52
Chawleigh. Devn 1H 11
Chawley. Oxon 5C 50
Chawston. Bed 5A 64
Chawton. Hants 3F 25
Chaxhill. Glos 4C 48
Cheadle. G Man 2C 84
Cheadle. Staf 1E 73
Cheadle Hulme. G Man 2C 84
Cheam. G Lon 4D 38
Cheapside. Wind 4A 38
Chearsley. Buck 4F 51
Chebsey. Staf 3C 72
Checkendon. Oxon 3E 37
Checkley. Ches E 1B 72
Checkley. Here 2A 48
Checkley. Staf 2E 73
Chedburgh. Suff 5G 65
Cheddar. Som 1H 21
Cheddington. Buck 4H 51
Cheddleton. Staf 5D 84
Cheddon Fitzpaine. Som 4F 21
Chedglow. Wilts 2E 35
Chedgrave. Norf 1F 67
Chedington. Dors 2H 13
Chediston. Suff 3F 67
Chediston Green. Suff 3F 67
Chedworth. Glos 4F 49
Chedzoy. Som 3G 21
Cheeseman's Green. Kent 2E 29
Cheetham Hill. G Man 4G 91
Cheglinch. Devn 2F 19
Cheldon. Devn 1H 11
Chelford. Ches E 3C 84
Chellaston. Derb 2A 74
Chellington. Bed 5G 63
Chelmarsh. Shrp 2B 60
Chelmick. Shrp 1G 59
Chelmondiston. Suff 2F 55
Chelmorton. Derbs 4F 85
Chelmsford. Essx 5H 53
Chelsea. G Lon 3D 38
Chelsfield. G Lon 4F 39
Chelsham. Surr 5E 39
Chelston. Som 4E 21
Chelsworth. Suff 1C 54
Cheltenham. Glos 192 (3E 49)
Chelveston. Nptn 4G 63
Chelvey. N Som 5H 33
Chelwood. Bath 5B 34
Chelwood Common. E Sus 3F 27
Chelwood Gate. E Sus 3F 27
Chelworth. Wilts 2E 35
Chelworth Lower Green. Wilts 2F 35
Chelworth Upper Green. Wilts 2F 35
Chelynch. Som 2B 22
Cheney Longville. Shrp 2G 59
Chenies. Buck 1B 38
Chepstow. Mon 2A 34
Chequerfield. W Yor 2E 93
Chequers Corner. Norf 5D 77
Cherhill. Wilts 4F 35
Cherington. Glos 2E 35
Cherington. Warw 2A 50
Cheriton. Devn 2H 19
Cheriton. Hants 4D 24
Cheriton. Kent 2G 29
Cheriton. Pemb 5D 43
Cheriton. Swan 3D 30
Cheriton Bishop. Devn 3A 12
Cheriton Cross. Devn 3A 12
Cheriton Fitzpaine. Devn 2B 12
Cherrington. Telf 3A 72
Cherrybank. Per 1D 136
Cherry Burton. E Yor 5D 101
Cherry Green. Herts 3D 52
Cherry Hinton. Cambs 5D 65
Cherry Willingham. Linc 3H 87
Chertsey. Surr 4B 38
Cheselbourne. Dors 3C 14
Chesham. Buck 5H 51
Chesham. G Man 3G 91
Chesham Bois. Buck 1A 38
Cheshunt. Herts 5D 52
Cheslyn Hay. Staf 5D 73
Chessetts Wood. Warw 3F 61
Chessington. G Lon 4C 38
Chester. Ches W 192 (4G 83)
Chesterblade. Som 2B 22
Chesterfield. Derbs 3A 86
Chesterfield. Staf 5F 73
Chesterhope. Nmbd 1B 114
Chester-le-Street. Dur 4F 115
Chester Moor. Dur 5F 115
Chesters. Bord 3A 120
Chesterton. Cambs
nr. Cambridge 4D 64
nr. Peterborough 1A 64
Chesterton. Glos 5F 49
Chesterton. Oxon 3D 50
Chesterton. Shrp 1B 60
Chesterton. Staf 1C 72
Chesterton Green. Warw 5H 61
Chesterwood. Nmbd 3B 114
Chestfield. Kent 4F 41
Cheston. Devn 3C 8
Cheswardine. Shrp 2B 72
Cheswell. Telf 4B 72
Cheswick. Nmbd 5G 131
Cheswick Green. W Mid 3F 61
Chetnole. Dors 2B 14
Chettiscombe. Devn 1C 12
Chettisham. Cambs 2E 65
Chettle. Dors 1E 15
Chetton. Shrp 1A 60
Chetwode. Buck 3E 51
Chetwynd Aston. Telf 4B 72
Cheveley. Cambs 4F 65
Chevening. Kent 5F 39
Chevington. Suff 5G 65
Chevithorne. Devn 1C 12
Chew Magna. Bath 5A 34
Chew Moor. G Man 4E 91
Chew Stoke. Bath 5A 34
Chewton Keynsham. Bath 5B 34
Chewton Mendip. Som 1A 22
Chichacott. Devn 3G 11
Chicheley. Mil 1H 51
Chichester. W Sus 2G 17
Chickerell. Dors 4B 14
Chickering. Suff 3E 66
Chicklade. Wilts 3E 23
Chicksands. C Beds 2B 52
Chickward. Here 5E 59
Chidden. Hants 1E 17
Chiddingfold. Surr 2A 26
Chiddingly. E Sus 4G 27
Chiddingstone. Kent 1G 27
Chiddingstone Causeway. Kent 1G 27
Chiddingstone Hoath. Kent 1F 27
Chideock. Dors 3H 13
Chidgley. Som 3D 20
Chidham. W Sus 2F 17
Chieveley. W Ber 4C 36
Chignal St James. Essx 5G 53
Chignal Smealy. Essx 4G 53
Chigwell. Essx 1F 39
Chigwell Row. Essx 1F 39
Chilbolton. Hants 2B 24
Chilcomb. Hants 4D 24
Chilcombe. Dors 3A 14
Chilcompton. Som 1B 22
Chilcote. Leics 4G 73
Childer Thornton. Ches W 3F 83
Child Okeford. Dors 1D 14
Childrey. Oxon 3B 36
Child's Ercall. Shrp 3A 72

Childswickham. *Worc* 2F 49
Childwall. *Mers* 2G 83
Childwick Green. *Herts* 4B 52
Chilfrome. *Dors* 3A 14
Chilgrove. *W Sus* 1G 17
Chilham. *Kent* 5E 41
Chilhampton. *Wilts* 3F 23
Chilla. *Devn* 2E 11
Chilland. *Hants* 3D 24
Chillaton. *Devn* 4E 11
Chillenden. *Kent* 5G 41
Chillerton. *IOW* 4C 16
Chillesford. *Suff* 5F 67
Chillingham. *Nmbd* 2E 121
Chillington. *Devn* 4D 9
Chillington. *Som* 1G 13
Chilmark. *Wilts* 3E 23
Chilmington Green. *Kent* 1D 28
Chilson. *Oxon* 4B 50
Chilsworthy. *Corn* 5E 11
Chilsworthy. *Devn* 2D 10
Chiltern Green. *C Beds* 4B 52
Chilthorne Domer. *Som* 1A 14
Chilton. *Buck* 4E 51
Chilton. *Devn* 2B 12
Chilton. *Dur* 2F 105
Chilton. *Oxon* 3C 36
Chilton Candover. *Hants* 2D 24
Chilton Cantelo. *Som* 4A 22
Chilton Foliat. *Wilts* 4B 36
Chilton Lane. *Dur* 1A 106
Chilton Polden. *Som* 3G 21
Chilton Street. *Suff* 1A 54
Chilton Trinity. *Som* 3F 21
Chilwell. *Notts* 2C 74
Chilworth. *Hants* 1C 16
Chilworth. *Surr* 1B 26
Chimney. *Oxon* 5B 50
Chimney Street. *Suff* 1H 53
Chineham. *Hants* 1E 25
Chingford. *G Lon* 1E 39
Chinley. *Derbs* 2E 85
Chinnor. *Oxon* 5F 51
Chipley. *Shrp* 4E 20
Chipnall. *Shrp* 2B 72
Chippenham. *Cambs* 4F 65
Chippenham. *Wilts* 4E 35
Chipperfield. *Herts* 5A 52
Chipping. *Herts* 2D 52
Chipping. *Lanc* 5F 97
Chipping Campden. *Glos* 2G 49
Chipping Hill. *Essx* 4B 54
Chipping Norton. *Oxon* 3B 50
Chipping Ongar. *Essx* 5F 53
Chipping Sodbury. *S Glo* 3C 34
Chipping Warden. *Nptn* 1C 50
Chipstable. *Som* 4D 20
Chipstead. *Kent* 5G 39
Chipstead. *Surr* 5D 38
Chirbury. *Shrp* 1E 59
Chirk. *Wrex* 2E 71
Chirmorie. *S Ayr* 2H 109
Chirnside. *Bord* 4E 131
Chirnsidebridge. *Bord* 4E 131
Chirton. *Wilts* 1F 23
Chisbridge Cross. *Buck* 3G 37
Chisbury. *Wilts* 5A 36
Chiselborough. *Som* 1H 13
Chiseldon. *Swin* 4G 35
Chiselhampton. *Oxon* 2D 36
Chiserley. *W Yor* 2A 92
Chislehurst. *G Lon* 3F 39
Chislet. *Kent* 4G 41
Chiswell. *Dors* 5B 14
Chiswell Green. *Herts* 5B 52
Chiswick. *G Lon* 3D 38
Chisworth. *Derbs* 1D 85
Chitcombe. *E Sus* 3C 28
Chithurst. *W Sus* 4G 25
Chittering. *Cambs* 4D 65
Chitterley. *Devn* 2C 12
Chitterne. *Wilts* 2E 23
Chittlehamholt. *Devn* 4G 19
Chittlehampton. *Devn* 4G 19
Chittoe. *Wilts* 5E 35
Chivelstone. *Devn* 5D 9
Chivenor. *Devn* 3F 19
Chobham. *Surr* 4A 38
Cholderton. *Wilts* 2H 23
Cholesbury. *Buck* 5H 51
Chollerford. *Nmbd* 2C 114
Chollerton. *Nmbd* 2C 114
Cholsey. *Oxon* 3D 36
Cholstrey. *Here* 5G 59
Chop Gate. *N Yor* 5C 106
Choppington. *Nmbd* 1F 115
Chopwell. *Tyne* 4E 115
Chorley. *Ches E* 5H 83
Chorley. *Lanc* 3D 90
Chorley. *Shrp* 2A 60
Chorley. *Staf* 4E 73
Chorleywood. *Herts* 1B 38
Chorlton. *Ches E* 5B 84
Chorlton-cum-Hardy. *G Man* 1C 84
Chorlton Lane. *Ches W* 1G 71
Choulton. *Shrp* 2F 59
Chrishall. *Essx* 2E 53
Christchurch. *Cambs* 1D 65
Christchurch. *Dors* 3G 15
Christchurch. *Glos* 4A 48
Christian Malford. *Wilts* 4E 35
Christleton. *Ches W* 4G 83
Christmas Common. *Oxon* 2F 37
Christon. *N Som* 1G 21
Christon Bank. *Nmbd* 2G 121
Christow. *Devn* 4B 12
Chryston. *N Lan* 2H 127
Chuck Hatch. *E Sus* 2F 27
Chudleigh. *Devn* 5B 12
Chudleigh Knighton. *Devn* 5B 12
Chulmleigh. *Devn* 1G 11

Chunal. *Derbs* 1E 85
Church. *Lanc* 2F 91
Churcham. *Glos* 4C 48
Church Aston. *Telf* 4B 72
Church Brampton. *Nptn* 4E 62
Church Brough. *Cumb* 3A 104
Church Broughton. *Derbs* 2G 73
Church Corner. *Suff* 2G 67
Church Crookham. *Hants* 1G 25
Churchdown. *Glos* 3D 49
Church Eaton. *Staf* 4C 72
Church End. *Cambs*
  nr. Cambridge 5D 65
  nr. Over 3C 64
  nr. Sawtry 2B 64
  nr. Wisbech 5C 76
Church End. *C Beds*
  nr. Stotfold 2B 52
  nr. Totternhoe 3H 51
Church End. *E Yor* 4E 101
Church End. *Essx*
  nr. Braintree 3H 53
  nr. Great Dunmow 3G 53
  nr. Saffron Walden 1F 53
Churchend. *Essx* 1E 40
Church End. *Glos* 5C 48
Church End. *Hants* 1E 25
Church End. *Linc*
  nr. Donington 2B 76
  nr. North Somercotes 1D 88
Church End. *Norf* 4E 77
Church End. *Warw*
  nr. Coleshill 1G 61
  nr. Nuneaton 1G 61
Church End. *Wilts* 4F 35
Church Enstone. *Oxon* 3B 50
Church Fenton. *N Yor* 1F 93
Church Green. *Devn* 3E 13
Church Gresley. *Derbs* 4G 73
Church Hanborough. *Oxon* 4C 50
Church Hill. *Ches W* 4A 84
Church Hill. *Worc* 4E 61
Church Hougham. *Kent* 1G 29
Church Houses. *N Yor* 5D 106
Churchill. *Devn*
  nr. Axminster 2G 13
  nr. Barnstaple 2F 19
Churchill. *N Som* 1H 21
Churchill. *Oxon* 3A 50
Churchill. *Worc*
  nr. Kidderminster 3C 60
  nr. Worcester 5D 60
Churchinford. *Som* 1F 13
Church Knowle. *Dors* 4E 15
Church Laneham. *Notts* 3F 87
Church Langley. *Essx* 5E 53
Church Langton. *Leics* 1E 62
Church Lawford. *Warw* 3B 62
Church Lawton. *Ches E* 5C 84
Church Leigh. *Staf* 2E 73
Church Lench. *Worc* 5E 61
Church Mayfield. *Staf* 1F 73
Church Minshull. *Ches E* 4A 84
Church Norton. *W Sus* 3G 17
Churchover. *Warw* 2C 62
Church Preen. *Shrp* 1H 59
Church Pulverbatch. *Shrp* 5G 71
Churchstanton. *Som* 1E 13
Church Stoke. *Powy* 1E 59
Churchstow. *Devn* 4D 8
Church Stowe. *Nptn* 5D 62
Church Street. *Kent* 3B 40
Church Stretton. *Shrp* 1G 59
Churchtown. *Cumb* 5E 113
Churchtown. *Derbs* 4G 85
Churchtown. *Devn* 2G 19
Churchtown. *IOM* 2D 108
Churchtown. *Lanc* 5D 97
Church Town. *Leics* 4A 74
Churchtown. *Mers* 3B 90
Church Town. *N Lin* 4A 94
Churchtown. *Shrp* 2E 59
Church Village. *Rhon* 3D 32
Church Warsop. *Notts* 4C 86
Church Westcote. *Glos* 3H 49
Church Wilne. *Derbs* 2B 74
Churnsike Lodge. *Nmbd* 2H 113
Churston Ferrers. *Torb* 3F 9
Churt. *Surr* 3G 25
Churton. *Ches W* 5G 83
Churwell. *W Yor* 2C 92
Chute Standen. *Wilts* 1B 24
Chwilog. *Gwyn* 2D 68
Chwitffordd. *Flin* 3D 82
Chyandour. *Corn* 3B 4
Cilan Uchaf. *Gwyn* 3B 68
Cilcain. *Flin* 4D 82
Cilcennin. *Cdgn* 4E 57
Cilfrew. *Neat* 5A 46
Cilfynydd. *Rhon* 2D 32
Cilgerran. *Pemb* 1B 44
Cilgeti. *Pemb* 4F 43
Cilgwyn. *Carm* 3H 45
Cilgwyn. *Pemb* 1E 43
Ciliau Aeron. *Cdgn* 5D 57
Cill Amhlaidh. *W Isl* 4C 170
Cill Donnain. *W Isl* 6C 170
Cille a' Bhacstair. *High* 2C 154
Cille Bhrighde. *W Isl* 7C 170
Cille Pheadair. *W Isl* 7C 170
Cilmaengwyn. *Neat* 5H 45
Cilmeri. *Powy* 5C 58
Cilmery. *Powy* 5C 58
Cilrhedyn. *Pemb* 1G 43
Cilsan. *Carm* 3F 45
Ciltalgarth. *Gwyn* 1A 70
Ciltwrch. *Powy* 1E 47
Cilybebyll. *Neat* 5H 45
Cilycwm. *Carm* 1A 46
Cimla. *Neat* 2A 32
Cinderford. *Glos* 4B 48

Cinderhill. *Derbs* 1A 74
Cippenham. *Slo* 2A 38
Cippyn. *Pemb* 1B 44
Cirbhig. *W Isl* 3D 171
Cirencester. *Glos* 5F 49
City, The. *Buck* 2F 37
City. *Powy* 1E 58
City. *V Glam* 4C 32
City Airport. *G Lon* 2F 39
City Centre. *Stoke* 211 (1C 72)
City Dulas. *IOA* 2D 80
Clabhach. *Arg* 3C 138
Clachaig. *Arg* 1C 126
Clachaig. *High*
  nr. Kinlochleven 3F 141
  nr. Nethy Bridge 2E 151
Clachamish. *High* 3C 154
Clachan. *Arg*
  on Kintyre 4F 125
  on Lismore 4C 140
Clachan. *High*
  nr. Bettyhill 2H 167
  nr. Staffin 2D 155
  nr. Uig 1D 154
  on Raasay 5E 155
Clachan Farm. *Arg* 2A 134
Clachan na Luib. *W Isl* 2D 170
Clachan of Campsie. *E Dun* 2H 127
Clachan of Glendaruel. *Arg* 1A 126
Clachan-Seil. *Arg* 2E 133
Clachan Shannda. *W Isl* 1D 170
Clachan Strachur. *Arg* 3H 133
Clachbreck. *Arg* 2F 125
Clachnaharry. *High* 4A 158
Clachtoll. *High* 1E 163
Clackmannan. *Clac* 4B 136
Clackmannanshire Bridge.
  Clac 1C 128
Clackmarras. *Mor* 3G 159
Clacton-on-Sea. *Essx* 4E 55
Cladach a Chaolais. *W Isl* 2C 170
Cladach Chairinis. *W Isl* 3D 170
Cladach Chirceboist. *W Isl* 2C 170
Cladach Iolaraigh. *W Isl* 2C 170
Cladich. *Arg* 1H 133
Cladswell. *Worc* 5E 61
Claggan. *High*
  nr. Fort William 1F 141
  nr. Lochaline 3B 140
Claigan. *High* 3B 154
Clandown. *Bath* 1B 22
Clanfield. *Hants* 1E 17
Clanfield. *Oxon* 5A 50
Clanville. *Hants* 2B 24
Clanville. *Som* 3B 22
Claonaig. *Arg* 4G 125
Clapgate. *Dors* 2F 15
Clapgate. *Herts* 3E 53
Clapham. *Bed* 5H 63
Clapham. *G Lon* 3D 39
Clapham. *N Yor* 3G 97
Clapham. *W Sus* 5B 26
Clap Hill. *Kent* 2E 29
Clappers. *Bord* 4F 131
Clappersgate. *Cumb* 4E 103
Clapphoull. *Shet* 9F 173
Clapton. *Som*
  nr. Crewkerne 2H 13
  nr. Radstock 1B 22
Clapton in Gordano. *N Som* 4H 33
Clapton-on-the-Hill. *Glos* 4G 49
Clapworthy. *Devn* 4G 19
Clara Vale. *Tyne* 3E 115
Clarbeston. *Pemb* 2E 43
Clarbeston Road. *Pemb* 2E 43
Clarborough. *Notts* 2E 87
Clare. *Suff* 1A 54
Clarebrand. *Dum* 3E 111
Clarencefield. *Dum* 3B 112
Clarilaw. *Bord* 3H 119
Clark's Green. *Surr* 2C 26
Clark's Hill. *Linc* 3C 76
Clarkston. *E Ren* 4G 127
Clasheddy. *High* 2G 167
Clashindarroch. *Abers* 5B 160
Clashmore. *High*
  nr. Dornoch 5E 165
  nr. Stoer 1E 163
Clashnessie. *High* 1E 163
Clashnoir. *Mor* 1G 151
Clate. *Shet* 5G 173
Clathick. *Per* 1H 135
Clathy. *Per* 2B 136
Clatt. *Abers* 1C 152
Clatter. *Powy* 1B 58
Clatterford. *IOW* 4C 16
Clatworthy. *Som* 3D 20
Claughton. *Lanc*
  nr. Caton 3E 97
  nr. Garstang 5E 97
Claughton. *Mers* 2E 83
Claverdon. *Warw* 4F 61
Claverham. *N Som* 5H 33
Clavering. *Essx* 2E 53
Claverley. *Shrp* 1B 60
Claverton. *Bath* 5C 34
Clawdd-coch. *V Glam* 4D 32
Clawdd-newydd. *Den* 5C 82
Clawson Hill. *Leics* 3E 75
Clawton. *Devn* 3D 10
Claxby. *Linc*
  nr. Alford 3D 88
  nr. Market Rasen 1A 88
Claxton. *Norf* 5F 79
Claxton. *N Yor* 3A 100
Claybrooke Magna. *Leics* 2B 62
Claybrooke Parva. *Leics* 2B 62
Clay Common. *Suff* 2G 67

Clay Coton. *Nptn* 3C 62
Clay Cross. *Derbs* 4A 86
Claydon. *Oxon* 5B 62
Claydon. *Suff* 5D 66
Clay End. *Herts* 3D 52
Claygate. *Dum* 2E 113
Claygate. *Kent* 1B 28
Claygate. *Surr* 4C 38
Claygate Cross. *Kent* 5H 39
Clayhall. *Hants* 3E 16
Clayhanger. *Devn* 4D 20
Clayhanger. *W Mid* 5E 73
Clayhidon. *Devn* 1E 13
Clay Hill. *Bris* 4B 34
Clayhill. *E Sus* 3C 28
Clayhill. *Hants* 2B 16
Clayhithe. *Cambs* 4E 65
Clayholes. *Ang* 5E 145
Clay Lake. *Linc* 3B 76
Clayock. *High* 3D 168
Claypits. *Glos* 5C 48
Claypole. *Linc* 1F 75
Claythorpe. *Linc* 3D 88
Clayton. *G Man* 1C 84
Clayton. *S Yor* 4E 93
Clayton. *Staf* 1C 72
Clayton. *W Sus* 4E 27
Clayton. *W Yor* 1B 92
Clayton Green. *Lanc* 2D 90
Clayton-le-Moors. *Lanc* 1F 91
Clayton-le-Woods. *Lanc* 2D 90
Clayton West. *W Yor* 3C 92
Clayworth. *Notts* 2E 87
Cleadale. *High* 5C 146
Cleadon. *Tyne* 3G 115
Clearbrook. *Devn* 2B 8
Clearwell. *Glos* 5A 48
Cleasby. *N Yor* 3F 105
Cleat. *Orkn*
  nr. Braehead 3D 172
  nr. St Margaret's Hope 9D 172
Cleatlam. *Dur* 3E 105
Cleator. *Cumb* 3B 102
Cleator Moor. *Cumb* 3B 102
Cleckheaton. *W Yor* 2B 92
Cleedownton. *Shrp* 2H 59
Cleehill. *Shrp* 3H 59
Cleekhimin. *N Lan* 4A 128
Clee St Margaret. *Shrp* 2H 59
Cleestanton. *Shrp* 3H 59
Cleethorpes. *NE Lin* 4G 95
Cleeton St Mary. *Shrp* 3A 60
Cleeve. *N Som* 5H 33
Cleeve. *Oxon* 3E 36
Cleeve Hill. *Glos* 3E 49
Cleeve Prior. *Worc* 1F 49
Clehonger. *Here* 2H 47
Cleigh. *Arg* 1F 133
Cleish. *Per* 4C 136
Cleland. *N Lan* 4B 128
Clench Common. *Wilts* 5G 35
Clenchwarton. *Norf* 3E 77
Clennell. *Nmbd* 4D 120
Clent. *Worc* 3D 60
Cleobury Mortimer. *Shrp* 3A 60
Cleobury North. *Shrp* 2A 60
Clephanton. *High* 3C 158
Clerkhill. *High* 2H 167
Clestrain. *Orkn* 7C 172
Clevancy. *Wilts* 4F 35
Clevedon. *N Som* 4H 33
Cleveley. *Oxon* 3B 50
Cleveleys. *Lanc* 5C 96
Clevelode. *Worc* 1D 48
Cleverton. *Wilts* 3E 35
Clewer. *Som* 1H 21
Cley next the Sea. *Norf* 1C 78
Cliaid. *W Isl* 8B 170
Cliasmol. *W Isl* 7C 171
Cliburn. *Cumb* 2G 103
Cliddesden. *Hants* 2E 25
Clieves Hills. *Lanc* 4B 90
Cliff. *Warw* 1G 61
Cliffburn. *Ang* 4F 145
Cliffe. *Medw* 3B 40
Cliffe. *N Yor*
  nr. Darlington 3F 105
  nr. Selby 1G 93
Cliff End. *E Sus* 4C 28
Cliffe Woods. *Medw* 3B 40
Clifford. *Here* 1F 47
Clifford. *W Yor* 5G 99
Clifford Chambers. *Warw* 5F 61
Clifford's Mesne. *Glos* 3C 48
Cliffsend. *Kent* 4H 41
Clifton. *Bris* 4A 34
Clifton. *C Beds* 2B 52
Clifton. *Cumb* 2G 103
Clifton. *Derbs* 1F 73
Clifton. *Devn* 2G 19
Clifton. *G Man* 4F 91
Clifton. *Lanc* 1C 90
Clifton. *Nmbd* 1F 115
Clifton. *N Yor* 5D 98
Clifton. *Nott* 2C 74
Clifton. *Oxon* 2C 50
Clifton. *S Yor* 1C 86
Clifton. *Stir* 5H 141
Clifton. *Worc* 1D 48
Clifton. *York* 4H 99
Clifton Campville. *Staf* 4G 73
Clifton Hampden. *Oxon* 2D 36
Clifton Hill. *Worc* 4B 60
Clifton Reynes. *Mil* 5G 63
Clifton upon Dunsmore. *Warw* 3C 62
Clifton upon Teme. *Worc* 4B 60
Cliftonville. *Kent* 3H 41
Cliftonville. *Norf* 2F 79
Climping. *W Sus* 5A 26

Climpy. *S Lan* 4C 128
Clink. *Som* 2C 22
Clint. *N Yor* 4E 99
Clint Green. *Norf* 4C 78
Clintmains. *Bord* 1A 120
Cliobh. *W Isl* 4C 171
Clipiau. *Gwyn* 4H 69
Clippesby. *Norf* 4G 79
Clippings Green. *Norf* 4C 78
Clipsham. *Rut* 4G 75
Clipston. *Nptn* 2E 62
Clipston. *Notts* 2D 74
Clipstone. *Notts* 4C 86
Clitheroe. *Lanc* 5G 97
Cliuthar. *W Isl* 8D 171
Clive. *Shrp* 3H 71
Clivocast. *Shet* 1G 173
Clixby. *Linc* 4D 94
Clocaenog. *Den* 5C 82
Clochan. *Mor* 2B 160
Clochforbie. *Abers* 3F 161
Clock Face. *Mers* 1H 83
Cloddiau. *Powy* 5E 70
Cloddymoss. *Mor* 2D 159
Clodock. *Here* 3G 47
Cloford. *Som* 2C 22
Clola. *Abers* 4H 161
Clophill. *C Beds* 2A 52
Clopton. *Nptn* 2H 63
Clopton Corner. *Suff* 5E 66
Clopton Green. *Suff* 5G 65
Close Clark. *IOM* 4B 108
Closeburn. *Dum* 5A 118
Closworth. *Som* 1A 14
Clothall. *Herts* 2C 52
Clotton. *Ches W* 4H 83
Clough. *G Man* 3H 91
Clough. *W Yor* 3A 92
Clough Foot. *W Yor* 2H 91
Cloughton. *N Yor* 5H 107
Cloughton Newlands. *N Yor* 5H 107
Clousta. *Shet* 6E 173
Clouston. *Orkn* 6B 172
Clova. *Abers* 1B 152
Clova. *Ang* 1C 144
Clovelly. *Devn* 4D 18
Clovenfords. *Bord* 1G 119
Clovenstone. *Abers* 2E 153
Clovullin. *High* 2E 141
Clowne. *Derbs* 3B 86
Clows Top. *Worc* 3B 60
Cloy. *Wrex* 1F 71
Cluanie Inn. *High* 2C 148
Cluanie Lodge. *High* 2C 148
Cluddley. *Telf* 4A 72
Y Clun. *Neat* 5B 46
Clun. *Shrp* 2F 59
Clunas. *High* 4C 158
Clunbury. *Shrp* 2F 59
Clunderwen. *Pemb* 3F 43
Clune. *High* 1B 150
Clunes. *High* 5E 148
Clungunford. *Shrp* 3F 59
Clunie. *Per* 4A 144
Clunton. *Shrp* 2F 59
Cluny. *Fife* 4E 137
Clutton. *Bath* 1B 22
Clutton. *Ches W* 5G 83
Clwt-y-bont. *Gwyn* 4E 81
Clwydfagwyr. *Mer T* 5D 46
Clydach. *Mon* 4F 47
Clydach. *Swan* 5G 45
Clydach Vale. *Rhon* 2C 32
Clydebank. *W Dun* 2G 127
Clydey. *Pemb* 1G 43
Clyffe Pypard. *Wilts* 4F 35
Clynder. *Arg* 1D 126
Clyne. *Neat* 5B 46
Clynelish. *High* 3F 165
Clynnog-fawr. *Gwyn* 1D 68
Clyro. *Powy* 1F 47
Clyst Honiton. *Devn* 3C 12
Clyst Hydon. *Devn* 2D 12
Clyst St George. *Devn* 4C 12
Clyst St Lawrence. *Devn* 2D 12
Clyst St Mary. *Devn* 3C 12
Clyth. *High* 5E 169
Cnip. *W Isl* 4C 171
Cnoc Amhlaigh. *W Isl* 4H 171
Cnwcau. *Pemb* 1C 44
Cnwch Coch. *Cdgn* 3F 57
Coad's Green. *Corn* 5C 10
Coal Aston. *Derbs* 3A 86
Coalbrookdale. *Telf* 5A 72
Coalbrookvale. *Blae* 5E 47
Coalburn. *S Lan* 1H 117
Coalburns. *Tyne* 3E 115
Coalcleugh. *Nmbd* 5B 114
Coaley. *Glos* 5C 48
Coalford. *Abers* 4F 153
Coalhall. *E Ayr* 3D 116
Coalhill. *Essx* 1B 40
Coalpit Heath. *S Glo* 3B 34
Coal Pool. *W Mid* 5E 73
Coalport. *Telf* 5B 72
Coalsnaughton. *Clac* 4B 136
Coaltown of Balgonie. *Fife* 4F 137
Coaltown of Wemyss. *Fife* 4F 137
Coalville. *Leics* 4B 74
Coalway. *Glos* 4A 48
Coanwood. *Nmbd* 4H 113
Coat. *Som* 4H 21
Coatbridge. *N Lan* 3A 128
Coatdyke. *N Lan* 3A 128
Coate. *Swin* 3G 35
Coate. *Wilts* 5F 35
Coates. *Cambs* 1C 64
Coates. *Glos* 5E 49
Coates. *Linc* 2G 87
Coates. *W Sus* 4A 26
Coatham. *Red C* 2C 106

Coatham Mundeville. *Darl* 2F **105**
Cobbaton. *Devn* 4G **19**
Coberley. *Glos* 4E **49**
Cobhall Common. *Here* 2H **47**
Cobham. *Kent* 4A **40**
Cobham. *Surr* 5C **38**
Cobnash. *Here* 4G **59**
Coburg. *Devn* 5B **12**
Cockayne. *N Yor* 5D **106**
Cockayne Hatley. *C Beds* 1C **52**
Cock Bank. *Wrex* 1F **71**
Cock Bridge. *Abers* 3G **151**
Cockburnspath. *Bord* 2D **130**
Cock Clarks. *Essx* 5B **54**
Cockenzie and Port Seton.
    E Lot 2H **129**
Cockerham. *Lanc* 4D **96**
Cockermouth. *Cumb* 1C **102**
Cockernhoe. *Herts* 3B **52**
Cockfield. *Dur* 2E **105**
Cockfield. *Suff* 5B **66**
Cockfosters. *G Lon* 1D **39**
Cock Gate. *Here* 4G **59**
Cock Green. *Essx* 4G **53**
Cocking. *W Sus* 1G **17**
Cocking Causeway. *W Sus* 1G **17**
Cockington. *Torb* 2E **9**
Cocklake. *Som* 2H **21**
Cocklaw. *Abers* 4H **161**
Cocklaw. *Nmbd* 2C **114**
Cockley Beck. *Cumb* 4D **102**
Cockley Cley. *Norf* 5G **77**
Cockmuir. *Abers* 3G **161**
Cockpole Green. *Wok* 3F **37**
Cockshutford. *Shrp* 2H **59**
Cockshutt. *Shrp* 3G **71**
Cockthorpe. *Norf* 1B **78**
Cockwood. *Devn* 4C **12**
Cockyard. *Derbs* 3E **85**
Cockyard. *Here* 2H **47**
Codda. *Corn* 5B **10**
Coddenham. *Suff* 5D **66**
Coddenham Green. *Suff* 5D **66**
Coddington. *Ches W* 5G **83**
Coddington. *Here* 1C **48**
Coddington. *Notts* 5F **87**
Codford. *Wilts* 3E **23**
Codicote. *Herts* 4C **52**
Codmore Hill. *W Sus* 3B **26**
Codnor. *Derbs* 1B **74**
Codrington. *S Glo* 4C **34**
Codsall. *Staf* 5C **72**
Codsall Wood. *Staf* 5C **72**
Coed Duon. *Cphy* 2E **33**
Coedely. *Rhon* 3D **32**
Coedglasson. *Powy* 4C **58**
Coedkernew. *Newp* 3F **33**
Coed Morgan. *Mon* 4G **47**
Coedpoeth. *Wrex* 5E **83**
Coedway. *Powy* 4F **71**
Coed-y-bryn. *Cdgn* 1D **44**
Coed-y-paen. *Mon* 2G **33**
Coed Ystumgwern. *Gwyn* 3E **69**
Coelbren. *Powy* 4B **46**
Coffinswell. *Devn* 2E **9**
Cofton Hackett. *Worc* 3E **61**
Cogan. *V Glam* 4E **33**
Cogenhoe. *Nptn* 4F **63**
Cogges. *Oxon* 5B **50**
Coggeshall. *Essx* 3B **54**
Coggeshall Hamlet. *Essx* 3B **54**
Coggins Mill. *E Sus* 3G **27**
Coignafearn Lodge. *High* 2A **150**
Coig Peighinnean. *W Isl* 1H **171**
Coig Peighinnean Bhuirgh.
    W Isl 2G **171**
Coilleag. *W Isl* 7C **170**
Coillemore. *High* 1A **158**
Coillore. *High* 5C **154**
Coire an Fhuarain. *W Isl* 4E **171**
Coity. *B'end* 3C **32**
Cokhay Green. *Derbs* 3G **73**
Col. *W Isl* 3G **171**
Colaboll. *High* 2C **164**
Colan. *Corn* 2C **6**
Colaton Raleigh. *Devn* 4D **12**
Colbost. *High* 4B **154**
Colburn. *N Yor* 5E **105**
Colby. *Cumb* 2H **103**
Colby. *IOM* 4B **108**
Colby. *Norf* 2E **78**
Colchester. *Essx* 3D **54**
Cold Ash. *W Ber* 5D **36**
Cold Ashby. *Nptn* 3D **62**
Cold Ashton. *S Glo* 4C **34**
Cold Aston. *Glos* 4G **49**
Coldbackie. *High* 3G **167**
Cold Blow. *Pemb* 3F **43**
Cold Brayfield. *Mil* 5G **63**
Cold Cotes. *N Yor* 2G **97**
Coldean. *Brig* 5E **27**
Coldeast. *Devn* 5B **12**
Colden. *W Yor* 2H **91**
Colden Common. *Hants* 4C **24**
Coldfair Green. *Suff* 4G **67**
Coldham. *Cambs* 5D **76**
Coldham. *Staf* 5C **72**
Cold Hanworth. *Linc* 2H **87**
Coldharbour. *Corn* 4B **6**
Cold Harbour. *Dors* 3E **15**
Coldharbour. *Glos* 5A **48**
Coldharbour. *Kent* 5G **39**
Coldharbour. *Surr* 1C **26**
Cold Hatton. *Telf* 3A **72**
Cold Hatton Heath. *Telf* 3A **72**
Cold Hesledon. *Dur* 5H **115**
Cold Hiendley. *W Yor* 3D **92**
Cold Higham. *Nptn* 5D **62**
Coldingham. *Bord* 3F **131**
Cold Kirby. *N Yor* 1H **99**
Coldmeece. *Staf* 2C **72**

Cold Northcott. *Corn* 4C **10**
Cold Norton. *Essx* 5B **54**
Cold Overton. *Leics* 4F **75**
Coldrain. *Per* 3C **136**
Coldred. *Kent* 1G **29**
Coldridge. *Devn* 1G **11**
Cold Row. *Lanc* 5C **96**
Coldstream. *Bord* 5E **131**
Coldwaltham. *W Sus* 4B **26**
Coldwell. *Here* 2H **47**
Coldwells. *Abers* 5H **161**
Coldwells Croft. *Abers* 1C **152**
Cole. *Shet* 5E **173**
Cole. *Som* 3B **22**
Colebatch. *Shrp* 2F **59**
Colebrook. *Devn* 2D **12**
Colebrooke. *Devn* 3A **12**
Coleburn. *Mor* 3G **159**
Coleby. *Linc* 4G **87**
Coleby. *N Lin* 3B **94**
Cole End. *Warw* 2G **61**
Coleford. *Devn* 2A **12**
Coleford. *Glos* 4A **48**
Coleford. *Som* 2B **22**
Colegate End. *Norf* 2D **66**
Cole Green. *Herts* 4C **52**
Cole Henley. *Hants* 1C **24**
Colehill. *Dors* 2F **15**
Coleman Green. *Herts* 4B **52**
Coleman's Hatch. *E Sus* 2F **27**
Colemere. *Shrp* 2G **71**
Colemore. *Hants* 3F **25**
Colemore Green. *Shrp* 1B **60**
Coleorton. *Leics* 4B **74**
Colerne. *Wilts* 4D **34**
Colesbourne. *Glos* 4F **49**
Colesden. *Bed* 5A **64**
Coles Green. *Worc* 5B **60**
Coleshill. *Buck* 1A **38**
Coleshill. *Oxon* 2H **35**
Coleshill. *Warw* 2G **61**
Colestocks. *Devn* 2D **12**
Colethrop. *Glos* 4D **48**
Coley. *Bath* 1A **22**
Colgate. *W Sus* 2D **26**
Colinsburgh. *Fife* 3G **137**
Colinton. *Edin* 3F **129**
Colintraive. *Arg* 2B **126**
Colkirk. *Norf* 3B **78**
Collace. *Per* 5B **144**
Collam. *W Isl* 8D **171**
Collaton. *Devn* 5D **8**
Collaton St Mary. *Torb* 2E **9**
College of Roseisle. *Mor* 2F **159**
Collessie. *Fife* 2E **137**
Collier Row. *G Lon* 1F **39**
Colliers End. *Herts* 3D **52**
Collier Street. *Kent* 1B **28**
Colliery Row. *Tyne* 5G **115**
Collieston. *Abers* 1H **153**
Collin. *Dum* 2B **112**
Collingbourne Ducis. *Wilts* 1H **23**
Collingbourne Kingston. *Wilts* 1H **23**
Collingham. *Notts* 4F **87**
Collingham. *W Yor* 5F **99**
Collingtree. *Nptn* 5E **63**
Collins Green. *Warr* 1H **83**
Collins Green. *Worc* 5B **60**
Colliston. *Ang* 4F **145**
Colliton. *Devn* 2D **12**
Collydean. *Fife* 3E **137**
Collyweston. *Nptn* 5G **75**
Colmonell. *S Ayr* 1G **109**
Colmworth. *Bed* 5A **64**
Colnbrook. *Slo* 3B **38**
Colne. *Cambs* 3C **64**
Colne. *Lanc* 5A **98**
Colne Engaine. *Essx* 2B **54**
Colney. *Norf* 5D **78**
Colney Heath. *Herts* 5C **52**
Colney Street. *Herts* 5B **52**
Coln Rogers. *Glos* 5F **49**
Coln St Aldwyns. *Glos* 5G **49**
Coln St Dennis. *Glos* 4F **49**
Colpitts Grange. *Nmbd* 4C **114**
Colpy. *Abers* 5D **160**
Colscott. *Devn* 1D **10**
Colsterdale. *N Yor* 1D **98**
Colsterworth. *Linc* 3G **75**
Colston Bassett. *Notts* 2E **74**
Colstoun House. *E Lot* 2B **130**
Coltfield. *Mor* 2F **159**
Colthouse. *Cumb* 5E **103**
Coltishall. *Norf* 4E **79**
Coltness. *N Lan* 4B **128**
Colton. *Cumb* 1C **96**
Colton. *Norf* 5D **78**
Colton. *N Yor* 5H **99**
Colton. *Staf* 3E **73**
Colton. *W Yor* 1D **92**
Col Uarach. *W Isl* 4G **171**
Colt's Hill. *Kent* 1H **27**
Colvend. *Dum* 4F **111**
Colvister. *Shet* 2G **173**
Colwall. *Here* 1C **48**
Colwall Green. *Here* 1C **48**
Colwell. *Nmbd* 2C **114**
Colwich. *Staf* 3E **73**
Colwick. *Notts* 1D **74**
Colwinston. *V Glam* 4C **32**
Colworth. *W Sus* 5A **26**
Colwyn Bay. *Cnwy* 3A **82**
Colyford. *Devn* 3F **13**
Colyton. *Devn* 3F **13**
Combe. *Devn* 2D **8**
Combe. *Here* 4F **59**
Combe. *Oxon* 4C **50**
Combe Almer. *Dors* 3E **15**
Combebow. *Devn* 4E **11**
Combe Down. *Bath* 5C **34**

Combe Fishacre. *Devn* 2E **9**
Combe Florey. *Som* 3E **21**
Combe Hay. *Bath* 5C **34**
Combeinteignhead. *Devn* 5C **12**
Combe Martin. *Devn* 2F **19**
Combe Moor. *Here* 4F **59**
Combe Raleigh. *Devn* 2E **13**
Comberbach. *Ches W* 3A **84**
Comberford. *Staf* 5F **73**
Comberton. *Cambs* 5C **64**
Comberton. *Here* 4G **59**
Combe St Nicholas. *Som* 1G **13**
Combpyne. *Devn* 3F **13**
Combridge. *Staf* 2E **73**
Combrook. *Warw* 5H **61**
Combs. *Derbs* 3E **85**
Combs. *Suff* 5C **66**
Combs Ford. *Suff* 5C **66**
Combwich. *Som* 2F **21**
Comers. *Abers* 3D **152**
Comhampton. *Worc* 4C **60**
Comins Coch. *Cdgn* 2F **57**
Comley. *Shrp* 1G **59**
Commercial End. *Cambs* 4E **65**
Commins. *Powy* 3D **70**
Commins Coch. *Powy* 5H **69**
Common, The. *Wilts*
    nr. Salisbury 3H **23**
    nr. Swindon 3F **35**
Commondale. *N Yor* 3D **106**
Common End. *Cumb* 2B **102**
Common Hill. *Here* 2A **48**
Common Moor. *Corn* 2G **7**
Commonside. *Ches W* 3H **83**
Common Side. *Derbs* 3H **85**
Commonside. *Derbs* 1G **73**
Compstall. *G Man* 1D **84**
Compton. *Devn* 2E **9**
Compton. *Hants* 4C **24**
Compton. *Staf* 2C **60**
Compton. *Surr* 1A **26**
Compton. *W Ber* 4D **36**
Compton. *W Sus* 1F **17**
Compton. *Wilts* 1G **23**
Compton Abbas. *Dors* 1D **15**
Compton Abdale. *Glos* 4F **49**
Compton Bassett. *Wilts* 4F **35**
Compton Beauchamp. *Oxon* 3A **36**
Compton Bishop. *Som* 1G **21**
Compton Chamberlayne. *Wilts* 4F **23**
Compton Dando. *Bath* 5B **34**
Compton Dundon. *Som* 3H **21**
Compton Greenfield. *S Glo* 3A **34**
Compton Martin. *Bath* 1A **22**
Compton Pauncefoot. *Som* 4B **22**
Compton Valence. *Dors* 3A **14**
Comrie. *Fife* 1D **128**
Comrie. *Per* 1G **135**
Conaglen. *High* 2E **141**
Conchra. *Arg* 1B **126**
Conchra. *High* 1A **148**
Conder Green. *Lanc* 4D **96**
Conderton. *Worc* 2E **49**
Condicote. *Glos* 3G **49**
Condorrat. *N Lan* 2A **128**
Condover. *Shrp* 5G **71**
Coneyhurst. *W Sus* 3C **26**
Coneysthorpe. *N Yor* 2B **100**
Coneythorpe. *N Yor* 4F **99**
Coney Weston. *Suff* 3B **66**
Conford. *Hants* 3G **25**
Congdon's Shop. *Corn* 5C **10**
Congerstone. *Leics* 5A **74**
Congham. *Norf* 3G **77**
Congleton. *Ches E* 4C **84**
Congl-y-wal. *Gwyn* 1G **69**
Congresbury. *N Som* 5H **33**
Congreve. *Staf* 4D **72**
Conham. *S Glo* 4B **34**
Conicaval. *Mor* 3D **159**
Coningsby. *Linc* 5B **88**
Conington. *Cambs*
    nr. Fenstanton 4C **64**
    nr. Sawtry 2A **64**
Conisbrough. *S Yor* 1C **86**
Conisby. *Arg* 3A **124**
Conisholme. *Linc* 1D **88**
Coniston. *Cumb* 5E **102**
Coniston. *E Yor* 1E **95**
Coniston Cold. *N Yor* 4B **98**
Conistone. *N Yor* 3B **98**
Connah's Quay. *Flin* 3E **83**
Connel. *Arg* 5D **140**
Connel Park. *E Ayr* 3F **117**
Connista. *High* 1D **154**
Connor Downs. *Corn* 3C **4**
Conock. *Wilts* 1F **23**
Conon Bridge. *High* 3H **157**
Cononley. *N Yor* 5B **98**
Cononsyth. *Ang* 4E **145**
Conordan. *High* 5E **155**
Consall. *Staf* 1D **72**
Consett. *Dur* 4E **115**
Constable Burton. *N Yor* 5E **105**
Constantine. *Corn* 4E **5**
Constantine Bay. *Corn* 1C **6**
Contin. *High* 3G **157**
Contullich. *High* 1A **158**
Conwy. *Cnwy* 3G **81**
Conyer. *Kent* 4D **40**
Conyer's Green. *Suff* 4A **66**
Cooden. *E Sus* 5B **28**
Cooil. *IOM* 4C **108**
Cookbury. *Devn* 2E **11**
Cookbury Wick. *Devn* 2D **11**
Cookham. *Wind* 3G **37**
Cookham Dean. *Wind* 3G **37**
Cookham Rise. *Wind* 3G **37**
Cookhill. *Worc* 5E **61**
Cookley. *Suff* 3F **67**
Cookley. *Worc* 2C **60**

Cookley Green. *Oxon* 2E **37**
Cookney. *Abers* 4F **153**
Cooksbridge. *E Sus* 4F **27**
Cooksey Green. *Worc* 4D **60**
Cookshill. *Staf* 1D **72**
Cooksmill Green. *Essx* 5G **53**
Coolham. *W Sus* 3C **26**
Cooling. *Medw* 3B **40**
Cooling Street. *Medw* 3B **40**
Coombe. *Corn*
    nr. Bude 1C **10**
    nr. St Austell 3D **6**
    nr. Truro 4C **6**
Coombe. *Devn*
    nr. Sidmouth 3E **12**
    nr. Teignmouth 5C **12**
Coombe. *Glos* 2C **34**
Coombe. *Hants* 4E **25**
Coombe. *Wilts* 1G **23**
Coombe Bissett. *Wilts* 4G **23**
Coombe Hill. *Glos* 3D **49**
Coombe Keynes. *Dors* 4D **14**
Coombes. *W Sus* 5C **26**
Coopersale. *Essx* 5E **53**
Coopersale Street. *Essx* 5E **53**
Cooper's Corner. *Kent* 1F **27**
Cooper Street. *Kent* 5H **41**
Cootham. *W Sus* 4B **26**
Copalder Corner. *Cambs* 1C **64**
Copdock. *Suff* 1E **54**
Copford. *Essx* 3C **54**
Copford Green. *Essx* 3C **54**
Copgrove. *N Yor* 3F **99**
Copister. *Shet* 4F **173**
Cople. *Bed* 1B **52**
Copley. *Dur* 2D **105**
Coplow Dale. *Derbs* 3F **85**
Copmanthorpe. *York* 5H **99**
Copp. *Lanc* 1C **90**
Coppathorne. *Corn* 2C **10**
Coppenhall. *Ches E* 5B **84**
Coppenhall. *Staf* 4D **72**
Coppenhall Moss. *Ches E* 5B **84**
Copperhouse. *Corn* 3C **4**
Coppicegate. *Shrp* 2B **60**
Coppingford. *Cambs* 2A **64**
Copplestone. *Devn* 2A **12**
Coppull. *Lanc* 3D **90**
Coppull Moor. *Lanc* 3D **90**
Copsale. *W Sus* 3C **26**
Copshaw Holm. *Bord* 1F **113**
Copster Green. *Lanc* 1E **91**
Copston Magna. *Warw* 2B **62**
Copt Green. *Warw* 4F **61**
Copthall Green. *Essx* 5E **53**
Copt Heath. *W Mid* 3F **61**
Copt Hewick. *N Yor* 2F **99**
Copthill. *Dur* 5B **114**
Copthorne. *W Sus* 2E **27**
Coptiviney. *Shrp* 2G **71**
Copy's Green. *Norf* 2B **78**
Copythorne. *Hants* 1B **16**
Corby. *Nptn* 2F **63**
Corby Glen. *Linc* 3G **75**
Cordon. *N Ayr* 2E **123**
Coreley. *Shrp* 3A **60**
Corfe. *Som* 1F **13**
Corfe Castle. *Dors* 4E **15**
Corfe Mullen. *Dors* 3E **15**
Corfton. *Shrp* 2G **59**
Corgarff. *Abers* 3G **151**
Corhampton. *Hants* 4E **24**
Corlae. *Dum* 5F **117**
Corlannau. *Neat* 2A **32**
Corley. *Warw* 2H **61**
Corley Ash. *Warw* 2G **61**
Corley Moor. *Warw* 2G **61**
Cormiston. *S Lan* 1C **118**
Cornaa. *IOM* 3D **108**
Cornaigbeg. *Arg* 4A **138**
Cornaigmore. *Arg*
    on Coll 2D **138**
    on Tiree 4A **138**
Corner Row. *Lanc* 1C **90**
Corney. *Cumb* 5C **102**
Cornforth. *Dur* 1A **106**
Cornhill. *Abers* 3C **160**
Cornhill. *High* 4C **164**
Cornhill-on-Tweed. *Nmbd* 1C **120**
Cornholme. *W Yor* 2H **91**
Cornish Hall End. *Essx* 2G **53**
Cornquoy. *Orkn* 7E **172**
Cornriggs. *Dur* 5B **114**
Cornsay. *Dur* 5E **115**
Cornsay Colliery. *Dur* 5E **115**
Corntown. *High* 3H **157**
Corntown. *V Glam* 4C **32**
Cornwell. *Oxon* 3A **50**
Cornwood. *Devn* 3C **8**
Cornworthy. *Devn* 3E **9**
Corpach. *High* 1E **141**
Corpusty. *Norf* 3D **78**
Corra. *Dum* 3F **111**
Corran. *High*
    nr. Arnisdale 2E **141**
    nr. Fort William 3A **148**
Corrany. *IOM* 3D **108**
Corribeg. *High* 1D **141**
Corrie. *N Ayr* 5B **126**
Corrie Common. *Dum* 1D **112**
Corriecravie. *N Ayr* 3D **122**
Corriekinloch. *High* 1A **164**
Corriemoillie. *High* 2F **157**
Corrievarkie Lodge. *Per* 1C **142**
Corrievorrie. *High* 1B **150**
Corrigall. *Orkn* 6C **172**
Corrimony. *High* 5F **157**
Corringham. *Linc* 1F **87**
Corringham. *Thur* 2B **40**
Corris. *Gwyn* 5G **69**

Corris Uchaf. *Gwyn* 5G **69**
Corrour Shooting Lodge.
    High .2B **142**
Corry. *High* 1E **147**
Corrybrough. *High* 1C **150**
Corrygills. *N Ayr* 2E **123**
Corry of Ardnagrask. *High* 4H **157**
Corsback. *High*
    nr. Dunnet 1E **169**
    nr. Halkirk 3E **169**
Corscombe. *Dors* 2A **14**
Corse. *Abers* 4D **160**
Corse. *Glos* 3C **48**
Corsehill. *Abers* 3G **161**
Corse Lawn. *Worc* 2D **48**
Corse of Kinnoir. *Abers* 4C **160**
Corsham. *Wilts* 4D **34**
Corsley. *Wilts* 2D **22**
Corsley Heath. *Wilts* 2D **22**
Corsock. *Dum* 2E **111**
Corston. *Bath* 5B **34**
Corston. *Wilts* 3E **35**
Corstorphine. *Edin* 2F **129**
Cortachy. *Ang* 3C **144**
Corton. *Suff* 1H **67**
Corton. *Wilts* 2E **23**
Corton Denham. *Som* 4B **22**
Corwar House. *S Ayr* 1H **109**
Corwen. *Den* 1C **70**
Coryates. *Dors* 4B **14**
Coryton. *Devn* 4E **11**
Coryton. *Thur* 2B **40**
Cosby. *Leics* 1C **62**
Coscote. *Oxon* 3D **36**
Coseley. *W Mid* 1D **60**
Cosgrove. *Nptn* 1F **51**
Cosham. *Port* 2E **17**
Cosheston. *Pemb* 4E **43**
Coskills. *N Lin* 3D **94**
Cosmeston. *V Glam* 5E **33**
Cossall. *Notts* 1B **74**
Cossington. *Leics* 4D **74**
Cossington. *Som* 2G **21**
Costa. *Orkn* 5C **172**
Costessey. *Norf* 4D **78**
Costock. *Notts* 3C **74**
Coston. *Leics* 3F **75**
Cote. *Oxon* 5B **50**
Cotebrook. *Ches W* 4H **83**
Cotehill. *Cumb* 4F **113**
Cotes. *Cumb* 1D **97**
Cotes. *Leics* 3C **74**
Cotes. *Staf* 2C **72**
Cotesbach. *Leics* 2C **62**
Cotes Heath. *Staf* 2C **72**
Cotford St Luke. *Som* 4E **21**
Cotgrave. *Notts* 2D **74**
Cothal. *Abers* 2F **153**
Cotham. *Notts* 1E **75**
Cothelstone. *Som* 3E **21**
Cotheridge. *Worc* 5B **60**
Cotherstone. *Dur* 3D **104**
Cothill. *Oxon* 2C **36**
Cotland. *Mon* 5A **48**
Cotleigh. *Devn* 2F **13**
Cotmanhay. *Derbs* 1B **74**
Coton. *Cambs* 5D **64**
Coton. *Nptn* 3D **62**
Coton. *Staf*
    nr. Gnosall 3C **72**
    nr. Stone 2D **73**
    nr. Tamworth 5F **73**
Coton Clanford. *Staf* 3C **72**
Coton Hayes. *Staf* 2D **73**
Coton Hill. *Shrp* 4G **71**
Coton in the Clay. *Staf* 3F **73**
Coton in the Elms. *Derbs* 4G **73**
Cotonwood. *Shrp* 2H **71**
Cotonwood. *Staf* 3C **72**
Cott. *Devn* 2D **9**
Cott. *Orkn* 5F **172**
Cottam. *E Yor* 3D **101**
Cottam. *Lanc* 1D **90**
Cottam. *Notts* 3F **87**
Cottartown. *High* 5E **159**
Cottarville. *Nptn* 4E **63**
Cottenham. *Cambs* 4D **64**
Cotterdale. *N Yor* 5B **104**
Cottered. *Herts* 3D **52**
Cotterstock. *Nptn* 1H **63**
Cottesbrooke. *Nptn* 3E **62**
Cottesmore. *Rut* 4G **75**
Cotteylands. *Devn* 1C **12**
Cottingham. *E Yor* 1D **94**
Cottingham. *Nptn* 1F **63**
Cottingley. *W Yor* 1B **92**
Cottisford. *Oxon* 2D **50**
Cotton. *Staf* 1E **73**
Cotton. *Suff* 4C **66**
Cotton End. *Bed* 1A **52**
Cottown. *Abers* 4F **161**
Cotts. *Devn* 2A **8**
Cotwalton. *Staf* 2D **72**
Couch's Mill. *Corn* 3F **7**
Coughton. *Here* 3A **48**
Coughton. *Warw* 4E **61**
Coulags. *High* 4B **156**
Coulby Newham. *Midd* 3C **106**
Coulderton. *Cumb* 4A **102**
Coulin Lodge. *High* 3C **156**
Coull. *Abers* 3C **152**
Coulport. *Arg* 1D **126**
Coulsdon. *G Lon* 5D **39**
Coulston. *Wilts* 1E **23**
Coulter. *S Lan* 1C **118**
Coultings. *Som* 2F **21**
Coulton. *N Yor* 2A **100**
Cound. *Shrp* 5H **71**
Coundon. *Dur* 2F **105**
Coundon Grange. *Dur* 2F **105**

Countersett—Crwbin

Countersett. *N Yor* 1B 98
Countess. *Wilts* 2G 23
Countess Cross. *Essx* 2B 54
Countesthorpe. *Leics* 1C 62
Countisbury. *Devn* 2H 19
Coupar Angus. *Per* 4B 144
Coupe Green. *Lanc* 2D 90
Coupland. *Cumb* 3A 104
Coupland. *Nmbd* 1D 120
Cour. *Arg* 5G 125
Courance. *Dum* 5C 118
Court-at-Street. *Kent* 2E 29
Courteachan. *High* 4E 147
Courteenhall. *Nptn* 5E 63
Court Henry. *Carm* 3F 45
Courtsend. *Essx* 1E 41
Courtway. *Som* 3F 21
Cousland. *Midl* 3G 129
Cousley Wood. *E Sus* 2A 28
Coustonn. *Arg* 2B 126
Cove. *Arg* 1D 126
Cove. *Devn* 1C 12
Cove. *Hants* 1G 25
Cove. *High* 4C 162
Cove. *Bord* 2D 130
Cove Bay. *Aber* 3G 153
Covehithe. *Suff* 2H 67
Coven. *Staf* 5D 72
Coveney. *Cambs* 2D 65
Covenham St Bartholomew. *Linc* 1C 88
Covenham St Mary. *Linc* 1C 88
Coven Heath. *Staf* 5D 72
Coventry. *W Mid* 192 (3H 61)
Coverack. *Corn* 5E 5
Coverham. *N Yor* 1D 98
Covesea. *Mor* 1F 159
Covingham. *Swin* 3G 35
Covington. *Cambs* 3H 63
Covington. *S Lan* 1B 118
Cowan Bridge. *Lanc* 2F 97
Cowan Head. *Cumb* 5F 103
Cowbar. *Red C* 3E 107
Cowbeech. *E Sus* 4H 27
Cowbit. *Linc* 4B 76
Cowbridge. *V Glam* 4C 32
Cowden. *Kent* 1F 27
Cowdenbeath. *Fife* 4D 136
Cowdenburn. *Bord* 4F 129
Cowdenend. *Fife* 4D 136
Cowers Lane. *Derbs* 1H 73
Cowes. *IOW* 3C 16
Cowesby. *N Yor* 1G 99
Cowfold. *W Sus* 3D 26
Cowfords. *Mor* 2H 159
Cowgill. *Cumb* 1G 97
Cowie. *Abers* 5F 153
Cowie. *Stir* 1B 128
Cowlam. *E Yor* 3D 100
Cowley. *Devn* 3C 12
Cowley. *Glos* 4E 49
Cowley. *G Lon* 2B 38
Cowley. *Oxon* 5D 50
Cowley. *Staf* 4C 72
Cowleymoor. *Devn* 1C 12
Cowling. *Lanc* 3D 90
Cowling. *N Yor*
nr. Bedale 1E 99
nr. Glusburn 5B 98
Cowlinge. *Suff* 5G 65
Cowmes. *W Yor* 3B 92
Cowpe. *Lanc* 2G 91
Cowpen. *Nmbd* 1F 115
Cowpen Bewley. *Stoc T* 2B 106
Cowplain. *Hants* 1E 17
Cowshill. *Dur* 5B 114
Cowslip Green. *N Som* 5H 33
Cowstrandburn. *Fife* 4C 136
Cowthorpe. *N Yor* 4G 99
Coxall. *Here* 3F 59
Coxbank. *Ches E* 1A 72
Coxbench. *Derbs* 1A 74
Cox Common. *Suff* 2G 67
Coxford. *Norf* 3H 77
Coxgreen. *Staf* 2C 60
Cox Green. *Surr* 2B 26
Cox Green. *Tyne* 4G 115
Coxheath. *Kent* 5B 40
Coxhoe. *Dur* 1A 106
Coxley. *Som* 2A 22
Coxwold. *N Yor* 2H 99
Coychurch. *B'end* 3C 32
Coylton. *S Ayr* 3D 116
Coylumbridge. *High* 2D 150
Coynach. *Abers* 3B 152
Coynachie. *Abers* 5B 160
Coytrahen. *B'end* 3B 32
Crabbs Cross. *Worc* 4E 61
Crabgate. *Norf* 3C 78
Crab Orchard. *Dors* 2F 15
Crabtree. *W Sus* 3D 26
Crabtree Green. *Wrex* 1F 71
Crackaig. *High* 2G 165
Crackenthorpe. *Cumb* 2H 103
Crackington Haven. *Corn* 3B 10
Crackley. *Staf* 5C 84
Crackley. *Warw* 3G 61
Crackleybank. *Shrp* 4B 72
Crackpot. *N Yor* 5C 104
Cracoe. *N Yor* 3B 98
Craddock. *Devn* 1D 12
Cradhlastadh. *W Isl* 4C 171
Cradley. *Here* 1C 48
Cradley. *W Mid* 2D 60
Cradoc. *Powy* 2D 46
Crafthole. *Corn* 3H 7
Crafton. *Buck* 4G 51
Cragabus. *Arg* 5B 124
Crag Foot. *Lanc* 2D 97
Craggan. *High* 1E 151
Cragganmore. *Mor* 5F 159
Cragganvallie. *High* 5H 157
Craggie. *High* 2F 165
Craggiemore. *High* 5B 158
Cragg Vale. *W Yor* 2A 92
Craghead. *Dur* 4F 115
Crai. *Powy* 3B 46
Craichie. *Ang* 4E 145
Craig. *Arg* 5E 141
Craig. *Dum* 2D 111
Craig. *High*
nr. Achnashellach 4C 156
nr. Lower Diabaig 2G 155
nr. Stromeferry 5H 155
Craiganour Lodge. *Per* 3D 142
Craigbrack. *Arg* 4A 134
Craig-Cefn-Parc. *Swan* 5G 45
Craigdallie. *Per* 1E 137
Craigdam. *Abers* 5F 161
Craigdarroch. *E Ayr* 4F 117
Craigdarroch. *High* 3G 157
Craigdhu. *High* 4G 157
Craigearn. *Abers* 2E 152
Craigellachie. *Mor* 4G 159
Craigend. *Per* 1D 136
Craigendoran. *Arg* 1E 126
Craigends. *Ren* 3F 127
Craigenputtock. *Dum* 1E 111
Craigens. *E Ayr* 3E 117
Craighall. *Edin* 2E 129
Craighead. *Fife* 2H 137
Craighouse. *Arg* 3D 124
Craigie. *Abers* 2G 153
Craigie. *D'dee* 5D 144
Craigie. *Per*
nr. Blairgowrie 4A 144
nr. Perth 1D 136
Craigie. *S Ayr* 1D 116
Craigielaw. *E Lot* 2A 130
Craiglemine. *Dum* 5B 110
Craig-llwyn. *Shrp* 3E 71
Craiglockhart. *Edin* 2F 129
Craig Lodge. *Arg* 2B 126
Craigmalloch. *E Ayr* 5D 117
Craigmaud. *Abers* 3F 161
Craigmill. *Stir* 4H 135
Craigmillar. *Edin* 2F 129
Craigmore. *Arg* 3C 126
Craigmuie. *Dum* 1E 111
Craignair. *Dum* 3F 111
Craignant. *Shrp* 2E 71
Craigneuk. *N Lan*
nr. Airdrie 3A 128
nr. Motherwell 4A 128
Craignure. *Arg* 5B 140
Craigo. *Ang* 2F 145
Craigrory. *High* 4A 158
Craigrothie. *Fife* 2F 137
Craigs. *Dum* 2D 112
Craigs, The. *High* 4B 164
Craigshill. *W Lot* 3D 128
Craigton. *Aber* 3F 153
Craigton. *Abers* 3E 152
Craigton. *Ang*
nr. Carnoustie 5E 145
nr. Kirriemuir 3C 144
Craigton. *High* 4A 158
Craigtown. *High* 3A 168
Craig-y-Duke. *Neat* 5H 45
Craig-y-nos. *Powy* 4B 46
Craik. *Bord* 4F 119
Crail. *Fife* 3H 137
Crailing. *Bord* 2A 120
Crailinghall. *Bord* 2A 120
Crakehill. *N Yor* 2G 99
Crakemarsh. *Staf* 2E 73
Crambe. *N Yor* 3B 100
Crambeck. *N Yor* 3B 100
Cramlington. *Nmbd* 2F 115
Cramond. *Edin* 2E 129
Cramond Bridge. *Edin* 2E 129
Cranage. *Ches E* 4B 84
Cranberry. *Staf* 2C 72
Cranborne. *Dors* 1F 15
Cranbourne. *Brac* 3A 38
Cranbrook. *Devn* 3D 12
Cranbrook. *Kent* 2B 28
Cranbrook Common. *Kent* 2B 28
Crane Moor. *S Yor* 4D 92
Crane's Corner. *Norf* 4B 78
Cranfield. *C Beds* 1H 51
Cranford. *G Lon* 3C 38
Cranford St Andrew. *Nptn* 3G 63
Cranford St John. *Nptn* 3G 63
Cranham. *Glos* 4D 49
Cranham. *G Lon* 2G 39
Crank. *Mers* 1H 83
Cranleigh. *Surr* 2B 26
Cranley. *Suff* 3D 66
Cranloch. *Mor* 3G 159
Cranmer Green. *Suff* 3C 66
Cranmore. *IOW* 3C 16
Cranmore. *Linc* 5A 76
Crannich. *Arg* 4G 139
Crannoch. *Mor* 3B 160
Cranoe. *Leics* 1E 63
Cransford. *Suff* 4F 67
Cranshaws. *Bord* 3C 130
Cranstal. *IOM* 1D 108
Crantock. *Corn* 2B 6
Cranwell. *Linc* 1H 75
Cranwich. *Norf* 1G 65
Cranworth. *Norf* 5B 78
Craobh Haven. *Arg* 3E 133
Craobhnaclag. *High* 4G 157
Crapstone. *Devn* 2B 8
Crarae. *Arg* 4G 133
Crask. *High*
nr. Bettyhill 2H 167
nr. Lairg 1C 164
Crask of Aigas. *High* 4G 157
Craster. *Nmbd* 2G 121
Craswall. *Here* 2F 47
Cratfield. *Suff* 3F 67
Crathes. *Abers* 4E 153
Crathie. *Abers* 4G 151
Crathie. *High* 4H 149
Crathorne. *N Yor* 4B 106
Craven Arms. *Shrp* 2G 59
Crawcrook. *Tyne* 3E 115
Crawford. *Lanc* 4C 90
Crawford. *S Lan* 2B 118
Crawforddyke. *S Lan* 4B 128
Crawfordjohn. *S Lan* 2A 118
Crawick. *Dum* 3G 117
Crawley. *Devn* 2F 13
Crawley. *Hants* 3C 24
Crawley. *Oxon* 4B 50
Crawley. *W Sus* 2D 26
Crawley Down. *W Sus* 2E 27
Crawley End. *Essx* 1E 53
Crawley Side. *Dur* 5C 114
Crawshawbooth. *Lanc* 2G 91
Crawton. *Abers* 5F 153
Cray. *N Yor* 2B 98
Cray. *Per* 2A 144
Crayford. *G Lon* 3G 39
Crayke. *N Yor* 2H 99
Craymere Beck. *Norf* 2C 78
Crays Hill. *Essx* 1B 40
Cray's Pond. *Oxon* 3E 37
Crazies Hill. *Wok* 3F 37
Creacombe. *Devn* 1B 12
Creagan. *Arg* 4D 140
Creag Aoil. *High* 1F 141
Creag Ghoraidh. *W Isl* 4C 170
Creaguaineach Lodge. *High* 2H 141
Creamore Bank. *Shrp* 2H 71
Creaton. *Nptn* 3E 62
Creca. *Dum* 2D 112
Credenhill. *Here* 1H 47
Crediton. *Devn* 2B 12
Creebridge. *Dum* 3B 110
Creech. *Dors* 4E 15
Creech Heathfield. *Som* 4F 21
Creech St Michael. *Som* 4F 21
Creed. *Corn* 4D 6
Creekmoor. *Pool* 3E 15
Creekmouth. *G Lon* 2F 39
Creeting St Mary. *Suff* 5C 66
Creeting St Peter. *Suff* 5C 66
Creeton. *Linc* 3H 75
Creetown. *Dum* 4B 110
Creggans. *Arg* 3H 133
Cregneash. *IOM* 5A 108
Cregrina. *Powy* 5D 58
Creich. *Arg* 2B 132
Creich. *Fife* 1F 137
Creighton. *Staf* 2E 73
Creigiau. *Card* 3D 32
Cremyll. *Corn* 3A 8
Crendell. *Dors* 1F 15
Crepkill. *High* 4D 154
Cressage. *Shrp* 5H 71
Cressbrook. *Derbs* 3F 85
Cresselly. *Pemb* 4E 43
Cressing. *Essx* 3A 54
Cresswell. *Nmbd* 5G 121
Cresswell. *Staf* 2D 73
Cresswell Quay. *Pemb* 4E 43
Creswell. *Derbs* 3C 86
Creswell Green. *Staf* 4E 73
Cretingham. *Suff* 4E 67
Crewe. *Ches E* 5B 84
Crewe-by-Farndon. *Ches W* 5G 83
Crewgreen. *Powy* 4F 71
Crewkerne. *Som* 2H 13
Crews Hill. *G Lon* 5D 52
Crewton. *Derb* 2A 74
Crianlarich. *Stir* 1C 134
Cribbs Causeway. *S Glo* 3A 34
Cribyn. *Cdgn* 5E 57
Criccieth. *Gwyn* 2D 69
Crich. *Derbs* 5A 86
Crichton. *Midl* 3G 129
Crick. *Mon* 2H 33
Crick. *Nptn* 3C 62
Crickadarn. *Powy* 1D 46
Cricket Hill. *Hants* 5G 37
Cricket Malherbie. *Som* 1G 13
Cricket St Thomas. *Som* 2G 13
Crickham. *Som* 2H 21
Crickheath. *Shrp* 3E 71
Crickhowell. *Powy* 4F 47
Cricklade. *Wilts* 2G 35
Cricklewood. *G Lon* 2D 38
Cridling Stubbs. *N Yor* 2F 93
Crieff. *Per* 1A 136
Criftins. *Shrp* 2F 71
Criggion. *Powy* 4E 71
Crigglestone. *W Yor* 3D 92
Crimchard. *Som* 2G 13
Crimdon Park. *Dur* 1B 106
Crimond. *Abers* 3H 161
Crimonmogate. *Abers* 3H 161
Crimplesham. *Norf* 5F 77
Crimscote. *Warw* 1H 49
Crinan. *Arg* 4E 133
Cringleford. *Norf* 5D 78
Crinow. *Pemb* 3F 43
Cripplesease. *Corn* 3C 4
Cripplestyle. *Dors* 1F 15
Cripp's Corner. *E Sus* 3B 28
Croanford. *Corn* 5A 10
Crockenhill. *Kent* 4G 39
Crocker End. *Oxon* 3F 37
Crockerhill. *Hants* 2D 16
Crockernwell. *Devn* 3A 12
Crocker's Ash. *Here* 4A 48
Crockerton. *Wilts* 2D 22
Crocketford. *Dum* 2F 111
Crockey Hill. *York* 5A 100
Crockham Hill. *Kent* 5F 39
Crockhurst Street. *Kent* 1H 27
Crockleford Heath. *Essx* 3D 54
Croeserw. *Neat* 2B 32
Croes-Goch. *Pemb* 1C 42
Croes Hywel. *Mon* 4G 47
Croes-lan. *Cdgn* 1D 45
Croesor. *Gwyn* 1F 69
Croesoswallt. *Shrp* 3E 71
Croesyceiliog. *Carm* 4E 45
Croesyceiliog. *Torf* 2G 33
Croes-y-mwyalch. *Torf* 2G 33
Croesywaun. *Gwyn* 5E 81
Croford. *Som* 4E 20
Croft. *Leics* 1C 62
Croft. *Linc* 4E 89
Croft. *Warr* 1A 84
Croftamie. *Stir* 1F 127
Croftfoot. *Glas* 3G 127
Croftmill. *Per* 5F 143
Crofton. *Cumb* 4E 112
Crofton. *W Yor* 3D 93
Crofton. *Wilts* 5A 36
Croft-on-Tees. *N Yor* 4F 105
Crofts. *Dum* 2E 111
Crofts of Benachielt. *High* 5D 169
Crofts of Dipple. *Mor* 3H 159
Crofty. *Swan* 3E 31
Croggan. *Arg* 1E 132
Croglin. *Cumb* 5G 113
Croich. *High* 4B 164
Croick. *High* 3A 168
Croig. *Arg* 3E 139
Cromarty. *High* 2B 158
Crombie. *Fife* 1D 128
Cromdale. *High* 1E 151
Cromer. *Herts* 3C 52
Cromer. *Norf* 1E 78
Cromford. *Derbs* 5G 85
Cromhall. *S Glo* 2B 34
Cromor. *W Isl* 5G 171
Cromra. *High* 5H 149
Cromwell. *Notts* 4E 87
Cronberry. *E Ayr* 2F 117
Crondall. *Hants* 2F 25
Cronk, The. *IOM* 2C 108
Cronk-y-Voddy. *IOM* 3C 108
Cronton. *Mers* 2G 83
Crook. *Cumb* 5F 103
Crook. *Dur* 1E 105
Crookdake. *Cumb* 5C 112
Crooke. *G Man* 4D 90
Crookedholm. *E Ayr* 1D 116
Crooked Soley. *Wilts* 4B 36
Crookes. *S Yor* 2H 85
Crookgate Bank. *Dur* 4E 115
Crookhall. *Dur* 4E 115
Crookham. *Nmbd* 1D 120
Crookham. *W Ber* 5D 36
Crookham Village. *Hants* 1F 25
Crooklands. *Cumb* 1E 97
Crook of Devon. *Per* 3C 136
Crookston. *Glas* 3G 127
Cropredy. *Oxon* 1C 50
Cropston. *Leics* 4C 74
Cropthorne. *Worc* 1E 49
Cropton. *N Yor* 1B 100
Cropwell Bishop. *Notts* 2D 74
Cropwell Butler. *Notts* 2D 74
Cros. *W Isl* 1H 171
Crosbie. *N Ayr* 4D 126
Crosbost. *W Isl* 5F 171
Crosby. *Cumb* 1B 102
Crosby. *IOM* 4C 108
Crosby. *Mers* 1F 83
Crosby. *N Lin* 3B 94
Crosby Court. *N Yor* 5A 106
Crosby Garrett. *Cumb* 4A 104
Crosby Ravensworth. *Cumb* 3H 103
Crosby Villa. *Cumb* 1B 102
Croscombe. *Som* 2A 22
Crosland Moor. *W Yor* 3B 92
Cross. *Som* 1H 21
Crossaig. *Arg* 4G 125
Crossapol. *Arg* 4A 138
Cross Ash. *Mon* 4H 47
Cross-at-Hand. *Kent* 1B 28
Crossbush. *W Sus* 5B 26
Crosscanonby. *Cumb* 1B 102
Crossdale Street. *Norf* 2E 79
Cross End. *Essx* 2B 54
Crossens. *Mers* 2B 90
Crossford. *Fife* 1D 128
Crossford. *S Lan* 5B 128
Cross Foxes. *Gwyn* 4G 69
Crossgate. *Orkn* 6D 172
Crossgate. *Staf* 2D 72
Crossgatehall. *E Lot* 3G 129
Crossgates. *Fife* 1E 129
Crossgates. *N Yor* 1E 101
Crossgates. *Powy* 4C 58
Cross Gates. *W Yor* 1D 92
Crossgill. *Lanc* 3E 97
Cross Green. *Devn* 4D 11
Cross Green. *Staf* 5D 72
Cross Green. *Suff*
nr. Cockfield 5A 66
nr. Hitcham 5B 66
Cross Hands. *Carm* 4F 45
Crosshands. *Carm* 2F 43
Crosshands. *E Ayr* 1D 117
Cross Hill. *Derbs* 1B 74
Crosshill. *E Ayr* 2D 117
Crosshill. *Fife* 4D 136
Cross Hill. *Glos* 2A 34
Crosshill. *S Ayr* 4C 116
Crosshills. *High* 1A 158
Cross Hills. *N Yor* 5C 98
Cross Holme. *N Yor* 5C 106
Crosshouse. *E Ayr* 1C 116
Cross Houses. *Shrp* 5H 71
Crossings. *Cumb* 2G 113
Cross in Hand. *E Sus* 3G 27
Cross Inn. *Cdgn*
nr. Aberaeron 4E 57
nr. New Quay 5C 56
Cross Inn. *Rhon* 3D 32
Crosskeys. *Cphy* 2F 33
Crosskirk. *High* 2C 168
Crosslands. *Cumb* 1C 96
Cross Lane Head. *Shrp* 1B 60
Cross Lanes. *Corn* 4D 5
Cross Lanes. *Dur* 3D 104
Cross Lanes. *N Yor* 3H 99
Crosslanes. *Shrp* 4F 71
Cross Lanes. *Wrex* 1F 71
Crosslee. *Ren* 3F 127
Crossmichael. *Dum* 3E 111
Crossmoor. *Lanc* 1C 90
Cross Oak. *Powy* 3E 46
Cross of Jackston. *Abers* 5E 161
Cross o' th' Hands. *Derbs* 1G 73
Crossroads. *Abers*
nr. Aberdeen 3G 153
nr. Banchory 4E 153
Crossroads. *E Ayr* 1D 116
Cross Side. *Devn* 4B 20
Cross Street. *Suff* 3D 66
Crosston. *Ang* 3E 145
Cross Town. *Ches E* 3B 84
Crossway. *Mon* 4H 47
Crossway. *Powy* 5C 58
Crossway Green. *Mon* 2A 34
Crossway Green. *Worc* 4C 60
Crossways. *Dors* 4C 14
Crosswell. *Pemb* 1F 43
Crosswood. *Cdgn* 3F 57
Crosthwaite. *Cumb* 5F 103
Croston. *Lanc* 3C 90
Crostwick. *Norf* 4E 79
Crostwight. *Norf* 3F 79
Crothair. *W Isl* 4D 171
Crouch. *Kent* 5H 39
Croucheston. *Wilts* 4F 23
Crouch Hill. *Dors* 1C 14
Croughton. *Nptn* 2D 50
Crovie. *Abers* 2F 161
Crow. *Hants* 2G 15
Crowan. *Corn* 3D 4
Crowborough. *E Sus* 2G 27
Crowcombe. *Som* 3E 21
Crowcroft. *Worc* 5B 60
Crowdecote. *Derbs* 4F 85
Crowden. *Derbs* 1E 85
Crowden. *Devn* 3E 11
Crowdhill. *Hants* 1C 16
Crowdon. *N Yor* 5G 107
Crow Edge. *S Yor* 4B 92
Crow End. *Cambs* 5C 64
Crowfield. *Nptn* 1E 50
Crowfield. *Suff* 5D 66
Crow Green. *Essx* 1G 39
Crow Hill. *Here* 3B 48
Crowhurst. *E Sus* 4B 28
Crowhurst. *Surr* 1E 27
Crowhurst Lane End. *Surr* 1E 27
Crowland. *Linc* 4B 76
Crowland. *Suff* 3C 66
Crowlas. *Corn* 3C 4
Crowle. *N Lin* 3A 94
Crowle. *Worc* 5D 60
Crowle Green. *Worc* 5D 60
Crowmarsh Gifford. *Oxon* 3E 36
Crown Corner. *Suff* 3E 67
Crownthorpe. *Norf* 5C 78
Crowntown. *Corn* 3D 4
Crows-an-wra. *Corn* 4A 4
Crowshill. *Norf* 5B 78
Crowthorne. *Brac* 5G 37
Crowton. *Ches W* 3H 83
Croxall. *Staf* 4F 73
Croxby. *Linc* 1A 88
Croxdale. *Dur* 1F 105
Croxden. *Staf* 2E 73
Croxley Green. *Herts* 1B 38
Croxton. *Cambs* 4B 64
Croxton. *Norf*
nr. Fakenham 2B 78
nr. Thetford 2A 66
Croxton. *N Lin* 3D 94
Croxton. *Staf* 2B 72
Croxtonbank. *Staf* 2B 72
Croxton Green. *Ches E* 5H 83
Croxton Kerrial. *Leics* 3F 75
Croy. *High* 4B 158
Croy. *N Lan* 2A 128
Croyde. *Devn* 3E 19
Croydon. *Cambs* 1D 52
Croydon. *G Lon* 4E 39
Crubenbeg. *High* 4A 150
Crubenmore Lodge. *High* 4A 150
Cruckmeole. *Shrp* 5G 71
Cruckton. *Shrp* 4G 71
Cruden Bay. *Abers* 5H 161
Crudgington. *Telf* 4A 72
Crudie. *Abers* 3E 161
Crudwell. *Wilts* 2E 35
Cruft. *Devn* 3F 11
Crug. *Powy* 3D 58
Crughywel. *Powy* 4F 47
Crugmeer. *Corn* 1D 6
Crugybar. *Carm* 2G 45
Crug-y-byddar. *Powy* 2D 58
Crulabhig. *W Isl* 4D 171
Crumlin. *Cphy* 2F 33
Crumpsall. *G Man* 4G 91
Crumpsbrook. *Shrp* 3A 60
Crundale. *Kent* 1E 29
Crundale. *Pemb* 3D 42
Cruwys Morchard. *Devn* 1B 12
Crux Easton. *Hants* 1C 24
Cruxton. *Dors* 3B 14
Crwbin. *Carm* 4E 45

Cryers Hill—Dibden Purlieu

Cryers Hill. *Buck* 2G **37**
Crymych. *Pemb* 1F **43**
Crynant. *Neat* 5A **46**
Crystal Palace. *G Lon* 3E **39**
Cuaich. *High* 5A **150**
Cuaig. *High* 3G **155**
Cuan. *Arg* 2E **133**
Cubbington. *Warw* 4H **61**
Cubert. *Corn* 3B **6**
Cubley. *S Yor* 4C **92**
Cubley Common. *Derbs* 2F **73**
Cublington. *Buck* 3G **51**
Cublington. *Here* 2G **47**
Cuckfield. *W Sus* 3E **27**
Cucklington. *Som* 4C **22**
Cuckney. *Notts* 3C **86**
Cuckron. *Shet* 6F **173**
Cuddesdon. *Oxon* 5E **50**
Cuddington. *Buck* 4F **51**
Cuddington. *Ches W* 3A **84**
Cuddington Heath. *Ches W* 1G **71**
Cuddy Hill. *Lanc* 1C **90**
Cudham. *G Lon* 5F **39**
Cudlipptown. *Devn* 5F **11**
Cudworth. *Som* 1G **13**
Cudworth. *S Yor* 4D **93**
Cudworth. *Surr* 1D **26**
Cuerdley Cross. *Warr* 2H **83**
Cuffley. *Herts* 5D **52**
Cuidhir. *W Isl* 8B **170**
Cuidhsiadar. *W Isl* 2H **171**
Cuidhtinis. *W Isl* 9C **171**
Culbo. *High* 2A **158**
Culbokie. *High* 3A **158**
Culburnie. *High* 4G **157**
Culcabock. *High* 4A **158**
Culcharry. *High* 3C **158**
Culcheth. *Warr* 1A **84**
Culduie. *High* 4G **155**
Culeave. *High* 4C **164**
Culford. *Suff* 3H **65**
Culgaith. *Cumb* 2H **103**
Culham. *Oxon* 2D **36**
Culkein. *High* 1E **163**
Culkein Drumbeg. *High* 5B **166**
Culkerton. *Glos* 2E **35**
Cullen. *Mor* 2C **160**
Cullercoats. *Tyne* 2G **115**
Cullicudden. *High* 2A **158**
Cullingworth. *W Yor* 1A **92**
Cullipool. *Arg* 2E **133**
Cullivoe. *Shet* 1G **173**
Culloch. *Per* 2G **135**
Culloden. *High* 4B **158**
Cullompton. *Devn* 2D **12**
Culm Davy. *Devn* 1E **13**
Culmington. *Shrp* 2G **59**
Culmstock. *Devn* 1E **12**
Cul na Caepaich. *High* 5E **147**
Culnacnoc. *High* 2E **155**
Culnacraig. *High* 3E **163**
Culrain. *High* 4C **164**
Culross. *Fife* 1C **128**
Culroy. *S Ayr* 3C **116**
Culswick. *Shet* 7D **173**
Cults. *Aber* 3F **153**
Cults. *Abers* 5C **160**
Cults. *Fife* 3F **137**
Cultybraggan Camp. *Per* 1G **135**
Culver. *Devn* 3B **12**
Culverlane. *Devn* 2D **8**
Culverstone Green. *Kent* 4H **39**
Culverthorpe. *Linc* 1H **75**
Culworth. *Nptn* 1D **50**
Culzie Lodge. *High* 1H **157**
Cumberlow Green. *Herts* 2D **52**
Cumbernauld. *N Lan* 2A **128**
Cumbernauld Village. *N Lan* 2A **128**
Cumberworth. *Linc* 3E **89**
Cumdivock. *Cumb* 5E **113**
Cuminestown. *Abers* 3F **161**
Cumledge Mill. *Bord* 4D **130**
Cumlewick. *Shet* 9F **173**
Cummersdale. *Cumb* 4E **113**
Cummertrees. *Dum* 3C **112**
Cummingstown. *Mor* 2F **159**
Cumnock. *E Ayr* 2E **117**
Cumnor. *Oxon* 5C **50**
Cumrew. *Cumb* 4G **113**
Cumwhinton. *Cumb* 4F **113**
Cumwhitton. *Cumb* 4G **113**
Cundall. *N Yor* 2G **99**
Cunninghamhead. *N Ayr* 5E **127**
Cunning Park. *S Ayr* 3C **116**
Cunningsburgh. *Shet* 9F **173**
Cunnister. *Shet* 2G **173**
Cupar. *Fife* 2F **137**
Cupar Muir. *Fife* 2F **137**
Cupernham. *Hants* 4B **24**
Curbar. *Derbs* 3G **85**
Curborough. *Staf* 4F **73**
Curbridge. *Hants* 1D **16**
Curbridge. *Oxon* 5B **50**
Curdridge. *Hants* 1D **16**
Curdworth. *Warw* 1F **61**
Curland. *Som* 1F **13**
Curland Common. *Som* 1F **13**
Curridge. *W Ber* 4C **36**
Currie. *Edin* 3E **129**
Curry Mallet. *Som* 4G **21**
Curry Rivel. *Som* 4G **21**
Curtisden Green. *Kent* 1B **28**
Curtisknowle. *Devn* 3D **8**
Cury. *Corn* 4D **5**
Cusgarne. *Corn* 4B **6**
Cusop. *Here* 1F **47**
Cusworth. *S Yor* 4F **93**
Cutcombe. *Som* 3C **20**
Cuthill. *E Lot* 2G **129**
Cutiau. *Gwyn* 4F **69**
Cutlers Green. *Essx* 2F **53**
Cutmadoc. *Corn* 2E **7**
Cutnall Green. *Worc* 4C **60**
Cutsdean. *Glos* 2F **49**
Cutthorpe. *Derbs* 3H **85**
Cuttiford's Door. *Som* 1G **13**
Cuttivett. *Corn* 2H **7**
Cutts. *Shet* 8E **173**
Cuttybridge. *Pemb* 3D **42**
Cuttyhill. *Abers* 3H **161**
Cuxham. *Oxon* 2E **37**
Cuxton. *Medw* 4B **40**
Cuxwold. *Linc* 4E **95**
Cwm. *Blae* 5E **47**
Cwm. *Den* 3C **82**
Cwm. *Powy* 1E **59**
Cwmafan. *Neat* 2A **32**
Cwmaman. *Rhon* 2C **32**
Cwmann. *Carm* 1F **45**
Cwmbach. *Carm* 2G **43**
Cwmbach. *Powy* 2E **47**
Cwmbach. *Rhon* 5D **46**
Cwmbach Llechrhyd. *Powy* 5C **58**
Cwmbelan. *Powy* 2B **58**
Cwmbran. *Torf* 2F **33**
Cwmbrwyno. *Cdgn* 2G **57**
Cwm Capel. *Carm* 5E **45**
Cwmcarn. *Cphy* 2F **33**
Cwmcarvan. *Mon* 5H **47**
Cwm-celyn. *Blae* 5F **47**
Cwmcerdinen. *Swan* 5G **45**
Cwm-Cewydd. *Gwyn* 4A **70**
Cwm-cou. *Cdgn* 1C **44**
Cwmcych. *Pemb* 1G **43**
Cwmdare. *Rhon* 5C **46**
Cwmdu. *Carm* 2G **45**
Cwmdu. *Powy* 3E **47**
Cwmduad. *Carm* 2D **45**
Cwm Dulais. *Swan* 5G **45**
Cwmerfyn. *Cdgn* 2F **57**
Cwmfelin. *B'end* 3B **32**
Cwmfelin Boeth. *Carm* 3F **43**
Cwmfelinfach. *Cphy* 2E **33**
Cwmfelin Mynach. *Carm* 2G **43**
Cwmffrwd. *Carm* 4E **45**
Cwmgiedd. *Powy* 4A **46**
Cwmgors. *Neat* 4H **45**
Cwmgwili. *Carm* 4F **45**
Cwmgwrach. *Neat* 5B **46**
Cwmhiraeth. *Carm* 1H **43**
Cwmifor. *Carm* 3G **45**
Cwmisfael. *Carm* 4E **45**
Cwm-Llinau. *Powy* 5H **69**
Cwmllynfell. *Neat* 4H **45**
Cwm-mawr. *Carm* 4F **45**
Cwm-miles. *Carm* 2F **43**
Cwmorgan. *Carm* 1G **43**
Cwmparc. *Rhon* 2C **32**
Cwm Penmachno. *Cnwy* 1G **69**
Cwmpennar. *Rhon* 5D **46**
Cwm Plysgog. *Pemb* 1B **44**
Cwmrhos. *Powy* 3E **47**
Cwmsychpant. *Cdgn* 1E **45**
Cwmsyfiog. *Cphy* 5E **47**
Cwmsymlog. *Cdgn* 2F **57**
Cwmtillery. *Blae* 5F **47**
Cwm-twrch Isaf. *Powy* 5A **46**
Cwm-twrch Uchaf. *Powy* 4A **46**
Cwmwysg. *Powy* 3B **46**
Cwm-y-glo. *Gwyn* 4E **81**
Cwmyoy. *Mon* 3F **47**
Cwmystwyth. *Cdgn* 3G **57**
Cwrt. *Gwyn* 5F **69**
Cwrtnewydd. *Cdgn* 1E **45**
Cwrt-y-Cadno. *Carm* 1G **45**
Cydweli. *Carm* 5E **45**
Cyffylliog. *Den* 5C **82**
Cymau. *Flin* 5E **83**
Cymer. *Neat* 2B **32**
Cymmer. *Neat* 2B **32**
Cymmer. *Rhon* 2D **32**
Cyncoed. *Card* 3E **33**
Cynghordy. *Carm* 2B **46**
Cynheidre. *Carm* 5E **45**
Cynonville. *Neat* 2B **32**
Cynwyd. *Den* 1C **70**
Cynwyl Elfed. *Carm* 3D **44**
Cywarch. *Gwyn* 4A **70**

D

Dacre. *Cumb* 2F **103**
Dacre. *N Yor* 3D **98**
Dacre Banks. *N Yor* 3D **98**
Daddry Shield. *Dur* 1B **104**
Dadford. *Buck* 2E **51**
Dadlington. *Leics* 1B **62**
Dafen. *Carm* 5F **45**
Daffy Green. *Norf* 5B **78**
Dagdale. *Staf* 2E **73**
Dagenham. *G Lon* 2F **39**
Daggons. *Dors* 1G **15**
Daglingworth. *Glos* 5E **49**
Dagnall. *Buck* 4H **51**
Dagtail End. *Worc* 4E **61**
Dail. *Arg* 5E **141**
Dail Beag. *W Isl* 3E **171**
Dail bho Dheas. *W Isl* 1G **171**
Dailly. *S Ayr* 4B **116**
Dail Mor. *W Isl* 3E **171**
Dairsie. *Fife* 2G **137**
Daisy Bank. *W Mid* 1E **61**
Daisy Hill. *G Man* 4E **91**
Daisy Hill. *W Yor* 1B **92**
Dalabrog. *W Isl* 6C **170**
Dalavich. *Arg* 2G **133**
Dalbeattie. *Dum* 3F **111**
Dalblair. *E Ayr* 3F **117**
Dalbury. *Derbs* 2G **73**
Dalby. *IOM* 4B **108**
Dalby Wolds. *Leics* 3D **74**
Dalchalm. *High* 3G **165**
Dalcharn. *High* 3G **167**
Dalchork. *High* 2C **164**
Dalchreichart. *High* 2E **149**
Dalchruin. *Per* 2G **135**
Dalcross. *High* 4B **158**
Dalderby. *Linc* 4B **88**
Dale. *Cumb* 5G **113**
Dale. *Pemb* 4C **42**
Dale Abbey. *Derbs* 2B **74**
Dalebank. *Derbs* 4A **86**
Dale Bottom. *Cumb* 2D **102**
Dale Head. *Cumb* 3F **103**
Dalehouse. *N Yor* 3E **107**
Dalelia. *High* 2B **140**
Dale of Walls. *Shet* 6C **173**
Dalgarven. *N Ayr* 5D **126**
Dalgety Bay. *Fife* 1E **129**
Dalginross. *Per* 1G **135**
Dalguise. *Per* 4G **143**
Dalhalvaig. *High* 3A **168**
Dalham. *Suff* 4G **65**
Dalintart. *Arg* 1F **133**
Dalkeith. *Midl* 3G **129**
Dallas. *Mor* 3F **159**
Dalleagles. *E Ayr* 3E **117**
Dall House. *Per* 3C **142**
Dallinghoo. *Suff* 5E **67**
Dallington. *E Sus* 4A **28**
Dallow. *N Yor* 2D **98**
Dalmally. *Arg* 1A **134**
Dalmarnock. *Glas* 3H **127**
Dalmellington. *E Ayr* 4D **117**
Dalmeny. *Edin* 2E **129**
Dalmigavie. *High* 2B **150**
Dalmilling. *S Ayr* 2C **116**
Dalmore. *High*
nr. Alness 2A **158**
nr. Rogart 3E **164**
Dalmuir. *W Dun* 2F **127**
Dalmunach. *Mor* 4G **159**
Dalnabreck. *High* 2B **140**
Dalnacardoch Lodge. *Per* 1E **142**
Dalnamein Lodge. *Per* 2E **143**
Dalnaspidal Lodge. *Per* 1D **142**
Dalnatrat. *High* 3D **140**
Dalnavie. *High* 1A **158**
Dalnawillan Lodge. *High* 4C **168**
Dalness. *High* 3F **141**
Dalnessie. *High* 2D **164**
Dalqueich. *Per* 3C **136**
Dalquhairn. *S Ayr* 5C **116**
Dalreavoch. *High* 3E **165**
Dalreoch. *Per* 2C **136**
Dalry. *Edin* 2F **129**
Dalry. *N Ayr* 5D **126**
Dalrymple. *E Ayr* 3C **116**
Dalscote. *Nptn* 5D **62**
Dalserf. *S Lan* 4B **128**
Dalsmirren. *Arg* 4A **122**
Dalston. *Cumb* 4E **113**
Dalswinton. *Dum* 1G **111**
Dalton. *Dum* 2C **112**
Dalton. *Lanc* 4C **90**
Dalton. *Nmbd*
nr. Hexham 4C **114**
nr. Ponteland 2E **115**
Dalton. *N Yor*
nr. Richmond 4E **105**
nr. Thirsk 2G **99**
Dalton. *S Lan* 4H **127**
Dalton. *S Yor* 1B **86**
Dalton-in-Furness.
Cumb 2B **96**
Dalton-le-Dale. *Dur* 5H **115**
Dalton Magna. *S Yor* 1B **86**
Dalton-on-Tees. *N Yor* 4F **105**
Dalton Piercy. *Hart* 1B **106**
Daltot. *Arg* 1F **125**
Dalvey. *High* 5F **159**
Dalwhinnie. *High* 5A **150**
Dalwood. *Devn* 2F **13**
Damerham. *Hants* 1G **15**
Damgate. *Norf*
nr. Acle 5G **79**
nr. Martham 4G **79**
Dam Green. *Norf* 2C **66**
Damhead. *Mor* 3E **159**
Danaway. *Kent* 4C **40**
Danbury. *Essx* 5A **54**
Danby. *N Yor* 4E **107**
Danby Botton. *N Yor* 4D **107**
Danby Wiske. *N Yor* 5A **106**
Danderhall. *Midl* 3G **129**
Danebank. *Ches E* 2D **85**
Danebridge. *Ches E* 4D **84**
Dane End. *Herts* 3D **52**
Danehill. *E Sus* 3F **27**
Danesford. *Shrp* 1B **60**
Daneshill. *Hants* 1E **25**
Danesmoor. *Derbs* 4B **86**
Danestone. *Aber* 2G **153**
Dangerous Corner. *Lanc* 3D **90**
Daniel's Water. *Kent* 1D **28**
Dan's Castle. *Dur* 1E **105**
Danzey Green. *Warw* 4F **61**
Dapple Heath. *Staf* 3E **73**
Daren. *Powy* 4F **47**
Darenth. *Kent* 3G **39**
Daresbury. *Hal* 2H **83**
Darfield. *S Yor* 4E **93**
Dargate. *Kent* 4E **41**
Dargill. *Per* 2A **136**
Darite. *Corn* 2G **7**
Darlaston. *W Mid* 1D **61**
Darley. *N Yor* 4E **98**
Darley Abbey. *Derb* 2H **73**
Darley Bridge. *Derbs* 4G **85**
Darley Dale. *Derbs* 4G **85**
Darley Head. *N Yor* 4D **98**
Darlingscott. *Warw* 1H **49**
Darlington. *Darl* 3F **105**
Darliston. *Shrp* 2H **71**
Darlton. *Notts* 3E **87**
Darmsden. *Suff* 5C **66**
Darnall. *S Yor* 2A **86**
Darnford. *Abers* 4E **153**
Darnford. *Staf* 5F **73**
Darnhall. *Ches W* 4A **84**
Darnick. *Bord* 1H **119**
Darowen. *Powy* 5H **69**
Darra. *Abers* 4E **161**
Darracott. *Devn* 3E **19**
Darras Hall. *Nmbd* 2E **115**
Darrington. *W Yor* 2E **93**
Darrow Green. *Norf* 2E **67**
Darsham. *Suff* 4G **67**
Dartfield. *Abers* 3H **161**
Dartford. *Kent* 3G **39**
Dartford-Thurrock River Crossing.
Kent 3G **39**
Dartington. *Devn* 2D **9**
Dartmeet. *Devn* 5G **11**
Dartmouth. *Devn* 3E **9**
Darton. *S Yor* 3D **92**
Darvel. *E Ayr* 1E **117**
Darwen. *Bkbn* 2E **91**
Dassels. *Herts* 3D **53**
Datchet. *Wind* 3A **38**
Datchworth. *Herts* 4C **52**
Datchworth Green. *Herts* 4C **52**
Daubhill. *G Man* 4F **91**
Dauntsey. *Wilts* 3E **35**
Dauntsey Green. *Wilts* 3E **35**
Dauntsey Lock. *Wilts* 3E **35**
Dava. *Mor* 5E **159**
Davenham. *Ches W* 3A **84**
Daventry. *Nptn* 4C **62**
Davidson's Mains. *Edin* 2F **129**
Davidston. *High* 2B **158**
Davidstow. *Corn* 4B **10**
David's Well. *Powy* 3C **58**
Davington. *Dum* 4E **119**
Daviot. *Abers* 1E **153**
Daviot. *High* 5B **158**
Davyhulme. *G Man* 1B **84**
Daw Cross. *N Yor* 4E **99**
Dawdon. *Dur* 5H **115**
Dawesgreen. *Surr* 1D **26**
Dawley. *Telf* 5A **72**
Dawlish. *Devn* 5C **12**
Dawlish Warren. *Devn* 5C **12**
Dawn. *Cnwy* 3A **82**
Daws Heath. *Essx* 2C **40**
Dawshill. *Worc* 5C **60**
Daw's House. *Corn* 4D **10**
Dawsmere. *Linc* 2D **76**
Dayhills. *Staf* 2D **72**
Dayhouse Bank. *Worc* 3D **60**
Daylesford. *Glos* 3H **49**
Daywall. *Shrp* 2E **71**
Ddol. *Flin* 3D **82**
Ddol Cownwy. *Powy* 4C **70**
Deadman's Cross. *C Beds* 1B **52**
Deadwater. *Nmbd* 5A **120**
Deaf Hill. *Dur* 1A **106**
Deal. *Kent* 5H **41**
Dean. *Cumb* 2B **102**
Dean. *Devn*
nr. Combe Martin 2G **19**
nr. Lynton 2H **19**
Dean. *Dors* 1E **15**
Dean. *Hants*
nr. Bishop's Waltham 1D **16**
nr. Winchester 3C **24**
Dean. *Oxon* 3B **50**
Dean. *Som* 2B **22**
Dean Bank. *Dur* 1F **105**
Deanburnhaugh. *Bord* 3F **119**
Dean Cross. *Devn* 2F **19**
Deane. *Hants* 1D **24**
Deanich Lodge. *High* 5A **164**
Deanland. *Dors* 1E **15**
Deanlane End. *W Sus* 1F **17**
Dean Park. *Shrp* 4A **60**
Dean Prior. *Devn* 2D **8**
Dean Row. *Ches E* 2C **84**
Deans. *W Lot* 3D **128**
Deanscales. *Cumb* 2B **102**
Deanshanger. *Nptn* 1F **51**
Deanston. *Stir* 3G **135**
Dearham. *Cumb* 1B **102**
Dearne Valley. *S Yor* 4D **93**
Debach. *Suff* 5E **67**
Debden. *Essx* 2F **53**
Debden Green. *Essx*
nr. Loughton 1F **39**
nr. Saffron Walden 2F **53**
Debenham. *Suff* 4D **66**
Dechmont. *W Lot* 2D **128**
Deddington. *Oxon* 2C **50**
Dedham. *Essx* 2D **54**
Dedham Heath. *Essx* 2D **54**
Deebank. *Abers* 4D **152**
Deene. *Nptn* 1G **63**
Deenethorpe. *Nptn* 1G **63**
Deepcar. *S Yor* 1G **85**
Deepcut. *Surr* 5A **38**
Deepdale. *Cumb* 1G **97**
Deepdale. *N Lin* 3D **94**
Deepdale. *N Yor* 2A **98**
Deeping Gate. *Pet* 5A **76**
Deeping St James. *Linc* 4A **76**
Deeping St Nicholas. *Linc* 4B **76**
Deerhill. *Mor* 3B **160**
Deerhurst. *Glos* 3D **48**
Deerhurst Walton. *Glos* 3D **49**
Deerness. *Orkn* 7E **172**
Defford. *Worc* 1E **49**
Defynnog. *Powy* 3C **46**
Deganwy. *Cnwy* 3G **81**
Deighton. *N Yor* 4A **106**
Deighton. *W Yor* 3B **92**
Deighton. *York* 5A **100**
Deiniolen. *Gwyn* 4E **81**
Delabole. *Corn* 4A **10**
Delamere. *Ches W* 4H **83**
Delfour. *High* 3C **150**
Dell, The. *Suff* 1G **67**
Delliefure. *High* 5E **159**
Delly End. *Oxon* 4B **50**
Delny. *High* 1B **158**
Delph. *G Man* 4H **91**
Delves. *Dur* 5E **115**
Delves, The. *W Mid* 1E **61**
Delvin End. *Essx* 2A **54**
Dembleby. *Linc* 2H **75**
Demelza. *Corn* 2D **6**
Den, The. *N Ayr* 4E **127**
Denaby Main. *S Yor* 1B **86**
Denbeath. *Fife* 4F **137**
Denbigh. *Den* 4C **82**
Denbury. *Devn* 2E **9**
Denby. *Derbs* 1A **74**
Denby Common. *Derbs* 1B **74**
Denby Dale. *W Yor* 4C **92**
Denchworth. *Oxon* 2B **36**
Dendron. *Cumb* 2B **96**
Deneside. *Dur* 5H **115**
Denford. *Nptn* 3G **63**
Dengie. *Essx* 5C **54**
Denham. *Buck* 2B **38**
Denham. *Suff*
nr. Bury St Edmunds 4G **65**
nr. Eye 3D **66**
Denham Green. *Buck* 2B **38**
Denham Street. *Suff* 3D **66**
Denhead. *Abers*
nr. Ellon 5G **161**
nr. Strichen 3G **161**
Denhead. *Fife* 2G **137**
Denholm. *Bord* 3H **119**
Denholme. *W Yor* 1A **92**
Denholme Clough.
W Yor 1A **92**
Denholme Gate. *W Yor* 1A **92**
Denio. *Gwyn* 2C **68**
Denmead. *Hants* 1E **17**
Dennington. *Suff* 4E **67**
Denny. *Falk* 1B **128**
Denny End. *Cambs* 4D **65**
Dennyloanhead. *Falk* 1B **128**
Den of Lindores. *Fife* 2E **137**
Denshaw. *G Man* 3H **91**
Denside. *Abers* 4F **153**
Densole. *Kent* 1G **29**
Denston. *Suff* 5G **65**
Denstone. *Staf* 1F **73**
Denstroude. *Kent* 4F **41**
Dent. *Cumb* 1G **97**
Denton. *Cambs* 2A **64**
Denton. *Darl* 3F **105**
Denton. *E Sus* 5F **27**
Denton. *G Man* 1D **84**
Denton. *Kent* 1G **29**
Denton. *Linc* 2F **75**
Denton. *Norf* 2E **67**
Denton. *Nptn* 5F **63**
Denton. *N Yor* 5D **98**
Denton. *Oxon* 5D **50**
Denver. *Norf* 5F **77**
Denwick. *Nmbd* 3G **121**
Deopham. *Norf* 5C **78**
Deopham Green. *Norf* 1C **66**
Depden. *Suff* 5G **65**
Depden Green. *Suff* 5G **65**
Deptford. *G Lon* 3E **39**
Deptford. *Wilts* 3F **23**
Derby. *Derb* **193** (2A **74**)
Derbyhaven. *IOM* 5B **108**
Derculich. *Per* 3F **143**
Dereham. *Norf* 4B **78**
Deri. *Cphy* 5E **47**
Derril. *Devn* 2D **10**
Derringstone. *Kent* 1G **29**
Derrington. *Shrp* 1A **60**
Derrington. *Staf* 3C **72**
Derriton. *Devn* 2D **10**
Derryguaig. *Arg* 5F **139**
Derry Hill. *Wilts* 4E **35**
Derrythorpe. *N Lin* 4B **94**
Dersingham. *Norf* 2F **77**
Dervaig. *Arg* 3F **139**
Derwen. *Den* 5C **82**
Derwen Gam. *Cdgn* 5D **56**
Derwenlas. *Powy* 1G **57**
Desborough. *Nptn* 2F **63**
Desford. *Leics* 5B **74**
Detchant. *Nmbd* 1E **121**
Dethick. *Derbs* 5H **85**
Detling. *Kent* 5B **40**
Deuchar. *Ang* 2D **144**
Deuddwr. *Powy* 4E **71**
Devauden. *Mon* 2H **33**
Devil's Bridge. *Cdgn* 3G **57**
Devitts Green. *Warw* 1G **61**
Devizes. *Wilts* 5F **35**
Devonport. *Plym* 3A **8**
Devonside. *Clac* 4B **136**
Devoran. *Corn* 5B **6**
Dewartown. *Midl* 3G **129**
Dewlish. *Dors* 3C **14**
Dewsall Court. *Here* 2H **47**
Dewsbury. *W Yor* 2C **92**
Dexbeer. *Devn* 2C **10**
Dhoon. *IOM* 3D **108**
Dhoor. *IOM* 2D **108**
Dhowin. *IOM* 1D **108**
Dial Green. *W Sus* 3A **26**
Dial Post. *W Sus* 4C **26**
Dibberford. *Dors* 2H **13**
Dibden. *Hants* 2C **16**
Dibden Purlieu. *Hants* 2C **16**

Dickleburgh—Dunton

Dickleburgh. Norf 2D 66
Didbrook. Glos 2F 49
Didcot. Oxon 2D 36
Diddington. Cambs 4A 64
Diddlebury. Shrp 2H 59
Didley. Here 2H 47
Didling. W Sus 1G 17
Didmarton. Glos 3D 34
Didsbury. G Man 1C 84
Didworthy. Devn 2C 8
Digby. Linc 5H 87
Digg. High 2D 154
Diggle. G Man 4A 92
Digmoor. Lanc 4C 90
Digswell. Herts 4C 52
Dihewyd. Cdgn 5D 57
Dilham. Norf 3F 79
Dilhorne. Staf 1D 72
Dillarburn. S Lan 5B 128
Dillington. Cambs 4A 64
Dilston. Nmbd 3C 114
Dilton Marsh. Wilts 2D 22
Dilwyn. Here 5G 59
Dimmer. Som 3B 22
Dimple. G Man 3F 91
Dinas. Carm 1G 43
Dinas. Gwyn
nr. Caernarfon 5D 81
nr. Tudweiliog 2B 68
Dinas Cross. Pemb 1E 43
Dinas Dinlle. Gwyn 5D 80
Dinas Mawddwy. Gwyn 4A 70
Dinas Powys. V Glam 4E 33
Dinbych. Den 4C 82
Dinbych-y-Pysgod. Pemb 4F 43
Dinckley. Lanc 1E 91
Dinder. Som 2A 22
Dinedor. Here 2A 48
Dinedor Cross. Here 2A 48
Dingestow. Mon 4H 47
Dingle. Mers 2F 83
Dingleden. Kent 2C 28
Dingleton. Bord 1H 119
Dingley. Nptn 2E 63
Dingwall. High 3H 157
Dinmael. Cnwy 1C 70
Dinnet. Abers 4B 152
Dinnington. Som 1H 13
Dinnington. S Yor 2C 86
Dinnington. Tyne 2F 115
Dinorwig. Gwyn 4E 81
Dinton. Buck 4F 51
Dinton. Wilts 3F 23
Dinworthy. Devn 1D 10
Dipley. Hants 1F 25
Dippen. Arg 2B 122
Dippenhall. Surr 2G 25
Dippertown. Devn 4E 11
Dippin. N Ayr 3E 123
Dipple. S Ayr 4B 116
Diptford. Devn 3D 8
Dipton. Dur 4E 115
Dirleton. E Lot 1B 130
Dirt Pot. Nmbd 5B 114
Discoed. Powy 4E 59
Diseworth. Leics 3B 74
Dishes. Orkn 5F 172
Dishforth. N Yor 2F 99
Disley. Ches E 2D 85
Diss. Norf 3D 66
Disserth. Powy 5C 58
Distington. Cumb 2B 102
Ditchampton. Wilts 3F 23
Ditcheat. Som 3B 22
Ditchingham. Norf 1F 67
Ditchling. E Sus 4E 27
Ditteridge. Wilts 5D 34
Dittisham. Devn 3E 9
Ditton. Hal 2G 83
Ditton. Kent 5B 40
Ditton Green. Cambs 5F 65
Ditton Priors. Shrp 2A 60
Divach. High 1G 149
Dixonfield. High 2D 168
Dixton. Glos 2E 49
Dixton. Mon 4A 48
Dizzard. Corn 3B 10
Dobcross. G Man 4H 91
Dobs Hill. Flin 4F 83
Dobson's Bridge. Shrp 2G 71
Dobwalls. Corn 2G 7
Doccombe. Devn 4A 12
Dochgarroch. High 4A 158
Docking. Norf 2G 77
Docklow. Here 5H 59
Dockray. Cumb 2E 103
Doc Penfro. Pemb 215 (4D 42)
Dodbrooke. Devn 4D 8
Doddenham. Worc 5B 60
Doddinghurst. Essx 1G 39
Doddington. Cambs 1C 64
Doddington. Kent 5D 40
Doddington. Linc 3G 87
Doddington. Nmbd 1D 121
Doddington. Shrp 3A 60
Doddiscombsleigh. Devn 4B 12
Doddshill. Norf 2G 77
Dodford. Nptn 4D 62
Dodford. Worc 3D 60
Dodington. Som 2E 21
Dodington. S Glo 3C 34
Dodleston. Ches W 4F 83
Dods Leigh. Staf 2E 73
Dodworth. S Yor 4D 92
Doe Lea. Derbs 4B 86
Dogdyke. Linc 5B 88
Dogmersfield. Hants 1F 25
Dogsthorpe. Pet 5B 76
Dog Village. Devn 3C 12
Dolanog. Powy 4C 70
Dolau. Powy 4D 58
Dolau. Rhon 3D 32
Dolbenmaen. Gwyn 1E 69
Doley. Staf 3B 72
Dol-fâch. Powy 5B 70
Dolfach. Powy 3B 58
Dolfor. Powy 2D 58
Dolgarrog. Cnwy 4G 81
Dolgellau. Gwyn 4G 69
Dolgoch. Gwyn 5F 69
Dol-gran. Carm 2E 45
Dolhelfa. Powy 3B 58
Doll. High 3F 165
Dollar. Clac 4B 136
Dolley Green. Powy 4E 59
Dollwen. Cdgn 2F 57
Dolphin. Flin 3D 82
Dolphinholme. Lanc 4E 97
Dolphinton. S Lan 5E 129
Dolton. Devn 1F 11
Dolwen. Cnwy 3A 82
Dolwyddelan. Cnwy 5G 81
Dol-y-Bont. Cdgn 2F 57
Dolyhir. Powy 5E 59
Domgay. Powy 4E 71
Doncaster. S Yor 4F 93
Doncaster Sheffield Airport.
S Yor 1D 86
Donhead St Andrew. Wilts 4E 23
Donhead St Mary. Wilts 4E 23
Doniford. Som 2D 20
Donington. Linc 2B 76
Donington. Shrp 5C 72
Donington Eaudike. Linc 2B 76
Donington le Heath. Leics 4B 74
Donington on Bain. Linc 2B 88
Donington South Ing. Linc 2B 76
Donisthorpe. Leics 4H 73
Donkey Street. Kent 2F 29
Donkey Town. Surr 4A 38
Donna Nook. Linc 1D 88
Donnington. Glos 3G 49
Donnington. Here 2C 48
Donnington. Shrp 5H 71
Donnington. Telf 4B 72
Donnington. W Ber 5C 36
Donnington. W Sus 2G 17
Donyatt. Som 1G 13
Doomsday Green. W Sus 3C 26
Doonfoot. S Ayr 3C 116
Doonholm. S Ayr 3C 116
Dorback Lodge. High 2E 151
Dorchester. Dors 3B 14
Dorchester on Thames. Oxon 2D 36
Dordon. Warw 5G 73
Dore. S Yor 2H 85
Dores. High 5H 157
Dorking. Surr 1C 26
Dorking Tye. Suff 2C 54
Dormansland. Surr 1F 27
Dormans Park. Surr 1E 27
Dormanstown. Red C 2C 106
Dormington. Here 1A 48
Dormston. Worc 5D 61
Dorn. Glos 2H 49
Dorney. Buck 3A 38
Dornie. High 1A 148
Dornoch. High 5E 165
Dornock. Dum 3D 112
Dorrery. High 3C 168
Dorridge. W Mid 3F 61
Dorrington. Linc 5H 87
Dorrington. Shrp 5G 71
Dorsington. Warw 1G 49
Dorstone. Here 1G 47
Dorton. Buck 4E 51
Dosthill. Staf 5G 73
Dotham. IOA 3C 80
Dottery. Dors 3H 13
Doublebois. Corn 2F 7
Dougarie. N Ayr 2C 122
Doughton. Glos 2D 35
Douglas. IOM 4C 108
Douglas. S Lan 1H 117
Douglastown. Ang 4D 144
Douglas Water. S Lan 1A 118
Doulting. Som 2B 22
Dounby. Orkn 5B 172
Doune. High
nr. Kingussie 2C 150
nr. Lairg 3B 164
Doune. Stir 3G 135
Dounie. High
nr. Bonar Bridge 4C 164
nr. Tain 5D 164
Dounreay. High 2B 168
Doura. N Ayr 5E 127
Dousland. Devn 2B 8
Dovaston. Shrp 3F 71
Dove Holes. Derbs 3E 85
Dovenby. Cumb 1B 102
Dover. Kent 193 (1H 29)
Dovercourt. Essx 2F 55
Doverdale. Worc 4C 60
Doveridge. Derbs 2F 73
Doversgreen. Surr 1D 26
Dowally. Per 4H 143
Dowbridge. Lanc 1C 90
Dowdeswell. Glos 4F 49
Dowlais. Mer T 5D 46
Dowland. Devn 1F 11
Dowlands. Devn 3F 13
Dowles. Worc 3B 60
Dowlesgreen. Wok 5G 37
Dowlish Wake. Som 1G 13
Down, The. Shrp 1A 60
Downall Green. Mers 4D 90
Down Ampney. Glos 2G 35
Downderry. Corn
nr. Looe 3H 7
nr. St Austell 3D 6
Downe. G Lon 4F 39
Downend. IOW 4D 16
Downend. S Glo 4B 34
Downend. W Ber 4C 36
Down Field. Cambs 3F 65
Downfield. D'dee 5C 144
Downgate. Corn
nr. Kelly Bray 5D 10
nr. Upton Cross 5C 10
Downham. Essx 1B 40
Downham. Lanc 5G 97
Downham. Nmbd 1C 120
Downham Market. Norf 5F 77
Down Hatherley. Glos 3D 48
Downhead. Som
nr. Frome 2B 22
nr. Yeovil 4A 22
Downholland Cross. Lanc 4B 90
Downholme. N Yor 5E 105
Downies. Abers 4G 153
Downley. Buck 2G 37
Down St Mary. Devn 2H 11
Downside. Som
nr. Chilcompton 1B 22
nr. Shepton Mallet 2B 22
Downside. Surr 5C 38
Down Thomas. Devn 3B 8
Downton. Hants 3A 16
Downton. Wilts 4G 23
Downton on the Rock. Here 3G 59
Dowsby. Linc 3A 76
Dowsdale. Linc 4B 76
Dowthwaitehead. Cumb 2E 103
Doxey. Staf 3D 72
Doxford. Nmbd 2F 121
Doynton. S Glo 4C 34
Drabblegate. Norf 3E 78
Draethen. Cphy 3F 33
Draffan. S Lan 5A 128
Dragonby. N Lin 3C 94
Dragon's Green. W Sus 3C 26
Drakelow. Worc 2C 60
Drakemyre. N Ayr 4D 126
Drakes Broughton. Worc 1E 49
Drakes Cross. Worc 3E 61
Drakewalls. Corn 5E 11
Draughton. Nptn 3E 63
Draughton. N Yor 4C 98
Drax. N Yor 2G 93
Draycot. Oxon 5E 51
Draycote. Warw 3B 62
Draycot Foliat. Swin 4G 35
Draycott. Derbs 2B 74
Draycott. Glos 2G 49
Draycott. Shrp 1C 60
Draycott. Som
nr. Cheddar 1H 21
nr. Yeovil 4A 22
Draycott. Worc 1D 48
Draycott in the Clay. Staf 3F 73
Draycott in the Moors. Staf 1D 73
Drayford. Devn 1A 12
Drayton. Leics 1F 63
Drayton. Linc 2B 76
Drayton. Norf 4D 78
Drayton. Nptn 4C 62
Drayton. Oxon
nr. Abingdon 2C 36
nr. Banbury 1C 50
Drayton. Port 2E 17
Drayton. Som 4H 21
Drayton. Warw 5F 61
Drayton. Worc 3D 60
Drayton Bassett. Staf 5F 73
Drayton Beauchamp. Buck 4H 51
Drayton Parslow. Buck 3G 51
Drayton St Leonard. Oxon 2D 36
Drebley. N Yor 4C 98
Dreenhill. Pemb 3D 42
Y Dref. Gwyn 2D 69
Drefach. Carm
nr. Meidrim 4F 45
nr. Newcastle Emlyn 2D 44
nr. Tumble 2G 43
Drefach. Cdgn 1E 45
Dreghorn. N Ayr 1C 116
Drellingore. Kent 1G 29
Drem. E Lot 2B 130
Y Drenewydd. Powy 1D 58
Dreumasdal. W Isl 5C 170
Drewsteignton. Devn 3H 11
Driby. Linc 3C 88
Driffield. E Yor 4E 101
Driffield. Glos 2F 35
Drift. Corn 4B 4
Drigg. Cumb 5B 102
Drighlington. W Yor 2C 92
Drimnin. High 3G 139
Drimpton. Dors 2H 13
Dringhoe. E Yor 4F 101
Drinisiadar. W Isl 8D 171
Drinkstone. Suff 4B 66
Drinkstone Green. Suff 4B 66
Drointon. Staf 3E 73
Droitwich Spa. Worc 4C 60
Droman. High 3B 166
Dron. Per 2D 136
Dronfield. Derbs 3A 86
Dronfield Woodhouse.
Derbs 3H 85
Drongan. E Ayr 3D 116
Dronley. Ang 5C 144
Droop. Dors 2C 14
Drope. V Glam 4E 32
Droxford. Hants 1E 16
Droylsden. G Man 1C 84
Druggers End. Worc 2C 48
Druid. Den 1C 70
Druid's Heath. W Mid 5E 73
Druidston. Pemb 3C 42
Druim. High 3D 158
Druimarbin. High 1E 141
Druim Fhearna. High 2E 147
Druimindarroch. High 5E 147
Druim Saighdinis. W Isl 2D 170
Drum. Per 3C 136
Drumbeg. High 5B 166
Drumblade. Abers 4C 160
Drumbuie. Dum 1C 110
Drumbuie. High 5G 155
Drumburgh. Cumb 4D 112
Drumburn. Dum 3A 112
Drumchapel. Glas 2G 127
Drumchardine. High 4H 157
Drumchork. High 5C 162
Drumclog. S Lan 1F 117
Drumeldrie. Fife 3G 137
Drumelzier. Bord 1D 118
Drumfearn. High 2E 147
Drumgask. High 4A 150
Drumgelloch. N Lan 3A 128
Drumgley. Ang 3D 144
Drumguish. High 4B 150
Drumin. Mor 5F 159
Drumindorsair. High 4G 157
Drumlamford House.
S Ayr 2H 109
Drumlasie. Abers 3D 152
Drumlemble. Arg 4A 122
Drumlithie. Abers 5E 153
Drummoddie. Dum 5A 110
Drummond. High 2A 158
Drummore. Dum 5E 109
Drummuir. Mor 4A 160
Drumnadrochit. High 5H 157
Drumnagorrach. Mor 3C 160
Drumoak. Abers 4E 153
Drumrunie. High 3F 163
Drumry. W Dun 2G 127
Drums. Abers 1G 153
Drumsleet. Dum 2G 111
Drumsmittal. High 4A 158
Drums of Park. Abers 3C 160
Drumsturdy. Ang 5D 145
Drumtochty Castle. Abers 5D 152
Drumuie. High 4D 154
Drumuillie. High 1D 150
Drumvaich. Stir 3F 135
Drumwhindle. Abers 5G 161
Drunkendub. Ang 4F 145
Drury. Flin 4E 83
Drury Square. Norf 4B 78
Drybeck. Cumb 3H 103
Drybridge. Mor 2B 160
Drybridge. N Ayr 1C 116
Drybrook. Glos 4B 48
Drybrook. Here 4A 48
Dryburgh. Bord 1H 119
Dry Doddington. Linc 1F 75
Dry Drayton. Cambs 4C 64
Drym. Corn 3D 4
Drymen. Stir 1F 127
Drymuir. Abers 4G 161
Drynachan Lodge. High 5C 158
Drynie Park. High 3H 157
Drynoch. High 5D 154
Dry Sandford. Oxon 5C 50
Dryslwyn. Carm 3F 45
Dry Street. Essx 2A 40
Dryton. Shrp 5H 71
Dubford. Abers 2E 161
Dubiton. Abers 3D 160
Dubton. Ang 3E 145
Duchally. High 2A 164
Duck End. Essx 3G 53
Duckington. Ches W 5G 83
Ducklington. Oxon 5B 50
Duckmanton. Derbs 3B 86
Duck Street. Hants 2B 24
Dudbridge. Glos 5D 48
Duddenhoe End. Essx 2E 53
Duddingston. Edin 2F 129
Duddington. Nptn 5G 75
Duddleswell. E Sus 3F 27
Duddo. Nmbd 5F 131
Duddon. Ches W 4H 83
Duddon Bridge. Cumb 1A 96
Dudleston. Shrp 2F 71
Dudleston Heath. Shrp 2F 71
Dudley. Tyne 2F 115
Dudley. W Mid 2D 60
Dudston. Shrp 1E 59
Dudwells. Pemb 2D 42
Duffield. Derbs 1H 73
Duffryn. Neat 2B 32
Dufftown. Mor 4H 159
Duffus. Mor 2F 159
Dufton. Cumb 2H 103
Duggleby. N Yor 3C 100
Duirinish. High 5G 155
Duisdalemore. High 2E 147
Duisdeil Mòr. High 2E 147
Duisky. High 1E 141
Dukesfield. Nmbd 4C 114
Dukestown. Blae 5E 47
Dukinfield. G Man 1D 84
Dulas. IOA 2D 81
Dulcote. Som 2A 22
Dulford. Devn 2D 12
Dull. Per 4F 143
Dullatur. N Lan 2A 128
Dullingham. Cambs 5F 65
Dullingham Ley. Cambs 5F 65
Dulnain Bridge. High 1D 151
Duloe. Bed 4A 64
Duloe. Corn 3G 7
Dulverton. Som 4C 20
Dulwich. G Lon 3E 39
Dumbarton. W Dun 2F 127
Dumbleton. Glos 2F 49
Dumfin. Arg 1E 127
Dumfries. Dum 193 (2A 112)
Dumgoyne. Stir 1G 127
Dummer. Hants 2D 24
Dumpford. W Sus 4G 25
Dun. Ang 2F 145
Dunagoil. Arg 4B 126
Dunalastair. Per 3E 142
Dunan. High 1D 147
Dunball. Som 2G 21
Dunbar. E Lot 2C 130
Dunbeath. High 5D 168
Dunbeg. Arg 5C 140
Dunblane. Stir 3G 135
Dunbog. Fife 2E 137
Dunbridge. Hants 4B 24
Duncanston. Abers 1C 152
Duncanston. High 3H 157
Dun Charlabhaigh. W Isl 3D 171
Dunchideock. Devn 4B 12
Dunchurch. Warw 3B 62
Duncote. Nptn 5D 62
Duncow. Dum 1A 112
Duncrievie. Per 3D 136
Duncton. W Sus 4A 26
Dundee. D'dee 194 (5D 144)
Dundee Airport. D'dee 1F 137
Dundon. Som 3H 21
Dundonald. S Ayr 1C 116
Dundonnell. High 5E 163
Dundraw. Cumb 5D 112
Dundreggan. High 2F 149
Dundrennan. Dum 5E 111
Dundridge. Hants 1D 16
Dundry. N Som 5A 34
Dunecht. Abers 3E 153
Dunfermline. Fife 1D 129
Dunford Bridge. S Yor 4B 92
Dungate. Kent 5D 40
Dunge. Wilts 1D 23
Dungeness. Kent 4E 29
Dungworth. S Yor 2G 85
Dunham-on-the-Hill.
Ches W 3G 83
Dunham-on-Trent. Notts 3F 87
Dunhampton. Worc 4C 60
Dunham Town. G Man 2B 84
Dunham Woodhouses.
G Man 2B 84
Dunholme. Linc 3H 87
Dunino. Fife 2H 137
Dunipace. Falk 1B 128
Dunira. Per 1G 135
Dunkeld. Per 4H 143
Dunkerton. Bath 1C 22
Dunkeswell. Devn 2E 13
Dunkeswick. N Yor 5F 99
Dunkirk. Kent 5E 41
Dunkirk. S Glo 3C 34
Dunkirk. Staf 5C 84
Dunkirk. Wilts 5E 35
Dunk's Green. Kent 5H 39
Dunlappie. Ang 2E 145
Dunley. Hants 1C 24
Dunley. Worc 4B 60
Dunlichity Lodge. High 5A 158
Dunlop. E Ayr 5F 127
Dunmaglass Lodge. High 1H 149
Dunmore. Arg 3F 125
Dunmore. Falk 1B 128
Dunmore. High 4H 157
Dunnet. High 1E 169
Dunnichen. Ang 4E 145
Dunning. Per 2C 136
Dunnington. E Yor 4F 101
Dunnington. Warw 5E 61
Dunnington. York 4A 100
Dunningwell. Cumb 1A 96
Dunnockshaw. Lanc 2G 91
Dunoon. Arg 2C 126
Dunphail. Mor 4E 159
Dunragit. Dum 4G 109
Dunrostan. Arg 1F 125
Duns. Bord 4D 130
Dunsby. Linc 3A 76
Dunscar. G Man 3F 91
Dunscore. Dum 1F 111
Dunscroft. S Yor 4G 93
Dunsdale. Red C 3D 106
Dunsden Green. Oxon 4F 37
Dunsfold. Surr 2B 26
Dunsford. Devn 4B 12
Dunshalt. Fife 2E 137
Dunshillock. Abers 4G 161
Dunsley. N Yor 3F 107
Dunsley. Staf 2C 60
Dunsmore. Buck 5G 51
Dunsop Bridge. Lanc 4F 97
Dunstable. C Beds 3A 52
Dunstal. Staf 3E 73
Dunstall. Staf 3F 73
Dunstall Green. Suff 4G 65
Dunstall Hill. W Mid 5D 72
Dunstan. Nmbd 3G 121
Dunster. Som 2C 20
Duns Tew. Oxon 3C 50
Dunston. Linc 4H 87
Dunston. Norf 5E 79
Dunston. Staf 4D 72
Dunston. Tyne 3F 115
Dunstone. Devn 3B 8
Dunston Heath. Staf 4D 72
Dunsville. S Yor 4G 93
Dunswell. E Yor 1D 94
Dunsyre. S Lan 5D 128
Dunterton. Devn 5D 11
Duntisbourne Abbots. Glos 5E 49
Duntisbourne Leer. Glos 5E 49
Duntisbourne Rouse. Glos 5E 49
Duntish. Dors 2B 14
Duntocher. W Dun 2F 127
Dunton. Buck 3G 51
Dunton. C Beds 1C 52
Dunton. Norf 2A 78

Dunton Bassett. *Leics* 1C **62**
Dunton Green. *Kent* 5G **39**
Dunton Patch. *Norf* 2A **78**
Duntulm. *High* 1D **154**
Dunure. *S Ayr* 3B **116**
Dunvant. *Swan* 3E **31**
Dunvegan. *High* 4B **154**
Dunwich. *Suff* 3G **67**
Dunwood. *Staf* 5D **84**
Durdar. *Cumb* 4F **113**
Durgates. *E Sus* 2H **27**
Durham. *Dur* **194** (5F **115**)
Durham Tees Valley Airport.
. . . . *Darl* 3A **106**
Durisdeer. *Dum* 4A **118**
Durisdeermill. *Dum* 4A **118**
Durkar. *W Yor* 3D **92**
Durleigh. *Som* 3F **21**
Durley. *Hants* 1D **16**
Durley. *Wilts* 5H **35**
Durley Street. *Hants* 1D **16**
Durlow Common. *Here* 2B **48**
Durnamuck. *High* 4E **163**
Durness. *High* 2E **166**
Durno. *Abers* 1E **152**
Durns Town. *Hants* 3A **16**
Duror. *High* 3D **141**
Durran. *Arg* 3G **133**
Durran. *High* 2D **169**
Durrant Green. *Kent* 2C **28**
Durrants. *Hants* 1F **17**
Durrington. *W Sus* 5C **26**
Durrington. *Wilts* 2G **23**
Dursley. *Glos* 2C **34**
Dursley Cross. *Glos* 4B **48**
Durston. *Som* 4F **21**
Durweston. *Dors* 2D **14**
Dury. *Shet* 6F **173**
Duston. *Nptn* 4E **63**
Duthil. *High* 1D **150**
Dutlas. *Powy* 3E **58**
Duton Hill. *Essx* 3G **53**
Dutson. *Corn* 4D **10**
Dutton. *Ches W* 3H **83**
Duxford. *Cambs* 1E **53**
Duxford. *Oxon* 2B **36**
Dwygyfylchi. *Cnwy* 3G **81**
Dwyran. *IOA* 4D **80**
Dyce. *Aber* 2F **153**
Dyffryn. *B'end* 2B **32**
Dyffryn. *Carm* 2H **43**
Dyffryn. *Pemb* 1D **42**
Dyffryn. *V Glam* 4D **32**
Dyffryn Ardudwy. *Gwyn* 3E **69**
Dyffryn Castell. *Cdgn* 2G **57**
Dyffryn Ceidrych. *Carm* 3H **45**
Dyffryn Cellwen. *Neat* 5B **46**
Dyke. *Linc* 3A **76**
Dyke. *Mor* 3D **159**
Dykehead. *Ang* 2C **144**
Dykehead. *N Lan* 3B **128**
Dykehead. *Stir* 4E **135**
Dykend. *Ang* 3B **144**
Dykesfield. *Cumb* 4E **112**
Dylife. *Powy* 1A **58**
Dymchurch. *Kent* 3F **29**
Dymock. *Glos* 2C **48**
Dyrham. *S Glo* 4C **34**
Dysart. *Fife* 4F **137**
Dyserth. *Den* 3C **82**

E

Eachwick. *Nmbd* 2E **115**
Eadar Dha Fhadhail. *W Isl* 4C **171**
Eagland Hill. *Lanc* 5D **96**
Eagle. *Linc* 4F **87**
Eagle Barnsdale. *Linc* 4F **87**
Eagle Moor. *Linc* 4F **87**
Eaglescliffe. *Stoc T* 3B **106**
Eaglesfield. *Cumb* 2B **102**
Eaglesfield. *Dum* 2D **112**
Eaglesham. *E Ren* 4G **127**
Eaglethorpe. *Nptn* 1H **63**
Eagley. *G Man* 3F **91**
Eairy. *IOM* 4B **108**
Eakley Lanes. *Mil* 5F **63**
Eakring. *Notts* 4D **86**
Ealand. *N Lin* 3A **94**
Ealing. *G Lon* 2C **38**
Eallabus. *Arg* 3B **124**
Eals. *Nmbd* 4H **113**
Eamont Bridge. *Cumb* 2G **103**
Earby. *Lanc* 5B **98**
Earcroft. *Bkbn* 2E **91**
Eardington. *Shrp* 1B **60**
Eardisland. *Here* 5G **59**
Eardisley. *Here* 1G **47**
Eardiston. *Shrp* 3F **71**
Eardiston. *Worc* 4A **60**
Earith. *Cambs* 3C **64**
Earlais. *High* 2C **154**
Earle. *Nmbd* 2D **121**
Earlesfield. *Linc* 2G **75**
Earlestown. *Mers* 1H **83**
Earley. *Wok* 4F **37**
Earlham. *Norf* 5D **78**
Earlish. *High* 2C **154**
Earls Barton. *Nptn* 4F **63**
Earls Colne. *Essx* 3B **54**
Earls Common. *Worc* 5D **60**
Earl's Croome. *Worc* 1D **48**
Earlsdon. *W Mid* 3H **61**
Earlsferry. *Fife* 3G **137**
Earlsford. *Abers* 5F **161**
Earl's Green. *Suff* 4C **66**
Earlsheaton. *W Yor* 2C **92**
Earl Shilton. *Leics* 1B **62**
Earl Soham. *Suff* 4E **67**
Earl Sterndale. *Derbs* 4E **85**

Earlston. *E Ayr* 1D **116**
Earlston. *Bord* 1H **119**
Earl Stonham. *Suff* 5D **66**
Earlstoun. *Dum* 1D **110**
Earlswood. *Mon* 2H **33**
Earlswood. *Warw* 3F **61**
Earnley. *W Sus* 3G **17**
Earsairidh. *W Isl* 9C **170**
Earsdon. *Tyne* 2G **115**
Earsham. *Norf* 2F **67**
Earsham Street. *Suff* 3E **67**
Earswick. *York* 4A **100**
Eartham. *W Sus* 5A **26**
Earthcott Green. *S Glo* 3B **34**
Easby. *N Yor*
. . . . . nr. Great Ayton 4C **106**
. . . . . nr. Richmond 4E **105**
Easdale. *Arg* 2E **133**
Easebourne. *W Sus* 4G **25**
Easenhall. *Warw* 3B **62**
Eashing. *Surr* 1A **26**
Easington. *Buck* 4E **51**
Easington. *Dur* 5H **115**
Easington. *E Yor* 3G **95**
Easington. *Nmbd* 1F **121**
Easington. *Oxon*
. . . . . nr. Banbury 2C **50**
. . . . . nr. Watlington 2E **37**
Easington. *Red C* 3E **107**
Easington Colliery. *Dur* 5H **115**
Easington Lane. *Tyne* 5G **115**
Easingwold. *N Yor* 2H **99**
Eassie. *Ang* 4C **144**
Eassie and Nevay. *Ang* 4C **144**
East Aberthaw. *V Glam* 5D **32**
Eastacombe. *Devn* 4F **19**
Eastacott. *Devn* 4G **19**
East Allington. *Devn* 4D **8**
East Anstey. *Devn* 4B **20**
East Anton. *Hants* 2B **24**
East Appleton. *N Yor* 5F **105**
East Ardsley. *W Yor* 2D **92**
East Ashley. *Devn* 1G **11**
East Ashling. *W Sus* 2G **17**
East Aston. *Hants* 2C **24**
East Ayton. *N Yor* 1D **101**
East Barkwith. *Linc* 2A **88**
East Barnby. *N Yor* 3F **107**
East Barnet. *G Lon* 1D **39**
East Barns. *E Lot* 2D **130**
East Barsham. *Norf* 2B **78**
East Beach. *W Sus* 3G **17**
East Beckham. *Norf* 2D **78**
East Bedfont. *G Lon* 3B **38**
East Bennan. *N Ayr* 3D **123**
East Bergholt. *Suff* 2D **54**
East Bierley. *W Yor* 2C **92**
East Bilney. *Norf* 4B **78**
East Blatchington. *E Sus* 5F **27**
East Bloxworth. *Dors* 3D **15**
East Boldre. *Hants* 2B **16**
East Bolton. *Nmbd* 3F **121**
Eastbourne. *Darl* 3F **105**
Eastbourne. *E Sus* **195** (5H **27**)
East Brent. *Som* 1G **21**
East Bridge. *Suff* 4G **67**
East Bridgford. *Notts* 1D **74**
East Briscoe. *Dur* 3C **104**
East Buckland. *Devn*
. . . . . nr. Barnstaple 3G **19**
. . . . . nr. Thurlestone 4C **8**
East Budleigh. *Devn* 4D **12**
Eastburn. *W Yor* 5C **98**
East Burnham. *Buck* 2A **38**
East Burrafirth. *Shet* 6E **173**
East Burton. *Dors* 4D **14**
Eastbury. *Herts* 1B **38**
Eastbury. *W Ber* 4B **36**
East Butsfield. *Dur* 5E **115**
East Butterleigh. *Devn* 2C **12**
East Butterwick. *N Lin* 4B **94**
Eastby. *N Yor* 4C **98**
East Calder. *W Lot* 3D **129**
East Carleton. *Norf* 5D **78**
East Carlton. *Nptn* 2F **63**
East Carlton. *W Yor* 5E **98**
East Chaldon. *Dors* 4C **14**
East Challow. *Oxon* 3B **36**
East Charleton. *Devn* 4D **8**
East Chelborough. *Dors* 2A **14**
East Chiltington. *E Sus* 4E **27**
East Chinnock. *Som* 1H **13**
East Chisenbury. *Wilts* 1G **23**
Eastchurch. *Kent* 3D **40**
East Clandon. *Surr* 5B **38**
East Claydon. *Buck* 3F **51**
East Clevedon. *N Som* 4H **33**
East Clyne. *High* 3F **165**
East Clyth. *High* 5E **169**
East Coker. *Som* 1A **14**
Eastcombe. *Glos* 5D **49**
East Combe. *Som* 3E **21**
East Common. *N Yor* 1G **93**
East Compton. *Som* 2B **22**
East Cornworthy. *Devn* 3E **9**
Eastcote. *G Lon* 2C **38**
Eastcote. *Nptn* 5D **62**
Eastcote. *W Mid* 3F **61**
Eastcott. *Corn* 1C **10**
Eastcott. *Wilts* 1F **23**
East Cottingwith. *E Yor* 5B **100**
Eastcourt. *Wilts*
. . . . . nr. Pewsey 5H **35**
. . . . . nr. Tetbury 2E **35**
East Cowes. *IOW* 3D **16**
East Cowick. *E Yor* 2G **93**
East Cowton. *N Yor* 4A **106**
East Cramlington. *Nmbd* 2F **115**
East Cranmore. *Som* 2B **22**
East Creech. *Dors* 4E **15**

East Croachy. *High* 1A **150**
East Dean. *E Sus* 5G **27**
East Dean. *Glos* 3B **48**
East Dean. *Hants* 4A **24**
East Dean. *W Sus* 4A **26**
East Down. *Devn* 2G **19**
East Drayton. *Notts* 3E **87**
East Dundry. *N Som* 5A **34**
East Ella. *Hull* 2D **94**
East End. *Cambs* 3C **64**
East End. *Dors* 3E **15**
East End. *E Yor*
. . . . . nr. Ulrome 4F **101**
. . . . . nr. Withernsea 2F **95**
East End. *Hants*
. . . . . nr. Lymington 3B **16**
. . . . . nr. Newbury 5C **36**
East End. *Herts* 3E **53**
East End. *Kent*
. . . . . nr. Minster 3D **40**
. . . . . nr. Tenterden 2C **28**
East End. *N Som* 4H **33**
East End. *Oxon* 4B **50**
East End. *Som* 1A **22**
East End. *Suff* 2E **54**
Easter Ardross. *High* 1A **158**
Easter Balgedie. *Per* 3D **136**
Easter Balmoral. *Abers* 4G **151**
Easter Brae. *High* 2A **158**
Easter Buckieburn. *Stir* 1A **128**
Easter Compton. *S Glo* 3A **34**
Easter Fearn. *High* 5D **164**
Easter Galcantray. *High* 4C **158**
Eastergate. *W Sus* 5A **26**
Easterhouse. *Glas* 3H **127**
Easter Howgate. *Midl* 3F **129**
Easter Kinkell. *High* 3H **157**
Easter Lednathie. *Ang* 2C **144**
Easter Ogil. *Ang* 2D **144**
Easter Ord. *Abers* 3F **153**
Easter Quarff. *Shet* 8F **173**
Easter Rhynd. *Per* 2D **136**
Easter Skeld. *Shet* 7E **173**
Easter Suddie. *High* 3A **158**
Easterton. *Wilts* 1F **23**
Eastertown. *Som* 1G **21**
Easter Tulloch. *Abers* 1G **145**
Easter Everleigh. *Wilts* 1H **23**
East Farleigh. *Kent* 5B **40**
East Farndon. *Nptn* 2E **62**
East Ferry. *Linc* 1F **87**
Eastfield. *N Lan*
. . . . . nr. Caldercruix 3B **128**
. . . . . nr. Harthill 3B **128**
Eastfield. *N Yor* 1E **101**
Eastfield. *S Lan* 3H **127**
Eastfield Hall. *Nmbd* 4G **121**
East Fortune. *E Lot* 2B **130**
East Garforth. *W Yor* 1E **93**
East Garston. *W Ber* 4B **36**
Eastgate. *Dur* 1C **104**
Eastgate. *Norf* 3D **78**
East Ginge. *Oxon* 3C **36**
East Gores. *Essx* 3B **54**
East Goscote. *Leics* 4D **74**
East Grafton. *Wilts* 5A **36**
East Green. *Suff* 5F **65**
East Grimstead. *Wilts* 4H **23**
East Grinstead. *W Sus* 2E **27**
East Guldeford. *E Sus* 3D **28**
East Haddon. *Nptn* 4D **62**
East Hagbourne. *Oxon* 3D **36**
East Halton. *N Lin* 2E **95**
East Ham. *G Lon* 2F **39**
Eastham. *Mers* 2F **83**
Eastham. *Worc* 4A **60**
Eastham Ferry. *Mers* 2F **83**
Easthampstead. *Brac* 5G **37**
Easthampton. *Here* 4G **59**
East Hanney. *Oxon* 2C **36**
East Hanningfield. *Essx* 5A **54**
East Hardwick. *W Yor* 3E **93**
East Harling. *Norf* 2B **66**
East Harlsey. *N Yor* 5B **106**
East Harptree. *Bath* 1A **22**
East Hartford. *Nmbd* 2F **115**
East Harting. *W Sus* 1G **17**
East Hatch. *Wilts* 4E **23**
East Hatley. *Cambs* 5B **64**
Easthaugh. *Norf* 4C **78**
East Hauxwell. *N Yor* 5E **105**
East Haven. *Ang* 5E **145**
Eastheath. *Wok* 5G **37**
East Heckington. *Linc* 1A **76**
East Hedleyhope. *Dur* 5E **115**
East Helmsdale. *High* 2H **165**
East Hendred. *Oxon* 3C **36**
East Heslerton. *N Yor* 2D **100**
East Hoathly. *E Sus* 4G **27**
East Holme. *Dors* 4D **15**
Easthope. *Shrp* 1H **59**
Easthorpe. *Essx* 3C **54**
Easthorpe. *Leics* 2F **75**
East Horrington. *Som* 2A **22**
East Horsley. *Surr* 5B **38**
East Horton. *Nmbd* 1E **121**
Easthouses. *Midl* 3G **129**
East Howe. *Bour* 3F **15**
East Huntspill. *Som* 2G **21**
East Hyde. *C Beds* 4B **52**
East Ilsley. *W Ber* 3C **36**
Eastington. *Devn* 2H **11**
Eastington. *Glos*
. . . . . nr. Northleach 4G **49**
. . . . . nr. Stonehouse 5C **48**
East Keal. *Linc* 4C **88**
East Kennett. *Wilts* 5G **35**
East Keswick. *W Yor* 5F **99**
East Kilbride. *S Lan* 4H **127**
East Kirkby. *Linc* 4C **88**
East Knapton. *N Yor* 2C **100**

East Knighton. *Dors* 4D **14**
East Knowstone. *Devn* 4B **20**
East Knoyle. *Wilts* 3D **23**
East Kyloe. *Nmbd* 1E **121**
East Lambrook. *Som* 1H **13**
East Langdon. *Kent* 1H **29**
East Langton. *Leics* 1E **63**
East Langwell. *High* 3E **164**
East Lavant. *W Sus* 2G **17**
East Lavington. *W Sus* 4A **26**
East Layton. *N Yor* 4E **105**
Eastleach Martin. *Glos* 5H **49**
Eastleach Turville. *Glos* 5G **49**
East Leake. *Notts* 3C **74**
East Learmouth. *Nmbd* 1C **120**
East Leigh. *Devn*
. . . . . nr. Crediton 2G **11**
. . . . . nr. Modbury 3C **8**
Eastleigh. *Devn* 4E **19**
Eastleigh. *Hants* 1C **16**
East Lexham. *Norf* 4A **78**
East Lilburn. *Nmbd* 2E **121**
Eastling. *Kent* 5D **40**
East Linton. *E Lot* 2B **130**
East Liss. *Hants* 4F **25**
East Lockinge. *Oxon* 3C **36**
East Looe. *Corn* 3G **7**
East Lound. *N Lin* 1E **87**
East Lulworth. *Dors* 4D **14**
East Lutton. *N Yor* 3D **100**
East Lydford. *Som* 3A **22**
East Lyng. *Som* 4G **21**
East Mains. *Abers* 4D **152**
East Malling. *Kent* 5B **40**
East Marden. *W Sus* 1G **17**
East Markham. *Notts* 3E **87**
East Marton. *N Yor* 4B **98**
East Meon. *Hants* 4E **25**
East Mersea. *Essx* 4D **54**
East Mey. *High* 1F **169**
East Midlands Airport.
. . . . *Leics* **216** (3B **74**)
East Molesey. *Surr* 4C **38**
Eastmoor. *Norf* 5G **77**
East Morden. *Dors* 3E **15**
East Morton. *W Yor* 5D **98**
East Ness. *N Yor* 2A **100**
East Newton. *E Yor* 1F **95**
East Newton. *N Yor* 2A **100**
Eastney. *Port* 3E **17**
Eastnor. *Here* 2C **48**
East Norton. *Leics* 5E **75**
East Nynehead. *Som* 4E **21**
East Oakley. *Hants* 1D **24**
Eastoft. *N Lin* 3B **94**
East Ogwell. *Devn* 5B **12**
Easton. *Cambs* 3A **64**
Easton. *Cumb*
. . . . . nr. Burgh by Sands 4D **112**
. . . . . nr. Longtown 2F **113**
Easton. *Devn* 4H **11**
Easton. *Dors* 5B **14**
Easton. *Hants* 3D **24**
Easton. *Linc* 3G **75**
Easton. *Norf* 4D **78**
Easton. *Som* 2A **22**
Easton. *Suff* 5E **67**
Easton. *Wilts* 4D **35**
Easton Grey. *Wilts* 3D **35**
Easton-in-Gordano. *N Som* 4A **34**
Easton Maudit. *Nptn* 5F **63**
Easton on the Hill. *Nptn* 5H **75**
Easton Royal. *Wilts* 5H **35**
East Orchard. *Dors* 1D **14**
East Ord. *Nmbd* 4F **131**
East Panson. *Devn* 3D **10**
East Peckham. *Kent* 1A **28**
East Pennard. *Som* 3A **22**
East Perry. *Cambs* 4A **64**
East Pitcorthie. *Fife* 3H **137**
East Portlemouth. *Devn* 5D **8**
East Prawle. *Devn* 5D **9**
East Preston. *W Sus* 5B **26**
East Putford. *Devn* 1D **10**
East Quantoxhead. *Som* 2E **21**
East Rainton. *Tyne* 5G **115**
East Ravendale. *NE Lin* 1B **88**
East Raynham. *Norf* 3A **78**
Eastrea. *Cambs* 1B **64**
East Rhidorroch Lodge.
. . . . *High* 4G **163**
Eastriggs. *Dum* 3D **112**
East Rigton. *W Yor* 5F **99**
Eastrington. *E Yor* 2A **94**
East Rounton. *N Yor* 4B **106**
East Row. *N Yor* 3F **107**
East Rudham. *Norf* 3H **77**
East Runton. *Norf* 1D **78**
East Ruston. *Norf* 3F **79**
Eastry. *Kent* 5H **41**
East Saltoun. *E Lot* 3A **130**
East Shaws. *Dur* 3D **105**
East Shefford. *W Ber* 4B **36**
Eastshore. *Shet* 10E **173**
East Sleekburn. *Nmbd* 1F **115**
East Somerton. *Norf* 4G **79**
East Stockwith. *Linc* 1E **87**
East Stoke. *Dors* 4D **14**
East Stoke. *Notts* 1E **75**
East Stoke. *Som* 1H **13**
East Stour. *Dors* 4D **22**
East Stourmouth. *Kent* 4G **41**
East Stowford. *Devn* 4G **19**
East Stratton. *Hants* 2D **24**
East Studdal. *Kent* 1H **29**
East Taphouse. *Corn* 2F **7**
East-the-Water. *Devn* 4E **19**
East Thirston. *Nmbd* 5F **121**
East Tilbury. *Thur* 3A **40**
East Tisted. *Hants* 3F **25**
East Torrington. *Linc* 2A **88**

East Tuddenham. *Norf* 4C **78**
East Tytherley. *Hants* 4A **24**
East Tytherton. *Wilts* 4E **35**
East Village. *Devn* 2B **12**
Eastville. *Linc* 5D **88**
East Wall. *Shrp* 1H **59**
East Walton. *Norf* 4G **77**
East Week. *Devn* 3G **11**
Eastwell. *Leics* 3E **75**
East Wellow. *Hants* 4B **24**
East Wemyss. *Fife* 4F **137**
East Whitburn. *W Lot* 3C **128**
Eastwick. *Herts* 4E **53**
Eastwick. *Shet* 4E **173**
East Williamston. *Pemb* 4E **43**
East Winch. *Norf* 4F **77**
East Winterslow. *Wilts* 3H **23**
East Wittering. *W Sus* 3F **17**
East Witton. *N Yor* 1D **98**
Eastwood. *Notts* 1B **74**
Eastwood. *S'end* 2C **40**
East Woodburn. *Nmbd* 1C **114**
Eastwood End. *Cambs* 1D **64**
East Woodhay. *Hants* 5C **36**
East Woodlands. *Som* 2C **22**
East Worldham. *Hants* 3F **25**
East Worlington. *Devn* 1A **12**
East Wretham. *Norf* 1B **66**
East Youlstone. *Devn* 1C **10**
Eathorpe. *Warw* 4A **62**
Eaton. *Ches E* 4C **84**
Eaton. *Ches W* 4H **83**
Eaton. *Leics* 3E **75**
Eaton. *Norf*
. . . . . nr. Heacham 2F **77**
. . . . . nr. Norwich 5E **78**
Eaton. *Notts* 3E **86**
Eaton. *Oxon* 5C **50**
Eaton. *Shrp*
. . . . . nr. Bishop's Castle 2F **59**
. . . . . nr. Church Stretton 2H **59**
Eaton Bishop. *Here* 2H **47**
Eaton Bray. *C Beds* 3H **51**
Eaton Constantine. *Shrp* 5H **71**
Eaton Hastings. *Oxon* 2A **36**
Eaton Socon. *Cambs* 5A **64**
Eaton upon Tern. *Shrp* 3A **72**
Eau Brink. *Norf* 4E **77**
Eaves Green. *W Mid* 2G **61**
Ebberley Hill. *Devn* 1F **11**
Ebberston. *N Yor* 1C **100**
Ebbesbourne Wake.
. . . . *Wilts* 4E **23**
Ebblake. *Dors* 2G **15**
Ebbsfleet. *Kent* 3H **39**
Ebbw Vale. *Blae* 5E **47**
Ebchester. *Dur* 4E **115**
Ebernoe. *W Sus* 3A **26**
Ebford. *Devn* 4C **12**
Ebley. *Glos* 5D **48**
Ebnal. *Ches W* 1G **71**
Ebrington. *Glos* 1G **49**
Ecchinswell. *Hants* 1D **24**
Ecclefechan. *Dum* 2C **112**
Eccles. *G Man* 1B **84**
Eccles. *Kent* 4B **40**
Eccles. *Bord* 5D **130**
Ecclesall. *S Yor* 2H **85**
Ecclesfield. *S Yor* 1A **86**
Eccles Green. *Here* 1G **47**
Eccleshall. *Staf* 3C **72**
Eccleshill. *W Yor* 1B **92**
Ecclesmachan. *W Lot* 2D **128**
Eccles on Sea. *Norf* 3G **79**
Eccles Road. *Norf* 1C **66**
Eccleston. *Ches W* 4G **83**
Eccleston. *Lanc* 3D **90**
Eccleston. *Mers* 1G **83**
Eccup. *W Yor* 5E **99**
Echt. *Abers* 3E **153**
Eckford. *Bord* 2B **120**
Eckington. *Derbs* 3B **86**
Eckington. *Worc* 1E **49**
Ecton. *Nptn* 4F **63**
Edale. *Derbs* 2F **85**
Eday Airport. *Orkn* 4E **172**
Edburton. *W Sus* 4D **26**
Edderside. *Cumb* 5C **112**
Edderton. *High* 5E **164**
Eddington. *Kent* 4F **41**
Eddington. *W Ber* 5B **36**
Eddleston. *Bord* 5F **129**
Eddlewood. *S Lan* 4A **128**
Edenbridge. *Kent* 1F **27**
Edendonich. *Arg* 1A **134**
Edenfield. *Lanc* 3F **91**
Edenhall. *Cumb* 1G **103**
Edenham. *Linc* 3H **75**
Edensor. *Derbs* 3G **85**
Edentaggart. *Arg* 4C **134**
Edenthorpe. *S Yor* 4G **93**
Eden Vale. *Dur* 1B **106**
Edern. *Gwyn* 2B **68**
Edgarley. *Som* 3A **22**
Edgbaston. *W Mid* 2E **61**
Edgcott. *Buck* 3E **51**
Edgcott. *Som* 3B **20**
Edge. *Glos* 5D **48**
Edge. *Shrp* 5F **71**
Edgebolton. *Shrp* 3H **71**
Edge End. *Glos* 4A **48**
Edgefield. *Norf* 2C **78**
Edgefield Street. *Norf* 2C **78**
Edge Green. *Ches W* 5G **83**
Edgehead. *Midl* 3G **129**
Edgeley. *Shrp* 1H **71**
Edgeside. *Lanc* 2G **91**
Edgeworth. *Glos* 5E **49**
Edgiock. *Worc* 4E **61**
Edgmond. *Telf* 4B **72**
Edgmond Marsh. *Telf* 3B **72**

Edgton—Farnborough

Edgton. Shrp 2F 59
Edgware. G Lon 1C 38
Edgworth. Bkbn 3F 91
Edinbane. High 3C 154
Edinburgh. Edin 194 (2F 129)
Edinburgh Airport. Edin 2E 129
Edingale. Staf 4G 73
Edingley. Notts 5D 86
Edingthorpe. Norf 2F 79
Edington. Som 3G 21
Edington. Wilts 1E 23
Edingworth. Som 1G 21
Edistone. Devn 4C 18
Edithmead. Som 2G 21
Edith Weston. Rut 5G 75
Edlaston. Derbs 1F 73
Edlesborough. Buck 4H 51
Edlingham. Nmbd 4F 121
Edlington. Linc 3B 88
Edmondsham. Dors 1F 15
Edmondsley. Dur 5F 115
Edmondthorpe. Leics 4F 75
Edmonstone. Orkn 5E 172
Edmonton. Corn 1D 6
Edmonton. G Lon 1E 39
Edmundbyers. Dur 4D 114
Ednam. Bord 1B 120
Ednaston. Derbs 1G 73
Edney Common. Essx 5G 53
Edrom. Bord 4E 131
Edstaston. Shrp 2H 71
Edstone. Warw 4F 61
Edwalton. Notts 2C 74
Edwardstone. Suff 1C 54
Edwardsville. Mer T 2D 32
Edwinsford. Carm 2G 45
Edwinstowe. Notts 4D 86
Edworth. C Beds 1C 52
Edwyn Ralph. Here 5A 60
Edzell. Ang 2F 145
Efail-fach. Neat 2A 32
Efail Isaf. Rhon 3D 32
Efailnewydd. Gwyn 2C 68
Efail-rhyd. Powy 3D 70
Efailwen. Carm 2F 43
Efenechtyd. Den 5D 82
Effingham. Surr 5C 38
Effingham Common. Surr 5C 38
Effirth. Shet 6E 173
Efflinch. Staf 4F 73
Efford. Devn 2B 12
Efstigarth. Shet 2F 173
Egbury. Hants 1C 24
Egdon. Worc 5D 60
Egerton. G Man 3F 91
Egerton. Kent 1D 28
Egerton Forstal. Kent 1C 28
Eggborough. N Yor 2F 93
Eggbuckland. Plym 3A 8
Eggesford. Devn 1G 11
Eggington. C Beds 3H 51
Egginton. Derbs 3G 73
Egglescliffe. Stoc T 3B 106
Eggleston. Dur 2C 104
Egham. Surr 3B 38
Egham Hythe. Surr 3B 38
Egleton. Rut 5F 75
Eglingham. Nmbd 3F 121
Egloshayle. Corn 5A 10
Egloskerry. Corn 4C 10
Eglwysbach. Cnwy 3H 81
Eglwys-Brewis. V Glam 5D 32
Eglwys Fach. Cdgn 1F 57
Eglwyswrw. Pemb 1F 43
Egmanton. Notts 4E 87
Egmere. Norf 2B 78
Egremont. Cumb 3B 102
Egremont. Mers 1F 83
Egton. N Yor 4F 107
Egton Bridge. N Yor 4F 107
Egypt. Buck 2A 38
Egypt. Hants 2C 24
Eight Ash Green. Essx 3C 54
Eight Mile Burn. Midl 4E 129
Eignaig. High 4B 140
Eilanreach. High 2G 147
Eildon. Bord 1H 119
Eileanach Lodge. High 2H 157
Eilean Fhlodaigh. W Isl 3D 170
Eilean Iarmain. High 2F 147
Einacleit. W Isl 5D 171
Eisgein. W Isl 6F 171
Eisingrug. Gwyn 2F 69
Elan Village. Powy 4B 58
Elberton. S Glo 3B 34
Elbridge. W Sus 5A 26
Elburton. Plym 3B 8
Elcho. Per 1D 136
Elcombe. Swin 3G 35
Elcot. W Ber 5B 36
Eldernell. Cambs 1C 64
Eldersfield. Worc 2D 48
Elderslie. Ren 3F 127
Elder Street. Essx 2F 53
Eldon. Dur 2F 105
Eldroth. N Yor 3G 97
Eldwick. W Yor 5D 98
Elfhowe. Cumb 5F 103
Elford. Nmbd 1F 121
Elford. Staf 4F 73
Elford Closes. Cambs 3D 65
Elgin. Mor 2G 159
Elgol. High 2D 146
Elham. Kent 1F 29
Elie. Fife 3G 137
Eling. Hants 1B 16
Eling. W Ber 4D 36
Elishaw. Nmbd 5C 120
Elizafield. Dum 2B 112
Elkesley. Notts 3D 86
Elkington. Nptn 3D 62
Elkins Green. Essx 5G 53
Elkstone. Glos 4E 49
Ellan. High 1C 150
Elland. W Yor 2B 92
Ellary. Arg 2F 125
Ellastone. Staf 1F 73
Ellbridge. Corn 2A 8
Ellel. Lanc 4D 97
Ellemford. Bord 3D 130
Ellenabeich. Arg 2E 133
Ellenborough. Cumb 1B 102
Ellenbrook. Herts 5C 52
Ellenhall. Staf 3C 72
Ellen's Green. Surr 2B 26
Ellerbeck. N Yor 5B 106
Ellerburn. N Yor 1C 100
Ellerby. N Yor 3E 107
Ellerdine. Telf 3A 72
Ellerdine Heath. Telf 3A 72
Ellerhayes. Devn 2C 12
Elleric. Arg 4E 141
Ellerker. E Yor 2C 94
Ellerton. E Yor 1H 93
Ellerton. Shrp 3B 72
Ellerton-on-Swale. N Yor 5F 105
Ellesborough. Buck 5G 51
Ellesmere. Shrp 2G 71
Ellesmere Port. Ches W 3G 83
Ellingham. Hants 2G 15
Ellingham. Norf 1F 67
Ellingham. Nmbd 2F 121
Ellingstring. N Yor 1D 98
Ellington. Cambs 3A 64
Ellington. Nmbd 5G 121
Ellington Thorpe. Cambs 3A 64
Elliot. Ang 5F 145
Ellisfield. Hants 2E 25
Ellishadder. High 2E 155
Ellistown. Leics 4B 74
Ellon. Abers 5G 161
Ellonby. Cumb 1F 103
Ellough. Suff 2G 67
Elloughton. E Yor 2C 94
Ellwood. Glos 5A 48
Elm. Cambs 5D 76
Elmbridge. Glos 4D 48
Elmbridge. Worc 4D 60
Elmdon. Essx 2E 53
Elmdon. W Mid 2F 61
Elmdon Heath. W Mid 2F 61
Elmesthorpe. Leics 1B 62
Elmfield. IOW 3E 16
Elm Hill. Dors 4D 22
Elmhurst. Staf 4F 73
Elmley Castle. Worc 1E 49
Elmley Lovett. Worc 4C 60
Elmore. Glos 4C 48
Elmore Back. Glos 4C 48
Elm Park. G Lon 2G 39
Elmscott. Devn 4C 18
Elmsett. Suff 1D 54
Elmstead. Essx 3D 54
Elmstead Heath. Essx 3D 54
Elmstead Market. Essx 3D 54
Elmsted. Kent 1F 29
Elmstone. Kent 4G 41
Elmstone Hardwicke. Glos 3E 49
Elmswell. E Yor 4D 101
Elmswell. Suff 4B 66
Elmton. Derbs 3C 86
Elphin. High 2G 163
Elphinstone. E Lot 2G 129
Elrick. Abers 3F 153
Elrick. Mor 1B 152
Elrig. Dum 5A 110
Elsdon. Nmbd 5D 120
Elsecar. S Yor 1A 86
Elsenham. Essx 3F 53
Elsfield. Oxon 4D 50
Elsham. N Lin 3D 94
Elsing. Norf 4C 78
Elslack. N Yor 5B 98
Elsrickle. S Lan 5D 128
Elstead. Surr 1A 26
Elsted. W Sus 1G 17
Elsted Marsh. W Sus 4G 25
Elsthorpe. Linc 3H 75
Elstob. Dur 2A 106
Elston. Devn 2A 12
Elston. Lanc 1E 90
Elston. Notts 1E 75
Elston. Wilts 2F 23
Elstone. Devn 1G 11
Elstow. Bed 1A 52
Elstree. Herts 1C 38
Elstronwick. E Yor 1F 95
Elswick. Lanc 1C 90
Elswick. Tyne 3F 115
Elsworth. Cambs 4C 64
Elterwater. Cumb 4E 103
Eltham. G Lon 3F 39
Eltisley. Cambs 5B 64
Elton. Cambs 1H 63
Elton. Ches W 3G 83
Elton. Derbs 4G 85
Elton. Glos 4C 48
Elton. G Man 3F 91
Elton. Here 3G 59
Elton. Notts 2E 75
Elton. Stoc T 3B 106
Elton Green. Ches W 3G 83
Eltringham. Nmbd 3D 115
Elvanfoot. S Lan 3B 118
Elvaston. Derbs 2B 74
Elveden. Suff 3H 65
Elvetham Heath. Hants 1F 25
Elvingston. E Lot 2A 130
Elvington. Kent 5G 41
Elvington. York 5B 100
Elwick. Hart 1B 106
Elwick. Nmbd 1F 121
Elworth. Ches E 4B 84
Elworth. Dors 4A 14
Elworthy. Som 3D 20
Ely. Cambs 2E 65
Ely. Card 4E 33
Emberton. Mil 1G 51
Embleton. Cumb 1C 102
Embleton. Hart 2B 106
Embleton. Nmbd 2G 121
Embo. High 4F 165
Emborough. Som 1B 22
Embo Street. High 4F 165
Embsay. N Yor 4C 98
Emery Down. Hants 2A 16
Emley. W Yor 3C 92
Emmbrook. Wok 5F 37
Emmer Green. Read 4F 37
Emmington. Oxon 5F 51
Emneth. Norf 5D 77
Emneth Hungate. Norf 5E 77
Empingham. Rut 5G 75
Empshott. Hants 3F 25
Emsworth. Hants 2F 17
Enborne. W Ber 5C 36
Enborne Row. W Ber 5C 36
Enchmarsh. Shrp 1H 59
Enderby. Leics 1C 62
Endmoor. Cumb 1E 97
Endon. Staf 5D 84
Endon Bank. Staf 5D 84
Enfield. G Lon 1E 39
Enfield Wash. G Lon 1E 39
Enford. Wilts 1G 23
Engine Common. S Glo 3B 34
Englefield. W Ber 4E 37
Englefield Green. Surr 3A 38
Englesea-brook. Ches E 5B 84
English Bicknor. Glos 4A 48
Englishcombe. Bath 5C 34
English Frankton. Shrp 3G 71
Enham Alamein. Hants 2B 24
Enmore. Som 3F 21
Ennerdale Bridge. Cumb 3B 102
Enniscaven. Corn 3D 6
Enoch. Dum 4A 118
Enochdhu. Per 2H 143
Ensay. Arg 4E 139
Ensbury. Bour 3F 15
Ensdon. Shrp 4G 71
Ensis. Devn 4F 19
Enson. Staf 3D 72
Enstone. Oxon 3B 50
Enterkinfoot. Dum 4A 118
Enville. Staf 2C 60
Eolaigearraidh. W Isl 8C 170
Eorabus. Arg 1A 132
Eoropaidh. W Isl 1H 171
Epney. Glos 4C 48
Epperstone. Notts 1D 74
Epping. Essx 5E 53
Epping Green. Essx 5E 53
Epping Green. Herts 5C 52
Epping Upland. Essx 5E 53
Eppleby. N Yor 3E 105
Eppleworth. E Yor 1D 94
Epsom. Surr 4D 38
Epwell. Oxon 1B 50
Epworth. N Lin 4A 94
Epworth Turbary. N Lin 4A 94
Erbistock. Wrex 1F 71
Erbusaig. High 1F 147
Erchless Castle. High 4G 157
Erdington. W Mid 1F 61
Eredine. Arg 3G 133
Eriboll. High 3E 167
Ericstane. Dum 3C 118
Eridge Green. E Sus 2G 27
Erines. Arg 2G 125
Eriswell. Suff 3G 65
Erith. G Lon 3G 39
Erlestoke. Wilts 1E 23
Ermine. Linc 3G 87
Ermington. Devn 3C 8
Ernesettle. Plym 3A 8
Erpingham. Norf 2D 78
Erriott Wood. Kent 5D 40
Errogie. High 1H 149
Errol. Per 1E 137
Errol Station. Per 1E 137
Erskine. Ren 2F 127
Erskine Bridge. Ren 2F 127
Ervie. Dum 3F 109
Erwarton. Suff 2F 55
Erwood. Powy 1D 46
Eryholme. N Yor 4A 106
Eryrys. Den 5E 82
Escalls. Corn 4A 4
Escomb. Dur 1E 105
Escrick. N Yor 5A 100
Esgair. Carm
nr. Carmarthen 3D 45
nr. St Clears 3G 43
Esgairgeiliog. Powy 5G 69
Esh. Dur 5E 115
Esher. Surr 4C 38
Esholt. W Yor 5D 98
Eshott. Nmbd 5G 121
Eshton. N Yor 4B 98
Esh Winning. Dur 5E 115
Eskadale. High 5G 157
Eskbank. Midl 3G 129
Eskdale Green. Cumb 4C 102
Eskdalemuir. Dum 5E 119
Eskham. Linc 1C 88
Esknish. Arg 3B 124
Esk Valley. N Yor 4F 107
Eslington Hall. Nmbd 3E 121
Esprick. Lanc 1C 90
Essendine. Rut 4H 75
Essendon. Herts 5C 52
Essich. High 5A 158
Essington. Staf 5D 72
Eston. Red C 3C 106
Estover. Plym 3B 8
Eswick. Shet 6F 173
Etal. Nmbd 1D 120
Etchilhampton. Wilts 5F 35
Etchingham. E Sus 3B 28
Etchinghill. Kent 2F 29
Etchinghill. Staf 4E 73
Etherley Dene. Dur 2E 105
Ethie Haven. Ang 4F 145
Etling Green. Norf 4C 78
Etloe. Glos 5B 48
Eton. Wind 3A 38
Eton Wick. Wind 3A 38
Etteridge. High 4A 150
Ettersgill. Dur 2B 104
Ettiley Heath. Ches E 4B 84
Ettington. Warw 1A 50
Etton. E Yor 5D 101
Etton. Pet 5A 76
Ettrick. Bord 3E 119
Ettrickbridge. Bord 2F 119
Etwall. Derbs 2G 73
Eudon Burnell. Shrp 2B 60
Eudon George. Shrp 2A 60
Euston. Suff 3A 66
Euxton. Lanc 3D 90
Evanstown. B'end 3C 32
Evanton. High 2A 158
Evedon. Linc 1H 75
Evelix. High 4E 165
Evendine. Here 1C 48
Evenjobb. Powy 4E 59
Evenley. Nptn 2D 50
Evenlode. Glos 3H 49
Even Swindon. Swin 3G 35
Evenwood. Dur 2E 105
Evenwood Gate. Dur 2E 105
Everbay. Orkn 5F 172
Evercreech. Som 3B 22
Everdon. Nptn 5C 62
Everingham. E Yor 5C 100
Everleigh. Wilts 1H 23
Everley. N Yor 1D 100
Eversholt. C Beds 2H 51
Evershot. Dors 2A 14
Eversley. Hants 5F 37
Eversley Centre. Hants 5F 37
Eversley Cross. Hants 5F 37
Everthorpe. E Yor 1C 94
Everton. C Beds 5B 64
Everton. Hants 3A 16
Everton. Mers 1F 83
Everton. Notts 1D 86
Evertown. Dum 2E 113
Evesbatch. Here 1B 48
Evesham. Worc 1F 49
Evington. Leic 5D 74
Ewden Village. S Yor 1G 85
Ewdness. Shrp 1B 60
Ewell. Surr 4D 38
Ewell Minnis. Kent 1G 29
Ewelme. Oxon 2E 37
Ewen. Glos 2F 35
Ewenny. V Glam 4C 32
Ewerby. Linc 1A 76
Ewes. Dum 5F 119
Ewesley. Nmbd 5E 121
Ewhurst. Surr 1B 26
Ewhurst Green. E Sus 3B 28
Ewhurst Green. Surr 2B 26
Ewlo. Flin 4E 83
Ewloe. Flin 4E 83
Ewood Bridge. Lanc 2F 91
Eworthy. Devn 3E 11
Ewshot. Hants 1G 25
Ewyas Harold. Here 3G 47
Exbourne. Devn 2G 11
Exbury. Hants 2C 16
Exceat. E Sus 5G 27
Exebridge. Som 4C 20
Exelby. N Yor 1E 99
Exeter. Devn 195 (3C 12)
Exeter Airport. Devn 3D 12
Exford. Som 3B 20
Exfords Green. Shrp 5G 71
Exhall. Warw 5F 61
Exlade Street. Oxon 3E 37
Exminster. Devn 4C 12
Exmouth. Devn 4D 12
Exnaboe. Shet 10E 173
Exning. Suff 4F 65
Exton. Devn 4C 12
Exton. Hants 4E 24
Exton. Rut 4G 75
Exton. Som 3C 20
Exwick. Devn 3C 12
Eyam. Derbs 3G 85
Eydon. Nptn 5C 62
Eye. Here 4G 59
Eye. Pet 5B 76
Eye. Suff 3D 66
Eye Green. Pet 5B 76
Eyemouth. Bord 3F 131
Eyeworth. C Beds 1C 52
Eyhorne Street. Kent 5C 40
Eyke. Suff 5F 67
Eynesbury. Cambs 5A 64
Eynort. High 1B 146
Eynsford. Kent 4G 39
Eynsham. Oxon 5C 50
Eyre. High
on Isle of Skye 3D 154
on Raasay 5E 155
Eythorne. Kent 1G 29
Eyton. Here 4G 59
Eyton. Shrp
nr. Bishop's Castle 2F 59
nr. Shrewsbury 4F 71
Eyton. Wrex 1F 71
Eyton on Severn. Shrp 5H 71
Eyton upon the Weald Moors. Telf 4A 72

F

Faccombe. Hants 1B 24
Faceby. N Yor 4B 106
Faddiley. Ches E 5H 83
Fadmoor. N Yor 1A 100
Fagwyr. Swan 5G 45
Faichem. High 3E 149
Faifley. W Dun 2G 127
Fail. S Ayr 2D 116
Failand. N Som 4A 34
Failford. S Ayr 2D 116
Failsworth. G Man 4H 91
Fairbourne. Gwyn 4F 69
Fairbourne Heath. Kent 5C 40
Fairburn. N Yor 2E 93
Fairfield. Derbs 3E 85
Fairfield. Kent 3D 28
Fairfield. Worc
nr. Bromsgrove 3D 60
nr. Evesham 1F 49
Fairford. Glos 5G 49
Fair Green. Norf 4F 77
Fair Hill. Cumb 1G 103
Fairhill. S Lan 4A 128
Fair Isle Airport. Shet 1B 172
Fairlands. Surr 5A 38
Fairlie. N Ayr 4D 126
Fairlight. E Sus 4C 28
Fairlight Cove. E Sus 4C 28
Fairmile. Devn 3D 12
Fairmile. Surr 4C 38
Fairmilehead. Edin 3F 129
Fair Oak. Devn 1D 12
Fair Oak. Hants
nr. Eastleigh 1C 16
nr. Kingsclere 5D 36
Fairoak. Staf 2B 72
Fair Oak Green. Hants 5E 37
Fairseat. Kent 4H 39
Fairstead. Essx 4A 54
Fairstead. Norf 4F 77
Fairwarp. E Sus 3F 27
Fairwater. Card 4E 33
Fairy Cross. Devn 4E 19
Fakenham. Norf 2B 78
Fakenham Magna. Suff 3B 66
Fala. Midl 3H 129
Fala Dam. Midl 3H 129
Falcon. Here 2B 48
Faldingworth. Linc 2H 87
Falfield. S Glo 2B 34
Y Fali. IOA 3B 80
Falkenham. Suff 2F 55
Falkirk. Falk 1B 128
Falkland. Fife 3E 137
Fallin. Stir 4H 135
Fallowfield. G Man 1C 84
Falmer. E Sus 5E 27
Falmouth. Corn 5C 6
Falsgrave. N Yor 1E 101
Falstone. Nmbd 1A 114
Fanagmore. High 4B 166
Fancott. C Beds 3A 52
Fanellan. High 4G 157
Fangdale Beck. N Yor 5C 106
Fangfoss. E Yor 4B 100
Fankerton. Falk 1A 128
Fanmore. Arg 4F 139
Fanner's Green. Essx 4G 53
Fannich Lodge. High 2E 156
Fans. Bord 5C 130
Farcet. Cambs 1B 64
Far Cotton. Nptn 5E 63
Fareham. Hants 2D 16
Farewell. Staf 4E 73
Far Forest. Worc 3B 60
Farforth. Linc 3C 88
Far Green. Glos 5C 48
Far Hoarcross. Staf 3F 73
Faringdon. Oxon 2A 36
Farington. Lanc 2D 90
Farlam. Cumb 4G 113
Farleigh. N Som 5H 33
Farleigh. Surr 4E 39
Farleigh Hungerford. Som 1D 22
Farleigh Wallop. Hants 2E 24
Farleigh Wick. Wilts 5D 34
Farlesthorpe. Linc 3D 88
Farleton. Cumb 1E 97
Farleton. Lanc 3E 97
Farley. High 4G 157
Farley. Shrp
nr. Shrewsbury 5F 71
nr. Telford 5A 72
Farley. Staf 1E 73
Farley. Wilts 4H 23
Farley Green. Suff 5G 65
Farley Green. Surr 1B 26
Farley Hill. Wok 5F 37
Farley's End. Glos 4C 48
Farlington. N Yor 3A 100
Farlington. Port 2E 17
Farlow. Shrp 2A 60
Farmborough. Bath 5B 34
Farmcote. Glos 3F 49
Farmcote. Shrp 1B 60
Farmington. Glos 4D 49
Far Moor. G Man 4D 90
Farmoor. Oxon 5C 50
Farmtown. Mor 3C 160
Farnah Green. Derbs 1H 73
Farnborough. G Lon 4F 39
Farnborough. Hants 1G 25
Farnborough. Warw 1C 50
Farnborough. W Ber 3C 36

Farncombe. Surr 1A 26
Farndish. Bed 4G 63
Farndon. Ches W 5G 83
Farndon. Notts 5E 87
Farnell. Ang 3F 145
Farnham. Dors 1E 15
Farnham. Essx 3E 53
Farnham. N Yor 3F 99
Farnham. Suff 4F 67
Farnham. Surr 2G 25
Farnham Common. Buck 2A 38
Farnham Green. Essx 3E 53
Farnham Royal. Buck 2A 38
Farnhill. N Yor 5C 98
Farningham. Kent 4G 39
Farnley. N Yor 5E 98
Farnley Tyas. W Yor 3B 92
Farnsfield. Notts 5D 86
Farnworth. G Man 4F 91
Farnworth. Hal 2H 83
Far Oakridge. Glos 5E 49
Farr. High
  nr. Bettyhill 2H 167
  nr. Inverness 5A 158
  nr. Kingussie 3C 150
Farraline. High 1H 149
Farringdon. Devn 3D 12
Farrington. Dors 1D 14
Farrington Gurney. Bath 1B 22
Far Sawrey. Cumb 5E 103
Farsley. W Yor 1C 92
Farthinghoe. Nptn 2D 50
Farthingstone. Nptn 5D 62
Farthorpe. Linc 3B 88
Fartown. W Yor 3B 92
Farway. Devn 3E 13
Fasag. High 3A 156
Fascadale. High 1G 139
Fasnacloich. Arg 4E 141
Fassfern. High 1E 141
Fatfield. Tyne 4G 115
Faugh. Cumb 4G 113
Fauld. Staf .3F 73
Fauldhouse. W Lot 3C 128
Faulkbourne. Essx 4A 54
Faulkland. Som 1C 22
Fauls. Shrp 2H 71
Faverdale. Darl 3F 105
Faversham. Kent 4E 40
Fawdington. N Yor 2G 99
Fawfieldhead. Staf 4E 85
Fawkham Green. Kent 4G 39
Fawler. Oxon 4B 50
Fawley. Buck 3F 37
Fawley. Hants 2C 16
Fawley. W Ber 3B 36
Fawley Chapel. Here 3A 48
Fawton. Corn 2F 7
Faxfleet. E Yor 2B 94
Faygate. W Sus 2D 26
Fazakerley. Mers 1F 83
Fazeley. Staf 5F 73
Feagour. High 4H 149
Fearann Dhomhnaill. High 3E 147
Fearby. N Yor 1D 98
Fearn. High 1C 158
Fearnan. Per 4E 142
Fearnbeg. High 3G 155
Fearnhead. Warr 1A 84
Fearnmore. High 2G 155
Featherstone. Staf 5D 72
Featherstone. W Yor 2E 93
Featherstone Castle. Nmbd 3H 113
Feckenham. Worc 4E 61
Feering. Essx 3B 54
Feetham. N Yor 5C 104
Feizor. N Yor 3G 97
Felbridge. Surr 2E 27
Felbrigg. Norf 2E 78
Felcourt. Surr 1E 27
Felden. Herts 5A 52
Felhampton. Shrp 2G 59
Felindre. Carm
  nr. Llandeilo 3F 45
  nr. Llandovery 2G 45
  nr. Newcastle Emlyn 2D 44
Felindre. Powy 2D 58
Felindre. Swan 5G 45
Felindre Farchog. Pemb 1F 43
Felinfach. Cdgn 5E 57
Felinfach. Powy 2D 46
Felinfoel. Carm 5F 45
Felingwmisaf. Carm 3F 45
Felingwmuchaf. Carm 3F 45
Y Felinheli. Gwyn 4E 81
Felin Newydd. Powy
  nr. Newtown 5C 70
  nr. Oswestry 3E 70
Felin Wnda. Cdgn 1D 44
Felixkirk. N Yor 1G 99
Felixstowe. Suff 2F 55
Felixstowe Ferry. Suff 2G 55
Felkington. Nmbd 5F 131
Fell End. Cumb 5A 104
Felling. Tyne 3F 115
Fell Side. Cumb 1E 102
Felmersham. Bed 5G 63
Felmingham. Norf 3E 79
Felpham. W Sus 3H 17
Felsham. Suff 5B 66
Felsted. Essx 3G 53
Feltham. G Lon 3C 38
Felthamhill. Surr 3B 38
Felthorpe. Norf 4D 78
Felton. Here 1A 48
Felton. N Som 5A 34
Felton. Nmbd 4F 121
Felton Butler. Shrp 4F 71
Feltwell. Norf 1G 65
Fenay Bridge. W Yor 3B 92

Fence. Lanc 1G 91
Fence Houses. Tyne 4G 115
Fencott. Oxon 4D 50
Fen Ditton. Cambs 4D 65
Fen Drayton. Cambs 4C 64
Fen End. Linc 3B 76
Fen End. W Mid 3G 61
Fenham. Nmbd 5G 131
Fenham. Tyne 3F 115
Fenhouses. Linc 1B 76
Feniscowles. Bkbn 2E 91
Feniton. Devn 3D 12
Fenn Green. Shrp 2B 60
Y Fenni. Mon 4G 47
Fenn's Bank. Wrex 2H 71
Fenn Street. Medw 3B 40
Fenny Bentley. Derbs 5F 85
Fenny Bridges. Devn 3E 12
Fenny Compton. Warw 5B 62
Fenny Drayton. Leics 1H 61
Fenny Stratford. Mil 2G 51
Fenrother. Nmbd 5F 121
Fenstanton. Cambs 4C 64
Fen Street. Norf 1C 66
Fenton. Cambs 3C 64
Fenton. Cumb 4G 113
Fenton. Linc
  nr. Caythorpe 5F 87
  nr. Saxilby 3F 87
Fenton. Nmbd 1D 120
Fenton. Notts 2E 87
Fenton. Stoke 1C 72
Fentonadle. Corn 5A 10
Fenton Barns. E Lot 1B 130
Fenwick. E Ayr 5F 127
Fenwick. Nmbd
  nr. Berwick-upon-Tweed 5G 131
  nr. Hexham 2D 114
Fenwick. S Yor 3F 93
Feochaig. Arg 4B 122
Feock. Corn 5C 6
Feolin Ferry. Arg 3C 124
Feorlan. Arg 5A 122
Ferindonald. High 3E 147
Feriniquarrie. High 3A 154
Fern. Ang 2D 145
Ferndale. Rhon 2C 32
Ferndown. Dors 2F 15
Ferness. High 4D 158
Fernham. Oxon 2A 36
Fernhill. W Sus 1E 27
Fernhill Heath. Worc 5C 60
Fernhurst. W Sus 4G 25
Fernieflatt. Abers 1H 145
Ferniegair. S Lan 4A 128
Fernilea. High 5C 154
Fernilee. Derbs 3E 85
Ferrensby. N Yor 3F 99
Ferriby Sluice. N Lin 2C 94
Ferring. W Sus 5B 26
Ferrybridge. W Yor 2E 93
Ferryden. Ang 3G 145
Ferryhill. Aber 3G 153
Ferry Hill. Cambs 2C 64
Ferryhill. Dur 1F 105
Ferryhill Station. Dur 1A 106
Ferryside. Carm 4D 44
Ferryton. High 2A 158
Fersfield. Norf 2C 66
Fersit. High .1A 142
Y Ferwig. Cdgn 1B 44
Feshiebridge. High 3C 150
Fetcham. Surr 5C 38
Fetterangus. Abers 3G 161
Fettercairn. Abers 1F 145
Fewcott. Oxon 3D 50
Fewston. N Yor 4D 98
Ffairfach. Carm 3G 45
Ffair Rhos. Cdgn 4G 57
Ffaldybrenin. Carm 1G 45
Ffarmers. Carm 1G 45
Ffawyddog. Powy 4F 47
Y Fflint. Flin 3E 83
Ffodun. Powy 5E 71
Ffont-y-gari. V Glam 5D 32
Y Ffor. Gwyn 2C 68
Fforest. Carm 5F 45
Fforest-fach. Swan 3F 31
Fforest Goch. Neat 5H 45
Ffostrasol. Cdgn 1D 44
Ffos-y-ffin. Cdgn 4D 56
Ffrith. Flin 5E 83
Ffwl-y-mwn. V Glam 5D 32
Ffynnon-ddrain. Carm 3E 45
Ffynnongroyw. Flin 2D 82
Ffynnon Gynydd. Powy 1E 47
Ffynnon-oer. Cdgn 5E 57
Fiag Lodge. High 1B 164
Fidden. Arg .2B 132
Fiddington. Glos 2E 49
Fiddington. Som 2F 21
Fiddleford. Dors 1D 14
Fiddlers Hamlet. Essx 5E 53
Field. Staf .2E 73
Field Assarts. Oxon 4B 50
Field Broughton. Cumb 1C 96
Field Dalling. Norf 2C 78
Field Head. Leics 5B 74
Fifehead Magdalen. Dors 4C 22
Fifehead Neville. Dors 1C 14
Fifehead St Quintin. Dors 1C 14
Fife Keith. Mor 3B 160
Fifield. Oxon 4H 49
Fifield. Wilts 1G 23
Fifield. Wind 3A 38
Fifield Bavant. Wilts 4F 23
Figheldean. Wilts 2G 23
Filands. Wilts 3E 35
Filby. Norf .4G 79
Filey. N Yor 1F 101
Filford. Dors 3H 13

Filgrave. Mil 1G 51
Filkins. Oxon 5H 49
Filleigh. Devn
  nr. Crediton 1H 11
  nr. South Molton 4G 19
Fillingham. Linc 2G 87
Fillongley. Warw 2G 61
Filton. S Glo 4B 34
Fimber. E Yor 3C 100
Finavon. Ang 3D 145
Fincham. Norf 5F 77
Finchampstead. Wok 5F 37
Fincharn. Arg 3G 133
Finchdean. Hants 1F 17
Finchingfield. Essx 2G 53
Finchley. G Lon 1D 38
Findern. Derbs 2H 73
Findhorn. Mor 2E 159
Findhorn Bridge. High 1C 150
Findochty. Mor 2B 160
Findo Gask. Per 1C 136
Findon. Abers 4G 153
Findon. W Sus 5C 26
Findon Mains. High 2A 158
Findon Valley. W Sus 5C 26
Finedon. Nptn 3G 63
Fingal Street. Suff 3E 66
Fingest. Buck 2F 37
Finghall. N Yor 1D 98
Fingland. Cumb 4D 112
Fingland. Dum 3G 117
Finglesham. Kent 5H 41
Fingringhoe. Essx 3D 54
Finiskaig. High 4A 148
Finmere. Oxon 2E 51
Finnart. Per 3C 142
Finningham. Suff 4C 66
Finningley. S Yor 1D 86
Finnygaud. Abers 3D 160
Finsbury. G Lon 2E 39
Finstall. Worc 4D 61
Finsthwaite. Cumb 1C 96
Finstock. Oxon 4B 50
Finstown. Orkn 6C 172
Fintry. Abers 3E 161
Fintry. D'dee 5D 144
Fintry. Stir .1H 127
Finton. C Beds 2A 52
Flitwick. C Beds 2A 52
Flixborough. N Lin 3B 94
Flixton. G Man 1B 84
Flixton. N Yor 2E 101
Flixton. Suff 2F 67
Flockton. W Yor 3C 92
Flodden. Nmbd 1D 120
Flodigarry. High 1D 154
Flood's Ferry. Cambs 1C 64
Flookburgh. Cumb 2C 96
Flordon. Norf 1D 66
Flore. Nptn .4D 62
Flotterton. Nmbd 4D 121
Flowton. Suff 1D 54
Flushing. Abers 4H 161
Flushing. Corn 5C 6
Fluxton. Devn 3D 12
Flyford Flavell. Worc 5D 61
Fobbing. Thur 2B 40
Fochabers. Mor 3H 159
Fochriw. Cphy 5E 46
Fockerby. N Lin 3B 94
Fodderty. High 3H 157
Foddington. Som 4A 22
Foel. Powy .4B 70
Foffarty. Ang 4D 144
Foggathorpe. E Yor 1A 94
Fogo. Bord .5D 130
Fogorig. Bord 5D 130
Foindle. High 4B 166
Folda. Ang .2A 144
Fole. Staf 2E 73
Foleshill. W Mid 2A 62
Foley Park. Worc 3C 60
Folke. Dors 1B 14
Folkestone. Kent 195 (2G 29)
Folkingham. Linc 2H 75
Folkington. E Sus 5G 27
Folksworth. Cambs 2A 64
Folkton. N Yor 2E 101
Folla Rule. Abers 5E 161
Follifoot. N Yor 4F 99
Folly, The. Herts 4B 52
Folly Cross. Devn 2E 11
Folly Gate. Devn 3F 11
Fonmon. V Glam 5D 32
Fonthill Bishop. Wilts 3E 23
Fonthill Gifford. Wilts 3E 23
Fontmell Magna. Dors 1D 14
Fontwell. W Sus 5A 26
Font-y-gary. V Glam 5D 32
Foodieash. Fife 2F 137
Foolow. Derbs 3F 85
Footdee. Aber 3G 153
Footherley. Staf 5F 73
Foots Cray. G Lon 3F 39
Forbestown. Abers 2A 152
Force Forge. Cumb 5E 103
Force Mills. Cumb 5E 103
Forcett. N Yor 3E 105
Ford. Arg 3F 133
Ford. Buck .5F 51
Ford. Derbs 2B 86
Ford. Devn
  nr. Bideford 4E 19
  nr. Holbeton 3C 8
  nr. Salcombe 4D 9
Ford. Nmbd 1D 120
Ford. Plym .3A 8
Ford. Shrp .4G 71
Ford. Som
  nr. Wells .1A 22
  nr. Wiveliscombe 4D 20

Flaunden. Herts 5A 52
Flawborough. Notts 1E 75
Flawith. N Yor 3G 99
Flax Bourton. N Som 5A 34
Flaxby. N Yor 4F 99
Flaxholme. Derbs 1H 73
Flaxley. Glos 4B 48
Flaxley Green. Staf 4E 73
Flaxpool. Som 3E 21
Flaxton. N Yor 3A 100
Fleck. Shet 10E 173
Fleckney. Leics 1D 62
Flecknoe. Warw 4C 62
Fledborough. Notts 3F 87
Fleet. Hants
  nr. Farnborough 1G 25
Fleet. Hants
  nr. South Hayling 2F 17
Fleet. Linc .3C 76
Fleet Hargate. Linc 3C 76
Fleetville. Herts 5B 52
Fleetwood. Lanc 5C 96
Fleggburgh. Norf 4G 79
Fleisirin. W Isl 4H 171
Flemingston. V Glam 5D 32
Flemington. S Lan
  nr. Glasgow 3H 127
  nr. Strathaven 5A 128
Flempton. Suff 4H 65
Fleoideabhagh. W Isl 9C 171
Fletcher's Green. Kent 1G 27
Fletchertown. Cumb 5D 112
Fletching. E Sus 3F 27
Fleuchary. High 4E 165
Flexbury. Corn 2C 10
Flexford. Surr 1A 26
Flimby. Cumb 1B 102
Flimwell. E Sus 2B 28
Flint. Flin 3E 83
Flintham. Notts 1E 75
Flint Mountain. Flin 3E 83
Flinton. E Yor 1F 95
Flintsham. Here 5F 59
Flishinghurst. Kent 2B 28
Flitcham. Norf 3G 77
Forgandenny. Per 2C 136
Forge, The. Here 5F 59
Forge. Powy 1G 57
Forge Side. Torf 5F 47
Forgewood. N Lan 4A 128
Forgie. Mor 3A 160
Forgue. Abers 4D 160
Formby. Mers 4B 90
Forncett End. Norf 1D 66
Forncett St Mary. Norf 1D 66
Forncett St Peter. Norf 1D 66
Forneth. Per 4H 143
Fornham All Saints. Suff 4H 65
Fornham St Martin. Suff 4A 66
Forres. Mor 3E 159
Forrestfield. N Lan 3B 128
Forrest Lodge. Dum 1C 110
Forsbrook. Staf 1D 72
Forse. High .5E 169
Forsinard. High 4A 168
Forss. High .2C 168
Forstal, The. Kent 2E 29
Forston. Dors 3B 14
Fort Augustus. High 3F 149
Forteviot. Per 2C 136
Fort George. High 3B 158
Forth. S Lan 4C 128
Forthampton. Glos 2D 48
Forthay. Glos 2C 34
Forth Road Bridge. Edin 2E 129
Fortingall. Per 4E 143
Fort Matilda. Inv 2D 126
Forton. Hants 2C 24
Forton. Lanc 4D 97
Forton. Shrp 4G 71
Forton. Som 2G 13
Forton. Staf 3B 72
Forton Heath. Shrp 4G 71
Fortrie. Abers 4D 160
Fortrose. High 3B 158
Fortuneswell. Dors 5B 14
Fort William. High 1F 141
Forty Green. Buck 1A 38
Forty Hill. G Lon 1E 39
Forward Green. Suff 5C 66
Fosbury. Wilts 1B 24
Foscot. Oxon 3H 49
Fosdyke. Linc 2C 76
Foss. Per 3E 143
Fossebridge. Glos 4F 49
Foster Street. Essx 5E 53
Foston. Derbs 2F 73
Foston. Leics 1D 62
Foston. Linc 1F 75
Foston. N Yor 3A 100
Foston on the Wolds. E Yor 4F 101
Fotherby. Linc 1C 88
Fothergill. Cumb 1B 102
Fotheringhay. Nptn 1H 63
Foubister. Orkn 7E 172
Foula Airport. Shet 8A 173
Foul Anchor. Cambs 4D 76
Foulbridge. Cumb 5F 113
Foulden. Norf 1G 65
Foulden. Bord 4F 131
Foul Mile. E Sus 4H 27
Foulridge. Lanc 5A 98
Foulsham. Norf 3C 78
Fountainhall. Bord 5H 129
Four Alls, The. Shrp 2A 72
Four Ashes. Staf
  nr. Cannock 5D 72
  nr. Kinver .2C 60
Four Ashes. Suff 3C 66

Four Crosses. *Powy*
   nr. Llanerfyl 5C 70
   nr. Llanymynech 4E 71
Four Crosses. *Staf* 5D 72
Four Elms. *Kent* 1F 27
Four Forks. *Som* 3F 21
Four Gotes. *Cambs* 4D 76
Four Lane End. *S Yor* 4C 92
Four Lane Ends. *Lanc* 4E 97
Four Lanes. *Corn* 5A 6
Fourlanes End. *Ches E* 5C 84
Four Marks. *Hants* 3E 25
Four Mile Bridge. *IOA* 3B 80
Four Oaks. *E Sus* 3C 28
Four Oaks. *Glos* 3B 48
Four Oaks. *W Mid* 2G 61
Four Roads. *Carm* 5E 45
Four Roads. *IOM* 5B 108
Fourstones. *Nmbd* 3B 114
Four Throws. *Kent* 3B 28
Fovant. *Wilts* 4F 23
Foveran. *Abers* 1G 153
Fowey. *Corn* 3F 7
Fowlershill. *Aber* 2G 153
Fowley Common. *Warr* 1A 84
Fowlis. *Ang* 5C 144
Fowlis Wester. *Per* 1B 136
Fowlmere. *Cambs* 1E 53
Fownhope. *Here* 2A 48
Fox Corner. *Surr* 5A 38
Foxcote. *Glos* 4F 49
Foxcote. *Som* 1C 22
Foxdale. *IOM* 4B 108
Foxearth. *Essx* 1B 54
Foxfield. *Cumb* 1B 96
Foxham. *Wilts* 4E 35
Fox Hatch. *Essx* 1G 39
Foxhole. *Corn* 3D 6
Foxholes. *N Yor* 2E 101
Foxhunt Green. *E Sus* 4G 27
Fox Lane. *Hants* 1G 25
Foxley. *Norf* 3C 78
Foxley. *Nptn* 5D 62
Foxley. *Wilts* 3D 35
Foxlydiate. *Worc* 4E 61
Fox Street. *Essx* 3D 54
Foxt. *Staf* 1E 73
Foxton. *Cambs* 1E 53
Foxton. *Dur* 2A 106
Foxton. *Leics* 2D 62
Foxton. *N Yor* 5B 106
Foxup. *N Yor* 2A 98
Foxwist Green. *Ches W* 4A 84
Foxwood. *Shrp* 3A 60
Foy. *Here* 3A 48
Foyers. *High* 1G 149
Foynesfield. *High* 3C 158
Fraddam. *Corn* 3C 4
Fraddon. *Corn* 3D 6
Fradley. *Staf* 4F 73
Fradley South. *Staf* 4F 73
Fradswell. *Staf* 2D 73
Fraisthorpe. *E Yor* 3F 101
Framfield. *E Sus* 3F 27
Framingham Earl. *Norf* 5E 79
Framingham Pigot. *Norf* 5E 79
Framlingham. *Suff* 4E 67
Frampton. *Dors* 3B 14
Frampton. *Linc* 2C 76
Frampton Cotterell. *S Glo* 3B 34
Frampton Mansell. *Glos* 5E 49
Frampton on Severn. *Glos* 5C 48
Frampton West End. *Linc* 1B 76
Framsden. *Suff* 5D 66
Framwellgate Moor. *Dur* 5F 115
Franche. *Worc* 3C 60
Frandley. *Ches W* 3A 84
Frankby. *Mers* 2E 83
Frankfort. *Norf* 3F 79
Frankley. *Worc* 2D 61
Frank's Bridge. *Powy* 5D 58
Frankton. *Warw* 3B 62
Frankwell. *Shrp* 4G 71
Frant. *E Sus* 2G 27
Fraserburgh. *Abers* 2G 161
Frating Green. *Essx* 3D 54
Fratton. *Port* 2E 17
Freathy. *Corn* 3A 8
Freckenham. *Suff* 3F 65
Freckleton. *Lanc* 2C 90
Freeby. *Leics* 3F 75
Freefolk Priors. *Hants* 2C 24
Freehay. *Staf* 1E 73
Freeland. *Oxon* 4C 50
Freester. *Shet* 6F 173
Freethorpe. *Norf* 5G 79
Freiston. *Linc* 1C 76
Freiston Shore. *Linc* 1C 76
Fremington. *Devn* 3F 19
Fremington. *N Yor* 5D 104
Frenchay. *S Glo* 4B 34
Frenchbeer. *Devn* 4G 11
Frenich. *Stir* 3D 134
Frensham. *Surr* 2G 25
Frenze. *Norf* 2D 66
Fresgoe. *High* 2B 168
Freshfield. *Mers* 4A 90
Freshford. *Bath* 5C 34
Freshwater. *IOW* 4B 16
Freshwater Bay. *IOW* 4B 16
Freshwater East. *Pemb* 5E 43
Fressingfield. *Suff* 3E 67
Freston. *Suff* 2E 55
Freswick. *High* 2F 169
Fretherne. *Glos* 5C 48
Frettenham. *Norf* 4E 79
Freuchie. *Fife* 3E 137
Freystrop. *Pemb* 3D 42
Friar's Gate. *E Sus* 2F 27
Friar Waddon. *Dors* 4B 14
Friday Bridge. *Cambs* 5D 76

Friday Street. *E Sus* 5H 27
Friday Street. *Surr* 1C 26
Fridaythorpe. *E Yor* 4C 100
Friden. *Derbs* 4F 85
Friern Barnet. *G Lon* 1D 39
Friesthorpe. *Linc* 2A 88
Frieston. *Linc* 1G 75
Frieth. *Buck* 2F 37
Friezeland. *Notts* 5B 86
Frilford. *Oxon* 2C 36
Frilsham. *W Ber* 4D 36
Frimley. *Surr* 1G 25
Frimley Green. *Surr* 1G 25
Frindsbury. *Medw* 4B 40
Fring. *Norf* 2G 77
Fringford. *Oxon* 3E 50
Frinsted. *Kent* 5C 40
Frinton-on-Sea. *Essx* 4F 55
Friockheim. *Ang* 4E 145
Friog. *Gwyn* 4F 69
Frisby. *Leics* 5E 74
Frisby on the Wreake. *Leics* 4D 74
Friskney. *Linc* 5D 88
Friskney Eaudyke. *Linc* 5D 88
Friston. *E Sus* 5G 27
Friston. *Suff* 4G 67
Fritchley. *Derbs* 5A 86
Frith Bank. *Linc* 1C 76
Frith Common. *Worc* 4A 60
Frithelstock. *Devn* 1E 11
Frithelstock Stone. *Devn* 1E 11
Frithsden. *Herts* 5A 52
Frithville. *Linc* 5C 88
Frittenden. *Kent* 1C 28
Frittiscombe. *Devn* 4E 9
Fritton. *Norf*
   nr. Great Yarmouth 5G 79
   nr. Long Stratton 1E 67
Fritwell. *Oxon* 3D 50
Frizinghall. *W Yor* 1B 92
Frizington. *Cumb* 3B 102
Frobost. *W Isl* 6C 170
Frocester. *Glos* 5C 48
Frochas. *Powy* 5H 71
Frodesley. *Shrp* 5H 71
Frodingham. *N Lin* 3C 94
Frodsham. *Ches W* 3H 83
Froggatt. *Derbs* 3G 85
Froghall. *Staf* 1E 73
Frogham. *Hants* 1G 15
Frogham. *Kent* 5G 41
Frogmore. *Devn* 4D 8
Frogmore. *Hants* 5G 37
Frogmore. *Herts* 5B 52
Frognall. *Linc* 4A 76
Frogshall. *Norf* 2E 79
Frogwell. *Corn* 2H 7
Frolesworth. *Leics* 1C 62
Frome. *Som* 2C 22
Fromefield. *Som* 2C 22
Frome St Quintin. *Dors* 2A 14
Fromes Hill. *Here* 1B 48
Fron. *Gwyn* 2C 68
Y Fron. *Gwyn* 5E 81
Fron. *Powy*
   nr. Llandrindod Wells 4C 58
   nr. Newtown 1D 58
   nr. Welshpool 5E 71
Froncysyllte. *Wrex* 1E 71
Frongoch. *Gwyn* 2B 70
Fron Isaf. *Wrex* 1E 71
Fronoleu. *Gwyn* 2G 69
Frosterley. *Dur* 1D 104
Frotoft. *Orkn* 5D 172
Froxfield. *C Beds* 2H 51
Froxfield. *Wilts* 5A 36
Froxfield Green. *Hants* 4F 25
Fryern Hill. *Hants* 4C 24
Fryerning. *Essx* 5G 53
Fryton. *N Yor* 2A 100
Fugglestone St Peter. *Wilts* 3G 23
Fulbeck. *Linc* 5G 87
Fulbourn. *Cambs* 5E 65
Fulbrook. *Oxon* 4A 50
Fulflood. *Hants* 3C 24
Fulford. *Som* 4F 21
Fulford. *Staf* 2D 72
Fulford. *York* 5A 100
Fulham. *G Lon* 3D 38
Fulking. *W Sus* 4D 26
Fuller's Moor. *Ches W* 5G 83
Fuller Street. *Essx* 4H 53
Fullerton. *Hants* 3B 24
Fulletby. *Linc* 3B 88
Full Sutton. *E Yor* 4B 100
Fullwood. *E Ayr* 4F 127
Fulmer. *Buck* 2A 38
Fulmodeston. *Norf* 2B 78
Fulnetby. *Linc* 3H 87
Fulney. *Linc* 3B 76
Fulstow. *Linc* 1C 88
Fulthorpe. *Stoc T* 2B 106
Fulwell. *Tyne* 4G 115
Fulwood. *Lanc* 1D 90
Fulwood. *Notts* 5B 86
Fulwood. *Som* 1F 13
Fulwood. *S Yor* 2G 85
Fundenhall. *Norf* 1D 66
Funtington. *W Sus* 2G 17
Funtley. *Hants* 2D 16
Funzie. *Shet* 2H 173
Furley. *Devn* 2F 13
Furnace. *Arg* 3H 133
Furnace. *Carm* 5F 45
Furnace. *Cdgn* 1F 57
Furner's Green. *E Sus* 3F 27
Furness Vale. *Derbs* 2E 85
Furneux Pelham. *Herts* 3E 53
Furzebrook. *Dors* 4E 15
Furzehill. *Devn* 2H 19

Furzehill. *Dors* 2F 15
Furzeley Corner. *Hants* 1E 17
Furzey Lodge. *Hants* 2B 16
Furzley. *Hants* 1A 16
Fyfield. *Essx* 5F 53
Fyfield. *Glos* 5H 49
Fyfield. *Hants* 2A 24
Fyfield. *Oxon* 2C 36
Fyfield. *Wilts* 5G 35
Fylde, The. *Lanc* 1C 90
Fylingthorpe. *N Yor* 4G 107
Fyning. *W Sus* 4G 25
Fyvie. *Abers* 5E 161

G

Gabhsann bho Dheas. *W Isl* 2G 171
Gabhsann bho Thuath. *W Isl* . . .2G 171
Gabroc Hill. *E Ayr* 4F 127
Gadbrook. *Surr* 1D 26
Gaddesby. *Leics* 4D 74
Gadfa. *IOA* 2D 80
Gadgirth. *S Ayr* 2D 116
Gaer. *Powy* 3E 47
Gaerwen. *IOA* 3D 81
Gagingwell. *Oxon* 3C 50
Gaick Lodge. *High* 5B 150
Gailey. *Staf* 4D 72
Gainford. *Dur* 3E 105
Gainsborough. *Linc* 1F 87
Gainsborough. *Suff* 1E 55
Gainsford End. *Essx* 2H 53
Gairletter. *Arg* 1C 126
Gairloch. *Abers* 3E 153
Gairloch. *High* 1H 155
Gairlochy. *High* 5D 148
Gairney Bank. *Per* 4D 136
Gairnshiel Lodge. *Abers* 3G 151
Gaisgill. *Cumb* 4H 103
Gaitsgill. *Cumb* 5E 113
Galashiels. *Bord* 1G 119
Galgate. *Lanc* 4D 97
Galhampton. *Som* 4B 22
Gallatown. *Fife* 4E 137
Galley Common. *Warw* 1H 61
Galleyend. *Essx* 5H 53
Galleywood. *Essx* 5H 53
Gallin. *Per* 4C 142
Gallowfauld. *Ang* 4D 144
Gallowhill. *Per* 5A 144
Gallowhill. *Ren* 3F 127
Gallowhills. *Abers* 3H 161
Gallows Green. *Staf* 1E 73
Gallows Green. *Worc* 4D 60
Gallowstree Common.
   Oxon 3E 37
Galltair. *High* 1G 147
Gallt Melyd. *Den* 2C 82
Galmington. *Som* 4F 21
Galmisdale. *High* 5C 146
Galmpton. *Devn* 4C 8
Galmpton. *Torb* 3E 9
Galmpton Warborough.
   Torb 3E 9
Galphay. *N Yor* 2E 99
Galston. *E Ayr* 1D 117
Galton. *Dors* 4C 14
Galtrigill. *High* 3A 154
Gamblesby. *Cumb* 1H 103
Gamelsby. *Cumb* 4D 112
Gamesley. *Derbs* 1E 85
Gamlingay. *Cambs* 5B 64
Gamlingay Cinques. *Cambs* 5B 64
Gamlingay Great Heath.
   Cambs 5B 64
Gammaton. *Devn* 4E 19
Gammersgill. *N Yor* 1C 98
Gamston. *Notts*
   nr. Nottingham 2D 74
   nr. Retford 3E 86
Ganarew. *Here* 4A 48
Ganavan. *Arg* 5C 140
Ganborough. *Glos* 3G 49
Gang. *Corn* 2H 7
Ganllwyd. *Gwyn* 3G 69
Gannochy. *Ang* 1E 145
Gannochy. *Per* 1D 136
Gansclet. *High* 4F 169
Ganstead. *E Yor* 1E 95
Ganthorpe. *N Yor* 2A 100
Ganton. *N Yor* 2D 101
Gants Hill. *G Lon* 2F 39
Gappah. *Devn* 5B 12
Garafad. *High* 2D 155
Garboldisham. *Norf* 2C 66
Garden City. *Flin* 4F 83
Gardeners Green. *Wok* 5G 37
Garden Village. *S Yor* 1G 85
Garden Village. *Swan* 3E 31
Garderhouse. *Shet* 7E 173
Gardham. *E Yor* 5D 100
Gardie. *Shet*
   on Papa Stour 5C 173
   on Unst 1H 173
Gardie Ho. *Shet* 7F 173
Gare Hill. *Wilts* 2C 22
Garelochhead. *Arg* 1B 134
Garford. *Oxon* 2C 36
Garforth. *W Yor* 1E 93
Gargrave. *N Yor* 4B 98
Gargunnock. *Stir* 4G 135
Garleffin. *S Ayr* 1F 109
Garlieston. *Dum* 5B 110
Garlinge Green. *Kent* 5F 41
Garlogie. *Abers* 3E 153
Garmelow. *Staf* 3B 72
Garmond. *Abers* 3F 161
Garmondsway. *Dur* 1A 106
Garmony. *Arg* 4A 140

Garmouth. *Mor* 2H 159
Garmston. *Shrp* 5A 72
Garnant. *Carm* 4G 45
Garndiffaith. *Torf* 5F 47
Garndolbenmaen. *Gwyn* 1D 69
Garnett Bridge. *Cumb* 5G 103
Garnfadryn. *Gwyn* 2B 68
Garnkirk. *N Lan* 3H 127
Garnlydan. *Blae* 4E 47
Garnsgate. *Linc* 3D 76
Garnswllt. *Swan* 5G 45
Garn yr Erw. *Torf* 4F 47
Garrabost. *W Isl* 4H 171
Garrallan. *E Ayr* 3E 117
Garras. *Corn* 4E 5
Garreg. *Gwyn* 1F 69
Garrigill. *Cumb* 5A 114
Garriston. *N Yor* 5E 105
Garrogie Lodge. *High* 2H 149
Garros. *High* 2D 155
Garrow. *Per* 4F 143
Garsdale. *Cumb* 1G 97
Garsdale Head. *Cumb* 5A 104
Garsdon. *Wilts* 3E 35
Garshall Green. *Staf* 2D 72
Garsington. *Oxon* 5D 50
Garstang. *Lanc* 5D 97
Garston. *Mers* 2G 83
Garswood. *Mers* 1H 83
Gartcosh. *N Lan* 3H 127
Garth. *B'end* 2B 32
Garth. *Cdgn* 2F 57
Garth. *Gwyn* 2E 69
Garth. *IOM* 4C 108
Garth. *Powy*
   nr. Builth Wells 1C 46
   nr. Knighton 3E 59
Garth. *Shet*
   nr. Sandness 6D 173
   nr. Skellister 6F 173
Garth. *Wrex* 1E 71
Garthamlock. *Glas* 3H 127
Garthbrengy. *Powy* 2D 46
Gartheli. *Cdgn* 5E 57
Garthmyl. *Powy* 1D 58
Garthorpe. *Leics* 3F 75
Garthorpe. *N Lin* 3B 94
Garth Owen. *Powy* 1D 58
Garth Place. *Cphy* 3E 33
Garth Row. *Cumb* 5G 103
Gartly. *Abers* 5C 160
Gartmore. *Stir* 4E 135
Gartness. *N Lan* 3A 128
Gartness. *Stir* 1G 127
Gartocharn. *W Dun* 1F 127
Garton. *E Yor* 1F 95
Garton-on-the-Wolds. *E Yor* 4D 101
Gartsherrie. *N Lan* 3A 128
Gartymore. *High* 2H 165
Garvald. *E Lot* 2B 130
Garvamore. *High* 4H 149
Garvard. *Arg* 4A 132
Garvault. *High* 5H 167
Garve. *High* 2F 157
Garvestone. *Norf* 5C 78
Garvie. *Arg* 4H 133
Garvock. *Abers* 1G 145
Garvock. *Inv* 2D 126
Garway. *Here* 3H 47
Garway Common. *Here* 3H 47
Garway Hill. *Here* 3H 47
Garwick. *Linc* 1A 76
Gaskan. *High* 1C 140
Gasper. *Wilts* 3C 22
Gastard. *Wilts* 5D 35
Gasthorpe. *Norf* 2B 66
Gatcombe. *IOW* 4C 16
Gateacre. *Mers* 2G 83
Gatebeck. *Cumb* 1E 97
Gate Burton. *Linc* 2F 87
Gateforth. *N Yor* 2F 93
Gatehead. *E Ayr* 1C 116
Gate Helmsley. *N Yor* 4A 100
Gatehouse. *Nmbd* 1A 114
Gatehouse of Fleet. *Dum* 4D 110
Gatelawbridge. *Dum* 5B 118
Gateley. *Norf* 3B 78
Gatenby. *N Yor* 1F 99
Gatesgarth. *Cumb* 3C 102
Gateshead. *Tyne* 3F 115
Gatesheath. *Ches W* 4G 83
Gateside. *Ang*
   nr. Forfar 4D 144
   nr. Kirriemuir 4C 144
Gateside. *Fife* 3D 136
Gateside. *N Ayr* 4E 127
Gathurst. *G Man* 4D 90
Gatley. *G Man* 2C 84
Gatton. *Surr* 5D 39
Gattonside. *Bord* 1H 119
Gatwick Airport. *W Sus* 216 (1D 27)
Gaufron. *Powy* 4B 58
Gaulby. *Leics* 5D 74
Gauldry. *Fife* 1F 137
Gaultree. *Norf* 5D 77
Gaunt's Common. *Dors* 2F 15
Gaunt's Earthcott. *S Glo* 3B 34
Gautby. *Linc* 3A 88
Gavinton. *Bord* 4D 130
Gawber. *S Yor* 4D 92
Gawcott. *Buck* 2E 51
Gawsworth. *Ches E* 4C 84
Gawthorpe. *W Yor* 2C 92
Gawthrop. *Cumb* 1F 97
Gawthwaite. *Cumb* 1B 96
Gay Bowers. *Essx* 5A 54
Gaydon. *Warw* 5A 62
Gayfield. *Orkn* 2D 172
Gayhurst. *Mil* 1G 51
Gayle. *N Yor* 1A 98
Gayles. *N Yor* 4E 105

Gay Street. *W Sus* 3B 26
Gayton. *Mers* 2E 83
Gayton. *Norf* 4G 77
Gayton. *Nptn* 5E 62
Gayton. *Staf* 3D 73
Gayton le Marsh. *Linc* 2D 88
Gayton le Wold. *Linc* 2B 88
Gayton Thorpe. *Norf* 4G 77
Gaywood. *Norf* 3F 77
Gazeley. *Suff* 4G 65
Geanies. *High* 1C 158
Gearraidh Bhailteas. *W Isl* 6C 170
Gearraidh Bhaird. *W Isl* 6F 171
Gearraidh ma Monadh. *W Isl* . . .7C 170
Gearraidh na h-Aibhne. *W Isl* . . .4E 171
Geary. *High* 2B 154
Geddes. *High* 3C 158
Gedding. *Suff* 5B 66
Geddington. *Nptn* 2F 63
Gedintailor. *High* 5E 155
Gedling. *Notts* 1D 74
Gedney. *Linc* 3D 76
Gedney Broadgate. *Linc* 3D 76
Gedney Drove End. *Linc* 3D 76
Gedney Dyke. *Linc* 3D 76
Gedney Hill. *Linc* 4C 76
Gee Cross. *G Man* 1D 84
Geeston. *Rut* 5G 75
Geilston. *Arg* 2E 127
Geirinis. *W Isl* 4C 170
Geise. *High* 2D 168
Geisiadar. *W Isl* 4D 171
Gelder Shiel. *Abers* 5G 151
Geldeston. *Norf* 1F 67
Gell. *Cnwy* 4A 82
Gelli. *Pemb* 2F 43
Gelli. *Rhon* 2C 32
Gellifor. *Den* 4D 82
Gelligaer. *Cphy* 2E 33
Y Gelli Gandryll. *Powy* 1F 47
Gellilydan. *Gwyn* 2F 69
Gellinudd. *Neat* 5H 45
Gellyburn. *Per* 5H 143
Gellywen. *Carm* 2G 43
Gelston. *Dum* 4E 111
Gelston. *Linc* 1G 75
Gembling. *E Yor* 4F 101
Gentleshaw. *Staf* 4E 73
Geneva. *Cdgn* 5D 56
Geocrab. *W Isl* 8D 171
George Green. *Buck* 2A 38
Georgeham. *Devn* 3E 19
George Nympton. *Devn* 4H 19
Georgetown. *Blae* 5E 47
Georgetown. *Ren* 3F 127
Georth. *Orkn* 5C 172
Gerlan. *Gwyn* 4F 81
Germansweek. *Devn* 3E 11
Germoe. *Corn* 4C 4
Gerrans. *Corn* 5C 6
Gerrard's Bromley. *Staf* 2B 72
Gerrards Cross. *Buck* 2A 38
Gerston. *High* 3D 168
Gestingthorpe. *Essx* 2B 54
Gethsemane. *Pemb* 1A 44
Geuffordd. *Powy* 4E 70
Gibraltar. *Buck* 4F 51
Gibraltar. *Linc* 5E 89
Gibraltar. *Suff* 5D 66
Gibsmere. *Notts* 1E 74
Giddeahall. *Wilts* 4D 34
Gidea Park. *G Lon* 2G 39
Gidleigh. *Devn* 4G 11
Giffnock. *E Ren* 4G 127
Gifford. *E Lot* 3B 130
Giffordtown. *Fife* 2E 137
Giggetty. *Staf* 1C 60
Giggleswick. *N Yor* 3H 97
Gignog. *Pemb* 2C 42
Gilberdyke. *E Yor* 2B 94
Gilbert's End. *Worc* 1D 48
Gilbert's Green. *Warw* 3F 61
Gilchriston. *E Lot* 3A 130
Gilcrux. *Cumb* 1C 102
Gildersome. *W Yor* 2C 92
Gildingwells. *S Yor* 2C 86
Gilesgate Moor. *Dur* 5F 115
Gileston. *V Glam* 5D 32
Gilfach. *Cphy* 2E 33
Gilfach Goch. *Rhon* 3C 32
Gilfachreda. *Cdgn* 5D 56
Gilgarran. *Cumb* 2B 102
Gillamoor. *N Yor* 5D 107
Gillan. *Corn* 4E 5
Gillar's Green. *Mers* 1G 83
Gillen. *High* 3B 154
Gilling East. *N Yor* 2A 100
Gillingham. *Dors* 4D 22
Gillingham. *Medw* 204 (4B 40)
Gillingham. *Norf* 1G 67
Gilling West. *N Yor* 4E 105
Gillock. *High* 3E 169
Gillow Heath. *Staf* 5C 84
Gills. *High* 1F 169
Gill's Green. *Kent* 2B 28
Gilmanscleuch. *Bord* 2F 119
Gilmerton. *Edin* 3F 129
Gilmerton. *Per* 1A 136
Gilmonby. *Dur* 3C 104
Gilmorton. *Leics* 2C 62
Gilsland. *Nmbd* 3H 113
Gilsland Spa. *Cumb* 3H 113
Gilston. *Bord* 4H 129
Giltbrook. *Notts* 1B 74
Gilwern. *Mon* 4F 47
Gimingham. *Norf* 2E 79
Giosla. *W Isl* 5D 171
Gipping. *Suff* 4C 66
Gipsey Bridge. *Linc* 1B 76
Gipton. *W Yor* 1D 92
Girdle Toll. *N Ayr* 5E 127

Girlsta. *Shet* 6F **173**
Girsby. *N Yor* 4A **106**
Girthon. *Dum* 4D **110**
Girton. *Cambs* 4D **64**
Girton. *Notts* 4F **87**
Girvan. *S Ayr* 5A **116**
Gisburn. *Lanc* 5H **97**
Gisleham. *Suff* 2H **67**
Gislingham. *Suff* 3C **66**
Gissing. *Norf* 2D **66**
Gittisham. *Devn* 3E **13**
Gladestry. *Powy* 5E **59**
Gladsmuir. *E Lot* 2A **130**
Glaichbea. *High* 5H **157**
Glais. *Swan* 5H **45**
Glaisdale. *N Yor* 4E **107**
Glame. *High* 4E **155**
Glamis. *Ang* 4C **144**
Glanaman. *Carm* 4G **45**
Glan-Conwy. *Cnwy* 5H **81**
Glandford. *Norf* 1C **78**
Glan Duar. *Carm* 1F **45**
Glandwr. *Blae* 5F **47**
Glandwr. *Pemb* 2F **43**
Glan-Dwyfach. *Gwyn* 1D **69**
Glandy Cross. *Carm* 2F **43**
Glandyfi. *Cdgn* 1F **57**
Glangrwyney. *Powy* 4F **47**
Glanmule. *Powy* 1D **58**
Glanrhyd. *Pemb* 2B **68**
Glan-rhyd. *Pemb* 1F **43**
Glanrhyd. *Pemb* 1B **44**
Glan-rhyd. *Powy* 5A **46**
Glanton. *Nmbd* 3E **121**
Glanton Pyke. *Nmbd* 3E **121**
Glanvilles Wootton. *Dors* 2B **14**
Glan-y-don. *Flin* 3D **82**
Glan-y-nant. *Powy* 2B **58**
Glan-yr-afon. *Gwyn* 1C **70**
Glan-yr-afon. *IOA* 2F **81**
Glan-yr-afon. *Powy* 5C **70**
Glan-y-wern. *Gwyn* 2F **69**
Glapthorn. *Nptn* 1H **63**
Glapwell. *Derbs* 4B **86**
Glas Aird. *Arg* 4A **132**
Glas-allt Shiel. *Abers* 5G **151**
Glasbury. *Powy* 2E **47**
Glaschoil. *High* 5E **159**
Glascoed. *Den* 3B **82**
Glascoed. *Mon* 5G **47**
Glascote. *Staf* 5G **73**
Glascwm. *Powy* 5D **58**
Glasfryn. *Cnwy* 5B **82**
Glasgow. *Glas* **196** (3G **127**)
Glasgow Airport. *Ren* **216** (3F **127**)
Glasgow Prestwick Airport.
  S Ayr 2C **116**
Glashvin. *High* 2D **154**
Glasinfryn. *Gwyn* 4E **81**
Glas na Cardaich. *High* 4E **147**
Glasnacardoch. *High* 4E **147**
Glasnakille. *High* 2D **146**
Glaspwll. *Cdgn* 1G **57**
Glassburn. *High* 5F **157**
Glassenbury. *Kent* 2B **28**
Glasserton. *Dum* 5B **110**
Glassford. *S Lan* 5A **128**
Glassgreen. *Mor* 2G **159**
Glasshouse. *Glos* 3C **48**
Glasshouses. *N Yor* 3D **98**
Glasson. *Cumb* 3D **112**
Glasson. *Lanc* 4D **96**
Glassonby. *Cumb* 1G **103**
Glasterlaw. *Ang* 3E **145**
Glaston. *Rut* 5F **75**
Glastonbury. *Som* 3H **21**
Glatton. *Cambs* 2A **64**
Glazebrook. *Warr* 1A **84**
Glazebury. *Warr* 1A **84**
Glazeley. *Shrp* 2B **60**
Gleadless. *S Yor* 2A **86**
Gleadsmoss. *Ches E* 4C **84**
Gleann Dail bho Dheas. *W Isl* 7C **170**
Gleann Tholastaidh. *W Isl* 3H **171**
Gleann Uige. *High* 1A **140**
Gleaston. *Cumb* 2B **96**
Glecknabae. *Arg* 3B **126**
Gledrid. *Shrp* 2E **71**
Gleiniant. *Powy* 1B **58**
Glemsford. *Suff* 1B **54**
Glen. *Dum* 4C **110**
Glenancross. *High* 4E **147**
Glen Auldyn. *IOM* 2D **108**
Glenbarr. *Arg* 2A **122**
Glenbeg. *High* 2G **139**
Glen Bernisdale. *High* 4D **154**
Glenbervie. *Abers* 5E **153**
Glenboig. *N Lan* 3A **128**
Glenborrodale. *High* 2A **140**
Glenbranter. *Arg* 4A **134**
Glenbreck. *Bord* 2C **118**
Glenbrein Lodge. *High* 2G **149**
Glenbrittle. *High* 1C **146**
Glenbuchat Lodge. *Abers* 2H **151**
Glenbuck. *E Ayr* 2G **117**
Glenburn. *Ren* 3F **127**
Glencalvie Lodge. *High* 5B **164**
Glencaple. *Dum* 3A **112**
Glencarron Lodge. *High* 3C **156**
Glencarse. *Per* 1D **136**
Glencassley Castle. *High* 3B **164**
Glencat. *Abers* 4C **152**
Glencoe. *High* 3F **141**
Glen Cottage. *High* 5E **147**
Glencraig. *Fife* 4D **136**
Glendale. *High* 4A **154**
Glendevon. *Per* 3B **136**
Glendoebeg. *High* 3G **149**
Glendoick. *Per* 1E **136**
Glendoune. *S Ayr* 5A **116**
Glenduckie. *Fife* 2E **137**

Gleneagles. *Per* 3B **136**
Glenegedale. *Arg* 4B **124**
Glenegedale Lots. *Arg* 4B **124**
Glenelg. *High* 2G **147**
Glenesslin. *Dum* 1F **111**
Glenfarg. *Per* 2D **136**
Glenfarquhar Lodge. *Abers* 5E **152**
Glenferness Mains. *High* 4D **158**
Glenfeshie Lodge. *High* 4C **150**
Glenfiddich Lodge. *Mor* 5H **159**
Glenfield. *Leics* 5C **74**
Glenfinnan. *High* 5B **148**
Glenfintaig Lodge. *High* 5E **148**
Glenfoot. *Per* 2D **136**
Glenfyne Lodge. *Arg* 2B **134**
Glengap. *Dum* 4D **110**
Glengarnock. *N Ayr* 4E **126**
Glengolly. *High* 2D **168**
Glengorm Castle. *Arg* 3F **139**
Glengrasco. *High* 4D **154**
Glenhead Farm. *Ang* 2B **144**
Glenholm. *Bord* 1D **118**
Glen House. *Bord* 1E **119**
Glenhurich. *High* 2C **140**
Glenkerry. *Bord* 3E **119**
Glenkiln. *Dum* 2F **111**
Glenkindie. *Abers* 2B **152**
Glenkinglass Lodge. *Arg* 5F **141**
Glenkirk. *Bord* 2C **118**
Glenlean. *Arg* 1B **126**
Glenlee. *Dum* 1D **110**
Glenleraig. *High* 5B **166**
Glenlichorn. *Per* 2G **135**
Glenlivet. *Mor* 1F **151**
Glenlochar. *Dum* 3E **111**
Glenlochsie Lodge. *Per* 1H **143**
Glenluce. *Dum* 4G **109**
Glenmarksie. *High* 3F **157**
Glenmassan. *Arg* 1C **126**
Glenmavis. *N Lan* 3A **128**
Glen Maye. *IOM* 4B **108**
Glenmazeran Lodge. *High* 1B **150**
Glenmidge. *Dum* 1F **111**
Glen Mona. *IOM* 3D **108**
Glenmore. *High*
  nr. Glenborrodale 2G **139**
  nr. Kingussie 3D **151**
  on Isle of Skye 4D **154**
Glenmoy. *Ang* 2D **144**
Glennoe. *Arg* 5E **141**
Glen of Coachford. *Abers* 4B **160**
Glenogil. *Ang* 2D **144**
Glen Parva. *Leics* 1C **62**
Glenprosen Village. *Ang* 2C **144**
Glenree. *N Ayr* 3D **122**
Glenridding. *Cumb* 3E **103**
Glenrosa. *N Ayr* 2E **123**
Glenrothes. *Fife* 3E **137**
Glensanda. *High* 4C **140**
Glensaugh. *Abers* 1F **145**
Glenshero Lodge. *High* 4H **149**
Glensluain. *Arg* 4H **133**
Glenstockadale. *Dum* 3F **109**
Glenstriven. *Arg* 2B **126**
Glen Tanar House. *Abers* 4B **152**
Glentham. *Linc* 1H **87**
Glenton. *Abers* 1D **152**
Glentress. *Bord* 1E **119**
Glentromie Lodge. *High* 4B **150**
Glentrool Lodge. *Dum* 1B **110**
Glentrool Village. *Dum* 2A **110**
Glentruim House. *High* 4A **150**
Glentworth. *Linc* 2G **87**
Glenuig. *High* 1A **140**
Glen Village. *Falk* 2B **128**
Glen Vine. *IOM* 4C **108**
Glenwhilly. *Dum* 2G **109**
Glenzierfoot. *Dum* 2E **113**
Glespin. *S Lan* 2H **117**
Goole. *E Yor* 2H **93**
Gloom's Hill. *Worc* 5E **61**
Goonabarn. *Corn* 3D **6**
Goonbell. *Corn* 4B **6**
Goonhavern. *Corn* 3B **6**
Goonlaze. *Corn* 5B **6**
Goonvrea. *Corn* 4B **6**
Goose Green. *Cumb* 1E **97**
Goose Green. *S Glo* 3C **34**
Gooseham. *Corn* 1C **10**
Goosewell. *Plym* 3B **8**
Goosey. *Oxon* 2B **36**
Goosnargh. *Lanc* 1D **90**
Goostrey. *Ches E* 3B **84**
Gorcott Hill. *Warw* 4E **61**
Gord. *Shet* 9F **173**
Gordon. *Bord* 5C **130**
Gordonbush. *High* 3F **165**
Gordonstown. *Abers*
  nr. Cornhill 3C **160**
  nr. Fyvie 5E **160**
Gorebridge. *Midl* 3G **129**
Gorefield. *Cambs* 4D **76**
Gores. *Wilts* 1G **23**
Gorgie. *Edin* 2F **129**
Goring. *Oxon* 3E **36**
Goring-by-Sea. *W Sus* 5C **26**
Goring Heath. *Oxon* 4E **37**
Gorleston-on-Sea. *Norf* 5H **79**
Gornalwood. *W Mid* 1D **60**
Gorran Churchtown. *Corn* 4D **6**
Gorran Haven. *Corn* 4E **6**
Gorran High Lanes. *Corn* 4D **6**
Gors. *Cdgn* 3F **57**
Gorsedd. *Flin* 3D **82**
Gorseinon. *Swan* 3E **31**
Gorseness. *Orkn* 6D **172**
Gorseybank. *Derbs* 5G **85**
Gorsgoch. *Cdgn* 5D **57**
Gorslas. *Carm* 4F **45**
Gorsley. *Glos* 3B **48**
Gorsley Common. *Here* 3B **48**

Gobernuisgach Lodge. *High* 4E **167**
Gobernuisgeach. *High* 5B **168**
Gobhaig. *W Isl* 7C **171**
Gobowen. *Shrp* 2F **71**
Godalming. *Surr* 1A **26**
Goddard's Corner. *Suff* 4E **67**
Goddard's Green. *Kent*
  nr. Benenden 2C **28**
  nr. Cranbrook 2B **28**
Goddards' Green. *W Sus* 3D **27**
Godford Cross. *Devn* 2E **13**
Godleybrook. *Staf* 1D **73**
Godmanchester. *Cambs* 3B **64**
Godmanstone. *Dors* 3B **14**
Godmersham. *Kent* 5E **41**
Godolphin Cross. *Corn* 3D **4**
Godre'r-graig. *Neat* 5A **46**
Godshill. *Hants* 1G **15**
Godshill. *IOW* 4D **16**
Godstone. *Staf* 2E **73**
Godstone. *Surr* 5E **39**
Goetre. *Mon* 5G **47**
Goff's Oak. *Herts* 5D **52**
Gogar. *Edin* 2E **129**
Goginan. *Cdgn* 2F **57**
Golan. *Gwyn* 1E **69**
Golant. *Corn* 3F **7**
Golberdon. *Corn* 5D **10**
Golborne. *G Man* 1A **84**
Golcar. *W Yor* 3A **92**
Goldcliff. *Newp* 3G **33**
Golden Cross. *E Sus* 4G **27**
Golden Green. *Kent* 1H **27**
Golden Grove. *Carm* 4F **45**
Golden Grove. *N Yor* 4F **107**
Golden Hill. *Pemb* 2D **43**
Goldenhill. *Stoke* 5C **84**
Golden Pot. *Hants* 2F **25**
Golden Valley. *Glos* 3E **49**
Golders Green. *G Lon* 2D **38**
Goldhanger. *Essx* 5C **54**
Gold Hill. *Norf* 1E **65**
Golding. *Shrp* 5H **71**
Goldington. *Bed* 5H **63**
Goldsborough. *N Yor*
  nr. Harrogate 4F **99**
  nr. Whitby 3F **107**
Goldsithney. *Corn* 3C **4**
Goldstone. *Kent* 4G **41**
Goldstone. *Shrp* 3B **72**
Goldthorpe. *S Yor* 4E **93**
Goldworthy. *Devn* 4D **19**
Golfa. *Powy* 3D **70**
Gollanfield. *High* 3C **158**
Gollinglith Foot. *N Yor* 1D **98**
Golsoncott. *Som* 3D **20**
Golspie. *High* 4F **165**
Gomeldon. *Wilts* 3G **23**
Gomersal. *W Yor* 2C **92**
Gometra House. *Arg* 4E **139**
Gomshall. *Surr* 1B **26**
Gonalston. *Notts* 1D **74**
Gonerby Hill Foot. *Linc* 2G **75**
Gonfirth. *Shet* 5E **173**
Good Easter. *Essx* 4G **53**
Gooderstone. *Norf* 5G **77**
Goodleigh. *Devn* 3G **19**
Goodmanham. *E Yor* 5C **100**
Goodmayes. *G Lon* 2F **39**
Goodnestone. *Kent*
  nr. Aylesham 5G **41**
  nr. Faversham 4E **41**
Goodrich. *Here* 4A **48**
Goodrington. *Torb* 3E **9**
Goodshaw. *Lanc* 2G **91**
Goodshaw Fold. *Lanc* 2G **91**
Goodstone. *Devn* 5A **12**
Goodwick. *Pemb* 1D **42**
Goodworth Clatford. *Hants* 2B **24**

Gorstan. *High* 2F **157**
Gorstella. *Ches W* 4F **83**
Gorsty Common. *Here* 2H **47**
Gorsty Hill. *Staf* 3F **73**
Gortantaoid. *Arg* 2B **124**
Gorteneorn. *High* 2A **140**
Gortenfern. *High* 2A **140**
Gorton. *G Man* 1C **84**
Gosbeck. *Suff* 5D **66**
Gosberton. *Linc* 2B **76**
Gosberton Cheal. *Linc* 3B **76**
Gosberton Clough. *Linc* 3A **76**
Goseley Dale. *Derbs* 3H **73**
Gosfield. *Essx* 3A **54**
Gosford. *Oxon* 4D **50**
Gosforth. *Cumb* 4B **102**
Gosforth. *Tyne* 3F **115**
Gosmore. *Herts* 3B **52**
Gospel End. *Staf* 1C **60**
Gosport. *Hants* 3E **16**
Gossabrough. *Shet* 3G **173**
Gossington. *Glos* 5C **48**
Gossops Green. *W Sus* 2D **26**
Goswick. *Nmbd* 5G **131**
Gotham. *Notts* 2C **74**
Gotherington. *Glos* 3E **49**
Gott. *Arg* 4B **138**
Gott. *Shet* 7F **173**
Goudhurst. *Kent* 2B **28**
Goulceby. *Linc* 3B **88**
Gourdon. *Abers* 1H **145**
Gourock. *Inv* 2D **126**
Govan. *Glas* 3G **127**
Govanhill. *Glas* 3G **127**
Goverton. *Notts* 1E **74**
Goveton. *Devn* 4D **8**
Govilon. *Mon* 4F **47**
Gowanhill. *Abers* 2H **161**
Gowdall. *E Yor* 2G **93**
Gowerton. *Swan* 3E **31**
Gowkhall. *Fife* 1D **128**
Gowthorpe. *E Yor* 4B **100**
Goxhill. *E Yor* 5F **101**
Goxhill. *N Lin* 2E **94**
Goxhill Haven. *N Lin* 2E **94**
Goytre. *Neat* 3A **32**
Grabhair. *W Isl* 6F **171**
Graby. *Linc* 3H **75**
Graffham. *W Sus* 4A **26**
Grafham. *Cambs* 4A **64**
Grafham. *Surr* 1B **26**
Grafton. *Here* 2H **47**
Grafton. *N Yor* 3G **99**
Grafton. *Oxon* 5A **50**
Grafton. *Shrp* 4G **71**
Grafton. *Worc*
  nr. Evesham 2E **49**
  nr. Leominster 4H **59**
Grafton Flyford. *Worc* 5D **60**
Grafton Regis. *Nptn* 1F **51**
Grafton Underwood. *Nptn* 2G **63**
Grafty Green. *Kent* 1C **28**
Graianrhyd. *Den* 5E **82**
Graig. *Carm* 5E **45**
Graig. *Cnwy* 3H **81**
Graig. *Den* 3C **82**
Graig-fechan. *Den* 5D **82**
Graig Penllyn. *V Glam* 4C **32**
Grain. *Medw* 3C **40**
Grainsby. *Linc* 1B **88**
Grainthorpe. *Linc* 1C **88**
Grainthorpe Fen. *Linc* 1C **88**
Gramasdail. *W Isl* 3D **170**
Grampound. *Corn* 4D **6**
Grampound Road. *Corn* 3D **6**
Granborough. *Buck* 3F **51**
Granby. *Notts* 2E **75**
Grandborough. *Warw* 4B **62**
Grandpont. *Oxon* 5D **50**
Grandtully. *Per* 3G **143**
Grange. *Cumb* 3D **102**
Grange. *E Ayr* 1D **116**
Grange. *Here* 3G **59**
Grange. *Mers* 2E **82**
Grange, The. *N Yor* 5C **106**
Grange. *Per* 1E **137**
Grange Crossroads. *Mor* 3B **160**
Grange Hill. *Essx* 1F **39**
Grangemill. *Derbs* 5G **85**
Grange Moor. *W Yor* 3C **92**
Grangemouth. *Falk* 1C **128**
Grange of Lindores. *Fife* 2E **137**
Grange-over-Sands. *Cumb* 2D **96**
Grangepans. *Falk* 1D **128**
Grangetown. *Card* 4E **33**
Grangetown. *Red C* 2C **106**
Grange Villa. *Dur* 4F **115**
Granish. *High* 2C **150**
Gransmoor. *E Yor* 4F **101**
Granston. *Pemb* 1C **42**
Grantchester. *Cambs* 5D **64**
Grantham. *Linc* 2G **75**
Grantley. *N Yor* 3E **99**
Grantlodge. *Abers* 2E **152**
Granton. *Edin* 2F **129**
Grantown-on-Spey. *High* 1E **151**
Grantshouse. *Bord* 3E **130**
Grappenhall. *Warr* 2A **84**
Grasby. *Linc* 4D **94**
Grasmere. *Cumb* 4E **103**
Grasscroft. *G Man* 4H **91**
Grassendale. *Mers* 2F **83**
Grassgarth. *Cumb* 5E **113**
Grassholme. *Dur* 2C **104**
Grassington. *N Yor* 3C **98**
Grassmoor. *Derbs* 4B **86**
Grassthorpe. *Notts* 4E **87**
Grateley. *Hants* 2A **24**
Gratton. *Devn* 1D **11**
Gratton. *Staf* 5D **84**

Gratwich. *Staf* 2E **73**
Graveley. *Cambs* 4B **64**
Graveley. *Herts* 3C **52**
Gravelhill. *Shrp* 4G **71**
Gravel Hole. *G Man* 4H **91**
Gravelly Hill. *W Mid* 1F **61**
Graven. *Shet* 4F **173**
Graveney. *Kent* 4E **41**
Gravesend. *Kent* 3H **39**
Grayingham. *Linc* 1G **87**
Grayrigg. *Cumb* 5G **103**
Grays. *Thur* 3H **39**
Grayshott. *Hants* 3G **25**
Grayson Green. *Cumb* 2A **102**
Grayswood. *Surr* 2A **26**
Graythorp. *Hart* 2C **106**
Grazeley. *Wok* 5E **37**
Grealin. *High* 2E **155**
Greasbrough. *S Yor* 1B **86**
Greasby. *Mers* 2E **83**
Great Abington. *Cambs* 1F **53**
Great Addington. *Nptn* 3G **63**
Great Alne. *Warw* 5F **61**
Great Altcar. *Lanc* 4B **90**
Great Amwell. *Herts* 4D **52**
Great Asby. *Cumb* 3H **103**
Great Ashfield. *Suff* 4B **66**
Great Ayton. *N Yor* 3C **106**
Great Baddow. *Essx* 5H **53**
Great Bardfield. *Essx* 2G **53**
Great Barford. *Bed* 5A **64**
Great Barr. *W Mid* 1E **61**
Great Barrington. *Glos* 4H **49**
Great Barrow. *Ches W* 4G **83**
Great Barton. *Suff* 4A **66**
Great Barugh. *N Yor* 2B **100**
Great Bavington. *Nmbd* 1C **114**
Great Bealings. *Suff* 1F **55**
Great Bedwyn. *Wilts* 5A **36**
Great Bentley. *Essx* 3E **54**
Great Billing. *Nptn* 4F **63**
Great Bircham. *Norf* 2G **77**
Great Blakenham. *Suff* 5D **66**
Great Blencow. *Cumb* 1F **103**
Great Bolas. *Telf* 3A **72**
Great Bookham. *Surr* 5C **38**
Great Bosullow. *Corn* 3B **4**
Great Bourton. *Oxon* 1C **50**
Great Bowden. *Leics* 2E **63**
Great Bradley. *Suff* 5F **65**
Great Braxted. *Essx* 4B **54**
Great Bricett. *Suff* 5C **66**
Great Brickhill. *Buck* 2H **51**
Great Bridgeford. *Staf* 3C **72**
Great Brington. *Nptn* 4D **62**
Great Bromley. *Essx* 3D **54**
Great Broughton. *Cumb* 1B **102**
Great Broughton. *N Yor* 4C **106**
Great Budworth. *Ches W* 3A **84**
Great Burdon. *Darl* 3A **106**
Great Burstead. *Essx* 1A **40**
Great Busby. *N Yor* 4C **106**
Great Canfield. *Essx* 4F **53**
Great Carlton. *Linc* 2D **88**
Great Casterton. *Rut* 5G **75**
Great Chalfield. *Wilts* 5D **34**
Great Chart. *Kent* 1D **28**
Great Chatwell. *Staf* 4B **72**
Great Chesterford. *Essx* 1F **53**
Great Cheverell. *Wilts* 1E **23**
Great Chilton. *Dur* 1F **105**
Great Chishill. *Cambs* 2E **53**
Great Clacton. *Essx* 4E **55**
Great Cliff. *W Yor* 3D **92**
Great Clifton. *Cumb* 2B **102**
Great Coates. *NE Lin* 3F **95**
Great Comberton. *Worc* 1E **49**
Great Corby. *Cumb* 4F **113**
Great Cornard. *Suff* 1B **54**
Great Cowden. *E Yor* 5G **101**
Great Coxwell. *Oxon* 2A **36**
Great Crakehall. *N Yor* 5F **105**
Great Cransley. *Nptn* 3F **63**
Great Cressingham. *Norf* 5A **78**
Great Crosby. *Mers* 4B **90**
Great Cubley. *Derbs* 2F **73**
Great Dalby. *Leics* 4E **75**
Great Doddington. *Nptn* 4F **63**
Great Doward. *Here* 4A **48**
Great Dunham. *Norf* 4A **78**
Great Dunmow. *Essx* 3G **53**
Great Durnford. *Wilts* 3G **23**
Great Easton. *Essx* 3G **53**
Great Easton. *Leics* 1F **63**
Great Eccleston. *Lanc* 5D **96**
Great Edstone. *N Yor* 1B **100**
Great Ellingham. *Norf* 1C **66**
Great Elm. *Som* 2C **22**
Great Eppleton. *Tyne* 5G **115**
Great Eversden. *Cambs* 5C **64**
Great Fencote. *N Yor* 5F **105**
Great Finborough. *Suff* 5C **66**
Greatford. *Linc* 4H **75**
Great Fransham. *Norf* 4A **78**
Great Gaddesden. *Herts* 4A **52**
Great Gate. *Staf* 1E **73**
Great Gidding. *Cambs* 2A **64**
Great Givendale. *E Yor* 4C **100**
Great Glemham. *Suff* 4F **67**
Great Glen. *Leics* 1D **62**
Great Gonerby. *Linc* 2F **75**
Great Gransden. *Cambs* 5B **64**
Great Green. *Norf* 2E **67**
Great Green. *Suff*
  nr. Lavenham 5B **66**
  nr. Palgrave 3D **66**
Great Habton. *N Yor* 2B **100**
Great Hale. *Linc* 1A **76**
Great Hallingbury. *Essx* 4F **53**
Greatham. *Hants* 3F **25**
Greatham. *Hart* 2B **106**

Greatham. W Sus 4B 26
Great Hampden. Buck 5G 51
Great Harrowden. Nptn 3F 63
Great Harwood. Lanc 1F 91
Great Haseley. Oxon 5E 51
Great Hatfield. E Yor 5F 101
Great Haywood. Staf 3D 73
Great Heath. W Mid 2H 61
Great Heck. N Yor 2F 93
Great Henny. Essx 2B 54
Great Hinton. Wilts 1E 23
Great Hockham. Norf 1B 66
Great Holland. Essx 4F 55
Great Horkesley. Essx 2C 54
Great Hormead. Herts 2E 53
Great Horton. W Yor 1B 92
Great Horwood. Buck 2F 51
Great Houghton. Nptn 5E 63
Great Houghton. S Yor 4E 93
Great Hucklow. Derbs 3F 85
Great Kelk. E Yor 4F 101
Great Kendale. E Yor 3E 101
Great Kimble. Buck 5G 51
Great Kingshill. Buck 2G 37
Great Langdale. Cumb 4D 102
Great Langton. N Yor 5F 105
Great Leighs. Essx 4H 53
Great Limber. Linc 4E 95
Great Linford. Mil 1G 51
Great Livermere. Suff 3A 66
Great Longstone. Derbs 3G 85
Great Lumley. Dur 5F 115
Great Lyth. Shrp 5G 71
Great Malvern. Worc 1C 48
Great Maplestead. Essx 2B 54
Great Marton. Bkpl 1B 90
Great Massingham. Norf 3G 77
Great Melton. Norf 5D 78
Great Milton. Oxon 5E 51
Great Missenden. Buck 5G 51
Great Mitton. Lanc 1F 91
Great Mongeham. Kent 5H 41
Great Moulton. Norf 1D 66
Great Munden. Herts 3D 52
Great Musgrave. Cumb 3A 104
Great Ness. Shrp 4F 71
Great Notley. Essx 3H 53
Great Oak. Mon 5G 47
Great Oakley. Essx 3E 55
Great Oakley. Nptn 2F 63
Great Offley. Herts 3B 52
Great Ormside. Cumb 3A 104
Great Orton. Cumb 4E 113
Great Ouseburn. N Yor 3G 99
Great Oxendon. Nptn 2E 63
Great Oxney Green. Essx 5G 53
Great Parndon. Essx 5E 53
Great Paxton. Cambs 4B 64
Great Plumpton. Lanc 1B 90
Great Plumstead. Norf 4F 79
Great Ponton. Linc 2G 75
Great Potheridge. Devn 1F 11
Great Preston. W Yor 2E 93
Great Raveley. Cambs 2B 64
Great Rissington. Glos 4G 49
Great Rollright. Oxon 2B 50
Great Ryburgh. Norf 3B 78
Great Ryle. Nmbd 3E 121
Great Ryton. Shrp 5G 71
Great Saling. Essx 3H 53
Great Salkeld. Cumb 1G 103
Great Sampford. Essx 2G 53
Great Sankey. Warr 2H 83
Great Saredon. Staf 5D 72
Great Saxham. Suff 4G 65
Great Shefford. W Ber 4B 36
Great Shelford. Cambs 5D 64
Great Shoddesden. Hants 2A 24
Great Smeaton. N Yor 4A 106
Great Snoring. Norf 2B 78
Great Somerford. Wilts 3E 35
Great Stainton. Darl 2A 106
Great Stambridge. Essx 1C 40
Great Staughton. Cambs 4A 64
Great Steeping. Linc 4D 88
Great Stonar. Kent 5H 41
Greatstone-on-Sea. Kent 3E 29
Great Strickland. Cumb 2G 103
Great Stukeley. Cambs 3B 64
Great Sturton. Linc 3B 88
Great Sutton. Ches W 3F 83
Great Sutton. Shrp 2H 59
Great Swinburne. Nmbd 2C 114
Great Tew. Oxon 3B 50
Great Tey. Essx 3B 54
Great Thirkleby. N Yor 2G 99
Great Thorness. IOW 3C 16
Great Thurlow. Suff 5F 65
Great Torr. Devn 4C 8
Great Torrington. Devn 1E 11
Great Tosson. Nmbd 4E 121
Great Totham North. Essx 4B 54
Great Totham South. Essx 4B 54
Great Tows. Linc 1B 88
Great Urswick. Cumb 2B 96
Great Wakering. Essx 2D 40
Great Waldingfield. Suff 1C 54
Great Walsingham. Norf 2B 78
Great Waltham. Essx 4G 53
Great Warley. Essx 1G 39
Great Washbourne. Glos 2E 49
Great Wenham. Suff 2D 54
Great Whelnetham. Suff 5A 66
Great Whittington. Nmbd 2D 114
Great Wigborough. Essx 4C 54
Great Wilbraham. Cambs 5E 65
Great Wilne. Derbs 2B 74
Great Wishford. Wilts 3F 23
Great Witchingham. Norf 3D 78
Great Witcombe. Glos 4E 49
Great Witley. Worc 4B 60

Great Wolford. Warw 2H 49
Greatworth. Nptn 1D 50
Great Wratting. Suff 1G 53
Great Wymondley. Herts 3C 52
Great Wytheford. Shrp 4H 71
Great Yarmouth. Norf 196 (5H 79)
Great Yeldham. Essx 2A 54
Grebby. Linc 4D 88
Greeba Castle. IOM 3C 108
Green, The. Cumb 1A 96
Green, The. Wilts 3D 22
Greenbank. Shet 1G 173
Greenbottom. Corn 4B 6
Greenburn. W Lot 3C 128
Greencroft. Dur 4E 115
Greendykes. Nmbd 2E 121
Green End. Bed
   nr. Bedford 1A 52
   nr. Little Staughton 4A 64
Green End. Herts
   nr. Buntingford 2D 52
   nr. Stevenage 3D 52
Green End. N Yor 4F 107
Green End. Warw 2G 61
Greenfield. Arg 4B 134
Greenfield. C Beds 2A 52
Greenfield. Flin 3D 82
Greenfield. G Man 4H 91
Greenfield. Oxon 2F 37
Greenfoot. N Lan 3A 128
Greenford. G Lon 2C 38
Greengairs. N Lan 2A 128
Greengate. Norf 4C 78
Greengill. Cumb 1C 102
Greenhalgh. Lanc 1C 90
Greenham. Dors 2H 13
Greenham. Som 4D 20
Greenham. W Ber 5C 36
Green Hammerton. N Yor 4G 99
Greenhaugh. Nmbd 1A 114
Greenhead. Nmbd 3H 113
Green Heath. Staf 4D 73
Greenhill. Dum 2C 112
Greenhill. Falk 2B 128
Greenhill. Kent 4F 41
Greenhill. S Yor 2H 85
Greenhill. Worc 3C 60
Greenhills. N Ayr 4E 127
Greenhithe. Kent 3G 39
Greenholm. E Ayr 1E 117
Greenhow Hill. N Yor 3D 98
Greenigoe. Orkn 7D 172
Greenland. High 2E 169
Greenland Mains. High 2E 169
Greenlands. Worc 4E 61
Green Lane. Shrp 3A 72
Green Lane. Worc 4E 61
Greenlaw. Bord 5D 130
Greenlea. Dum 2B 112
Greenloaning. Per 3H 135
Greenmount. G Man 3F 91
Greenmow. Shet 9F 173
Greenock. Inv 2D 126
Greenock Mains. E Ayr 2F 117
Greenodd. Cumb 1C 96
Green Ore. Som 1A 22
Greenrow. Cumb 4C 112
Greens. Abers 4F 161
Greensgate. Norf 4D 78
Greenside. Tyne 3E 115
Greensidehill. Nmbd 3D 121
Greens Norton. Nptn 1E 51
Greenstead Green. Essx 3B 54
Greensted Green. Essx 5F 53
Green Street. Herts 1C 38
Green Street. Suff 3D 66
Green Street Green. G Lon 4F 39
Green Street Green. Kent 3G 39
Greenstreet Green. Suff 1D 54
Green Tye. Herts 4E 53
Greenwall. Orkn 7E 172
Greenway. Pemb 1E 43
Greenway. V Glam 4D 32
Greenwell. Cumb 4G 113
Greenwich. G Lon 3E 39
Greet. Glos 2F 49
Greete. Shrp 3H 59
Greetham. Linc 3C 88
Greetham. Rut 4G 75
Greetland. W Yor 2A 92
Gregson Lane. Lanc 2D 90
Grein. W Isl 8B 170
Greinetobht. W Isl 1D 170
Greinton. Som 3H 21
Gremista. Shet 7F 173
Grenaby. IOM 4B 108
Grendon. Nptn 4F 63
Grendon. Warw 1G 61
Grendon Common. Warw 1G 61
Grendon Green. Here 5H 59
Grendon Underwood. Buck 3E 51
Grenofen. Devn 5E 11
Grenoside. S Yor 1H 85
Greosabhagh. W Isl 8D 171
Gresford. Wrex 5F 83
Gresham. Norf 2D 78
Greshornish. High 3C 154
Gressenhall. Norf 4B 78
Gressingham. Lanc 3E 97
Greta Bridge. Dur 3D 105
Gretna. Dum 3E 112
Gretna Green. Dum 3E 112
Gretton. Glos 2F 49
Gretton. Nptn 1G 63
Gretton. Shrp 1H 59
Grewelthorpe. N Yor 2E 99
Greygarth. N Yor 2D 98
Grey Green. N Lin 4A 94
Greylake. Som 3G 21

Greysouthen. Cumb 2B 102
Greystoke. Cumb 1F 103
Greystoke Gill. Cumb 2F 103
Greystone. Ang 4E 145
Greywell. Hants 1F 25
Grianan. W Isl 4G 171
Grianan. W Isl 4G 171
Gribthorpe. E Yor 1A 94
Gribun. Arg 5F 139
Griff. Warw 2A 62
Griffithstown. Torf 2F 33
Griffydam. Leics 4B 74
Griggs Green. Hants 3G 25
Grimbister. Orkn 6C 172
Grimeford Village. Lanc 3E 90
Grimeston. Orkn 6C 172
Grimethorpe. S Yor 4E 93
Griminis. W Isl
   on Benbecula 3C 170
   on North Uist 1C 170
Grimister. Shet 2F 173
Grimley. Worc 4C 60
Grimness. Orkn 8D 172
Grimoldby. Linc 2C 88
Grimpo. Shrp 3F 71
Grimsargh. Lanc 1D 90
Grimsbury. Oxon 1C 50
Grimsby. NE Lin 4F 95
Grimscote. Nptn 5D 62
Grimscott. Corn 2C 10
Grimshaw. Bkbn 2F 91
Grimshaw Green. Lanc 3C 90
Grimsthorpe. Linc 3H 75
Grimston. E Yor 1F 95
Grimston. Leics 3D 74
Grimston. Norf 3G 77
Grimston. York 4A 100
Grimstone. Dors 3B 14
Grimstone End. Suff 4B 66
Grinacombe Moor. Devn 3E 11
Grindale. E Yor 2F 101
Grindhill. Devn 3E 11
Grindiscol. Shet 8F 173
Grindle. Shrp 5B 72
Grindleford. Derbs 3G 85
Grindleton. Lanc 5G 97
Grindley. Staf 3E 73
Grindley Brook. Shrp 1H 71
Grindlow. Derbs 3F 85
Grindon. Nmbd 5F 131
Grindon. Staf 5E 85
Gringley on the Hill. Notts 1E 87
Grinsdale. Cumb 4E 113
Grinshill. Shrp 3H 71
Grinton. N Yor 5D 104
Griomsidar. W Isl 5G 171
Grishipoll. Arg 3C 138
Grisling Common. E Sus 3F 27
Gristhorpe. N Yor 1E 101
Griston. Norf 1B 66
Gritley. Orkn 7E 172
Grittenham. Wilts 3F 35
Grittleton. Wilts 3D 34
Grizebeck. Cumb 1B 96
Grizedale. Cumb 5E 103
Grobister. Orkn 5F 172
Grobsness. Shet 5E 173
Groby. Leics 5C 74
Groes. Cnwy 4C 82
Groes. Neat 3A 32
Groes-faen. Rhon 3D 32
Groesffordd. Gwyn 2B 68
Groesffordd. Powy 3D 46
Groeslon. Gwyn 5D 81
Groes-lwyd. Powy 4E 70
Groes-wen. Cphy 3E 33
Grogport. Arg 5G 125
Groigearraidh. W Isl 4C 170
Gromford. Suff 5F 67
Gronant. Flin 2C 82
Groombridge. E Sus 2G 27
Grosmont. Mon 3H 47
Grosmont. N Yor 4F 107
Groton. Suff 1C 54
Grove. Dors 5B 14
Grove, The. Dum 2A 112
Grove. Kent 4G 41
Grove. Notts 3E 87
Grove. Oxon 2B 36
Grove, The. Worc 1D 48
Grovehill. E Yor 1D 94
Grove Park. G Lon 3F 39
Grovesend. Swan 5F 45
Grub Street. Staf 3B 72
Grudie. High 2F 157
Gruids. High 3C 164
Gruinard House. High 4D 162
Gruinart. Arg 3A 124
Grulinbeg. Arg 3A 124
Gruline. Arg 4G 139
Grummore. High 5G 167
Grundisburgh. Suff 5E 66
Gruting. Shet 7D 173
Grutness. Shet 10F 173
Gualachulain. High 4F 141
Gualin House. High 3D 166
Guardbridge. Fife 2G 137
Guarlford. Worc 1D 48
Guay. Per 4H 143
Gubblecote. Herts 4H 51
Guestling Green. E Sus 4C 28
Guestling Thorn. E Sus 4C 28
Guestwick. Norf 3C 78
Guestwick Green. Norf 3C 78
Guide. Bkbn 2F 91
Guide Post. Nmbd 1F 115
Guilden Down. Shrp 2F 59
Guilden Morden. Cambs 1C 52
Guilden Sutton. Ches W 4G 83
Guildford. Surr 197 (1A 26)

Guildtown. Per 5A 144
Guilsborough. Nptn 3D 62
Guilsfield. Powy 4E 70
Guineaford. Devn 3F 19
Guisborough. Red C 3D 106
Guiseley. W Yor 5D 98
Guist. Norf 3B 78
Guiting Power. Glos 3F 49
Gulberwick. Shet 8F 173
Gullane. E Lot 1A 130
Gulling Green. Suff 5H 65
Gulval. Corn 3B 4
Gulworthy. Devn 5E 11
Gumfreston. Pemb 4F 43
Gumley. Leics 1D 62
Gunby. E Yor 1H 93
Gunby. Linc 3G 75
Gundleton. Hants 3E 24
Gun Green. Kent 2B 28
Gunn. Devn 3G 19
Gunnerside. N Yor 5C 104
Gunnerton. Nmbd 2C 114
Gunness. N Lin 3B 94
Gunnislake. Corn 5E 11
Gunnista. Shet 7F 173
Gunsgreenhill. Bord 3F 131
Gunstone. Staf 5C 72
Gunthorpe. Norf 2C 78
Gunthorpe. N Lin 1F 87
Gunthorpe. Notts 1D 74
Gunthorpe. Pet 5A 76
Gunville. IOW 4C 16
Gupworthy. Som 3C 20
Gurnard. IOW 3C 16
Gurney Slade. Som 2B 22
Gurnos. Powy 5A 46
Gussage All Saints. Dors 1F 15
Gussage St Andrew. Dors 1E 15
Gussage St Michael. Dors 1E 15
Guston. Kent 1H 29
Gutcher. Shet 2G 173
Guthram Gowt. Linc 3A 76
Guthrie. Ang 3E 145
Guyhirn. Cambs 5D 76
Guyhirn Gull. Cambs 5C 76
Guy's Head. Linc 3D 77
Guy's Marsh. Dors 4D 22
Guyzance. Nmbd 4G 121
Gwaelod-y-garth. Card 3E 32
Gwaenynog Bach. Den 4C 82
Gwaenysgor. Flin 2C 82
Gwalchmai. IOA 3C 80
Gwastad. Pemb 2E 43
Gwaun-Cae-Gurwen. Neat 4H 45
Gwbert. Cdgn 1B 44
Gweek. Corn 4E 5
Gwehelog. Mon 5G 47
Gwenddwr. Powy 1D 46
Gwennap. Corn 4B 6
Gwenter. Corn 5E 5
Gwernaffield. Flin 4E 82
Gwernesney. Mon 5H 47
Gwernogle. Carm 2F 45
Gwern-y-go. Powy 1E 58
Gwernymynydd. Flin 4E 82
Gwersyllt. Wrex 5F 83
Gwespyr. Flin 2D 82
Gwinear. Corn 3C 4
Gwithian. Corn 2C 4
Gwredog. IOA 2D 80
Gwyddelwern. Den 1C 70
Gwyddgrug. Carm 2E 45
Gwynfryn. Wrex 5E 83
Gwystre. Powy 4C 58
Gwytherin. Cnwy 4A 82
Gyfelia. Wrex 1F 71
Gyffin. Cnwy 3G 81

H

Haa of Houlland. Shet 1G 173
Habberley. Shrp 5G 71
Habblesthorpe. Notts 2E 87
Habergham. Lanc 1G 91
Habin. W Sus 4G 25
Habrough. NE Lin 3E 95
Haceby. Linc 2H 75
Hacheston. Suff 5F 67
Hackenthorpe. S Yor 2B 86
Hackford. Norf 5C 78
Hackforth. N Yor 5F 105
Hackland. Orkn 5C 172
Hackleton. Nptn 5F 63
Hackman's Gate. Worc 3C 60
Hackness. N Yor 5G 107
Hackness. Orkn 8C 172
Hackney. G Lon 2E 39
Hackthorn. Linc 2G 87
Hackthorpe. Cumb 2G 103
Haclait. W Isl 4D 170
Haconby. Linc 3A 76
Hadden. Bord 1B 120
Haddenham. Buck 5F 51
Haddenham. Cambs 3D 64
Haddenham End Field.
   Cambs 3D 64
Haddington. E Lot 2B 130
Haddington. Linc 4G 87
Haddiscoe. Norf 1G 67
Haddo. Abers 5F 161
Haddon. Cambs 1A 64
Hademore. Staf 5F 73
Hadfield. Derbs 1E 85
Hadham Cross. Herts 4E 53
Hadham Ford. Herts 3E 53
Hadleigh. Essx 2C 40
Hadleigh. Suff 1D 54
Hadleigh Heath. Suff 1C 54
Hadley. Telf 4A 72

Hadley. Worc 4C 60
Hadley End. Staf 3F 73
Hadley Wood. G Lon 1D 38
Hadnall. Shrp 3H 71
Hadstock. Essx 1F 53
Hadston. Nmbd 4G 121
Hady. Derbs 3A 86
Hadzor. Worc 4D 60
Haffenden Quarter. Kent 1C 28
Haggate. Lanc 1G 91
Haggbeck. Cumb 2F 113
Haggersta. Shet 7E 173
Haggerston. Nmbd 5G 131
Haggrister. Shet 4E 173
Hagley. Here 1A 48
Hagley. Worc 2D 60
Hagnaby. Linc 4C 88
Hagworthingham. Linc 4C 88
Haigh. G Man 4E 90
Haigh Moor. W Yor 2C 92
Haighton Green. Lanc 1D 90
Haile. Cumb 4B 102
Hailes. Glos 2F 49
Hailey. Herts 4D 52
Hailey. Oxon 4B 50
Hailsham. E Sus 5G 27
Hail Weston. Cambs 4A 64
Hainault. G Lon 1F 39
Hainford. Norf 4E 78
Hainton. Linc 2A 88
Hainworth. W Yor 1A 92
Haisthorpe. E Yor 3F 101
Hakin. Pemb 4C 42
Halam. Notts 5D 86
Halbeath. Fife 1E 129
Halberton. Devn 1D 12
Halcro. High 2E 169
Hale. Cumb 2E 97
Hale. G Man 2B 84
Hale. Hal 2G 83
Hale. Hants 1G 15
Hale. Surr 2G 25
Halebarns. G Man 2B 84
Hales. Norf 1F 67
Hales. Staf 2B 72
Halesgate. Linc 3C 76
Hales Green. Derbs 1F 73
Halesowen. W Mid 2D 60
Hale Street. Kent 1A 28
Halesworth. Suff 3F 67
Halewood. Mers 2G 83
Halford. Shrp 2G 59
Halford. Warw 1A 50
Halfpenny. Cumb 1E 97
Halfpenny Furze. Carm 3G 43
Halfpenny Green. Staf 1C 60
Halfway. Carm
   nr. Llandeilo 2G 45
   nr. Llandovery 2B 46
Halfway. S Yor 2B 86
Halfway. W Ber 5C 36
Halfway House. Shrp 4F 71
Halfway Houses. Kent 3D 40
Halgabron. Corn 4A 10
Halifax. W Yor 2A 92
Halistra. High 3B 154
Halket. E Ayr 4F 127
Halkirk. High 3D 168
Halkyn. Flin 3E 82
Hallam Fields. Derbs 1B 74
Halland. E Sus 4G 27
Hallands, The. N Lin 2D 94
Hallaton. Leics 1E 63
Hallatrow. Bath 1B 22
Hallbank. Cumb 5H 103
Hallbankgate. Cumb 4G 113
Hall Dunnerdale. Cumb 5D 102
Hallen. S Glo 3A 34
Hall End. Bed 1A 52
Hallgarth. Dur 5G 115
Hall Green. Ches E 5C 84
Hall Green. Norf 2D 66
Hall Green. W Mid 2F 61
Hall Green. W Yor 3D 92
Hall Green. Wrex 1G 71
Halliburton. Bord 5C 130
Hallin. High 3B 154
Halling. Medw 4B 40
Hallington. Linc 2C 88
Hallington. Nmbd 2C 114
Halloughton. Notts 5D 86
Hallow. Worc 5C 60
Hallow Heath. Worc 5C 60
Hallowsgate. Ches W 4H 83
Hallsands. Devn 5E 9
Hall's Green. Herts 3C 52
Hallspill. Devn 4E 19
Hallthwaites. Cumb 1A 96
Hall Waberthwaite. Cumb 5C 102
Hallwood Green. Glos 2B 48
Hallworthy. Corn 4B 10
Hallyne. Bord 5E 129
Halmer End. Staf 1C 72
Halmond's Frome. Here 1B 48
Halmore. Glos 5B 48
Halnaker. W Sus 5A 26
Halsall. Lanc 3B 90
Halse. Nptn 1D 50
Halse. Som 4E 21
Halsetown. Corn 3C 4
Halsham. E Yor 2F 95
Halsinger. Devn 3F 19
Halstead. Essx 2B 54
Halstead. Kent 4F 39
Halstead. Leics 5E 75
Halstock. Dors 2A 14
Halsway. Som 3E 21

Haltcliff Bridge. *Cumb* 1E **103**
Haltham. *Linc* 4B **88**
Haltoft End. *Linc* 1C **76**
Halton. *Buck* 5G **51**
Halton. *Hal* 2H **83**
Halton. *Lanc* 3E **97**
Halton. *Nmbd* 3C **114**
Halton. *W Yor* 1D **92**
Halton. *Wrex* 2F **71**
Halton East. *N Yor* 4C **98**
Halton Fenside. *Linc* 4D **88**
Halton Gill. *N Yor* 2A **98**
Halton Holegate. *Linc* 4D **88**
Halton Lea Gate. *Nmbd* 4H **113**
Halton Moor. *W Yor* 1D **92**
Halton Shields. *Nmbd* 3D **114**
Halton West. *N Yor* 4H **97**
Haltwhistle. *Nmbd* 3A **114**
Halvergate. *Norf* 5G **79**
Halwell. *Devn* 3D **9**
Halwill. *Devn* 3E **11**
Halwill Junction. *Devn* 3E **11**
Ham. *Devn* 2F **13**
Ham. *Glos* 2B **34**
Ham. *G Lon* 3C **38**
Ham. *High* 1E **169**
Ham. *Kent* 5H **41**
Ham. *Plym* 3A **8**
Ham. *Shet* 8A **173**
Ham. *Som*
   nr. Ilminster 1F **13**
   nr. Taunton 4F **21**
   nr. Wellington 4E **21**
Ham. *Wilts* 5B **36**
Hambleden. *Buck* 3F **37**
Hambledon. *Hants* 1E **17**
Hambledon. *Surr* 2A **26**
Hamble-le-Rice. *Hants* 2C **16**
Hambleton. *Lanc* 5C **96**
Hambleton. *N Yor* 1F **93**
Hambridge. *Som* 4G **21**
Hambrook. *S Glo* 4B **34**
Hambrook. *W Sus* 2F **17**
Ham Common. *Dors* 4D **22**
Hameringham. *Linc* 4C **88**
Hamerton. *Cambs* 3A **64**
Ham Green. *Here* 1C **48**
Ham Green. *Kent* 4C **40**
Ham Green. *N Som* 4A **34**
Ham Green. *Worc* 4E **61**
Ham Hill. *Kent* 4A **40**
Hamilton. *Leic* 5D **74**
Hamilton. *S Lan* 4A **128**
Hamister. *Shet* 5G **173**
Hammer. *W Sus* 3G **25**
Hammersmith. *G Lon* 3D **38**
Hammerwich. *Staf* 5E **73**
Hammerwood. *E Sus* 2F **27**
Hammill. *Kent* 5G **41**
Hammond Street. *Herts* 5D **52**
Hammoon. *Dors* 1D **14**
Hamnavoe. *Shet*
   nr. Braehoulland 3D **173**
   nr. Burland 8E **173**
   nr. Lunna 4F **173**
   on Yell 3F **173**
Hamp. *Som* 3G **21**
Hampden Park. *E Sus* 5G **27**
Hampen. *Glos* 4F **49**
Hamperden End. *Essx* 2F **53**
Hamperley. *Shrp* 2G **59**
Hampnett. *Glos* 4F **49**
Hampole. *S Yor* 3F **93**
Hampreston. *Dors* 3F **15**
Hampstead. *G Lon* 2D **38**
Hampstead Norreys. *W Ber* 4D **36**
Hampsthwaite. *N Yor* 4E **99**
Hampton. *Devn* 3F **13**
Hampton. *G Lon* 3C **38**
Hampton. *Kent* 4F **41**
Hampton. *Shrp* 2B **60**
Hampton. *Swin* 2G **35**
Hampton. *Worc* 1F **49**
Hampton Bishop. *Here* 2A **48**
Hampton Fields. *Glos* 2D **35**
Hampton Hargate. *Pet* 1A **64**
Hampton Heath. *Ches W* 1H **71**
Hampton in Arden. *W Mid* 2G **61**
Hampton Loade. *Shrp* 2B **60**
Hampton Lovett. *Worc* 4C **60**
Hampton Lucy. *Warw* 5G **61**
Hampton Magna. *Warw* 4G **61**
Hampton on the Hill. *Warw* 4G **61**
Hampton Poyle. *Oxon* 4D **50**
Hampton Wick. *G Lon* 4C **38**
Hamptworth. *Wilts* 1H **15**
Hamrow. *Norf* 3B **78**
Hamsey. *E Sus* 4F **27**
Hamsey Green. *Surr* 5E **39**
Hamstall Ridware. *Staf* 4F **73**
Hamstead. *IOW* 3C **16**
Hamstead. *W Mid* 1E **61**
Hamstead Marshall.
   W Ber 5C **36**
Hamsterley. *Dur*
   nr. Consett 4E **121**
   nr. Wolsingham 1E **105**
Hamsterley Mill. *Dur* 4E **115**
Hamstreet. *Kent* 2E **28**
Ham Street. *Som* 3A **22**
Hamworthy. *Pool* 3E **15**
Hanbury. *Staf* 3F **73**
Hanbury. *Worc* 4D **60**
Hanbury Woodend. *Staf* 3F **73**
Hanby. *Linc* 2H **75**
Hanchurch. *Staf* 1C **72**
Hand and Pen. *Devn* 3D **12**
Handbridge. *Ches W* 4G **83**
Handforth. *Ches E* 2C **84**
Handley. *Ches W* 5G **83**

Handley. *Derbs* 4A **86**
Handsacre. *Staf* 4E **73**
Handsworth. *S Yor* 2B **86**
Handsworth. *W Mid* 1E **61**
Handy Cross. *Buck* 2G **37**
Hanford. *Dors* 1D **14**
Hanford. *Stoke* 1C **72**
Hangersley. *Hants* 2G **15**
Hanging Houghton. *Nptn* 3E **63**
Hanging Langford. *Wilts* 3F **23**
Hangleton. *Brig* 5D **26**
Hangleton. *W Sus* 5B **26**
Hanham. *S Glo* 4B **34**
Hanham Green. *S Glo* 4B **34**
Hankelow. *Ches E* 1A **72**
Hankerton. *Wilts* 2E **35**
Hankham. *E Sus* 5H **27**
Hanley. *Stoke* **211** (1C **72**)
Hanley Castle. *Worc* 1D **48**
Hanley Childe. *Worc* 4A **60**
Hanley Swan. *Worc* 1D **48**
Hanley William. *Worc* 4A **60**
Hanlith. *N Yor* 3B **98**
Hanmer. *Wrex* 2G **71**
Hannaborough. *Devn* 2F **11**
Hannaford. *Devn* 4G **19**
Hannah. *Linc* 3E **89**
Hannington. *Hants* 1D **24**
Hannington. *Nptn* 3F **63**
Hannington. *Swin* 2G **35**
Hannington Wick. *Swin* 2G **35**
Hanscombe End. *C Beds* 2B **52**
Hanslope. *Mil* 1G **51**
Hanthorpe. *Linc* 3H **75**
Hanwell. *G Lon* 2C **38**
Hanwell. *Oxon* 1C **50**
Hanwood. *Shrp* 5G **71**
Hanworth. *G Lon* 3C **38**
Hanworth. *Norf* 2D **78**
Happas. *Ang* 4D **144**
Happendon. *S Lan* 1A **118**
Happisburgh. *Norf* 2F **79**
Happisburgh Common. *Norf* 3F **79**
Hapsford. *Ches W* 3G **83**
Hapton. *Lanc* 1F **91**
Hapton. *Norf* 1D **66**
Harberton. *Devn* 3D **9**
Harbertonford. *Devn* 3D **9**
Harbledown. *Kent* 5F **41**
Harborne. *W Mid* 2E **61**
Harborough Magna. *Warw* 3B **62**
Harbottle. *Nmbd* 4D **120**
Harbourneford. *Devn* 2D **8**
Harbours Hill. *Worc* 4D **60**
Harbridge. *Hants* 1G **15**
Harbury. *Warw* 4A **62**
Harby. *Leics* 2E **75**
Harby. *Notts* 3F **87**
Harcombe. *Devn* 3E **13**
Harcombe Bottom. *Devn* 3G **13**
Harcourt. *Corn* 5C **6**
Harden. *W Yor* 1A **92**
Hardenhuish. *Wilts* 4E **35**
Hardgate. *Abers* 3E **153**
Hardgate. *Dum* 3F **111**
Hardham. *W Sus* 4B **26**
Hardingham. *Norf* 5C **78**
Hardingstone. *Nptn* 5E **63**
Hardings Wood. *Staf* 5C **84**
Hardington. *Som* 1C **22**
Hardington Mandeville. *Som* 1A **14**
Hardington Marsh. *Som* 2A **14**
Hardington Moor. *Som* 1A **14**
Hardley. *Hants* 2C **16**
Hardley Street. *Norf* 5F **79**
Hardmead. *Mil* 1H **51**
Hardraw. *N Yor* 5B **104**
Hardstoft. *Derbs* 4B **86**
Hardway. *Hants* 2E **16**
Hardway. *Som* 3C **22**
Hardwick. *Buck* 4G **51**
Hardwick. *Cambs* 5C **64**
Hardwick. *Norf* 2E **66**
Hardwick. *Oxon*
   nr. Bicester 3D **50**
   nr. Witney 5B **50**
Hardwick. *Shrp* 1F **59**
Hardwick. *S Yor* 2B **86**
Hardwick. *Stoc T* 2B **106**
Hardwick. *W Mid* 1E **61**
Hardwicke. *Glos*
   nr. Cheltenham 3E **49**
   nr. Gloucester 4C **48**
Hardwicke. *Here* 1F **47**
Hardwick Village. *Notts* 3D **86**
Hardy's Green. *Essx* 3C **54**
Hare. *Som* 1F **13**
Hareby. *Linc* 4C **88**
Hareden. *Lanc* 4F **97**
Harefield. *G Lon* 1B **38**
Hare Green. *Essx* 3D **54**
Hare Hatch. *Wok* 4G **37**
Harehill. *Derbs* 2F **73**
Harehills. *W Yor* 1D **92**
Harehope. *Nmbd* 2E **121**
Harelaw. *Dum* 2F **113**
Harelaw. *Dur* 4E **115**
Hareplain. *Kent* 2C **28**
Haresceugh. *Cumb* 5H **113**
Harescombe. *Glos* 4D **48**
Haresfield. *Glos* 4D **48**
Hareshaw. *N Lan* 3B **128**
Hare Street. *Essx* 5E **53**
Hare Street. *Herts* 3D **53**
Harewood. *W Yor* 5F **99**
Harewood End. *Here* 3A **48**
Harford. *Devn* 3C **8**
Hargate. *Norf* 1D **66**
Hargatewall. *Derbs* 3F **85**

Hargrave. *Ches W* 4G **83**
Hargrave. *Nptn* 3H **63**
Hargrave. *Suff* 5G **65**
Harker. *Cumb* 3E **113**
Harkland. *Shet* 3F **173**
Harkstead. *Suff* 2E **55**
Harlaston. *Staf* 4G **73**
Harlaxton. *Linc* 2F **75**
Harlech. *Gwyn* 2E **69**
Harlequin. *Notts* 2D **74**
Harlescott. *Shrp* 4H **71**
Harleston. *Devn* 4D **9**
Harleston. *Norf* 2E **67**
Harleston. *Suff* 4C **66**
Harlestone. *Nptn* 4E **62**
Harley. *Shrp* 5H **71**
Harley. *S Yor* 1A **86**
Harling Road. *Norf* 2B **66**
Harlington. *C Beds* 2A **52**
Harlington. *G Lon* 3B **38**
Harlington. *S Yor* 4E **93**
Harlosh. *High* 4B **154**
Harlow. *Essx* 4E **53**
Harlow Hill. *Nmbd* 3D **115**
Harlsey Castle. *N Yor* 5B **106**
Harlthorpe. *E Yor* 1H **93**
Harlton. *Cambs* 5C **64**
Harlyn Bay. *Corn* 1C **6**
Harman's Cross. *Dors* 4E **15**
Harmby. *N Yor* 1D **98**
Harmer Green. *Herts* 4C **52**
Harmer Hill. *Shrp* 3G **71**
Harmondsworth. *G Lon* 3B **38**
Harmston. *Linc* 4G **87**
Harnage. *Shrp* 5H **71**
Harnham. *Nmbd* 1D **115**
Harnham. *Wilts* 4G **23**
Harnhill. *Glos* 5F **49**
Harold Hill. *G Lon* 1G **39**
Haroldston West. *Pemb* 3C **42**
Haroldswick. *Shet* 1H **173**
Harold Wood. *G Lon* 1G **39**
Harome. *N Yor* 1A **100**
Harpenden. *Herts* 4B **52**
Harpford. *Devn* 3D **12**
Harpham. *E Yor* 3E **101**
Harpley. *Norf* 3G **77**
Harpley. *Worc* 4A **60**
Harpole. *Nptn* 4D **62**
Harpsdale. *High* 3D **168**
Harpsden. *Oxon* 3F **37**
Harpswell. *Linc* 2G **87**
Harpurhey. *G Man* 4G **91**
Harpur Hill. *Derbs* 3E **85**
Harraby. *Cumb* 4F **113**
Harracott. *Devn* 4F **19**
Harrapool. *High* 1E **147**
Harrapul. *High* 1E **147**
Harrietfield. *Per* 1B **136**
Harrietsham. *Kent* 5C **40**
Harrington. *Cumb* 2A **102**
Harrington. *Linc* 3C **88**
Harrington. *Nptn* 2E **63**
Harringworth. *Nptn* 1G **63**
Harriseahead. *Staf* 5C **84**
Harriston. *Cumb* 5C **112**
Harrogate. *N Yor* **197** (4F **99**)
Harrold. *Bed* 5G **63**
Harrop Dale. *G Man* 4A **92**
Harrow. *G Lon* 2C **38**
Harrowbarrow. *Corn* 2H **7**
Harrowden. *Bed* 1A **52**
Harrowgate Hill. *Darl* 3F **105**
Harrow on the Hill. *G Lon* 2C **38**
Harrow Weald. *G Lon* 1C **38**
Harry Stoke. *S Glo* 4B **34**
Harston. *Cambs* 5D **64**
Harston. *Leics* 2F **75**
Harswell. *E Yor* 5C **100**
Hart. *Hart* 1B **106**
Hartburn. *Nmbd* 1D **115**
Hartburn. *Stoc T* 3B **106**
Hartest. *Suff* 5H **65**
Hartfield. *E Sus* 2F **27**
Hartford. *Cambs* 3B **64**
Hartford. *Ches W* 3A **84**
Hartford. *Som* 4C **20**
Hartford Bridge. *Hants* 1F **25**
Hartford End. *Essx* 4G **53**
Harthill. *Ches W* 5H **83**
Harthill. *N Lan* 3C **128**
Harthill. *S Yor* 2B **86**
Hartington. *Derbs* 4F **85**
Hartland. *Devn* 4C **18**
Hartland Quay. *Devn* 4C **18**
Hartle. *Worc* 3D **60**
Hartlebury. *Worc* 3C **60**
Hartlepool. *Hart* 1C **106**
Hartley. *Cumb* 4A **104**
Hartley. *Kent*
   nr. Cranbrook 2B **28**
   nr. Dartford 4H **39**
Hartley. *Nmbd* 2G **115**
Hartley Green. *Staf* 3D **73**
Hartley Mauditt. *Hants* 3F **25**
Hartley Wespall. *Hants* 1E **25**
Hartley Wintney. *Hants* 1F **25**
Hartlip. *Kent* 4C **40**
Hartmount Holdings. *High* 1B **158**
Hartoft End. *N Yor* 5E **107**
Harton. *N Yor* 3B **100**
Harton. *Shrp* 2G **59**
Harton. *Tyne* 3G **115**
Hartpury. *Glos* 3D **48**
Hartshead. *W Yor* 2B **92**
Hartshill. *Warw* 1H **61**
Hartshorne. *Derbs* 3H **73**
Hartsop. *Cumb* 3F **103**
Hart Station. *Hart* 1B **106**
Hartswell. *Som* 4D **20**
Hartwell. *Nptn* 5E **63**

Hartwood. *Lanc* 3D **90**
Hartwood. *N Lan* 4B **128**
Harvel. *Kent* 4A **40**
Harvington. *Worc*
   nr. Evesham 1F **49**
   nr. Kidderminster 3C **60**
Harwell. *Oxon* 3C **36**
Harwich. *Essx* **215** (2F **55**)
Harwood. *Dur* 1B **104**
Harwood. *G Man* 3F **91**
Harwood Dale. *N Yor* 5G **107**
Harworth. *Notts* 1D **86**
Hascombe. *Surr* 2A **26**
Haselbech. *Nptn* 3E **62**
Haselbury Plucknett. *Som* 1H **13**
Haseley. *Warw* 4G **61**
Hasfield. *Glos* 3D **48**
Hasguard. *Pemb* 4C **42**
Haskayne. *Lanc* 4B **90**
Hasketon. *Suff* 5E **67**
Hasland. *Derbs* 4A **86**
Haslemere. *Surr* 2A **26**
Haslingden. *Lanc* 2F **91**
Haslingfield. *Cambs* 5D **64**
Haslington. *Ches E* 5B **84**
Hassall. *Ches E* 5B **84**
Hassall Green. *Ches E* 5B **84**
Hassell Street. *Kent* 1E **29**
Hassendean. *Bord* 2H **119**
Hassingham. *Norf* 5F **79**
Hassness. *Cumb* 3C **102**
Hassocks. *W Sus* 4E **27**
Hassop. *Derbs* 3G **85**
Haster. *High* 3F **169**
Hasthorpe. *Linc* 4D **89**
Hastigrow. *High* 2E **169**
Hastingleigh. *Kent* 1E **29**
Hastings. *E Sus* 5C **28**
Hastingwood. *Essx* 5E **53**
Hastoe. *Herts* 5H **51**
Haston. *Shrp* 3H **71**
Haswell. *Dur* 5G **115**
Haswell Plough. *Dur* 5G **115**
Hatch. *C Beds* 1B **52**
Hatch Beauchamp. *Som* 4G **21**
Hatch End. *G Lon* 1C **38**
Hatch Green. *Som* 1G **13**
Hatching Green. *Herts* 4B **52**
Hatchmere. *Ches W* 3H **83**
Hatch Warren. *Hants* 2E **24**
Hatcliffe. *NE Lin* 4F **95**
Hatfield. *Here* 5H **59**
Hatfield. *Herts* 5C **52**
Hatfield. *S Yor* 4G **93**
Hatfield. *Worc* 5C **60**
Hatfield Broad Oak. *Essx* 4F **53**
Hatfield Garden Village. *Herts* 5C **52**
Hatfield Heath. *Essx* 4F **53**
Hatfield Hyde. *Herts* 4C **52**
Hatfield Peverel. *Essx* 4A **54**
Hatfield Woodhouse. *S Yor* 4G **93**
Hatford. *Oxon* 2B **36**
Hatherden. *Hants* 1B **24**
Hatherleigh. *Devn* 2F **11**
Hathern. *Leics* 3B **74**
Hatherop. *Glos* 5G **49**
Hathersage. *Derbs* 2G **85**
Hathersage Booths. *Derbs* 2G **85**
Hatherton. *Ches E* 1A **72**
Hatherton. *Staf* 4D **72**
Hatley St George. *Cambs* 5B **64**
Hatt. *Corn* 2H **7**
Hattersley. *G Man* 1D **85**
Hattingley. *Hants* 3E **25**
Hatton. *Abers* 5H **161**
Hatton. *Derbs* 2G **73**
Hatton. *G Lon* 3B **38**
Hatton. *Linc* 3A **88**
Hatton. *Shrp* 1G **59**
Hatton. *Warr* 2A **84**
Hatton. *Warw* 4G **61**
Hattoncrook. *Abers* 1F **153**
Hatton Heath. *Ches W* 4G **83**
Hatton of Fintray. *Abers* 2F **153**
Haugh. *E Ayr* 2D **117**
Haugh. *Linc* 3D **88**
Haugham. *Linc* 2C **88**
Haugh Head. *Nmbd* 2E **121**
Haughley. *Suff* 4C **66**
Haughley Green. *Suff* 4C **66**
Haugh of Ballechin. *Per* 3G **143**
Haugh of Glass. *Mor* 5B **160**
Haugh of Urr. *Dum* 3F **111**
Haughton. *Ches E* 5H **83**
Haughton. *Notts* 3D **86**
Haughton. *Shrp*
   nr. Bridgnorth 1A **60**
   nr. Oswestry 3F **71**
   nr. Shifnal 5B **72**
   nr. Shrewsbury 4H **71**
Haughton. *Staf* 3C **72**
Haughton Green. *G Man* 1D **84**
Haughton le Skerne. *Darl* 3A **106**
Haultwick. *Herts* 3D **52**
Haunn. *Arg* 4E **139**
Haunn. *W Isl* 7C **170**
Haunton. *Staf* 4G **73**
Hauxton. *Cambs* 5D **64**
Havannah. *Ches E* 4C **84**
Havant. *Hants* 2F **17**
Haven. *Here* 5G **59**
Haven, The. *W Sus* 2B **26**
Haven Bank. *Linc* 5B **88**
Havenstreet. *IOW* 3D **16**
Havercroft. *W Yor* 3D **93**
Haverfordwest. *Pemb* 3D **42**
Haverhill. *Suff* 1G **53**
Haverigg. *Cumb* 2A **96**
Havering-Atte-Bower.
   G Lon 1G **39**
Havering's Grove. *Essx* 1A **40**

Haversham. *Mil* 1G **51**
Haverthwaite. *Cumb* 1C **96**
Haverton Hill. *Stoc T* 2B **106**
Havyatt. *Som* 3A **22**
Hawarden. *Flin* 4F **83**
Hawbridge. *Worc* 1E **49**
Hawcoat. *Cumb* 2B **96**
Hawcross. *Glos* 2C **48**
Hawen. *Cdgn* 1D **44**
Hawes. *N Yor* 1A **98**
Hawes Green. *Norf* 1E **67**
Hawick. *Bord* 3H **119**
Hawkchurch. *Devn* 2G **13**
Hawkedon. *Suff* 5G **65**
Hawkenbury. *Kent* 1C **28**
Hawkeridge. *Wilts* 1D **22**
Hawkerland. *Devn* 4D **12**
Hawkesbury. *S Glo* 3C **34**
Hawkesbury. *Warw* 2A **62**
Hawkesbury Upton. *S Glo* 3C **34**
Hawkes End. *W Mid* 2G **61**
Hawk Green. *G Man* 2D **84**
Hawkhurst. *Kent* 2B **28**
Hawkhurst Common. *E Sus* 4G **27**
Hawkinge. *Kent* 1G **29**
Hawkley. *Hants* 4F **25**
Hawkridge. *Som* 3B **20**
Hawksdale. *Cumb* 5E **113**
Hawkshaw. *G Man* 3F **91**
Hawkshead. *Cumb* 5E **103**
Hawkshead Hill. *Cumb* 5E **103**
Hawkswick. *N Yor* 2B **98**
Hawksworth. *Notts* 1E **75**
Hawksworth. *W Yor* 5D **98**
Hawkwell. *Essx* 1C **40**
Hawley. *Hants* 1G **25**
Hawley. *Kent* 3G **39**
Hawling. *Glos* 3F **49**
Hawnby. *N Yor* 1H **99**
Haworth. *W Yor* 1A **92**
Hawstead. *Suff* 5A **66**
Hawthorn. *Dur* 5H **115**
Hawthorn Hill. *Brac* 4G **37**
Hawthorn Hill. *Linc* 5B **88**
Hawthorpe. *Linc* 3H **75**
Hawton. *Notts* 5E **87**
Haxby. *York* 4A **100**
Haxey. *N Lin* 1E **87**
Haybridge. *Shrp* 3A **60**
Haybridge. *Som* 2A **22**
Haydock. *Mers* 1H **83**
Haydon. *Bath* 1B **22**
Haydon. *Dors* 1B **14**
Haydon. *Som* 4F **21**
Haydon Bridge. *Nmbd* 3B **114**
Haydon Wick. *Swin* 3G **35**
Haye. *Corn* 2H **7**
Hayes. *G Lon*
   nr. Bromley 4F **39**
   nr. Uxbridge 2B **38**
Hayfield. *Derbs* 2E **85**
Hay Green. *Norf* 4E **77**
Hayhill. *E Ayr* 3D **116**
Haylands. *IOW* 3D **16**
Hayle. *Corn* 3C **4**
Hayley Green. *W Mid* 2D **60**
Hayling Island. *Hants* 3F **17**
Hayne. *Devn* 3B **12**
Haynes. *C Beds* 1A **52**
Haynes West End. *C Beds* 1A **52**
Hay-on-Wye. *Powy* 1F **47**
Hayscastle. *Pemb* 2C **42**
Hayscastle Cross. *Pemb* 2D **42**
Hayshead. *Ang* 4F **145**
Hay Street. *Herts* 3D **53**
Hayton. *Aber* 3G **153**
Hayton. *Cumb*
   nr. Aspatria 5C **112**
   nr. Brampton 4G **113**
Hayton. *E Yor* 5C **100**
Hayton. *Notts* 2E **87**
Hayton's Bent. *Shrp* 2H **59**
Haytor Vale. *Devn* 5A **12**
Haywood. *S Lan* 4C **128**
Haywards Heath. *W Sus* 3E **27**
Haywood. *S Lan* 4C **128**
Hazelbank. *S Lan* 5B **128**
Hazelbury Bryan. *Dors* 2C **14**
Hazeleigh. *Essx* 5B **54**
Hazeley. *Hants* 1F **25**
Hazel Grove. *G Man* 2D **84**
Hazelhead. *S Yor* 4B **92**
Hazelslade. *Staf* 4E **73**
Hazel Street. *Kent* 2A **28**
Hazelton Walls. *Fife* 1F **137**
Hazelwood. *Derbs* 1H **73**
Hazlemere. *Buck* 2G **37**
Hazler. *Shrp* 1G **59**
Hazlerigg. *Tyne* 2F **115**
Hazles. *Staf* 1E **73**
Hazleton. *Glos* 4F **49**
Hazon. *Nmbd* 4F **121**
Heacham. *Norf* 2F **77**
Headbourne Worthy. *Hants* 3C **24**
Headcorn. *Kent* 1C **28**
Headingley. *W Yor* 1C **92**
Headington. *Oxon* 5D **50**
Headlam. *Dur* 3E **105**
Headless Cross. *Worc* 4E **61**
Headley. *Hants*
   nr. Haslemere 3G **25**
   nr. Kingsclere 5D **36**
Headley. *Surr* 5D **38**
Headley Down. *Hants* 3G **25**
Headley Heath. *Worc* 3E **61**
Headley Park. *Bris* 5A **34**
Headon. *Notts* 3E **87**
Heads Nook. *Cumb* 4F **113**
Heage. *Derbs* 5A **86**

Healaugh. N Yor
  nr. Grinton 5D 104
  nr. York 5H 99
Heald Green. G Man 2C 84
Heale. Devn 2G 19
Healey. G Man 3G 91
Healey. Nmbd 4D 114
Healey. N Yor 1D 98
Healeyfield. Dur 5D 114
Healing. NE Lin 3F 95
Heamoor. Corn 3B 4
Heanish. Arg 4B 138
Heanor. Derbs 1B 74
Heanton Punchardon. Devn . .3F 19
Heapham. Linc 2F 87
Heartsease. Powy 4D 58
Heasley Mill. Devn 3A 19
Heaste. High 2E 147
Heath. Derbs 4B 86
Heath, The. Norf
  nr. Buxton 3E 79
  nr. Fakenham 3B 78
  nr. Hevingham 3D 78
Heath, The. Staf 2E 73
Heath, The. Suff 2E 55
Heath and Reach. C Beds . . .3H 51
Heath Common. W Sus 4C 26
Heathcote. Derbs 4F 85
Heath Cross. Devn 3H 11
Heathencote. Nptn 1F 51
Heath End. Hants 5D 36
Heath End. Leics 3A 74
Heath End. W Mid 5E 73
Heather. Leics 4A 74
Heatherfield. High 4D 155
Heatherton. Derb 2H 73
Heathfield. Cambs 1E 53
Heathfield. Cumb 5C 112
Heathfield. Devn 5B 12
Heathfield. E Sus 3G 27
Heathfield. Ren 3E 126
Heathfield. Som
  nr. Lydeard St Lawrence . .3E 21
  nr. Norton Fitzwarren 4E 21
Heath Green. Worc 3E 61
Heathhall. Dum 2A 112
Heath Hayes. Staf 4E 73
Heath Hill. Shrp 4B 72
Heath House. Som 2H 21
Heathrow Airport.
  G Lon 216 (3B 38)
Heathstock. Devn 2F 13
Heathton. Shrp 1C 60
Heathtop. Derb 2G 73
Heath Town. W Mid 1D 60
Heatley. Staf 3E 73
Heatley. Warr 2B 84
Heaton. Lanc 3D 96
Heaton. Staf 4D 84
Heaton. Tyne 3F 115
Heaton. W Yor 1B 92
Heaton Moor. G Man 1C 84
Heaton's Bridge. Lanc 3C 90
Heaverham. Kent 5G 39
Heavitree. Devn 3C 12
Hebburn. Tyne 3G 115
Hebden. N Yor 3C 98
Hebden Bridge. W Yor 2H 91
Hebden Green. Ches W 4A 84
Hebing End. Herts 3D 52
Hebron. Carm 2F 43
Hebron. Nmbd 1E 115
Heck. Dum 1B 112
Heckdyke. Notts 1E 87
Heckfield. Hants 5F 37
Heckfield Green. Suff 3D 66
Heckfordbridge. Essx 3C 54
Heckington. Linc 1A 76
Heckmondwike. W Yor 2C 92
Heddington. Wilts 5E 35
Heddle. Orkn 6C 172
Heddon. Devn 4G 19
Heddon-on-the-Wall. Nmbd . .3E 115
Hedenham. Norf 1F 67
Hedge End. Hants 1C 16
Hedgerley. Buck 2A 38
Hedging. Som 4G 21
Hedley on the Hill. Nmbd 4D 115
Hednesford. Staf 4E 73
Hedon. E Yor 2E 95
Hegdon Hill. Here 5H 59
Heglibister. Shet 6E 173
Heighington. Darl 2F 105
Heighington. Linc 4H 87
Heightington. Worc 3B 60
Heights of Brae. High 2H 157
Heights of Fodderty. High . . .2H 157
Heights of Kinlochewe. High . .2C 156
Heiton. Bord 1B 120
Hele. Devn
  nr. Exeter 2C 12
  nr. Holsworthy 3D 10
  nr. Ilfracombe 2F 19
Hele. Torb 2F 9
Helensburgh. Arg 1D 126
Helford. Corn 4E 5
Helhoughton. Norf 3A 78
Helions Bumpstead. Essx 1G 53
Helland. Corn 5A 10
Helland. Som 4G 21
Hellandbridge. Corn 5A 10
Hellesdon. Norf 4E 78
Hellesveor. Corn 2C 4
Hellidon. Nptn 5C 62
Hellifield. N Yor 4A 98
Hellingly. E Sus 4G 27
Hellington. Norf 5F 79
Hellister. Shet 7E 173
Helmdon. Nptn 1D 50
Helmingham. Suff 5D 66
Helmington Row. Dur 1E 105

Helmsdale. High 2H 165
Helmshore. Lanc 2F 91
Helmsley. N Yor 1A 100
Helperby. N Yor 3G 99
Helperthorpe. N Yor 2D 100
Helpringham. Linc 1A 76
Helpston. Pet 5A 76
Helsby. Ches W 3G 83
Helsey. Linc 3E 89
Helston. Corn 4D 4
Helstone. Corn 4A 10
Helton. Cumb 2G 103
Helwith. N Yor 4D 105
Helwith Bridge. N Yor 3H 97
Helygain. Flin 3E 82
Hem, The. Shrp 5B 72
Hemblington. Norf 4F 79
Hemerdon. Devn 3B 8
Hemingbrough. N Yor 1G 93
Hemingby. Linc 3B 88
Hemingfield. S Yor 4D 93
Hemingford Abbots. Cambs . .3B 64
Hemingford Grey. Cambs 3B 64
Hemingstone. Suff 5D 66
Hemington. Leics 3B 74
Hemington. Nptn 2H 63
Hemington. Som 1C 22
Hemley. Suff 1F 55
Hemlington. Midd 3B 106
Hempholme. E Yor 4E 101
Hempnall. Norf 1E 67
Hempnall Green. Norf 1E 67
Hempriggs. High 4F 169
Hemp's Green. Essx 3C 54
Hempstead. Essx 2G 53
Hempstead. Medw 4B 40
Hempstead. Norf
  nr. Holt 2D 78
  nr. Stalham 3G 79
Hempsted. Glos 4D 48
Hempton. Norf 3B 78
Hempton. Oxon 2C 50
Hemsby. Norf 4G 79
Hemswell. Linc 1G 87
Hemswell Cliff. Linc 2G 87
Hemsworth. Dors 2E 15
Hemsworth. W Yor 3E 93
Hemyock. Devn 1E 13
Henallt. Carm 3E 45
Henbury. Bris 4A 34
Henbury. Ches E 3C 84
Hendomen. Powy 1E 58
Hendon. G Lon 2D 38
Hendon. Tyne 4H 115
Hendra. Corn 3D 6
Hendre. B'end 3C 32
Hendreforgan. Rhon 3C 32
Hendy. Carm 5F 45
Heneglwys. IOA 3D 80
Henfeddau Fawr. Pemb 1G 43
Henfield. S Glo 4B 34
Henfield. W Sus 4D 26
Henford. Devn 3D 10
Hengoed. Cphy 2E 33
Hengoed. Shrp 2E 71
Hengrave. Suff 4H 65
Henham. Essx 3F 53
Heniarth. Powy 5D 70
Henlade. Som 4F 21
Henley. Dors 2B 14
Henley. Shrp
  nr. Church Stretton 2G 59
  nr. Ludlow 3H 59
Henley. Som 3H 21
Henley. Suff 5D 66
Henley. W Sus 4G 25
Henley Down. E Sus 4B 28
Henley-in-Arden. Warw 4F 61
Henley-on-Thames. Oxon 3F 37
Henley Street. Kent 4A 40
Henllan. Cdgn 1D 44
Henllan. Den 4C 82
Henllan. Mon 3F 47
Henllan Amgoed. Carm 2F 33
Henllys. Torf 2F 33
Henlow. C Beds 2B 52
Hennock. Devn 4B 12
Henny Street. Essx 2B 54
Henryd. Cnwy 3G 81
Henry's Moat. Pemb 2E 43
Hensall. N Yor 2F 93
Henshaw. Nmbd 3A 114
Hensingham. Cumb 3A 102
Henstead. Suff 2G 67
Hensting. Hants 4C 24
Henstridge. Som 1C 14
Henstridge Ash. Som 4C 22
Henstridge Bowden. Som 4B 22
Henstridge Marsh. Som 4C 22
Henton. Oxon 5F 51
Henton. Som 2H 21
Henwood. Corn 5C 10
Heogan. Shet 7F 173
Heolgerrig. Mer T 5D 46
Heol Senni. Powy 3C 46
Heol-y-Cyw. B'end 3C 32
Hepburn. Nmbd 2E 121
Hepple. Nmbd 4D 121
Hepscott. Nmbd 1F 115
Heptonstall. W Yor 2H 91
Hepworth. Suff 3B 66
Hepworth. W Yor 4B 92
Herbrandston. Pemb 4C 42
Hereford. Here 197 (2A 48)
Heribusta. High 1D 154
Heriot. Bord 4H 129
Hermiston. Edin 2E 129
Hermitage. Dors 2B 14
Hermitage. Bord 5H 119
Hermitage. W Ber 4D 36

Hermitage. W Sus 2F 17
Hermon. Carm
  nr. Llandeilo 3G 45
  nr. Newcastle Emlyn 2D 44
Hermon. IOA 4C 80
Hermon. Pemb 1G 43
Herne. Kent 4F 41
Herne Bay. Kent 4F 41
Herne Common. Kent 4F 41
Herne Pound. Kent 5A 40
Herner. Devn 4F 19
Hernhill. Kent 4E 41
Herodsfoot. Corn 2G 7
Heronden. Kent 5G 41
Herongate. Essx 1H 39
Heronsford. S Ayr 1G 109
Heronsgate. Herts 1B 38
Heron's Ghyll. E Sus 3F 27
Herra. Shet 2H 173
Herriard. Hants 2E 25
Herringfleet. Suff 1G 67
Herringswell. Suff 4G 65
Herrington. Tyne 4G 115
Hersden. Kent 4G 41
Hersham. Corn 2C 10
Hersham. Surr 4C 38
Herstmonceux. E Sus 4H 27
Herston. Dors 5F 15
Herston. Orkn 8D 172
Hertford. Herts 4D 52
Hertford Heath. Herts 4D 52
Hertingfordbury. Herts 4D 52
Hesketh. Lanc 2C 90
Hesketh Bank. Lanc 2C 90
Hesketh Lane. Lanc 5F 97
Hesket Newmarket. Cumb . . .1E 103
Heskin Green. Lanc 3D 90
Hesleden. Dur 1B 106
Hesleyside. Nmbd 1B 114
Heslington. York 4A 100
Hessay. York 4H 99
Hessenford. Corn 3H 7
Hessett. Suff 4B 66
Hessilhead. N Ayr 4E 127
Hessle. E Yor 2D 94
Hestaford. Shet 6D 173
Hest Bank. Lanc 3D 96
Hester's Way. Glos 3E 49
Hestinsetter. Shet 7D 173
Heston. G Lon 3C 38
Hestwall. Orkn 6B 172
Heswall. Mers 2E 83
Hethe. Oxon 3D 50
Hethelpit Cross. Glos 3C 48
Hethersett. Norf 5D 78
Hethersgill. Cumb 3F 113
Hetherside. Cumb 3F 113
Hethpool. Nmbd 2C 120
Hett. Dur 1F 105
Hetton. N Yor 4B 98
Hetton-le-Hole. Tyne 5G 115
Hetton Steads. Nmbd 1E 121
Heugh. Nmbd 2D 115
Heugh-head. Abers 2A 152
Heveningham. Suff 3F 67
Hever. Kent 1F 27
Heversham. Cumb 1D 97
Hevingham. Norf 3D 78
Hewas Water. Corn 4D 6
Hewelsfield. Glos 5A 48
Hewish. N Som 5H 33
Hewish. Som 2H 13
Hewood. Dors 2G 13
Heworth. York 4A 100
Hexham. Nmbd 3C 114
Hextable. Kent 3G 39
Hexton. Herts 2B 52
Hexworthy. Devn 5G 11
Heybridge. Essx
  nr. Brentwood 1H 39
  nr. Maldon 5B 54
Heybridge Basin. Essx 5B 54
Heybrook Bay. Devn 4A 8
Heydon. Cambs 1E 53
Heydon. Norf 3D 78
Heydour. Linc 2H 75
Heylipol. Arg 4A 138
Heyop. Powy 3E 59
Heysham. Lanc 3D 96
Heyshott. W Sus 1G 17
Heytesbury. Wilts 2E 23
Heythrop. Oxon 3B 50
Heywood. G Man 3G 91
Heywood. Wilts 1D 22
Hibaldstow. N Lin 4C 94
Hickleton. S Yor 4E 93
Hickling. Norf 3G 79
Hickling. Notts 3D 74
Hickling Green. Norf 3G 79
Hickling Heath. Norf 3G 79
Hickstead. W Sus 3D 26
Hidcote Bartrim. Glos 1G 49
Hidcote Boyce. Glos 1G 49
Higford. Shrp 5B 72
High Ackworth. W Yor 3E 93
Higham. Derbs 5A 86
Higham. Kent 3B 40
Higham. Lanc 1G 91
Higham. S Yor 4D 92
Higham. Suff
  nr. Ipswich 2D 54
  nr. Newmarket 4G 65
Higham Dykes. Nmbd 2E 115
Higham Ferrers. Nptn 4G 63
Higham Gobion. C Beds 2B 52
Higham on the Hill. Leics 1A 62
Highampton. Devn 2E 11
Higham Wood. Kent 1H 27
High Angerton. Nmbd 1D 115
High Auldgirth. Dum 1G 111
High Bankhill. Cumb 5G 113

High Banton. N Lan 1A 128
High Barnet. G Lon 1D 38
High Beech. Essx 1F 39
High Bentham. N Yor 3F 97
High Bickington. Devn 4G 19
High Biggins. Cumb 2E 97
High Birkwith. N Yor 2G 97
High Blantyre. S Lan 4H 127
High Bonnybridge. Falk 2B 128
High Borrans. Cumb 4F 103
High Bradfield. S Yor 1G 85
High Bray. Devn 3G 19
Highbridge. Cumb 5E 113
Highbridge. High 5E 148
Highbridge. Som 2G 21
Highbrook. W Sus 2E 27
High Brooms. Kent 1G 27
High Bullen. Devn 4F 19
Highburton. W Yor 3B 92
Highbury. Som 2B 22
High Buston. Nmbd 4G 121
High Callerton. Nmbd 2E 115
High Carlingill. Cumb 4H 103
High Catton. E Yor 4B 100
High Church. Nmbd 1E 115
Highclere. Hants 5C 36
Highcliffe. Dors 3H 15
High Cogges. Oxon 5B 50
High Common. Norf 5B 78
High Coniscliffe. Darl 3F 105
High Crosby. Cumb 4F 113
High Cross. Hants 4F 25
High Cross. Herts 4D 52
High Easter. Essx 4G 53
High Eggborough. N Yor 2F 93
High Ellington. N Yor 1D 98
Higher Alham. Som 2B 22
Higher Ansty. Dors 2C 14
Higher Ashton. Devn 4B 12
Higher Ballam. Lanc 1B 90
Higher Bartle. Lanc 1D 90
Higher Bockhampton. Dors . . .3C 14
Higher Bojewyan. Corn 3A 4
Higher Cheriton. Devn 2E 12
Higher Clovelly. Devn 4D 18
Higher Compton. Plym 3A 8
Higher Dean. Devn 2D 8
Higher Dinting. Derbs 1E 85
Higher Dunstone. Devn 5H 11
Higher End. G Man 4D 90
Higherford. Lanc 5A 98
Higher Gabwell. Devn 2F 9
Higher Halstock Leigh. Dors . .2A 14
Higher Heysham. Lanc 3D 96
Higher Hurdsfield. Ches E 3D 84
Higher Kingcombe. Dors 3A 14
Higher Kinnerton. Flin 4F 83
Higher Melcombe. Dors 2C 14
Higher Penwortham. Lanc 2D 90
Higher Porthpean. Corn 3E 7
Higher Poynton. Ches E 2D 84
Higher Shotton. Flin 4F 83
Higher Shurlach. Ches W 3A 84
Higher Slade. Devn 2F 19
Higher Tale. Devn 2D 12
Higher Town. Corn 4C 6
Higher Town. IOS 1B 4
Higher Town. Som 2C 20
Higher Vexford. Som 3E 20
Higher Walton. Lanc 2D 90
Higher Walton. Warr 2H 83
Higher Whatcombe. Dors 2D 14
Higher Wheelton. Lanc 2E 90
Higher Whiteleigh. Corn 3C 10
Higher Whitley. Ches W 2A 84
Higher Wincham. Ches W 3A 84
Higher Wraxall. Dors 2A 14
Higher Wych. Ches W 1G 71
High Ercall. Telf 4H 71
High Etherley. Dur 2E 105
High Ferry. Linc 1C 76
Highfield. E Yor 1H 93
Highfield. N Ayr 4E 126
Highfield. Tyne 4E 115
Highfields Caldecote. Cambs . .5C 64
High Gallowhill. E Dun 2H 127
High Garrett. Essx 3A 54
Highgate. G Lon 2D 39
Highgate. N Ayr 4E 127
Highgate. Powy 1D 58
High Grange. Dur 1E 105
High Green. Cumb 4F 103
High Green. Norf 5D 78
High Green. Shrp 2B 60
High Green. S Yor 1H 85
High Green. W Yor 3B 92
High Green. Worc 1D 49
Highgreen Manor. Nmbd 5C 120
High Halden. Kent 2C 28
High Halstow. Medw 3B 40
High Ham. Som 3H 21
High Harrington. Cumb 2B 102
High Haswell. Dur 5G 115
High Hatton. Shrp 3A 72
High Hawsker. N Yor 4G 107
High Hesket. Cumb 5F 113
High Hesleden. Dur 1B 106
High Hoyland. S Yor 3C 92
High Hunsley. E Yor 1C 94
High Hurstwood. E Sus 3F 27
High Hutton. N Yor 3B 100
High Ireby. Cumb 1D 102
High Keil. Arg 5A 122
High Kelling. Norf 2D 78
High Kilburn. N Yor 2H 99
High Knipe. Cumb 3G 103
High Lands. Dur 2E 105
Highlands, The. Shrp 2A 60
Highlane. Ches E 4C 84
Highlane. Derbs 2B 86

High Lane. G Man 2D 84
High Lane. Worc 4A 60
High Laver. Essx 5F 53
Highlaws. Cumb 5C 112
Highleadon. Glos 3C 48
High Legh. Ches E 2B 84
Highleigh. W Sus 3G 17
High Leven. Stoc T 3B 106
Highley. Shrp 2B 60
High Littleton. Bath 1B 22
High Longthwaite. Cumb 5D 112
High Lorton. Cumb 2C 102
High Marishes. N Yor 2C 100
High Marnham. Notts 3F 87
High Melton. S Yor 4F 93
Highmoor. Cumb 5D 112
High Moor. Lanc 3D 90
Highmoor. Oxon 3F 37
Highmoor Cross. Oxon 3F 37
Highmoor Hill. Mon 3H 33
Highnam. Glos 4C 48
High Newport. Tyne 4G 115
High Newton. Cumb 1D 96
High Newton-by-the-Sea.
  Nmbd 2G 121
High Nibthwaite. Cumb 1B 96
High Offley. Staf 3B 72
High Ongar. Essx 5F 53
High Onn. Staf 4C 72
High Orchard. Glos 4D 48
High Park. Mers 3B 90
High Roding. Essx 4G 53
High Row. Cumb 1E 103
High Salvington. W Sus 5C 26
High Scales. Cumb 5C 112
High Shaw. N Yor 5B 104
High Shincliffe. Dur 5F 115
High Side. Cumb 1D 102
High Spen. Tyne 3E 115
Highsted. Kent 4D 40
High Stoop. Dur 5E 115
High Street. Corn 3D 6
High Street. Suff
  nr. Aldeburgh 5G 67
  nr. Bungay 2F 67
  nr. Yoxford 3G 67
Highstreet Green. Essx 2A 54
High Street Green. Suff 5C 66
Highstreet Green. Surr 2A 26
Hightae. Dum 2B 112
High Throston. Hart 1B 106
Hightown. Ches E 4C 84
Hightown. Mers 4A 90
High Town. Staf 4D 73
Hightown Green. Suff 5B 66
High Toynton. Linc 4B 88
High Trewhitt. Nmbd 4E 121
High Valleyfield. Fife 1D 128
Highway. Here 1H 47
Highweek. Devn 5B 12
High Westwood. Dur 4E 115
Highwood. Staf 2E 73
Highwood. Worc 4A 60
High Worsall. N Yor 4A 106
Highworth. Swin 2H 35
High Wray. Cumb 5E 103
High Wych. Herts 4E 53
High Wycombe. Buck 2G 37
Hilborough. Norf 5H 77
Hilcott. Wilts 1G 23
Hildenborough. Kent 1G 27
Hildersham. Cambs 1F 53
Hilderstone. Staf 2D 72
Hilderthorpe. E Yor 3F 101
Hilfield. Dors 2B 14
Hilgay. Norf 1F 65
Hill, The. Cumb 1A 96
Hill. S Glo 2B 34
Hill. Warw 4B 62
Hill. Worc 1E 49
Hillam. N Yor 2F 93
Hillbeck. Cumb 3A 104
Hillberry. IOM 4C 108
Hillborough. Kent 4G 41
Hillbourne. Pool 3F 15
Hillbrae. Abers
  nr. Aberchirder 4D 160
  nr. Inverurie 1E 153
  nr. Methlick 5F 161
Hill Brow. Hants 4F 25
Hillbutts. Dors 2E 15
Hillcliffelane. Derbs 1G 73
Hillcommon. Som 4E 21
Hill Deverill. Wilts 2D 22
Hilldyke. Linc 1C 76
Hill End. Dur 1D 104
Hill End. Fife 4C 136
Hillend. Fife 1E 129
Hillend. N Lan 3B 128
Hill End. N Yor 4C 98
Hillend. N Lan 1C 60
Hillend. Shrp 3D 30
Hillend. Swan 4A 48
Hillersland. Glos 4A 48
Hillerton. Devn 3H 11
Hillesden. Buck 3E 51
Hillesley. Glos 3C 34
Hillfarrance. Som 4E 21
Hill Gate. Here 3H 47
Hill Green. Essx 2E 53
Hill Green. W Ber 4C 36
Hillhead. Abers 5C 160
Hillhead. Devn 3F 9
Hill Head. Hants 2D 16
Hillhead. S Ayr 3D 116
Hillhead of Auchentumb.
  Abers 3G 161
Hilliard's Cross. Staf 4F 73
Hilliclay. High 2D 168
Hillingdon. G Lon 2B 38
Hillington. Glas 3G 127

Hillington. *Norf* 3G 77
Hillmorton. *Warw* 3C 62
Hill of Beath. *Fife* 4D 136
Hill of Fearn. *High* 1C 158
Hill of Fiddes. *Abers* 1G 153
Hill of Keillor. *Ang* 4B 144
Hill of Overbrae. *Abers* 2F 161
Hill Ridware. *Staf* 4E 73
Hillsborough. *S Yor* 1H 85
Hillside. *Abers* 4G 153
Hillside. *Ang* 2G 145
Hillside. *Devn* 2D 8
Hillside. *Mers* 3B 90
Hillside. *Orkn* 5C 172
Hillside. *Shet* 5F 173
Hillside. *Shrp* 2A 60
Hill Side. *W Yor* 3B 92
Hillside. *Worc* 4B 60
Hillside of Prieston. *Ang* 5C 144
Hill Somersal. *Derbs* 2F 73
Hillstown. *Derbs* 4B 86
Hillstreet. *Hants* 1B 16
Hillswick. *Shet* 4D 173
Hill Top. *Dur*
   nr. Barnard Castle 2C 104
   nr. Durham 5F 115
   nr. Stanley 4E 115
Hill View. *Dors* 3E 15
Hillwell. *Shet* 10E 173
Hill Wootton. *Warw* 4H 61
Hillyland. *Per* 1C 136
Hilmarton. *Wilts* 4F 35
Hilperton. *Wilts* 1D 22
Hilperton Marsh. *Wilts* 1D 22
Hilsea. *Port* 2E 17
Hilston. *E Yor* 1F 95
Hiltingbury. *Hants* 4C 24
Hilton. *Cambs* 4B 64
Hilton. *Cumb* 2A 104
Hilton. *Derbs* 2G 73
Hilton. *Dors* 2C 14
Hilton. *Dur* 2E 105
Hilton. *High* 5E 165
Hilton. *Shrp* 1B 60
Hilton. *Staf* 5E 73
Hilton. *Stoc T* 3B 106
Hilton of Cadboll. *High* 1C 158
Himbleton. *Worc* 5D 60
Himley. *Staf* 1C 60
Hincaster. *Cumb* 1E 97
Hinchwick. *Glos* 3G 49
Hinckley. *Leics* 1B 62
Hinderclay. *Suff* 3C 66
Hinderwell. *N Yor* 3E 107
Hindford. *Shrp* 2F 71
Hindhead. *Surr* 3G 25
Hindley. *G Man* 4E 90
Hindley. *Nmbd* 4D 114
Hindley Green. *G Man* 4E 91
Hindlip. *Worc* 5C 60
Hindolveston. *Norf* 3C 78
Hindon. *Wilts* 3E 23
Hindringham. *Norf* 2B 78
Hingham. *Norf* 5C 78
Hinksford. *Staf* 2C 60
Hinstock. *Shrp* 3A 72
Hintlesham. *Suff* 1D 54
Hinton. *Hants* 3H 15
Hinton. *Here* 2G 47
Hinton. *Nptn* 5C 62
Hinton. *Shrp* 5G 71
Hinton. *S Glo* 4C 34
Hinton Ampner. *Hants* 4D 24
Hinton Blewett. *Bath* 1A 22
Hinton Charterhouse. *Bath* 1C 22
Hinton-in-the-Hedges. *Nptn* . . .2D 50
Hinton Martell. *Dors* 2F 15
Hinton on the Green. *Worc* 1F 49
Hinton Parva. *Swin* 3H 35
Hinton St George. *Som* 1H 13
Hinton St Mary. *Dors* 1C 14
Hinton Waldrist. *Oxon* 2B 36
Hints. *Shrp* 3A 60
Hints. *Staf* 5F 73
Hinwick. *Bed* 4G 63
Hinxhill. *Kent* 1E 29
Hinxton. *Cambs* 1E 53
Hinxworth. *Herts* 1C 52
Hipley. *Hants* 1E 16
Hipperholme. *W Yor* 2B 92
Hipsburn. *Nmbd* 3G 121
Hipswell. *N Yor* 5E 105
Hiraeth. *Carm* 2F 43
Hirn. *Abers* 3E 153
Hirnant. *Powy* 3C 70
Hirst. *N Lan* 3B 128
Hirst. *Nmbd* 1F 115
Hirst Courtney. *N Yor* 2G 93
Hirwaen. *Den* 4D 82
Hirwaun. *Rhon* 5C 46
Hiscott. *Devn* 4F 19
Histon. *Cambs* 4D 64
Hitcham. *Suff* 5B 66
Hitchin. *Herts* 3B 52
Hittisleigh. *Devn* 3H 11
Hittisleigh Barton. *Devn* 3H 11
Hive. *E Yor* 1B 94
Hixon. *Staf* 3E 73
Hoaden. *Kent* 5G 41
Hoar Cross. *Staf* 3F 73
Hoarwithy. *Here* 3A 48
Hoath. *Kent* 4G 41
Yr Hôb. *Flin* 5F 83
Hobarris. *Shrp* 3F 59
Hobbister. *Orkn* 7C 172
Hobbles Green. *Suff* 5G 65
Hobbs Cross. *Essx* 1F 39
Hobkirk. *Bord* 3H 119
Hobson. *Dur* 4E 115
Hoby. *Leics* 4D 74
Hockering. *Norf* 4C 78

Hockering Heath. *Norf* 4C 78
Hockerton. *Notts* 5E 86
Hockley. *Essx* 1C 40
Hockley. *Staf* 5G 73
Hockley. *W Mid* 3G 61
Hockley Heath. *W Mid* 3F 61
Hockliffe. *C Beds* 3H 51
Hockwold cum Wilton. *Norf* 2G 65
Hockworthy. *Devn* 1D 12
Hoddesdon. *Herts* 5D 52
Hoddlesden. *Bkbn* 2F 91
Hoddomcross. *Dum* 2C 112
Hodgeston. *Pemb* 5E 43
Hodley. *Powy* 1D 58
Hodnet. *Shrp* 3A 72
Hodsoll Street. *Kent* 4H 39
Hodson. *Swin* 3G 35
Hodthorpe. *Derbs* 3C 86
Hoe. *Norf* 4B 78
Hoe, The. *Plym* 3A 8
Hoe Gate. *Hants* 1E 17
Hoff. *Cumb* 3H 103
Hoffleet Stow. *Linc* 2B 76
Hogaland. *Shet* 4E 173
Hogben's Hill. *Kent* 5E 41
Hoggard's Green. *Suff* 5A 66
Hoggeston. *Buck* 3G 51
Hoggrill's End. *Warw* 1G 61
Hogha Gearraidh. *W Isl* 1C 170
Hoghton. *Lanc* 2E 90
Hoghton Bottoms. *Lanc* 2E 91
Hognaston. *Derbs* 5G 85
Hogsthorpe. *Linc* 3E 89
Hogstock. *Dors* 2E 15
Holbeach. *Linc* 3C 76
Holbeach Bank. *Linc* 3C 76
Holbeach Clough. *Linc* 3C 76
Holbeach Drove. *Linc* 4C 76
Holbeach Hurn. *Linc* 3C 76
Holbeach St Johns. *Linc* 4C 76
Holbeach St Marks. *Linc* 2C 76
Holbeach St Matthew. *Linc* 2D 76
Holbeck. *Notts* 3C 86
Holbeck. *W Yor* 1C 92
Holbeck Woodhouse.
   Notts 3C 86
Holberrow Green. *Worc* 5E 61
Holbeton. *Devn* 3C 8
Holborn. *G Lon* 2E 39
Holbrook. *Derbs* 1A 74
Holbrook. *S Yor* 2B 86
Holbrook. *Suff* 2E 55
Holburn. *Nmbd* 1E 121
Holbury. *Hants* 2C 16
Holcombe. *Devn* 5C 12
Holcombe. *G Man* 3F 91
Holcombe. *Som* 2B 22
Holcombe Brook. *G Man* 3F 91
Holcombe Rogus. *Devn* 1D 12
Holcot. *Nptn* 4E 63
Holden. *Lanc* 5G 97
Holdenby. *Nptn* 4D 62
Holder's Green. *Essx* 3G 53
Holdgate. *Shrp* 2H 59
Holdingham. *Linc* 1H 75
Holditch. *Dors* 2G 13
Holemoor. *Devn* 2E 11
Hole Street. *W Sus* 4C 26
Holford. *Som* 2E 21
Holker. *Cumb* 2C 96
Holkham. *Norf* 1A 78
Hollacombe. *Devn* 2D 11
Holland. *Orkn*
   on Papa Westray 2D 172
   on Stronsay 5F 172
Holland Fen. *Linc* 1B 76
Holland Lees. *Lanc* 4D 90
Holland-on-Sea. *Essx* 4F 55
Holland Park. *W Mid* 5E 73
Hollandstoun. *Orkn* 2G 172
Hollesley. *Suff* 1G 55
Hollinfare. *Warr* 1A 84
Hollingbourne. *Kent* 5C 40
Hollingbury. *Brig* 5E 27
Hollingdon. *Buck* 3G 51
Hollingrove. *E Sus* 3A 28
Hollington. *Derbs* 2G 73
Hollington. *E Sus* 4B 28
Hollington. *Staf* 2E 73
Hollington Grove. *Derbs* 2G 73
Hollingworth. *G Man* 1E 85
Hollins. *Derbs* 3H 85
Hollins. *G Man*
   nr. Bury 4G 91
   nr. Middleton 4G 91
Hollinsclough. *Staf* 4E 85
Hollinswood. *Telf* 5B 72
Hollinthorpe. *W Yor* 1D 93
Hollinwood. *G Man* 4H 91
Hollinwood. *Shrp* 2H 71
Hollocombe. *Devn* 1G 11
Holloway. *Derbs* 5H 85
Hollowell. *Nptn* 3D 62
Hollow Meadows. *S Yor* 2G 85
Hollows. *Dum* 2E 113
Hollybush. *Cphy* 5E 47
Hollybush. *E Ayr* 3C 116
Hollybush. *Worc* 2C 48
Holly End. *Norf* 5D 77
Holly Hill. *N Yor* 4E 105
Hollym. *E Yor* 2G 95
Hollyhurst. *Shrp* 1H 71
Holmacott. *Devn* 4F 19
Holmbridge. *W Yor* 4B 92
Holmbury St Mary. *Surr* 1C 26
Holmcroft. *Staf* 3D 72
Holme. *Cambs* 2A 64
Holme. *Cumb* 2E 97
Holme. *N Lin* 4C 94

Holme. *N Yor* 1F 99
Holme. *Notts* 5F 87
Holme. *W Yor* 4B 92
Holmebridge. *Dors* 4D 15
Holme Chapel. *Lanc* 2G 91
Holme Hale. *Norf* 5A 78
Holme Lacy. *Here* 2A 48
Holme Marsh. *Here* 5F 59
Holmend. *Dum* 4C 118
Holme next the Sea. *Norf* 1G 77
Holme-on-Spalding-Moor.
   E Yor 1B 94
Holme on the Wolds. *E Yor* 5D 100
Holme Pierrepont. *Notts* 2D 74
Holmer. *Here* 1A 48
Holmer Green. *Buck* 1A 38
Holmes. *Lanc* 3C 90
Holme St Cuthbert. *Cumb* 5C 112
Holmes Chapel. *Ches E* 4B 84
Holmesfield. *Derbs* 3H 85
Holmeswood. *Lanc* 3C 90
Holmewood. *Derbs* 4B 86
Holmfirth. *W Yor* 4B 92
Holmhead. *E Ayr* 2E 117
Holmisdale. *High* 4A 154
Holm of Drumlanrig.
   Dum 5H 117
Holmpton. *E Yor* 2G 95
Holmrook. *Cumb* 5B 102
Holmsgarth. *Shet* 7F 173
Holmside. *Dur* 5F 115
Holmwrangle. *Cumb* 5G 113
Holne. *Devn* 2D 8
Holsworthy. *Devn* 2D 10
Holsworthy Beacon.
   Devn 2D 10
Holt. *Dors* 2F 15
Holt. *Norf* 2C 78
Holt. *Wilts* 5D 34
Holt. *Worc* 4C 60
Holt. *Wrex* 5G 83
Holtby. *York* 4A 100
Holt End. *Hants* 3E 25
Holt End. *Worc* 4E 61
Holt Fleet. *Worc* 4C 60
Holt Green. *Lanc* 4B 90
Holt Heath. *Dors* 2F 15
Holt Heath. *Worc* 4C 60
Holton. *Oxon* 5D 50
Holton. *Som* 4B 22
Holton. *Suff* 3F 67
Holton cum Beckering.
   Linc 2A 88
Holton Heath. *Dors* 3E 15
Holton le Clay. *Linc* 4F 95
Holton le Moor. *Linc* 1H 87
Holton St Mary. *Suff* 2D 54
Holt Pound. *Hants* 2G 25
Holtsemere End. *Herts* 4A 52
Holtye. *E Sus* 2F 27
Holwell. *Dors* 1C 14
Holwell. *Herts* 2B 52
Holwell. *Leics* 3E 75
Holwell. *Oxon* 5H 49
Holwell. *Som* 2C 22
Holwick. *Dur* 2C 104
Holworth. *Dors* 4C 14
Holybourne. *Hants* 2F 25
Holy City. *Devn* 2G 13
Holy Cross. *Worc* 3D 60
Holyfield. *Essx* 5D 53
Holyhead. *IOA* 2B 80
Holy Island. *Nmbd* 5H 131
Holymoorside. *Derbs* 4H 85
Holyport. *Wind* 4G 37
Holystone. *Nmbd* 4D 120
Holytown. *N Lan* 3A 128
Holywell. *Cambs* 3C 64
Holywell. *Corn* 3B 6
Holywell. *Dors* 2A 14
Holywell. *Flin* 3D 82
Holywell. *Glos* 2C 34
Holywell. *Nmbd* 2G 115
Holywell. *Warw* 4F 61
Holywell Green. *W Yor* 3A 92
Holywell Lake. *Som* 4E 20
Holywell Row. *Suff* 3G 65
Holywood. *Dum* 1G 111
Homer. *Shrp* 5A 72
Homer Green. *Mers* 4B 90
Homersfield. *Suff* 2E 67
Hom Green. *Here* 3A 48
Homington. *Wilts* 4G 23
Honeyborough. *Pemb* 4D 42
Honeybourne. *Worc* 1G 49
Honeychurch. *Devn* 2G 11
Honeydon. *Bed* 5A 64
Honey Hill. *Kent* 4F 41
Honey Street. *Wilts* 5G 35
Honey Tye. *Suff* 2C 54
Honeywick. *C Beds* 3H 51
Honiley. *Warw* 3G 61
Honing. *Norf* 3F 79
Honingham. *Norf* 4D 78
Honington. *Linc* 1G 75
Honington. *Suff* 3B 66
Honington. *Warw* 1A 50
Honiton. *Devn* 2E 13
Honley. *W Yor* 3B 92
Honnington. *Telf* 4B 72
Hoo. *Suff* 5E 67
Hoobrook. *Worc* 3C 60
Hood Green. *S Yor* 4D 92
Hooe. *Plym* 3B 8
Hooe. *E Sus* 5A 28
Hooe Common. *E Sus* 4A 28
Hoo Green. *Ches E* 2B 84
Hoohill. *Bkpl* 1B 90
Hook. *Cambs* 1D 64
Hook. *E Yor* 2A 94
Hook. *G Lon* 4C 38

Hook. *Hants*
   nr. Basingstoke 1F 25
   nr. Fareham 2D 16
Hook. *Pemb* 3D 43
Hook. *Wilts* 3F 35
Hook-a-Gate. *Shrp* 5G 71
Hook Bank. *Worc* 1D 48
Hooke. *Dors* 2A 14
Hooker Gate. *Tyne* 4E 115
Hookgate. *Staf* 2B 72
Hook Green. *Kent*
   nr. Lamberhurst 2A 28
   nr. Meopham 4H 39
   nr. Southfleet 3H 39
Hook Norton. *Oxon* 2B 50
Hook's Cross. *Herts* 3C 52
Hook Street. *Glos* 2B 34
Hookway. *Devn* 3B 12
Hookwood. *Surr* 1D 26
Hoole. *Ches W* 4G 83
Hooley. *Surr* 5D 39
Hooley Bridge. *G Man* 3G 91
Hooley Brow. *G Man* 3G 91
Hoo St Werburgh. *Medw* 3B 40
Hooton. *Ches W* 3F 83
Hooton Levitt. *S Yor* 1C 86
Hooton Pagnell. *S Yor* 4E 93
Hooton Roberts. *S Yor* 1B 86
Hoove. *Shet* 7E 173
Hope. *Derbs* 2F 85
Hope. *Flin* 5F 83
Hope. *High* 2E 167
Hope. *Powy* 5E 71
Hope. *Shrp* 5F 71
Hope. *Staf* 5F 85
Hope Bagot. *Shrp* 3H 59
Hope Bowdler. *Shrp* 1G 59
Hopedale. *Staf* 5F 85
Hope Green. *Ches E* 2D 84
Hopeman. *Mor* 2F 159
Hope Mansell. *Here* 4B 48
Hopesay. *Shrp* 2F 59
Hope's Green. *Essx* 2B 40
Hopetown. *W Yor* 2D 93
Hope under Dinmore. *Here* 5H 59
Hopley's Green. *Here* 5F 59
Hopperton. *N Yor* 4G 99
Hop Pole. *Linc* 4A 76
Hopstone. *Shrp* 1B 60
Hopton. *Derbs* 5G 85
Hopton. *Powy* 1E 59
Hopton. *Shrp*
   nr. Oswestry 3F 71
   nr. Wem 3H 71
Hopton. *Staf* 3D 72
Hopton. *Suff* 3B 66
Hopton Cangeford. *Shrp* 2H 59
Hopton Castle. *Shrp* 3F 59
Hoptonheath. *Shrp* 3F 59
Hopton Heath. *Staf* 3D 72
Hopton on Sea. *Norf* 5H 79
Hopton Wafers. *Shrp* 3A 60
Hopwas. *Staf* 5F 73
Hopwood. *Worc* 3E 61
Horam. *E Sus* 4G 27
Horbling. *Linc* 2A 76
Horbury. *W Yor* 3C 92
Horcott. *Glos* 5G 49
Horden. *Dur* 5H 115
Horderley. *Shrp* 2G 59
Hordle. *Hants* 3A 16
Hordley. *Shrp* 2F 71
Horeb. *Carm*
   nr. Brechfa 3F 45
   nr. Llanelli 5E 45
Horeb. *Cdgn* 1D 45
Horfield. *Bris* 4A 34
Horgabost. *W Isl* 8C 171
Horham. *Suff* 3E 66
Horkstow. *N Lin* 3C 94
Horley. *Oxon* 1C 50
Horley. *Surr* 1D 27
Horn Ash. *Dors* 2G 13
Hornblotton Green. *Som* 3A 22
Hornby. *Lanc* 3E 97
Hornby. *N Yor*
   nr. Appleton Wiske 4A 106
   nr. Catterick Garrison 5F 105
Horncastle. *Linc* 4B 88
Hornchurch. *G Lon* 2G 39
Horncliffe. *Nmbd* 5F 131
Horndean. *Hants* 1F 17
Horndean. *Bord* 5E 131
Horndon. *Devn* 4F 11
Horndon on the Hill. *Thur* 2A 40
Horne. *Surr* 1E 27
Horner. *Som* 2C 20
Horning. *Norf* 4F 79
Horninghold. *Leics* 1F 63
Horninglow. *Staf* 3G 73
Horningsea. *Cambs* 4D 65
Horningsham. *Wilts* 2D 22
Horningtoft. *Norf* 3B 78
Hornsbury. *Som* 1G 13
Hornsby. *Cumb* 4G 113
Hornsbygate. *Cumb* 4G 113
Horns Corner. *Kent* 3B 28
Horns Cross. *Devn* 4D 19
Hornsea. *E Yor* 5G 101
Hornsea Burton. *E Yor* 5G 101
Hornsey. *G Lon* 2E 39
Hornton. *Oxon* 1B 50
Horpit. *Swin* 3H 35
Horrabridge. *Devn* 2B 8
Horringer. *Suff* 4H 65
Horringford. *IOW* 4D 16
Horrocks Fold. *G Man* 3F 91
Horrocksford. *Lanc* 5G 97
Horsbrugh Ford. *Bord* 1E 119
Horsebridge. *Devn* 5E 11
Horsebridge. *Hants* 3B 24

Horsebrook. *Staf* 4C 72
Horsecastle. *N Som* 5H 33
Horsehay. *Telf* 5A 72
Horseheath. *Cambs* 1G 53
Horsehouse. *N Yor* 1C 98
Horsell. *Surr* 5A 38
Horseman's Green. *Wrex* 1G 71
Horsenden. *Buck* 5F 51
Horseway. *Cambs* 2D 64
Horsey. *Norf* 3G 79
Horsey. *Som* 3G 21
Horsford. *Norf* 4D 78
Horsforth. *W Yor* 1C 92
Horsham. *W Sus* 2C 26
Horsham. *Worc* 5B 60
Horsham St Faith. *Norf* 4E 78
Horsington. *Linc* 4A 88
Horsington. *Som* 4C 22
Horsley. *Derbs* 1A 74
Horsley. *Glos* 2D 34
Horsley. *Nmbd*
   nr. Prudhoe 3D 115
   nr. Rochester 5C 120
Horsley Cross. *Essx* 3E 54
Horsleycross Street. *Essx* 3E 54
Horsleyhill. *Bord* 3H 119
Horsleyhope. *Dur* 5D 114
Horsley Woodhouse. *Derbs* 1A 74
Horsmonden. *Kent* 1A 28
Horspath. *Oxon* 5D 50
Horstead. *Norf* 4E 79
Horsted Keynes. *W Sus* 3E 27
Horton. *Buck* 4H 51
Horton. *Dors* 2F 15
Horton. *Lanc* 4A 98
Horton. *Nptn* 5F 63
Horton. *Shrp* 2G 71
Horton. *Som* 1G 13
Horton. *S Glo* 3C 34
Horton. *Staf* 5D 84
Horton. *Swan* 4D 30
Horton. *Wilts* 5F 35
Horton. *Wind* 3B 38
Horton Cross. *Som* 1G 13
Horton-cum-Studley. *Oxon* 4D 50
Horton Grange. *Nmbd* 2F 115
Horton Green. *Ches W* 1G 71
Horton Heath. *Hants* 1C 16
Horton in Ribblesdale. *N Yor* 2H 97
Horton Kirby. *Kent* 4G 39
Hortonwood. *Telf* 4A 72
Horwich. *G Man* 3E 91
Horwich End. *Derbs* 2E 85
Horwood. *Devn* 4F 19
Hoscar. *Lanc* 3C 90
Hose. *Leics* 3E 75
Hosh. *Per* 1A 136
Hosta. *W Isl* 1C 170
Hoswick. *Shet* 9F 173
Hotham. *E Yor* 1B 94
Hothfield. *Kent* 1D 28
Hoton. *Leics* 3C 74
Houbie. *Shet* 2H 173
Hough. *Arg* 4A 138
Hough. *Ches E*
   nr. Crewe 5B 84
   nr. Wilmslow 3C 84
Hougham. *Linc* 1F 75
Hough Green. *Hal* 2G 83
Hough-on-the-Hill. *Linc* 1G 75
Houghton. *Cambs* 3B 64
Houghton. *Cumb* 4F 113
Houghton. *Hants* 3B 24
Houghton. *Nmbd* 3E 115
Houghton. *Pemb* 4D 43
Houghton. *W Sus* 4B 26
Houghton Bank. *Darl* 2F 105
Houghton Conquest. *C Beds* 1A 52
Houghton Green. *E Sus* 3D 28
Houghton Green. *Warr* 1A 84
Houghton-le-Side. *Darl* 2F 105
Houghton-le-Spring. *Tyne* 4G 115
Houghton on the Hill. *Leics* 5D 74
Houghton Regis. *C Beds* 3A 52
Houghton St Giles. *Norf* 2B 78
Houlland. *Shet*
   on Mainland 6E 173
   on Yell 4G 173
Houlsyke. *N Yor* 4E 107
Hound. *Hants* 2C 16
Hound Green. *Hants* 1F 25
Houndslow. *Bord* 5C 130
Houndsmoor. *Som* 4E 21
Houndwood. *Bord* 3E 131
Hounsdown. *Hants* 1B 16
Hounslow. *G Lon* 3C 38
Housabister. *Shet* 6F 173
Housay. *Shet* 4H 173
Househill. *High* 3C 158
Housetter. *Shet* 3E 173
Houss. *Shet* 8E 173
Houston. *Ren* 3F 127
Housty. *High* 5D 168
Houton. *Orkn* 7C 172
Hove. *Brig* 189 (5D 27)
Hoveringham. *Notts* 1D 74
Hoveton. *Norf* 4F 79
Hovingham. *N Yor* 2A 100
How. *Cumb* 4G 113
How Caple. *Here* 2B 48
Howden. *E Yor* 2H 93
Howden-le-Wear. *Dur* 1E 105
Howe, The. *Cumb* 1D 96
Howe. *High* 2F 169
Howe, The. *IOM* 5A 108
Howe. *Norf* 5E 79
Howe. *N Yor* 1F 99
Howe Green. *Essx* 5H 53
Howegreen. *Essx* 5B 54
Howe Green. *Warw* 2H 61
Howell. *Linc* 1A 76
How End. *C Beds* 1A 52

Howe of Teuchar. *Abers* 4E **161**
Howes. *Dum* 3C **112**
Howe Street. *Essx*
  nr. Chelmsford 4G **53**
  nr. Finchingfield 2G **53**
Howey. *Powy* 5C **58**
Howgate. *Midl* 4F **129**
Howgill. *Lanc* 5H **97**
Howgill. *N Yor* 4C **98**
How Green. *Kent* 1F **27**
How Hill. *Norf* 4F **79**
Howick. *Nmbd* 3G **121**
Howle. *Telf* 3A **72**
Howle Hill. *Here* 3B **48**
Howleigh. *Som* 1F **13**
Howlett End. *Essx* 2F **53**
Howley. *Som* 2F **13**
Howley. *Warr* 2A **84**
Hownam. *Bord* 3B **120**
Howsham. *N Lin* 4D **94**
Howsham. *N Yor* 3B **100**
Howtel. *Nmbd* 1C **120**
Howt Green. *Kent* 4C **40**
Howton. *Here* 3H **47**
Howwood. *Ren* 3E **127**
Hoxne. *Suff* 3D **66**
Hoylake. *Mers* 2E **82**
Hoyland. *S Yor* 4D **92**
Hoylandswaine. *S Yor* 4C **92**
Hoyle. *W Sus* 4A **26**
Hubberholme. *N Yor* 2B **98**
Hubberston. *Pemb* 4C **42**
Hubbert's Bridge. *Linc* 1B **76**
Huby. *N Yor*
  nr. Harrogate 5E **99**
  nr. York 3H **99**
Hucclecote. *Glos* 4D **48**
Hucking. *Kent* 5C **40**
Hucknall. *Notts* 1C **74**
Huddersfield. *W Yor* 3B **92**
Huddington. *Worc* 5D **60**
Huddlesford. *Staf* 5F **73**
Hudswell. *N Yor* 4E **105**
Huggate. *E Yor* 4C **100**
Hugglescote. *Leics* 4B **74**
Hughenden Valley. *Buck* 2G **37**
Hughley. *Shrp* 1H **59**
Hughton. *High* 4G **157**
Hugh Town. *IOS* 1B **4**
Hugus. *Corn* 4B **6**
Huish. *Devn* 1F **11**
Huish. *Wilts* 5G **35**
Huish Champflower. *Som* . . .4D **20**
Huish Episcopi. *Som* 4H **21**
Huisinis. *W Isl* 6B **171**
Hulcote. *Nptn* 1F **51**
Hulcott. *Buck* 4G **51**
Hulham. *Devn* 4D **12**
Hull. *Hull* **199** (2E **94**)
Hulland. *Derbs* 1G **73**
Hulland Moss. *Derbs* 1G **73**
Hulland Ward. *Derbs* 1G **73**
Hullavington. *Wilts* 3D **35**
Hullbridge. *Essx* 1C **40**
Hulme. *G Man* 1C **84**
Hulme. *Staf* 1D **72**
Hulme End. *Staf* 5F **85**
Hulme Walfield. *Ches E* 4C **84**
Hulverstone. *IOW* 4B **16**
Hulver Street. *Suff* 2G **67**
Humber. *Devn* 5C **12**
Humber. *Here* 5H **59**
Humber Bridge. *N Lin* 2D **94**
Humberside Airport. *N Lin* . . .3D **94**
Humberston. *NE Lin* 4G **95**
Humberstone. *Leic* 5D **74**
Humbie. *E Lot* 3A **130**
Humbleton. *E Yor* 1F **95**
Humbleton. *Nmbd* 2D **121**
Humby. *Linc* 2H **75**
Hume. *Bord* 5D **130**
Humshaugh. *Nmbd* 2C **114**
Huna. *High* 1F **169**
Huncoat. *Lanc* 1F **91**
Huncote. *Leics* 1C **62**
Hundall. *Derbs* 3A **86**
Hunderthwaite. *Dur* 2C **104**
Hundleby. *Linc* 4C **88**
Hundle Houses. *Linc* 5B **88**
Hundleton. *Pemb* 4D **42**
Hundon. *Suff* 1H **53**
Hundred, The. *Here* 4H **59**
Hundred Acres. *Hants* 1D **16**
Hundred House. *Powy* 5D **58**
Hungarton. *Leics* 5D **74**
Hungerford. *Hants* 1G **15**
Hungerford. *Shrp* 2H **59**
Hungerford. *Som* 2D **20**
Hungerford. *W Ber* 5B **36**
Hungerford Newtown. *W Ber* .4B **36**
Hunger Hill. *G Man* 4E **91**
Hungerton. *Linc* 2F **75**
Hungladder. *High* 1C **154**
Hungryhatton. *Shrp* 3A **72**
Hunmanby. *N Yor* 2E **101**
Hunmanby Sands. *N Yor* . . .2F **101**
Hunningham. *Warw* 4A **62**
Hunnington. *Worc* 2D **60**
Hunny Hill. *IOW* 4C **16**
Hunsdon. *Herts* 4E **53**
Hunsdonbury. *Herts* 4E **53**
Hunsingore. *N Yor* 4G **99**
Hunslet. *W Yor* 1D **92**
Hunslet Carr. *W Yor* 1D **92**
Hunsonby. *Cumb* 1G **103**
Hunspow. *High* 1E **169**
Hunstanton. *Norf* 1F **77**
Hunstanworth. *Dur* 5C **114**
Hunston. *Suff* 4B **66**
Hunston. *W Sus* 2G **17**
Hunstrete. *Bath* 5B **34**

Hunt End. *Worc* 4E **61**
Hunterfield. *Midl* 3G **129**
Hunters Forstal. *Kent* 4F **41**
Hunter's Quay. *Arg* 2C **126**
Huntham. *Som* 4G **21**
Hunthill Lodge. *Ang* 1D **144**
Huntingdon. *Cambs* 3B **64**
Huntingfield. *Suff* 3F **67**
Huntingford. *Wilts* 4D **22**
Huntington. *Ches W* 4G **83**
Huntington. *E Lot* 2A **130**
Huntington. *Here* 5E **59**
Huntington. *Staf* 4D **72**
Huntington. *Telf* 5A **72**
Huntington. *York* 4A **100**
Huntingtower. *Per* 1C **136**
Huntley. *Glos* 4C **48**
Huntly. *Staf* 1E **73**
Huntly. *Abers* 5C **160**
Huntlywood. *Bord* 5C **130**
Hunton. *Hants* 3C **24**
Hunton. *Kent* 1B **28**
Hunton. *N Yor* 5E **105**
Hunton Bridge. *Herts* 1B **38**
Hunt's Corner. *Norf* 2C **66**
Huntscott. *Som* 2C **20**
Hunt's Cross. *Mers* 2G **83**
Hunts Green. *Warw* 1F **61**
Huntsham. *Devn* 4D **20**
Huntshaw. *Devn* 4F **19**
Huntspill. *Som* 2G **21**
Huntstile. *Som* 3F **21**
Huntworth. *Som* 3G **21**
Hunwick. *Dur* 1E **105**
Hunworth. *Norf* 2C **78**
Hurcott. *Som*
  nr. Ilminster 1G **13**
  nr. Somerton 4A **22**
Hurdcott. *Wilts* 3G **23**
Hurdley. *Powy* 1E **59**
Hurdsfield. *Ches E* 3D **84**
Hurlet. *Glas* 3G **127**
Hurley. *Warw* 1G **61**
Hurley. *Wind* 3G **37**
Hurlford. *E Ayr* 1D **116**
Hurliness. *Orkn* 9B **172**
Hurlston Green. *Lanc* 3C **90**
Hurn. *Dors* 3G **15**
Hursey. *Dors* 2H **13**
Hursley. *Hants* 4C **24**
Hurst. *G Man* 4H **91**
Hurst. *N Yor* 4D **104**
Hurst. *Som* 1H **13**
Hurst. *Wok* 4F **37**
Hurstbourne Priors. *Hants* 2C **24**
Hurstbourne Tarrant. *Hants* . . .1B **24**
Hurst Green. *Ches E* 1H **71**
Hurst Green. *E Sus* 3B **28**
Hurst Green. *Essx* 4D **54**
Hurst Green. *Lanc* 1E **91**
Hurst Green. *Surr* 5E **39**
Hurstley. *Here* 1G **47**
Hurstpierpoint. *W Sus* 4D **27**
Hurstway Common. *Here* 1G **47**
Hurst Wickham. *W Sus* 4D **27**
Hurstwood. *Lanc* 1G **91**
Hurtmore. *Surr* 1A **26**
Hurworth-on-Tees. *Darl* 3A **106**
Hurworth Place. *Darl* 4F **105**
Hury. *Dur* 3C **104**
Husbands Bosworth. *Leics* . . .2D **62**
Husborne Crawley. *C Beds* . . .2H **51**
Husthwaite. *N Yor* 2H **99**
Hutcherleigh. *Devn* 3D **9**
Hut Green. *N Yor* 2F **93**
Huthwaite. *Notts* 5B **86**
Huttoft. *Linc* 3E **89**
Hutton. *Cumb* 2F **103**
Hutton. *E Yor* 4E **101**
Hutton. *Essx* 1H **39**
Hutton. *Lanc* 2C **90**
Hutton. *N Som* 1G **21**
Hutton. *Bord* 4F **131**
Hutton Bonville. *N Yor* 4A **106**
Hutton Buscel. *N Yor* 1D **100**
Hutton Conyers. *N Yor* 2F **99**
Hutton Cranswick. *E Yor* 4E **101**
Hutton End. *Cumb* 1F **103**
Hutton Gate. *Red C* 3C **106**
Hutton Henry. *Dur* 1B **106**
Hutton-le-Hole. *N Yor* 1B **100**
Hutton Magna. *Dur* 3E **105**
Hutton Mulgrave. *N Yor* 4F **107**
Hutton Roof. *Cumb*
  nr. Kirkby Lonsdale 2E **97**
  nr. Penrith 1E **103**
Hutton Rudby. *N Yor* 4B **106**
Huttons Ambo. *N Yor* 3B **100**
Hutton Sessay. *N Yor* 2G **99**
Hutton Village. *Red C* 3D **106**
Hutton Wandesley. *N Yor* 4H **99**
Huxham. *Devn* 3C **12**
Huxham Green. *Som* 3A **22**
Huxley. *Ches W* 4H **83**
Huxter. *Shet*
  on Mainland 6C **173**
  on Whalsay 5G **173**
Huyton. *Mers* 1G **83**
Hwlffordd. *Pemb* 3D **42**
Hycemoor. *Cumb* 1A **96**
Hyde. *Glos*
  nr. Stroud 5D **49**
  nr. Winchcombe 3F **49**
Hyde. *G Man* 1D **84**
Hyde Heath. *Buck* 5H **51**
Hyde Lea. *Staf* 4D **72**
Hyde Park. *S Yor* 4F **93**
Hydestile. *Surr* 1A **26**
Hyndford Bridge. *S Lan* 5C **128**
Hynish. *Arg* 5A **138**
Hyssington. *Powy* 1F **59**

Hythe. *Hants* 2C **16**
Hythe. *Kent* 2F **29**
Hythe End. *Wind* 3B **38**
Hythie. *Abers* 3H **161**
Hyton. *Cumb* 1A **96**

I

Ianstown. *Mor* 2B **160**
Iarsiadar. *W Isl* 4D **171**
Ibberton. *Dors* 2C **14**
Ible. *Derbs* 5G **85**
Ibrox. *Glas* 3G **127**
Ibsley. *Hants* 2G **15**
Ibstock. *Leics* 4B **74**
Ibstone. *Buck* 2F **37**
Ibthorpe. *Hants* 1B **24**
Iburndale. *N Yor* 4F **107**
Ibworth. *Hants* 1D **24**
Icelton. *N Som* 5G **33**
Ichrachan. *Arg* 5E **141**
Ickburgh. *Norf* 1H **65**
Ickenham. *G Lon* 2B **38**
Ickenthwaite. *Cumb* 1C **96**
Ickford. *Buck* 5E **51**
Ickham. *Kent* 5G **41**
Ickleford. *Herts* 2B **52**
Icklesham. *E Sus* 4C **28**
Ickleton. *Cambs* 1E **53**
Icklingham. *Suff* 3G **65**
Ickwell. *C Beds* 1B **52**
Icomb. *Glos* 3H **49**
Idbury. *Oxon* 4H **49**
Iddesleigh. *Devn* 2F **11**
Ide. *Devn* 3B **12**
Ideford. *Devn* 5B **12**
Ide Hill. *Kent* 5F **39**
Iden. *E Sus* 3D **28**
Iden Green. *Kent*
  nr. Benenden 2C **28**
  nr. Goudhurst 2B **28**
Idle. *W Yor* 1B **92**
Idless. *Corn* 4C **6**
Idlicote. *Warw* 1A **50**
Idmiston. *Wilts* 3G **23**
Idole. *Carm* 4E **45**
Idridgehay. *Derbs* 1G **73**
Idrigill. *High* 2C **154**
Idstone. *Oxon* 3A **36**
Iffley. *Oxon* 5D **50**
Ifield. *W Sus* 2D **26**
Ifieldwood. *W Sus* 2D **26**
Ifold. *W Sus* 2B **26**
Iford. *E Sus* 5F **27**
Ifton Heath. *Shrp* 2F **71**
Ightfield. *Shrp* 2H **71**
Ightham. *Kent* 5G **39**
Iken. *Suff* 5G **67**
Ilam. *Staf* 5F **85**
Ilchester. *Som* 4A **22**
Ilderton. *Nmbd* 2E **121**
Ilford. *G Lon* 2F **39**
Ilford. *Som* 1G **13**
Ilfracombe. *Devn* 2F **19**
Ilkeston. *Derbs* 1B **74**
Ilketshall St Andrew. *Suff* 2F **67**
Ilketshall St Lawrence. *Suff* . . .2F **67**
Ilketshall St Margaret. *Suff* . . .2F **67**
Ilkley. *W Yor* 5D **98**
Illand. *Corn* 5C **10**
Illey. *W Mid* 2D **61**
Illidge Green. *Ches E* 4B **84**
Illington. *Norf* 2B **66**
Illingworth. *W Yor* 2A **92**
Illogan. *Corn* 4A **6**
Illogan Highway. *Corn* 4A **6**
Illston on the Hill. *Leics* 1E **62**
Ilmer. *Buck* 5F **51**
Ilmington. *Warw* 1H **49**
Ilminster. *Som* 1G **13**
Ilsington. *Devn* 5A **12**
Ilsington. *Dors* 3C **14**
Ilston. *Swan* 3E **31**
Ilton. *N Yor* 2D **98**
Ilton. *Som* 1G **13**
Imachar. *N Ayr* 5G **125**
Immingham. *NE Lin* 3E **95**
Immingham Dock. *NE Lin* 3F **95**
Impington. *Cambs* 4D **64**
Ince. *Ches W* 3G **83**
Ince Blundell. *Mers* 4B **90**
Ince-in-Makerfield. *G Man* . .4D **90**
Inchbae Lodge. *High* 2G **157**
Inchbare. *Ang* 2F **145**
Inchberry. *Mor* 3H **159**
Inchbraoch. *Ang* 3G **145**
Inchbrook. *Glos* 5D **48**
Incheril. *High* 2C **156**
Inchinnan. *Ren* 3F **127**
Inchlaggan. *High* 3D **148**
Inchmichael. *Per* 1E **137**
Inchnadamph. *High* 1G **163**
Inchree. *High* 2E **141**
Inchture. *Per* 1E **137**
Inchyra. *Per* 1D **136**
Indian Queens. *Corn* 3D **6**
Ingatestone. *Essx* 1H **39**
Ingbirchworth. *S Yor* 4C **92**
Ingestre. *Staf* 3D **73**
Ingham. *Linc* 2G **87**
Ingham. *Norf* 3F **79**
Ingham. *Suff* 3A **66**
Ingham Corner. *Norf* 3F **79**
Ingleborough. *Norf* 4D **76**
Ingleby. *Derbs* 3H **73**
Ingleby Arncliffe. *N Yor* 4B **106**
Ingleby Barwick. *Stoc T* 3B **106**
Ingleby Greenhow. *N Yor* 4C **106**
Ingleigh Green. *Devn* 2G **11**

Inglemire. *Hull* 1D **94**
Inglesbatch. *Bath* 5C **34**
Ingleton. *Dur* 2E **105**
Ingleton. *N Yor* 2F **97**
Inglewhite. *Lanc* 5E **97**
Ingoe. *Nmbd* 2D **114**
Ingol. *Lanc* 1D **90**
Ingoldisthorpe. *Norf* 2F **77**
Ingoldmells. *Linc* 4E **89**
Ingoldsby. *Linc* 2H **75**
Ingon. *Warw* 5G **61**
Ingram. *Nmbd* 3E **121**
Ingrave. *Essx* 1H **39**
Ingrow. *W Yor* 1A **92**
Ings. *Cumb* 5F **103**
Ingst. *S Glo* 3A **34**
Ingthorpe. *Rut* 5G **75**
Ingworth. *Norf* 3D **78**
Inkberrow. *Worc* 5E **61**
Inkford. *Worc* 3E **61**
Inkpen. *W Ber* 5B **36**
Inkstack. *High* 1E **169**
Innellan. *Arg* 3C **126**
Inner Hope. *Devn* 5C **8**
Innerleith. *Fife* 2E **137**
Innerleithen. *Bord* 1F **119**
Innerleven. *Fife* 3F **137**
Innermessan. *Dum* 3F **109**
Innerwick. *E Lot* 2D **130**
Innerwick. *Per* 4C **142**
Innsworth. *Glos* 3D **48**
Insch. *Abers* 1D **152**
Insh. *High* 3C **150**
Inshegra. *High* 3C **166**
Inshore. *High* 1D **166**
Inskip. *Lanc* 1C **90**
Instow. *Devn* 3E **19**
Intwood. *Norf* 5D **78**
Inver. *Abers* 4G **151**
Inver. *High* 5F **165**
Inver. *Per* 4H **143**
Inverailort. *High* 5F **147**
Inveralligin. *High* 3H **155**
Inverallochy. *Abers* 2H **161**
Inveramsay. *Abers* 1E **153**
Inveran. *High* 4C **164**
Inveraray. *Arg* 3H **133**
Inverarish. *High* 5E **155**
Inverarity. *Ang* 4D **144**
Inverarnan. *Stir* 2C **134**
Inverarnie. *High* 5A **158**
Inverbeg. *Arg* 4C **134**
Inverbervie. *Abers* 1H **145**
Inverboyndie. *Abers* 2D **160**
Invercassley. *High* 3B **164**
Invercharnan. *High* 4F **141**
Inverchoran. *High* 3E **157**
Invercreran. *Arg* 4E **141**
Inverdruie. *High* 2D **150**
Inverebrie. *Abers* 5G **161**
Invereck. *Arg* 1C **126**
Inveresk. *E Lot* 2G **129**
Inveresragan. *Arg* 5D **141**
Inverey. *Abers* 5E **151**
Inverfarigaig. *High* 1H **149**
Invergarry. *High* 3F **149**
Invergeldie. *Per* 1G **135**
Invergordon. *High* 2B **158**
Invergowrie. *Per* 5C **144**
Inverguseran. *High* 3F **147**
Inverharroch. *Mor* 5A **160**
Inverie. *High* 3F **147**
Inverinan. *Arg* 2G **133**
Inverinate. *High* 1B **148**
Inverkeilor. *Ang* 4F **145**
Inverkeithing. *Fife* 1E **129**
Inverkeithny. *Abers* 4D **160**
Inverkip. *Inv* 2D **126**
Inverkirkaig. *High* 1E **163**
Inverlael. *High* 5F **163**
Inverliever Lodge. *Arg* 3F **133**
Inverliver. *Arg* 5E **141**
Inverlochlarig. *Stir* 2D **134**
Inverlochy. *High* 1F **141**
Inverlussa. *Arg* 1E **125**
Inver Mallie. *High* 5D **148**
Invermarkie. *Abers* 5B **160**
Invermoriston. *High* 2G **149**
Invernaver. *High* 2H **167**
Inverneil House. *Arg* 1G **125**
Inverness. *High* **198** (4A **158**)
Inverness Airport. *High* 3B **158**
Invernettie. *Abers* 4H **161**
Inverpolly Lodge. *High* 2E **163**
Inverquhomery. *Abers* 4H **161**
Inverroy. *High* 5E **149**
Inversanda. *High* 3D **140**
Invershiel. *High* 2B **148**
Invershin. *High* 4C **164**
Invershore. *High* 5E **169**
Inversnaid. *Stir* 3C **134**
Inveruglas. *Arg* 3C **134**
Inverurie. *Abers* 1E **153**
Invervar. *Per* 4D **142**
Inverythan. *Abers* 4E **161**
Inwardleigh. *Devn* 3F **11**
Inworth. *Essx* 4B **54**
Iochdar. *W Isl* 4C **170**
Iping. *W Sus* 4G **25**
Ipplepen. *Devn* 2E **9**
Ipsden. *Oxon* 3E **37**
Ipstones. *Staf* 1E **73**
Ipswich. *Suff* **198** (1E **55**)
Irby. *Mers* 2E **83**
Irby in the Marsh. *Linc* 4D **88**
Irby upon Humber. *NE Lin* . . .4E **95**
Irchester. *Nptn* 4G **63**
Ireby. *Cumb* 1D **102**
Ireby. *Lanc* 2F **97**
Ireland. *Shet* 9E **173**

Ireleth. *Cumb* 2B **96**
Ireshopeburn. *Dur* 1B **104**
Ireton Wood. *Derbs* 1G **73**
Irlam. *G Man* 1B **84**
Irnham. *Linc* 3H **75**
Iron Acton. *S Glo* 3B **34**
Iron Bridge. *Cambs* 1D **65**
Ironbridge. *Telf* 5A **72**
Iron Cross. *Warw* 5E **61**
Ironville. *Derbs* 5B **86**
Irstead. *Norf* 3F **79**
Irthington. *Cumb* 3F **113**
Irthlingborough. *Nptn* 3G **63**
Irton. *N Yor* 1E **101**
Irvine. *N Ayr* 1C **116**
Irvine Mains. *N Ayr* 1C **116**
Isabella Pit. *Nmbd* 1G **115**
Isauld. *High* 2B **168**
Isbister. *Orkn* 6C **172**
Isbister. *Shet*
  on Mainland 2E **173**
  on Whalsay 5G **173**
Isfield. *E Sus* 4F **27**
Isham. *Nptn* 3F **63**
Island Carr. *N Lin* 4C **94**
Islay Airport. *Arg* 4B **124**
Isle Abbotts. *Som* 4G **21**
Isle Brewers. *Som* 4G **21**
Isleham. *Cambs* 3F **65**
Isle of Man Airport. *IOM* 5B **108**
Isle of Thanet. *Kent* 4H **41**
Isle of Whithorn. *Dum* 5B **110**
Isle of Wight. *IOW* 4C **16**
Isleornsay. *High* 2F **147**
Islesburgh. *Shet* 5E **173**
Isles of Scilly (St Mary's) Airport.
  IOS 1B **4**
Islesteps. *Dum* 2A **112**
Isleworth. *G Lon* 3C **38**
Isley Walton. *Leics* 3B **74**
Islibhig. *W Isl* 5B **171**
Islington. *G Lon* 2E **39**
Islington. *Telf* 3B **72**
Islip. *Nptn* 3G **63**
Islip. *Oxon* 4D **50**
Isombridge. *Telf* 4A **72**
Istead Rise. *Kent* 4H **39**
Itchen. *Sotn* 1C **16**
Itchen Abbas. *Hants* 3D **24**
Itchenor. *W Sus* 2F **17**
Itchen Stoke. *Hants* 3D **24**
Itchingfield. *W Sus* 3C **26**
Itchington. *S Glo* 3B **34**
Itlaw. *Abers* 3D **160**
Itteringham. *Norf* 2D **78**
Itteringham Common. *Norf* . . .3D **78**
Itton. *Devn* 3G **11**
Itton Common. *Mon* 2H **33**
Ivegill. *Cumb* 5F **113**
Ivelet. *N Yor* 5C **104**
Iverchaolain. *Arg* 2B **126**
Iver Heath. *Buck* 2B **38**
Iveston. *Dur* 4E **115**
Ivetsey Bank. *Staf* 4C **72**
Ivinghoe. *Buck* 4H **51**
Ivinghoe Aston. *Buck* 4H **51**
Ivington. *Here* 5G **59**
Ivington Green. *Here* 5G **59**
Ivybridge. *Devn* 3C **8**
Ivychurch. *Kent* 3E **29**
Ivy Hatch. *Kent* 5G **39**
Ivy Todd. *Norf* 5A **78**
Iwade. *Kent* 4D **40**
Iwerne Courtney. *Dors* 1D **14**
Iwerne Minster. *Dors* 1D **14**
Ixworth. *Suff* 3B **66**
Ixworth Thorpe. *Suff* 3B **66**

J

Jackfield. *Shrp* 5A **72**
Jack Hill. *N Yor* 4D **98**
Jacksdale. *Notts* 5B **86**
Jackton. *S Lan* 4G **127**
Jacobstow. *Corn* 3B **10**
Jacobstowe. *Devn* 2F **11**
Jacobs Well. *Surr* 5A **38**
Jameston. *Pemb* 5E **43**
Jamestown. *Dum* 5F **119**
Jamestown. *Fife* 1E **129**
Jamestown. *High* 3G **157**
Jamestown. *W Dun* 1E **127**
Janetstown. *High*
  nr. Thurso 2C **168**
  nr. Wick 3F **169**
Jarrow. *Tyne* 3G **115**
Jarvis Brook. *E Sus* 3G **27**
Jasper's Green. *Essx* 3H **53**
Jaywick. *Essx* 4E **55**
Jedburgh. *Bord* 2A **120**
Jeffreyston. *Pemb* 4E **43**
Jemimaville. *High* 2B **158**
Jenkins Park. *High* 3F **149**
Jersey Marine. *Neat* 3G **31**
Jesmond. *Tyne* 3F **115**
Jevington. *E Sus* 5G **27**
Jingle Street. *Mon* 4H **47**
Jockey End. *Herts* 4A **52**
Jodrell Bank. *Ches E* 3B **84**
Johnby. *Cumb* 1F **103**
John O'Gaunts. *W Yor* 2D **92**
John o' Groats. *High* 1F **169**
John's Cross. *E Sus* 3B **28**
Johnshaven. *Abers* 2G **145**
Johnson Street. *Norf* 4F **79**
Johnston. *Pemb* 3D **42**
Johnstone. *Ren* 3F **127**
Johnstonebridge. *Dum* 5C **118**
Johnstown. *Carm* 4E **45**
Johnstown. *Wrex* 1F **71**

Joppa. *Edin* 2G **129**
Joppa. *S Ayr* 3D **116**
Jordan Green. *Norf* 3C **78**
Jordans. *Buck* 1A **38**
Jordanston. *Pemb* 1D **42**
Jump. *S Yor* 4D **93**
Jumpers Common. *Dors* 3G **15**
Juniper. *Nmbd* 4C **114**
Juniper Green. *Edin* 3E **129**
Jurby East. *IOM* 2C **108**
Jurby West. *IOM* 2C **108**
Jury's Gap. *E Sus* 4D **28**

K

Kaber. *Cumb* 3A **104**
Kaimend. *S Lan* 5C **128**
Kaimes. *Edin* 3F **129**
Kaimrig End. *Bord* 5D **129**
Kames. *Arg* 2A **126**
Kames. *E Ayr* 2F **117**
Kea. *Corn* 4C **6**
Keadby. *N Lin* 3B **94**
Keal Cotes. *Linc* 4C **88**
Kearsley. *G Man* 4F **91**
Kearsney. *Kent* 1G **29**
Kearstwick. *Cumb* 1F **97**
Kearton. *N Yor* 5C **104**
Kearvaig. *High* 1C **166**
Keasden. *N Yor* 3G **97**
Keason. *Corn* 2H **7**
Keckwick. *Hal* 2H **83**
Keddington. *Linc* 2C **88**
Keddington Corner. *Linc* 2C **88**
Kedington. *Suff* 1H **53**
Kedleston. *Derbs* 1H **73**
Kedlock Feus. *Fife* 2F **137**
Keekle. *Cumb* 3B **102**
Keelby. *Linc* 3E **95**
Keele. *Staf* 1C **72**
Keeley Green. *Bed* 1A **52**
Keeston. *Pemb* 3D **42**
Keevil. *Wilts* 1E **23**
Kegworth. *Leics* 3B **74**
Kehelland. *Corn* 2D **4**
Keig. *Abers* 2D **152**
Keighley. *W Yor* 5C **98**
Keilarsbrae. *Clac* 4A **136**
Keillmore. *Arg* 1E **125**
Keillor. *Per* 4B **144**
Keilour. *Per* 1B **136**
Keills. *Arg* 3C **124**
Keiloch. *Abers* 4F **151**
Keils. *Arg* 3D **124**
Keinton Mandeville. *Som* 3A **22**
Keir Mill. *Dum* 5A **118**
Keirsleywell Row. *Nmbd* 4A **114**
Keisby. *Linc* 3H **75**
Keisley. *Cumb* 2A **104**
Keiss. *High* 2F **169**
Keith. *Mor* 3B **160**
Keith Inch. *Abers* 4H **161**
Kelbrook. *Lanc* 5B **98**
Kelby. *Linc* 1H **75**
Keld. *Cumb* 3G **103**
Keld. *N Yor* 4B **104**
Keldholme. *N Yor* 1B **100**
Kelfield. *N Lin* 4B **94**
Kelfield. *N Yor* 1F **93**
Kelham. *Notts* 5E **87**
Kellacott. *Devn* 4E **11**
Kellan. *Arg* 4G **139**
Kellas. *Ang* 5D **144**
Kellas. *Mor* 3F **159**
Kellaton. *Devn* 5E **9**
Kelleth. *Cumb* 4H **103**
Kelling. *Norf* 1C **78**
Kellingley. *N Yor* 2F **93**
Kellington. *N Yor* 2F **93**
Kelloe. *Dur* 1A **106**
Kelloholm. *Dum* 3G **117**
Kells. *Cumb* 3A **102**
Kelly. *Devn* 4D **11**
Kelly Bray. *Corn* 5D **10**
Kelmarsh. *Nptn* 3E **63**
Kelmscott. *Oxon* 2H **35**
Kelsale. *Suff* 4F **67**
Kelsall. *Ches W* 4H **83**
Kelshall. *Herts* 2D **52**
Kelsick. *Cumb* 4C **112**
Kelso. *Bord* 1B **120**
Kelstedge. *Derbs* 4H **85**
Kelstern. *Linc* 1B **88**
Kelsterton. *Flin* 3E **83**
Kelston. *Bath* 5C **34**
Keltneyburn. *Per* 4E **143**
Kelton. *Dum* 2A **112**
Kelton Hill. *Dum* 4E **111**
Kelty. *Fife* 4D **136**
Kelvedon. *Essx* 4B **54**
Kelvedon Hatch. *Essx* 1G **39**
Kelvinside. *Glas* 3G **127**
Kelynack. *Corn* 3A **4**
Kemback. *Fife* 2G **137**
Kemberton. *Shrp* 5B **72**
Kemble. *Glos* 2E **35**
Kemerton. *Worc* 2E **49**
Kemeys Commander. *Mon* 5G **47**
Kemnay. *Abers* 2E **153**
Kempe's Corner. *Kent* 1E **29**
Kempley. *Glos* 3B **48**
Kempley Green. *Glos* 3B **48**
Kempsey. *Worc* 1D **48**
Kempsford. *Glos* 2G **35**
Kemps Green. *Warw* 3F **61**
Kempshott. *Hants* 2E **24**
Kempston. *Bed* 1A **52**
Kempston Hardwick. *Bed* 1A **52**
Kempton. *Shrp* 2F **59**
Kemp Town. *Brig* 5E **27**

Kemsing. *Kent* 5G **39**
Kemsley. *Kent* 4D **40**
Kenardington. *Kent* 2D **28**
Kenchester. *Here* 1H **47**
Kencot. *Oxon* 5A **50**
Kendal. *Cumb* 5G **103**
Kendleshire. *S Glo* 4B **34**
Kendray. *S Yor* 4D **92**
Kenfig. *B'end* 3B **32**
Kenfig Hill. *B'end* 3B **32**
Kengharair. *Arg* 4F **139**
Kenilworth. *Warw* 3G **61**
Kenknock. *Stir* 5B **142**
Kenley. *G Lon* 5E **39**
Kenley. *Shrp* 5H **71**
Kenmore. *High* 3G **155**
Kenmore. *Per* 4E **143**
Kenn. *Devn* 4C **12**
Kenn. *N Som* 5H **33**
Kennacraig. *Arg* 3G **125**
Kenneggy Downs. *Corn* 4C **4**
Kennerleigh. *Devn* 2B **12**
Kennet. *Clac* 4B **136**
Kennethmont. *Abers* 1C **152**
Kennett. *Cambs* 4G **65**
Kennford. *Devn* 4C **12**
Kenninghall. *Norf* 2C **66**
Kennington. *Kent* 1E **28**
Kennington. *Oxon* 5D **50**
Kennoway. *Fife* 3F **137**
Kennyhill. *Suff* 3F **65**
Kennythorpe. *N Yor* 3B **100**
Kenovay. *Arg* 4A **138**
Kensaleyre. *High* 3D **154**
Kensington. *G Lon* 3D **38**
Kenstone. *Shrp* 3H **71**
Kensworth. *C Beds* 4A **52**
Kensworth Common. *C Beds* 4A **52**
Kentallen. *High* 3E **141**
Kentchurch. *Here* 3H **47**
Kentford. *Suff* 4G **65**
Kentisbeare. *Devn* 2D **12**
Kentisbury. *Devn* 2G **19**
Kentisbury Ford. *Devn* 2G **19**
Kentmere. *Cumb* 4F **103**
Kenton. *Devn* 4C **12**
Kenton. *G Lon* 2C **38**
Kenton. *Suff* 4D **66**
Kenton Bankfoot. *Tyne* 3F **115**
Kentra. *High* 2A **140**
Kentrigg. *Cumb* 5G **103**
Kents Bank. *Cumb* 2C **96**
Kent's Green. *Glos* 3C **48**
Kent's Oak. *Hants* 4B **24**
Kent Street. *E Sus* 4B **28**
Kent Street. *Kent* 5A **40**
Kent Street. *W Sus* 3D **26**
Kenton. *Suff* 4D **66**
Kenwick. *Shrp* 2G **71**
Kenwyn. *Corn* 4C **6**
Kenyon. *Warr* 1A **84**
Keoldale. *High* 2D **166**
Keppoch. *High* 1B **148**
Keresley. *W Mid* 2H **61**
Keresley Newland. *Warw* 2H **61**
Keristal. *IOM* 4C **108**
Kerne Bridge. *Here* 4A **48**
Kerridge. *Ches E* 3D **84**
Kerris. *Corn* 4B **4**
Kerrow. *High* 5F **157**
Kerry. *Powy* 2D **58**
Kerrycroy. *Arg* 3C **126**
Kerry's Gate. *Here* 2G **47**
Kersall. *Notts* 4E **86**
Kersbrook. *Devn* 4D **12**
Kerse. *Ren* 4E **127**
Kersey. *Suff* 1D **54**
Kershopefoot. *Cumb* 1F **113**
Kersoe. *Worc* 1E **49**
Kerswell. *Devn* 2D **12**
Kerswell Green. *Worc* 1D **48**
Kesgrave. *Suff* 1F **55**
Kessingland. *Suff* 2H **67**
Kessingland Beach. *Suff* 2H **67**
Kestle. *Corn* 4D **6**
Kestle Mill. *Corn* 3C **6**
Keston. *G Lon* 4F **39**
Keswick. *Cumb* 2D **102**
Keswick. *Norf*
    nr. North Walsham 2F **79**
    nr. Norwich 5E **78**
Ketsby. *Linc* 3C **88**
Kettering. *Nptn* 3F **63**
Ketteringham. *Norf* 5D **78**
Kettins. *Per* 5B **144**
Kettlebaston. *Suff* 5B **66**
Kettlebridge. *Fife* 3F **137**
Kettlebrook. *Staf* 5G **73**
Kettleburgh. *Suff* 4E **67**
Kettleholm. *Dum* 2C **112**
Kettleness. *N Yor* 3F **107**
Kettleshulme. *Ches E* 3D **85**
Kettlesing. *N Yor* 4E **98**
Kettlesing Bottom. *N Yor* 4E **99**
Kettlestone. *Norf* 2B **78**
Kettlethorpe. *Linc* 3F **87**
Kettletoft. *Orkn* 4F **172**
Kettlewell. *N Yor* 2B **98**
Ketton. *Rut* 5G **75**
Kew. *G Lon* 3C **38**
Kewaigue. *IOM* 4C **108**
Kewstoke. *N Som* 5G **33**
Kexbrough. *S Yor* 4C **92**
Kexby. *Linc* 2F **87**
Kexby. *York* 4B **100**
Keyford. *Som* 2C **22**
Key Green. *Ches E* 4C **84**
Key Green. *N Yor* 4F **107**
Keyham. *Leics* 5D **74**
Keyhaven. *Hants* 3B **16**
Keyhead. *Abers* 3H **161**

Keyingham. *E Yor* 2F **95**
Keymer. *W Sus* 4E **27**
Keynsham. *Bath* 5B **34**
Keysoe. *Bed* 4H **63**
Keysoe Row. *Bed* 4H **63**
Key's Toft. *Linc* 5D **89**
Keyston. *Cambs* 3H **63**
Key Street. *Kent* 4C **40**
Keyworth. *Notts* 2D **74**
Kibblesworth. *Tyne* 4F **115**
Kibworth Beauchamp. *Leics* 1D **62**
Kibworth Harcourt. *Leics* 1D **62**
Kidbrooke. *G Lon* 3F **39**
Kidburngill. *Cumb* 2B **102**
Kiddemore Green. *Staf* 5C **72**
Kidderminster. *Worc* 3C **60**
Kiddington. *Oxon* 3C **50**
Kidd's Moor. *Norf* 5D **78**
Kidlington. *Oxon* 4C **50**
Kidmore End. *Oxon* 4E **37**
Kidnal. *Ches W* 1G **71**
Kidsgrove. *Staf* 5C **84**
Kidstones. *N Yor* 1B **98**
Kidwelly. *Carm* 5E **45**
Kiel Crofts. *Arg* 5D **140**
Kielder. *Nmbd* 5A **120**
Kilbagie. *Fife* 4B **136**
Kilbarchan. *Ren* 3F **127**
Kilbeg. *High* 3E **147**
Kilberry. *Arg* 3F **125**
Kilbirnie. *N Ayr* 4E **126**
Kilbride. *Arg* 1F **133**
Kilbride. *High* 1D **147**
Kilbucho Place. *Bord* 1C **118**
Kilburn. *Derbs* 1A **74**
Kilburn. *G Lon* 2D **38**
Kilburn. *N Yor* 2H **99**
Kilby. *Leics* 1D **62**
Kilchattan. *Arg* 4A **132**
Kilchattan Bay. *Arg* 4C **126**
Kilchenzie. *Arg* 3A **122**
Kilcheran. *Arg* 5C **140**
Kilchiaran. *Arg* 3A **124**
Kilchoan. *High*
    nr. Inverie 4F **147**
    nr. Tobermory 2F **139**
Kilchoman. *Arg* 3A **124**
Kilchrenan. *Arg* 1H **133**
Kilconquhar. *Fife* 3G **137**
Kilcot. *Glos* 3B **48**
Kilcoy. *High* 3H **157**
Kilcreggan. *Arg* 1D **126**
Kildale. *N Yor* 4D **106**
Kildary. *High* 1B **158**
Kildermorie Lodge. *High* 1H **157**
Kildonan. *Dum* 4F **109**
Kildonan. *High*
    nr. Helmsdale 1G **165**
    on Isle of Skye 3C **154**
Kildonan. *N Ayr* 3E **123**
Kildonnan. *High* 5C **146**
Kildrummy. *Abers* 2B **152**
Kildwick. *N Yor* 5C **98**
Kilfillan. *Dum* 4H **109**
Kilfinan. *Arg* 2H **125**
Kilfinnan. *High* 4E **149**
Kilgetty. *Pemb* 4F **43**
Kilgour. *Fife* 3E **136**
Kilgrammie. *S Ayr* 4B **116**
Kilham. *E Yor* 3E **101**
Kilham. *Nmbd* 1C **120**
Kilkenneth. *Arg* 4A **138**
Kilkhampton. *Corn* 1C **10**
Killamarsh. *Derbs* 2B **86**
Killandrist. *Arg* 4C **140**
Killay. *Swan* 3F **31**
Killean. *Arg* 5E **125**
Killearn. *Stir* 1G **127**
Killellan. *Arg* 4A **122**
Killen. *High* 3A **158**
Killerby. *Darl* 3E **105**
Killichonan. *Per* 3C **142**
Killiechronan. *Arg* 4G **139**
Killiecrankie. *Per* 2G **143**
Killilan. *High* 5B **156**
Killimster. *High* 3F **169**
Killin. *Stir* 5C **142**
Killinghall. *N Yor* 4E **99**
Killington. *Cumb* 1F **97**
Killingworth. *Tyne* 2F **115**
Killin Lodge. *High* 3H **149**
Killinochonoch. *Arg* 4F **133**
Killochyett. *Bord* 5A **130**
Killundine. *High* 4G **139**
Kilmacolm. *Inv* 3E **127**
Kilmahog. *Stir* 3F **135**
Kilmahumaig. *Arg* 4E **133**
Kilmalieu. *High* 3C **140**
Kilmaluag. *High* 1D **154**
Kilmany. *Fife* 1F **137**
Kilmarie. *High* 2D **146**
Kilmarnock. *E Ayr* **198** (1D **116**)
Kilmaron. *Fife* 2F **137**
Kilmartin. *Arg* 4F **133**
Kilmaurs. *E Ayr* 5F **127**
Kilmelford. *Arg* 2F **133**
Kilmeny. *Arg* 3B **124**
Kilmersdon. *Som* 1B **22**
Kilmeston. *Hants* 4D **24**
Kilmichael Glassary. *Arg* 4F **133**
Kilmichael of Inverlussa. *Arg* . . .1F **125**
Kilmington. *Devn* 3F **13**
Kilmington. *Wilts* 3C **22**
Kilmoluaig. *Arg* 4A **138**
Kilmorack. *High* 4G **157**
Kilmore. *Arg* 1F **133**
Kilmore. *High* 3E **147**
Kilmory. *Arg* 3F **125**
Kilmory. *High*
    nr. Kilchoan 1G **139**
    on Rùm 3B **146**

Kilmory. *N Ayr* 3D **122**
Kilmory Lodge. *Arg* 3E **132**
Kilmote. *High* 2G **165**
Kilmuir. *High*
    nr. Dunvegan 4B **154**
    nr. Invergordon 1B **158**
    nr. Inverness 4A **158**
    nr. Uig 1C **154**
Kilmun. *Arg* 1C **126**
Kilnave. *Arg* 2A **124**
Kilncadzow. *S Lan* 5B **128**
Kilndown. *Kent* 2B **28**
Kiln Green. *Here* 4B **48**
Kiln Green. *Wok* 4G **37**
Kilnhill. *Cumb* 1D **102**
Kilnhurst. *S Yor* 1B **86**
Kilninian. *Arg* 4E **139**
Kilninver. *Arg* 1F **133**
Kiln Pit Hill. *Nmbd* 4D **114**
Kilnsea. *E Yor* 3H **95**
Kilnsey. *N Yor* 3B **98**
Kilnwick. *E Yor* 5D **101**
Kiloran. *Arg* 4A **132**
Kilpatrick. *N Ayr* 3D **122**
Kilpeck. *Here* 2H **47**
Kilpin. *E Yor* 2A **94**
Kilpin Pike. *E Yor* 2A **94**
Kilrenny. *Fife* 3H **137**
Kilsby. *Nptn* 3C **62**
Kilspindie. *Per* 1E **136**
Kilsyth. *N Lan* 2A **128**
Kiltarlity. *High* 4H **157**
Kilton. *Som* 2E **21**
Kilton Thorpe. *Red C* 3D **107**
Kilvaxter. *High* 2C **154**
Kilve. *Som* 2E **21**
Kilvington. *Notts* 1F **75**
Kilwinning. *N Ayr* 5D **126**
Kimberley. *Norf* 5C **78**
Kimberley. *Notts* 1B **74**
Kimblesworth. *Dur* 5F **115**
Kimble Wick. *Buck* 5G **51**
Kimbolton. *Cambs* 4H **63**
Kimbolton. *Here* 4H **59**
Kimcote. *Leics* 2C **62**
Kimmeridge. *Dors* 5E **15**
Kimmerston. *Nmbd* 1D **120**
Kimpton. *Hants* 2A **24**
Kimpton. *Herts* 4B **52**
Kinbeachie. *High* 2A **158**
Kinbrace. *High* 5A **168**
Kinbuck. *Stir* 3G **135**
Kincaple. *Fife* 2G **137**
Kincardine. *Fife* 1C **128**
Kincardine. *High* 5D **164**
Kincardine Bridge. *Falk* 1C **128**
Kincardine O'Neil. *Abers* 4C **152**
Kinchrackine. *Arg* 1A **134**
Kincorth. *Aber* 3G **153**
Kincraig. *High* 3C **150**
Kincraigie. *Per* 4G **143**
Kindallachan. *Per* 3G **143**
Kineton. *Glos* 3F **49**
Kineton. *Warw* 5H **61**
Kinfauns. *Per* 1D **136**
Kingairloch. *High* 3C **140**
Kingarth. *Arg* 4B **126**
Kingcoed. *Mon* 5H **47**
King Edward. *Abers* 3E **160**
Kingerby. *Linc* 1H **87**
Kingham. *Oxon* 3A **50**
Kingholm Quay. *Dum* 2A **112**
Kinghorn. *Fife* 1F **129**
Kingie. *High* 3D **148**
Kinglassie. *Fife* 4E **137**
Kingledores. *Bord* 2D **118**
King o' Muirs. *Clac* 4A **136**
Kingoodie. *Per* 1F **137**
King's Acre. *Here* 1H **47**
Kingsand. *Corn* 3A **8**
Kingsash. *Buck* 5G **51**
Kingsbarns. *Fife* 2H **137**
Kingsbridge. *Devn* 4D **8**
Kingsbridge. *Som* 3C **20**
King's Bromley. *Staf* 4F **73**
Kingsburgh. *High* 3C **154**
Kingsbury. *G Lon* 2C **38**
Kingsbury. *Warw* 1G **61**
Kingsbury Episcopi. *Som* 4H **21**
Kings Caple. *Here* 3A **48**
Kingscavil. *W Lot* 2D **128**
Kingsclere. *Hants* 1D **24**
King's Cliffe. *Nptn* 1H **63**
Kings Clipstone. *Notts* 4D **86**
Kingscote. *Glos* 2D **34**
Kingscott. *Devn* 1F **11**
Kings Coughton. *Warw* 5E **61**
Kingscross. *N Ayr* 3E **123**
Kingsdon. *Som* 4A **22**
Kingsdown. *Kent* 1H **29**
Kingsdown. *Swin* 3G **35**
Kingsdown. *Wilts* 5D **34**
Kingseat. *Fife* 4D **136**
Kingsey. *Buck* 5F **51**
Kingsfold. *Lanc* 2D **90**
Kingsfold. *W Sus* 2C **26**
Kingsford. *E Ayr* 5F **127**
Kingsford. *Worc* 2C **60**
Kingsforth. *N Lin* 3D **94**
Kingsgate. *Kent* 3H **41**
King's Green. *Glos* 2C **48**
Kingshall Street. *Suff* 4B **66**
Kingsheanton. *Devn* 3F **19**
King's Heath. *W Mid* 2E **61**
Kings Hill. *Kent* 5A **40**
Kingsholm. *Glos* 4D **48**
Kingshouse. *High* 3G **141**
Kingshouse. *Stir* 1E **135**
Kingshurst. *W Mid* 2F **61**
Kingskerswell. *Devn* 2E **9**
Kingskettle. *Fife* 3F **137**

Kingsland. *Here* 4G **59**
Kingsland. *IOA* 2B **80**
Kings Langley. *Herts* 5A **52**
Kingsley. *Ches W* 3H **83**
Kingsley. *Hants* 3F **25**
Kingsley. *Staf* 1E **73**
Kingsley Green. *W Sus* 3G **25**
Kingsley Holt. *Staf* 1E **73**
King's Lynn. *Norf* 3F **77**
King's Meaburn. *Cumb* 2H **103**
King's Moss. *Mers* 4D **90**
Kingsmuir. *Ang* 4D **145**
Kingsmuir. *Fife* 3H **137**
Kings Muir. *Bord* 1E **119**
King's Newnham. *Warw* 3B **62**
King's Newton. *Derbs* 3A **74**
Kingsnorth. *Kent* 2E **28**
Kingsnorth. *Medw* 3C **40**
King's Norton. *Leics* 5D **74**
King's Norton. *W Mid* 3E **61**
King's Nympton. *Devn* 1G **11**
King's Pyon. *Here* 5G **59**
Kings Ripton. *Cambs* 3B **64**
King's Somborne. *Hants* 3B **24**
King's Stag. *Dors* 1C **14**
King's Stanley. *Glos* 5D **48**
King's Sutton. *Nptn* 2C **50**
Kingstanding. *W Mid* 1E **61**
Kingsteignton. *Devn* 5B **12**
King Sterndale. *Derbs* 3E **85**
Kingsthorpe. *Nptn* 4E **63**
Kingston. *Cambs* 5C **64**
Kingston. *Devn* 4C **8**
Kingston. *Dors*
    nr. Sturminster Newton 2C **14**
    nr. Swanage 5E **15**
Kingston. *E Lot* 1B **130**
Kingston. *Hants* 2G **15**
Kingston. *IOW* 4C **16**
Kingston. *Kent* 5F **41**
Kingston. *Mor* 2H **159**
Kingston. *W Sus* 5B **26**
Kingston Bagpuize. *Oxon* 2C **36**
Kingston Blount. *Oxon* 2F **37**
Kingston by Sea. *W Sus* 5D **26**
Kingston Deverill. *Wilts* 3D **22**
Kingstone. *Here* 2H **47**
Kingstone. *Som* 1G **13**
Kingstone. *Staf* 3E **73**
Kingston Lisle. *Oxon* 3B **36**
Kingston Maurward. *Dors* 3C **14**
Kingston near Lewes. *E Sus* 5E **27**
Kingston on Soar. *Notts* 3C **74**
Kingston Russell. *Dors* 3A **14**
Kingston St Mary. *Som* 4F **21**
Kingston Seymour. *N Som* 5H **33**
Kingston Stert. *Oxon* 5F **51**
Kingston upon Hull.
    Hull **199** (2E **94**)
Kingston upon Thames. *G Lon* . .4C **38**
King's Walden. *Herts* 3B **52**
Kingswear. *Devn* 3E **9**
Kingswells. *Aber* 3F **153**
Kingswinford. *W Mid* 2C **60**
Kingswood. *Buck* 4E **51**
Kingswood. *Glos* 2C **34**
Kingswood. *Here* 5E **59**
Kingswood. *Kent* 5C **40**
Kingswood. *Per* 5H **143**
Kingswood. *Powy* 5E **71**
Kingswood. *Som* 3E **20**
Kingswood. *S Glo* 4B **34**
Kingswood. *Surr* 5D **38**
Kingswood. *Warw* 3F **61**
Kingswood Common. *Staf* 5C **72**
Kings Worthy. *Hants* 3C **24**
Kingthorpe. *Linc* 3A **88**
Kington. *Here* 5E **59**
Kington. *S Glo* 2B **34**
Kington. *Worc* 5D **60**
Kington Langley. *Wilts* 4E **35**
Kington Magna. *Dors* 4C **22**
Kington St Michael. *Wilts* 4E **35**
Kingussie. *High* 3B **150**
Kingweston. *Som* 3A **22**
Kinharrachie. *Abers* 5G **161**
Kinhrive. *High* 1A **158**
Kinkell Bridge. *Per* 2B **136**
Kinknockie. *Abers* 4H **161**
Kinkry Hill. *Cumb* 2G **113**
Kinlet. *Shrp* 2B **60**
Kinloch. *High*
    nr. Lochaline 3A **140**
    nr. Loch More 5D **166**
    on Rùm 4B **146**
Kinloch. *Per* 4A **144**
Kinlochard. *Stir* 3D **134**
Kinlochbervie. *High* 3C **166**
Kinlocheil. *High* 1D **140**
Kinlochewe. *High* 2C **156**
Kinloch Hourn. *High* 3B **148**
Kinloch Laggan. *High* 5H **149**
Kinlochleven. *High* 2F **141**
Kinloch Lodge. *High* 3F **167**
Kinlochmoidart. *High* 1B **140**
Kinlochmore. *High* 2F **141**
Kinloch Rannoch. *Per* 3D **142**
Kinlochspelve. *Arg* 1D **132**
Kinloid. *High* 5E **147**
Kinloss. *Mor* 2E **159**
Kinmel Bay. *Cnwy* 2B **82**
Kinmuck. *Abers* 2F **153**
Kinnadie. *Abers* 4G **161**
Kinnaird. *Per* 1E **137**
Kinneff. *Abers* 1H **145**
Kinnelhead. *Dum* 4C **118**
Kinnell. *Ang* 3F **145**
Kinnerley. *Shrp* 3F **71**
Kinnernie. *Abers* 3E **152**

Kinnersley. Here 1G 47
Kinnersley. Worc 1D 48
Kinnerton. Powy 4E 59
Kinnerton. Shrp 1F 59
Kinnesswood. Per 3D 136
Kinninvie. Dur 2D 104
Kinnordy. Ang 3C 144
Kinoulton. Notts 2D 74
Kinross. Per 3D 136
Kinrossie. Per 5A 144
Kinsbourne Green. Herts 4B 52
Kinsey Heath. Ches E 1A 72
Kinsham. Here 4F 59
Kinsham. Worc 2E 49
Kinsley. W Yor 3E 93
Kinson. Bour 3F 15
Kintbury. W Ber 5B 36
Kintessack. Mor 2E 159
Kintillo. Per 2D 136
Kinton. Here 3G 59
Kinton. Shrp 4F 71
Kintore. Abers 2E 153
Kintour. Arg 4C 124
Kintra. Arg 2B 132
Kintraw. Arg 3F 133
Kinveachy. High 2D 150
Kinver. Staf 2C 60
Kinwarton. Warw 5F 61
Kiplingcotes. E Yor 5D 100
Kippax. W Yor 1E 93
Kippen. Stir 4F 135
Kippford. Dum 4F 111
Kipping's Cross. Kent 1H 27
Kirbister. Orkn
  nr. Hobbister 7C 172
  nr. Quholm 6B 172
Kirbuster. Orkn 5F 172
Kirby Bedon. Norf 5E 79
Kirby Bellars. Leics 4E 74
Kirby Cane. Norf 1F 67
Kirby Cross. Essx 3F 55
Kirby Fields. Leics 5C 74
Kirby Green. Norf 1F 67
Kirby Grindalythe. N Yor 3D 100
Kirby Hill. N Yor
  nr. Richmond 4E 105
  nr. Ripon 3F 99
Kirby Knowle. N Yor 1G 99
Kirby-le-Soken. Essx 3F 55
Kirby Misperton. N Yor 2B 100
Kirby Muxloe. Leics 5C 74
Kirby Sigston. N Yor 5B 106
Kirby Underdale. E Yor 4C 100
Kirby Wiske. N Yor 1F 99
Kirdford. W Sus 3B 26
Kirk. High 3E 169
Kirkabister. Shet
  on Bressay 8F 173
  on Mainland 6F 173
Kirkandrews. Dum 5D 110
Kirkandrews-on-Eden. Cumb . .4E 113
Kirkapol. Arg 4B 138
Kirkbampton. Cumb 4E 112
Kirkbean. Dum 4A 112
Kirk Bramwith. S Yor 3G 93
Kirkbride. Cumb 4D 112
Kirkbridge. N Yor 5F 105
Kirkbuddo. Ang 4E 145
Kirkburn. E Yor 4D 101
Kirkburton. W Yor 3B 92
Kirkby. Linc 1H 87
Kirkby. Mers 1G 83
Kirkby. N Yor 4C 106
Kirkby Fenside. Linc 4C 88
Kirkby Fleetham. N Yor 5F 105
Kirkby Green. Linc 5H 87
Kirkby-in-Ashfield. Notts 5C 86
Kirkby-in-Furness. Cumb 1B 96
Kirkby la Thorpe. Linc 1A 76
Kirkby Lonsdale. Cumb 2F 97
Kirkby Malham. N Yor 3A 98
Kirkby Mallory. Leics 5B 74
Kirkby Malzeard. N Yor 2E 99
Kirkby Mills. N Yor 1B 100
Kirkbymoorside. N Yor 1A 100
Kirkby on Bain. Linc 4B 88
Kirkby Overblow. N Yor 5F 99
Kirkby Stephen. Cumb 4A 104
Kirkby Thore. Cumb 2H 103
Kirkby Underwood. Linc 3H 75
Kirkby Wharfe. N Yor 5H 99
Kirkcaldy. Fife 4E 137
Kirkcambeck. Cumb 3G 113
Kirkcolm. Dum 3F 109
Kirkconnel. Dum 3G 117
Kirkconnell. Dum 3A 112
Kirkcowan. Dum 3A 110
Kirkcudbright. Dum 4D 111
Kirkdale. Mers 1F 83
Kirk Deighton. N Yor 4F 99
Kirk Ella. E Yor 2D 94
Kirkfieldbank. S Lan 5B 128
Kirkforthar Feus. Fife 3E 137
Kirkgunzeon. Dum 3F 111
Kirk Hallam. Derbs 1B 74
Kirkham. Lanc 1C 90
Kirkham. N Yor 3B 100
Kirkhamgate. W Yor 2C 92
Kirk Hammerton. N Yor 4G 99
Kirkharle. Nmbd 1D 114
Kirkheaton. Nmbd 2D 114
Kirkheaton. W Yor 3B 92
Kirkhill. Ang 2F 145
Kirkhill. High 4H 157
Kirkhope. S Lan 4B 118
Kirkhouse. Bord 1F 119
Kirkibost. High 2D 146
Kirkinch. Ang 4C 144
Kirkinner. Dum 4B 110
Kirkintilloch. E Dun 2H 127
Kirk Ireton. Derbs 5G 85

Kirkland. Cumb
  nr. Cleator Moor 3B 102
  nr. Penrith 1H 103
  nr. Wigton 5D 112
Kirkland. Dum
  nr. Kirkconnel 3G 117
  nr. Moniaive 5H 117
Kirkland Guards. Cumb 5C 112
Kirk Langley. Derbs 2G 73
Kirklauchline. Dum 4F 109
Kirkleatham. Red C 2C 106
Kirklevington. Stoc T 4B 106
Kirkley. Suff 1H 67
Kirklington. N Yor 1F 99
Kirklington. Notts 5D 86
Kirklinton. Cumb 3F 113
Kirkliston. Edin 2E 129
Kirkmabreck. Dum 4B 110
Kirkmaiden. Dum 5E 109
Kirk Merrington. Dur 1F 105
Kirk Michael. IOM 2C 108
Kirkmichael. Per 2H 143
Kirkmichael. S Ayr 4C 116
Kirkmuirhill. S Lan 5A 128
Kirknewton. Nmbd 1D 120
Kirknewton. W Lot 3E 129
Kirkney. Abers 5C 160
Kirk of Shotts. N Lan 3B 128
Kirkoswald. Cumb 5G 113
Kirkoswald. S Ayr 4B 116
Kirkpatrick. Dum 5B 118
Kirkpatrick Durham. Dum 2E 111
Kirkpatrick-Fleming. Dum 2D 112
Kirk Sandall. S Yor 4G 93
Kirksanton. Cumb 1A 96
Kirk Smeaton. N Yor 3F 93
Kirkstall. W Yor 1C 92
Kirkstile. Dum 5F 119
Kirkstyle. High 1F 169
Kirkthorpe. W Yor 2D 92
Kirkton. Abers
  nr. Alford 2D 152
  nr. Insch 1D 152
  nr. Turriff 4F 161
Kirkton. Ang
  nr. Dundee 5D 144
  nr. Forfar 4D 144
  nr. Tarfside 5B 152
Kirkton. Dum 1A 112
Kirkton. Fife 1F 137
Kirkton. High
  nr. Golspie 4E 165
  nr. Kyle of Lochalsh 1G 147
  nr. Lochcarron 4B 156
Kirkton. Bord 3H 119
Kirkton. S Lan 2B 118
Kirktonhill. W Dun 2E 127
Kirkton Manor. Bord 1E 118
Kirkton of Airlie. Ang 3C 144
Kirkton of Auchterhouse.
  Ang 5C 144
Kirkton of Bourtie. Abers 1F 153
Kirkton of Collace. Per 5A 144
Kirkton of Craig. Ang 3G 145
Kirkton of Culsalmond. Abers . .5D 160
Kirkton of Durris. Abers 4E 153
Kirkton of Glenbuchat. Abers . .2A 152
Kirkton of Glenisla. Ang 2B 144
Kirkton of Kingoldrum. Ang 3C 144
Kirkton of Largo. Fife 3G 137
Kirkton of Lethendy. Per 4A 144
Kirkton of Logie Buchan.
  Abers 1G 153
Kirkton of Maryculter. Abers . . .4F 153
Kirkton of Menmuir. Ang 2E 145
Kirkton of Monikie. Ang 5E 145
Kirkton of Oyne. Abers 1D 152
Kirkton of Rayne. Abers 5D 160
Kirkton of Skene. Abers 3F 153
Kirktown. Abers
  nr. Fraserburgh 2G 161
  nr. Peterhead 3H 161
Kirktown of Alvah. Abers 2D 160
Kirktown of Auchterless.
  Abers 4E 160
Kirktown of Deskford. Mor 2C 160
Kirktown of Fetteresso. Abers . .5F 153
Kirktown of Mortlach. Mor 5H 159
Kirktown of Slains. Abers 1H 153
Kirkurd. Bord 5E 129
Kirkwall. Orkn 6D 172
Kirkwall Airport. Orkn 7D 172
Kirkwhelpington. Nmbd 1C 114
Kirk Yetholm. Bord 2C 120
Kirmington. N Lin 3E 94
Kirmond le Mire. Linc 1A 88
Kirn. Arg 2C 126
Kirriemuir. Ang 3C 144
Kirstead Green. Norf 1E 67
Kirtlebridge. Dum 2D 112
Kirtleton. Dum 2D 112
Kirtling. Cambs 5F 65
Kirtling Green. Cambs 5F 65
Kirtlington. Oxon 4D 50
Kirtomy. High 2H 167
Kirton. Linc 2C 76
Kirton. Notts 4D 86
Kirton. Suff 2F 55
Kirton End. Linc 1B 76
Kirton Holme. Linc 1B 76
Kirton in Lindsey. N Lin 1G 87
Kishorn. High 4H 155
Kislingbury. Nptn 5D 62
Kites Hardwick. Warw 4B 62
Kittisford. Som 4D 20
Kittle. Swan 4E 31
Kittybrewster. Aber 3G 153
Kitwood. Hants 3E 25
Kivernoll. Here 2H 47
Kiveton Park. S Yor 2B 86
Knaith. Linc 2F 87

Knaith Park. Linc 2F 87
Knaphill. Surr 5A 38
Knapp. Hants 4C 24
Knapp. Per 5B 144
Knapp. Som 4G 21
Knapperfield. High 3E 169
Knapton. Norf 2F 79
Knapton. York 4H 99
Knapton Green. Here 5G 59
Knapwell. Cambs 4C 64
Knaresborough. N Yor 4F 99
Knarsdale. Nmbd 4H 113
Knatts Valley. Kent 4G 39
Knaven. Abers 4F 161
Knayton. N Yor 1G 99
Knebworth. Herts 3C 52
Knedlington. E Yor 2H 93
Kneesall. Notts 4E 86
Kneesworth. Cambs 1D 52
Kneeton. Notts 1E 74
Knelston. Swan 4D 30
Knenhall. Staf 2D 72
Knightacott. Devn 3G 19
Knightcote. Warw 5B 62
Knightcott. N Som 1G 21
Knightley. Staf 3C 72
Knightley Dale. Staf 3C 72
Knightlow Hill. Warw 3B 62
Knighton. Devn 4B 8
Knighton. Dors 1B 14
Knighton. Leic 5C 74
Knighton. Powy 3E 59
Knighton. Som 2E 21
Knighton. Staf
  nr. Eccleshall 3B 72
  nr. Woore 1B 72
Knighton. Wilts 4A 36
Knighton. Worc 5E 61
Knighton Common. Worc 3A 60
Knightswood. Glas 3G 127
Knightwick. Worc 5B 60
Knill. Here 4E 59
Knipton. Leics 2F 75
Knitsley. Dur 5E 115
Kniveton. Derbs 5G 85
Knock. Arg 5G 139
Knock. Cumb 2H 103
Knock. Mor 3C 160
Knockally. High 5D 168
Knockan. Arg 1B 132
Knockan. High 2G 163
Knockandhu. Mor 1G 151
Knockando. Mor 4F 159
Knockarthur. High 3E 165
Knockbain. High 3A 158
Knockbreck. High 2B 154
Knockdee. High 2D 168
Knockdolian. S Ayr 1G 109
Knockdon. S Ayr 3C 116
Knockdown. Glos 3D 34
Knockenbaird. Abers 1D 152
Knockenkelly. N Ayr 3E 123
Knockentiber. E Ayr 1C 116
Knockfarrel. High 3H 157
Knockglass. High 2C 168
Knockholt. Kent 5F 39
Knockholt Pound. Kent 5F 39
Knockie Lodge. High 2G 149
Knockin. Shrp 3F 71
Knockinlaw. E Ayr 1D 116
Knockinnon. High 5D 169
Knockrome. Arg 2D 124
Knocksharry. IOM 3B 108
Knockshinnoch. E Ayr 3D 116
Knockvennie. Dum 2E 111
Knockvologan. Arg 3B 132
Knodishall. Suff 4G 67
Knole. Som 4H 21
Knollbury. Mon 3H 33
Knolls Green. Ches E 3C 84
Knolton. Wrex 2F 71
Knook. Wilts 2E 23
Knossington. Leics 5F 75
Knott. High 3C 154
Knott End-on-Sea. Lanc 5C 96
Knotting. Bed 4H 63
Knotting Green. Bed 4H 63
Knottingley. W Yor 2E 93
Knotts. Cumb 2F 103
Knotty Ash. Mers 1G 83
Knotty Green. Buck 1A 38
Knowbury. Shrp 3H 59
Knowe. Dum 2A 110
Knowefield. Cumb 4F 113
Knowehead. Dum 5F 117
Knowes. E Lot 2C 130
Knowesgate. Nmbd 1C 114
Knoweside. S Ayr 3B 116
Knowes of Elrick. Abers 3D 160
Knowle. Bris 4B 34
Knowle. Devn
  nr. Braunton 3E 19
  nr. Budleigh Salterton 4D 12
  nr. Crediton 2A 12
Knowle. Devn 3H 59
Knowle. Shrp 3H 59
Knowle. W Mid 3F 61
Knowle Green. Lanc 1E 91
Knowle St Giles. Som 1G 13
Knowlesands. Shrp 1B 60
Knowle Village. Hants 2D 16
Knowl Hill. Wind 4G 37
Knowlton. Kent 5G 41
Knowsley. Mers 1G 83
Knucklas. Powy 3E 59
Knuston. Nptn 4G 63
Knutsford. Ches E 3B 84
Knypersley. Staf 5C 84
Krumlin. W Yor 3A 92
Kuggar. Corn 5E 5

Kyleakin. High 1F 147
Kyle of Lochalsh. High 1F 147
Kylerhea. High 1F 147
Kylesku. High 5C 166
Kylesmorar. High 4G 147
Kylestrome. High 5C 166
Kymin. Mon 4A 48
Kynaston. Here 2B 48
Kynaston. Shrp 3F 71
Kynnersley. Telf 4A 72
Kyre Green. Worc 4A 60
Kyre Park. Worc 4A 60
Kyrewood. Worc 4A 60

L

Labost. W Isl 3E 171
Lacasaidh. W Isl 5F 171
Lacasdail. W Isl 4G 171
Laceby. NE Lin 4F 95
Lacey Green. Buck 5G 51
Lach Dennis. Ches W 3B 84
Lache. Ches W 4F 83
Lackford. Suff 3G 65
Lacock. Wilts 5E 35
Ladbroke. Warw 5B 62
Laddingford. Kent 1A 28
Lade Bank. Linc 5C 88
Ladock. Corn 3C 6
Lady. Orkn 3F 172
Ladybank. Fife 2F 137
Ladycross. Corn 4D 10
Lady Green. Mers 4B 90
Lady Hall. Cumb 1A 96
Ladykirk. Bord 5E 131
Ladysford. Abers 2G 161
Ladywood. W Mid 2E 61
Ladywood. Worc 4C 60
Laga. High 2A 140
Lagavulin. Arg 5C 124
Lagg. Arg 2D 125
Lagg. N Ayr 3D 122
Laggan. Arg 4A 124
Laggan. High
  nr. Fort Augustus 4E 149
  nr. Newtonmore 4A 150
Laggan. Mor 5H 159
Lagganlia. High 3C 150
Lagganulva. Arg 4F 139
Laglingarten. Arg 3A 134
Lagness. W Sus 2G 17
Laid. High 3E 166
Laide. High 4C 162
Laigh Fenwick. E Ayr 5F 127
Laindon. Essx 2A 40
Lairg. High 3C 164
Lairg Muir. High 3C 164
Laithes. Cumb 1F 103
Laithkirk. Dur 2C 104
Lake. Devn 3F 19
Lake. IOW 4D 16
Lake. Wilts 3G 23
Lakenham. Norf 5E 79
Lakenheath. Suff 2G 65
Lakesend. Norf 1E 65
Lakeside. Cumb 1C 96
Laleham. Surr 4B 38
Laleston. B'end 3B 32
Lamancha. Bord 4F 129
Lamarsh. Essx 2B 54
Lamas. Norf 3E 79
Lamb Corner. Essx 2D 54
Lambden. Bord 5D 130
Lamberhead Green. G Man 4D 90
Lamberhurst. Kent 2A 28
Lamberhurst Quarter. Kent 2A 28
Lamberton. Bord 4F 131
Lambeth. G Lon 3E 39
Lambfell Moar. IOM 3B 108
Lambhill. Glas 3G 127
Lambley. Nmbd 4H 113
Lambley. Notts 1D 74
Lamborough. Bord 2F 103
Lambourn. W Ber 4B 36
Lambourne End. Essx 1F 39
Lambourn Woodlands. W Ber . .4B 36
Lambs Green. Dors 3E 15
Lambs Green. W Sus 2D 26
Lambston. Pemb 3D 42
Lamellion. Corn 2G 7
Lamerton. Devn 5E 11
Lamesley. Tyne 4F 115
Laminess. Orkn 4F 172
Lamington. High 1B 158
Lamington. S Lan 1B 118
Lamlash. N Ayr 2E 123
Lamonby. Cumb 1F 103
Lamorick. Corn 2E 7
Lamorna. Corn 4B 4
Lamorran. Corn 4C 6
Lampeter. Cdgn 1F 45
Lampeter Velfrey. Pemb 3F 43
Lamphey. Pemb 4E 43
Lamplugh. Cumb 2B 102
Lamport. Nptn 3E 63
Lamyatt. Som 3B 22
Lana. Devn
  nr. Ashwater 3D 10
  nr. Holsworthy 2D 10
Lanark. S Lan 5B 128
Lanarth. Corn 4E 5
Lancaster. Lanc 3D 97
Lanchester. Dur 5E 115
Lancing. W Sus 5C 26
Landbeach. Cambs 4D 65
Landcross. Devn 4E 19
Landerberry. Abers 3E 153
Landford. Wilts 1A 16
Land Gate. G Man 4D 90
Landhallow. High 5D 169

Landimore. Swan 3D 30
Landkey. Devn 3F 19
Landkey Newland. Devn 3F 19
Landore. Swan 3F 31
Landport. Port 2E 17
Landrake. Corn 2H 7
Landscove. Devn 2D 9
Land's End (St Just) Airport.
  Corn 4A 4
Landshipping. Pemb 3E 43
Landulph. Corn 2A 8
Landywood. Staf 5D 73
Lane. Corn 2C 6
Laneast. Corn 4C 10
Lane Bottom. Lanc 1G 91
Lane End. Buck 2G 37
Lane End. Hants 4D 24
Lane End. IOW 4E 17
Lane End. Wilts 2D 22
Lane Ends. Derbs 2G 73
Lane Ends. Dur 1E 105
Lane Ends. Lanc 4G 97
Laneham. Notts 3F 87
Lane Head. Dur
  nr. Hutton Magna 3E 105
  nr. Woodland 2D 105
Lanehead. Dur 5B 114
Lane Head. G Man 1A 84
Lanehead. Nmbd 1A 114
Lane Head. W Yor 4B 92
Lane Heads. Lanc 1C 90
Lanercost. Cumb 3G 113
Laneshaw Bridge. Lanc 5B 98
Laney Green. Staf 5D 72
Langais. W Isl 2D 170
Langal. High 2B 140
Langar. Notts 2E 74
Langbank. Ren 2E 127
Langbar. N Yor 4C 98
Langburnshiels. Bord 4H 119
Langcliffe. N Yor 3H 97
Langdale End. N Yor 5G 107
Langdon. Corn 3C 10
Langdon Beck. Dur 1B 104
Langdon Cross. Corn 4D 10
Langdon Hills. Essx 2A 40
Langdown. Hants 2C 16
Langdyke. Fife 3F 137
Langenhoe. Essx 4D 54
Langford. C Beds 1B 52
Langford. Devn 2D 12
Langford. Essx 5B 54
Langford. Notts 5F 87
Langford. Oxon 5H 49
Langford. Som 4F 21
Langford Budville. Som 4E 20
Langham. Dors 4C 22
Langham. Essx 2D 54
Langham. Norf 1C 78
Langham. Rut 4F 75
Langham. Suff 4B 66
Langho. Lanc 1F 91
Langholm. Dum 1E 113
Langland. Swan 4F 31
Langleeford. Nmbd 2D 120
Langley. Ches E 3D 84
Langley. Derbs 1B 74
Langley. Essx 2E 53
Langley. Glos 3F 49
Langley. Hants 2C 16
Langley. Herts 3C 52
Langley. Kent 5C 40
Langley. Nmbd 3B 114
Langley. Slo 3B 38
Langley. Som 4D 20
Langley. Warw 4F 61
Langley. W Sus 4G 25
Langley Burrell. Wilts 4E 35
Langley Common. Derbs 2G 73
Langley Green. Derbs 2G 73
Langley Green. Norf 5F 79
Langley Green. Warw 4F 61
Langley Green. W Sus 2D 26
Langley Heath. Kent 5C 40
Langley Marsh. Som 4D 20
Langley Moor. Dur 5F 115
Langley Park. Dur 5F 115
Langley Street. Norf 5F 79
Langney. E Sus 5H 27
Langold. Notts 2C 86
Langore. Corn 4C 10
Langport. Som 4H 21
Langrick. Linc 1B 76
Langridge. Bath 5C 34
Langridgeford. Devn 4F 19
Langrigg. Cumb 5C 112
Langrish. Hants 4F 25
Langsett. S Yor 4C 92
Langshaw. Bord 1H 119
Langstone. Hants 2F 17
Langthorne. N Yor 5F 105
Langthorpe. N Yor 3F 99
Langthwaite. N Yor 4D 104
Langtoft. E Yor 3E 101
Langtoft. Linc 4A 76
Langton. Dur 3E 105
Langton. Linc
  nr. Horncastle 4B 88
  nr. Spilsby 3C 88
Langton. N Yor 3B 100
Langton by Wragby. Linc 3A 88
Langton Green. Kent 2G 27
Langton Herring. Dors 4B 14
Langton Long Blandford. Dors . .2D 15
Langton Matravers. Dors 5E 15
Langtree. Devn 1E 11
Langwathby. Cumb 1G 103
Langwith. Derbs 4C 86
Langworth. Linc 3H 87
Lanivet. Corn 2E 7

Lanjeth. *Corn* 3D **6**
Lank. *Corn* 5A **10**
Lanlivery. *Corn* 3E **7**
Lanner. *Corn* 5B **6**
Lanreath. *Corn* 3F **7**
Lansallos. *Corn* 3F **7**
Lansdown. *Bath* 5C **34**
Lansdown. *Glos* 3E **49**
Lanteglos Highway. *Corn* 3F **7**
Lanton. *Nmbd* 1D **120**
Lanton. *Bord* 2A **120**
Lapford. *Devn* 2H **11**
Lapford Cross. *Devn* 2H **11**
Laphroaig. *Arg* 5B **124**
Lapley. *Staf* 4C **72**
Lapworth. *Warw* 3F **61**
Larachbeg. *High* 4A **140**
Larbert. *Falk* 1B **128**
Larden Green. *Ches E* 5H **83**
Larel. *High* 3D **169**
Largie. *Abers* 5D **160**
Largiemore. *Arg* 1H **125**
Largoward. *Fife* 3G **137**
Largs. *N Ayr* 4D **126**
Largue. *Abers* 4D **160**
Largybeg. *N Ayr* 3E **123**
Largymeanoch. *N Ayr* 3E **123**
Largymore. *N Ayr* 3E **123**
Larkfield. *Inv* 2D **126**
Larkfield. *Kent* 5B **40**
Larkhall. *Bath* 5C **34**
Larkhall. *S Lan* 4A **128**
Larkhill. *Wilts* 2G **23**
Larling. *Norf* 2B **66**
Larport. *Here* 2A **48**
Lartington. *Dur* 3D **104**
Lary. *Abers* 3H **151**
Lasham. *Hants* 2E **25**
Lashenden. *Kent* 1C **28**
Lasswade. *Midl* 3G **129**
Lastingham. *N Yor* 5E **107**
Latchford. *Herts* 3D **53**
Latchford. *Oxon* 5E **51**
Latchingdon. *Essx* 5B **54**
Latchley. *Corn* 5E **11**
Latchmere Green. *Hants* 1E **25**
Lathbury. *Mil* 1G **51**
Latheron. *High* 5D **169**
Latheronwheel. *High* 5D **169**
Lathom. *Lanc* 4C **90**
Lathones. *Fife* 3G **137**
Latimer. *Buck* 1B **38**
Latteridge. *S Glo* 3B **34**
Lattiford. *Som* 4B **22**
Latton. *Wilts* 2F **35**
Laudale House. *High* 3B **140**
Lauder. *Bord* 5B **130**
Laugharne. *Carm* 3H **43**
Laughterton. *Linc* 3F **87**
Laughton. *E Sus* 4G **27**
Laughton. *Leics* 2D **62**
Laughton. *Linc*
 nr. Gainsborough 1F **87**
 nr. Grantham 2H **75**
Laughton Common. *S Yor* 2C **86**
Laughton en le Morthen. *S Yor* .2C **86**
Launcells. *Corn* 2C **10**
Launceston. *Corn* 4D **10**
Launcherley. *Som* 2A **22**
Launton. *Oxon* 3E **50**
Laurencekirk. *Abers* 1G **145**
Laurieston. *Dum* 3D **111**
Laurieston. *Falk* 2C **128**
Lavendon. *Mil* 5G **63**
Lavenham. *Suff* 1C **54**
Laverhay. *Dum* 5D **118**
Laversdale. *Cumb* 3F **113**
Laverstock. *Wilts* 3G **23**
Laverstoke. *Hants* 2C **24**
Laverton. *Glos* 2F **49**
Laverton. *N Yor* 2E **99**
Laverton. *Som* 1C **22**
Lavister. *Wrex* 5F **83**
Law. *S Lan* 4B **128**
Lawers. *Per* 5D **142**
Lawford. *Essx* 2D **54**
Lawhitton. *Corn* 4D **10**
Lawkland. *N Yor* 3G **97**
Lawley. *Telf* 5A **72**
Lawnhead. *Staf* 3C **72**
Lawrenny. *Pemb* 4E **43**
Lawshall. *Suff* 5A **66**
Lawton. *Here* 5G **59**
Laxey. *IOM* 3D **108**
Laxfield. *Suff* 3E **67**
Laxfirth. *Shet* 6F **173**
Laxo. *Shet* 5F **173**
Laxton. *E Yor* 2A **94**
Laxton. *Nptn* 1G **63**
Laxton. *Notts* 4E **86**
Laycock. *W Yor* 5C **98**
Layer Breton. *Essx* 4C **54**
Layer-de-la-Haye. *Essx* 3C **54**
Layer Marney. *Essx* 4C **54**
Laymore. *Dors* 2G **13**
Laysters Pole. *Here* 4H **59**
Layter's Green. *Buck* 1A **38**
Laytham. *E Yor* 1H **93**
Lazenby. *Red C* 3C **106**
Lazonby. *Cumb* 1G **103**
Lea. *Derbs* 5H **85**
Lea. *Here* 3B **48**
Lea. *Linc* 2F **87**
Lea. *Shrp*
 nr. Bishop's Castle 2F **59**
 nr. Shrewsbury 5G **71**
Lea. *Wilts* 3E **35**
Leabrooks. *Derbs* 5B **86**
Leac a Li. *W Isl* 8D **171**
Leachd. *Arg* 4H **133**
Leachkin. *High* 4A **158**

Leachpool. *Pemb* 3D **42**
Leadburn. *Midl* 4F **129**
Leaden Roding. *Essx* 4F **53**
Leadgate. *Cumb* 5A **114**
Leadgate. *Dur* 4E **115**
Leadgate. *Nmbd* 4E **115**
Leadhills. *S Lan* 3A **118**
Leadingcross Green. *Kent* 5C **40**
Leafield. *Oxon* 4B **50**
Leagrave. *Lutn* 3A **52**
Lea Hall. *W Mid* 2F **61**
Lea Heath. *Staf* 3E **73**
Leake. *N Yor* 5B **106**
Leake Common Side. *Linc* 5C **88**
Leake Fold Hill. *Linc* 5D **88**
Leake Hurn's End. *Linc* 1D **76**
Lealholm. *N Yor* 4E **107**
Lealt. *Arg* 4D **132**
Lealt. *High* 2E **155**
Leam. *Derbs* 3G **85**
Lea Marston. *Warw* 1G **61**
Leamington Hastings. *Warw* . . .4B **62**
Leamington Spa, Royal.
 Warw 4H **61**
Leamonsley. *Staf* 5F **73**
Leamside. *Dur* 5G **115**
Leargybreck. *Arg* 2D **124**
Lease Rigg. *N Yor* 4F **107**
Leasgill. *Cumb* 1D **97**
Leasingham. *Linc* 1H **75**
Leasingthorne. *Dur* 1F **105**
Leasowe. *Mers* 1E **83**
Leatherhead. *Surr* 5C **38**
Leathley. *N Yor* 5E **99**
Leaths. *Dum* 3E **111**
Leaton. *Shrp* 4G **71**
Leaton. *Telf* 4A **72**
Lea Town. *Lanc* 1C **90**
Leaveland. *Kent* 5E **40**
Leavenheath. *Suff* 2C **54**
Leavening. *N Yor* 3B **100**
Leaves Green. *G Lon* 4F **39**
Lea Yeat. *Cumb* 1G **97**
Leazes. *Dur* 4E **115**
Lebberston. *N Yor* 1E **101**
Lechlade on Thames. *Glos* 2H **35**
Leck. *Lanc* 2F **97**
Leckford. *Hants* 3B **24**
Leckfurin. *High* 3H **167**
Leckgruinart. *Arg* 3A **124**
Leckhampstead. *Buck* 2F **51**
Leckhampstead. *W Ber* 4C **36**
Leckhampton. *Glos* 4E **49**
Leckmelm. *High* 4F **163**
Leckwith. *V Glam* 4E **33**
Leconfield. *E Yor* 5E **101**
Ledaig. *Arg* 5D **140**
Ledburn. *Buck* 3H **51**
Ledbury. *Here* 2C **48**
Ledgemoor. *Here* 5G **59**
Ledgowan. *High* 3D **156**
Ledicot. *Here* 4G **59**
Ledmore. *High* 2G **163**
Lednabirichen. *High* 4E **165**
Lednagullin. *High* 2A **168**
Ledsham. *Ches W* 3F **83**
Ledsham. *W Yor* 2E **93**
Ledston. *W Yor* 2E **93**
Ledstone. *Devn* 4D **8**
Ledwell. *Oxon* 3C **50**
Lee. *The. Buck* 5H **51**
Lee. *Devn*
 nr. Ilfracombe 2E **19**
 nr. South Molton 4B **20**
Lee. *G Lon* 3E **39**
Lee. *Hants* 1B **16**
Lee. *Lanc* 4E **97**
Lee. *Shrp* 2G **71**
Leeans. *Shet* 7E **173**
Leebotten. *Shet* 9F **173**
Leebotwood. *Shrp* 1G **59**
Lee Brockhurst. *Shrp* 3H **71**
Leece. *Cumb* 3B **96**
Leechpool. *Mon* 3A **34**
Lee Clump. *Buck* 5H **51**
Leeds. *Kent* 5C **40**
Leeds. *W Yor* **199** (1C **92**)
Leeds Bradford Airport.
 W Yor 5E **99**
Leedstown. *Corn* 3D **4**
Leegomery. *Telf* 4A **72**
Lee Head. *Derbs* 1E **85**
Leek. *Staf* 5D **85**
Leekbrook. *Staf* 5D **85**
Leek Wootton. *Warw* 4G **61**
Lee Mill. *Devn* 3B **8**
Leeming. *N Yor* 1E **99**
Leeming Bar. *N Yor* 5F **105**
Lee Moor. *Devn* 2B **8**
Lee Moor. *W Yor* 2D **92**
Lee-on-the-Solent. *Hants* 2D **16**
Lees. *Derbs* 2G **73**
Lees. *G Man* 4H **91**
Lees. *The. Kent* 5E **40**
Lees. *W Yor* 1A **92**
Leeswood. *Flin* 4E **83**
Leetown. *Per* 1E **136**
Leftwich. *Ches W* 3A **84**
Legbourne. *Linc* 2C **88**
Legburthwaite. *Cumb* 3E **102**
Legerwood. *Bord* 5B **130**
Legsby. *Linc* 2A **88**
Leicester. *Leic* **200** (5C **74**)
Leicester Forest East. *Leics* . . .5C **74**
Leigh. *Dors* 2B **14**
Leigh, *The. Glos* 3D **48**
Leigh. *G Man* 4E **91**
Leigh. *Kent* 1G **27**

Leigh. *Shrp* 5F **71**
Leigh. *Surr* 1D **26**
Leigh. *Wilts* 2F **35**
Leigh. *Worc* 5B **60**
Leigham. *Plym* 3B **8**
Leigh Beck. *Essx* 2C **40**
Leigh Common. *Som* 4C **22**
Leigh Delamere. *Wilts* 4D **35**
Leigh Green. *Kent* 2D **28**
Leighland Chapel. *Som* 3D **20**
Leigh-on-Sea. *S'end* 2C **40**
Leigh Park. *Hants* 2F **17**
Leigh Sinton. *Worc* 5B **60**
Leighton. *Glos* 2D **34**
Leighton. *N Yor* 2D **98**
Leighton. *Powy* 5E **71**
Leighton. *Shrp* 5A **72**
Leighton. *Som* 2C **22**
Leighton Bromswold.
 Cambs 3A **64**
Leighton Buzzard. *C Beds* . . .3H **51**
Leigh-upon-Mendip. *Som* 2B **22**
Leinthall Earls. *Here* 4G **59**
Leinthall Starkes. *Here* 4G **59**
Leintwardine. *Here* 3G **59**
Leire. *Leics* 1C **62**
Leirinmore. *High* 2E **166**
Leishmore. *High* 4G **157**
Leiston. *Suff* 4G **67**
Leitfie. *Per* 4B **144**
Leith. *Edin* 2F **129**
Leitholm. *Bord* 5D **130**
Lelant. *Corn* 3C **4**
Lelant Downs. *Corn* 3C **4**
Lelley. *E Yor* 1F **95**
Lem Hill. *Shrp* 3B **60**
Lemington. *Tyne* 3E **115**
Lempitlaw. *Bord* 1B **120**
Lemsford. *Herts* 4C **52**
Lenacre. *Cumb* 1F **97**
Lenchie. *Abers* 5C **160**
Lenchwick. *Worc* 1F **49**
Lendalfoot. *S Ayr* 1G **109**
Lendrick. *Stir* 3E **135**
Lenham. *Kent* 5C **40**
Lenham Heath. *Kent* 1D **28**
Lenimore. *N Ayr* 5G **125**
Lennel. *Bord* 5E **131**
Lennoxtown. *E Dun* 2H **127**
Lenton. *Linc* 2H **75**
Lentran. *High* 4H **157**
Lenwade. *Norf* 4C **78**
Lenzie. *E Dun* 2H **127**
Leochel Cushnie. *Abers* 2C **152**
Leogh. *Shet* 1B **172**
Leominster. *Here* 5G **59**
Leonard Stanley. *Glos* 5D **48**
Lepe. *Hants* 3C **16**
Lephenstrath. *Arg* 5A **122**
Lephin. *High* 4A **154**
Lephinchapel. *Arg* 4G **133**
Lephinmore. *Arg* 4G **133**
Leppington. *N Yor* 3B **100**
Lepton. *W Yor* 3C **92**
Lerryn. *Corn* 3F **7**
Lerwick. *Shet* 7F **173**
Lerwick (Tingwall) Airport.
 Shet 7F **173**
Lesbury. *Nmbd* 3G **121**
Leslie. *Abers* 1C **152**
Leslie. *Fife* 3E **137**
Lesmahagow. *S Lan* 1H **117**
Lesnewth. *Corn* 3B **10**
Lessingham. *Norf* 3F **79**
Lessonhall. *Cumb* 4D **112**
Leswalt. *Dum* 3F **109**
Letchmore Heath. *Herts* 1C **38**
Letchworth Garden City.
 Herts 2C **52**
Letcombe Bassett. *Oxon* 3B **36**
Letcombe Regis. *Oxon* 3B **36**
Letham. *Ang* 4E **145**
Letham. *Falk* 1B **128**
Letham. *Fife* 2F **137**
Lethanhill. *E Ayr* 3D **116**
Lethenty. *Abers* 4F **161**
Letheringham. *Suff* 5E **67**
Letheringsett. *Norf* 2C **78**
Lettaford. *Devn* 4H **11**
Lettan. *Orkn* 3G **172**
Letter. *Abers* 2E **153**
Letterewe. *High* 1B **156**
Letterfearn. *High* 1A **148**
Lettermore. *Arg* 4F **139**
Letters. *High* 5F **163**
Letterston. *Pemb* 2D **42**
Letton. *Here*
 nr. Kington 1G **47**
 nr. Leintwardine 3F **59**
Letty Green. *Herts* 4C **52**
Letwell. *S Yor* 2C **86**
Leuchars. *Fife* 1G **137**
Leumrabhagh. *W Isl* 6F **171**
Leusdon. *Devn* 5H **11**
Levaneap. *Shet* 5F **173**
Levedale. *Staf* 4C **72**
Leven. *E Yor* 5F **101**
Leven. *Fife* 3F **137**
Levencorroch. *N Ayr* 3E **123**
Levenhall. *E Lot* 2G **129**
Levens. *Cumb* 1D **97**
Levens Green. *Herts* 3D **52**
Levenshulme. *G Man* 1C **84**
Levenwick. *Shet* 9F **173**
Leverburgh. *W Isl* 9G **171**
Leverington. *Cambs* 4D **76**
Leverton. *Linc* 1C **76**
Leverton. *W Ber* 4B **36**
Leverton Lucasgate. *Linc* 1D **76**
Leverton Outgate. *Linc* 1D **76**
Levington. *Suff* 2F **55**

Levisham. *N Yor* 5F **107**
Levishie. *High* 2G **149**
Lew. *Oxon* 5B **50**
Lewaigue. *IOM* 2D **108**
Lewannick. *Corn* 4C **10**
Lewdown. *Devn* 4E **11**
Lewes. *E Sus* 4F **27**
Leweston. *Pemb* 2D **42**
Lewisham. *G Lon* 3E **39**
Lewiston. *High* 1H **149**
Lewistown. *B'end* 3C **32**
Lewknor. *Oxon* 2F **37**
Leworthy. *Devn*
 nr. Barnstaple 3G **19**
 nr. Holsworthy 2D **10**
Lewson Street. *Kent* 4D **40**
Lewthorn Cross. *Devn* 5A **12**
Lewtrenchard. *Devn* 4E **11**
Ley. *Corn* 2F **7**
Leybourne. *Kent* 5A **40**
Leyburn. *N Yor* 5E **105**
Leycett. *Staf* 1B **72**
Leyfields. *Staf* 5G **73**
Ley Green. *Herts* 3B **52**
Ley Hill. *Buck* 5H **51**
Leyland. *Lanc* 2D **90**
Leylodge. *Abers* 2E **153**
Leymoor. *W Yor* 3B **92**
Leys. *Per* 5B **144**
Leysdown-on-Sea. *Kent* 3E **41**
Leysmill. *Ang* 4F **145**
Leyton. *G Lon* 2E **39**
Leytonstone. *G Lon* 2F **39**
Lezant. *Corn* 5D **10**
Leziate. *Norf* 4F **77**
Lhanbryde. *Mor* 2G **159**
Lhen, *The. IOM* 1C **108**
Liatrie. *High* 5E **157**
Libanus. *Powy* 3C **46**
Libberton. *S Lan* 5C **128**
Libbery. *Worc* 5D **60**
Liberton. *Edin* 3F **129**
Liceasto. *W Isl* 8D **171**
Lichfield. *Staf* 5F **73**
Lickey. *Worc* 3D **61**
Lickey End. *Worc* 3D **60**
Lickfold. *W Sus* 3A **26**
Liddaton. *Devn* 4E **11**
Liddington. *Swin* 3H **35**
Liddle. *Orkn* 9D **172**
Lidgate. *Suff* 5G **65**
Lidgett. *Notts* 4D **86**
Lidham Hill. *E Sus* 4C **28**
Lidlington. *C Beds* 2H **51**
Lidsey. *W Sus* 5A **26**
Lidstone. *Oxon* 3B **50**
Lienassie. *High* 1B **148**
Liff. *Ang* 5C **144**
Lifford. *W Mid* 2E **61**
Lifton. *Devn* 4D **11**
Liftondown. *Devn* 4D **10**
Lighthorne. *Warw* 5H **61**
Light Oaks. *Stoke* 5D **84**
Lightwater. *Surr* 4A **38**
Lightwood. *Staf* 1E **73**
Lightwood. *Stoke* 1D **72**
Lightwood Green. *Ches E* 1A **72**
Lightwood Green. *Wrex* 1F **71**
Lilbourne. *Nptn* 3C **62**
Lilburn Tower. *Nmbd* 2E **121**
Lillesdon. *Som* 4G **21**
Lilleshall. *Telf* 4B **72**
Lilley. *Herts* 3B **52**
Lilliesleaf. *Bord* 2H **119**
Lillingstone Dayrell. *Buck* 2F **51**
Lillingstone Lovell. *Buck* 1F **51**
Lillington. *Dors* 1B **14**
Lilstock. *Som* 2E **21**
Lilybank. *Inv* 2E **126**
Lilyhurst. *Shrp* 4B **72**
Limbrick. *Lanc* 3E **90**
Limbury. *Lutn* 3A **52**
Limekilnburn. *S Lan* 4A **128**
Limekilns. *Fife* 1D **129**
Limerigg. *Falk* 2B **128**
Limestone Brae. *Nmbd* 5A **114**
Lime Street. *Worc* 2D **48**
Limington. *Som* 4A **22**
Limpenhoe. *Norf* 5F **79**
Limpley Stoke. *Wilts* 5C **34**
Limpsfield. *Surr* 5F **39**
Limpsfield Chart. *Surr* 5F **39**
Linburn. *W Lot* 3E **129**
Linby. *Notts* 5C **86**
Linchmere. *W Sus* 3G **25**
Lincluden. *Dum* 2A **112**
Lincoln. *Linc* **198** (3G **87**)
Lincomb. *Worc* 4C **60**
Lindale. *Cumb* 1D **96**
Lindal in Furness. *Cumb* 2B **96**
Lindean. *Bord* 1G **119**
Linden. *Glos* 4D **48**
Lindfield. *W Sus* 3E **27**
Lindford. *Hants* 3G **25**
Lindores. *Fife* 2E **137**
Lindridge. *Worc* 4A **60**
Lindsell. *Essx* 3G **53**
Lindsey. *Suff* 1C **54**
Lindsey Tye. *Suff* 1C **54**
Linford. *Hants* 2G **15**
Linford. *Thur* 3A **40**
Lingague. *IOM* 4B **108**
Lingdale. *Red C* 3D **106**
Lingen. *Here* 4F **59**
Lingfield. *Surr* 1E **27**
Lingreabhagh. *W Isl* 9C **171**
Lingwood. *Norf* 5F **79**
Lingy Close. *Cumb* 4E **113**
Liniclate. *W Isl* 4C **170**
Linicro. *High* 2C **154**
Linkend. *Worc* 2D **48**
Linkenholt. *Hants* 1B **24**

Linkinhorne. *Corn* 5D **10**
Linklater. *Orkn* 9D **172**
Linksness. *Orkn* 6E **172**
Linktown. *Fife* 4E **137**
Linkwood. *Mor* 2G **159**
Linley. *Shrp*
 nr. Bishop's Castle 1F **59**
 nr. Bridgnorth 1A **60**
Linley Green. *Here* 5A **60**
Linlithgow. *W Lot* 2C **128**
Linlithgow Bridge. *Falk* 2C **128**
Linneraineach. *High* 3F **163**
Linshiels. *Nmbd* 4C **120**
Linsiadar. *W Isl* 4E **171**
Linsidemore. *High* 4C **164**
Linslade. *C Beds* 3H **51**
Linstead Parva. *Suff* 3F **67**
Linstock. *Cumb* 4F **113**
Linthwaite. *W Yor* 3B **92**
Lintlaw. *Bord* 4E **131**
Lintmill. *Mor* 2C **160**
Linton. *Cambs* 1F **53**
Linton. *Derbs* 4G **73**
Linton. *Here* 3B **48**
Linton. *Kent* 1B **28**
Linton. *N Yor* 3B **98**
Linton. *Bord* 2B **120**
Linton. *W Yor* 5F **99**
Linton Colliery. *Nmbd* 5G **121**
Linton Hill. *Here* 3B **48**
Linton-on-Ouse. *N Yor* 3G **99**
Lintzford. *Dur* 4E **115**
Lintzgarth. *Dur* 5C **114**
Linwood. *Hants* 2G **15**
Linwood. *Linc* 2A **88**
Linwood. *Ren* 3F **127**
Lionacleit. *W Isl* 4C **170**
Lionacro. *High* 2C **154**
Lionacuidhe. *W Isl* 4C **170**
Lional. *W Isl* 1H **171**
Liphook. *Hants* 3G **25**
Liplate. *Edin* 3F **129**
Lipley. *Shrp* 2B **72**
Lipyeate. *Som* 1B **22**
Liquo. *N Lan* 4B **128**
Liscard. *Mers* 1F **83**
Liscombe. *Som* 3B **20**
Liskeard. *Corn* 2G **7**
Lisle Court. *Hants* 3B **16**
Liss. *Hants* 4F **25**
Lissett. *E Yor* 4F **101**
Liss Forest. *Hants* 4F **25**
Lissington. *Linc* 2A **88**
Liston. *Essx* 1B **54**
Lisvane. *Card* 3E **33**
Liswerry. *Newp* 3G **33**
Litcham. *Norf* 4A **78**
Litchard. *B'end* 3C **32**
Litchborough. *Nptn* 5D **62**
Litchfield. *Hants* 1C **24**
Litherland. *Mers* 1F **83**
Litlington. *Cambs* 1D **52**
Litlington. *E Sus* 5G **27**
Littlemill. *Nmbd* 3G **121**
Litterty. *Abers* 3E **161**
Little Abington. *Cambs* 1F **53**
Little Addington. *Nptn* 3G **63**
Little Airmyn. *N Yor* 2H **93**
Little Alne. *Warw* 4F **61**
Little Ardo. *Abers* 5F **161**
Little Asby. *Cumb* 4H **103**
Little Aston. *Staf* 5E **73**
Little Atherfield. *IOW* 4C **16**
Little Ayton. *N Yor* 3C **106**
Little Baddow. *Essx* 5A **54**
Little Badminton. *S Glo* 3D **34**
Little Ballinluig. *Per* 3G **143**
Little Bampton. *Cumb* 4D **112**
Little Bardfield. *Essx* 2G **53**
Little Barford. *Bed* 5A **64**
Little Barningham. *Norf* 2D **78**
Little Barrington. *Glos* 4H **49**
Little Barrow. *Ches W* 4G **83**
Little Barugh. *N Yor* 2B **100**
Little Bavington. *Nmbd* 2C **114**
Little Bealings. *Suff* 1F **55**
Littlebeck. *Cumb* 3H **103**
Little Bedwyn. *Wilts* 5A **36**
Little Bentley. *Essx* 3E **54**
Little Berkhamsted. *Herts* 5C **52**
Little Billing. *Nptn* 4F **63**
Little Billington. *C Beds* 3H **51**
Little Birch. *Here* 2A **48**
Little Bispham. *Bkpl* 5C **96**
Little Blakenham. *Suff* 1E **54**
Little Blencow. *Cumb* 1F **103**
Little Bognor. *W Sus* 3B **26**
Little Bolas. *Shrp* 3A **72**
Little Bollington. *Ches E* 2B **84**
Little Bookham. *Surr* 5C **38**
Littleborough. *Devn* 1B **12**
Littleborough. *G Man* 3H **91**
Littleborough. *Notts* 2F **87**
Littlebourne. *Kent* 5G **41**
Little Bourton. *Oxon* 1C **50**
Little Bowden. *Leics* 2E **63**
Little Bradley. *Suff* 5F **65**
Little Brampton. *Shrp* 2F **59**
Little Brechin. *Ang* 2E **145**
Littlebredy. *Dors* 4A **14**
Little Brickhill. *Mil* 2H **51**
Little Bridgeford. *Staf* 3C **72**
Little Brington. *Nptn* 4D **62**
Little Bromley. *Essx* 3D **54**
Little Broughton. *Cumb* 1B **102**
Little Budworth. *Ches W* 4H **83**
Little Burstead. *Essx* 1A **40**
Little Burton. *E Yor* 5F **101**
Littlebury. *Essx* 2F **53**
Littlebury Green. *Essx* 2E **53**
Little Bytham. *Linc* 4H **75**
Little Canfield. *Essx* 3F **53**

Little Canford. *Dors* 3F **15**
Little Carlton. *Linc* 2C **88**
Little Carlton. *Notts* 5E **87**
Little Casterton. *Rut* 5H **75**
Little Catwick. *E Yor* 5F **101**
Little Catworth. *Cambs* 3A **64**
Little Cawthorpe. *Linc* 2C **88**
Little Chalfont. *Buck* 1A **38**
Little Chart. *Kent* 1D **28**
Little Chesterton. *Essx* 1F **53**
Little Cheverell. *Wilts* 1E **23**
Little Chishill. *Cambs* 2E **53**
Little Clacton. *Essx* 4E **55**
Little Clanfield. *Oxon* 5A **50**
Little Clifton. *Cumb* 2B **102**
Little Coates. *NE Lin* 4F **95**
Little Comberton. *Worc* 1E **49**
Little Common. *E Sus* 5B **28**
Little Compton. *Warw* 2A **50**
Little Cornard. *Suff* 2B **54**
Littlecote. *Buck* 3G **51**
Littlecott. *Wilts* 1G **23**
Little Cowarne. *Here* 5A **60**
Little Coxwell. *Oxon* 2A **36**
Little Crakehall. *N Yor* 5F **105**
Little Crawley. *Mil* 1H **51**
Little Creich. *High* 5D **164**
Little Cressingham. *Norf* 5A **78**
Little Crosby. *Mers* 4B **90**
Little Crosthwaite. *Cumb* 2D **102**
Little Cubley. *Derbs* 2F **73**
Little Dalby. *Leics* 4E **75**
Little Dawley. *Telf* 5A **72**
Littledean. *Glos* 4B **48**
Little Dens. *Abers* 4H **161**
Little Dewchurch. *Here* 2A **48**
Little Ditton. *Cambs* 5F **65**
Little Down. *Hants* 1B **24**
Little Downham. *Cambs* 2E **65**
Little Drayton. *Shrp* 2A **72**
Little Driffield. *E Yor* 4E **101**
Little Dunham. *Norf* 4A **78**
Little Dunkeld. *Per* 4H **143**
Little Dunmow. *Essx* 3G **53**
Little Easton. *Essx* 3G **53**
Little Eaton. *Derbs* 1A **74**
Little Eccleston. *Lanc* 5D **96**
Little Ellingham. *Norf* 1C **66**
Little Elm. *Som* 2C **22**
Little End. *Essx* 5F **53**
Little Everdon. *Nptn* 5C **62**
Little Eversden. *Cambs* 5C **64**
Little Faringdon. *Oxon* 5H **49**
Little Fencote. *N Yor* 5F **105**
Little Fenton. *N Yor* 1F **93**
Littleferry. *High* 4F **165**
Little Fransham. *Norf* 4B **78**
Little Gaddesden. *Herts* 4H **51**
Little Garway. *Here* 3H **47**
Little Gidding. *Cambs* 2A **64**
Little Glemham. *Suff* 5F **67**
Little Glenshee. *Per* 5G **143**
Little Gransden. *Cambs* 5B **64**
Little Green. *Suff* 3C **66**
Little Green. *Wrex* 1G **71**
Little Grimsby. *Linc* 1C **88**
Little Habton. *N Yor* 2B **100**
Little Hadham. *Herts* 3E **53**
Little Hale. *Linc* 1A **76**
Little Hallingbury. *Essx* 4E **53**
Littleham. *Devn*
  nr. Bideford 4E **19**
  nr. Exmouth 4D **12**
Little Hampden. *Buck* 5G **51**
Littlehampton. *W Sus* 5B **26**
Little Haresfield. *Glos* 5D **48**
Little Harrowden. *Nptn* 3F **63**
Little Haseley. *Oxon* 5E **51**
Little Hatfield. *E Yor* 5F **101**
Little Hautbois. *Norf* 3E **79**
Little Haven. *Pemb* 3C **42**
Little Hay. *Staf* 5F **73**
Little Hayfield. *Derbs* 2E **85**
Little Haywood. *Staf* 3E **73**
Little Heath. *W Mid* 2H **61**
Little Heck. *N Yor* 2F **93**
Littlehempston. *Devn* 2E **9**
Little Herbert's. *Glos* 4E **49**
Little Hereford. *Here* 4H **59**
Little Horkesley. *Essx* 2C **54**
Little Hormead. *Herts* 3D **53**
Little Horsted. *E Sus* 4F **27**
Little Horton. *W Yor* 1B **92**
Little Horwood. *Buck* 2F **51**
Little Houghton. *Nptn* 5F **63**
Littlehoughton. *Nmbd* 3G **121**
Little Houghton. *S Yor* 4E **93**
Little Hucklow. *Derbs* 3F **85**
Little Hulton. *G Man* 4F **91**
Little Irchester. *Nptn* 4G **63**
Little Kelk. *E Yor* 3E **101**
Little Kimble. *Buck* 5G **51**
Little Kineton. *Warw* 5H **61**
Little Kingshill. *Buck* 2G **37**
Little Langdale. *Cumb* 4E **102**
Little Langford. *Wilts* 3F **23**
Little Laver. *Essx* 5F **53**
Little Lawford. *Warw* 3B **62**
Little Leigh. *Ches W* 3A **84**
Little Leighs. *Essx* 4H **53**
Little Leven. *E Yor* 5E **101**
Little Lever. *G Man* 4F **91**
Little Linford. *Mil* 1G **51**
Little London. *Buck* 4E **51**
Little London. *E Sus* 4G **27**
Little London. *Hants*
  nr. Andover 2B **24**
  nr. Basingstoke 1E **24**
Little London. *Linc*
  nr. Long Sutton 3D **76**
  nr. Spalding 3B **76**

Little London. *Norf*
  nr. North Walsham 2E **79**
  nr. Northwold 1G **65**
  nr. Saxthorpe 2D **78**
  nr. Southery 1F **65**
Little London. *Powy* 2C **58**
Little Longstone. *Derbs* 3F **85**
Little Malvern. *Worc* 1C **48**
Little Maplestead. *Essx* 2B **54**
Little Marcle. *Here* 2B **48**
Little Marlow. *Buck* 3G **37**
Little Massingham. *Norf* 3G **77**
Little Melton. *Norf* 5D **78**
Littlemill. *Abers* 4H **151**
Littlemill. *E Ayr* 3D **116**
Littlemill. *High* 4D **158**
Little Mill. *Mon* 5G **47**
Little Milton. *Oxon* 5E **50**
Little Missenden. *Buck* 1A **38**
Littlemoor. *Derbs* 4A **86**
Littlemoor. *Dors* 4B **14**
Littlemore. *Oxon* 5D **50**
Little Mountain. *Flin* 4E **83**
Little Musgrave. *Cumb* 3A **104**
Little Ness. *Shrp* 4G **71**
Little Neston. *Ches W* 3E **83**
Little Newcastle. *Pemb* 2D **43**
Little Newsham. *Dur* 3E **105**
Little Oakley. *Essx* 3F **55**
Little Oakley. *Nptn* 2F **63**
Little Onn. *Staf* 4C **72**
Little Ormside. *Cumb* 3A **104**
Little Orton. *Cumb* 4E **113**
Little Orton. *Leics* 5H **73**
Little Ouse. *Cambs* 2F **65**
Little Ouseburn. *N Yor* 3G **99**
Little Packington. *Warw* 2G **61**
Little Paxton. *Cambs* 4A **64**
Little Petherick. *Corn* 1D **6**
Little Plumpton. *Lanc* 1B **90**
Little Plumstead. *Norf* 4F **79**
Little Ponton. *Linc* 2G **75**
Littleport. *Cambs* 2E **65**
Little Posbrook. *Hants* 2D **16**
Little Potheridge. *Devn* 1F **11**
Little Preston. *Nptn* 5C **62**
Little Raveley. *Cambs* 3B **64**
Little Reynoldston. *Swan* 4D **31**
Little Ribston. *N Yor* 4F **99**
Little Rissington. *Glos* 4G **49**
Little Rogart. *High* 3E **165**
Little Rollright. *Oxon* 2A **50**
Little Ryburgh. *Norf* 3B **78**
Little Ryle. *Nmbd* 3E **121**
Little Ryton. *Shrp* 5G **71**
Little Salkeld. *Cumb* 1G **103**
Little Sampford. *Essx* 2G **53**
Little Sandhurst. *Brac* 5G **37**
Little Saredon. *Staf* 5D **72**
Little Saxham. *Suff* 4G **65**
Little Scatwell. *High* 3F **157**
Little Shelford. *Cambs* 5D **64**
Little Shoddesden. *Hants* 2A **24**
Little Singleton. *Lanc* 1B **90**
Little Smeaton. *N Yor* 3F **93**
Little Snoring. *Norf* 2B **78**
Little Sodbury. *S Glo* 3C **34**
Little Somborne. *Hants* 3B **24**
Little Somerford. *Wilts* 3E **35**
Little Soudley. *Shrp* 3B **72**
Little Stainforth. *N Yor* 3H **97**
Little Stainton. *Darl* 3A **106**
Little Stanney. *Ches W* 3G **83**
Little Staughton. *Bed* 4A **64**
Little Steeping. *Linc* 4D **88**
Littlester. *Shet* 3G **173**
Little Stoke. *Staf* 2D **72**
Littlestone-on-Sea. *Kent* 3E **29**
Little Stonham. *Suff* 4D **66**
Little Stretton. *Leics* 5D **74**
Little Stretton. *Shrp* 1G **59**
Little Strickland. *Cumb* 3G **103**
Little Stukeley. *Cambs* 3B **64**
Little Sugnall. *Staf* 2C **72**
Little Sutton. *Ches W* 3F **83**
Little Sutton. *Linc* 3D **76**
Little Swinburne. *Nmbd* 2C **114**
Little Tew. *Oxon* 3B **50**
Little Tey. *Essx* 3B **54**
Little Thetford. *Cambs* 3E **65**
Little Thirkleby. *N Yor* 2G **99**
Little Thornage. *Norf* 2C **78**
Little Thornton. *Lanc* 5C **96**
Littlethorpe. *Leics* 1C **62**
Littlethorpe. *N Yor* 3F **99**
Little Thorpe. *W Yor* 2B **92**
Little Thurlow. *Suff* 5F **65**
Little Thurrock. *Thur* 3H **39**
Littleton. *Ches W* 4G **83**
Littleton. *Hants* 3C **24**
Littleton. *Som* 3H **21**
Littleton. *Surr*
  nr. Guildford 1A **26**
  nr. Staines 4B **38**
Littleton Drew. *Wilts* 3D **34**
Littleton Pannell. *Wilts* 1F **23**
Littleton-upon-Severn. *S Glo* 3A **34**
Little Torboll. *High* 4E **165**
Little Torrington. *Devn* 1E **11**
Little Totham. *Essx* 4B **54**
Little Town. *Cumb* 3D **102**
Littletown. *Dur* 5G **115**
Littletown. *High* 5E **165**
Little Town. *Lanc* 1E **91**
Little Twycross. *Leics* 5H **73**
Little Urswick. *Cumb* 2B **96**
Little Wakering. *Essx* 2D **40**
Little Walden. *Essx* 1F **53**
Little Waldingfield. *Suff* 1C **54**
Little Walsingham. *Norf* 2B **78**

Little Waltham. *Essx* 4H **53**
Little Warley. *Essx* 1H **39**
Little Weighton. *E Yor* 1C **94**
Little Wenham. *Suff* 2D **54**
Little Wenlock. *Telf* 5A **72**
Little Whelnetham. *Suff* 4A **66**
Little Whittingham Green. *Suff* . . .3E **67**
Littlewick Green. *Wind* 4G **37**
Little Wilbraham. *Cambs* 5E **65**
Littlewindsor. *Dors* 2H **13**
Little Wisbeach. *Linc* 2A **76**
Little Witcombe. *Glos* 4E **49**
Little Witley. *Worc* 4B **60**
Little Wittenham. *Oxon* 2D **36**
Little Wolford. *Warw* 2A **50**
Littleworth. *Bed* 1A **52**
Littleworth. *Glos* 5D **48**
Littleworth. *Oxon* 2B **36**
Littleworth. *Staf*
  nr. Cannock 4E **73**
  nr. Eccleshall 3B **72**
  nr. Stafford 3D **72**
Littleworth. *W Sus* 3C **26**
Littleworth. *Worc*
  nr. Redditch 4D **61**
  nr. Worcester 5C **60**
Little Wratting. *Suff* 1G **53**
Little Wymondley. *Herts* 3C **52**
Little Wyrley. *Staf* 5E **73**
Little Yeldham. *Essx* 2A **54**
Littley Green. *Essx* 4G **53**
Litton. *Derbs* 3F **85**
Litton. *N Yor* 2B **98**
Litton. *Som* 1A **22**
Litton Cheney. *Dors* 3A **14**
Liurbost. *W Isl* 5F **171**
Liverpool. *Mers* **200** (1F **83**)
Liverpool John Lennon Airport.
  Mers 2G **83**
Liversedge. *W Yor* 2B **92**
Liverton. *Devn* 5B **12**
Liverton. *Red C* 3E **107**
Liverton Mines. *Red C* 3E **107**
Livingston. *W Lot* 3D **128**
Livingston Village. *W Lot* 3D **128**
Lixwm. *Flin* 3D **82**
Lizard. *Corn* 5E **5**
Llaingoch. *IOA* 2B **80**
Llaithddu. *Powy* 2C **58**
Llampha. *V Glam* 4C **32**
Llan. *Powy* 5A **70**
Llanaber. *Gwyn* 4F **69**
Llanaelhaearn. *Gwyn* 1C **68**
Llanaeron. *Cdgn* 4F **57**
Llanafan. *Cdgn* 3F **57**
Llanafan-fawr. *Powy* 5B **58**
Llanafan-fechan. *Powy* 5B **58**
Llanallgo. *IOA* 2D **81**
Llanandras. *Powy* 4F **59**
Llananno. *Powy* 3C **58**
Llanarmon. *Gwyn* 2D **68**
Llanarmon Dyffryn Ceiriog.
  Wrex 2D **70**
Llanarmon-yn-Ial. *Den* 5D **82**
Llanarth. *Cdgn* 5D **56**
Llanarth. *Mon* 4G **47**
Llanarthne. *Carm* 3F **45**
Llanasa. *Flin* 2D **82**
Llanbabo. *IOA* 2C **80**
Llanbadarn Fawr. *Cdgn* 2F **57**
Llanbadarn Fynydd. *Powy* 3D **58**
Llanbadarn-y-garreg. *Powy* 1D **46**
Llanbadoc. *Mon* 5G **47**
Llanbadrig. *IOA* 1C **80**
Llanbeder. *Newp* 2G **33**
Llanbedr. *Gwyn* 3E **69**
Llanbedr. *Powy*
  nr. Crickhowell 3F **47**
  nr. Hay-on-Wye 1E **47**
Llanbedr-Dyffryn-Clwyd. *Den* . . .5D **82**
Llanbedrgoch. *IOA* 2E **81**
Llanbedrog. *Gwyn* 2C **68**
Llanbedr Pont Steffan. *Cdgn* 1F **45**
Llanbedr-y-cennin. *Cnwy* 4G **81**
Llanberis. *Gwyn* 4E **81**
Llanbethery. *V Glam* 5D **32**
Llanbister. *Powy* 3D **58**
Llanblethian. *V Glam* 4C **32**
Llanboidy. *Carm* 2G **43**
Llanbradach. *Cphy* 2E **33**
Llanbrynmair. *Powy* 5A **70**
Llanbydderi. *V Glam* 5D **32**
Llancadle. *V Glam* 5D **32**
Llancarfan. *V Glam* 4D **32**
Llancatal. *V Glam* 5D **32**
Llancayo. *Mon* 5G **47**
Llancloudy. *Here* 3H **47**
Llancoch. *Powy* 3E **59**
Llancynfelyn. *Cdgn* 1F **57**
Llandaff. *Card* 4E **33**
Llandanwg. *Gwyn* 3E **69**
Llandarcy. *Neat* 3G **31**
Llandawke. *Carm* 3G **43**
Llanddaniel Fab. *IOA* 3D **81**
Llanddarog. *Carm* 4F **45**
Llanddeiniol. *Cdgn* 3E **57**
Llanddeiniolen. *Gwyn* 4E **81**
Llandderfel. *Gwyn* 2B **70**
Llanddeusant. *Carm* 3A **46**
Llanddeusant. *IOA* 2C **80**
Llanddew. *Powy* 2D **46**
Llanddewi. *Swan* 4D **30**
Llanddewi Brefi. *Cdgn* 5F **57**
Llanddewi'r Cwm. *Powy* 1D **46**
Llanddewi Rhydderch. *Mon* 4G **47**
Llanddewi Velfrey. *Pemb* 3F **43**
Llanddewi Ystradenni. *Powy* 4D **58**
Llanddoged. *Cnwy* 4H **81**
Llanddona. *IOA* 3E **81**
Llanddowror. *Carm* 3G **43**
Llanddulas. *Cnwy* 3B **82**

Llanddwywe. *Gwyn* 3E **69**
Llanddyfnan. *IOA* 3E **81**
Llandecwyn. *Gwyn* 2F **69**
Llandefaelog Fach. *Powy* 2D **46**
Llandefaelog-tre'r-graig. *Powy* . . .2E **47**
Llandefalle. *Powy* 2E **46**
Llandegfan. *IOA* 3E **81**
Llandegla. *Den* 5D **82**
Llandegley. *Powy* 4D **58**
Llandegveth. *Mon* 2G **33**
Llandeilo. *Carm* 3G **45**
Llandeilo Graban. *Powy* 1D **46**
Llandeilo'r Fan. *Powy* 2B **46**
Llandeloy. *Pemb* 2C **42**
Llandenny. *Mon* 5H **47**
Llandevaud. *Newp* 2H **33**
Llandevenny. *Mon* 3H **33**
Llandilo. *Pemb* 2F **43**
Llandinabo. *Here* 3A **48**
Llandinam. *Powy* 2C **58**
Llandissilio. *Pemb* 2F **43**
Llandogo. *Mon* 5A **48**
Llandough. *V Glam*
  nr. Cowbridge 4C **32**
  nr. Penarth 4E **33**
Llandovery. *Carm* 2A **46**
Llandow. *V Glam* 4C **32**
Llandre. *Cdgn* 2F **57**
Llandrillo. *Den* 2C **70**
Llandrillo-yn-Rhos. *Cnwy* 2H **81**
Llandrindod Wells. *Powy* 4C **58**
Llandrinio. *Powy* 4E **71**
Llandudno. *Cnwy* 2G **81**
Llandudno Junction. *Cnwy* 3G **81**
Llandudoch. *Pemb* 1B **44**
Llandw. *V Glam* 4C **32**
Llandwrog. *Gwyn* 5D **80**
Llandybie. *Carm* 4G **45**
Llandyfaelog. *Carm* 4E **45**
Llandyfan. *Carm* 4G **45**
Llandyfriog. *Cdgn* 1D **44**
Llandyfrydog. *IOA* 2D **80**
Llandygai. *Gwyn* 3F **81**
Llandygwydd. *Cdgn* 1C **44**
Llandynan. *Den* 1D **70**
Llandyrnog. *Den* 4D **82**
Llandysilio. *Powy* 4E **71**
Llandyssil. *Powy* 1D **58**
Llandysul. *Cdgn* 1E **45**
Llanedeyrn. *Card* 3F **33**
Llaneglwys. *Powy* 2D **46**
Llanegryn. *Gwyn* 5F **69**
Llanegwad. *Carm* 3F **45**
Llaneilian. *IOA* 1D **80**
Llanelian-yn-Rhos. *Cnwy* 3A **82**
Llanelidan. *Den* 5D **82**
Llanelieu. *Powy* 2E **47**
Llanellen. *Mon* 4G **47**
Llanelli. *Carm* 3E **31**
Llanelltyd. *Gwyn* 4G **69**
Llanelly. *Mon* 4F **47**
Llanelly Hill. *Mon* 4F **47**
Llanelwedd. *Powy* 5C **58**
Llan-Elwy. *Den* 3C **82**
Llanenddwyn. *Gwyn* 3E **69**
Llanengan. *Gwyn* 3B **68**
Llanerch. *Powy* 1F **59**
Llanerchymedd. *IOA* 2D **80**
Llanerfyl. *Powy* 5C **70**
Llaneuddog. *IOA* 2D **80**
Llanfachraeth. *IOA* 2C **80**
Llanfachreth. *Gwyn* 3G **69**
Llanfaelog. *IOA* 3C **80**
Llanfaelrhys. *Gwyn* 3B **68**
Llanfaenor. *Mon* 4H **47**
Llanfaes. *IOA* 3F **81**
Llanfaes. *Powy* 3D **46**
Llanfaethlu. *IOA* 2C **80**
Llanfaglan. *Gwyn* 4D **80**
Llanfair. *Gwyn* 3E **69**
Llanfair. *Here* 1F **47**
Llanfair Caereinion. *Powy* 5D **70**
Llanfair Clydogau. *Cdgn* 5F **57**
Llanfair Dyffryn Clwyd. *Den* 5D **82**
Llanfairfechan. *Cnwy* 3F **81**
Llanfair-Nant-Gwyn. *Pemb* 1F **43**
Llanfair Pwllgwyngyll. *IOA* 3E **81**
Llanfair Talhaiarn. *Cnwy* 3B **82**
Llanfair Waterdine. *Shrp* 3E **59**
Llanfair-ym-Muallt. *Powy* 5C **58**
Llanfairyneubwll. *IOA* 3C **80**
Llanfairynghornwy. *IOA* 1C **80**
Llanfallteg. *Carm* 3F **43**
Llanfallteg West. *Carm* 3F **43**
Llanfaredd. *Powy* 5C **58**
Llanfarian. *Cdgn* 3E **57**
Llanfechain. *Powy* 3D **70**
Llanfechell. *IOA* 1C **80**
Llanfendigaid. *Gwyn* 5E **69**
Llanferres. *Den* 4D **82**
Llan Ffestiniog. *Gwyn* 1G **69**
Llanfflewyn. *IOA* 2C **80**
Llanfihangel-ar-Arth. *Carm* 2E **45**
Llanfihangel Glyn Myfyr. *Cnwy* . .1B **70**
Llanfihangel Nant Bran. *Powy* . . .2C **46**
Llanfihangel-Nant-Melan.
  Powy 5D **58**
Llanfihangel near Rogiet. *Mon* . . .3H **33**
Llanfihangel Rhydithon. *Powy* . . .4D **58**
Llanfihangel Tal-y-llyn. *Powy* 3E **46**
Llanfihangel-uwch-Gwili. *Carm* . .3E **45**
Llanfihangel-y-Creuddyn. *Cdgn* . .3F **57**
Llanfihangel-yng-Ngwynfa.
  Powy 4C **70**
Llanfihangel-y Nhowyn. *IOA* 3C **80**
Llanfihangel-y-pennant. *Gwyn*
  nr. Golan 1E **69**
  nr. Tywyn 5F **69**
Llanfihangel-y-traethau. *Gwyn* . . .2E **69**
Llanfilo. *Powy* 2E **47**

Llanfleiddan. *V Glam* 4C **32**
Llanfoist. *Mon* 4F **47**
Llanfor. *Gwyn* 2B **70**
Llanfrechfa. *Torf* 2G **33**
Llanfrothen. *Gwyn* 1F **69**
Llanfrynach. *Powy* 3D **46**
Llanfwrog. *Den* 5D **82**
Llanfwrog. *IOA* 2C **80**
Llanfyllin. *Powy* 3F **45**
Llanfynydd. *Carm* 5E **83**
Llanfynydd. *Flin* 5E **83**
Llanfyrnach. *Pemb* 1G **43**
Llangadfan. *Powy* 4C **70**
Llangadog. *Carm*
  nr. Llandovery 3H **45**
  nr. Llanelli 5E **45**
Llangadwaladr. *IOA* 4C **80**
Llangadwaladr. *Powy* 2D **70**
Llangaffo. *IOA* 4D **80**
Llangain. *Carm* 4D **45**
Llangammarch Wells. *Powy* 1C **46**
Llangan. *V Glam* 4C **32**
Llangarron. *Here* 3A **48**
Llangasty-Talyllyn. *Powy* 3E **47**
Llangathen. *Carm* 3F **45**
Llangattock. *Powy* 4F **47**
Llangattock Lingoed. *Mon* 3G **47**
Llangattock-Vibon-Avel. *Mon* 4H **47**
Llangedwyn. *Powy* 3D **70**
Llangefni. *IOA* 3D **80**
Llangeinor. *B'end* 3C **32**
Llangeitho. *Cdgn* 5F **57**
Llangeler. *Carm* 2D **44**
Llangelynin. *Gwyn* 5E **69**
Llangendeirne. *Carm* 4E **45**
Llangennech. *Carm* 5F **45**
Llangennith. *Swan* 3D **30**
Llangenny. *Powy* 4F **47**
Llangernyw. *Cnwy* 4A **82**
Llangian. *Gwyn* 3B **68**
Llangiwg. *Neat* 5H **45**
Llangloffan. *Pemb* 1D **42**
Llanglydwen. *Carm* 2F **43**
Llangoed. *IOA* 3F **81**
Llangoedmor. *Cdgn* 1B **44**
Llangollen. *Den* 1E **70**
Llangolman. *Pemb* 2F **43**
Llangorse. *Powy* 3E **47**
Llangorwen. *Cdgn* 2F **57**
Llangovan. *Mon* 5H **47**
Llangower. *Gwyn* 2B **70**
Llangranog. *Cdgn* 5C **56**
Llangristiolus. *IOA* 3D **80**
Llangrove. *Here* 4A **48**
Llangua. *Mon* 3G **47**
Llangunllo. *Powy* 3E **58**
Llangunnor. *Carm* 3E **45**
Llangurig. *Powy* 3B **58**
Llangwm. *Cnwy* 1B **70**
Llangwm. *Mon* 5H **47**
Llangwm. *Pemb* 4D **43**
Llangwm-isaf. *Mon* 5H **47**
Llangwnnadl. *Gwyn* 2B **68**
Llangwyfan. *Den* 4D **82**
Llangwyfan-isaf. *IOA* 4C **80**
Llangwyllog. *IOA* 3D **80**
Llangwyryfon. *Cdgn* 3F **57**
Llangybi. *Cdgn* 5F **57**
Llangybi. *Gwyn* 1D **68**
Llangybi. *Mon* 2G **33**
Llangyfelach. *Swan* 3F **31**
Llangynhafal. *Den* 4D **82**
Llangynidr. *Powy* 4E **47**
Llangynin. *Carm* 3G **43**
Llangynog. *Carm* 3H **43**
Llangynog. *Powy* 3C **70**
Llangynwyd. *B'end* 3B **32**
Llanhamlach. *Powy* 3D **46**
Llanharan. *Rhon* 3D **32**
Llanharry. *Rhon* 3D **32**
Llanhennock. *Mon* 2G **33**
Llanhilleth. *Blae* 5F **47**
Llanidloes. *Powy* 2B **58**
Llaniestyn. *Gwyn* 2B **68**
Llanigon. *Powy* 1F **47**
Llanilar. *Cdgn* 3F **57**
Llanilid. *Rhon* 3C **32**
Llanilltud Fawr. *V Glam* 5C **32**
Llanishen. *Card* 3E **33**
Llanishen. *Mon* 5H **47**
Llanllawddog. *Carm* 3E **45**
Llanllechid. *Gwyn* 4F **81**
Llanllowell. *Mon* 2G **33**
Llanllugan. *Powy* 5C **70**
Llanllwch. *Carm* 4D **45**
Llanllwchaiarn. *Powy* 1D **58**
Llanllwni. *Carm* 2E **45**
Llanllyfni. *Gwyn* 5D **80**
Llanmadoc. *Swan* 3D **30**
Llanmaes. *V Glam* 5C **32**
Llanmartin. *Newp* 3G **33**
Llanmerwig. *Powy* 1D **58**
Llanmihangel. *V Glam* 4C **32**
Llan-mill. *Pemb* 3F **43**
Llanmiloe. *Carm* 4G **43**
Llanmorlais. *Swan* 3E **31**
Llannefydd. *Cnwy* 3B **82**
Llannon. *Carm* 5F **45**
Llan-non. *Cdgn* 4E **57**
Llannor. *Gwyn* 2C **68**
Llanover. *Mon* 5G **47**
Llanpumsaint. *Carm* 3E **45**
Llanrhaeadr. *Den* 4C **82**
Llanrhaeadr-ym-Mochnant.
  Powy 3D **70**
Llanrhian. *Pemb* 1C **42**
Llanrhidian. *Swan* 3D **31**
Llanrhos. *Cnwy* 2G **81**
Llanrhyddlad. *IOA* 2C **80**
Llanrhystud. *Cdgn* 4E **57**
Llanrothal. *Here* 4H **47**

Llanrug. Gwyn 4E **81**
Llanrumney. Card 3F **33**
Llanrwst. Cnwy 4G **81**
Llansadurnen. Carm 3G **43**
Llansadwrn. Carm 2G **45**
Llansadwrn. IOA 3E **81**
Llansaint. Carm 5D **45**
Llansamlet. Swan 3F **31**
Llansanffraid Glan Conwy.
    Cnwy 3H **81**
Llansannan. Cnwy 4B **82**
Llansannor. V Glam 4C **32**
Llansantffraed. Cdgn 4E **57**
Llansantffraed. Powy 3E **46**
Llansantffraed Cwmdeuddwr.
    Powy 4B **58**
Llansantffraed-in-Elwel. Powy . .5C **58**
Llansantffraid-ym-Mechain.
    Powy 3E **70**
Llansawel. Carm 2G **45**
Llansawel. Neat 3G **31**
Llansilin. Powy 3E **70**
Llansoy. Mon 5H **47**
Llanspyddid. Powy 3D **46**
Llanstadwell. Pemb 4D **42**
Llansteffan. Carm 4D **44**
Llanstephan. Powy 1E **46**
Llantarnam. Torf 2G **33**
Llanteg. Pemb 3F **43**
Llanthony. Mon 3F **47**
Llantilio Crossenny. Mon 4G **47**
Llantilio Pertholey. Mon 4G **47**
Llantood. Pemb 1B **44**
Llantrisant. Mon 2G **33**
Llantrisant. Rhon 3D **32**
Llantrithyd. V Glam 4D **32**
Llantwit Fardre. Rhon 3D **32**
Llantwit Major. V Glam 5C **32**
Llanuwchllyn. Gwyn 2A **70**
Llanvaches. Newp 2H **33**
Llanvair Discoed. Mon 2H **33**
Llanvapley. Mon 4G **47**
Llanvetherine. Mon 4G **47**
Llanveynoe. Here 2G **47**
Llanvihangel Crucorney. Mon . .3G **47**
Llanvihangel Gobion. Mon 5G **47**
Llanvihangel Ystern-Llewern.
    Mon 4H **47**
Llanwarne. Here 3A **48**
Llanwddyn. Powy 4C **70**
Llanwenarth. Mon 4F **47**
Llanwenog. Cdgn 1E **45**
Llanwern. Newp 3G **33**
Llanwinio. Carm 2G **43**
Llanwnda. Gwyn 5D **80**
Llanwnda. Pemb 1D **42**
Llanwnnen. Cdgn 1F **45**
Llanwnog. Powy 1C **58**
Llanwrda. Carm 2H **45**
Llanwrin. Powy 5G **69**
Llanwrthwl. Powy 4B **58**
Llanwrtud. Powy 1B **46**
Llanwrtyd. Powy 1B **46**
Llanwrtyd Wells. Powy 1B **46**
Llanwyddelan. Powy 5C **70**
Llanyblodwel. Shrp 3E **71**
Llanybri. Carm 3H **43**
Llanybydder. Carm 1F **45**
Llanycefn. Pemb 2E **43**
Llanychaer. Pemb 1D **43**
Llanycil. Gwyn 2B **70**
Llanymawddwy. Gwyn 4B **70**
Llanymddyfri. Carm 2A **46**
Llanymynech. Powy 3E **71**
Llanynghenedl. IOA 2C **80**
Llanynys. Den 4D **82**
Llan-y-pwll. Wrex 5F **83**
Llanyrafon. Torf 2G **33**
Llanyre. Powy 4C **58**
Llanystumdwy. Gwyn 2D **68**
Llanywern. Powy 3E **46**
Llawhaden. Pemb 3E **43**
Llawndy. Flin 2D **82**
Llawnt. Shrp 2E **71**
Llawr Dref. Gwyn 3B **68**
Llawryglyn. Powy 1B **58**
Llay. Wrex 5F **83**
Llechfaen. Powy 3D **46**
Llechryd. Cphy 5E **46**
Llechryd. Cdgn 1C **44**
Llechrydau. Wrex 2E **71**
Lledrod. Cdgn 3F **57**
Llethrid. Swan 3E **31**
Llidiad-Nenog. Carm 2F **45**
Llidiardau. Gwyn 2A **70**
Llidiart y Parc. Den 1D **70**
Llithfaen. Gwyn 1C **68**
Lloc. Flin 3D **82**
Llong. Flin 4E **83**
Llowes. Powy 1E **47**
Lloyney. Powy 3E **59**
Llundain-fach. Cdgn 5E **57**
Llwydcoed. Rhon 5C **46**
Llwyncelyn. Cdgn 5D **56**
Llwyncelyn. Swan 5G **45**
Llwyndafydd. Cdgn 5C **56**
Llwynderw. Powy 5E **70**
Llwyn-du. Mon 4F **47**
Llwyngwril. Gwyn 5E **69**
Llwynhendy. Carm 3E **31**
Llwynmawr. Wrex 2E **71**
Llwyn-on Village. Mer T 4D **46**
Llwyn-têg. Carm 5F **45**
Llwyn-y-brain. Carm 3F **43**
Llwynygog. Powy 1A **58**
Llwyn-y-groes. Cdgn 5E **57**
Llwynypia. Rhon 2C **32**
Llynclys. Shrp 3E **71**
Llynfaes. IOA 3D **80**
Llysfaen. Cnwy 3A **82**
Llyswen. Powy 2E **47**

Llysworney. V Glam 4C **32**
Llys-y-fran. Pemb 2E **43**
Llywel. Powy 2B **46**
Llywernog. Cdgn 2G **57**
Loan. Falk 2C **128**
Loanend. Nmbd 4F **131**
Loanhead. Midl 3F **129**
Loaningfoot. Dum 4A **112**
Loanreoch. High 1A **158**
Loans. S Ayr 1C **116**
Loansdean. Nmbd 1E **115**
Lobb. Devn 3E **19**
Lobhillcross. Devn 4E **11**
Lochaber. Mor 3E **159**
Loch a Charnain. W Isl 4D **170**
Loch a Ghainmhich. W Isl 5E **171**
Lochailort. High 5F **147**
Lochaline. High 4A **140**
Lochans. Dum 4F **109**
Locharbriggs. Dum 1A **112**
Lochardil. High 4A **158**
Lochassynt Lodge. High 1F **163**
Lochavich. Arg 2G **133**
Lochawe. Arg 1A **134**
Loch Baghasdail. W Isl 7C **170**
Lochboisdale. W Isl 7C **170**
Lochbuie. Arg 1D **132**
Lochcarron. High 5A **156**
Loch Choire Lodge. High 5G **167**
Lochdochart House. Stir 1D **134**
Lochdon. Arg 5B **140**
Lochearnhead. Stir 1E **135**
Lochee. D'dee 5C **144**
Lochend. High
    nr. Inverness 5H **157**
    nr. Thurso 2E **169**
Locherben. Dum 5B **118**
Loch Euphort. W Isl 2D **170**
Lochfoot. Dum 2F **111**
Lochgair. Arg 4G **133**
Lochgarthside. High 2H **149**
Lochgelly. Fife 4D **136**
Lochgilphead. Arg 1G **125**
Lochgoilhead. Arg 3A **134**
Loch Head. Dum 5A **110**
Lochhill. Mor 2G **159**
Lochindorb Lodge. High 5D **158**
Lochinver. High 1E **163**
Lochlane. Per 1H **135**
Loch Lomond. Arg 3C **134**
Loch Loyal Lodge. High 4G **167**
Lochluichart. High 2F **157**
Lochmaben. Dum 1B **112**
Lochmaddy. W Isl 2E **170**
Loch nam Madadh. W Isl 2E **170**
Lochore. Fife 4D **136**
Lochportain. W Isl 1E **170**
Lochranza. N Ayr 4H **125**
Loch Sgioport. W Isl 5D **170**
Lochside. Abers 2G **145**
Lochside. High
    nr. Achentoul 5A **168**
    nr. Nairn 3C **158**
Lochslin. High 5F **165**
Lochstack Lodge. High 4C **166**
Lochton. Abers 4E **153**
Lochty. Fife 3H **137**
Lochuisge. High 3B **140**
Lochussie. High 3G **157**
Lochwinnoch. Ren 4E **127**
Lochyside. High 1F **141**
Lockengate. Corn 2E **7**
Lockerbie. Dum 1C **112**
Lockeridge. Wilts 5G **35**
Lockerley. Hants 4A **24**
Lockhills. Cumb 5G **113**
Locking. N Som 1G **21**
Lockington. E Yor 5D **101**
Lockington. Leics 3B **74**
Lockleywood. Shrp 3A **72**
Locksgreen. IOW 3C **16**
Locks Heath. Hants 2D **16**
Lockton. N Yor 5F **107**
Loddington. Leics 5E **75**
Loddington. Nptn 3F **63**
Loddiswell. Devn 4D **8**
Loddon. Norf 1F **67**
Lode. Cambs 4E **65**
Loders. Dors 3H **13**
Lodsworth. W Sus 3A **26**
Lofthouse. N Yor 2D **98**
Lofthouse. W Yor 2D **92**
Lofthouse Gate. W Yor 2D **92**
Loftus. Red C 3E **107**
Logan. E Ayr 2E **117**
Loganlea. W Lot 3C **128**
Logaston. Here 5F **59**
Loggerheads. Staf 2B **72**
Loggie. High 4F **163**
Logie. Ang 2F **145**
Logie. Fife 1G **137**
Logie. Mor 3E **159**
Logie Coldstone. Abers 3B **152**
Logie Pert. Ang 2F **145**
Logierait. Per 3G **143**
Login. Carm 2F **43**
Lolworth. Cambs 4C **64**
Lonbain. High 3F **155**
Londesborough. E Yor 5C **100**
London. G Lon . . .**202-203** (2E **39**)
London Apprentice. Corn 3E **6**
London Ashford Airport. Kent . .3E **29**
London City Airport. G Lon 2F **39**
London Colney. Herts 5B **52**
Londonderry. N Yor 1F **99**
London Gatwick Airport.
    W Sus **216** (1D **26**)
London Heathrow Airport.
    G Lon **216** (3B **38**)
London Luton Airport.
    Lutn **216** (3B **52**)

London Southend Airport. Essx . . .2C **40**
London Stansted Airport.
    Essx **216** (3F **53**)
Londonthorpe. Linc 2G **75**
Londubh. High 5C **162**
Lone. High 4D **166**
Lonemore. High
    nr. Dornoch 5E **165**
    nr. Gairloch 1G **155**
Long Ashton. N Som 4A **34**
Long Bank. Worc 3B **60**
Longbar. N Ayr 4E **127**
Long Bennington. Linc 1F **75**
Longborough. Glos 3G **49**
Long Bredy. Dors 3A **14**
Longbridge. Warw 4G **61**
Longbridge. W Mid 3E **61**
Longbridge Deverill. Wilts 2D **22**
Long Buckby. Nptn 4D **62**
Long Buckby Wharf. Nptn 4D **62**
Longburgh. Cumb 4E **112**
Longburton. Dors 1B **14**
Long Clawson. Leics 3E **74**
Longcliffe. Derbs 5G **85**
Long Common. Hants 1D **16**
Long Compton. Staf 3C **72**
Long Compton. Warw 2A **50**
Longcot. Oxon 2A **36**
Long Crendon. Buck 5E **51**
Long Crichel. Dors 1E **15**
Longcroft. Cumb 4D **112**
Longcroft. Falk 2A **128**
Longcross. Surr 4A **38**
Longdale. Cumb 4H **103**
Longdales. Cumb 5G **113**
Longden. Shrp 5G **71**
Longden Common. Shrp 5G **71**
Long Ditton. Surr 4C **38**
Longdon. Staf 4E **73**
Longdon. Worc 2D **48**
Longdon Green. Staf 4E **73**
Longdon on Tern. Telf 4A **72**
Longdown. Devn 3B **12**
Longdowns. Corn 5B **6**
Long Drax. N Yor 2G **93**
Long Duckmanton. Derbs 3B **86**
Long Eaton. Derbs 2B **74**
Longfield. Kent 4H **39**
Longfield. Shet 10E **173**
Longfield Hill. Kent 4H **39**
Longford. Derbs 2G **73**
Longford. Glos 3D **48**
Longford. G Lon 3B **38**
Longford. Shrp 2A **72**
Longford. Telf 4B **72**
Longford. W Mid 2A **62**
Longforgan. Per 5C **144**
Longformacus. Bord 4C **130**
Longframlington. Nmbd 4F **121**
Long Gardens. Essx 2B **54**
Long Green. Ches W 3G **83**
Long Green. Worc 2D **48**
Longham. Dors 3F **15**
Longham. Norf 4B **78**
Long Hanborough. Oxon 4C **50**
Longhedge. Wilts 2D **22**
Longhill. Abers 3H **161**
Longhirst. Nmbd 1F **115**
Longhope. Glos 4B **48**
Longhope. Orkn 8C **172**
Longhorsley. Nmbd 5F **121**
Longhoughton. Nmbd 3G **121**
Long Itchington. Warw 4B **62**
Longlands. Cumb 1D **102**
Longlane. Derbs 2G **73**
Long Lane. Telf 4A **72**
Longlane. W Ber 4C **36**
Long Lawford. Warw 3B **62**
Long Lease. N Yor 4G **107**
Longley Green. Worc 5B **60**
Long Load. Som 4H **21**
Longmanhill. Abers 2E **161**
Long Marston. Herts 4G **51**
Long Marston. N Yor 4H **99**
Long Marston. Warw 1G **49**
Long Marton. Cumb 2H **103**
Long Meadow. Cambs 4E **65**
Long Meadowend. Shrp 2G **59**
Long Melford. Suff 1B **54**
Longmoor Camp. Hants 3F **25**
Longmorn. Mor 3G **159**
Longmoss. Ches E 3C **84**
Long Newnton. Glos 2E **35**
Longnewton. Bord 2H **119**
Long Newton. Stoc T 3A **106**
Longney. Glos 4C **48**
Longniddry. E Lot 2H **129**
Longnor. Shrp 5G **71**
Longnor. Staf
    nr. Leek 4E **85**
    nr. Stafford 4C **72**
Longparish. Hants 2C **24**
Longpark. Cumb 3F **113**
Long Preston. N Yor 4H **97**
Longridge. Lanc 1E **90**
Longridge. Staf 4D **72**
Longridge. W Lot 3C **128**
Longriggend. N Lan 2A **128**
Long Riston. E Yor 5F **101**
Longrock. Corn 3C **4**
Longsdon. Staf 5D **84**
Longshaw. G Man 4D **90**
Longshaw. Staf 1E **73**
Longside. Abers 4H **161**
Longslow. Shrp 2A **72**
Longstanton. Cambs 4C **64**
Longstock. Hants 3B **24**
Longstowe. Cambs 5C **64**
Long Stratton. Norf 1D **66**
Long Street. Mil 1F **51**

Longstreet. Wilts 1G **23**
Long Sutton. Hants 2F **25**
Long Sutton. Linc 3D **76**
Long Sutton. Som 4H **21**
Longthorpe. Pet 1A **64**
Long Thurlow. Suff 4C **66**
Longthwaite. Cumb 2F **103**
Longton. Lanc 2C **90**
Longton. Stoke 1D **72**
Longtown. Cumb 3E **113**
Longtown. Here 3G **47**
Longville in the Dale. Shrp 1H **59**
Long Whatton. Leics 3B **74**
Longwick. Buck 5F **51**
Long Wittenham. Oxon 2D **36**
Longwitton. Nmbd 1D **115**
Longworth. Oxon 2B **36**
Longyester. E Lot 3B **130**
Lonmore. High 4B **154**
Looe. Corn 3G **7**
Loose. Kent 5B **40**
Loosegate. Linc 3C **76**
Loosley Row. Buck 5G **51**
Lopcombe Corner. Wilts 3A **24**
Lopen. Som 1H **13**
Loppington. Shrp 3G **71**
Lorbottle. Nmbd 4E **121**
Lordington. W Sus 2F **17**
Loscoe. Derbs 1B **74**
Loscombe. Dors 3A **14**
Losgaintir. W Isl 8C **171**
Lossiemouth. Mor 2G **159**
Lossit. Arg 4A **124**
Lostock Gralam. Ches W 3A **84**
Lostock Green. Ches W 3A **84**
Lostock Hall. Lanc 2D **90**
Lostock Junction. G Man 4E **91**
Lostwithiel. Corn 3F **7**
Lothbeg. High 2G **165**
Lothersdale. N Yor 5B **98**
Lothianbridge. Midl 3G **129**
Lothianburn. Midl 3F **129**
Lothmore. High 2G **165**
Lottisham. Som 3A **22**
Loudwater. Buck 1A **38**
Loughborough. Leics 4C **74**
Loughor. Swan 3E **31**
Loughton. Essx 1F **39**
Loughton. Mil 2G **51**
Loughton. Shrp 2A **60**
Lound. Linc 4H **75**
Lound. Notts 2D **86**
Lound. Suff 1H **67**
Lount. Leics 4A **74**
Louth. Linc 2C **88**
Love Clough. Lanc 2G **91**
Lovedean. Hants 1E **17**
Lover. Wilts 4H **23**
Loversall. S Yor 1C **86**
Loves Green. Essx 5G **53**
Loveston. Pemb 4E **43**
Lovington. Som 3A **22**
Low Ackworth. W Yor 3E **93**
Low Angerton. Nmbd 1D **115**
Low Ardwell. Dum 5F **109**
Low Ballochdowan. S Ayr 2F **109**
Lowbands. Glos 2C **48**
Low Barlings. Linc 3H **87**
Low Bell End. N Yor 5E **107**
Low Bentham. N Yor 3F **97**
Low Borrowbridge. Cumb 4H **103**
Low Bradfield. S Yor 1G **85**
Low Bradley. N Yor 5C **98**
Low Braithwaite. Cumb 5F **113**
Low Brunton. Nmbd 2C **114**
Low Burnham. N Lin 4A **94**
Lowca. Cumb 2A **102**
Low Catton. E Yor 4B **100**
Low Coniscliffe. Darl 3F **105**
Low Coylton. S Ayr 3D **116**
Low Crosby. Cumb 4F **113**
Low Dalby. N Yor 1C **100**
Lowdham. Notts 1D **74**
Low Dinsdale. Darl 3A **106**
Lowe. Shrp 2H **71**
Low Ellington. N Yor 1E **98**
Lower Amble. Corn 1D **6**
Lower Ansty. Dors 2C **14**
Lower Arboll. High 5F **165**
Lower Arncott. Oxon 4E **50**
Lower Ashton. Devn 4B **12**
Lower Assendon. Oxon 3F **37**
Lower Auchenreath. Mor 2A **160**
Lower Badcall. High 4B **166**
Lower Ballam. Lanc 1B **90**
Lower Basildon. W Ber 4E **36**
Lower Beeding. W Sus 3D **26**
Lower Benefield. Nptn 2G **63**
Lower Bentley. Worc 4D **61**
Lower Beobridge. Shrp 1B **60**
Lower Bockhampton. Dors 3C **14**
Lower Boddington. Nptn 5B **62**
Lower Bordean. Hants 4E **25**
Lower Brailes. Warw 2B **50**
Lower Breakish. High 1E **147**
Lower Broadheath. Worc 5C **60**
Lower Brynamman. Neat 4H **45**
Lower Bullingham. Here 2A **48**
Lower Bullington. Hants 2C **24**
Lower Burgate. Hants 1G **15**
Lower Cam. Glos 5C **48**
Lower Catesby. Nptn 5C **62**
Lower Chapel. Powy 2D **46**
Lower Cheriton. Devn 2E **12**
Lower Chicksgrove. Wilts 3E **23**
Lower Chute. Wilts 1B **24**
Lower Clopton. Warw 5F **61**
Lower Common. Hants 2E **25**
Lower Crossings. Derbs 2E **85**
Lower Cumberworth. W Yor 4C **92**
Lower Darwen. Bkbn 2E **91**

Lower Dean. Bed 4H **63**
Lower Dean. Devn 2D **8**
Lower Diabaig. High 2G **155**
Lower Dicker. E Sus 4G **27**
Lower Dounreay. High 2B **168**
Lower Down. Shrp 2F **59**
Lower Dunsforth. N Yor 3G **99**
Lower East Carleton. Norf 5D **78**
Lower Egleton. Here 1B **48**
Lower Ellastone. Staf 1F **73**
Lower End. Nptn 4F **63**
Lower Everleigh. Wilts 1G **23**
Lower Eype. Dors 3H **13**
Lower Failand. N Som 4A **34**
Lower Faintree. Shrp 2A **60**
Lower Farringdon. Hants 3F **25**
Lower Foxdale. IOM 4B **108**
Lower Frankton. Shrp 2F **71**
Lower Froyle. Hants 2F **25**
Lower Gabwell. Devn 2F **9**
Lower Gledfield. High 4C **164**
Lower Godney. Som 2H **21**
Lower Gravenhurst. C Beds 2B **52**
Lower Green. Essx 2E **53**
Lower Green. Norf 2B **78**
Lower Green. W Ber 5B **36**
Lower Halstow. Kent 4C **40**
Lower Hardres. Kent 5F **41**
Lower Hardwick. Here 5G **59**
Lower Hartshay. Derbs 5A **86**
Lower Hawthwaite. Cumb 1B **96**
Lower Haysden. Kent 1G **27**
Lower Hayton. Shrp 2H **59**
Lower Hergest. Here 5E **59**
Lower Heyford. Oxon 3C **50**
Lower Heysham. Lanc 3D **96**
Lower Higham. Kent 3B **40**
Lower Holbrook. Suff 2E **55**
Lower Holditch. Dors 2G **13**
Lower Hordley. Shrp 3F **71**
Lower Horncroft. W Sus 4B **26**
Lower Horsebridge. E Sus 4G **27**
Lower Kilcott. Glos 3C **34**
Lower Killeyan. Arg 5A **124**
Lower Kingcombe. Dors 3A **14**
Lower Kingswood. Surr 5D **38**
Lower Kinnerton. Ches W 4F **83**
Lower Langford. N Som 5H **33**
Lower Largo. Fife 3G **137**
Lower Layham. Suff 1D **54**
Lower Ledwyche. Shrp 3H **59**
Lower Leigh. Staf 2E **73**
Lower Lemington. Glos 2H **49**
Lower Lenie. High 1H **149**
Lower Ley. Glos 4C **48**
Lower Llanfadog. Powy 4B **58**
Lower Lode. Glos 2D **49**
Lower Lovacott. Devn 4F **19**
Lower Loxhore. Devn 3G **19**
Lower Loxley. Staf 2E **73**
Lower Lydbrook. Glos 4A **48**
Lower Lye. Here 4G **59**
Lower Machen. Newp 3F **33**
Lower Maes-coed. Here 2G **47**
Lower Meend. Glos 5A **48**
Lower Midway. Derbs 3H **73**
Lower Milovaig. High 3A **154**
Lower Moor. Worc 1E **49**
Lower Morton. S Glo 2B **34**
Lower Mountain. Flin 5F **83**
Lower Nazeing. Essx 5D **53**
Lower Netchwood. Shrp 1A **60**
Lower Nyland. Dors 4C **22**
Lower Oakfield. Fife 4D **136**
Lower Oddington. Glos 3H **49**
Lower Ollach. High 5E **155**
Lower Penarth. V Glam 5E **33**
Lower Penn. Staf 1C **60**
Lower Pennington. Hants 3B **16**
Lower Peover. Ches W 3B **84**
Lower Pilsley. Derbs 4B **86**
Lower Pitkerrie. High 1C **158**
Lower Place. G Man 3H **91**
Lower Quinton. Warw 1G **49**
Lower Rainham. Medw 4C **40**
Lower Raydon. Suff 2D **54**
Lower Seagry. Wilts 3E **35**
Lower Shelton. C Beds 1H **51**
Lower Shiplake. Oxon 4F **37**
Lower Shuckburgh. Warw 4B **62**
Lower Sketty. Swan 3F **31**
Lower Slade. Devn 2F **19**
Lower Slaughter. Glos 3G **49**
Lower Soudley. Glos 4B **48**
Lower Stanton St Quintin. Wilts . .3E **35**
Lower Stoke. Medw 3C **40**
Lower Stondon. C Beds 2B **52**
Lower Stonnall. Staf 5E **73**
Lower Stow Bedon. Norf 1B **66**
Lower Street. Norf 2E **79**
Lower Strensham. Worc 1E **49**
Lower Sundon. C Beds 3A **52**
Lower Swanwick. Hants 2C **16**
Lower Swell. Glos 3G **49**
Lower Tale. Devn 2D **12**
Lower Tean. Staf 2E **73**
Lower Thurlton. Norf 1G **67**
Lower Thurnham. Lanc 4D **96**
Lower Thurvaston. Derbs 2G **73**
Lowertown. Corn 4D **4**
Lower Town. Here 1B **48**
Lower Town. IOS 1B **4**
Lowertown. Orkn 8D **172**
Lower Town. Pemb 1D **42**
Lower Tysoe. Warw 1B **50**
Lower Upham. Hants 1D **16**
Lower Upnor. Medw 3B **40**
Lower Vexford. Som 3E **20**
Lower Walton. Warr 2A **84**
Lower Wear. Devn 4C **12**
Lower Weare. Som 1H **21**

Lower Welson—Marston Jabbett

Lower Welson. Here 5E 59
Lower Whatcombe. Dors 2D 14
Lower Whitley. Ches W 3A 84
Lower Wield. Hants 2E 25
Lower Withington. Ches E 4C 84
Lower Woodend. Buck 3G 37
Lower Woodford. Wilts 3G 23
Lower Wraxall. Dors 2A 14
Lower Wych. Ches W 1G 71
Lower Wyche. Worc 1C 48
Lowesby. Leics 5E 74
Lowestoft. Suff 1H 67
Loweswater. Cumb 2C 102
Low Etherley. Dur 2E 105
Lowfield Heath. W Sus 1D 26
Lowford. Hants 1C 16
Low Fulney. Linc 3B 76
Low Gate. Nmbd 3C 114
Lowgill. Cumb 5H 103
Lowgill. Lanc 3F 97
Low Grantley. N Yor 2E 99
Low Green. N Yor 4E 98
Low Habberley. Worc 3C 60
Low Ham. Som 4H 21
Low Hameringham. Linc 4C 88
Low Hawsker. N Yor 4G 107
Low Hesket. Cumb 5F 113
Low Hesleyhurst. Nmbd 5E 121
Lowick. Cumb 1B 96
Lowick. Nptn 2G 63
Lowick. Nmbd 1E 121
Lowick Bridge. Cumb 1B 96
Lowick Green. Cumb 1B 96
Low Knipe. Cumb 2G 103
Low Leighton. Derbs 2E 85
Low Lorton. Cumb 2C 102
Low Marishes. N Yor 2C 100
Low Marnham. Notts 4F 87
Low Mill. N Yor 5D 106
Low Moor. Lanc 5G 97
Low Moor. W Yor 2B 92
Low Moorsley. Tyne 5G 115
Low Newton-by-the-Sea.
  Nmbd 2G 121
Lownie Moor. Ang 4D 145
Lowood. Bord 1H 119
Low Row. Cumb
  nr. Brampton 3G 113
  nr. Wigton 5C 112
Low Row. N Yor 5C 104
Lowsonford. Warw 4F 61
Low Street. Norf 5C 78
Lowther. Cumb 2G 103
Lowthorpe. E Yor 3E 101
Lowton. Devn 2G 11
Lowton. G Man 1A 84
Lowton. Som 1E 13
Lowton Common. G Man 1A 84
Low Torry. Fife 1D 128
Low Toynton. Linc 3B 88
Low Valleyfield. Fife 1C 128
Low Westwood. Dur 4E 115
Low Whinnow. Cumb 4E 112
Low Wood. Cumb 1C 96
Low Worsall. N Yor 4A 106
Low Wray. Cumb 4E 103
Loxbeare. Devn 1C 12
Loxhill. Surr 2B 26
Loxhore. Devn 3G 19
Loxley. S Yor 2H 85
Loxley. Warw 5G 61
Loxley Green. Staf 2E 73
Loxton. N Som 1G 21
Loxwood. W Sus 2B 26
Lubcroy. High 3A 164
Lubenham. Leics 2E 62
Lubinvullin. High 2F 167
Luccombe. Som 2C 20
Luccombe Village. IOW 4D 16
Lucker. Nmbd 1F 121
Luckett. Corn 5D 11
Luckington. Wilts 3D 34
Lucklawhill. Fife 1G 137
Luckwell Bridge. Som 3C 20
Lucton. Here 4G 59
Ludag. W Isl 7C 170
Ludborough. Linc 1B 88
Ludchurch. Pemb 3F 43
Luddenden. W Yor 2A 92
Luddenden Foot. W Yor 2A 92
Luddenham. Kent 4D 40
Ludderburn. Cumb 5F 103
Luddesdown. Kent 4A 40
Luddington. N Lin 3B 94
Luddington. Warw 5F 61
Luddington in the Brook. Nptn 2A 64
Ludford. Linc 2A 88
Ludford. Shrp 3H 59
Ludgershall. Buck 4E 51
Ludgershall. Wilts 1A 24
Ludgvan. Corn 3C 4
Ludham. Norf 4F 79
Ludlow. Shrp 3H 59
Ludstone. Shrp 1C 60
Ludwell. Wilts 4E 23
Ludworth. Dur 5G 115
Luffenhall. Herts 3C 52
Luffincott. Devn 3D 10
Lugar. E Ayr 2E 117
Luggate Burn. E Lot 2C 130
Lugg Green. Here 4G 59
Luggiebank. N Lan 2A 128
Lugton. E Ayr 4F 127
Lugwardine. Here 1A 48
Luib. High 1D 146
Luib. Stir 1D 135
Lulham. Here 1H 47
Lullington. Derbs 4G 73
Lullington. E Sus 5G 27
Lullington. Som 1C 22
Lulsgate Bottom. N Som 5A 34
Lulsley. Worc 5B 60
Lulworth Camp. Dors 4D 14
Lumb. Lanc 2G 91
Lumby. N Yor 1E 93
Lumphanan. Abers 3C 152
Lumphinnans. Fife 4D 136
Lumsdaine. Bord 3E 131
Lumsden. Abers 1B 152
Lunan. Ang 3F 145
Lunanhead. Ang 3D 145
Luncarty. Per 1C 136
Lund. E Yor 5D 100
Lund. N Yor 1G 93
Lundie. Ang 5B 144
Lundin Links. Fife 3G 137
Lundy Green. Norf 1E 67
Lunna. Shet 5F 173
Lunning. Shet 5G 173
Lunnon. Swan 4E 31
Lunsford. Kent 5A 40
Lunsford's Cross. E Sus 4B 28
Lunt. Mers 4B 90
Luppitt. Devn 2E 13
Lupridge. Devn 3D 8
Lupset. W Yor 3D 92
Lupton. Cumb 1E 97
Lurgashall. W Sus 3A 26
Lurley. Devn 1C 12
Lusby. Linc 4C 88
Luscombe. Devn 3D 9
Luson. Devn 4C 8
Luss. Arg 4C 134
Lussagiven. Arg 1E 125
Lusta. High 3B 154
Lustleigh. Devn 4A 12
Luston. Here 4G 59
Luthermuir. Abers 2F 145
Luthrie. Fife 2F 137
Lutley. Staf 2C 60
Luton. Devn
  nr. Honiton 2D 12
  nr. Teignmouth 5C 12
Luton. Lutn **201** (3A 52)
Luton Airport. Lutn **216** (3B 52)
Lutterworth. Leics 2C 62
Lutton. Devn
  nr. Ivybridge 3B 8
  nr. South Brent 2C 8
Lutton. Linc 3D 76
Lutton. Nptn 2A 64
Lutton Gowts. Linc 3D 76
Lutworthy. Devn 1A 12
Luxborough. Som 3C 20
Luxley. Glos 3B 48
Luxulyan. Corn 3E 7
Lybster. High 5E 169
Lydbury North. Shrp 2F 59
Lydcott. Devn 3G 19
Lydd. Kent 3E 29
Lydd Airport. Kent 3E 29
Lydden. Kent
  nr. Dover 1G 29
  nr. Margate 4H 41
Lyddington. Rut 1F 63
Lydd-on-Sea. Kent 3E 29
Lydeard St Lawrence. Som 3E 21
Lyde Green. Hants 1F 25
Lydford. Devn 4F 11
Lydford Fair Place. Som 3A 22
Lydgate. G Man 4H 91
Lydgate. W Yor 2H 91
Lydham. Shrp 1F 59
Lydiard Millicent. Wilts 3F 35
Lydiate. Mers 4B 90
Lydiate Ash. Worc 3D 61
Lydlinch. Dors 1C 14
Lydmarsh. Som 2G 13
Lydney. Glos 5B 48
Lydstep. Pemb 5E 43
Lye, The. Shrp 1A 60
Lye. W Mid 2D 60
Lye Green. Buck 5H 51
Lye Green. E Sus 2G 27
Lye Head. Worc 3B 60
Lyford. Oxon 2B 36
Lyham. Nmbd 1E 121
Lylestone. N Ayr 5E 127
Lymbridge Green. Kent 1F 29
Lyme Regis. Dors 3G 13
Lyminge. Kent 1F 29
Lymington. Hants 3B 16
Lyminster. W Sus 5B 26
Lymm. Warr 2A 84
Lymore. Hants 3A 16
Lympne. Kent 2F 29
Lympsham. Som 1G 21
Lympstone. Devn 4C 12
Lynaberack Lodge. High 4B 150
Lynbridge. Devn 2H 19
Lynch. Som 2C 20
Lynchat. High 3B 150
Lynch Green. Norf 5D 78
Lyndhurst. Hants 2B 16
Lyndon. Rut 5G 75
Lyne. Bord 5F 129
Lyne. Surr 4B 38
Lyneal. Shrp 2G 71
Lyne Down. Here 2B 48
Lyneham. Oxon 3A 50
Lyneham. Wilts 4F 35
Lyneholmeford. Cumb 2G 113
Lynemouth. Nmbd 5G 121
Lyne of Gorthleck. High 1H 149
Lyne of Skene. Abers 2E 153
Lynesack. Dur 2D 105
Lyness. Orkn 8C 172
Lyng. Norf 4C 78
Lyngate. Norf
  nr. North Walsham 2E 79
  nr. Worstead 3F 79
Lynmouth. Devn 2H 19
Lynn. Staf 5E 73
Lynn. Telf 4B 72
Lynsted. Kent 4D 40
Lynstone. Corn 2C 10
Lynton. Devn 2H 19
Lynwilg. High 2C 150
Lyon's Gate. Dors 2B 14
Lyonshall. Here 5F 59
Lytchett Matravers. Dors 3E 15
Lytchett Minster. Dors 3E 15
Lyth. High 2E 169
Lytham. Lanc 2B 90
Lytham St Anne's. Lanc 2B 90
Lythe. N Yor 3F 107
Lythes. Orkn 9D 172
Lythmore. High 2C 168

M

Mabe Burnthouse. Corn 5B 6
Mabie. Dum 2A 112
Mablethorpe. Linc 2E 89
Macbiehill. Bord 4E 129
Macclesfield. Ches E 3D 84
Macclesfield Forest. Ches E 3D 84
Macduff. Abers 2E 160
Machan. S Lan 4A 128
Macharioch. Arg 5B 122
Machen. Cphy 3F 33
Machrie. N Ayr 2C 122
Machrihanish. Arg 3A 122
Machroes. Gwyn 3C 68
Machynlleth. Powy 5G 69
Mackerye End. Herts 4B 52
Mackworth. Derb 2H 73
Macmerry. E Lot 2H 129
Madderty. Per 1B 136
Maddington. Wilts 2F 23
Maddiston. Falk 2C 128
Madehurst. W Sus 4A 26
Madeley. Staf 1B 72
Madeley. Telf 5A 72
Madeley Heath. Staf 1B 72
Madeley Heath. Worc 3D 60
Madford. Devn 1E 13
Madingley. Cambs 4C 64
Madley. Here 2H 47
Madresfield. Worc 1D 48
Madron. Corn 3B 4
Maenaddwyn. IOA 2D 80
Maenclochog. Pemb 2E 43
Maendy. V Glam 4D 32
Maenporth. Corn 4E 5
Maentwrog. Gwyn 1F 69
Maen-y-groes. Cdgn 5C 56
Maer. Staf 2B 72
Maerdy. Carm 3G 45
Maerdy. Cnwy 1C 70
Maerdy. Rhon 2C 32
Maesbrook. Shrp 3F 71
Maesbury. Shrp 3F 71
Maesbury Marsh. Shrp 3F 71
Maes-glas. Flin 3D 82
Maesgwyn-Isaf. Powy 4D 70
Maeshafn. Den 4E 82
Maes Llyn. Cdgn 1D 44
Maesmynis. Powy 1D 46
Maesteg. B'end 2B 32
Maestir. Cdgn 1F 45
Maesybont. Carm 4F 45
Maesycrugiau. Carm 1E 45
Maesycwmmer. Cphy 2E 33
Maesyrhandir. Powy 1C 58
Magdalen Laver. Essx 5F 53
Maggieknockater. Mor 4H 159
Magham Down. E Sus 4H 27
Maghull. Mers 4B 90
Magna Park. Leics 2C 62
Magor. Mon 3H 33
Magpie Green. Suff 3C 66
Magwyr. Mon 3H 33
Maidenbower. W Sus 2D 27
Maiden Bradley. Wilts 3D 22
Maidencombe. Torb 2F 9
Maidenhayne. Devn 3F 13
Maidenhead. Wind 3G 37
Maiden Law. Dur 5E 115
Maiden Newton. Dors 3A 14
Maidens. S Ayr 4B 116
Maiden's Green. Brac 4G 37
Maidensgrove. Oxon 3F 37
Maidenwell. Corn 5B 10
Maidenwell. Linc 3C 88
Maiden Wells. Pemb 5D 42
Maidford. Nptn 5D 62
Maids Moreton. Buck 2F 51
Maidstone. Kent 5B 40
Maidwell. Nptn 3E 63
Mail. Shet 9F 173
Maindee. Newp 3G 33
Mainsforth. Dur 1A 106
Mains of Auchindachy. Mor 4B 160
Mains of Auchnagatt. Abers 4G 161
Mains of Drum. Abers 4F 153
Mains of Edingight. Mor 3C 160
Mainsriddle. Dum 4G 111
Mainstone. Shrp 2E 59
Maisemore. Glos 3D 48
Major's Green. Worc 3F 61
Makeney. Derbs 1A 74
Makerstoun. Bord 1A 120
Malacleit. W Isl 1C 170
Malaig. High 4E 147
Malaig Bheag. High 4E 147
Malborough. Devn 5D 8
Malcoff. Derbs 2E 85
Malcolmburn. Mor 3A 160
Malden Rushett. G Lon 5C 38
Maldon. Essx 5B 54
Malham. N Yor 3B 98
Maligar. High 2D 155
Malinslee. Telf 5A 72
Mallaig. High 4E 147
Malleny Mills. Edin 3E 129
Mallows Green. Essx 3E 53
Malltraeth. IOA 4D 80
Mallwyd. Gwyn 4A 70
Malmesbury. Wilts 3E 35
Malmsmead. Devn 2A 20
Malpas. Ches W 1G 71
Malpas. Corn 4C 6
Malpas. Newp 2G 33
Malswick. Glos 3C 48
Maltby. S Yor 1C 86
Maltby. Stoc T 3B 106
Maltby le Marsh. Linc 2D 88
Malt Lane. Arg 3H 133
Maltman's Hill. Kent 1D 28
Malton. N Yor 2B 100
Malvern Link. Worc 1C 48
Malvern Wells. Worc 1C 48
Mamble. Worc 3A 60
Mamhilad. Mon 5G 47
Manaccan. Corn 4E 5
Manafon. Powy 5D 70
Manais. W Isl 9D 171
Manaton. Devn 4A 12
Manby. Linc 2C 88
Mancetter. Warw 1H 61
Manchester. G Man **201** (1C 84)
Manchester Airport.
  G Man **216** (2C 84)
Mancot. Flin 4F 83
Manea. Cambs 2D 65
Maney. W Mid 1F 61
Manfield. N Yor 3F 105
Mangotsfield. S Glo 4B 34
Mangurstadh. W Isl 4C 171
Mankinholes. W Yor 2H 91
Manley. Ches W 3H 83
Manmoel. Cphy 5E 47
Mannal. Arg 4A 138
Mannerston. Falk 2D 128
Manningford Bohune. Wilts 1G 23
Manningford Bruce. Wilts 1G 23
Manningham. W Yor 1B 92
Mannings Heath. W Sus 3D 26
Mannington. Dors 2F 15
Manningtree. Essx 2E 54
Mannofield. Aber 3G 153
Manorbier. Pemb 5E 43
Manorbier Newton. Pemb 5E 43
Manordeilo. Carm 3G 45
Manorowen. Pemb 1D 42
Manor Park. G Lon 2F 39
Mansell Gamage. Here 1G 47
Mansell Lacy. Here 1H 47
Mansergh. Cumb 1F 97
Mansewood. Glas 3G 127
Mansfield. E Ayr 3F 117
Mansfield. Notts 4C 86
Mansfield Woodhouse. Notts 4C 86
Mansriggs. Cumb 1B 96
Manston. Dors 1D 14
Manston. Kent 4H 41
Manston. W Yor 1D 92
Manswood. Dors 2E 15
Manthorpe. Linc
  nr. Bourne 4H 75
  nr. Grantham 2G 75
Manton. N Lin 4C 94
Manton. Notts 3C 86
Manton. Rut 5F 75
Manton. Wilts 5G 35
Manuden. Essx 3E 53
Maperton. Som 4B 22
Maplebeck. Notts 4E 86
Maple Cross. Herts 1B 38
Mapledurham. Oxon 4E 37
Mapledurwell. Hants 1E 25
Maplehurst. W Sus 3C 26
Maplescombe. Kent 4G 39
Mapleton. Derbs 1F 73
Mapperley. Derbs 1B 74
Mapperley. Nott 1C 74
Mapperley Park. Nott 1C 74
Mapperton. Dors
  nr. Beaminster 3A 14
  nr. Poole 3E 15
Mappleborough Green.
  Warw 4E 61
Mappleton. E Yor 5G 101
Mapplewell. S Yor 4D 92
Mappowder. Dors 2C 14
Maraig. W Isl 7E 171
Marazion. Corn 3C 4
Marbhig. W Isl 6G 171
Marbury. Ches E 1H 71
March. Cambs 1D 64
Marcham. Oxon 2C 36
Marchamley. Shrp 3H 71
Marchington. Staf 2F 73
Marchington Woodlands.
  Staf 3F 73
Marchwiel. Wrex 1F 71
Marchwood. Hants 1B 16
Marcross. V Glam 5C 32
Marden. Here 1A 48
Marden. Kent 1B 28
Marden. Wilts 1F 23
Marden Beech. Kent 1B 28
Marden Thorn. Kent 1B 28
Mardu. Shrp 2E 59
Mardy. Mon 4G 47
Marefield. Leics 5E 75
Mareham le Fen. Linc 4B 88
Mareham on the Hill. Linc 4B 88
Marehay. Derbs 1B 74
Marehill. W Sus 4B 26
Maresfield. E Sus 3F 27
Marfleet. Hull 2E 95
Marford. Wrex 5F 83
Margam. Neat 3A 32
Margaret Marsh. Dors 1D 14
Margaret Roding. Essx 4F 53
Margaretting. Essx 5G 53
Margaretting Tye. Essx 5G 53
Margate. Kent 3H 41
Margery. Surr 5D 38
Margnaheglish. N Ayr 2E 123
Marham. Norf 5G 77
Marhamchurch. Corn 2C 10
Marholm. Pet 5A 76
Marian Cwm. Den 3C 82
Mariandyrys. IOA 2F 81
Marian-glas. IOA 2E 81
Mariansleigh. Devn 4H 19
Marian-y-de. Gwyn 2C 68
Marian-y-mor. Gwyn 2C 68
Marine Town. Kent 3D 40
Marishader. High 2D 155
Marjoriebanks. Dum 1B 112
Mark. Dum 4G 109
Mark. Som 2G 21
Markbeech. Kent 1F 27
Markby. Linc 3D 89
Mark Causeway. Som 2G 21
Mark Cross. E Sus 2G 27
Markeaton. Derb 2H 73
Market Bosworth. Leics 5B 74
Market Deeping. Linc 4A 76
Market Drayton. Shrp 2A 72
Market End. Warw 2H 61
Market Harborough. Leics 2E 63
Markethill. Per 5B 144
Market Lavington. Wilts 1F 23
Market Overton. Rut 4F 75
Market Rasen. Linc 2A 88
Market Stainton. Linc 2B 88
Market Weighton. E Yor 5C 100
Market Weston. Suff 3B 66
Markfield. Leics 4B 74
Markham. Cphy 5E 47
Markinch. Fife 3E 137
Markington. N Yor 3E 99
Marksbury. Bath 5B 34
Mark's Corner. IOW 3C 16
Marks Tey. Essx 3C 54
Markwell. Corn 3H 7
Markyate. Herts 4A 52
Marlborough. Wilts 5G 35
Marlcliff. Warw 5E 61
Marldon. Devn 2E 9
Marle Green. E Sus 4G 27
Marlesford. Suff 5F 67
Marley Green. Ches E 1H 71
Marley Hill. Tyne 4F 115
Marlingford. Norf 5D 78
Mar Lodge. Abers 5E 151
Marloes. Pemb 4B 42
Marlow. Buck 3G 37
Marlow. Here 3F 59
Marlow Bottom. Buck 3G 37
Marlow Common. Buck 3G 37
Marlpit Hill. Kent 1F 27
Marlpits. E Sus 3F 27
Marlpool. Derbs 1B 74
Marnhull. Dors 1C 14
Marnoch. Abers 3C 160
Marnock. N Lan 3A 128
Marple. G Man 2D 84
Marr. S Yor 4F 93
Marrel. High 2H 165
Marrick. N Yor 5D 105
Marrister. Shet 5G 173
Marros. Carm 4G 43
Marsden. Tyne 3G 115
Marsden. W Yor 3A 92
Marsett. N Yor 1B 98
Marsh. Buck 5G 51
Marsh. Devn 1F 13
Marsh, The. Powy 1F 59
Marsh, The. Shrp 3A 72
Marshall Meadows. Nmbd 4F 131
Marshalsea. Dors 2G 13
Marshalswick. Herts 5B 52
Marsham. Norf 3D 78
Marshaw. Lanc 4E 97
Marsh Baldon. Oxon 2D 36
Marsh Benham. W Ber 5C 36
Marshborough. Kent 5H 41
Marshbrook. Shrp 2G 59
Marshchapel. Linc 1C 88
Marshfield. Newp 3F 33
Marshfield. S Glo 4C 34
Marshgate. Corn 3B 10
Marsh Gibbon. Buck 3E 51
Marsh Green. Devn 3D 12
Marsh Green. Kent 1F 27
Marsh Green. Staf 5C 84
Marsh Green. Telf 4A 72
Marsh Lane. Derbs 3B 86
Marshside. Kent 4G 41
Marshside. Mers 3B 90
Marsh Side. Norf 1G 77
Marsh Street. Som 2C 20
Marshwood. Dors 3G 13
Marske. N Yor 4E 105
Marske-by-the-Sea. Red C 2D 106
Marston. Ches W 3A 84
Marston. Here 5F 59
Marston. Linc 1F 75
Marston. Oxon 5D 50
Marston. Staf
  nr. Stafford 3D 72
  nr. Wheaton Aston 4C 72
Marston. Warw 1G 61
Marston. Wilts 1E 23
Marston Doles. Warw 5B 62
Marston Green. W Mid 2F 61
Marston Hill. Glos 2G 35
Marston Jabbett. Warw 2A 62

Marston Magna. *Som* 4A **22**
Marston Meysey. *Wilts* 2G **35**
Marston Montgomery. *Derbs* . . .2F **73**
Marston Moretaine. *C Beds* 1H **51**
Marston on Dove. *Derbs* 3G **73**
Marston St Lawrence. *Nptn* 1D **50**
Marston Stannett. *Here* 5H **59**
Marston Trussell. *Nptn* 2D **62**
Marstow. *Here* 4A **48**
Marsworth. *Buck* 4H **51**
Marten. *Wilts* 1A **24**
Marthall. *Ches E* 3C **84**
Martham. *Norf* 4G **79**
Marthwaite. *Cumb* 5H **103**
Martin. *Hants* 1F **15**
Martin. *Kent* 1H **29**
Martin. *Linc*
  nr. Horncastle 4B **88**
  nr. Metheringham 5A **88**
Martindale. *Cumb* 3F **103**
Martin Dales. *Linc* 4A **88**
Martin Drove End. *Hants* 4F **23**
Martinhoe. *Devn* 2G **19**
Martinhoe Cross. *Devn* 2G **19**
Martin Hussingtree. *Worc* 4C **60**
Martin Mill. *Kent* 1H **29**
Martinscroft. *Warr* 2A **84**
Martin's Moss. *Ches E* 4C **84**
Martinstown. *Dors* 4B **14**
Martlesham. *Suff* 1F **55**
Martlesham Heath. *Suff* 1F **55**
Martletwy. *Pemb* 3E **43**
Martley. *Worc* 4B **60**
Martock. *Som* 1H **13**
Marton. *Ches E* 4C **84**
Marton. *Cumb* 2B **96**
Marton. *E Yor*
  nr. Bridlington 3G **101**
  nr. Hull 1E **95**
Marton. *Linc* 2F **87**
Marton. *Midd* 3C **106**
Marton. *N Yor*
  nr. Boroughbridge 3G **99**
  nr. Pickering 1B **100**
Marton. *Shrp*
  nr. Myddle 3G **71**
  nr. Worthen 5E **71**
Marton. *Warw* 4B **62**
Marton Abbey. *N Yor* 3H **99**
Marton-le-Moor. *N Yor* 2F **99**
Martyr's Green. *Surr* 5B **38**
Martyr Worthy. *Hants* 3D **24**
Marwick. *Orkn* 5B **172**
Marwood. *Devn* 3F **19**
Marybank. *High*
  nr. Dingwall 3G **157**
  nr. Invergordon 1B **158**
Maryburgh. *High* 3H **157**
Maryfield. *Corn* 3A **8**
Maryhill. *Glas* 3G **127**
Marykirk. *Abers* 2F **145**
Marylebone. *G Lon* 2D **39**
Marylebone. *G Man* 4D **90**
Marypark. *Mor* 5F **159**
Maryport. *Cumb* 1B **102**
Maryport. *Dum* 5E **109**
Marystow. *Devn* 4E **11**
Mary Tavy. *Devn* 5F **11**
Maryton. *Ang*
  nr. Kirriemuir 3C **144**
  nr. Montrose 3F **145**
Marywell. *Abers* 4C **152**
Marywell. *Ang* 4F **145**
Masham. *N Yor* 1E **98**
Mashbury. *Essx* 4G **53**
Masongill. *N Yor* 2F **97**
Masons Lodge. *Abers* 3F **153**
Mastin Moor. *Derbs* 3B **86**
Mastrick. *Aber* 3G **153**
Matching. *Essx* 4F **53**
Matching Green. *Essx* 4F **53**
Matching Tye. *Essx* 4F **53**
Matfen. *Nmbd* 2D **114**
Matfield. *Kent* 1A **28**
Mathern. *Mon* 2A **34**
Mathon. *Here* 1C **48**
Mathry. *Pemb* 1C **42**
Matlaske. *Norf* 2D **78**
Matlock. *Derbs* 5G **85**
Matlock Bath. *Derbs* 5G **85**
Matterdale End. *Cumb* 2E **103**
Mattersey. *Notts* 2D **86**
Mattersey Thorpe. *Notts* 2D **86**
Mattingley. *Hants* 1F **25**
Mattishall. *Norf* 4C **78**
Mattishall Burgh. *Norf* 4C **78**
Mauchline. *E Ayr* 2D **117**
Maud. *Abers* 4G **161**
Maudlin. *Corn* 2E **7**
Maugersbury. *Glos* 3G **49**
Maughold. *IOM* 2D **108**
Maulden. *C Beds* 2A **52**
Maulds Meaburn. *Cumb* 3H **103**
Maunby. *N Yor* 1F **99**
Maund Bryan. *Here* 5H **59**
Mautby. *Norf* 4G **79**
Mavesyn Ridware. *Staf* 4E **73**
Mavis Enderby. *Linc* 4C **88**
Mawbray. *Cumb* 5B **112**
Mawdesley. *Lanc* 3C **90**
Mawdlam. *B'end* 3B **32**
Mawgan. *Corn* 4E **5**
Mawgan Porth. *Corn* 2C **6**
Maw Green. *Ches E* 5B **84**
Mawla. *Corn* 4B **6**
Mawnan. *Corn* 4E **5**
Mawnan Smith. *Corn* 4E **5**
Mawsley Village. *Nptn* 3E **63**
Mawthorpe. *Linc* 3D **88**
Maxey. *Pet* 5A **76**
Maxstoke. *Warw* 2G **61**

Maxted Street. *Kent* 1F **29**
Maxton. *Kent* 1G **29**
Maxton. *Bord* 1A **120**
Maxwellheugh. *Bord* 1B **120**
Maxwelltown. *Dum* 2A **112**
Maxworthy. *Corn* 3C **10**
Mayals. *Swan* 4F **31**
Maybole. *S Ayr* 3C **116**
Maybush. *Sotn* 1B **16**
Mayes Green. *Surr* 2C **26**
Mayfield. *E Sus* 3G **27**
Mayfield. *Midl* 3G **129**
Mayfield. *Per* 1C **136**
Mayfield. *Staf* 1F **73**
Mayford. *Surr* 5A **38**
Mayhill. *Swan* 3F **31**
Mayland. *Essx* 5C **54**
Maylandsea. *Essx* 5C **54**
Maynard's Green. *E Sus* 4G **27**
Maypole. *IOS* 1B **4**
Maypole. *Kent* 4G **41**
Maypole. *Mon* 4H **47**
Maypole Green. *Norf* 1G **67**
Maypole Green. *Suff* 5B **66**
Maywick. *Shet* 9E **173**
Mead. *Devn* 1C **10**
Meadgate. *Bath* 1B **22**
Meadle. *Buck* 5G **51**
Meadowbank. *Ches W* 4A **84**
Meadowfield. *Dur* 1F **105**
Meadow Green. *Here* 5B **60**
Meadowmill. *E Lot* 2H **129**
Meadows. *Nott* 2C **74**
Meadowtown. *Shrp* 5F **71**
Meadwell. *Devn* 4E **11**
Meaford. *Staf* 2C **72**
Mealabost. *W Isl*
  nr. Borgh 2G **171**
  nr. Stornoway 4G **171**
Mealasta. *W Isl* 5B **171**
Meal Bank. *Cumb* 5G **103**
Mealrigg. *Cumb* 5C **112**
Mealsgate. *Cumb* 5D **112**
Meanwood. *W Yor* 1C **92**
Mearbeck. *N Yor* 3H **97**
Meare. *Som* 2H **21**
Meare Green. *Som*
  nr. Curry Mallet 4F **21**
  nr. Stoke St Gregory 4G **21**
Mears Ashby. *Nptn* 4F **63**
Measham. *Leics* 4H **73**
Meath Green. *Surr* 1D **27**
Meathop. *Cumb* 1D **96**
Meaux. *E Yor* 1D **94**
Meavy. *Devn* 2B **8**
Medbourne. *Leics* 1E **63**
Medburn. *Nmbd* 2E **115**
Meddon. *Devn* 1C **10**
Meden Vale. *Notts* 4C **86**
Medlam. *Linc* 5C **88**
Medlicott. *Shrp* 1G **59**
Medmenham. *Buck* 3G **37**
Medomsley. *Dur* 4E **115**
Medstead. *Hants* 3E **25**
Medway Towns. *Medw* **204** (4B **40**)
Meerbrook. *Staf* 4D **85**
Meer End. *W Mid* 3G **61**
Meers Bridge. *Linc* 2D **89**
Meesden. *Herts* 2E **53**
Meeson. *Telf* 3A **72**
Meeth. *Devn* 2F **11**
Meeting Green. *Suff* 5G **65**
Meeting House Hill. *Norf* 3F **79**
Meidrim. *Carm* 2G **43**
Meifod. *Powy* 4D **70**
Meigle. *Per* 4B **144**
Meikle Earnock. *S Lan* 4A **128**
Meikle Kilchattan Butts. *Arg* . . .4B **126**
Meikleour. *Per* 5A **144**
Meikle Tarty. *Abers* 1G **153**
Meikle Wartle. *Abers* 5E **160**
Meinciau. *Carm* 4E **45**
Meir. *Stoke* 1D **72**
Meir Heath. *Staf* 1D **72**
Melbourn. *Cambs* 1D **53**
Melbourne. *Derbs* 3A **74**
Melbourne. *E Yor* 5B **100**
Melbury Abbas. *Dors* 4D **23**
Melbury Bubb. *Dors* 2A **14**
Melbury Osmond. *Dors* 2A **14**
Melbury Sampford. *Dors* 2A **14**
Melby. *Shet* 6C **173**
Melchbourne. *Bed* 4H **63**
Melcombe Bingham. *Dors* 2C **14**
Melcombe Regis. *Dors* 4B **14**
Meldon. *Devn* 3F **11**
Meldon. *Nmbd* 1E **115**
Meldreth. *Cambs* 1D **53**
Melfort. *Arg* 2F **133**
Melgarve. *High* 4G **149**
Meliden. *Den* 2C **82**
Melinbyrhedyn. *Powy* 1H **57**
Melincourt. *Neat* 5B **46**
Melin-y-coed. *Cnwy* 4H **81**
Melin-y-ddol. *Powy* 5C **70**
Melin-y-wig. *Den* 1C **70**
Melkington. *Nmbd* 5E **131**
Melkinthorpe. *Cumb* 2G **103**
Melkridge. *Nmbd* 3A **114**
Melksham. *Wilts* 5E **35**
Mellangaun. *High* 5C **162**
Melldalloch. *Arg* 2H **125**
Mellguards. *Cumb* 5F **113**
Melling. *Lanc* 2E **97**
Melling. *Mers* 4B **90**
Melling Mount. *Mers* 4C **90**
Mellis. *Suff* 3C **66**
Mellon Charles. *High* 4C **162**
Mellon Udrigle. *High* 4C **162**
Mellor. *G Man* 2D **85**
Mellor. *Lanc* 1E **91**

Mellor Brook. *Lanc* 1E **91**
Mells. *Som* 2C **22**
Melmerby. *Cumb* 1H **103**
Melmerby. *N Yor*
  nr. Middleham 1C **98**
  nr. Ripon 2F **99**
Melpash. *Dors* 3H **13**
Melrose. *Bord* 1H **119**
Melsetter. *Orkn* 9B **172**
Melsonby. *N Yor* 4E **105**
Meltham. *W Yor* 3B **92**
Meltham Mills. *W Yor* 3B **92**
Melton. *E Yor* 2C **94**
Melton. *Suff* 5E **67**
Meltonby. *E Yor* 4B **100**
Melton Constable. *Norf* 2C **78**
Melton Mowbray. *Leics* 4E **75**
Melton Ross. *N Lin* 3D **94**
Melvaig. *High* 5B **162**
Melverley. *Shrp* 4F **71**
Melverley Green. *Shrp* 4F **71**
Melvich. *High* 2A **168**
Membury. *Devn* 2F **13**
Memsie. *Abers* 2G **161**
Memus. *Ang* 3D **144**
Menabilly. *Corn* 3E **7**
Menai Bridge. *IOA* 3E **81**
Mendham. *Suff* 2E **67**
Mendlesham. *Suff* 4D **66**
Mendlesham Green.
  Suff 4C **66**
Menethorpe. *N Yor* 3B **100**
Menheniot. *Corn* 2G **7**
Menithwood. *Worc* 4B **60**
Menna. *Corn* 3D **6**
Menston. *W Yor* 5D **98**
Menstrie. *Clac* 4H **135**
Menthorpe. *N Yor* 1H **93**
Mentmore. *Buck* 4H **51**
Meole Brace. *Shrp* 4G **71**
Meols. *Mers* 1E **83**
Meon. *Hants* 2D **16**
Meonstoke. *Hants* 1E **16**
Meopham. *Kent* 4H **39**
Meopham Green. *Kent* 4H **39**
Meopham Station. *Kent* 4H **39**
Mepal. *Cambs* 2D **64**
Meppershall. *C Beds* 2B **52**
Merbach. *Here* 1G **47**
Mercaston. *Derbs* 1G **73**
Merchiston. *Edin* 2F **129**
Mere. *Ches E* 2B **84**
Mere. *Wilts* 3D **22**
Mere Brow. *Lanc* 3C **90**
Mereclough. *Lanc* 1G **91**
Mere Green. *W Mid* 1F **61**
Mere Green. *Worc* 4D **60**
Mere Heath. *Ches W* 3A **84**
Mereside. *Bkpl* 1B **90**
Meretown. *Staf* 3B **72**
Mereworth. *Kent* 5A **40**
Meriden. *W Mid* 2G **61**
Merkadale. *High* 5C **154**
Merkland. *S Ayr* 5B **116**
Merkland Lodge. *High* 1A **164**
Merley. *Pool* 3F **15**
Merlin's Bridge. *Pemb* 3D **42**
Merridge. *Som* 3F **21**
Merrington. *Shrp* 3G **71**
Merrion. *Pemb* 5D **42**
Merriott. *Som* 1H **13**
Merrivale. *Devn* 5F **11**
Merrow. *Surr* 5B **38**
Merrybent. *Darl* 3F **105**
Merry Lees. *Leics* 5B **74**
Merrymeet. *Corn* 2G **7**
Mersham. *Kent* 2E **29**
Merstham. *Surr* 5D **39**
Merston. *W Sus* 2G **17**
Merstone. *IOW* 4D **16**
Merther. *Corn* 4C **6**
Merthyr. *Carm* 3D **44**
Merthyr Cynog. *Powy* 2C **46**
Merthyr Dyfan. *V Glam* 4E **32**
Merthyr Mawr. *B'end* 4B **32**
Merthyr Tudful. *Mer T* 5D **46**
Merthyr Tydfil. *Mer T* 5D **46**
Merthyr Vale. *Mer T* 5D **46**
Merton. *Devn* 1F **11**
Merton. *G Lon* 4D **38**
Merton. *Norf* 1B **66**
Merton. *Oxon* 4D **50**
Meshaw. *Devn* 1A **12**
Messing. *Essx* 4B **54**
Messingham. *N Lin* 4B **94**
Metcombe. *Devn* 3D **12**
Metfield. *Suff* 2E **67**
Metherell. *Corn* 2A **8**
Metheringham. *Linc* 4H **87**
Methil. *Fife* 4F **137**
Methilhill. *Fife* 4F **137**
Methley. *W Yor* 2D **93**
Methley Junction. *W Yor* 2D **93**
Methlick. *Abers* 5F **161**
Methven. *Per* 1C **136**
Methwold. *Norf* 1G **65**
Methwold Hythe. *Norf* 1G **65**
Mettingham. *Suff* 2F **67**
Metton. *Norf* 2D **78**
Mevagissey. *Corn* 4E **6**
Mey. *High* 1E **169**
Meysey Hampton. *Glos* 2G **35**
Miabhag. *W Isl* 8D **171**
Miabhaig. *W Isl*
  nr. Cliasmol 7C **171**
  nr. Timsgearraidh 4C **171**
Mial. *High* 1G **155**
Michaelchurch. *Here* 3A **48**
Michaelchurch Escley. *Here* 2G **47**

Michaelchurch-on-Arrow.
  Powy 5E **59**
Michaelston-le-Pit. *V Glam* 4E **33**
Michaelston-y-Fedw. *Newp* 3F **33**
Michaelstow. *Corn* 5A **10**
Michelcombe. *Devn* 2C **8**
Micheldever. *Hants* 3D **24**
Micheldever Station. *Hants* 2D **24**
Michelmersh. *Hants* 4B **24**
Mickfield. *Suff* 4D **66**
Micklebring. *S Yor* 1C **86**
Mickleby. *N Yor* 3F **107**
Micklefield. *W Yor* 1E **93**
Micklefield Green. *Herts* 1B **38**
Mickleham. *Surr* 5C **38**
Mickleover. *Derb* 2H **73**
Micklethwaite. *Cumb* 4D **112**
Micklethwaite. *W Yor* 5D **98**
Mickleton. *Dur* 2C **104**
Mickleton. *Glos* 1G **49**
Mickletown. *W Yor* 2D **93**
Mickle Trafford. *Ches W* 4G **83**
Mickley. *N Yor* 2E **99**
Mickley Green. *Suff* 5H **65**
Mickley Square. *Nmbd* 3D **115**
Mid Ardlaw. *Abers* 2G **161**
Midbea. *Orkn* 3D **172**
Mid Beltie. *Abers* 3D **152**
Mid Calder. *W Lot* 3D **129**
Mid Clyth. *High* 5E **169**
Middle Assendon. *Oxon* 3F **37**
Middle Aston. *Oxon* 3C **50**
Middle Barton. *Oxon* 3C **50**
Middlebie. *Dum* 2D **112**
Middle Chinnock. *Som* 1H **13**
Middle Claydon. *Buck* 3F **51**
Middlecliffe. *S Yor* 4E **93**
Middlecott. *Devn* 4H **11**
Middle Drums. *Ang* 3E **145**
Middle Duntisbourne. *Glos* 5E **49**
Middle Essie. *Abers* 3H **161**
Middleforth Green. *Lanc* 2D **90**
Middleham. *N Yor* 1D **98**
Middle Handley. *Derbs* 3B **86**
Middle Harling. *Norf* 2B **66**
Middlehope. *Shrp* 2G **59**
Middle Littleton. *Worc* 1F **49**
Middle Maes-coed. *Here* 2G **47**
Middlemarsh. *Dors* 2B **14**
Middle Marwood. *Devn* 3F **19**
Middlemoor. *Devn* 5E **11**
Middlemuir. *Abers*
  nr. New Deer 4F **161**
  nr. Strichen 3G **161**
Middle Rainton. *Tyne* 5G **115**
Middle Rasen. *Linc* 2H **87**
Middles, The. *Dur* 4F **115**
Middlesbrough. *Midd* **201** (3B **106**)
Middlesceugh. *Cumb* 5E **113**
Middleshaw. *Cumb* 1E **97**
Middlesmoor. *N Yor* 2C **98**
Middlestone. *Dur* 1F **105**
Middlestone Moor. *Dur* 1F **105**
Middle Stoughton. *Som* 2H **21**
Middlestown. *W Yor* 3C **92**
Middle Street. *Glos* 5C **48**
Middle Taphouse. *Corn* 2F **7**
Middleton. *Ang* 4E **145**
Middleton. *Arg* 4A **138**
Middleton. *Cumb* 1F **97**
Middleton. *Derbs*
  nr. Bakewell 4F **85**
  nr. Wirksworth 5G **85**
Middleton. *Essx* 2B **54**
Middleton. *G Man* 4G **91**
Middleton. *Hants* 2C **24**
Middleton. *Hart* 1C **106**
Middleton. *Here* 4H **59**
Middleton. *IOW* 4B **16**
Middleton. *Lanc* 4D **96**
Middleton. *Midl* 4G **129**
Middleton. *Norf* 4F **77**
Middleton. *Nptn* 2F **63**
Middleton. *Nmbd*
  nr. Belford 1F **121**
  nr. Morpeth 1D **114**
Middleton. *N Yor*
  nr. Ilkley 5D **98**
  nr. Pickering 1B **100**
Middleton. *Per* 3D **136**
Middleton. *Shrp*
  nr. Ludlow 3H **59**
  nr. Oswestry 3F **71**
Middleton. *Suff* 4G **67**
Middleton. *Swan* 4D **30**
Middleton. *Warw* 1F **61**
Middleton. *W Yor* 2C **92**
Middleton Cheney. *Nptn* 1D **50**
Middleton Green. *Staf* 2D **73**
Middleton-in-Teesdale. *Dur* 2C **104**
Middleton One Row. *Darl* 3A **106**
Middleton-on-Leven. *N Yor* 4B **106**
Middleton-on-Sea. *W Sus* 5A **26**
Middleton on the Hill. *Here* 4H **59**
Middleton-on-the-Wolds.
  E Yor 5D **100**
Middleton Priors. *Shrp* 1A **60**
Middleton Quernhow. *N Yor* 2F **99**
Middleton St George. *Darl* 3A **106**
Middleton Scriven. *Shrp* 2A **60**
Middleton Stoney. *Oxon* 3D **50**
Middleton Tyas. *N Yor* 4F **105**
Middletown. *Cumb* 4A **102**
Middle Town. *IOS* 1B **4**
Middletown. *Powy* 4F **71**
Middle Tysoe. *Warw* 1B **50**
Middle Wallop. *Hants* 3A **24**
Middlewich. *Ches E* 4B **84**
Middle Winterslow. *Wilts* 3H **23**
Middlewood. *Corn* 5C **10**

Middlewood. *S Yor* 1H **85**
Middle Woodford. *Wilts* 3G **23**
Middlewood Green. *Suff* 4C **66**
Middleyard. *Glos* 5D **48**
Middlezoy. *Som* 3G **21**
Middridge. *Dur* 2F **105**
Midfield. *High* 2F **167**
Midford. *Bath* 5C **34**
Mid Garrary. *Dum* 2C **110**
Midge Hall. *Lanc* 2D **90**
Midgeholme. *Cumb* 4H **113**
Midgham. *W Ber* 5D **36**
Midgley. *W Yor*
  nr. Halifax 2A **92**
  nr. Horbury 3C **92**
Mid Ho. *Shet* 2G **173**
Midhopestones. *S Yor* 1G **85**
Midhurst. *W Sus* 4G **25**
Mid Kirkton. *N Ayr* 4C **126**
Mid Lambrook. *Som* 1H **13**
Midland. *Orkn* 7C **172**
Mid Lavant. *W Sus* 2G **17**
Midlem. *Bord* 2H **119**
Midney. *Som* 4A **22**
Midsomer Norton. *Bath* 1B **22**
Midton. *Inv* 2D **126**
Midtown. *High*
  nr. Poolewe 5C **162**
  nr. Tongue 2F **167**
Midville. *Linc* 5C **88**
Mid Walls. *Shet* 7C **173**
Mid Yell. *Shet* 2G **173**
Migdale. *High* 4D **164**
Migvie. *Abers* 3B **152**
Milborne Port. *Som* 1B **14**
Milborne St Andrew. *Dors* 3D **14**
Milborne Wick. *Som* 4B **22**
Milbourne. *Nmbd* 2E **115**
Milbourne. *Wilts* 3E **35**
Milburn. *Cumb* 2H **103**
Milbury Heath. *S Glo* 2B **34**
Milby. *N Yor* 3G **99**
Milcombe. *Oxon* 2C **50**
Milden. *Suff* 1C **54**
Mildenhall. *Suff* 3G **65**
Mildenhall. *Wilts* 5H **35**
Milebush. *Kent* 1B **28**
Mile End. *Cambs* 2F **65**
Mile End. *Essx* 3C **54**
Mileham. *Norf* 4B **78**
Mile Oak. *Brig* 5D **26**
Miles Green. *Staf* 5C **84**
Miles Hope. *Here* 4H **59**
Milesmark. *Fife* 1D **128**
Mile Town. *Kent* 3D **40**
Milfield. *Nmbd* 1D **120**
Milford. *Derbs* 1A **74**
Milford. *Devn* 4C **18**
Milford. *Powy* 1C **58**
Milford. *Staf* 3D **72**
Milford. *Surr* 1A **26**
Milford Haven. *Pemb* 4D **42**
Milford on Sea. *Hants* 3A **16**
Milkwall. *Glos* 5A **48**
Milkwell. *Wilts* 4E **23**
Milland. *W Sus* 4G **25**
Millbank. *High* 2D **168**
Mill Bank. *W Yor* 2A **92**
Millbeck. *Cumb* 2D **102**
Millbounds. *Orkn* 4E **172**
Millbreck. *Abers* 4H **161**
Millbridge. *Surr* 2G **25**
Millbrook. *C Beds* 2A **52**
Millbrook. *Corn* 3A **8**
Millbrook. *G Man* 1D **85**
Millbrook. *Sotn* 1B **16**
Mill Common. *Suff* 2G **67**
Mill Corner. *E Sus* 3C **28**
Milldale. *Staf* 5F **85**
Milden Lodge. *Ang* 1E **145**
Milldens. *Ang* 3E **145**
Millearn. *Per* 2B **136**
Mill End. *Buck* 3F **37**
Mill End. *Cambs* 5F **65**
Mill End. *Glos* 4G **49**
Millend. *Glos* 2C **34**
Mill End. *Herts* 2D **52**
Millerhill. *Midl* 3G **129**
Miller's Dale. *Derbs* 3F **85**
Millers Green. *Derbs* 5G **85**
Millerston. *Glas* 3H **127**
Millfield. *Abers* 4B **152**
Millfield. *Pet* 5A **76**
Millgate. *Lanc* 3G **91**
Mill Green. *Essx* 5G **53**
Mill Green. *Norf* 2D **66**
Mill Green. *Shrp* 3A **72**
Mill Green. *Staf* 3E **73**
Mill Green. *Suff* 1C **54**
Millhalf. *Here* 1F **47**
Millhall. *E Ren* 4G **127**
Millhayes. *Devn*
  nr. Honiton 2F **13**
  nr. Wellington 1E **13**
Millhead. *Lanc* 2D **97**
Millheugh. *S Lan* 4A **128**
Mill Hill. *Bkbn* 2E **91**
Mill Hill. *G Lon* 1D **38**
Millholme. *Cumb* 5G **103**
Millhouse. *Arg* 2A **126**
Millhouse. *Cumb* 1E **103**
Millhouse. *Cumb* 1C **112**
Millhousebridge. *Dum* 1C **112**
Millhouses. *S Yor* 2H **85**
Millikenpark. *Ren* 3F **127**
Millington. *E Yor* 4C **100**
Millington Green. *Derbs* 1G **73**
Mill Knowe. *Arg* 3B **122**
Mill Lane. *Hants* 1F **25**
Millmeece. *Staf* 2C **72**

Mill of Craigievar—Mungrisdale

Mill of Craigievar. *Abers* 2C 152
Mill of Fintray. *Abers* 2F 153
Mill of Haldane. *W Dun* 1F 127
Millom. *Cumb* 1A 96
Millow. *C Beds* 1C 52
Millpool. *Corn* 5B 10
Millport. *N Ayr* 4C 126
Mill Side. *Cumb* 1D 96
Mill Street. *Norf*
nr. Lyng 4C 78
nr. Swanton Morley 4C 78
Millthorpe. *Derbs* 3H 85
Millthorpe. *Linc* 2A 76
Millthrop. *Cumb* 5H 103
Milltimber. *Aber* 3F 153
Milltown. *Abers*
nr. Corgarff 3G 151
nr. Lumsden 2B 152
Milltown. *Corn* 3F 7
Milltown. *Derbs* 4A 86
Milltown. *Devn* 3F 19
Milltown. *Dum* 2E 113
Milltown of Aberdalgie. *Per* 1C 136
Milltown of Auchindoun. *Mor* 4A 160
Milltown of Campfield. *Abers* 3D 152
Milltown of Edinvillie. *Mor* 4G 159
Milltown of Rothiemay. *Mor* 4C 160
Milltown of Towie. *Abers* 2B 152
Milnacraig. *Ang* 3B 144
Milnathort. *Per* 3D 136
Milngavie. *E Dun* 2G 127
Milnholm. *Stir* 1A 128
Milnrow. *G Man* 3H 91
Milnthorpe. *Cumb* 1D 97
Milnthorpe. *W Yor* 3D 92
Milson. *Shrp* 3A 60
Milstead. *Kent* 5D 40
Milston. *Wilts* 2G 23
Milthorpe. *Nptn* 1D 50
Milton. *Ang* 4C 144
Milton. *Cambs* 4D 65
Milton. *Cumb*
nr. Brampton 3G 113
nr. Crooklands 1E 97
Milton. *Derbs* 3H 73
Milton. *Dum*
nr. Crocketford 2F 111
nr. Glenluce 4H 109
Milton. *Glas* 3G 127
Milton. *High*
nr. Achnasheen 3F 157
nr. Applecross 4G 155
nr. Drumnadrochit 5G 157
nr. Invergordon 1B 158
nr. Inverness 4H 157
nr. Wick 3F 169
Milton. *Mor*
nr. Cullen 2C 160
nr. Tomintoul 2F 151
Milton. *N Som* 5G 33
Milton. *Notts* 3E 86
Milton. *Oxon*
nr. Bloxham 2C 50
nr. Didcot 2C 36
Milton. *Pemb* 4E 43
Milton. *Port* 3E 17
Milton. *Som* 4H 21
Milton. *S Ayr* 2D 116
Milton. *Stir*
nr. Aberfoyle 3E 135
nr. Drymen 4D 134
Milton. *Stoke* 5D 84
Milton. *W Dun* 2F 127
Milton Abbas. *Dors* 2D 14
Milton Abbot. *Devn* 5E 11
Milton Auchlossan. *Abers* 3C 152
Milton Bridge. *Midl* 3F 129
Milton Bryan. *C Beds* 2H 51
Milton Clevedon. *Som* 3B 22
Milton Coldwells. *Abers* 5G 161
Milton Combe. *Devn* 2A 8
Milton Common. *Oxon* 5E 51
Milton Damerel. *Devn* 1D 11
Miltonduff. *Mor* 2F 159
Milton End. *Glos* 5G 49
Milton Ernest. *Bed* 5H 63
Milton Green. *Ches W* 5G 83
Milton Hill. *Devn* 5C 12
Milton Hill. *Oxon* 2C 36
Milton Keynes. *Mil* 204 (2G 51)
Milton Keynes Village. *Mil* 2G 51
Milton Lilbourne. *Wilts* 5G 35
Milton Malsor. *Nptn* 5E 63
Milton Morenish. *Per* 5D 142
Milton of Auchinhove. *Abers* 3C 152
Milton of Balgonie. *Fife* 3F 137
Milton of Barras. *Abers* 1H 145
Milton of Campsie. *E Dun* 2H 127
Milton of Cultoquhey. *Per* 1A 136
Milton of Cushnie. *Abers* 2C 152
Milton of Finavon. *Ang* 3D 145
Milton of Gollanfield. *High* 3B 158
Milton of Lesmore. *Abers* 1B 152
Milton of Leys. *High* 4A 158
Milton of Tullich. *Abers* 4A 152
Milton on Stour. *Dors* 4C 22
Milton Regis. *Kent* 4C 40
Milton Street. *E Sus* 5G 27
Milton-under-Wychwood. *Oxon* 4A 50
Milverton. *Som* 4E 20
Milverton. *Warw* 4H 61
Milwich. *Staf* 2D 72
Mimbridge. *Surr* 4A 38
Minard. *Arg* 4G 133
Minchington. *Dors* 1E 15
Minchinhampton. *Glos* 5D 48
Mindrum. *Nmbd* 1C 120
Minehead. *Som* 2C 20
Minera. *Wrex* 5E 83
Minety. *Wilts* 2F 35
Minffordd. *Gwyn* 2E 69
Mingarrypark. *High* 2A 140
Mingary. *High* 2G 139
Mingearraidh. *W Isl* 6C 170
Miningsby. *Linc* 4C 88
Minions. *Corn* 5C 10
Minishant. *S Ayr* 3C 116
Minllyn. *Gwyn* 4A 70
Minnigaff. *Dum* 3B 110
Minorca. *IOM* 3D 108
Minskip. *N Yor* 3F 99
Minstead. *Hants* 1A 16
Minsted. *W Sus* 4G 25
Minster. *Kent*
nr. Ramsgate 4H 41
Minster. *Kent*
nr. Sheerness 3D 40
Minsteracres. *Nmbd* 4D 114
Minsterley. *Shrp* 5F 71
Minster Lovell. *Oxon* 4B 50
Minsterworth. *Glos* 4C 48
Minterne Magna. *Dors* 2B 14
Minterne Parva. *Dors* 2B 14
Minting. *Linc* 3A 88
Mintlaw. *Abers* 4H 161
Minto. *Bord* 2H 119
Minton. *Shrp* 1G 59
Minwear. *Pemb* 3E 43
Minworth. *W Mid* 1F 61
Miodar. *Arg* 4B 138
Mirbister. *Orkn* 5C 172
Mirehouse. *Cumb* 3A 102
Mireland. *High* 2F 169
Mirfield. *W Yor* 3C 92
Miserden. *Glos* 5E 49
Miskin. *Rhon* 3D 32
Misson. *Notts* 1D 86
Misterton. *Leics* 2C 62
Misterton. *Notts* 1E 87
Misterton. *Som* 2H 13
Mistley. *Essx* 2E 54
Mistley Heath. *Essx* 2E 55
Mitcham. *G Lon* 4D 39
Mitcheldean. *Glos* 4B 48
Mitchell. *Corn* 3C 6
Mitchel Troy. *Mon* 4H 47
Mitcheltroy Common. *Mon* 5H 47
Mitford. *Nmbd* 1E 115
Mithian. *Corn* 3B 6
Mitton. *Staf* 4C 72
Mixbury. *Oxon* 2E 50
Mixenden. *W Yor* 2A 92
Mixon. *Staf* 5E 85
Moaness. *Orkn* 7B 172
Moarfield. *Shet* 1G 173
Moat. *Cumb* 2F 113
Moats Tye. *Suff* 5C 66
Mobberley. *Ches E* 3B 84
Mobberley. *Staf* 1E 73
Moccas. *Here* 1G 47
Mochdre. *Cnwy* 3H 81
Mochdre. *Powy* 2C 58
Mochrum. *Dum* 5A 110
Mockbeggar. *Hants* 2G 15
Mockerkin. *Cumb* 2B 102
Modbury. *Devn* 3C 8
Moddershall. *Staf* 2D 72
Modsarie. *High* 2G 167
Moelfre. *Cnwy* 3B 82
Moelfre. *IOA* 2E 81
Moelfre. *Powy* 3D 70
Moffat. *Dum* 4C 118
Moggerhanger. *C Beds* 1B 52
Mogworthy. *Devn* 1B 12
Moira. *Leics* 4H 73
Molash. *Kent* 5E 41
Mol-chlach. *High* 2C 146
Mold. *Flin* 4E 83
Molehill Green. *Essx* 3F 53
Molescroft. *E Yor* 5E 101
Molesden. *Nmbd* 1E 115
Molesworth. *Cambs* 3H 63
Moll. *High* 1D 146
Molland. *Devn* 4B 20
Mollington. *Ches W* 3F 83
Mollington. *Oxon* 1C 50
Mollinsburn. *N Lan* 2A 128
Monachty. *Cdgn* 4E 57
Monachyle. *Stir* 2D 135
Monar Lodge. *High* 4E 156
Monaughty. *Powy* 4E 59
Monewden. *Suff* 5E 67
Moneydie. *Per* 1C 136
Moneyrow Green. *Wind* 4G 37
Moniaive. *Dum* 5G 117
Monifieth. *Ang* 5E 145
Monikie. *Ang* 5E 145
Monimail. *Fife* 2E 137
Monington. *Pemb* 1B 44
Monk Bretton. *S Yor* 4D 92
Monken Hadley. *G Lon* 1D 38
Monk Fryston. *N Yor* 2F 93
Monk Hesleden. *Dur* 1B 106
Monkhide. *Here* 1B 48
Monkhill. *Cumb* 4E 113
Monkhopton. *Shrp* 1A 60
Monkland. *Here* 5G 59
Monkleigh. *Devn* 4E 19
Monknash. *V Glam* 4C 32
Monkokehampton. *Devn* 2F 11
Monkseaton. *Tyne* 2G 115
Monks Eleigh. *Suff* 1C 54
Monk's Gate. *W Sus* 3D 26
Monk's Heath. *Ches E* 3C 84
Monk Sherborne. *Hants* 1E 24
Monkshill. *Abers* 4E 161
Monksilver. *Som* 3D 20
Monks Kirby. *Warw* 2B 62
Monk Soham. *Suff* 4E 66
Monk Soham Green. *Suff* 4E 66
Monkspath. *W Mid* 3F 61
Monks Risborough. *Buck* 5G 51
Monksthorpe. *Linc* 4D 88
Monk Street. *Essx* 3G 53
Monkswood. *Mon* 5G 47
Monkton. *Devn* 2E 13
Monkton. *Kent* 4G 41
Monkton. *Pemb* 4D 42
Monkton. *S Ayr* 2C 116
Monkton Combe. *Bath* 5C 34
Monkton Deverill. *Wilts* 3D 22
Monkton Farleigh. *Wilts* 5D 34
Monkton Heathfield. *Som* 4F 21
Monktonhill. *S Ayr* 2C 116
Monkton Up Wimborne. *Dors* 1F 15
Monkton Wyld. *Dors* 3G 13
Monkwearmouth. *Tyne* 4G 115
Monkwood. *Dors* 3H 13
Monkwood. *Hants* 3E 25
Monmarsh. *Here* 1A 48
Monmouth. *Mon* 4A 48
Monnington on Wye. *Here* 1G 47
Monreith. *Dum* 5A 110
Montacute. *Som* 1H 13
Montford. *Arg* 3C 126
Montford. *Shrp* 4G 71
Montford Bridge. *Shrp* 4G 71
Montgarrie. *Abers* 2C 152
Montgarswood. *E Ayr* 2E 117
Montgomery. *Powy* 1E 58
Montgreenan. *N Ayr* 5E 127
Montrave. *Fife* 3F 137
Montrose. *Ang* 3G 145
Monxton. *Hants* 2B 24
Monyash. *Derbs* 4F 85
Monymusk. *Abers* 2D 152
Monzie. *Per* 1A 136
Moodiesburn. *N Lan* 2H 127
Moon's Green. *Kent* 3C 28
Moonzie. *Fife* 2F 137
Moor, The. *Kent* 3B 28
Moor. *Som* 1H 13
Moor Allerton. *W Yor* 1C 92
Moorbath. *Dors* 3H 13
Moorbrae. *Shet* 3F 173
Moorby. *Linc* 4B 88
Moorcot. *Here* 5F 59
Moor Crichel. *Dors* 2E 15
Moor Cross. *Devn* 3C 8
Moordown. *Bour* 3F 15
Moore. *Hal* 2H 83
Moorend. *Dum* 2D 112
Moor End. *E Yor* 1B 94
Moorend. *Glos*
nr. Dursley 5C 48
nr. Gloucester 4D 48
Moorends. *S Yor* 3G 93
Moorgate. *S Yor* 1B 86
Moorgreen. *Hants* 1C 16
Moorgreen. *Notts* 1B 74
Moor Green. *Wilts* 5D 34
Moorhaigh. *Notts* 4C 86
Moorhall. *Derbs* 3H 85
Moorhampton. *Here* 1G 47
Moorhouse. *Cumb*
nr. Carlisle 4E 113
nr. Wigton 4D 112
Moorhouse. *Notts* 4E 87
Moorhouse. *Surr* 5F 39
Moorhouses. *Linc* 5B 88
Moorland. *Som* 3G 21
Moorlinch. *Som* 3H 21
Moor Monkton. *N Yor* 4H 99
Moor of Granary. *Mor* 3E 159
Moor Row. *Cumb*
nr. Whitehaven 3B 102
nr. Wigton 5D 112
Moorsholm. *Red C* 3D 107
Moorside. *Dors* 1C 14
Moorside. *G Man* 4H 91
Moortown. *Devn* 3D 10
Moortown. *Hants* 2G 15
Moortown. *IOW* 4C 16
Moortown. *Linc* 1H 87
Moortown. *Telf* 4A 72
Moortown. *W Yor* 1D 92
Morangie. *High* 5E 165
Morar. *High* 4E 147
Morborne. *Cambs* 1A 64
Morchard Bishop. *Devn* 2A 12
Morcombelake. *Dors* 3H 13
Morcott. *Rut* 5G 75
Morda. *Shrp* 3E 71
Morden. *G Lon* 4D 38
Mordiford. *Here* 2A 48
Mordon. *Dur* 2A 106
More. *Shrp* 1F 59
Morebath. *Devn* 4C 20
Morebattle. *Bord* 2B 120
Morecambe. *Lanc* 3D 96
Morefield. *High* 4F 163
Moreleigh. *Devn* 3D 8
Morenish. *Per* 5C 142
Moresby Parks. *Cumb* 3A 102
Morestead. *Hants* 4D 24
Moreton. *Dors* 4D 14
Moreton. *Essx* 5F 53
Moreton. *Here* 4H 59
Moreton. *Mers* 1E 83
Moreton. *Oxon* 5E 51
Moreton. *Staf* 4B 72
Moreton Corbet. *Shrp* 3H 71
Moretonhampstead. *Devn* 4A 12
Moreton-in-Marsh. *Glos* 2H 49
Moreton Jeffries. *Here* 1B 48
Moreton Morrell. *Warw* 5H 61
Moreton on Lugg. *Here* 1A 48
Moreton Pinkney. *Nptn* 1D 50
Moreton Say. *Shrp* 2A 72
Moreton Valence. *Glos* 5C 48
Morfa. *Cdgn* 5C 56
Morfa Bach. *Carm* 4D 44
Morfa Bychan. *Gwyn* 2E 69
Morfa Glas. *Neat* 5B 46
Morfa Nefyn. *Gwyn* 1B 68
Morganstown. *Card* 3E 33
Morgan's Vale. *Wilts* 4G 23
Morham. *E Lot* 2B 130
Moriah. *Cdgn* 3F 57
Morland. *Cumb* 2G 103
Morley. *Ches E* 2C 84
Morley. *Derbs* 1A 74
Morley. *Dur* 2E 105
Morley. *W Yor* 2C 92
Morley St Botolph. *Norf* 1C 66
Morningside. *Edin* 2F 129
Morningside. *N Lan* 4B 128
Morningthorpe. *Norf* 1E 66
Morpeth. *Nmbd* 1F 115
Morrey. *Staf* 4F 73
Morridge Side. *Staf* 5E 85
Morridge Top. *Staf* 4E 85
Morrington. *Dum* 1F 111
Morris Green. *Essx* 2H 53
Morriston. *Swan* 3F 31
Morston. *Norf* 1C 78
Mortehoe. *Devn* 2E 19
Morthen. *S Yor* 2B 86
Mortimer. *W Ber* 5E 37
Mortimer's Cross. *Here* 4G 59
Mortimer West End. *Hants* 5E 37
Mortomley. *S Yor* 1H 85
Morton. *Cumb*
nr. Calthwaite 1F 103
nr. Carlisle 4E 113
Morton. *Derbs* 4B 86
Morton. *Linc*
nr. Bourne 3H 75
nr. Gainsborough 1F 87
nr. Lincoln 4F 87
Morton. *Norf* 4D 78
Morton. *Notts* 5E 87
Morton. *Shrp* 3E 71
Morton. *S Glo* 2B 34
Morton Bagot. *Warw* 4F 61
Morton Mill. *Shrp* 3H 71
Morton-on-Swale. *N Yor* 5A 106
Morton Tinmouth. *Dur* 2E 105
Morvah. *Corn* 3B 4
Morval. *Corn* 3G 7
Morvich. *High*
nr. Golspie 3E 165
nr. Shiel Bridge 1B 148
Morvil. *Pemb* 1E 43
Morville. *Shrp* 1A 60
Morwenstow. *Corn* 1C 10
Morwick. *Nmbd* 4G 121
Mosborough. *S Yor* 2B 86
Moscow. *E Ayr* 5F 127
Mose. *Shrp* 1B 60
Mosedale. *Cumb* 1E 103
Moseley. *W Mid*
nr. Birmingham 2E 61
nr. Wolverhampton 5D 72
Moseley. *Worc* 5C 60
Moss. *Arg* 4A 138
Moss. *High* 2A 140
Moss. *S Yor* 3F 93
Moss. *Wrex* 5F 83
Mossatt. *Abers* 2B 152
Moss Bank. *Mers* 1H 83
Mossbank. *Shet* 4F 173
Mossblown. *S Ayr* 2D 116
Mossbrow. *G Man* 2B 84
Mossburnford. *Bord* 3A 120
Mossdale. *Dum* 2D 110
Mossedge. *Cumb* 3F 113
Mossend. *N Lan* 3A 128
Mossgate. *Staf* 2D 72
Moss Lane. *Ches E* 3D 84
Mossley. *Ches E* 4C 84
Mossley. *G Man* 4H 91
Mossley Hill. *Mers* 2F 83
Moss of Barmuckity. *Mor* 2G 159
Mosspark. *Glas* 3G 127
Mosspaul. *Bord* 5G 119
Moss Side. *Cumb* 4C 112
Moss Side. *G Man* 1C 84
Moss-side. *High* 3C 158
Moss Side. *Lanc*
nr. Blackpool 1B 90
nr. Preston 2D 90
Moss Side. *Mers* 4B 90
Moss-side of Cairness. *Abers* 2H 161
Mosstodloch. *Mor* 2H 159
Mosswood. *Nmbd* 4D 114
Mossy Lea. *Lanc* 3D 90
Mosterton. *Dors* 2H 13
Moston. *Shrp* 3H 71
Moston Green. *Ches E* 4B 84
Mostyn. *Flin* 2D 82
Mostyn Quay. *Flin* 2D 82
Motcombe. *Dors* 4D 22
Mothecombe. *Devn* 4C 8
Motherby. *Cumb* 2F 103
Motherwell. *N Lan* 4A 128
Mottingham. *G Lon* 3F 39
Mottisfont. *Hants* 4B 24
Mottistone. *IOW* 4C 16
Mottram in Longdendale. *G Man* 1D 85
Mottram St Andrew. *Ches E* 3C 84
Mott's Mill. *E Sus* 2G 27
Mouldsworth. *Ches W* 3H 83
Moulin. *Per* 3G 143
Moulsecoomb. *Brig* 5E 27
Moulsford. *Oxon* 3D 36
Moulsoe. *Mil* 1H 51
Moulton. *Ches W* 4A 84
Moulton. *Linc* 3C 76
Moulton. *Nptn* 4E 63
Moulton. *N Yor* 4F 105
Moulton. *Suff* 4F 65
Moulton. *V Glam* 4D 32
Moulton Chapel. *Linc* 4B 76
Moulton Eaugate. *Linc* 4C 76
Moulton St Mary. *Norf* 5F 79
Moulton Seas End. *Linc* 3C 76
Mount. *Corn*
nr. Bodmin 2F 7
nr. Newquay 3B 6
Mountain Ash. *Rhon* 2D 32
Mountain Cross. *Bord* 5E 129
Mountain Street. *Kent* 5E 41
Mountain Water. *Pemb* 2D 42
Mount Ambrose. *Corn* 4B 6
Mountbenger. *Bord* 2F 119
Mountblow. *W Dun* 2F 127
Mount Bures. *Essx* 2C 54
Mountfield. *E Sus* 3B 28
Mountgerald. *High* 2H 157
Mount Hawke. *Corn* 4B 6
Mount High. *High* 2A 158
Mountjoy. *Corn* 2C 6
Mount Lothian. *Midl* 4F 129
Mountnessing. *Essx* 1H 39
Mounton. *Mon* 2A 34
Mount Pleasant. *Buck* 2E 51
Mount Pleasant. *Ches E* 5C 84
Mount Pleasant. *Derbs*
nr. Derby 1H 73
nr. Swadlincote 4G 73
Mount Pleasant. *E Sus* 4F 27
Mount Pleasant. *Hants* 3A 16
Mount Pleasant. *Norf* 1B 66
Mount Skippett. *Oxon* 4B 50
Mountsorrel. *Leics* 4C 74
Mount Stuart. *Arg* 4C 126
Mousehole. *Corn* 4B 4
Mouswald. *Dum* 2B 112
Mow Cop. *Ches E* 5C 84
Mowden. *Darl* 3F 105
Mowhaugh. *Bord* 2C 120
Mowmacre Hill. *Leic* 5C 74
Mowsley. *Leics* 2D 62
Moy. *High* 5B 158
Moylgrove. *Pemb* 1B 44
Moy Lodge. *High* 5G 149
Muasdale. *Arg* 5E 125
Muchalls. *Abers* 4G 153
Much Birch. *Here* 2A 48
Much Cowarne. *Here* 1B 48
Much Dewchurch. *Here* 2H 47
Muchelney. *Som* 4H 21
Muchelney Ham. *Som* 4H 21
Much Hadham. *Herts* 4E 53
Much Hoole. *Lanc* 2C 90
Muchlarnick. *Corn* 3G 7
Much Marcle. *Here* 2B 48
Muchrachd. *High* 5E 157
Much Wenlock. *Shrp* 5A 72
Mucking. *Thur* 2A 40
Muckle Breck. *Shet* 5G 173
Muckleford. *Dors* 3B 14
Mucklestone. *Staf* 2B 72
Muckleton. *Norf* 2H 77
Muckleton. *Shrp* 3H 71
Muckley. *Shrp* 1A 60
Muckley Corner. *Staf* 5E 73
Muckton. *Linc* 2C 88
Mudale. *High* 5F 167
Muddiford. *Devn* 3F 19
Mudeford. *Dors* 3G 15
Mudford. *Som* 1A 14
Mudgley. *Som* 2H 21
Mugdock. *Stir* 2G 127
Mugeary. *High* 5D 154
Muggington. *Derbs* 1G 73
Muggintonlane End. *Derbs* 1G 73
Muggleswick. *Dur* 4D 114
Mugswell. *Surr* 5D 38
Muie. *High* 3D 164
Muirden. *Abers* 3E 160
Muirdrum. *Ang* 5E 145
Muiredge. *Per* 1E 137
Muirend. *Glas* 3G 127
Muirhead. *Ang* 5C 144
Muirhead. *Fife* 3E 137
Muirhead. *N Lan* 3H 127
Muirhouses. *Falk* 1D 128
Muirkirk. *E Ayr* 2F 117
Muir of Alford. *Abers* 2C 152
Muir of Fairburn. *High* 3G 157
Muir of Fowlis. *Abers* 2C 152
Muir of Miltonduff. *Mor* 3F 159
Muir of Ord. *High* 3H 157
Muir of Tarradale. *High* 3H 157
Muirshearlich. *High* 5D 148
Muirtack. *Abers* 5G 161
Muirton. *High* 2B 158
Muirton. *Per* 1D 136
Muirton of Ardblair. *Per* 4A 144
Muirtown. *Per* 2B 136
Muiryfold. *Abers* 3E 161
Muker. *N Yor* 5C 104
Mulbarton. *Norf* 5D 78
Mulben. *Mor* 3A 160
Mulindry. *Arg* 4B 124
Mulla. *Shet* 5F 173
Mullach Charlabhaigh. *W Isl* 3E 171
Mullacott. *Devn* 2F 19
Mullion. *Corn* 5D 5
Mullion Cove. *Corn* 5D 4
Mumbles. *Swan* 4F 31
Mumby. *Linc* 3E 89
Munderfield Row. *Here* 5A 60
Munderfield Stocks. *Here* 5A 60
Mundesley. *Norf* 2F 79
Mundford. *Norf* 1H 65
Mundham. *Norf* 1F 67
Mundon. *Essx* 5B 54
Munerigie. *High* 3E 149
Muness. *Shet* 1H 173
Mungasdale. *High* 4D 162
Mungrisdale. *Cumb* 1E 103

Munlochy—Newstreet Lane

Munlochy. *High* 3A 158
Munsley. *Here* 1B 48
Munslow. *Shrp* 2H 59
Murchington. *Devn* 4G 11
Murcot. *Worc* 1F 49
Murcott. *Oxon* 4D 50
Murdishaw. *Hal* 2H 83
Murieston. *W Lot* 3D 128
Murkle. *High* 2D 168
Murlaggan. *High* 4C 148
Murra. *Orkn* 7B 172
Murray, The. *S Lan* 4H 127
Murrayfield. *Edin* 2F 129
Murrell Green. *Hants* 1F 25
Murroes. *Ang* 5D 144
Murrow. *Cambs* 5C 76
Mursley. *Buck* 3G 51
Murthly. *Per* 5H 143
Murton. *Cumb* 2A 104
Murton. *Dur* 5G 115
Murton. *Nmbd* 5F 131
Murton. *Swan* 4E 31
Murton. *York* 4A 100
Musbury. *Devn* 3F 13
Muscoates. *N Yor* 1A 100
Muscott. *Nptn* 4D 62
Musselburgh. *E Lot* 2G 129
Muston. *Leics* 2F 75
Muston. *N Yor* 2E 101
Mustow Green. *Worc* 3C 60
Muswell Hill. *G Lon* 2D 39
Mutehill. *Dum* 5D 111
Mutford. *Suff* 2G 67
Muthill. *Per* 2A 136
Mutterton. *Devn* 2D 12
Muxton. *Telf* 4B 72
Mwmbwls. *Swan* 4F 31
Mybster. *High* 3D 168
Myddfai. *Carm* 2A 46
Myddle. *Shrp* 3G 71
Mydroilyn. *Cdgn* 5D 56
Myerscough. *Lanc* 1C 90
Mylor Bridge. *Corn* 5C 6
Mylor Churchtown. *Corn* 5C 6
Mynachlog-ddu. *Pemb* 1F 43
Mynydd-bach. *Mon* 2H 33
Mynydd Isa. *Flin* 4E 83
Mynyddislwyn. *Cphy* 2E 33
Mynydd Llandegai. *Gwyn* 4F 81
Mynydd Mechell. *IOA* 1C 80
Mynydd-y-briw. *Powy* 3D 70
Mynyddygarreg. *Carm* 5E 45
Mynytho. *Gwyn* 2C 68
Myrebird. *Abers* 4E 153
Myrelandhorn. *High* 3E 169
Mytchett. *Surr* 1G 25
Mythe, The. *Glos* 2D 49
Mytholmroyd. *W Yor* 2A 92
Myton-on-Swale. *N Yor* 3G 99
Mytton. *Shrp* 4G 71

N

Naast. *High* 5C 162
Na Buirgh. *W Isl* 8C 171
Naburn. *York* 5H 99
Nab Wood. *W Yor* 1B 92
Nackington. *Kent* 5F 41
Nacton. *Suff* 1F 55
Nafferton. *E Yor* 4E 101
Na Gearrannan. *W Isl* 3D 171
Nailbridge. *Glos* 4B 48
Nailsbourne. *Som* 4F 21
Nailsea. *N Som* 4H 33
Nailstone. *Leics* 5B 74
Nailsworth. *Glos* 2D 34
Nairn. *High* 3C 158
Nalderswood. *Surr* 1D 26
Nancegollan. *Corn* 3D 4
Nancledra. *Corn* 3B 4
Nangreaves. *G Man* 3G 91
Nanhyfer. *Pemb* 1E 43
Nannerch. *Flin* 4D 82
Nanpantan. *Leics* 4C 74
Nanpean. *Corn* 3D 6
Nanstallon. *Corn* 2E 7
Nant-ddu. *Powy* 4D 46
Nanternis. *Cdgn* 5C 56
Nantgaredig. *Carm* 3E 45
Nantgarw. *Rhon* 3E 33
Nant Glas. *Powy* 4B 58
Nantglyn. *Den* 4C 82
Nantgwyn. *Powy* 3B 58
Nantlle. *Gwyn* 5E 81
Nantmawr. *Shrp* 3E 71
Nantmel. *Powy* 4C 58
Nantmor. *Gwyn* 1F 69
Nant Peris. *Gwyn* 5F 81
Nantwich. *Ches E* 5A 84
Nant-y-bai. *Carm* 1A 46
Nant-y-bwch. *Blae* 4E 47
Nant-y-Derry. *Mon* 5G 47
Nant-y-dugoed. *Powy* 4B 70
Nant-y-felin. *Cnwy* 3F 81
Nantyffyllon. *B'end* 2B 32
Nantyglo. *Blae* 4E 47
Nant-y-meichiaid. *Powy* 4D 70
Nant-y-moel. *B'end* 2C 32
Nant-y-pandy. *Cnwy* 3F 81
Naphill. *Buck* 2G 37
Nappa. *N Yor* 4A 98
Napton on the Hill. *Warw* 4B 62
Narberth. *Pemb* 3F 43
Narberth Bridge. *Pemb* 3F 43
Narborough. *Leics* 1C 62
Narborough. *Norf* 4G 77
Narkurs. *Corn* 3H 7
Narth, The. *Mon* 5A 48
Narthwaite. *Cumb* 5A 104
Nasareth. *Gwyn* 5D 80
Naseby. *Nptn* 3D 62
Nash. *Buck* 2F 51
Nash. *Here* 4F 59
Nash. *Kent* 5G 41
Nash. *Newp* 3G 33
Nash. *Shrp* 3A 60
Nash Lee. *Buck* 5G 51
Nassington. *Nptn* 1H 63
Nasty. *Herts* 3D 52
Natcott. *Devn* 4C 18
Nateby. *Cumb* 4A 104
Nateby. *Lanc* 5D 96
Nately Scures. *Hants* 1F 25
Natland. *Cumb* 1E 97
Naughton. *Suff* 1D 54
Naunton. *Glos* 3G 49
Naunton. *Worc* 2D 49
Naunton Beauchamp. *Worc* 5D 60
Navenby. *Linc* 5G 87
Navestock. *Essx* 1G 39
Navestock Side. *Essx* 1G 39
Navidale. *High* 2H 165
Nawton. *N Yor* 1A 100
Nayland. *Suff* 2C 54
Nazeing. *Essx* 5E 53
Neacroft. *Hants* 3G 15
Nealhouse. *Cumb* 4E 113
Neal's Green. *Warw* 2H 61
Near Sawrey. *Cumb* 5E 103
Neasden. *G Lon* 2D 38
Neasham. *Darl* 3A 106
Neath. *Neat* 2A 32
Neath Abbey. *Neat* 3G 31
Neatishead. *Norf* 3F 79
Neaton. *Norf* 5B 78
Nebo. *Cdgn* 4E 57
Nebo. *Cnwy* 5H 81
Nebo. *Gwyn* 5D 81
Nebo. *IOA* 1D 80
Necton. *Norf* 5A 78
Nedd. *High* 5B 166
Nedderton. *Nmbd* 1F 115
Nedging. *Suff* 1D 54
Nedging Tye. *Suff* 1D 54
Needham. *Norf* 2E 67
Needham Market. *Suff* 5C 66
Needham Street. *Suff* 4G 65
Needingworth. *Cambs* 3C 64
Needwood. *Staf* 3F 73
Neen Savage. *Shrp* 3A 60
Neen Sollars. *Shrp* 3A 60
Neenton. *Shrp* 2A 60
Nefyn. *Gwyn* 1C 68
Neilston. *E Ren* 4F 127
Neithrop. *Oxon* 1C 50
Nelly Andrews Green. *Powy* 5E 71
Nelson. *Cphy* 2E 32
Nelson. *Lanc* 1G 91
Nelson Village. *Nmbd* 2F 115
Nemphlar. *S Lan* 5B 128
Nempnett Thrubwell. *Bath* 5A 34
Nene Terrace. *Linc* 5B 76
Nenthall. *Cumb* 5A 114
Nenthead. *Cumb* 5A 114
Nenthorn. *Bord* 1A 120
Nercwys. *Flin* 4E 83
Neribus. *Arg* 4A 124
Nerston. *S Lan* 4H 127
Nesbit. *Nmbd* 1D 121
Nesfield. *N Yor* 5C 98
Ness. *Ches W* 3F 83
Nesscliffe. *Shrp* 4F 71
Ness of Tenston. *Orkn* 6B 172
Neston. *Ches W* 3E 83
Neston. *Wilts* 5D 34
Nethanfoot. *S Lan* 5B 128
Nether Alderley. *Ches E* 3C 84
Netheravon. *Wilts* 2G 23
Nether Blainslie. *Bord* 5B 130
Netherbrae. *Abers* 3E 161
Netherbrough. *Orkn* 6C 172
Nether Broughton. *Leics* 3D 74
Netherburn. *S Lan* 5B 128
Nether Burrow. *Lanc* 2F 97
Netherbury. *Dors* 3H 13
Netherby. *Cumb* 2E 113
Nether Careston. *Ang* 3E 145
Nether Cerne. *Dors* 3B 14
Nether Compton. *Dors* 1A 14
Nethercote. *Glos* 3G 49
Nethercote. *Warw* 4C 62
Nethercott. *Devn* 3E 19
Nethercott. *Oxon* 3C 50
Nether Dallachy. *Mor* 2A 160
Nether Durdie. *Per* 1E 136
Nether End. *Derbs* 3G 85
Netherend. *Glos* 5A 48
Nether Exe. *Devn* 2C 12
Netherfield. *E Sus* 4B 28
Netherfield. *Notts* 1D 74
Nethergate. *Norf* 3C 78
Netherhampton. *Wilts* 4G 23
Nether Handley. *Derbs* 3B 86
Nether Haugh. *S Yor* 1B 86
Nether Heage. *Derbs* 5A 86
Nether Heyford. *Nptn* 5D 62
Netherhouses. *Cumb* 1B 96
Nether Howcleugh. *S Lan* 3C 118
Nether Kellet. *Lanc* 3E 97
Nether Kinmundy. *Abers* 4H 161
Netherland Green. *Staf* 2F 73
Nether Langwith. *Notts* 3C 86
Netherlaw. *Dum* 5E 111
Netherley. *Abers* 4F 153
Nethermill. *Dum* 1B 112
Nethermills. *Mor* 3C 160
Nether Moor. *Derbs* 4A 86
Nether Padley. *Derbs* 3G 85
Netherplace. *E Ren* 4G 127
Nether Poppleton. *York* 4H 99
Netherseal. *Derbs* 4G 73
Nether Silton. *N Yor* 5B 106
Nether Stowey. *Som* 3E 21
Nether Street. *Essx* 4F 53
Netherstreet. *Wilts* 5E 35
Netherthird. *E Ayr* 3E 117
Netherthong. *W Yor* 4B 92
Netherton. *Ang* 3E 145
Netherton. *Cumb* 1B 102
Netherton. *Devn* 5B 12
Netherton. *Hants* 1B 24
Netherton. *Here* 3A 48
Netherton. *Mers* 1F 83
Netherton. *N Lan* 4A 128
Netherton. *Nmbd* 4D 121
Netherton. *Per* 3A 144
Netherton. *Shrp* 2B 60
Netherton. *Stir* 2G 127
Netherton. *W Mid* 2D 60
Netherton. *W Yor*
  nr. Armitage Bridge 3B 92
  nr. Horbury 3C 92
Netherton. *Worc* 1E 49
Nethertown. *Cumb* 4A 102
Nethertown. *High* 1F 169
Nethertown. *Staf* 4F 73
Nether Urquhart. *Fife* 3D 136
Nether Wallop. *Hants* 3B 24
Nether Wasdale. *Cumb* 4C 102
Nether Welton. *Cumb* 5E 113
Nether Westcote. *Glos* 3H 49
Nether Whitacre. *Warw* 1G 61
Nether Winchendon. *Buck* 4F 51
Netherwitton. *Nmbd* 5F 121
Nether Worton. *Oxon* 2C 50
Nethy Bridge. *High* 1E 151
Netley. *Shrp* 5G 71
Netley Abbey. *Hants* 2C 16
Netley Marsh. *Hants* 1B 16
Nettlebed. *Oxon* 3F 37
Nettlebridge. *Som* 2B 22
Nettlecombe. *Dors* 3A 14
Nettlecombe. *IOW* 5D 16
Nettleden. *Herts* 4A 52
Nettleham. *Linc* 3H 87
Nettlestead. *Kent* 5A 40
Nettlestead Green. *Kent* 5A 40
Nettlestone. *IOW* 3E 16
Nettlesworth. *Dur* 5F 115
Nettleton. *Linc* 4E 94
Nettleton. *Wilts* 4D 34
Netton. *Devn* 4B 8
Netton. *Wilts* 3G 23
Neuadd. *Powy* 5C 70
Neuk, The. *Abers* 4E 153
Nevendon. *Essx* 1B 40
Nevern. *Pemb* 1E 43
New Abbey. *Dum* 3A 112
New Aberdour. *Abers* 2F 161
New Addington. *G Lon* 4E 39
Newall. *W Yor* 5E 98
New Alresford. *Hants* 3D 24
New Alyth. *Per* 4B 144
Newark. *Orkn* 3G 172
Newark. *Pet* 5B 76
Newark-on-Trent. *Notts* 5E 87
New Arley. *Warw* 2G 61
Newarthill. *N Lan* 4A 128
New Ash Green. *Kent* 4H 39
New Balderton. *Notts* 5F 87
New Barn. *Kent* 4H 39
New Barnetby. *N Lin* 3D 94
Newbattle. *Midl* 3G 129
New Bewick. *Nmbd* 2E 121
Newbie. *Dum* 3C 112
Newbiggin. *Cumb*
  nr. Appleby 2H 103
  nr. Barrow-in-Furness 3B 96
  nr. Cumrew 5G 113
  nr. Penrith 2F 103
  nr. Seascale 5B 102
Newbiggin. *Dur*
  nr. Consett 5E 115
  nr. Holwick 2C 104
Newbiggin. *Nmbd* 5C 114
Newbiggin. *N Yor*
  nr. Askrigg 5C 104
  nr. Filey 1F 101
  nr. Thoralby 1B 98
Newbiggin-by-the-Sea. *Nmbd* 1G 115
Newbigging. *Ang*
  nr. Monikie 5D 145
  nr. Newtyle 4B 144
  nr. Tealing 5D 144
Newbigging. *Edin* 2E 129
Newbigging. *S Lan* 5D 128
Newbiggin-on-Lune. *Cumb* 4A 104
Newbold. *Derbs* 3A 86
Newbold. *Leics* 4B 74
Newbold on Avon. *Warw* 3B 62
Newbold on Stour. *Warw* 1H 49
Newbold Pacey. *Warw* 5G 61
Newbold Verdon. *Leics* 5B 74
New Bolingbroke. *Linc* 5C 88
Newborough. *IOA* 4D 80
Newborough. *Pet* 5B 76
Newborough. *Staf* 3F 73
Newbottle. *Nptn* 2D 50
Newbottle. *Tyne* 4G 115
New Boultham. *Linc* 3G 87
Newbourne. *Suff* 1F 55
New Brancepeth. *Dur* 5F 115
Newbridge. *Cphy* 2F 33
Newbridge. *Cdgn* 5E 57
Newbridge. *Corn* 3B 4
New Bridge. *Dum* 2G 111
Newbridge. *Edin* 2E 129
Newbridge. *Hants* 1A 16
Newbridge. *IOW* 4C 16
Newbridge. *N Yor* 1C 100
Newbridge. *Pemb* 1D 42
Newbridge. *Wrex* 1E 71
Newbridge Green. *Worc* 2D 48
Newbridge-on-Usk. *Mon* 2G 33
Newbridge on Wye. *Powy* 5C 58
New Brighton. *Flin* 4E 83
New Brighton. *Hants* 2F 17
New Brighton. *Mers* 1F 83
New Brinsley. *Notts* 5B 86
Newbrough. *Nmbd* 3B 114
New Broughton. *Wrex* 5F 83
New Buckenham. *Norf* 1C 66
Newbuildings. *Devn* 2A 12
Newburgh. *Abers* 1G 153
Newburgh. *Fife* 2E 137
Newburgh. *Lanc* 3C 90
Newburn. *Tyne* 3E 115
Newbury. *W Ber* 5C 36
Newbury. *Wilts* 2D 22
Newby. *Cumb* 2G 103
Newby. *N Yor*
  nr. Ingleton 2G 97
  nr. Scarborough 1E 101
  nr. Stokesley 3C 106
Newby Bridge. *Cumb* 1C 96
Newby Cote. *N Yor* 2G 97
Newby East. *Cumb* 4F 113
Newby Head. *Cumb* 2G 103
New Byth. *Abers* 3F 161
Newby West. *Cumb* 4E 113
Newby Wiske. *N Yor* 1F 99
Newcastle. *B'end* 3B 32
Newcastle. *Mon* 4H 47
Newcastle. *Shrp* 2E 59
Newcastle Emlyn. *Carm* 1D 44
Newcastle International Airport. *Tyne* 2E 115
Newcastleton. *Bord* 1F 113
Newcastle-under-Lyme. *Staf* 1C 72
Newcastle upon Tyne. *Tyne* 205 (3F 115)
Newchapel. *Pemb* 1G 43
Newchapel. *Powy* 2B 58
Newchapel. *Staf* 5C 84
Newchapel. *Surr* 1E 27
New Cheriton. *Hants* 4D 24
Newchurch. *Carm* 3D 45
Newchurch. *Here* 5F 59
Newchurch. *IOW* 4D 16
Newchurch. *Kent* 2E 29
Newchurch. *Lanc* 2G 91
Newchurch. *Mon* 2H 33
Newchurch. *Powy* 5E 58
Newchurch. *Staf* 3F 73
Newchurch in Pendle. *Lanc* 1G 91
New Costessey. *Norf* 4D 78
Newcott. *Devn* 2F 13
New Cowper. *Cumb* 5C 112
Newcraighall. *Edin* 2G 129
New Crofton. *W Yor* 3D 93
New Cross. *Cdgn* 3F 57
New Cross. *Som* 1H 13
New Cumnock. *E Ayr* 3F 117
New Deer. *Abers* 4F 161
New Denham. *Buck* 2B 38
Newdigate. *Surr* 1C 26
New Duston. *Nptn* 4E 62
New Earswick. *York* 4A 100
New Edlington. *S Yor* 1C 86
New Elgin. *Mor* 2G 159
New Ellerby. *E Yor* 1E 95
Newell Green. *Brac* 4G 37
New Eltham. *G Lon* 3F 39
New End. *Warw* 4F 61
New End. *Worc* 5E 61
Newenden. *Kent* 3C 28
New England. *Essx* 1H 53
New England. *Pet* 5A 76
Newent. *Glos* 3C 48
New Ferry. *Mers* 2F 83
Newfield. *Dur*
  nr. Chester-le-Street 4F 115
  nr. Willington 1F 105
Newfound. *Hants* 1D 24
New Fryston. *W Yor* 2E 93
Newgale. *Pemb* 2C 42
New Galloway. *Dum* 2D 110
Newgate. *Norf* 1C 78
Newgate Street. *Herts* 5D 52
New Greens. *Herts* 5B 52
New Grimsby. *IOS* 1A 4
New Hainford. *Norf* 4E 78
Newhall. *Ches E* 1A 72
Newhall. *Derbs* 3G 73
Newham. *Nmbd* 2F 121
New Hartley. *Nmbd* 2G 115
Newhaven. *Derbs* 4F 85
Newhaven. *E Sus* 215 (5F 27)
Newhaven. *Edin* 2F 129
New Haw. *Surr* 4B 38
New Hedges. *Pemb* 4F 43
New Herrington. *Tyne* 4G 115
Newhey. *G Man* 3H 91
New Holkham. *Norf* 2A 78
New Holland. *N Lin* 2D 94
Newholm. *N Yor* 3F 107
New Houghton. *Derbs* 4C 86
New Houghton. *Norf* 3G 77
Newhouse. *N Lan* 3A 128
New Houses. *N Yor* 2H 97
New Hutton. *Cumb* 5G 103
New Hythe. *Kent* 5B 40
Newick. *E Sus* 3F 27
Newingreen. *Kent* 2F 29
Newington. *Edin* 2F 129
Newington. *Kent*
  nr. Folkestone 2F 29
  nr. Sittingbourne 4C 40
Newington. *Notts* 1D 86
Newington. *Oxon* 2E 36
Newington Bagpath. *Glos* 2D 34
New Inn. *Carm* 2E 45
New Inn. *Mon* 5H 47
New Inn. *N Yor* 2H 97
New Inn. *Torf* 2G 33
New Invention. *Shrp* 3E 59
New Kelso. *High* 4B 156
New Lanark. *S Lan* 5B 128
Newland. *Glos* 5A 48
Newland. *Hull* 1D 94
Newland. *N Yor* 2G 93
Newland. *Som* 3B 20
Newland. *Worc* 1C 48
Newlandrig. *Midl* 3G 129
Newlands. *Cumb* 1E 103
Newlands. *High* 4B 158
Newlands. *Nmbd* 4D 115
Newlands. *Staf* 3E 73
Newlands of Geise. *High* 2C 168
Newlands of Tynet. *Mor* 2A 160
Newlands Park. *IOA* 2B 80
New Lane. *Lanc* 3C 90
New Lane End. *Warr* 1A 84
New Langholm. *Dum* 1E 113
New Leake. *Linc* 5D 88
New Leeds. *Abers* 3G 161
New Lenton. *Nott* 2C 74
New Longton. *Lanc* 2D 90
Newlot. *Orkn* 6E 172
New Luce. *Dum* 3G 109
Newlyn. *Corn* 4B 4
Newmachar. *Abers* 2F 153
Newmains. *N Lan* 4B 128
New Mains of Ury. *Abers* 5F 153
New Malden. *G Lon* 4D 38
Newman's Green. *Suff* 1B 54
Newmarket. *Suff* 4F 65
Newmarket. *W Isl* 4G 171
New Marske. *Red C* 2D 106
New Marton. *Shrp* 2F 71
New Micklefield. *W Yor* 1E 93
New Mill. *Abers* 4E 160
New Mill. *Corn* 3B 4
New Mill. *Herts* 4H 51
Newmill. *Mor* 3B 160
Newmill. *Bord* 3G 119
New Mill. *W Yor* 4B 92
New Mill. *Wilts* 5G 35
Newmillerdam. *W Yor* 3D 92
New Mills. *Corn* 3C 6
New Mills. *Derbs* 2E 85
Newmills. *Fife* 1D 128
Newmills. *High* 2A 158
New Mills. *Mon* 5A 48
New Mills. *Powy* 5C 70
Newmiln. *Per* 5A 144
Newmilns. *E Ayr* 1E 117
New Milton. *Hants* 3H 15
New Mistley. *Essx* 2E 54
New Moat. *Pemb* 2E 43
Newmore. *High*
  nr. Dingwall 3H 157
  nr. Invergordon 1A 158
Newnham. *Cambs* 5D 64
Newnham. *Glos* 4B 48
Newnham. *Hants* 1F 25
Newnham. *Herts* 2C 52
Newnham. *Kent* 5D 40
Newnham. *Nptn* 5C 62
Newnham. *Warw* 4F 61
Newnham Bridge. *Worc* 4A 60
New Ollerton. *Notts* 4D 86
New Oscott. *W Mid* 1E 61
Newpark. *Fife* 2G 137
New Park. *N Yor* 4E 99
New Pitsligo. *Abers* 3F 161
New Polzeath. *Corn* 1D 6
Newport. *Corn* 4D 10
Newport. *Devn* 3F 19
Newport. *E Yor* 1B 94
Newport. *Essx* 2F 53
Newport. *Glos* 2B 34
Newport. *High* 1H 165
Newport. *IOW* 4D 16
Newport. *Newp* 205 (3G 33)
Newport. *Norf* 4H 79
Newport. *Pemb* 1E 43
Newport. *Som* 4G 21
Newport. *Telf* 4B 72
Newport-on-Tay. *Fife* 1G 137
Newport Pagnell. *Mil* 1G 51
Newpound Common. *W Sus* 3B 26
New Prestwick. *S Ayr* 2C 116
New Quay. *Cdgn* 5C 56
Newquay. *Corn* 2C 6
Newquay Cornwall Airport. *Corn* 2C 6
New Rackheath. *Norf* 4E 79
New Radnor. *Powy* 4E 58
New Rent. *Cumb* 1F 103
New Ridley. *Nmbd* 4D 114
New Romney. *Kent* 3E 29
New Rossington. *S Yor* 1D 86
New Row. *Cdgn* 3G 57
New Sauchie. *Clac* 4A 136
Newsbank. *Ches E* 4C 84
Newseat. *Abers* 5E 160
Newsham. *Lanc* 1D 90
Newsham. *Nmbd* 2G 115
Newsham. *N Yor*
  nr. Richmond 3E 105
  nr. Thirsk 1F 99
New Sharlston. *W Yor* 2D 93
Newsholme. *E Yor* 2H 93
Newsholme. *Lanc* 4H 97
New Shoreston. *Nmbd* 1F 121
New Springs. *G Man* 4D 90
Newstead. *Notts* 5C 86
Newstead. *Bord* 1H 119
New Stevenston. *N Lan* 4A 128
New Street. *Here* 5F 59
Newstreet Lane. *Shrp* 2A 72

New Swanage. *Dors* 4F **15**
New Swannington. *Leics* 4B **74**
Newthorpe. *N Yor* 1E **93**
Newthorpe. *Notts* 1B **74**
Newton. *Arg* 4H **133**
Newton. *B'end* 4B **32**
Newton. *Cambs*
  nr. Cambridge 1E **53**
  nr. Wisbech 4D **76**
Newton. *Ches W*
  nr. Chester 4G **83**
  nr. Tattenhall 5H **83**
Newton. *Cumb* 2B **96**
Newton. *Derbs* 5B **86**
Newton. *Dors* 1C **14**
Newton. *Dum*
  nr. Annan 2D **112**
  nr. Moffat 5D **118**
Newton. *G Man* 1D **84**
Newton. *Here*
  nr. Ewyas Harold 2G **47**
  nr. Leominster 5H **59**
Newton. *High*
  nr. Cromarty 2B **158**
  nr. Inverness 4B **158**
  nr. Kylestrome 5C **166**
  nr. Wick 4F **169**
Newton. *Lanc*
  nr. Blackpool 1B **90**
  nr. Carnforth 2E **97**
  nr. Clitheroe 4F **97**
Newton. *Linc* 2H **75**
Newton. *Mers* 2E **83**
Newton. *Mor* 2F **159**
Newton. *Norf* 4H **77**
Newton. *Nptn* 2F **63**
Newton. *Nmbd* 3D **114**
Newton. *Notts* 1D **74**
Newton. *Bord* 2A **120**
Newton. *Shet* 8E **173**
Newton. *Shrp*
  nr. Bridgnorth 1B **60**
  nr. Wem 2G **71**
Newton. *Som* 3E **20**
Newton. *S Lan*
  nr. Glasgow 3H **127**
  nr. Lanark 1B **118**
Newton. *Staf* 3E **73**
Newton. *Suff* 1C **54**
Newton. *Swan* 4F **31**
Newton. *Warw* 3C **62**
Newton. *W Lot* 2D **129**
Newton. *Wilts* 4H **23**
Newton Abbot. *Devn* 5B **12**
Newtonairds. *Dum* 1F **111**
Newton Arlosh. *Cumb* 4D **112**
Newton Aycliffe. *Dur* 2F **105**
Newton Bewley. *Hart* 2B **106**
Newton Blossomville. *Mil* 5G **63**
Newton Bromswold. *Nptn* 4G **63**
Newton Burgoland. *Leics* 5A **74**
Newton by Toft. *Linc* 2H **87**
Newton Ferrers. *Devn* 4B **8**
Newton Flotman. *Norf* 1E **66**
Newtongrange. *Midl* 3G **129**
Newton Green. *Mon* 2A **34**
Newton Hall. *Dur* 5F **115**
Newton Hall. *Nmbd* 3D **114**
Newton Harcourt. *Leics* 1D **62**
Newton Heath. *G Man* 4G **91**
Newtonhill. *Abers* 4G **153**
Newtonhill. *High* 4H **157**
Newton Hill. *W Yor* 2D **92**
Newton Ketton. *Darl* 2A **106**
Newton Kyme. *N Yor* 5G **99**
Newton-le-Willows. *Mers* 1H **83**
Newton-le-Willows. *N Yor* 1E **98**
Newton Longville. *Buck* 2G **51**
Newton Mearns. *E Ren* 4G **127**
Newtonmore. *High* 4B **150**
Newton Morrell. *N Yor* 4F **105**
Newton Mulgrave. *N Yor* 3E **107**
Newton of Ardtoe. *High* 1A **140**
Newton of Balcanquhal. *Per* 2D **136**
Newton of Beltrees. *Ren* 4E **127**
Newton of Falkland. *Fife* 3E **137**
Newton of Mountblairy.
  Abers 3D **160**
Newton of Pitcairns. *Per* 2C **136**
Newton-on-Ouse. *N Yor* 4H **99**
Newton-on-Rawcliffe.
  N Yor 5F **107**
Newton on the Hill. *Shrp* 3G **71**
Newton-on-the-Moor.
  Nmbd 4F **121**
Newton on Trent. *Linc* 3F **87**
Newton Poppleford. *Devn* 4D **12**
Newton Purcell. *Oxon* 2E **51**
Newton Regis. *Warw* 5G **73**
Newton Reigny. *Cumb* 1F **103**
Newton Rigg. *Cumb* 1F **103**
Newton St Cyres. *Devn* 3B **12**
Newton St Faith. *Norf* 4E **78**
Newton St Loe. *Bath* 5C **34**
Newton St Petrock. *Devn* 1E **11**
Newton Solney. *Derbs* 3G **73**
Newton Stacey. *Hants* 2C **24**
Newton Stewart. *Dum* 3B **110**
Newton Tony. *Wilts* 2H **23**
Newton Tony. *Wilts* 2H **23**
Newton Tracey. *Devn* 4F **19**
Newton under Roseberry.
  Red C 3C **106**
Newton upon Ayr. *S Ayr* 2C **116**
Newton upon Derwent.
  E Yor 5B **100**
Newton Valence. *Hants* 3F **25**
Newton-with-Scales. *Lanc* 1C **90**
Newtown. *Abers* 2E **160**
Newtown. *Cambs* 4H **63**
Newtown. *Corn* 5C **10**

Newtown. *Cumb*
  nr. Aspatria 5B **112**
  nr. Brampton 3G **113**
  nr. Penrith 2G **103**
Newtown. *Derbs* 2D **85**
Newtown. *Devn* 4A **20**
New Town. *Dors* 1E **15**
Newtown. *Dors* 2H **13**
New Town. *E Lot* 2H **129**
Newtown. *Falk* 1C **128**
Newtown. *Glos*
  nr. Lydney 5B **48**
  nr. Tewkesbury 2E **49**
Newtown. *Hants*
  nr. Bishop's Waltham 1D **16**
  nr. Liphook 3G **25**
  nr. Lyndhurst 1A **16**
  nr. Newbury 5C **36**
  nr. Romsey 4B **24**
  nr. Warsash 2C **16**
  nr. Wickham 1E **16**
Newtown. *Here*
  nr. Little Dewchurch 2A **48**
  nr. Stretton Grandison 1B **48**
Newtown. *High* 3F **149**
Newtown. *IOM* 4C **108**
Newtown. *IOW* 3C **16**
Newtown. *Lanc* 3D **90**
New Town. *Lutn* 3A **52**
Newtown. *Nmbd*
  nr. Rothbury 4E **121**
  nr. Wooler 2E **121**
Newtown. *Pool* 3F **15**
Newtown. *Powy* 1D **58**
Newtown. *Rhon* 2D **32**
Newtown. *Shet* 3F **173**
Newtown. *Shrp* 2G **71**
Newtown. *Som* 1F **13**
Newtown. *Staf*
  nr. Biddulph 4D **84**
  nr. Cannock 5D **73**
  nr. Longnor 4E **85**
New Town. *W Yor* 2E **93**
Newtown. *Wilts* 4E **23**
Newtown-in-St Martin. *Corn* 4E **5**
Newtown Linford. *Leics* 5C **74**
Newtown St Boswells. *Bord* 1H **119**
Newtown Unthank. *Leics* 5B **74**
New Tredegar. *Cphy* 5E **47**
Newtyle. *Ang* 4B **144**
New Village. *E Yor* 1D **94**
New Village. *S Yor* 4F **93**
New Walsoken. *Cambs* 5D **76**
New Waltham. *NE Lin* 4F **95**
New Winton. *E Lot* 2H **129**
New World. *Cambs* 1C **64**
New Yatt. *Oxon* 4B **50**
Newyears Green. *G Lon* 2B **38**
New York. *Linc* 5B **88**
New York. *Tyne* 2G **115**
Nextend. *Here* 5F **59**
Neyland. *Pemb* 4D **42**
Nib Heath. *Shrp* 4G **71**
Nicholashayne. *Devn* 1E **12**
Nicholaston. *Swan* 4E **31**
Nidd. *N Yor* 3F **99**
Niddrie. *Edin* 2G **129**
Niddry. *W Lot* 2D **129**
Nigg. *Aber* 3G **153**
Nigg. *High* 1C **158**
Nigg Ferry. *High* 2B **158**
Nightcott. *Som* 4B **20**
Nimmer. *Som* 1G **13**
Nine Ashes. *Essx* 5F **53**
Ninebanks. *Nmbd* 4A **114**
Nine Elms. *Swin* 3G **35**
Ninemile Bar. *Dum* 2F **111**
Nine Mile Burn. *Midl* 4E **129**
Ninfield. *E Sus* 4B **28**
Ningwood. *IOW* 4C **16**
Nisbet. *Bord* 2A **120**
Nisbet Hill. *Bord* 4D **130**
Niton. *IOW* 5D **16**
Nitshill. *Glas* 3G **127**
Niwbwrch. *IOA* 4D **80**
Noak Hill. *G Lon* 1G **39**
Nobold. *Shrp* 4G **71**
Nobottle. *Nptn* 4D **62**
Nocton. *Linc* 4H **87**
Nogdam End. *Norf* 5F **79**
Noke. *Oxon* 4D **50**
Nolton. *Pemb* 3C **42**
Nolton Haven. *Pemb* 3C **42**
No Man's Heath. *Ches W* 1H **71**
No Man's Heath. *Warw* 5G **73**
Nomansland. *Devn* 1B **12**
Nomansland. *Wilts* 1A **16**
Noneley. *Shrp* 3G **71**
Noness. *Shet* 9F **173**
Nonikilin. *High* 1A **158**
Nonington. *Kent* 5G **41**
Nook. *Cumb*
  nr. Longtown 2F **113**
  nr. Milnthorpe 1E **97**
Noranside. *Ang* 2D **144**
Norbreck. *Bkpl* 5C **96**
Norbridge. *Here* 1C **48**
Norbury. *Ches E* 1H **71**
Norbury. *Derbs* 1F **73**
Norbury. *Shrp* 1F **59**
Norbury. *Staf* 3B **72**
Norby. *N Yor* 1G **99**
Norby. *Shet* 6C **173**
Norcross. *Lanc* 5C **96**
Nordelph. *Norf* 5E **77**
Norden. *G Man* 3G **91**
Nordley. *Shrp* 1A **60**
Norham. *Nmbd* 5F **131**
Norland Town. *W Yor* 2A **92**
Norley. *Ches W* 3H **83**
Norleywood. *Hants* 3B **16**

Normanby. *N Lin* 3B **94**
Normanby. *N Yor* 1B **100**
Normanby. *Red C* 3C **106**
Normanby-by-Spital. *Linc* 2H **87**
Normanby le Wold. *Linc* 1A **88**
Norman Cross. *Cambs* 1A **64**
Norman's Bay. *E Sus* 5A **28**
Norman's Green. *Devn* 2D **12**
Normanton. *Derb* 2H **73**
Normanton. *Leics* 1F **75**
Normanton. *Notts* 5E **86**
Normanton. *W Yor* 2D **93**
Normanton le Heath. *Leics* 4A **74**
Normanton-on-Cliffe. *Linc* 1G **75**
Normanton on Soar. *Notts* 3C **74**
Normanton-on-the-Wolds.
  Notts 2D **74**
Normanton on Trent. *Notts* 4E **87**
Normoss. *Lanc* 1B **90**
Norrington Common. *Wilts* 5D **35**
Norris Green. *Mers* 1F **83**
Norris Hill. *Leics* 4H **73**
Norristhorpe. *W Yor* 2C **92**
Northacre. *Norf* 1B **66**
Northall. *Buck* 3H **51**
Northallerton. *N Yor* 5A **106**
Northam. *Devn* 4E **19**
Northam. *Sotn* 1C **16**
Northampton. *Nptn* **206** (4E **63**)
North Anston. *S Yor* 2C **86**
North Ascot. *Brac* 4A **38**
North Aston. *Oxon* 3C **50**
Northaw. *Herts* 5C **52**
Northay. *Som* 1F **13**
North Baddesley. *Hants* 4B **24**
North Balfern. *Dum* 4B **110**
North Ballachulish. *High* 2E **141**
North Barrow. *Som* 4B **22**
North Barsham. *Norf* 2B **78**
Northbeck. *Linc* 1H **75**
North Benfleet. *Essx* 2B **40**
North Bersted. *W Sus* 5A **26**
North Berwick. *E Lot* 1B **130**
North Bitchburn. *Dur* 1E **105**
North Blyth. *Nmbd* 1G **115**
North Boarhunt. *Hants* 1E **16**
North Bockhampton. *Dors* 3G **15**
Northborough. *Pet* 5A **76**
Northbourne. *Kent* 5H **41**
Northbourne. *Oxon* 3D **36**
North Bovey. *Devn* 4H **11**
North Bowood. *Dors* 3H **13**
North Bradley. *Wilts* 1D **22**
North Brentor. *Devn* 4E **11**
North Brewham. *Som* 3C **22**
Northbrook. *Oxon* 3C **50**
North Brook End. *Cambs* 1C **52**
North Broomhill. *Nmbd* 4G **121**
North Buckland. *Devn* 2E **19**
North Burlingham. *Norf* 4F **79**
North Cadbury. *Som* 4B **22**
North Carlton. *Linc* 3G **87**
North Cave. *E Yor* 1B **94**
North Cerney. *Glos* 5F **49**
North Chailey. *E Sus* 3E **27**
Northchapel. *W Sus* 3A **26**
North Charford. *Hants* 1G **15**
North Charlton. *Nmbd* 2F **121**
North Cheriton. *Som* 4B **22**
North Chideock. *Dors* 3H **13**
Northchurch. *Herts* 5H **51**
North Cliffe. *E Yor* 1B **94**
North Clifton. *Notts* 3F **87**
North Close. *Dur* 1F **105**
North Cockerington. *Linc* 1C **88**
North Coker. *Som* 1A **14**
North Collafirth. *Shet* 3E **173**
North Common. *E Sus* 3E **27**
North Commonty. *Abers* 4F **161**
North Coombe. *Devn* 1B **12**
North Cornelly. *B'end* 3B **32**
North Cotes. *Linc* 4G **95**
Northcott. *Devn*
  nr. Boyton 3D **10**
  nr. Culmstock 1D **12**
Northcourt. *Oxon* 2D **36**
North Cove. *Suff* 2G **67**
North Cowton. *N Yor* 4F **105**
North Craigo. *Ang* 2F **145**
North Crawley. *Mil* 1H **51**
North Cray. *G Lon* 3F **39**
North Creake. *Norf* 2A **78**
North Curry. *Som* 4G **21**
North Dalton. *E Yor* 4D **100**
North Deighton. *N Yor* 4F **99**
North Dronley. *Ang* 5C **144**
North Duffield. *N Yor* 1G **93**
Northdyke. *Orkn* 5B **172**
Northedge. *Derbs* 4A **86**
North Elkington. *Linc* 1B **88**
North Elmham. *Norf* 3B **78**
North Elmsall. *W Yor* 3E **93**
Northend. *Buck* 2F **37**
North End. *E Yor* 1F **95**
North End. *Essx*
  nr. Great Dunmow 4G **53**
  nr. Great Yeldham 2A **54**
North End. *Hants* 5C **36**
North End. *Leics* 4C **74**
North End. *Linc* 1B **76**
North End. *Norf* 1B **66**
North End. *N Som* 5H **33**
North End. *Port* 2E **17**
Northend. *Warw* 5A **62**
North End. *W Sus* 5C **26**
North End. *Wilts* 2F **35**
North Erradale. *High* 5B **162**
North Evington. *Leic* 5D **74**
North Fambridge. *Essx* 1C **40**
North Fearns. *High* 5E **155**

North Featherstone. *W Yor* 2E **93**
North Ferriby. *E Yor* 2C **94**
North Feorline. *N Ayr* 3D **122**
Northfield. *Aber* 3F **153**
Northfield. *E Yor* 2D **94**
Northfield. *Som* 3F **21**
Northfield. *W Mid* 3E **61**
Northfleet. *Kent* 3H **39**
North Frodingham. *E Yor* 4F **101**
Northgate. *Linc* 3A **76**
North Gluss. *Shet* 4E **173**
North Gorley. *Hants* 1G **15**
North Green. *Norf* 2E **66**
North Green. *Suff*
  nr. Framlingham 4F **67**
  nr. Halesworth 3F **67**
  nr. Saxmundham 4F **67**
North Greetwell. *Linc* 3H **87**
North Grimston. *N Yor* 3C **100**
North Halling. *Medw* 4B **40**
North Hayling. *Hants* 2F **17**
North Hazelrigg. *Nmbd* 1E **121**
North Heasley. *Devn* 3H **19**
North Heath. *W Sus* 3B **26**
North Hill. *Corn* 5C **10**
North Holmwood. *Surr* 1C **26**
North Huish. *Devn* 3D **8**
North Hykeham. *Linc* 4G **87**
Northiam. *E Sus* 3C **28**
Northill. *C Beds* 1B **52**
Northington. *Hants* 3D **24**
North Kelsey. *Linc* 4D **94**
North Kelsey Moor. *Linc* 4D **94**
North Kessock. *High* 4A **158**
North Killingholme. *N Lin* 3E **95**
North Kilvington. *N Yor* 1G **99**
North Kilworth. *Leics* 2D **62**
North Kyme. *Linc* 5A **88**
North Lancing. *W Sus* 5C **26**
Northlands. *Linc* 5C **88**
Northleach. *Glos* 4G **49**
North Lee. *Buck* 5G **51**
North Lees. *N Yor* 2E **99**
Northleigh. *Devn*
  nr. Barnstaple 3G **19**
  nr. Honiton 3E **13**
North Leigh. *Kent* 1F **29**
North Leigh. *Oxon* 4B **50**
North Leverton. *Notts* 2E **87**
Northlew. *Devn* 3F **11**
North Littleton. *Worc* 1F **49**
North Lopham. *Norf* 2C **66**
North Luffenham. *Rut* 5G **75**
North Marden. *W Sus* 1G **17**
North Marston. *Buck* 3F **51**
North Middleton. *Midl* 4G **129**
North Middleton. *Nmbd* 2E **121**
North Molton. *Devn* 4H **19**
North Moor. *N Yor* 1D **100**
Northmoor. *Oxon* 5C **50**
Northmoor Green. *Som* 3G **21**
North Moreton. *Oxon* 3D **36**
Northmuir. *Ang* 3C **144**
North Mundham. *W Sus* 2G **17**
North Murie. *Per* 1E **137**
North Muskham. *Notts* 5E **87**
North Ness. *Orkn* 8C **172**
North Newbald. *E Yor* 1C **94**
North Newington. *Oxon* 2C **50**
North Newnton. *Wilts* 1G **23**
North Newton. *Som* 3F **21**
Northney. *Hants* 2F **17**
North Nibley. *Glos* 2C **34**
North Oakley. *Hants* 1D **24**
North Ockendon. *G Lon* 2G **39**
Northolt. *G Lon* 2C **38**
Northop. *Flin* 4E **83**
Northop Hall. *Flin* 4E **83**
North Ormesby. *Midd* 3C **106**
North Ormsby. *Linc* 1B **88**
Northorpe. *Linc*
  nr. Bourne 4H **75**
  nr. Donington 2B **76**
  nr. Gainsborough 1F **87**
North Otterington. *N Yor* 1F **99**
Northover. *Som*
  nr. Glastonbury 3H **21**
  nr. Yeovil 4A **22**
North Owersby. *Linc* 1H **87**
Northowram. *W Yor* 2B **92**
North Perrott. *Som* 2H **13**
North Petherton. *Som* 3F **21**
North Petherwin. *Corn* 4C **10**
North Pickenham. *Norf* 5A **78**
North Piddle. *Worc* 5D **60**
North Poorton. *Dors* 3A **14**
North Port. *Arg* 1H **133**
Northport. *Dors* 4E **15**
North Queensferry. *Fife* 1E **129**
North Radworthy. *Devn* 3A **20**
North Rauceby. *Linc* 1H **75**
Northrepps. *Norf* 2E **79**
North Rigton. *N Yor* 5E **99**
North Rode. *Ches E* 4C **84**
North Roe. *Shet* 3E **173**
North Ronaldsay Airport.
  Orkn 2G **172**
North Row. *Cumb* 1D **102**
North Runcton. *Norf* 4F **77**
North Sannox. *N Ayr* 5B **126**
North Scale. *Cumb* 2A **96**
North Scarle. *Linc* 4F **87**
North Seaton. *Nmbd* 1F **115**
North Seaton Colliery. *Nmbd* . . .1F **115**
North Sheen. *G Lon* 3C **38**
North Shian. *Arg* 4D **140**
North Shields. *Tyne* 3G **115**
North Shoebury. *S'end* 2D **40**
North Shore. *Bkpl* 1B **90**
North Side. *Cumb* 2B **102**
North Skelton. *Red C* 3D **106**

North Somercotes. *Linc* 1D **88**
North Stainley. *N Yor* 2E **99**
North Stainmore. *Cumb* 3B **104**
North Stifford. *Thur* 2H **39**
North Stoke. *Bath* 5C **34**
North Stoke. *Oxon* 3E **36**
North Stoke. *W Sus* 4B **26**
Northstowe. *Cambs* 4D **64**
North Street. *Hants* 3E **25**
North Street. *Kent* 5E **40**
North Street. *Medw* 3C **40**
North Street. *W Ber* 4E **37**
North Sunderland. *Nmbd* 1G **121**
North Tamerton. *Corn* 3D **10**
North Tawton. *Devn* 2G **11**
North Thoresby. *Linc* 1B **88**
North Tidworth. *Wilts* 2H **23**
North Town. *Devn* 2F **11**
Northtown. *Orkn* 8D **172**
North Town. *Shet* 10E **173**
North Walbottle. *Tyne* 3E **115**
Northwall. *Orkn* 3G **172**
North Walney. *Cumb* 3A **96**
North Walsham. *Norf* 2E **79**
North Waltham. *Hants* 2D **24**
North Warnborough. *Hants* 1F **25**
North Water Bridge. *Ang* 2F **145**
North Watten. *High* 3E **169**
Northway. *Glos* 2E **49**
Northway. *Swan* 4E **31**
North Weald Bassett. *Essx* 5F **53**
North Weston. *N Som* 4H **33**
North Weston. *Oxon* 5E **51**
North Wheatley. *Notts* 2E **87**
North Whilborough. *Devn* 2E **9**
Northwich. *Ches W* 3A **84**
North Wick. *Bath* 5A **34**
Northwick. *Som* 2G **21**
Northwick. *S Glo* 3A **34**
North Widcombe. *Bath* 1A **22**
North Willingham. *Linc* 2A **88**
North Wingfield. *Derbs* 4B **86**
North Witham. *Linc* 3G **75**
Northwold. *Norf* 1G **65**
Northwood. *Derbs* 4G **85**
Northwood. *G Lon* 1B **38**
Northwood. *IOW* 3C **16**
Northwood. *Kent* 4H **41**
Northwood. *Shrp* 2G **71**
Northwood. *Stoke* 1C **72**
Northwood Green. *Glos* 4C **48**
North Wootton. *Dors* 1B **14**
North Wootton. *Norf* 3F **77**
North Wootton. *Som* 2A **22**
North Wraxall. *Wilts* 4D **34**
North Wroughton. *Swin* 3G **35**
North Yardhope. *Nmbd* 4D **120**
Norton. *Devn* 3E **9**
Norton. *Glos* 3D **48**
Norton. *Hal* 2H **83**
Norton. *Herts* 2C **52**
Norton. *IOW* 4B **16**
Norton. *Mon* 3H **47**
Norton. *Nptn* 4D **62**
Norton. *Notts* 3C **86**
Norton. *Powy* 4F **59**
Norton. *Shrp*
  nr. Ludlow 2G **59**
  nr. Madeley 5B **72**
  nr. Shrewsbury 5H **71**
Norton. *S Yor*
  nr. Askern 3F **93**
  nr. Sheffield 2A **86**
Norton. *Stoc T* 2B **106**
Norton. *Suff* 4B **66**
Norton. *Swan* 4F **31**
Norton. *W Sus*
  nr. Selsey 3G **17**
  nr. Westergate 5A **26**
Norton. *Wilts* 3D **35**
Norton. *Worc*
  nr. Evesham 1F **49**
  nr. Worcester 5C **60**
Norton Bavant. *Wilts* 2E **23**
Norton Bridge. *Staf* 2C **72**
Norton Canes. *Staf* 5E **73**
Norton Canon. *Here* 1G **47**
Norton Corner. *Norf* 3C **78**
Norton Disney. *Linc* 5F **87**
Norton East. *Staf* 5E **73**
Norton Ferris. *Wilts* 3C **22**
Norton Fitzwarren. *Som* 4F **21**
Norton Green. *IOW* 4B **16**
Norton Green. *Stoke* 5D **84**
Norton Hawkfield. *Bath* 5A **34**
Norton Heath. *Essx* 5F **53**
Norton in Hales. *Shrp* 2B **72**
Norton in the Moors. *Stoke* 5C **84**
Norton-Juxta-Twycross. *Leics* . . .5H **73**
Norton-le-Clay. *N Yor* 2G **99**
Norton Lindsey. *Warw* 4G **61**
Norton Little Green. *Suff* 4B **66**
Norton Malreward. *Bath* 5B **34**
Norton Mandeville. *Essx* 5F **53**
Norton-on-Derwent. *N Yor* 2B **100**
Norton St Philip. *Som* 1C **22**
Norton Subcourse. *Norf* 1G **67**
Norton sub Hamdon. *Som* 1H **13**
Norton Woodseats. *S Yor* 2A **86**
Norwell. *Notts* 4E **87**
Norwell Woodhouse. *Notts* 4E **87**
Norwich. *Norf* **205** (5E **79**)
Norwich Airport. *Norf* 4E **79**
Norwick. *Shet* 1H **173**
Norwood. *Derbs* 2B **86**
Norwood Green. *W Yor* 2B **92**
Norwood Hill. *Surr* 1D **26**
Norwood Park. *Som* 3A **22**
Norwoodside. *Cambs* 1D **64**
Noseley. *Leics* 1E **63**

Noss. Shet ...10E 173
Noss Mayo. Devn ...4B 8
Nosterfield. N Yor ...1E 99
Nostie. High ...1A 148
Notgrove. Glos ...3G 49
Nottage. B'end ...4B 32
Nottingham. Nott ...**206** (1C 74)
Nottington. Dors ...4B 14
Notton. Dors ...3B 14
Notton. W Yor ...3D 92
Notton. Wilts ...5E 35
Nounsley. Essx ...4A 54
Noutard's Green. Worc ...4B 60
Nox. Shrp ...4G 71
Noyadd Trefawr. Cdgn ...1C 44
Nuffield. Oxon ...3E 37
Nunburnholme. E Yor ...5C 100
Nuncargate. Notts ...5C 86
Nunclose. Cumb ...5F 113
Nuneaton. Warw ...1A 62
Nuneham Courtenay. Oxon ...2D 36
Nun Monkton. N Yor ...4H 99
Nunnerie. S Lan ...3B 118
Nunney. Som ...2C 22
Nunnington. N Yor ...2A 100
Nunnykirk. Nmbd ...5E 121
Nunsthorpe. NE Lin ...4F 95
Nunthorpe. Midd ...3C 106
Nunthorpe. York ...4H 99
Nunton. Wilts ...4G 23
Nunwick. Nmbd ...2B 114
Nunwick. N Yor ...2F 99
Nupend. Glos ...5C 48
Nursling. Hants ...1B 16
Nursted. Hants ...4F 25
Nursteed. Wilts ...5F 35
Nurston. V Glam ...5D 32
Nutbourne. W Sus
  nr. Chichester ...2F 17
  nr. Pulborough ...4B 26
Nutfield. Surr ...5E 39
Nuthall. Notts ...1C 74
Nuthampstead. Herts ...2E 53
Nuthurst. Warw ...3F 61
Nuthurst. W Sus ...3C 26
Nutley. E Sus ...3F 27
Nuttall. G Man ...3F 91
Nutwell. S Yor ...4G 93
Nybster. High ...2F 169
Nyetimber. W Sus ...3G 17
Nyewood. W Sus ...4G 25
Nymet Rowland. Devn ...2H 11
Nymet Tracey. Devn ...2H 11
Nympsfield. Glos ...5D 48
Nynehead. Som ...4E 21
Nyton. W Sus ...5A 26

O

Oadby. Leics ...5D 74
Oad Street. Kent ...4C 40
Oakamoor. Staf ...1E 73
Oakbank. Arg ...5B 140
Oakbank. W Lot ...3D 129
Oakdale. Cphy ...2E 33
Oakdale. Pool ...3F 15
Oake. Som ...4E 21
Oaken. Staf ...5C 72
Oakenclough. Lanc ...5E 97
Oakengates. Telf ...4A 72
Oakenholt. Flin ...3E 83
Oakenshaw. Dur ...1F 105
Oakenshaw. W Yor ...2B 92
Oakerthorpe. Derbs ...5A 86
Oakford. Cdgn ...5D 56
Oakford. Devn ...4C 20
Oakfordbridge. Devn ...4C 20
Oakgrove. Ches E ...4D 84
Oakham. Rut ...5F 75
Oakhanger. Ches E ...5B 84
Oakhanger. Hants ...3F 25
Oakhill. Som ...2B 22
Oakington. Cambs ...4D 64
Oaklands. Powy ...5C 58
Oakle Street. Glos ...4C 48
Oakley. Bed ...5H 63
Oakley. Buck ...4E 51
Oakley. Fife ...1D 128
Oakley. Hants ...1D 24
Oakley. Suff ...3D 66
Oakley Green. Wind ...3A 38
Oakley Park. Powy ...2B 58
Oakmere. Ches W ...4H 83
Oakridge Lynch. Glos ...5E 49
Oaks. Shrp ...5G 71
Oaksey. Wilts ...2E 35
Oaks Green. Derbs ...2F 73
Oakshaw Ford. Cumb ...2G 113
Oakshott. Hants ...4F 25
Oakthorpe. Leics ...4H 73
Oak Tree. Darl ...3A 106
Oakwood. Derb ...2A 74
Oakwood. W Yor ...1D 92
Oakwoodhill. Surr ...2C 26
Oakworth. W Yor ...1A 92
Oape. High ...3B 164
Oare. Kent ...4E 40
Oare. Som ...2B 20
Oare. W Ber ...4D 36
Oare. Wilts ...5G 35
Oareford. Som ...2B 20
Oasby. Linc ...2H 75
Oath. Som ...4G 21
Oathlaw. Ang ...3D 145
Oatlands. N Yor ...4F 99
Oban. Arg ...**206** (1F 133)
Oban. W Isl ...7D 171
Oborne. Dors ...1B 14
Obsdale. High ...2A 158
Obthorpe. Linc ...4H 75

Occlestone Green. Ches W ...4A 84
Occold. Suff ...3D 66
Ochiltree. E Ayr ...2E 117
Ochtermuthill. Per ...2H 135
Ochtertyre. Per ...1H 135
Ockbrook. Derbs ...2B 74
Ockeridge. Worc ...4B 60
Ockham. Surr ...5B 38
Ockle. High ...1G 139
Ockley. Surr ...1C 26
Ocle Pychard. Here ...1A 48
Octofad. Arg ...4A 124
Octomore. Arg ...4A 124
Octon. E Yor ...3E 101
Odcombe. Som ...1A 14
Odd Down. Bath ...5C 34
Oddingley. Worc ...5D 60
Oddington. Oxon ...4D 50
Oddsta. Shet ...2G 173
Odell. Bed ...5G 63
Odie. Orkn ...5F 172
Odiham. Hants ...1F 25
Odsey. Cambs ...2C 52
Odstock. Wilts ...4G 23
Odstone. Leics ...5A 74
Offchurch. Warw ...4A 62
Offenham. Worc ...1F 49
Offenham Cross. Worc ...1F 49
Offerton. G Man ...2D 84
Offerton. Tyne ...4G 115
Offham. E Sus ...4E 27
Offham. Kent ...5A 40
Offham. W Sus ...5B 26
Offleyhay. Staf ...3C 72
Offley Hoo. Herts ...3B 52
Offleymarsh. Staf ...3B 72
Offord Cluny. Cambs ...4B 64
Offord D'Arcy. Cambs ...4B 64
Offton. Suff ...1D 54
Offwell. Devn ...3E 13
Ogbourne Maizey. Wilts ...4G 35
Ogbourne St Andrew.
  Wilts ...4G 35
Ogbourne St George.
  Wilts ...4H 35
Ogden. G Man ...3H 91
Ogle. Nmbd ...2E 115
Ogmore. V Glam ...4B 32
Ogmore-by-Sea. V Glam ...4B 32
Ogmore Vale. B'end ...2C 32
Okeford Fitzpaine. Dors ...1D 14
Okehampton. Devn ...3F 11
Okehampton Camp. Devn ...3F 11
Okraquoy. Shet ...8F 173
Okus. Swin ...3G 35
Old. Nptn ...3E 63
Old Aberdeen. Aber ...3G 153
Old Alresford. Hants ...3D 24
Oldany. High ...5B 166
Old Arley. Warw ...1G 61
Old Basford. Nott ...1C 74
Old Basing. Hants ...1E 25
Oldberrow. Warw ...4F 61
Old Bewick. Nmbd ...2E 121
Old Bexley. G Lon ...3F 39
Old Blair. Per ...2F 143
Old Bolingbroke. Linc ...4C 88
Oldborough. Devn ...2A 12
Old Brampton. Derbs ...3H 85
Old Bridge of Tilt. Per ...2F 143
Old Bridge of Urr. Dum ...3E 111
Old Brumby. N Lin ...4B 94
Old Buckenham. Norf ...1C 66
Old Burghclere. Hants ...1C 24
Oldbury. Shrp ...1B 60
Oldbury. Warw ...1H 61
Oldbury. W Mid ...2D 61
Oldbury-on-Severn. S Glo ...2B 34
Oldbury on the Hill. Glos ...3D 34
Old Byland. N Yor ...1H 99
Old Cassop. Dur ...1A 106
Oldcastle. Mon ...3G 47
Oldcastle Heath. Ches W ...1G 71
Old Catton. Norf ...4E 79
Old Clee. NE Lin ...4F 95
Old Cleeve. Som ...2D 20
Old Colwyn. Cnwy ...3A 82
Oldcotes. Notts ...2C 86
Old Coulsdon. G Lon ...5E 39
Old Dailly. S Ayr ...5B 116
Old Dalby. Leics ...3D 74
Old Dam. Derbs ...3F 85
Old Deer. Abers ...4G 161
Old Dilton. Wilts ...2D 22
Old Down. S Glo ...3B 34
Oldeamere. Cambs ...1C 64
Old Edlington. S Yor ...1C 86
Old Eldon. Dur ...2F 105
Old Ellerby. E Yor ...1E 95
Old Fallings. W Mid ...5D 72
Oldfallow. Staf ...4D 73
Old Felixstowe. Suff ...2G 55
Oldfield. Shrp ...2A 60
Oldfield. Worc ...4C 60
Old Fletton. Pet ...1A 64
Oldford. Som ...1C 22
Old Forge. Here ...4A 48
Old Glossop. Derbs ...1E 85
Old Goole. E Yor ...2H 93
Old Gore. Here ...3B 48
Old Graitney. Dum ...3E 112
Old Grimsby. IOS ...1A 4
Oldhall. High ...3E 169
Old Hall Street. Norf ...2F 79
Oldham. G Man ...4H 91
Oldhamstocks. E Lot ...2D 130
Old Heathfield. E Sus ...3G 27
Old Hill. W Mid ...2D 60
Old Hunstanton. Norf ...1F 77
Oldhurst. Cambs ...3B 64
Old Hutton. Cumb ...1E 97

Old Kea. Corn ...4C 6
Old Kilpatrick. W Dun ...2F 127
Old Kinnernie. Abers ...3E 152
Old Knebworth. Herts ...3C 52
Oldland. S Glo ...4B 34
Old Laxey. IOM ...3D 108
Old Leake. Linc ...5D 88
Old Lenton. Nott ...2C 74
Old Llanberis. Gwyn ...5F 81
Old Malton. N Yor ...2B 100
Oldmeldrum. Abers ...1F 153
Old Micklefield. W Yor ...1E 93
Old Mill. Corn ...5D 10
Oldmixon. N Som ...1G 21
Old Monkland. N Lan ...3A 128
Old Newton. Suff ...4C 66
Old Park. Telf ...5A 72
Old Pentland. Midl ...3F 129
Old Philpstoun. W Lot ...2D 128
Old Quarrington. Dur ...1A 106
Old Radnor. Powy ...5E 59
Old Rayne. Abers ...1D 152
Oldridge. Devn ...3B 12
Old Romney. Kent ...3E 29
Old Scone. Per ...1D 136
Oldshore Beg. High ...3B 166
Oldshoremore. High ...3C 166
Old Snydale. W Yor ...2E 93
Old Sodbury. S Glo ...3C 34
Old Somerby. Linc ...2G 75
Old Spital. Dur ...3C 104
Oldstead. N Yor ...1H 99
Old Stratford. Nptn ...1F 51
Old Swan. Mers ...1F 83
Old Swarland. Nmbd ...4F 121
Old Tebay. Cumb ...4H 103
Old Town. Cumb ...5F 113
Old Town. E Sus ...5G 27
Oldtown. High ...5C 164
Old Town. IOS ...1B 4
Old Trafford. G Man ...1C 84
Old Tupton. Derbs ...4A 86
Oldwall. Cumb ...3F 113
Oldwalls. Swan ...3D 31
Old Warden. C Beds ...1B 52
Oldways End. Som ...4B 20
Old Westhall. Abers ...1D 152
Old Weston. Cambs ...3H 63
Oldwhat. Abers ...3F 161
Old Windsor. Wind ...3A 38
Old Wives Lees. Kent ...5E 41
Old Woking. Surr ...5B 38
Oldwood Common. Worc ...4H 59
Old Woodstock. Oxon ...4C 50
Olgrinmore. High ...3C 168
Oliver's Battery. Hants ...4C 24
Ollaberry. Shet ...3E 173
Ollerton. Ches E ...3B 84
Ollerton. Notts ...4D 86
Ollerton. Shrp ...3A 72
Olmarch. Cdgn ...5F 57
Olmstead Green. Cambs ...1G 53
Olney. Mil ...5F 63
Olrig. High ...2D 169
Olton. W Mid ...2F 61
Olveston. S Glo ...3B 34
Ombersley. Worc ...4C 60
Ompton. Notts ...4D 86
Omunsgarth. Shet ...7E 173
Onchan. IOM ...4D 108
Onecote. Staf ...5E 85
Onehouse. Suff ...5C 66
Onen. Mon ...4H 47
Ongar Hill. Norf ...3E 77
Ongar Street. Here ...4F 59
Onibury. Shrp ...3G 59
Onich. High ...2E 141
Onllwyn. Neat ...4B 46
Onneley. Staf ...1B 72
Onslow Green. Essx ...4G 53
Onslow Village. Surr ...1A 26
Onthank. E Ayr ...1D 116
Openwoodgate. Derbs ...1A 74
Opinan. High
  nr. Gairloch ...1G 155
  nr. Laide ...4C 162
Orasaigh. W Isl ...6F 171
Orbost. High ...4B 154
Orby. Linc ...4D 89
Orchard Hill. Devn ...4E 19
Orchard Portman.
  Som ...4F 21
Orcheston. Wilts ...2F 23
Orcop. Here ...3H 47
Orcop Hill. Here ...3H 47
Ord. High ...2E 147
Ordale. Shet ...1H 173
Ordhead. Abers ...2D 152
Ordie. Abers ...3B 152
Ordiquish. Mor ...3H 159
Ordley. Nmbd ...4C 114
Ordsall. Notts ...3E 86
Ore. E Sus ...4C 28
Oreton. Shrp ...2A 60
Orford. Suff ...1H 55
Orford. Warr ...1A 84
Organford. Dors ...3E 15
Orgil. Orkn ...7B 172
Orgreave. Staf ...4F 73
Oridge Street. Glos ...3C 48
Orlestone. Kent ...2D 28
Orleton. Here ...4G 59
Orleton. Worc ...4A 60
Orleton Common. Here ...4G 59
Orlingbury. Nptn ...3F 63
Ormacleit. W Isl ...5C 170
Ormathwaite. Cumb ...2D 102
Ormesby. Red C ...3C 106
Ormesby St Margaret.
  Norf ...4G 79

Ormesby St Michael.
  Norf ...4G 79
Ormiscaig. High ...4C 162
Ormiston. E Lot ...3H 129
Ormsaigbeg. High ...2F 139
Ormsaigmore. High ...2F 139
Ormsary. Arg ...2F 125
Ormsgill. Cumb ...2A 96
Ormskirk. Lanc ...4C 90
Orphir. Orkn ...7C 172
Orpington. G Lon ...4F 39
Orrell. G Man ...4D 90
Orrell. Mers ...1F 83
Orrisdale. IOM ...2C 108
Orsett. Thur ...2H 39
Orslow. Staf ...4C 72
Orston. Notts ...1E 75
Orthwaite. Cumb ...1D 102
Orton. Cumb ...4H 103
Orton. Mor ...3H 159
Orton. Nptn ...3F 63
Orton. Staf ...1C 60
Orton Longueville. Pet ...1A 64
Orton-on-the-Hill. Leics ...5H 73
Orton Waterville. Pet ...1A 64
Orton Wistow. Pet ...1A 64
Orwell. Cambs ...5C 64
Osbaldeston. Lanc ...1E 91
Osbaldwick. York ...4A 100
Osbaston. Leics ...5B 74
Osbaston. Shrp ...3F 71
Osbournby. Linc ...2H 75
Osclay. High ...5E 169
Oscroft. Ches W ...4H 83
Ose. High ...4C 154
Osgathorpe. Leics ...4B 74
Osgodby. Linc ...1H 87
Osgodby. N Yor
  nr. Scarborough ...1E 101
  nr. Selby ...1G 93
Oskaig. High ...5E 155
Oskamull. Arg ...5F 139
Osleston. Derbs ...2G 73
Osmaston. Derb ...2A 74
Osmaston. Derbs ...1G 73
Osmington. Dors ...4C 14
Osmington Mills. Dors ...4C 14
Osmondthorpe. W Yor ...1D 92
Osmondwall. Orkn ...9C 172
Osmotherley. N Yor ...5B 106
Osnaburgh. Fife ...2G 137
Ospisdale. High ...5E 164
Ospringe. Kent ...4E 40
Ossett. W Yor ...2C 92
Ossington. Notts ...4E 87
Ostend. Essx ...1D 40
Ostend. Norf ...2F 79
Osterley. G Lon ...3C 38
Oswaldkirk. N Yor ...2A 100
Oswaldtwistle. Lanc ...2F 91
Oswestry. Shrp ...3E 71
Otby. Linc ...1A 88
Otford. Kent ...5G 39
Otham. Kent ...5B 40
Otherton. Staf ...4D 72
Othery. Som ...3G 21
Otley. Suff ...5E 66
Otley. W Yor ...5E 98
Otterbourne. Hants ...4C 24
Otterburn. Nmbd ...5C 120
Otterburn. N Yor ...4A 98
Otterburn Camp.
  Nmbd ...5C 120
Otterburn Hall. Nmbd ...5C 120
Otter Ferry. Arg ...1H 125
Otterford. Som ...1F 13
Otterham. Corn ...3B 10
Otterhampton. Som ...2F 21
Otterham Quay. Medw ...4C 40
Ottershaw. Surr ...4B 38
Otterspool. Mers ...2F 83
Otterswick. Shet ...3G 173
Otterton. Devn ...4D 12
Otterwood. Hants ...2C 16
Ottery St Mary. Devn ...3D 12
Ottinge. Kent ...1F 29
Ottringham. E Yor ...2F 95
Oughterby. Cumb ...4D 112
Oughtershaw. N Yor ...1A 98
Oughterside. Cumb ...5C 112
Oughtibridge. S Yor ...1H 85
Oughtrington. Warr ...2A 84
Oulston. N Yor ...2H 99
Oulton. Cumb ...4D 112
Oulton. Norf ...3D 78
Oulton. Staf
  nr. Gnosall Heath ...3B 72
  nr. Stone ...2B 72
Oulton. Suff ...1H 67
Oulton. W Yor ...2D 92
Oulton Broad. Suff ...1H 67
Oulton Street. Norf ...3D 78
Oundle. Nptn ...2H 63
Ousby. Cumb ...1H 103
Ousdale. High ...2H 165
Ousden. Suff ...5G 65
Ousefleet. E Yor ...2B 94
Ouston. Dur ...4F 115
Ouston. Nmbd
  nr. Bearsbridge ...4A 114
  nr. Stamfordham ...2D 114
Outer Hope. Devn ...4C 8
Outertown. Orkn ...6B 172
Outgate. Cumb ...5E 103
Outhgill. Cumb ...4A 104
Outlands. Staf ...2B 72
Outlane. W Yor ...3A 92
Out Newton. E Yor ...2G 95
Out Rawcliffe. Lanc ...5D 96
Outwell. Norf ...5E 77
Outwick. Hants ...1G 15

Outwood. Surr ...1E 27
Outwood. W Yor ...2D 92
Outwood. Worc ...3D 60
Outwoods. Leics ...4B 74
Outwoods. Staf ...4B 72
Ouzlewell Green.
  W Yor ...2D 92
Ovenden. W Yor ...2A 92
Over. Cambs ...3C 64
Over. Ches W ...4A 84
Over. Glos ...4D 48
Over. S Glo ...3A 34
Overbister. Orkn ...3F 172
Overbury. Worc ...2E 49
Overcombe. Dors ...4B 14
Over Compton. Dors ...1A 14
Over End. Cambs ...1H 63
Over Finlarg. Ang ...4D 144
Overgreen. Derbs ...3H 85
Over Green. Warw ...1F 61
Over Haddon. Derbs ...4G 85
Over Hulton. G Man ...4E 91
Over Kellet. Lanc ...2E 97
Over Kiddington. Oxon ...3C 50
Overleigh. Som ...3H 21
Overley. Staf ...4F 73
Over Monnow. Mon ...4A 48
Over Norton. Oxon ...3B 50
Over Peover. Ches E ...3B 84
Overpool. Ches W ...3F 83
Overscaig. High ...1B 164
Overseal. Derbs ...4G 73
Over Silton. N Yor ...5B 106
Oversland. Kent ...5E 41
Overstone. Nptn ...4F 63
Over Stowey. Som ...3E 21
Overstrand. Norf ...1E 79
Over Stratton. Som ...1H 13
Over Street. Wilts ...3F 23
Overthorpe. Nptn ...1C 50
Overton. Aber ...2F 153
Overton. Ches W ...3H 83
Overton. Hants ...2D 24
Overton. Lanc ...4D 96
Overton. N Yor ...4H 99
Overton. Shrp
  nr. Bridgnorth ...2A 60
  nr. Ludlow ...3H 59
Overton. Swan ...4D 30
Overton. Wrex ...1F 71
Overtown. Lanc ...2F 97
Overtown. N Lan ...4B 128
Overtown. Swin ...4G 35
Over Wallop. Hants ...3A 24
Over Whitacre. Warw ...1G 61
Over Worton. Oxon ...3C 50
Oving. Buck ...3F 51
Oving. W Sus ...5A 26
Ovingdean. Brig ...5E 27
Ovingham. Nmbd ...3D 115
Ovington. Dur ...3E 105
Ovington. Essx ...1A 54
Ovington. Hants ...3D 24
Ovington. Norf ...5B 78
Ovington. Nmbd ...3D 114
Owen's Bank. Staf ...3G 73
Ower. Hants
  nr. Holbury ...2C 16
  nr. Totton ...1B 16
Owermoigne. Dors ...4C 14
Owlbury. Shrp ...1F 59
Owler Bar. Derbs ...3G 85
Owlerton. S Yor ...1H 85
Owlsmoor. Brac ...5G 37
Owlswick. Buck ...5F 51
Owmby. Linc ...4D 94
Owmby-by-Spital. Linc ...2H 87
Ownham. W Ber ...4C 36
Owrytn. Wrex ...1F 71
Owslebury. Hants ...4D 24
Owston. Leics ...5E 75
Owston. S Yor ...3F 93
Owston Ferry. N Lin ...4B 94
Owstwick. E Yor ...1F 95
Owthorne. E Yor ...2G 95
Owthorpe. Notts ...2D 74
Owton Manor. Hart ...2B 106
Oxborough. Norf ...5G 77
Oxbridge. Dors ...3H 13
Oxcombe. Linc ...3C 88
Oxen End. Essx ...3G 53
Oxenhall. Glos ...3C 48
Oxenholme. Cumb ...5G 103
Oxenhope. W Yor ...1A 92
Oxen Park. Cumb ...1C 96
Oxenpill. Som ...2H 21
Oxenton. Glos ...2E 49
Oxenwood. Wilts ...1B 24
Oxford. Oxon ...**207** (5D 50)
Oxgangs. Edin ...3F 129
Oxhey. Herts ...1C 38
Oxhill. Warw ...1B 50
Oxley. W Mid ...5D 72
Oxley Green. Essx ...4C 54
Oxley's Green. E Sus ...3A 28
Oxlode. Cambs ...2D 65
Oxnam. Bord ...3B 120
Oxshott. Surr ...4C 38
Oxspring. S Yor ...4C 92
Oxted. Surr ...5E 39
Oxton. Mers ...2F 83
Oxton. N Yor ...5H 99
Oxton. Notts ...5D 86
Oxton. Bord ...4A 130
Oxwich. Swan ...4D 31
Oxwich Green. Swan ...4D 31
Oxwick. Norf ...3B 78
Oykel Bridge. High ...3A 164

Oyne. Abers 1D 152
Oystermouth. Swan 4F 31
Ozleworth. Glos 2C 34

P

Pabail Iarach. W Isl 4H 171
Pabail Uarach. W Isl 4H 171
Pachesham Park. Surr 5C 38
Packers Hill. Dors 1C 14
Packington. Leics 4A 74
Packmoor. Stoke 5C 84
Packmores. Warw 4G 61
Packwood. W Mid 3F 61
Packwood Gullet. W Mid 3F 61
Padanaram. Ang 3D 144
Padbury. Buck 2F 51
Paddington. G Lon 2D 38
Paddington. Warr 2A 84
Paddlesworth. Kent 2F 29
Paddock. Kent 5D 40
Paddockhole. Dum 1D 112
Paddock Wood. Kent 1A 28
Paddolgreen. Shrp 2H 71
Padeswood. Flin 4E 83
Padiham. Lanc 1F 91
Padside. N Yor 4D 98
Padson. Devn 3F 11
Padstow. Corn 1D 6
Padworth. W Ber 5E 36
Page Bank. Dur 1F 105
Pagham. W Sus 3G 17
Paglesham Churchend. Essx 1D 40
Paglesham Eastend. Essx 1D 40
Paibeil. W Isl
  on North Uist 2C 170
  on Taransay 8C 171
Paiblesgearraidh. W Isl 2C 170
Paignton. Torb 2E 9
Pailton. Warw 2B 62
Paine's Corner. E Sus 3H 27
Painleyhill. Staf 2E 73
Painscastle. Powy 1E 47
Painshawfield. Nmbd 3D 114
Painsthorpe. E Yor 4C 100
Painswick. Glos 5D 48
Painter's Forstal. Kent 5D 40
Painthorpe. W Yor 3D 92
Pairc Shiaboist. W Isl 3E 171
Paisley. Ren 207 (3F 127)
Pakefield. Suff 1H 67
Pakenham. Suff 4B 66
Pale. Gwyn 2B 70
Palehouse Common. E Sus 4F 27
Palestine. Hants 2A 24
Paley Street. Wind 4G 37
Palgowan. Dum 1A 110
Palgrave. Suff 3D 66
Pallington. Dors 3C 14
Palmarsh. Kent 2F 29
Palmer Moor. Derbs 2F 73
Palmers Cross. W Mid 5C 72
Palmerstown. V Glam 5E 33
Palnackie. Dum 4F 111
Palnure. Dum 3B 110
Palterton. Derbs 4B 86
Pamber End. Hants 1E 24
Pamber Green. Hants 1E 24
Pamber Heath. Hants 5E 36
Pamington. Glos 2E 49
Pamphill. Dors 2E 15
Pampisford. Cambs 1E 53
Panborough. Som 2H 21
Panbride. Ang 5E 145
Pancrasweek. Devn 2C 10
Pandy. Gwyn
  nr. Bala 2A 70
  nr. Tywyn 5F 69
Pandy. Mon 3G 47
Pandy. Powy 5B 70
Pandy. Wrex 2D 70
Pandy Tudur. Cnwy 4A 82
Panfield. Essx 3H 53
Pangbourne. W Ber 4E 37
Pannal. N Yor 4F 99
Pannal Ash. N Yor 4F 99
Pannanich. Abers 4A 152
Pant. Shrp 3E 71
Pant. Wrex 1E 71
Pantasaph. Flin 3D 82
Pant Glas. Gwyn 1D 68
Pant-glas. Shrp 2E 71
Pantgwyn. Carm 3F 45
Pantgwyn. Cdgn 1C 44
Pant-lasau. Swan 5G 45
Panton. Linc 3A 88
Pant-pastynog. Den 4C 82
Pantperthog. Gwyn 5G 69
Pant-teg. Carm 3E 45
Pant-y-Caws. Carm 2F 43
Pant-y-dwr. Powy 3B 58
Pant-y-ffridd. Powy 5D 70
Pantyffynnon. Carm 4G 45
Pantygasseg. Torf 5F 47
Pant-yr-awel. B'end 3C 32
Pant y Wacco. Flin 3D 82
Panxworth. Norf 4F 79
Papa Stour Airport. Shet 6C 173
Papa Westray Airport. Orkn 2D 172
Papcastle. Cumb 1C 102
Papigoe. High 3F 169
Papil. Shet 8E 173
Papple. E Lot 2B 130
Papplewick. Notts 5C 86
Papworth Everard. Cambs 4B 64
Papworth St Agnes. Cambs 4B 64
Par. Corn 3E 7
Paramour Street. Kent 4G 41
Parbold. Lanc 3C 90

Parbrook. Som 3A 22
Parbrook. W Sus 3B 26
Parc. Gwyn 2A 70
Parclyn. Cdgn 5B 56
Parc-Seymour. Newp 2H 33
Pardown. Hants 2D 24
Pardshaw. Cumb 2B 102
Parham. Suff 4F 67
Park. Abers 4E 153
Park. Arg 4D 140
Park. Dum 5B 118
Park Bottom. Corn 4A 6
Parkburn. Abers 5E 161
Park Corner. E Sus 2G 27
Park Corner. Oxon 3E 37
Parkend. Glos 5B 48
Park End. Nmbd 2B 114
Parkeston. Essx 2F 55
Parkfield. Corn 2H 7
Parkgate. Ches W 3E 83
Parkgate. Cumb 5D 112
Parkgate. Dum 1B 112
Park Gate. Hants 2D 16
Parkgate. Surr 1D 26
Park Gate. Worc 3D 60
Parkhall. W Dun 2F 127
Parkham. Devn 4D 19
Parkham Ash. Devn 4D 18
Parkhead. Cumb 5E 113
Parkhead. Glas 3H 127
Park Hill. Mers 4C 90
Parkhouse. Mon 5A 48
Parkhurst. IOW 3C 16
Park Lane. G Man 4F 91
Park Lane. Staf 5C 72
Parkmill. W Yor 3C 92
Parkneuk. Abers 1G 145
Parkside. N Lan 4B 128
Parkstone. Pool 3F 15
Park Street. Herts 5B 52
Park Street. W Sus 2C 26
Park Town. Oxon 5D 50
Park Village. Nmbd 3H 113
Parkway. Here 2C 48
Parley Cross. Dors 3F 15
Parmoor. Buck 3F 37
Parr. Mers 1H 83
Parracombe. Devn 2G 19
Parrog. Pemb 1E 43
Parsonage Green. Essx 4H 53
Parsonby. Cumb 1C 102
Parson Cross. S Yor 1H 85
Parson Drove. Cambs 5C 76
Partick. Glas 3G 127
Partington. G Man 1B 84
Partney. Linc 4D 88
Parton. Cumb
  nr. Whitehaven 2A 102
  nr. Wigton 4D 112
Parton. Dum 2D 111
Partridge Green. W Sus 4C 26
Parwich. Derbs 5F 85
Passenham. Nptn 2F 51
Passfield. Hants 3G 25
Passingford Bridge. Essx 1G 39
Paston. Norf 2F 79
Pasturefields. Staf 3D 73
Patchacott. Devn 3E 11
Patcham. Brig 5E 27
Patchetts Green. Herts 1C 38
Patching. W Sus 5B 26
Patchole. Devn 2G 19
Patchway. S Glo 3B 34
Pateley Bridge. N Yor 3D 98
Pathe. Som 3G 21
Pathfinder Village. Devn 3B 12
Pathhead. Abers 2G 145
Pathhead. E Ayr 3F 117
Pathhead. Fife 4E 137
Pathhead. Midl 3G 129
Pathlow. Warw 5F 61
Path of Condie. Per 2C 136
Pathstruie. Per 2C 136
Patmore Heath. Herts 3E 53
Patna. E Ayr 3D 116
Patney. Wilts 1F 23
Patrick. IOM 3B 108
Patrick Brompton. N Yor 5F 105
Patrington. E Yor 2G 95
Patrington Haven. E Yor 2G 95
Patrixbourne. Kent 5F 41
Patterdale. Cumb 3E 103
Pattiesmuir. Fife 1D 129
Pattingham. Staf 1C 60
Pattishall. Nptn 5D 62
Pattiswick. Essx 3B 54
Patton Bridge. Cumb 5G 103
Paul. Corn 4B 4
Paulerspury. Nptn 1F 51
Paull. E Yor 2E 95
Paulton. Bath 1B 22
Pauperhaugh. Nmbd 5F 121
Pave Lane. Telf 4B 72
Pavenham. Bed 5G 63
Pawlett. Som 2F 21
Pawston. Nmbd 1C 120
Paxford. Glos 2G 49
Paxton. Bord 4F 131
Payhembury. Devn 2D 12
Paythorne. Lanc 4H 97
Payton. Som 4E 20
Peacehaven. E Sus 5F 27
Peak Dale. Derbs 3E 85
Peak Forest. Derbs 3F 85
Peak Hill. Linc 4B 76
Peakirk. Pet 5A 76
Pearsie. Ang 3C 144
Peasedown St John. Bath 1C 22
Peaseland Green. Norf 4C 78
Peasemore. W Ber 4C 36

Peasenhall. Suff 4F 67
Pease Pottage. W Sus 2D 26
Peaslake. Surr 1B 26
Peasley Cross. Mers 1H 83
Peasmarsh. E Sus 3C 28
Peasmarsh. Som 1G 13
Peasmarsh. Surr 1A 26
Peaston. E Lot 3H 129
Peastonbank. E Lot 3H 129
Peathill. Abers 2G 161
Peat Inn. Fife 3G 137
Peatling Magna. Leics 1C 62
Peatling Parva. Leics 2C 62
Peaton. Arg 1D 126
Peaton. Shrp 2H 59
Peats Corner. Suff 4D 66
Pebmarsh. Essx 2B 54
Pebworth. Worc 1G 49
Pecket Well. W Yor 2H 91
Peckforton. Ches E 5H 83
Peckham Bush. Kent 5A 40
Peckleton. Leics 5B 74
Pedair-ffordd. Powy 3D 70
Pedham. Norf 4F 79
Pedlinge. Kent 2F 29
Pedmore. W Mid 2D 60
Pedwell. Som 3H 21
Peebles. Bord 5F 129
Peel. IOM 3B 108
Peel. Bord 1G 119
Peel Common. Hants 2D 16
Peening Quarter. Kent 3C 28
Peggs Green. Leics 4B 74
Pegsdon. C Beds 2B 52
Pegswood. Nmbd 1F 115
Peinchorran. High 5E 155
Peinlich. High 3D 154
Pelaw. Tyne 3F 115
Pelcomb Bridge. Pemb 3D 42
Pelcomb Cross. Pemb 3D 42
Peldon. Essx 4C 54
Pelutho. Cumb 5C 112
Pelton. Dur 4F 115
Pelynt. Corn 3G 7
Pemberton. Carm 5F 45
Pembrey. Carm 5E 45
Pembridge. Here 5F 59
Pembroke. Pemb 4D 43
Pembroke Dock. Pemb 215 (4D 42)
Pembroke Ferry. Pemb 4D 42
Pembury. Kent 1H 27
Penallt. Mon 4A 48
Penally. Pemb 5F 43
Penalt. Here 3A 48
Penalum. Pemb 5F 43
Penare. Corn 4D 6
Penarth. V Glam 4E 33
Penbeagle. Corn 3C 4
Penberth. Corn 4B 4
Pen-bont Rhydybeddau. Cdgn 2F 57
Penbryn. Cdgn 5B 56
Pencader. Carm 2E 45
Pen-cae. Cdgn 5D 56
Pencaenewydd. Gwyn 1D 68
Pencaerau. Neat 3G 31
Pencaitland. E Lot 3H 129
Pencarnisiog. IOA 3C 80
Pencarreg. Carm 1F 45
Pencarrow. Corn 4B 10
Pencelli. Powy 3D 46
Pen-clawdd. Swan 3E 31
Pencoed. B'end 3C 32
Pencombe. Here 5H 59
Pencraig. Here 3A 48
Pencraig. Powy 3C 70
Pendeen. Corn 3A 4
Penderyn. Rhon 5C 46
Pendine. Carm 4G 43
Pendlebury. G Man 4F 91
Pendleton. G Man 1C 84
Pendleton. Lanc 1F 91
Pendock. Worc 2C 48
Pendoggett. Corn 5A 10
Pendomer. Som 1A 14
Pendoylan. V Glam 4D 32
Pendre. B'end 3C 32
Penegoes. Powy 5G 69
Penelewey. Corn 4C 6
Penffordd. Pemb 2E 43
Penffordd-Lâs. Powy 1A 58
Penfro. Pemb 4D 42
Pengam. Cphy 2E 33
Pengam. Card 4F 33
Penge. G Lon 4E 39
Pengelly. Corn 4A 10
Pengenffordd. Powy 2E 47
Pengersick. Corn 4C 4
Pengorffwysfa. IOA 1D 80
Pengover Green. Corn 2G 7
Pengwern. Den 3C 82
Penhale. Corn
  nr. Mullion 5D 5
  nr. St Austell 3D 6
Penhale Camp. Corn 3B 6
Penhallow. Corn 3B 6
Penhalvean. Corn 5B 6
Penhelig. Gwyn 1F 57
Penhill. Swin 3G 35
Penhow. Newp 2H 33
Penhurst. E Sus 4A 28
Peniarth. Gwyn 5F 69
Penicuik. Midl 3F 129
Peniel. Carm 3E 45
Penifiler. High 4D 155
Peninver. Arg 3B 122
Penisa'r Waun. Gwyn 4E 81
Penistone. S Yor 4C 92
Penketh. Warr 2H 83
Penkill. S Ayr 5B 116

Penkridge. Staf 4D 72
Penley. Wrex 2G 71
Penllech. Gwyn 2B 68
Penllergaer. Swan 3F 31
Pen-llyn. IOA 2C 80
Penmachno. Cnwy 5G 81
Penmaen. Swan 4E 31
Penmaenmawr. Cnwy 3G 81
Penmaenpool. Gwyn 4F 69
Penmaen Rhos. Cnwy 3A 82
Pen-marc. V Glam 5D 32
Penmark. V Glam 5D 32
Penmon. IOA 2F 81
Penmorfa. Gwyn 1E 69
Penmynydd. IOA 3E 81
Penn. Buck 1A 38
Penn. Dors 3G 13
Penn. W Mid 1C 60
Pennal. Gwyn 5G 69
Pennan. Abers 2F 161
Pennant. Cdgn 4E 57
Pennant. Den 2C 70
Pennant. Gwyn 3B 70
Pennant. Powy 1A 58
Pennant Melangell. Powy 3C 70
Pennar. Pemb 4D 42
Pennard. Swan 4E 31
Pennerley. Shrp 1F 59
Pennington. Cumb 2B 96
Pennington. G Man 1A 84
Pennington. Hants 3B 16
Pennorth. Powy 3E 46
Penn Street. Buck 1A 38
Pennsylvania. Devn 3C 12
Pennsylvania. S Glo 4C 34
Penny Bridge. Cumb 1C 96
Pennycross. Plym 3A 8
Pennygate. Norf 3F 79
Pennyghael. Arg 1C 132
Penny Hill. Linc 3C 76
Pennylands. Lanc 4C 90
Pennymoor. Devn 1B 12
Pennyvenie. E Ayr 4D 117
Pennywell. Tyne 4G 115
Penparc. Cdgn 1C 44
Penparcau. Cdgn 2E 57
Pen-pedair-heol. Cphy 2E 33
Penperlleni. Mon 5G 47
Penpillick. Corn 3E 7
Penpol. Corn 5C 6
Penpoll. Corn 3F 7
Penponds. Corn 3D 4
Penpont. Corn 5A 10
Penpont. Dum 5H 117
Penpont. Powy 3C 46
Penprysg. B'end 3C 32
Penquit. Devn 3C 8
Penrherber. Carm 1G 43
Penrhiw. Pemb 1C 44
Penrhiwceiber. Rhon 2D 32
Pen-Rhiw-fawr. Neat 4H 45
Penrhiw-llan. Cdgn 1D 44
Penrhiw-pal. Cdgn 1D 44
Penrhos. Gwyn 2C 68
Penrhos. Here 5F 59
Penrhos. IOA 2B 80
Penrhos. Mon 4H 47
Penrhos. Powy 4B 46
Penrhos Garnedd. Gwyn 3E 81
Penrhyn. IOA 1C 80
Penrhyn Bay. Cnwy 2H 81
Penrhyn-coch. Cdgn 2F 57
Penrhyndeudraeth. Gwyn 2F 69
Penrhyn-side. Cnwy 2H 81
Penrice. Swan 4D 31
Penrith. Cumb 2G 103
Penrose. Corn 1C 6
Penruddock. Cumb 2F 103
Penryn. Corn 5B 6
Pen-sarn. Carm 4E 45
Pen-sarn. Gwyn 3E 69
Pensax. Worc 4B 60
Pensby. Mers 2E 83
Penselwood. Som 3C 22
Pensford. Bath 5B 34
Pensham. Worc 1E 49
Penshaw. Tyne 4G 115
Penshurst. Kent 1G 27
Pensilva. Corn 2G 7
Pensnett. W Mid 2D 60
Penston. E Lot 2H 129
Penstone. Devn 2A 12
Pentewan. Corn 4E 6
Pentir. Gwyn 4E 81
Pentire. Corn 2B 6
Pentlepoir. Pemb 4F 43
Pentlow. Essx 1B 54
Pentney. Norf 4G 77
Penton Mewsey. Hants 2B 24
Pentraeth. IOA 3E 81
Pentre. Powy
  nr. Church Stoke 1E 59
  nr. Kerry 2D 58
  nr. Mochdre 2C 58
Pentre. Rhon 2C 32
Pentre. Shrp 4F 71
Pentre. Wrex
  nr. Chirk 1E 71
  nr. Llanarmon Dyffryn Ceiriog 2D 70
Pentrebach. Carm 2B 46
Pentre-bach. Cdgn 1F 45
Pentrebach. Mer T 5D 46
Pentrebach. Powy 2C 46
Pentrebach. Swan 5G 45
Pentre Berw. IOA 3D 80
Pentre-bont. Cnwy 5G 81
Pentrecagal. Carm 1D 44
Pentre-celyn. Den 5D 82
Pentre-clawdd. Shrp 2E 71

Pentreclwydau. Neat 5B 46
Pentre-cwrt. Carm 2D 45
Pentre Dolau Honddu. Powy 1C 46
Pentre-dwr. Swan 3F 31
Pentrefelin. Carm 3F 45
Pentrefelin. Cdgn 1G 45
Pentrefelin. Cnwy 3H 81
Pentrefelin. Gwyn 2E 69
Pentrefoelas. Cnwy 5A 82
Pentre Galar. Pemb 1F 43
Pentregat. Cdgn 5C 56
Pentre Gwenlais. Carm 4G 45
Pentre Gwynfryn. Gwyn 3E 69
Pentre Halkyn. Flin 3E 82
Pentre Hodre. Shrp 3F 59
Pentre-Llanrhaeadr. Den 4C 82
Pentre Llifior. Powy 1D 58
Pentrellwyn. IOA 2E 81
Pentre-llwyn-llwyd. Powy 5B 58
Pentre-llyn-cymmer. Cnwy 5B 82
Pentre Meyrick. V Glam 4C 32
Pentre-piod. Gwyn 2A 70
Pentre-poeth. Newp 3F 33
Pentre'r beirdd. Powy 4D 70
Pentre'r-felin. Powy 2C 46
Pentre-tafarn-y-fedw. Cnwy 4H 81
Pentre-ty-gwyn. Carm 2B 46
Pentre-uchaf. Gwyn 2C 68
Pentrich. Derbs 5A 86
Pentridge. Dors 1F 15
Pen-twyn. Cphy 5F 47
Pentwyn. Cphy 5E 46
Pentwyn. Card 3F 33
Pentyrch. Card 3E 32
Pentywyn. Carm 4G 43
Penuwch. Cdgn 4E 57
Penwithick. Corn 3E 7
Penwyllt. Powy 4B 46
Pen-y-banc. Carm 3G 45
Penybanc. Carm 4G 45
Pen-y-bont. Carm 2B 46
Pen-y-bont. Powy 3E 70
Penybont. Powy 4D 58
Pen-y-Bont Ar Ogwr. B'end 3C 32
Penybontfawr. Powy 3C 70
Penybryn. Cphy 2E 33
Pen-y-bryn. Pemb 1B 44
Pen-y-bryn. Wrex 1E 71
Pen-y-cae. Powy 4B 46
Penycae. Wrex 1E 71
Pen-y-cae mawr. Mon 2H 33
Penycaerau. Gwyn 3A 68
Pen-y-cefn. Flin 3D 82
Pen-y-clawdd. Mon 5H 47
Pen-y-coedcae. Rhon 3D 32
Penycwm. Pemb 2C 42
Pen-y-Darren. Mer T 5D 46
Pen-y-fai. B'end 3B 32
Pen-y-ffordd. Flin 2D 82
Penyffordd. Flin 4F 83
Penyffridd. Gwyn 5E 81
Pen-y-garn. Cdgn 2F 57
Pen-y-garnedd. IOA 3E 81
Penygarnedd. Powy 3D 70
Pen-y-graig. Gwyn 2B 68
Penygraig. Rhon 2C 32
Penygraigwen. IOA 2D 80
Pen-y-groes. Carm 4F 45
Penygroes. Gwyn 5D 80
Penygroes. Pemb 1F 43
Pen-y-Mynydd. Carm 5E 45
Penymynydd. Flin 4F 83
Pen-yr-heol. Mon 4H 47
Penyrheol. Cphy 3E 33
Pen-yr-heol. Mon 4H 47
Penyrheol. Swan 3E 31
Pensarn. IOA 1D 80
Pen-y-stryt. Den 5D 82
Penywaun. Rhon 5C 46
Penzance. Corn 3B 4
Peopleton. Worc 5D 60
Peover Heath. Ches E 3B 84
Peper Harow. Surr 1A 26
Peplow. Shrp 3A 72
Pepper Arden. N Yor 4F 105
Perceton. N Ayr 5E 127
Percyhorner. Abers 2G 161
Perham Down. Wilts 2A 24
Periton. Som 2C 20
Perkinsville. Dur 4F 115
Perlethorpe. Notts 3D 86
Perranarworthal. Corn 5B 6
Perranporth. Corn 3B 6
Perranuthnoe. Corn 4C 4
Perranwell. Corn 5B 6
Perranzabuloe. Corn 3B 6
Perrott's Brook. Glos 5F 49
Perry. W Mid 1E 61
Perry Barr. W Mid 1E 61
Perry Crofts. Staf 5G 73
Perry Green. Essx 3B 54
Perry Green. Herts 4E 53
Perry Green. Wilts 3E 35
Perry Street. Kent 3H 39
Perry Street. Som 2G 13
Perrywood. Kent 5E 41
Pershall. Staf 3C 72
Pershore. Worc 1E 49
Pertenhall. Bed 4H 63
Perth. Per 207 (1D 136)
Perthy. Shrp 2F 71
Perton. Staf 1C 60
Pertwood. Wilts 3D 23
Peterborough. Pet 208 (1A 64)
Peterburn. High 5B 162
Peterchurch. Here 2G 47
Peterculter. Aber 3F 153
Peterhead. Abers 4H 161
Peterlee. Dur 5H 115
Petersfield. Hants 4F 25
Petersfinger. Wilts 4G 23
Peters Green. Herts 4B 52

Peters Marland. *Devn* 1E **11**
Peterstone Wentlooge. *Newp* 3F **33**
Peterston-super-Ely. *V Glam* 4D **32**
Peterstow. *Here* 3A **48**
Peters Village. *Kent* 4B **40**
Peter Tavy. *Devn* 5F **11**
Petertown. *Orkn* 7C **172**
Petham. *Kent* 5F **41**
Petherwin Gate. *Corn* 4C **10**
Petrockstowe. *Devn* 2F **11**
Petsoe End. *Mil* 1G **51**
Pett. *E Sus* 4C **28**
Pettaugh. *Suff* 5D **66**
Pett Bottom. *Kent* 5F **41**
Petteridge. *Kent* 1A **28**
Pettinain. *S Lan* 5C **128**
Pettistree. *Suff* 5E **67**
Petton. *Devn* 4D **20**
Petton. *Shrp* 3G **71**
Petts Wood. *G Lon* 4F **39**
Pettycur. *Fife* 1F **129**
Pettywell. *Norf* 3C **78**
Petworth. *W Sus* 3A **26**
Pevensey. *E Sus* 5H **27**
Pevensey Bay. *E Sus* 5A **28**
Pewsey. *Wilts* 5G **35**
Pheasants Hill. *Buck* 3F **37**
Philadelphia. *Tyne* 4G **115**
Philham. *Devn* 4C **18**
Philiphaugh. *Bord* 2G **119**
Phillack. *Corn* 3C **4**
Philleigh. *Corn* 5C **6**
Philpstoun. *W Lot* 2D **128**
Phocle Green. *Here* 3B **48**
Phoenix Green. *Hants* 1F **25**
Pibsbury. *Som* 4H **21**
Pibwrlwyd. *Carm* 4E **45**
Pica. *Cumb* 2B **102**
Piccadilly. *Warw* 1G **61**
Piccadilly Corner. *Norf* 2E **67**
Piccotts End. *Herts* 5A **52**
Pickering. *N Yor* 1B **100**
Picket Piece. *Hants* 2B **24**
Picket Post. *Hants* 2G **15**
Pickford. *W Mid* 2G **61**
Pickhill. *N Yor* 1F **99**
Picklenash. *Glos* 3C **48**
Picklescott. *Shrp* 1G **59**
Pickletillem. *Fife* 1G **137**
Pickmere. *Ches E* 3A **84**
Pickstock. *Telf* 3B **72**
Pickwell. *Devn* 2E **19**
Pickwell. *Leics* 4E **75**
Pickworth. *Linc* 2H **75**
Pickworth. *Rut* 4G **75**
Picton. *Ches W* 3G **83**
Picton. *Flin* 2D **82**
Picton. *N Yor* 4B **106**
Pict's Hill. *Som* 4H **21**
Piddinghoe. *E Sus* 5F **27**
Piddington. *Buck* 2G **37**
Piddington. *Nptn* 5F **63**
Piddington. *Oxon* 4E **51**
Piddlehinton. *Dors* 3C **14**
Piddletrenthide. *Dors* 2C **14**
Pidley. *Cambs* 3C **64**
Pidney. *Dors* 2C **14**
Pie Corner. *Here* 4A **60**
Piercebridge. *Darl* 3F **105**
Pierowall. *Orkn* 3D **172**
Pigdon. *Nmbd* 1E **115**
Pightley. *Som* 3F **21**
Pikehall. *Derbs* 5F **85**
Pikeshill. *Hants* 2A **16**
Pilford. *Dors* 2F **15**
Pilgrims Hatch. *Essx* 1G **39**
Pilham. *Linc* 1F **87**
Pill, The. *Mon* 3H **33**
Pill. *N Som* 4A **34**
Pillaton. *Corn* 2H **7**
Pillaton. *Staf* 4D **72**
Pillerton Hersey. *Warw* 1B **50**
Pillerton Priors. *Warw* 1A **50**
Pilleth. *Powy* 4E **59**
Pilley. *Hants* 3B **16**
Pilley. *S Yor* 4D **92**
Pillgwenlly. *Newp* 3G **33**
Pilling. *Lanc* 5D **96**
Pilling Lane. *Lanc* 5C **96**
Pillowell. *Glos* 5B **48**
Pillwell. *Dors* 1C **14**
Pilning. *S Glo* 3A **34**
Pilsbury. *Derbs* 4F **85**
Pilsdon. *Dors* 3H **13**
Pilsgate. *Pet* 5H **75**
Pilsley. *Derbs*
  nr. Bakewell 3G **85**
  nr. Clay Cross 4B **86**
Pilson Green. *Norf* 4F **79**
Piltdown. *E Sus* 3F **27**
Pilton. *Edin* 2F **129**
Pilton. *Nptn* 2H **63**
Pilton. *Rut* 5G **75**
Pilton. *Som* 2A **22**
Pilton Green. *Swan* 4D **30**
Pimperne. *Dors* 2E **15**
Pinchbeck. *Linc* 3B **76**
Pinchbeck Bars. *Linc* 3A **76**
Pinchbeck West. *Linc* 3B **76**
Pinfold. *Lanc* 3B **90**
Pinford End. *Suff* 5H **65**
Pinged. *Carm* 5E **45**
Pinhoe. *Devn* 3C **12**
Pinkerton. *E Lot* 2D **130**
Pinkneys Green. *Wind* 3G **37**
Pinley. *W Mid* 3A **62**
Pinley Green. *Warw* 4G **61**
Pinmill. *Suff* 2F **55**
Pinmore. *S Ayr* 5B **116**
Pinner. *G Lon* 2C **38**
Pins Green. *Worc* 1C **48**

Pinsley Green. *Ches E* 1H **71**
Pinvin. *Worc* 1E **49**
Pinwherry. *S Ayr* 1G **109**
Pinxton. *Derbs* 5B **86**
Pipe and Lyde. *Here* 1A **48**
Pipe Aston. *Here* 3G **59**
Pipehill. *Staf* 5E **73**
Piperhill. *High* 3C **158**
Pipers Pool. *Corn* 4C **10**
Pipewell. *Nptn* 2F **63**
Pippacott. *Devn* 3F **19**
Pipton. *Powy* 2E **47**
Pirbright. *Surr* 5A **38**
Pirnmill. *N Ayr* 5G **125**
Pirton. *Herts* 2B **52**
Pirton. *Worc* 1D **49**
Pisgah. *Stir* 3G **135**
Pishill. *Oxon* 3F **37**
Pistyll. *Gwyn* 1C **68**
Pitagowan. *Per* 2F **143**
Pitcairn. *Per* 3F **143**
Pitcairngreen. *Per* 1C **136**
Pitcalnie. *High* 1C **158**
Pitcaple. *Abers* 1E **152**
Pitchcombe. *Glos* 5D **48**
Pitchcott. *Buck* 3F **51**
Pitchford. *Shrp* 5H **71**
Pitch Green. *Buck* 5F **51**
Pitch Place. *Surr* 5A **38**
Pitcombe. *Som* 3B **22**
Pitcox. *E Lot* 2C **130**
Pitcur. *Per* 5B **144**
Pitfichie. *Abers* 2D **152**
Pitgrudy. *High* 4E **165**
Pitkennedy. *Ang* 3E **145**
Pitlessie. *Fife* 3F **137**
Pitlochry. *Per* 3G **143**
Pitmachie. *Abers* 1D **152**
Pitmaduthy. *High* 1B **158**
Pitmedden. *Abers* 1F **153**
Pitminster. *Som* 1F **13**
Pitnacree. *Per* 3G **143**
Pitney. *Som* 4H **21**
Pitroddie. *Per* 1E **136**
Pitscottie. *Fife* 2G **137**
Pitsea. *Essx* 2B **40**
Pitsford. *Nptn* 4E **63**
Pitsford Hill. *Som* 3E **20**
Pitsmoor. *S Yor* 2A **86**
Pitstone. *Buck* 4H **51**
Pitt. *Hants* 4C **24**
Pitt Court. *Glos* 2C **34**
Pittentrail. *High* 3E **164**
Pittenweem. *Fife* 3H **137**
Pittington. *Dur* 5G **115**
Pitton. *Swan* 4D **30**
Pitton. *Wilts* 3H **23**
Pittswood. *Kent* 1H **27**
Pittulie. *Abers* 2G **161**
Pittville. *Glos* 3E **49**
Pityme. *Corn* 1D **6**
Pity Me. *Dur* 5F **115**
Pixey Green. *Suff* 3E **67**
Pixley. *Here* 2B **48**
Place Newton. *N Yor* 2C **100**
Plaidy. *Abers* 3E **161**
Plaidy. *Corn* 3G **7**
Plain Dealings. *Pemb* 3E **43**
Plains. *N Lan* 3A **128**
Plainsfield. *Som* 3E **21**
Plaish. *Shrp* 1H **59**
Plaistow. *Here* 2B **48**
Plaistow. *W Sus* 2B **26**
Plaitford. *Wilts* 1A **16**
Plastow Green. *Hants* 5D **36**
Plas yn Cefn. *Den* 3C **82**
Platt, The. *E Sus* 2G **27**
Platt Bridge. *G Man* 4E **90**
Platt Lane. *Shrp* 2H **71**
Platts Common. *S Yor* 4D **92**
Platt's Heath. *Kent* 5C **40**
Plawsworth. *Dur* 5F **115**
Plaxtol. *Kent* 5H **39**
Playden. *E Sus* 3D **28**
Playford. *Suff* 1F **55**
Play Hatch. *Oxon* 4F **37**
Playing Place. *Corn* 4C **6**
Playley Green. *Glos* 2C **48**
Plealey. *Shrp* 5G **71**
Plean. *Stir* 1B **128**
Pleasington. *Bkbn* 2E **91**
Pleasley. *Derbs* 4C **86**
Pledgdon Green. *Essx* 3F **53**
Plenmeller. *Nmbd* 3A **114**
Pleshey. *Essx* 4G **53**
Plockton. *High* 5H **155**
Plocrapol. *W Isl* 8D **171**
Ploughfield. *Here* 1G **47**
Plowden. *Shrp* 2F **59**
Ploxgreen. *Shrp* 5F **71**
Pluckley. *Kent* 1D **28**
Plucks Gutter. *Kent* 4G **41**
Plumbland. *Cumb* 1C **102**
Plumgarths. *Cumb* 5F **103**
Plumley. *Ches E* 3B **84**
Plummers Plain. *W Sus* 3D **26**
Plumpton. *Cumb* 1F **103**
Plumpton. *E Sus* 4E **27**
Plumpton. *Nptn* 1D **50**
Plumpton Foot. *Cumb* 1F **103**
Plumpton Green. *E Sus* 4E **27**
Plumpton Head. *Cumb* 1G **103**
Plumstead. *G Lon* 3F **39**
Plumstead. *Norf* 2D **78**
Plumtree. *Notts* 2D **74**
Plumtree Park. *Notts* 2D **74**
Plungar. *Leics* 2E **75**
Plush. *Dors* 2C **14**

Plushabridge. *Corn* 5D **10**
Plwmp. *Cdgn* 5C **56**
Plymouth. *Plym* **208** (3A **8**)
Plympton. *Plym* 3B **8**
Plymstock. *Plym* 3B **8**
Plymtree. *Devn* 2D **12**
Pockley. *N Yor* 1A **100**
Pocklington. *E Yor* 5C **100**
Pode Hole. *Linc* 3B **76**
Podimore. *Som* 4A **22**
Podington. *Bed* 4G **63**
Podmore. *Staf* 2B **72**
Poffley End. *Oxon* 4B **50**
Point Clear. *Essx* 4D **54**
Pointon. *Linc* 2A **76**
Pokesdown. *Bour* 3G **15**
Polbae. *Dum* 2H **109**
Polbain. *High* 3E **163**
Polbathic. *Corn* 3H **7**
Polbeth. *W Lot* 3D **128**
Polbrock. *Corn* 2E **6**
Polchar. *High* 3C **150**
Polebrook. *Nptn* 2H **63**
Pole Elm. *Worc* 1D **48**
Polegate. *E Sus* 5G **27**
Pole Moor. *W Yor* 3A **92**
Poles. *High* 4E **165**
Polesworth. *Warw* 5G **73**
Polglass. *High* 3E **163**
Polgooth. *Corn* 3D **6**
Poling. *W Sus* 5B **26**
Poling Corner. *W Sus* 5B **26**
Polio. *High* 1B **158**
Polkerris. *Corn* 3E **7**
Polla. *High* 3D **166**
Pollard Street. *Norf* 2F **79**
Pollicott. *Buck* 4F **51**
Pollington. *E Yor* 3G **93**
Polloch. *High* 2B **140**
Pollok. *Glas* 3G **127**
Pollokshaws. *Glas* 3G **127**
Pollokshields. *Glas* 3G **127**
Polmaily. *High* 5G **157**
Polmassick. *Corn* 4D **6**
Polmont. *Falk* 2C **128**
Polnessan. *E Ayr* 3D **116**
Polnish. *High* 5F **147**
Polperro. *Corn* 3G **7**
Polruan. *Corn* 3F **7**
Polscoe. *Corn* 2F **7**
Polsham. *Som* 2A **22**
Polskeoch. *Dum* 4F **117**
Polstead. *Suff* 2C **54**
Polstead Heath. *Suff* 1C **54**
Poltesco. *Corn* 5E **5**
Poltimore. *Devn* 3C **12**
Polton. *Midl* 3F **129**
Polwarth. *Bord* 4D **130**
Polyphant. *Corn* 4C **10**
Polzeath. *Corn* 1D **6**
Ponde. *Powy* 2E **46**
Pondersbridge. *Cambs* 1B **64**
Ponders End. *G Lon* 1E **39**
Pond Street. *Essx* 2E **53**
Pondtail. *Hants* 1G **25**
Ponsanooth. *Corn* 5B **6**
Ponsongath. *Corn* 5E **5**
Ponsworthy. *Devn* 5H **11**
Pontamman. *Carm* 4G **45**
Pontantwn. *Carm* 4E **45**
Pontardawe. *Neat* 5H **45**
Pontarddulais. *Swan* 5F **45**
Pontarfynach. *Cdgn* 3G **57**
Pont-ar-gothi. *Carm* 3F **45**
Pont ar Hydfer. *Powy* 3B **46**
Pontarllechau. *Carm* 3H **45**
Pontarsais. *Carm* 3E **45**
Pontblyddyn. *Flin* 4E **83**
Pontbren Llwyd. *Rhon* 5C **46**
Pont-Cyfyng. *Cnwy* 5G **81**
Pontdolgoch. *Powy* 1C **58**
Pontefract. *W Yor* 2E **93**
Ponteland. *Nmbd* 2E **115**
Ponterwyd. *Cdgn* 2G **57**
Pontesbury. *Shrp* 5G **71**
Pontesford. *Shrp* 5G **71**
Pontfadog. *Wrex* 2E **71**
Pontfaen. *Pemb* 1E **43**
Pont-faen. *Powy* 2C **46**
Pont-Faen. *Shrp* 2E **71**
Pontgarreg. *Cdgn* 5C **56**
Pont-Henri. *Carm* 5E **45**
Ponthir. *Torf* 2G **33**
Ponthirwaun. *Cdgn* 1C **44**
Pont-iets. *Carm* 5E **45**
Pontllanfraith. *Cphy* 2E **33**
Pontlliw. *Swan* 5G **45**
Pont Llogel. *Powy* 4C **70**
Pontllyfni. *Gwyn* 5D **80**
Pontlottyn. *Cphy* 5E **46**
Pontneddfechan. *Powy* 5C **46**
Pont-newydd. *Carm* 5E **45**
Pont-newydd. *Flin* 4D **82**
Pontnewydd. *Torf* 2F **33**
Ponton. *Shet* 6E **173**
Pont Pen-y-benglog. *Gwyn* 4F **81**
Pontrhydfendigaid. *Cdgn* 4G **57**
Pont Rhyd-y-cyff. *B'end* 3B **32**
Pontrhydyfen. *Neat* 2A **32**
Pont-rhyd-y-groes. *Cdgn* 3G **57**
Pontrhydyrun. *Torf* 2F **33**
Pont-Rhythallt. *Gwyn* 4E **81**
Pontrilas. *Here* 3G **47**
Pontrilas Road. *Here* 3G **47**
Pontrobert. *Powy* 4D **70**
Pont-rug. *Gwyn* 4E **81**
Ponts Green. *E Sus* 4A **28**
Pontshill. *Here* 3B **48**
Pont-Sian. *Cdgn* 1E **45**
Pontsticill. *Mer T* 4D **46**
Pont-Walby. *Neat* 5B **46**

Pontwelly. *Carm* 2E **45**
Pontwgan. *Cnwy* 3G **81**
Pontyates. *Carm* 5E **45**
Pontyberem. *Carm* 4F **45**
Pontybodkin. *Flin* 5E **83**
Pontyclun. *Rhon* 3D **32**
Pontycymer. *B'end* 2C **32**
Pontyglazier. *Pemb* 1F **43**
Pontygwaith. *Rhon* 2D **32**
Pont-y-pant. *Cnwy* 5G **81**
Pontypool. *Torf* 2F **33**
Pontypridd. *Rhon* 3D **32**
Pontypwl. *Torf* 2F **33**
Pontywaun. *Cphy* 2F **33**
Pooksgreen. *Hants* 1B **16**
Pool. *Corn* 4A **6**
Pool. *W Yor* 5E **99**
Poole. *N Yor* 2E **93**
Poole. *Pool* **215** (3F **15**)
Poole. *Som* 4E **21**
Poole Keynes. *Glos* 2E **35**
Poolend. *Staf* 5D **84**
Poolewe. *High* 5C **162**
Pooley Bridge. *Cumb* 2F **103**
Poolfold. *Staf* 5C **84**
Pool Head. *Here* 5H **59**
Pool Hey. *Lanc* 3B **90**
Poolhill. *Glos* 3C **48**
Poolmill. *Here* 3A **48**
Pool o' Muckhart. *Clac* 3C **136**
Pool Quay. *Powy* 4E **71**
Poolsbrook. *Derbs* 3B **86**
Pool Street. *Essx* 2A **54**
Pootings. *Kent* 1F **27**
Pope Hill. *Pemb* 3D **42**
Pope's Hill. *Glos* 4B **48**
Popeswood. *Brac* 5G **37**
Popham. *Hants* 2D **24**
Poplar. *G Lon* 2E **39**
Popley. *Hants* 1E **25**
Porchfield. *IOW* 3C **16**
Porin. *High* 3F **157**
Poringland. *Norf* 5E **79**
Porkellis. *Corn* 5A **6**
Porlock. *Som* 2B **20**
Porlock Weir. *Som* 2B **20**
Portachoillan. *Arg* 4F **125**
Port Adhair Bheinn na Faoghla.
  W Isl 3C **170**
Port Adhair Thirlodh. *Arg* 4B **138**
Port Ann. *Arg* 1H **125**
Port Appin. *Arg* 4D **140**
Port Asgaig. *Arg* 3C **124**
Port Askaig. *Arg* 3C **124**
Portavadie. *Arg* 3H **125**
Port Bannatyne. *Arg* 3B **126**
Portbury. *N Som* 4A **34**
Port Carlisle. *Cumb* 3D **112**
Port Charlotte. *Arg* 4A **124**
Portchester. *Hants* 2E **16**
Port Clarence. *Stoc T* 2B **106**
Port Driseach. *Arg* 2A **126**
Port Dundas. *Glas* 3G **127**
Port Ellen. *Arg* 5B **124**
Port Elphinstone. *Abers* 1E **153**
Portencalzie. *Dum* 2F **109**
Portencross. *N Ayr* 5C **126**
Port Erin. *IOM* 5A **108**
Port Erroll. *Abers* 5H **161**
Porter's Fen Corner. *Norf* 5E **77**
Porterstown. *Dors* 4B **14**
Portessie. *Mor* 2B **160**
Port e Vullen. *IOM* 2D **108**
Port-Eynon. *Swan* 4D **30**
Portfield. *Som* 4H **21**
Portfield Gate. *Pemb* 3D **42**
Portgate. *Devn* 4E **11**
Port Gaverne. *Corn* 4A **10**
Port Glasgow. *Inv* 2E **127**
Portgordon. *Mor* 2A **160**
Portgower. *High* 2H **165**
Porth. *Corn* 2C **6**
Porth. *Rhon* 2D **32**
Porthaethwy. *IOA* 3E **81**
Porthallow. *Corn*
  nr. Looe 3G **7**
  nr. St Keverne 4E **5**
Porthcawl. *B'end* 4B **32**
Porthceri. *V Glam* 5D **32**
Porthcothan. *Corn* 1C **6**
Porthcurno. *Corn* 4A **4**
Port Henderson. *High* 1G **155**
Porthgain. *Pemb* 1C **42**
Porthgwarra. *Corn* 4A **4**
Porthill. *Shrp* 4G **71**
Porthkerry. *V Glam* 5D **32**
Porthleven. *Corn* 4D **4**
Porthllechog. *IOA* 1D **80**
Porthmadog. *Gwyn* 2E **69**
Porthmeor. *Corn* 3B **4**
Porth Navas. *Corn* 4E **5**
Portholland. *Corn* 4D **6**
Porthoustock. *Corn* 4F **5**
Porthtowan. *Corn* 4A **6**
Porth Tywyn. *Carm* 5E **45**
Porth-y-felin. *IOA* 2B **80**
Porthyrhyd. *Carm*
  nr. Carmarthen 4F **45**
  nr. Llandovery 2H **45**
Porth-y-waen. *Shrp* 3E **71**
Portincaple. *Arg* 4B **134**
Portington. *E Yor* 1A **94**
Portinnisherrich. *Arg* 2G **133**
Portinscale. *Cumb* 2D **102**
Port Isaac. *Corn* 1D **6**
Portishead. *N Som* 4H **33**
Portknockie. *Mor* 2B **160**
Portlethen. *Abers* 4G **153**
Portlethen Village. *Abers* 4G **153**
Portling. *Dum* 4F **111**

Port Lion. *Pemb* 4D **43**
Portloe. *Corn* 5D **6**
Port Logan. *Dum* 5F **109**
Portmahomack. *High* 5G **165**
Portmead. *Swan* 3F **31**
Portmeirion. *Gwyn* 2E **69**
Portmellon. *Corn* 4E **6**
Port Mholair. *W Isl* 4H **171**
Port Mor. *High* 1F **139**
Portmore. *Hants* 3B **16**
Port Mulgrave. *N Yor* 3E **107**
Portnacroish. *Arg* 4D **140**
Portnahaven. *Arg* 4A **124**
Portnalong. *High* 5C **154**
Portnaluchaig. *High* 5E **147**
Portnancon. *High* 2E **167**
Port Nan Giuran. *W Isl* 4H **171**
Port nan Long. *W Isl* 1D **170**
Port Nis. *W Isl* 1H **171**
Portobello. *Edin* 2G **129**
Portobello. *W Yor* 3D **92**
Port of Menteith. *Stir* 3E **135**
Porton. *Wilts* 3G **23**
Portormin. *High* 5D **168**
Portpatrick. *Dum* 4F **109**
Port Quin. *Corn* 1D **6**
Port Ramsay. *Arg* 4C **140**
Portreath. *Corn* 4A **6**
Portree. *High* 4D **155**
Port Righ. *High* 4D **155**
Port St Mary. *IOM* 5B **108**
Portscatho. *Corn* 5C **6**
Portsea. *Port* 2E **17**
Port Seton. *E Lot* 2H **129**
Portskerra. *High* 2A **168**
Portskewett. *Mon* 3A **34**
Portslade-by-Sea. *Brig* 5D **26**
Portsmouth. *Port* **209** (2E **17**)
Portsmouth. *W Yor* 2H **91**
Port Soderick. *IOM* 4C **108**
Port Solent. *Port* 2E **17**
Portsonachan. *Arg* 1H **133**
Portsoy. *Abers* 2C **160**
Port Sunlight. *Mers* 2F **83**
Portswood. *Sotn* 1C **16**
Port Talbot. *Neat* 3A **32**
Porttannachy. *Mor* 2A **160**
Port Tennant. *Swan* 3F **31**
Portuairk. *High* 2F **139**
Portway. *Here* 1H **47**
Portway. *Worc* 3E **61**
Port Wemyss. *Arg* 4A **124**
Port William. *Dum* 5A **110**
Portwrinkle. *Corn* 3H **7**
Poslingford. *Suff* 1A **54**
Postbridge. *Devn* 5G **11**
Postcombe. *Oxon* 2F **37**
Post Green. *Dors* 3E **15**
Postling. *Kent* 2F **29**
Postlip. *Glos* 3F **49**
Post-Mawr. *Cdgn* 5D **56**
Postwick. *Norf* 5E **79**
Potarch. *Abers* 4D **152**
Potsgrove. *C Beds* 3H **51**
Potten End. *Herts* 5A **52**
Potter Brompton. *N Yor* 2D **101**
Pottergate Street. *Norf* 1D **66**
Potterhanworth. *Linc* 4H **87**
Potterhanworth Booths. *Linc* . . .4H **87**
Potter Heigham. *Norf* 4G **79**
Potter Hill. *Leics* 3E **75**
Potteries, The. *Stoke* 1C **72**
Potterne. *Wilts* 1E **23**
Potterne Wick. *Wilts* 1F **23**
Potternewton. *W Yor* 1D **92**
Potters Bar. *Herts* 5C **52**
Potters Brook. *Lanc* 4D **97**
Potter's Cross. *Staf* 2C **60**
Potters Crouch. *Herts* 5B **52**
Potter Somersal. *Derbs* 2F **73**
Potterspury. *Nptn* 1F **51**
Potter Street. *Essx* 5E **53**
Potterton. *Abers* 2G **153**
Potthorpe. *Norf* 3B **78**
Pottle Street. *Wilts* 2D **22**
Potto. *N Yor* 4B **106**
Potton. *C Beds* 1C **52**
Pott Row. *Norf* 3G **77**
Pott Shrigley. *Ches E* 3D **84**
Poughill. *Corn* 2C **10**
Poughill. *Devn* 2B **12**
Poulner. *Hants* 2G **15**
Poulshot. *Wilts* 1E **23**
Poulton. *Glos* 5G **49**
Poulton-le-Fylde. *Lanc* 1B **90**
Pound Bank. *Worc* 3B **60**
Poundbury. *Dors* 3B **14**
Poundfield. *E Sus* 2G **27**
Poundgate. *E Sus* 3F **27**
Pound Green. *E Sus* 3G **27**
Pound Green. *Suff* 5G **65**
Pound Hill. *W Sus* 2D **27**
Poundland. *S Ayr* 1G **109**
Poundon. *Buck* 3E **51**
Poundsgate. *Devn* 5H **11**
Poundstock. *Corn* 3C **10**
Pound Street. *Hants* 5C **36**
Pounsley. *E Sus* 3G **27**
Powburn. *Nmbd* 3E **121**
Powderham. *Devn* 4C **12**
Powerstock. *Dors* 3A **14**
Powfoot. *Dum* 3C **112**
Powick. *Worc* 5C **60**
Powmill. *Per* 4C **136**
Poxwell. *Dors* 4C **14**
Poyle. *Slo* 3B **38**
Poynings. *W Sus* 4D **26**
Poyntington. *Dors* 1B **14**
Poynton. *Ches E* 2D **84**
Poynton. *Telf* 4H **71**
Poynton Green. *Telf* 4H **71**

Poystreet Green—Rhemore

Poystreet Green. *Suff* 5B **66**
Praa Sands. *Corn* 4C **4**
Pratt's Bottom. *G Lon* 4F **39**
Praze-an-Beeble. *Corn* 3D **4**
Prees. *Shrp* 2H **71**
Preesall. *Lanc* 5C **96**
Preesall Park. *Lanc* 5C **96**
Prees Green. *Shrp* 2H **71**
Prees Higher Heath. *Shrp* 2H **71**
Prendergast. *Pemb* 3D **42**
Prendwick. *Nmbd* 3E **121**
Pren-gwyn. *Cdgn* 1E **45**
Prenteg. *Gwyn* 1E **69**
Prenton. *Mers* 2F **83**
Prescot. *Mers* 1G **83**
Prescott. *Devn* 1D **12**
Prescott. *Shrp* 3G **71**
Preshute. *Wilts* 5G **35**
Pressen. *Nmbd* 1C **120**
Prestatyn. *Den* 2C **82**
Prestbury. *Ches E* 3D **84**
Prestbury. *Glos* 3E **49**
Presteigne. *Powy* 4F **59**
Presthope. *Shrp* 1H **59**
Prestleigh. *Som* 2B **22**
Preston. *Brig* 5E **27**
Preston. *Devn* 5B **12**
Preston. *Dors* 4C **14**
Preston. *E Lot*
nr. East Linton 2B **130**
nr. Prestonpans 2G **129**
Preston. *E Yor* 1E **95**
Preston. *Glos* 5F **49**
Preston. *Herts* 3B **52**
Preston. *Kent*
nr. Canterbury 4G **41**
nr. Faversham 4E **41**
Preston. *Lanc* **208** (2D **90**)
Preston. *Nmbd* 2F **121**
Preston. *Rut* 5F **75**
Preston. *Bord* 4D **130**
Preston. *Shrp* 4H **71**
Preston. *Suff* 5B **66**
Preston. *Wilts*
nr. Aldbourne 4A **36**
nr. Lyneham 4F **35**
Preston Bagot. *Warw* 4F **61**
Preston Bissett. *Buck* 3E **51**
Preston Bowyer. *Som* 4E **21**
Preston Brockhurst. *Shrp* 3H **71**
Preston Brook. *Hal* 2H **83**
Preston Candover. *Hants* 2E **24**
Preston Capes. *Nptn* 5C **62**
Preston Cross. *Glos* 2B **48**
Preston Gubbals. *Shrp* 4G **71**
Preston-le-Skerne. *Dur* 2A **106**
Preston Marsh. *Here* 1A **48**
Prestonmill. *Dum* 4A **112**
Preston on Stour. *Warw* 1H **49**
Preston on the Hill. *Hal* 2H **83**
Preston on Wye. *Here* 1G **47**
Prestonpans. *E Lot* 2G **129**
Preston Plucknett. *Som* 1A **14**
Preston-under-Scar. *N Yor* 5D **104**
Preston upon the Weald Moors. *Telf* 4A **72**
Preston Wynne. *Here* 1A **48**
Prestwich. *G Man* 4G **91**
Prestwick. *Nmbd* 2E **115**
Prestwick. *S Ayr* 2C **116**
Prestwold. *Leics* 3C **74**
Prestwood. *Buck* 5G **51**
Prestwood. *Staf* 1F **73**
Price Town. *B'end* 2C **32**
Prickwillow. *Cambs* 2E **65**
Priddy. *Som* 1A **22**
Priestcliffe. *Derbs* 3F **85**
Priesthill. *Glas* 3G **127**
Priest Hutton. *Lanc* 2E **97**
Priestland. *E Ayr* 1E **117**
Priest Weston. *Shrp* 1E **59**
Priestwood. *Brac* 4G **37**
Priestwood. *Kent* 4A **40**
Primethorpe. *Leics* 1C **62**
Primrose Green. *Norf* 4C **78**
Primrose Hill. *Glos* 5B **48**
Primrose Hill. *Lanc* 4B **90**
Primrose Valley. *N Yor* 2F **101**
Primsidemill. *Bord* 2C **120**
Princes Gate. *Pemb* 3F **43**
Princes Risborough. *Buck* 5G **51**
Princethorpe. *Warw* 3B **62**
Princetown. *Devn* 5F **11**
Prinsted. *W Sus* 2F **17**
Prion. *Den* 4C **82**
Prior Muir. *Fife* 2H **137**
Prior's Frome. *Here* 2A **48**
Priors Halton. *Shrp* 3G **59**
Priors Hardwick. *Warw* 5B **62**
Priorslee. *Telf* 4B **72**
Priors Marston. *Warw* 5B **62**
Prior's Norton. *Glos* 3D **48**
Priory, The. *W Ber* 5B **36**
Priory Wood. *Here* 1F **47**
Priston. *Bath* 5B **34**
Pristow Green. *Norf* 2D **66**
Prittlewell. *S'end* 2C **40**
Privett. *Hants* 4E **25**
Prixford. *Devn* 3F **19**
Probus. *Corn* 4C **6**
Prospect. *Cumb* 5C **112**
Prospect Village. *Staf* 4E **73**
Provanmill. *Glas* 3H **127**
Prudhoe. *Nmbd* 3D **115**
Publow. *Bath* 5B **34**
Puckeridge. *Herts* 3D **53**
Puckington. *Som* 1G **13**
Pucklechurch. *S Glo* 4B **34**
Puckrup. *Glos* 2D **49**
Puddinglake. *Ches W* 4B **84**
Puddington. *Ches W* 3F **83**
Puddington. *Devn* 1B **12**
Puddlebrook. *Glos* 4B **48**
Puddledock. *Norf* 1C **66**
Puddletown. *Dors* 3C **14**
Pudleston. *Here* 5H **59**
Pudsey. *W Yor* 1C **92**
Pulborough. *W Sus* 4B **26**
Puleston. *Telf* 3B **72**
Pulford. *Ches W* 5F **83**
Pulham. *Dors* 2C **14**
Pulham Market. *Norf* 2D **66**
Pulham St Mary. *Norf* 2E **66**
Pulley. *Shrp* 5G **71**
Pulloxhill. *C Beds* 2A **52**
Pulpit Hill. *Arg* 1F **133**
Pulverbatch. *Shrp* 5G **71**
Pumpherston. *W Lot* 3D **128**
Pumsaint. *Carm* 1G **45**
Puncheston. *Pemb* 2E **43**
Puncknowle. *Dors* 4A **14**
Punnett's Town. *E Sus* 3H **27**
Purbrook. *Hants* 2E **17**
Purfleet. *Thur* 3G **39**
Puriton. *Som* 2G **21**
Purleigh. *Essx* 5B **54**
Purley. *G Lon* 4E **39**
Purley on Thames. *W Ber* 4E **37**
Purlogue. *Shrp* 3E **59**
Purl's Bridge. *Cambs* 2D **65**
Purse Caundle. *Dors* 1B **14**
Purslow. *Shrp* 2F **59**
Purston Jaglin. *W Yor* 3E **93**
Purtington. *Som* 2G **13**
Purton. *Glos*
nr. Lydney 5B **48**
nr. Sharpness 5B **48**
Purton. *Wilts* 3F **35**
Purton Stoke. *Wilts* 2F **35**
Pury End. *Nptn* 1F **51**
Pusey. *Oxon* 2B **36**
Putley. *Here* 2B **48**
Putney. *G Lon* 3D **38**
Putsborough. *Devn* 2E **19**
Puttenham. *Herts* 4G **51**
Puttenham. *Surr* 1A **26**
Puttock End. *Essx* 1B **54**
Puttock's End. *Essx* 4F **53**
Puxey. *Dors* 1C **14**
Puxton. *N Som* 5H **33**
Pwll. *Carm* 5E **45**
Pwll. *Powy* 5D **70**
Pwllcrochan. *Pemb* 4D **42**
Pwll-glas. *Den* 5D **82**
Pwllgloyw. *Powy* 2D **46**
Pwllheli. *Gwyn* 2C **68**
Pwllmeyric. *Mon* 2A **34**
Pwlltrap. *Carm* 3G **43**
Pwll-y-glaw. *Neat* 2A **32**
Pyecombe. *W Sus* 4D **27**
Pye Corner. *Herts* 4E **53**
Pye Corner. *Newp* 3G **33**
Pye Green. *Staf* 4D **73**
Pyewipe. *NE Lin* 3F **95**
Pyle. *B'end* 3B **32**
Pyle. *IOW* 5C **16**
Pyle Hill. *Surr* 5A **38**
Pylle. *Som* 3B **22**
Pymoor. *Cambs* 2D **65**
Pymore. *Dors* 3H **13**
Pyrford. *Surr* 5B **38**
Pyrford Village. *Surr* 5B **38**
Pyrton. *Oxon* 2E **37**
Pytchley. *Nptn* 3F **63**
Pyworthy. *Devn* 2D **10**

Q

Quabbs. *Shrp* 2E **58**
Quadring. *Linc* 2B **76**
Quadring Eaudike. *Linc* 2B **76**
Quainton. *Buck* 3F **51**
Quaking Houses. *Dur* 4E **115**
Quarley. *Hants* 2A **24**
Quarndon. *Derbs* 1H **73**
Quarrendon. *Buck* 4G **51**
Quarrier's Village. *Inv* 3E **127**
Quarrington. *Linc* 1H **75**
Quarrington Hill. *Dur* 1A **106**
Quarry, The. *Glos* 2C **34**
Quarry Bank. *W Mid* 2D **60**
Quarrywood. *Mor* 2F **159**
Quartalehouse. *Abers* 4G **161**
Quarter. *N Ayr* 3C **126**
Quarter. *S Lan* 4A **128**
Quatford. *Shrp* 1B **60**
Quatt. *Shrp* 2B **60**
Quebec. *Dur* 5E **115**
Quedgeley. *Glos* 4D **48**
Queen Adelaide. *Cambs* 2E **65**
Queenborough. *Kent* 3D **40**
Queen Camel. *Som* 4A **22**
Queen Charlton. *Bath* 5B **34**
Queen Dart. *Devn* 1B **12**
Queenhill. *Worc* 2D **48**
Queen Oak. *Dors* 3C **22**
Queensbury. *W Yor* 1B **92**
Queensferry Crossing. *Edin* 2E **129**
Queensferry. *Flin* 4F **83**
Queenstown. *Bkpl* 1B **90**
Queen Street. *Kent* 1A **28**
Queenzieburn. *N Lan* 2H **127**
Quemerford. *Wilts* 5F **35**
Quendale. *Shet* 10E **173**
Quendon. *Essx* 2F **53**
Queniborough. *Leics* 4D **74**
Quenington. *Glos* 5G **49**
Quernmore. *Lanc* 3E **97**
Quethiock. *Corn* 2H **7**
Quholm. *Orkn* 6B **172**
Quick's Green. *W Ber* 4D **36**
Quidenham. *Norf* 2C **66**
Quidhampton. *Hants* 1D **24**
Quidhampton. *Wilts* 3G **23**
Quilquox. *Abers* 5G **161**
Quina Brook. *Shrp* 2H **71**
Quindry. *Orkn* 8D **172**
Quine's Hill. *IOM* 4C **108**
Quinton. *Nptn* 5E **63**
Quinton. *W Mid* 2D **61**
Quintrell Downs. *Corn* 2C **6**
Quixhill. *Staf* 1F **73**
Quoditch. *Devn* 3E **11**
Quorn. *Leics* 4C **74**
Quorndon. *Leics* 4C **74**
Quothquan. *S Lan* 1B **118**
Quoyloo. *Orkn* 5B **172**
Quoyness. *Orkn* 7B **172**
Quoys. *Shet*
on Mainland 5F **173**
on Unst 1H **173**

R

Rableyheath. *Herts* 4C **52**
Raby. *Cumb* 4C **112**
Raby. *Mers* 3F **83**
Rachan Mill. *Bord* 1D **118**
Rachub. *Gwyn* 4F **81**
Rack End. *Oxon* 5C **50**
Rackenford. *Devn* 1B **12**
Rackham. *W Sus* 4B **26**
Rackheath. *Norf* 4E **79**
Racks. *Dum* 2B **112**
Rackwick. *Orkn*
on Hoy 8B **172**
on Westray 3D **172**
Radbourne. *Derbs* 2G **73**
Radcliffe. *G Man* 4F **91**
Radcliffe. *Nmbd* 4G **121**
Radcliffe on Trent. *Notts* 2D **74**
Radclive. *Buck* 2E **51**
Radernie. *Fife* 3G **137**
Radfall. *Kent* 4F **41**
Radford. *Bath* 1B **22**
Radford. *Nott* 1C **74**
Radford. *Oxon* 3C **50**
Radford. *W Mid* 2H **61**
Radford. *Worc* 5E **61**
Radford Semele. *Warw* 4H **61**
Radipole. *Dors* 4B **14**
Radlett. *Herts* 1C **38**
Radley. *Oxon* 2D **36**
Radnage. *Buck* 2F **37**
Radstock. *Bath* 1B **22**
Radstone. *Nptn* 1D **50**
Radway. *Warw* 1B **50**
Radway Green. *Ches E* 5B **84**
Radwell. *Bed* 5H **63**
Radwell. *Herts* 2C **52**
Radwinter. *Essx* 2G **53**
Radyr. *Card* 3E **33**
RAF Coltishall. *Norf* 3E **79**
Rafford. *Mor* 3E **159**
Ragdale. *Leics* 4D **74**
Ragdon. *Shrp* 1G **59**
Ragged Appleshaw. *Hants* 2B **24**
Raggra. *High* 4F **169**
Raglan. *Mon* 5H **47**
Ragnall. *Notts* 3F **87**
Raigbeg. *High* 1C **150**
Rainford. *Mers* 4C **90**
Rainford Junction. *Mers* 4C **90**
Rainham. *G Lon* 2G **39**
Rainham. *Medw* 4C **40**
Rainhill. *Mers* 1G **83**
Rainow. *Ches E* 3D **84**
Rainton. *N Yor* 2F **99**
Rainworth. *Notts* 5C **86**
Raisbeck. *Cumb* 4H **103**
Raise. *Cumb* 5A **114**
Rait. *Per* 1E **137**
Raithby. *Linc* 2C **88**
Raithby by Spilsby. *Linc* 4C **88**
Raithwaite. *N Yor* 3F **107**
Rake. *W Sus* 4G **25**
Rake End. *Staf* 4E **73**
Rakeway. *Staf* 1E **73**
Rakewood. *G Man* 3H **91**
Ralia. *High* 4B **150**
Ram Alley. *Wilts* 5H **35**
Ramasaig. *High* 4A **154**
Rame. *Corn*
nr. Millbrook 4A **8**
nr. Penryn 5B **6**
Ram Lane. *Kent* 1D **28**
Ramnageo. *Shet* 1H **173**
Rampisham. *Dors* 2A **14**
Rampside. *Cumb* 3B **96**
Rampton. *Cambs* 4D **64**
Rampton. *Notts* 3E **87**
Ramsbottom. *G Man* 3F **91**
Ramsburn. *Mor* 3C **160**
Ramsbury. *Wilts* 4A **36**
Ramscraigs. *High* 1H **165**
Ramsdean. *Hants* 4F **25**
Ramsdell. *Hants* 1D **24**
Ramsden. *Oxon* 4B **50**
Ramsden. *Worc* 1E **49**
Ramsden Bellhouse. *Essx* 1B **40**
Ramsden Heath. *Essx* 1B **40**
Ramsey. *Cambs* 2B **64**
Ramsey. *Essx* 2F **55**
Ramsey. *IOM* 2D **108**
Ramsey Forty Foot. *Cambs* 2C **64**
Ramsey Heights. *Cambs* 2B **64**
Ramsey Island. *Essx* 5C **54**
Ramsey Mereside. *Cambs* 2B **64**
Ramsey St Mary's. *Cambs* 2B **64**
Ramsgate. *Kent* 4H **41**
Ramsgill. *N Yor* 2D **98**
Ramshaw. *Dur* 5C **114**
Ramshorn. *Staf* 1E **73**
Ramsley. *Devn* 3G **11**
Ramsnest Common. *Surr* 2A **26**
Ramstone. *Abers* 2D **152**
Ranais. *W Isl* 5G **171**
Ranby. *Linc* 3B **88**
Ranby. *Notts* 2D **86**
Rand. *Linc* 3A **88**
Randwick. *Glos* 5D **48**
Ranfurly. *Ren* 3E **127**
Rangag. *High* 4D **169**
Rangemore. *Staf* 3F **73**
Rangeworthy. *S Glo* 3B **34**
Rankinston. *E Ayr* 3D **116**
Rank's Green. *Essx* 4H **53**
Ranmore Common. *Surr* 5C **38**
Rannoch Station. *Per* 3B **142**
Ranochan. *High* 5G **147**
Ranskill. *Notts* 2D **86**
Ranton. *Staf* 3C **72**
Ranton Green. *Staf* 3C **72**
Ranworth. *Norf* 4F **79**
Raploch. *Stir* 4G **135**
Rapness. *Orkn* 3E **172**
Rapps. *Som* 1G **13**
Rascal Moor. *E Yor* 1B **94**
Rascarrel. *Dum* 5E **111**
Rashfield. *Arg* 1C **126**
Rashwood. *Worc* 4D **60**
Raskelf. *N Yor* 2G **99**
Rassau. *Blae* 4E **47**
Rastrick. *W Yor* 2B **92**
Ratagan. *High* 2B **148**
Ratby. *Leics* 5C **74**
Ratcliffe Culey. *Leics* 1H **61**
Ratcliffe on Soar. *Notts* 3B **74**
Ratcliffe on the Wreake. *Leics* 4D **74**
Rathen. *Abers* 2H **161**
Rathillet. *Fife* 1F **137**
Rathmell. *N Yor* 3H **97**
Ratho. *Edin* 2E **129**
Ratho Station. *Edin* 2E **129**
Rathven. *Mor* 2B **160**
Ratley. *Hants* 4B **24**
Ratley. *Warw* 1B **50**
Ratlinghope. *Shrp* 1G **59**
Rattar. *High* 1E **169**
Ratten Row. *Cumb* 5E **113**
Ratten Row. *Lanc* 5D **96**
Rattery. *Devn* 2D **8**
Rattlesden. *Suff* 5B **66**
Ratton Village. *E Sus* 5G **27**
Rattray. *Abers* 3H **161**
Rattray. *Per* 4A **144**
Raughton. *Cumb* 5E **113**
Raughton Head. *Cumb* 5E **113**
Raunds. *Nptn* 3G **63**
Ravenfield. *S Yor* 1B **86**
Ravenfield Common. *S Yor* 1B **86**
Ravenglass. *Cumb* 5B **102**
Ravenhills Green. *Worc* 5B **60**
Raveningham. *Norf* 1F **67**
Ravenscar. *N Yor* 4G **107**
Ravensdale. *IOM* 2C **108**
Ravensden. *Bed* 5H **63**
Ravenseat. *N Yor* 4B **104**
Ravenshead. *Notts* 5C **86**
Ravensmoor. *Ches E* 5A **84**
Ravensthorpe. *Nptn* 3D **62**
Ravensthorpe. *W Yor* 2C **92**
Ravenstone. *Leics* 4B **74**
Ravenstone. *Mil* 5F **63**
Ravenstonedale. *Cumb* 4A **104**
Ravenstown. *Cumb* 2C **96**
Ravenstruther. *S Lan* 5C **128**
Ravensworth. *N Yor* 4E **105**
Raw. *N Yor* 4G **107**
Rawcliffe. *E Yor* 2G **93**
Rawcliffe. *York* 4H **99**
Rawcliffe Bridge. *E Yor* 2G **93**
Rawdon. *W Yor* 1C **92**
Rawgreen. *Nmbd* 4C **114**
Rawmarsh. *S Yor* 1B **86**
Rawnsley. *Staf* 4E **73**
Rawreth. *Essx* 1B **40**
Rawridge. *Devn* 2F **13**
Rawson Green. *Derbs* 1A **74**
Rawtenstall. *Lanc* 2G **91**
Raydon. *Suff* 2D **54**
Raylees. *Nmbd* 5D **120**
Rayleigh. *Essx* 1C **40**
Raymond's Hill. *Devn* 3G **13**
Rayne. *Essx* 3H **53**
Rayners Lane. *G Lon* 2C **38**
Reach. *Cambs* 4E **65**
Read. *Lanc* 1F **91**
Reading. *Read* **209** (4F **37**)
Reading Green. *Suff* 3D **66**
Reading Street. *Kent* 2D **28**
Readymoney. *Corn* 3F **7**
Reagill. *Cumb* 3H **103**
Rearquhar. *High* 4E **165**
Rearsby. *Leics* 4D **74**
Reasby. *Linc* 3H **87**
Reaseheath. *Ches E* 5A **84**
Reaster. *High* 2E **169**
Reawick. *Shet* 7E **173**
Reay. *High* 2B **168**
Rechullin. *High* 3A **156**
Reculver. *Kent* 4G **41**
Redberth. *Pemb* 4E **43**
Redbourn. *Herts* 4B **52**
Redbourne. *N Lin* 4C **94**
Redbrook. *Glos* 5A **48**
Redbrook. *Wrex* 1H **71**
Redburn. *High* 4D **158**
Redburn. *Nmbd* 3A **114**
Redcar. *Red C* 2D **106**
Redcastle. *High* 4H **157**
Redcliffe Bay. *N Som* 4H **33**
Red Dial. *Cumb* 5D **112**
Redding. *Falk* 2C **128**
Reddingmuirhead. *Falk* 2C **128**
Reddings, The. *Glos* 3E **49**
Reddish. *G Man* 1C **84**
Redditch. *Worc* 4E **61**
Rede. *Suff* 5H **65**
Redenhall. *Norf* 2E **67**
Redesdale Camp. *Nmbd* 5C **120**
Redesmouth. *Nmbd* 1B **114**
Redford. *Ang* 4E **145**
Redford. *Dur* 1D **105**
Redford. *W Sus* 4G **25**
Redfordgreen. *Bord* 3F **119**
Redgate. *Corn* 2G **7**
Redgrave. *Suff* 3C **66**
Redhill. *Abers* 3E **153**
Redhill. *Herts* 2C **52**
Redhill. *N Som* 5A **34**
Redhill. *Shrp* 4B **72**
Redhill. *Surr* 5D **39**
Red Hill. *Warw* 5F **61**
Red Hill. *W Yor* 2E **93**
Redhouses. *Arg* 3B **124**
Redisham. *Suff* 2G **67**
Redland. *Bris* 4A **34**
Redland. *Orkn* 5C **172**
Redlingfield. *Suff* 3D **66**
Red Lodge. *Suff* 3F **65**
Redlynch. *Som* 3C **22**
Redlynch. *Wilts* 4H **23**
Redmain. *Cumb* 1C **102**
Redmarley. *Worc* 4B **60**
Redmarley D'Abitot. *Glos* 2C **48**
Redmarshall. *Stoc T* 2A **106**
Redmile. *Leics* 2E **75**
Redmire. *N Yor* 5D **104**
Rednal. *Shrp* 3F **71**
Redpath. *Bord* 1H **119**
Redpoint. *High* 2G **155**
Red Post. *Corn* 2C **10**
Red Rock. *G Man* 4D **90**
Red Roses. *Carm* 3G **43**
Red Row. *Nmbd* 5G **121**
Redruth. *Corn* 4B **6**
Red Street. *Staf* 5C **84**
Redvales. *G Man* 4G **91**
Red Wharf Bay. *IOA* 2E **81**
Redwick. *Newp* 3H **33**
Redwick. *S Glo* 3A **34**
Redworth. *Darl* 2F **105**
Reed. *Herts* 2D **52**
Reed End. *Herts* 2D **52**
Reedham. *Linc* 5B **88**
Reedham. *Norf* 5G **79**
Reedness. *E Yor* 2B **94**
Reeds Beck. *Linc* 4B **88**
Reemshill. *Abers* 4E **161**
Reepham. *Linc* 3H **87**
Reepham. *Norf* 3C **78**
Reeth. *N Yor* 5D **104**
Regaby. *IOM* 2D **108**
Regil. *N Som* 5A **34**
Regoul. *High* 3C **158**
Reiff. *High* 2D **162**
Reigate. *Surr* 5D **38**
Reighton. *N Yor* 2F **101**
Reilth. *Shrp* 2E **59**
Reinigeadal. *W Isl* 7E **171**
Reisque. *Abers* 2F **153**
Reiss. *High* 3F **169**
Rejerrah. *Corn* 3B **6**
Releath. *Corn* 5A **6**
Relubbus. *Corn* 3C **4**
Relugas. *Mor* 4D **159**
Remenham. *Wok* 3F **37**
Remenham Hill. *Wok* 3F **37**
Rempstone. *Notts* 3C **74**
Rendcomb. *Glos* 5F **49**
Rendham. *Suff* 4F **67**
Rendlesham. *Suff* 5F **67**
Renfrew. *Ren* 3G **127**
Renhold. *Bed* 5H **63**
Renishaw. *Derbs* 3B **86**
Rennington. *Nmbd* 3G **121**
Renton. *W Dun* 2E **127**
Renwick. *Cumb* 5G **113**
Repps. *Norf* 4G **79**
Repton. *Derbs* 3H **73**
Rescassa. *Corn* 4D **6**
Rescobie. *Ang* 3E **145**
Rescorla. *Corn*
nr. Penwithick 3E **7**
nr. Sticker 4D **6**
Resipole. *High* 2B **140**
Resolfen. *Neat* 5B **46**
Resolis. *High* 2A **158**
Resolven. *Neat* 5B **46**
Rest and be thankful. *Arg* 3B **134**
Reston. *Bord* 3E **131**
Restrop. *Wilts* 3F **35**
Retford. *Notts* 2E **86**
Retire. *Corn* 2E **6**
Rettendon. *Essx* 1B **40**
Revesby. *Linc* 4B **88**
Rew. *Devn* 5D **8**
Rewe. *Devn* 3C **12**
Rew Street. *IOW* 3C **16**
Rexon. *Devn* 4E **11**
Reybridge. *Wilts* 5E **35**
Reydon. *Suff* 3H **67**
Reymerston. *Norf* 5C **78**
Reynalton. *Pemb* 4E **43**
Reynoldston. *Swan* 4D **31**
Rezare. *Corn* 5D **10**
Rhadyr. *Mon* 5G **47**
Rhaeadr Gwy. *Powy* 4B **58**
Rhandirmwyn. *Carm* 1A **46**
Rhayader. *Powy* 4B **58**
Rheindown. *High* 4H **157**
Rhemore. *High* 3G **139**

Rhenetra—Rugby

Rhenetra. High 3D 154
Rhewl. Den
nr. Llangollen 1D 70
nr. Ruthin 4D 82
Rhewl. Shrp 2F 71
Rhewl-Mostyn. Flin 2D 82
Rhian. High 2C 164
Rhian Breck. High 3C 164
Rhicarn. High 1E 163
Rhiconich. High 3C 166
Rhicullen. High 1A 158
Rhidorroch. High 4F 163
Rhifail. High 4H 167
Rhigos. Rhon 5C 46
Rhilochan. High 3E 165
Rhiroy. High 5F 163
Rhitongue. High 3G 167
Rhiw. Gwyn 3B 68
Rhiwabon. Wrex 1F 71
Rhiwbina. Card 3E 33
Rhiwbryfdir. Gwyn 1F 69
Rhiwderin. Newp 3F 33
Rhiwlas. Gwyn
nr. Bala 2B 70
nr. Bangor 4E 81
Rhiwlas. Powy 2D 70
Rhodes. G Man 4G 91
Rhodesia. Notts 2C 86
Rhodes Minnis. Kent 1F 29
Rhodiad-y-Brenin. Pemb 2B 42
Rhondda. Rhon 2C 32
Rhonehouse. Dum 4E 111
Rhoose. V Glam 5D 32
Rhos. Carm 2D 45
Rhos. Neat 5H 45
Rhos, The. Pemb 3E 43
Rhosaman. Carm 4H 45
Rhoscefnhir. IOA 3E 81
Rhoscolyn. IOA 3B 80
Rhos Common. Powy 4E 71
Rhoscrowther. Pemb 4D 42
Rhos-ddu. Gwyn 2B 68
Rhosdylluan. Gwyn 3A 70
Rhosesmor. Flin 4E 82
Rhos-fawr. Gwyn 2C 68
Rhosgadfan. Gwyn 5E 81
Rhosgoch. IOA 2D 80
Rhosgoch. Powy 1E 47
Rhos Haminiog. Cdgn 4E 57
Rhos-hill. Pemb 1B 44
Rhoshirwaun. Gwyn 3A 68
Rhoslan. Gwyn 1D 69
Rhoslefain. Gwyn 5E 69
Rhosllanerchrugog. Wrex 1E 71
Rhôs Lligwy. IOA 2D 81
Rhosmaen. Carm 3G 45
Rhosmeirch. IOA 3D 80
Rhosneigr. IOA 3C 80
Rhôs-on-Sea. Cnwy 2H 81
Rhossili. Swan 4D 30
Rhosson. Pemb 2B 42
Rhostrenwfa. IOA 3D 80
Rhostryfan. Gwyn 5D 81
Rhostyllen. Wrex 1F 71
Rhoswiel. Shrp 2E 71
Rhosybol. IOA 2D 80
Rhos-y-brithdir. Powy 3D 70
Rhos-y-garth. Cdgn 3F 57
Rhos-y-gwaliau. Gwyn 2B 70
Rhos-y-llan. Gwyn 2B 68
Rhos-y-meirch. Powy 4E 59
Rhu. Arg 1D 126
Rhualt. Den 3C 82
Rhubha Stoer. High 1E 163
Rhubodach. Arg 2B 126
Rhuddall Heath. Ches W 4H 83
Rhuddlan. Cdgn 1E 45
Rhuddlan. Den 3C 82
Rhue. High 4E 163
Rhulen. Powy 1E 47
Rhunahaorine. Arg 5F 125
Rhuthun. Den 5D 82
Rhuvoult. High 3C 166
Y Rhws. V Glam 5D 32
Rhyd. Gwyn 1F 69
Rhydaman. Carm 4G 45
Rhydargaeau. Carm 3E 45
Rhydcymerau. Carm 2F 45
Rhydd. Worc 1D 48
Rhyd-Ddu. Gwyn 5E 81
Rhydding. Neat 3G 31
Rhydfudr. Cdgn 4E 57
Rhydlanfair. Cnwy 5H 81
Rhydlewis. Cdgn 1D 44
Rhydlios. Gwyn 2A 68
Rhydlydan. Cnwy 5A 82
Rhyd-meirionydd. Cdgn 2F 57
Rhydowen. Cdgn 1E 45
Rhyd-Rosser. Cdgn 4E 57
Rhydspence. Here 1F 47
Rhydtalog. Flin 5E 83
Rhyd-uchaf. Gwyn 2B 70
Rhydwyn. IOA 2C 80
Rhyd-y-clafdy. Gwyn 2C 68
Rhydycroesau. Powy 2E 71
Rhydyfelin. Cdgn 3E 57
Rhydyfelin. Rhon 3D 32
Rhyd-y-foel. Cnwy 3B 82
Rhyd-y-fro. Neat 5H 45
Rhydymain. Gwyn 3H 69
Rhyd-y-meudwy. Den 5D 82
Rhydymwyn. Flin 4E 82
Rhyd-yr-onen. Gwyn 5F 69
Rhyd-y-sarn. Gwyn 1F 69
Rhyl. Den 2C 82
Rhymney. Cphy 5E 46
Rhymni. Cphy 5E 46
Rhynd. Per 1D 136
Rhynie. Abers 1B 152
Ribbesford. Worc 3B 60
Ribbleton. Lanc 1D 90
Ribby. Lanc 1C 90
Ribchester. Lanc 1E 91
Riber. Derbs 5H 85
Ribigill. High 3F 167
Riby. Linc 4E 95
Riccall. N Yor 1G 93
Riccarton. E Ayr 1D 116
Richards Castle. Here 4G 59
Richborough Port. Kent 4H 41
Richings Park. Buck 3B 38
Richmond. G Lon 3C 38
Richmond. N Yor 4E 105
Rickarton. Abers 5F 153
Rickerby. Cumb 4F 113
Rickerscote. Staf 3D 72
Rickford. N Som 1H 21
Rickham. Devn 5D 8
Rickinghall. Suff 3C 66
Rickleton. Tyne 4F 115
Rickling. Essx 2E 53
Rickling Green. Essx 3F 53
Rickmansworth. Herts 1B 38
Riddings. Derbs 5B 86
Riddlecombe. Devn 1G 11
Riddlesden. W Yor 5C 98
Ridge. Dors 4E 15
Ridge. Herts 5C 52
Ridge. Wilts 3E 23
Ridgebourne. Powy 4C 58
Ridge Lane. Warw 1G 61
Ridgeway. Derbs
nr. Alfreton 5A 86
nr. Sheffield 2B 86
Ridgeway. Staf 5C 84
Ridgeway Cross. Here 1C 48
Ridgeway Moor. Derbs 2B 86
Ridgewell. Essx 1H 53
Ridgewood. E Sus 3F 27
Ridgmont. C Beds 2H 51
Ridgwardine. Shrp 2A 72
Riding Mill. Nmbd 3D 114
Ridley. Kent 4H 39
Ridley. Nmbd 3A 114
Ridlington. Norf 2F 79
Ridlington. Rut 5F 75
Ridsdale. Nmbd 1C 114
Riemore Lodge. Per 4H 143
Rievaulx. N Yor 1H 99
Rift House. Hart 1B 106
Rigg. Dum 3D 112
Riggend. N Lan 2A 128
Rigsby. Linc 3D 88
Rigside. S Lan 1A 118
Riley Green. Lanc 2E 90
Rileyhill. Staf 4F 73
Rilla Mill. Corn 5C 10
Rillington. N Yor 2C 100
Rimington. Lanc 5H 97
Rimpton. Som 4B 22
Rimsdale. High 4H 167
Rimswell. E Yor 2G 95
Ringasta. Shet 10E 173
Ringford. Dum 4D 111
Ringing Hill. Leics 4B 74
Ringinglow. S Yor 2G 85
Ringland. Norf 4D 78
Ringlestone. Kent 5C 40
Ringmer. E Sus 4F 27
Ringmore. Devn
nr. Kingsbridge 4C 8
nr. Teignmouth 5C 12
Ring o' Bells. Lanc 3C 90
Ring's End. Cambs 5C 76
Ringsfield. Suff 2G 67
Ringsfield Corner. Suff 2G 67
Ringshall. Buck 4H 51
Ringshall. Suff 5C 66
Ringshall Stocks. Suff 5C 66
Ringstead. Norf 1G 77
Ringstead. Nptn 3G 63
Ringwood. Hants 2G 15
Ringwould. Kent 1H 29
Rinmore. Abers 2B 152
Rinnigill. Orkn 8C 172
Rinsey. Corn 4C 4
Riof. W Isl 4D 171
Ripe. E Sus 4G 27
Ripley. Derbs 5B 86
Ripley. Hants 3G 15
Ripley. N Yor 3E 99
Ripley. Surr 5B 38
Riplingham. E Yor 1C 94
Ripon. N Yor 2F 99
Rippingale. Linc 3H 75
Ripple. Kent 1H 29
Ripple. Worc 2D 48
Ripponden. W Yor 3A 92
Rireavach. High 4E 163
Risabus. Arg 5B 124
Risbury. Here 5H 59
Risby. E Yor 1D 94
Risby. N Lin 3C 94
Risby. Suff 4G 65
Risca. Cphy 2F 33
Rise. E Yor 5F 101
Riseden. E Sus 2H 27
Riseden. Kent 2B 28
Rise End. Derbs 5G 85
Risegate. Linc 3B 76
Riseholme. Linc 3G 87
Riseley. Bed 4H 63
Riseley. Wok 5F 37
Rishangles. Suff 4D 66
Rishton. Lanc 1F 91
Rishworth. W Yor 3A 92
Risley. Derbs 2B 74
Risley. Warr 1A 84
Risplith. N Yor 3E 99
Rispond. High 2E 167
Rivar. Wilts 5B 36
Rivenhall. Essx 4B 54
Rivenhall End. Essx 4B 54
River. Kent 1G 29
River. W Sus 3A 26
River Bank. Cambs 4E 65
Riverhead. Kent 5G 39
Rivington. Lanc 3E 91
Roach Bridge. Lanc 2D 90
Roachill. Devn 4B 20
Roade. Nptn 5E 63
Road Green. Norf 1E 67
Roadhead. Cumb 2G 113
Roadmeetings. S Lan 5B 128
Roadside. High 2D 168
Roadside of Catterline. Abers 1H 145
Roadside of Kinneff. Abers 1H 145
Roadwater. Som 3D 20
Road Weedon. Nptn 5D 62
Roag. High 4B 154
Roa Island. Cumb 3B 96
Roath. Card 4E 33
Roberton. Bord 3G 119
Roberton. S Lan 2B 118
Robertsbridge. E Sus 3B 28
Robertstown. Mor 4G 159
Robertstown. Rhon 5C 46
Roberttown. W Yor 2B 92
Robeston Back. Pemb 3E 43
Robeston Wathen. Pemb 3E 43
Robeston West. Pemb 4C 42
Robin Hood. Lanc 3D 90
Robin Hood. W Yor 2D 92
Robinhood End. Essx 2H 53
Robin Hood's Bay. N Yor 4G 107
Roborough. Devn
nr. Great Torrington 1F 11
nr. Plymouth 2B 8
Rob Roy's House. Arg 2A 134
Roby Mill. Lanc 4D 90
Rocester. Staf 2F 73
Roch. Pemb 2C 42
Rochdale. G Man 3G 91
Roche. Corn 2D 6
Rochester. Medw 204 (4B 40)
Rochester. Nmbd 5C 120
Rochford. Essx 1C 40
Rock. Corn 1D 6
Rock. Nmbd 2G 121
Rock. W Sus 4C 26
Rock. Worc 3B 60
Rockbeare. Devn 3D 12
Rockbourne. Hants 1G 15
Rockcliffe. Cumb 3E 113
Rockcliffe. Dum 4F 111
Rockcliffe Cross. Cumb 3E 113
Rock Ferry. Mers 2F 83
Rockfield. High 5G 165
Rockfield. Mon 4H 47
Rockford. Hants 2G 15
Rockgreen. Shrp 3H 59
Rockhampton. S Glo 2B 34
Rockhead. Corn 4A 10
Rockingham. Nptn 1F 63
Rockland All Saints. Norf 1B 66
Rockland St Mary. Norf 5F 79
Rockland St Peter. Norf 1B 66
Rockley. Wilts 4G 35
Rockwell End. Buck 3F 37
Rockwell Green. Som 1E 13
Rodborough. Glos 5D 48
Rodbourne. Wilts 3E 35
Rodd. Here 4F 59
Roddam. Nmbd 2E 121
Rodden. Dors 4B 14
Roddenloft. E Ayr 2D 117
Roddymoor. Dur 1E 105
Rode. Som 1D 22
Rode Heath. Ches E 5C 84
Rodeheath. Ches E 4C 84
Rodel. W Isl 9C 171
Roden. Telf 4H 71
Rodhuish. Som 3D 20
Rodington. Telf 4H 71
Rodington Heath. Telf 4H 71
Rodley. Glos 4C 48
Rodmarton. Glos 2E 35
Rodmell. E Sus 5F 27
Rodmersham. Kent 4D 40
Rodmersham Green. Kent 4D 40
Rodney Stoke. Som 2H 21
Rodsley. Derbs 1G 73
Rodway. Som 3F 21
Rodway. Telf 4A 72
Rodwell. Dors 5B 14
Roecliffe. N Yor 3F 99
Roe Green. Herts 2D 52
Roehampton. G Lon 3D 38
Roesound. Shet 5E 173
Roffey. W Sus 2C 26
Rogart. High 3E 165
Rogate. W Sus 4G 25
Roger Ground. Cumb 5E 103
Rogerstone. Newp 3F 33
Rogiet. Mon 3H 33
Rogue's Alley. Cambs 5C 76
Roke. Oxon 2E 37
Rokemarsh. Oxon 2E 36
Roker. Tyne 4H 115
Rollesby. Norf 4G 79
Rolleston. Leics 5E 75
Rolleston. Notts 5E 87
Rolleston on Dove. Staf 3G 73
Rolston. E Yor 5G 101
Rolvenden. Kent 2C 28
Rolvenden Layne. Kent 2C 28
Romaldkirk. Dur 2C 104
Roman Bank. Shrp 1H 59
Romanby. N Yor 5A 106
Romannobridge. Bord 5E 129
Romansleigh. Devn 4H 19
Romers Common. Worc 4H 59
Romesdal. High 3D 154
Romford. Dors 2F 15
Romford. G Lon 2G 39
Romiley. G Man 1D 84
Romsey. Hants 4B 24
Romsley. Shrp 2B 60
Romsley. Worc 3D 60
Ronague. IOM 4B 108
Ronaldsvoe. Orkn 8D 172
Rookby. Cumb 3B 104
Rookhope. Dur 5C 114
Rooking. Cumb 3F 103
Rookley. IOW 4D 16
Rooks Bridge. Som 1G 21
Rooksey Green. Suff 5B 66
Rook's Nest. Som 3D 20
Rookwood. W Sus 3F 17
Roos. E Yor 1F 95
Roosebeck. Cumb 3B 96
Roosecote. Cumb 3B 96
Rootfield. High 3H 157
Rootham's Green. Bed 5A 64
Rootpark. S Lan 4C 128
Ropley. Hants 3E 25
Ropley Dean. Hants 3E 25
Ropsley. Linc 2G 75
Rora. Abers 3H 161
Rorandle. Abers 2D 152
Rorrington. Shrp 5F 71
Rose. Corn 3B 6
Roseacre. Lanc 1C 90
Rose Ash. Devn 4A 20
Rosebank. S Lan 5B 128
Rosebush. Pemb 2E 43
Rosedale Abbey. N Yor 5E 107
Roseden. Nmbd 2E 121
Rose Green. Essx 3B 54
Rose Green. Suff 1C 54
Rosehall. High 3B 164
Rosehearty. Abers 2G 161
Rose Hill. E Sus 4F 27
Rose Hill. Lanc 1G 91
Rosehill. Shrp
nr. Market Drayton 2A 72
nr. Shrewsbury 4G 71
Roseisle. Mor 2F 159
Rosemarket. Pemb 4D 42
Rosemarkie. High 3B 158
Rosemary Lane. Devn 1E 13
Rosemount. Per 4A 144
Rosenannon. Corn 2D 6
Roser's Cross. E Sus 3G 27
Rosevean. Corn 3E 6
Rosewell. Midl 3F 129
Roseworth. Stoc T 2B 106
Roseworthy. Corn 3D 4
Rosgill. Cumb 3G 103
Roshven. High 1B 140
Roskhill. High 4B 154
Roskorwell. Corn 4E 5
Rosley. Cumb 5E 112
Roslin. Midl 3F 129
Rosliston. Derbs 4G 73
Rosneath. Arg 1D 126
Ross. Dum 5D 110
Ross. Nmbd 1F 121
Ross. Per 1G 135
Ross. Bord 3F 131
Rossendale. Lanc 2F 91
Rossett. Wrex 5F 83
Rossington. S Yor 1D 86
Rosskeen. High 2A 158
Rossland. Ren 2F 127
Ross-on-Wye. Here 3B 48
Roster. High 5E 169
Rostherne. Ches E 2B 84
Rostholme. S Yor 4F 93
Rosthwaite. Cumb 3D 102
Roston. Derbs 1F 73
Rosudgeon. Corn 4C 4
Rosyth. Fife 1E 129
Rothbury. Nmbd 4E 121
Rotherby. Leics 4D 74
Rotherfield. E Sus 3G 27
Rotherfield Greys. Oxon 3F 37
Rotherfield Peppard. Oxon 3F 37
Rotherham. S Yor 1B 86
Rothersthorpe. Nptn 5E 62
Rotherwick. Hants 1F 25
Rothes. Mor 4G 159
Rothesay. Arg 3B 126
Rothienorman. Abers 5E 160
Rothiesholm. Orkn 5F 172
Rothley. Leics 4C 74
Rothley. Nmbd 1D 114
Rothwell. Linc 1A 88
Rothwell. Nptn 2F 63
Rothwell. W Yor 2D 92
Rotsea. E Yor 4E 101
Rottal. Ang 2C 144
Rotten End. Suff 4F 67
Rotten Row. Norf 4C 78
Rotten Row. W Ber 4D 36
Rotten Row. W Mid 3F 61
Rottingdean. Brig 5E 27
Rottington. Cumb 3A 102
Roud. IOW 4D 16
Rougham. Norf 3H 77
Rougham. Suff 4B 66
Rough Close. Staf 2D 72
Rough Common. Kent 5F 41
Roughcote. Staf 1D 72
Rough Haugh. High 4H 167
Rough Hay. Staf 3G 73
Roughlee. Lanc 5H 97
Roughley. W Mid 1F 61
Roughsike. Cumb 2G 113
Roughton. Linc 4B 88
Roughton. Norf 2E 78
Roughton. Shrp 1B 60
Roundbush Green. Essx 4F 53
Roundham. Som 2H 13
Roundhay. W Yor 1D 92
Round Hill. Torb 2E 9
Roundhurst. W Sus 2A 26
Round Maple. Suff 1C 54
Round Oak. Shrp 2F 59
Roundstreet Common. W Sus 3B 26
Roundthwaite. Cumb 4H 103
Roundway. Wilts 5F 35
Roundyhill. Ang 3C 144
Rousdon. Devn 3F 13
Rousham. Oxon 3C 50
Rous Lench. Worc 5E 61
Routh. E Yor 5E 101
Rout's Green. Buck 2F 37
Row. Corn 5A 10
Row. Cumb
nr. Kendal 1D 96
nr. Penrith 1H 103
Row, The. Lanc 2D 96
Rowanburn. Dum 2F 113
Rowanhill. Abers 3H 161
Rowardennan. Stir 4C 134
Rowarth. Derbs 2E 85
Row Ash. Hants 1D 16
Rowberrow. Som 1H 21
Rowde. Wilts 5E 35
Rowden. Devn 3G 11
Rowen. Cnwy 3G 81
Rowfoot. Nmbd 3H 113
Row Green. Essx 3H 53
Row Heath. Essx 4E 55
Rowhedge. Essx 3D 54
Rowhook. W Sus 2C 26
Rowington. Warw 4G 61
Rowland. Derbs 3G 85
Rowlands Castle. Hants 1F 17
Rowlands Gill. Tyne 4E 115
Rowledge. Hants 2G 25
Rowley. Dur 5D 115
Rowley. E Yor 1C 94
Rowley. Shrp 5F 71
Rowley Hill. W Yor 3B 92
Rowley Regis. W Mid 2D 60
Rowlstone. Here 3G 47
Rowly. Surr 1B 26
Rowner. Hants 2D 16
Rowney Green. Worc 3E 61
Rownhams. Hants 1B 16
Rowrah. Cumb 3B 102
Rowsham. Buck 4G 51
Rowsley. Derbs 4G 85
Rowstock. Oxon 3C 36
Rowston. Linc 5H 87
Rowthorne. Derbs 4B 86
Rowton. Ches W 4G 83
Rowton. Shrp
nr. Ludlow 2G 59
nr. Shrewsbury 4F 71
Rowton. Telf 4A 72
Row Town. Surr 4B 38
Roxburgh. Bord 1B 120
Roxby. N Lin 3C 94
Roxby. N Yor 3E 107
Roxton. Bed 5A 64
Roxwell. Essx 5G 53
Royal Leamington Spa. Warw 4H 61
Royal Oak. Darl 2F 105
Royal Oak. Lanc 4C 90
Royal Oak. N Yor 2F 101
Royal's Green. Ches E 1A 72
Royal Sutton Coldfield. W Mid 1F 61
Royal Tunbridge Wells. Kent 2G 27
Royal Wootton Bassett. Wilts 3F 35
Roybridge. High 5E 149
Roydon. Essx 4E 53
Roydon. Norf
nr. Diss 2C 66
nr. King's Lynn 3G 77
Roydon Hamlet. Essx 5E 53
Royston. Herts 1D 52
Royston. S Yor 3D 92
Royston Water. Som 1F 13
Royton. G Man 4H 91
Ruabon. Wrex 1F 71
Ruaig. Arg 4B 138
Ruan High Lanes. Corn 5D 6
Ruan Lanihorne. Corn 4C 6
Ruan Major. Corn 5E 5
Ruan Minor. Corn 5E 5
Ruarach. High 1B 148
Ruardean. Glos 4B 48
Ruardean Hill. Glos 4B 48
Ruardean Woodside. Glos 4B 48
Rubery. Worc 3D 61
Ruchazie. Glas 3H 127
Ruckcroft. Cumb 5G 113
Ruckinge. Kent 2E 29
Ruckland. Linc 3C 88
Rucklers Lane. Herts 5A 52
Ruckley. Shrp 5H 71
Rudbaxton. Pemb 2D 42
Rudby. N Yor 4B 106
Ruddington. Notts 2C 74
Rudford. Glos 3C 48
Rudge. Shrp 1C 60
Rudge. Wilts 1D 22
Rudge Heath. Shrp 1B 60
Rudgeway. S Glo 3B 34
Rudgwick. W Sus 2B 26
Rudhall. Here 3B 48
Rudheath. Ches W 3A 84
Rudley Green. Essx 5B 54
Rudloe. Wilts 4D 34
Rudry. Cphy 3F 33
Rudston. E Yor 3E 101
Rudyard. Staf 5D 84
Rufford. Lanc 3C 90
Rufforth. York 4H 99
Rugby. Warw 3C 62

Rugeley. *Staf* 4E 73
Ruglen. *S Ayr* 4B 116
Ruilick. *High* 4H 157
Ruisaurie. *High* 4G 157
Ruishton. *Som* 4F 21
Ruisigearraidh. *W Isl* 1E 170
Ruislip. *G Lon* 2B 38
Ruislip Common. *G Lon* 2B 38
Rumbling Bridge. *Per* 4C 136
Rumburgh. *Suff* 2F 67
Rumford. *Corn* 1C 6
Rumford. *Falk* 2C 128
Rumney. *Card* 4F 33
Rumwell. *Som* 4E 21
Runcorn. *Hal* 2H 83
Runcton. *W Sus* 2G 17
Runcton Holme. *Norf* 5F 77
Rundlestone. *Devn* 5F 11
Runfold. *Surr* 2G 25
Runhall. *Norf* 5C 78
Runham. *Norf* 4G 79
Runnington. *Som* 4E 20
Runshaw Moor. *Lanc* 3D 90
Runswick. *N Yor* 3F 107
Runtaleave. *Ang* 2B 144
Runwell. *Essx* 1B 40
Ruscombe. *Wok* 4F 37
Rushall. *Here* 2B 48
Rushall. *Norf* 2D 66
Rushall. *W Mid* 5E 73
Rushall. *Wilts* 1G 23
Rushbrooke. *Suff* 4A 66
Rushbury. *Shrp* 1H 59
Rushden. *Herts* 2D 52
Rushden. *Nptn* 4G 63
Rushenden. *Kent* 3D 40
Rushford. *Devn* 5E 11
Rushford. *Suff* 2B 66
Rush Green. *Herts* 3C 52
Rushlake Green. *E Sus* 4H 27
Rushmere. *Suff* 2G 67
Rushmere St Andrew. *Suff* 1F 55
Rushmoor. *Surr* 2G 25
Rushock. *Worc* 3C 60
Rusholme. *G Man* 1C 84
Rushton. *Ches W* 4H 83
Rushton. *Nptn* 2F 63
Rushton. *Shrp* 5A 72
Rushton Spencer. *Staf* 4D 84
Rushwick. *Worc* 5C 60
Rushyford. *Dur* 2F 105
Ruskie. *Stir* 3E 135
Ruskington. *Linc* 5H 87
Rusland. *Cumb* 1C 96
Rusper. *W Sus* 2D 26
Ruspidge. *Glos* 4B 48
Russell's Water. *Oxon* 3F 37
Russel's Green. *Suff* 3E 67
Russ Hill. *Surr* 1D 26
Russland. *Orkn* 6C 172
Rusthall. *Kent* 2G 27
Rustington. *W Sus* 5B 26
Ruston. *N Yor* 1D 100
Ruston Parva. *E Yor* 3E 101
Ruswarp. *N Yor* 4F 107
Rutherglen. *S Lan* 3H 127
Ruthernbridge. *Corn* 2E 6
Ruthin. *Den* 5D 82
Ruthin. *V Glam* 4C 32
Ruthrieston. *Aber* 3G 153
Ruthven. *Abers* 4C 160
Ruthven. *Ang* 4B 144
Ruthven. *High*
  nr. Inverness 5C 158
  nr. Kingussie 4B 150
Ruthvoes. *Corn* 2D 6
Ruthwaite. *Cumb* 1D 102
Ruthwell. *Dum* 3C 112
Ruxton Green. *Here* 4A 48
Ruyton-XI-Towns. *Shrp* 3F 71
Ryal. *Nmbd* 2D 114
Ryall. *Dors* 3H 13
Ryall. *Worc* 1D 48
Ryarsh. *Kent* 5A 40
Rychraggan. *High* 5G 157
Rydal. *Cumb* 4E 103
Ryde. *IOW* 3D 16
Rye. *E Sus* 3D 28
Ryecroft Gate. *Staf* 4D 84
Ryeford. *Here* 3B 48
Rye Foreign. *E Sus* 3D 28
Rye Harbour. *E Sus* 4D 28
Ryehill. *E Yor* 2F 95
Rye Street. *Worc* 2C 48
Ryhall. *Rut* 4H 75
Ryhill. *W Yor* 3D 93
Ryhope. *Tyne* 4H 115
Ryhope Colliery. *Tyne* 4H 115
Rylands. *Notts* 2C 74
Rylstone. *N Yor* 4B 98
Ryme Intrinseca. *Dors* 1A 14
Ryther. *N Yor* 1F 93
Ryton. *Glos* 2C 48
Ryton. *N Yor* 2B 100
Ryton. *Shrp* 5B 72
Ryton. *Tyne* 3E 115
Ryton. *Warw* 2B 62
Ryton-on-Dunsmore. *Warw* 3A 62
Ryton Woodside. *Tyne* 3E 115

S

Saasaig. *High* 3E 147
Sabden. *Lanc* 1F 91
Sacombe. *Herts* 4D 52
Sacriston. *Dur* 5F 115
Sadberge. *Darl* 3A 106
Saddell. *Arg* 2B 122
Saddington. *Leics* 1D 62
Saddle Bow. *Norf* 4F 77

Saddlescombe. *W Sus* 4D 26
Saddleworth. *G Man* 4H 91
Sadgill. *Cumb* 4F 103
Saffron Walden. *Essx* 2F 53
Sageston. *Pemb* 4E 43
Saham Hills. *Norf* 5B 78
Saham Toney. *Norf* 5A 78
Saighdinis. *W Isl* 2D 170
Saighton. *Ches W* 4G 83
Sain Dunwyd. *V Glam* 5C 32
Sain Hilari. *V Glam* 4D 32
St Abbs. *Bord* 3F 131
St Agnes. *Corn* 3B 6
St Albans. *Herts* 5B 52
St Andrews. *Fife* **209** (2H 137)
St Andrews Major. *V Glam* 4E 33
St Anne's. *Lanc* 2B 90
St Ann's. *Dum* 5C 118
St Ann's Chapel. *Corn* 5E 11
St Ann's Chapel. *Devn* 4C 8
St Anthony. *Corn* 5C 6
St Anthony-in-Meneage. *Corn* 4E 5
St Arvans. *Mon* 2A 34
St Asaph. *Den* 3C 82
Sain Tathan. *V Glam* 5D 32
St Athan. *V Glam* 5D 32
St Austell. *Corn* 3E 6
St Bartholomew's Hill. *Wilts* 4E 23
St Bees. *Cumb* 3A 102
St Blazey. *Corn* 3E 7
St Blazey Gate. *Corn* 3E 7
St Boswells. *Bord* 1H 119
St Breock. *Corn* 1D 6
St Breward. *Corn* 5A 10
St Briavels. *Glos* 5A 48
St Brides. *Pemb* 3B 42
St Brides Major. *V Glam* 4B 32
St Bride's Netherwent. *Mon* 3H 33
St Brides-super-Ely. *V Glam* 4D 32
St Brides Wentlooge. *Newp* 3F 33
St Budeaux. *Plym* 3A 8
Saintbury. *Glos* 2G 49
St Buryan. *Corn* 4B 4
St Catherine. *Bath* 4C 34
St Catherines. *Arg* 3A 134
St Clears. *Carm* 3G 43
St Cleer. *Corn* 2G 7
St Clement. *Corn* 4C 6
St Clether. *Corn* 4C 10
St Colmac. *Arg* 3B 126
St Columb Major. *Corn* 2D 6
St Columb Minor. *Corn* 2C 6
St Columb Road. *Corn* 3D 6
St Combs. *Abers* 2H 161
St Cross. *Hants* 4C 24
St Cross South Elmham.
  Suff 2E 67
St Cyrus. *Abers* 2G 145
St Davids. *Pemb* 2B 42
St David's. *Per* 1B 136
St Day. *Corn* 4B 6
St Dennis. *Corn* 3D 6
St Dogmaels. *Pemb* 1B 44
St Dominick. *Corn* 2H 7
St Donat's. *V Glam* 5C 32
St Edith's Marsh. *Wilts* 5E 35
St Endellion. *Corn* 1D 6
St Enoder. *Corn* 3C 6
St Erme. *Corn* 4C 6
St Erney. *Corn* 3H 7
St Erth. *Corn* 3C 4
St Erth Praze. *Corn* 3C 4
St Ervan. *Corn* 1C 6
St Eval. *Corn* 2C 6
St Ewe. *Corn* 4D 6
St Fagans. *Card* 4E 32
St Fergus. *Abers* 3H 161
St Fillans. *Per* 1F 135
St Florence. *Pemb* 4E 43
St Gennys. *Corn* 3B 10
St George. *Cnwy* 3B 82
St George's. *N Som* 5G 33
St Georges. *V Glam* 4D 32
St George's Hill. *Surr* 4B 38
St Germans. *Corn* 3H 7
St Giles in the Wood. *Devn* 1F 11
St Giles on the Heath. *Devn* 3D 10
St Giles's Hill. *Hants* 4C 24
St Gluvias. *Corn* 5B 6
St Harmon. *Powy* 3B 58
St Helena. *Warw* 5G 73
St Helen Auckland. *Dur* 2E 105
St Helens. *Cumb* 1B 102
St Helen's. *E Sus* 4C 28
St Helen's. *IOW* 4E 17
St Helens. *Mers* 1H 83
St Hilary. *Corn* 3C 4
St Hilary. *V Glam* 4D 32
Saint Hill. *Devn* 2D 12
Saint Hill. *W Sus* 2E 27
St Illtyd. *Blae* 5F 47
St Ippolyts. *Herts* 3B 52
St Ishmael. *Carm* 5D 44
St Ishmael's. *Pemb* 4C 42
St Issey. *Corn* 1D 6
St Ive. *Corn* 2H 7
St Ives. *Cambs* 3C 64
St Ives. *Corn* 2C 4
St Ives. *Dors* 2G 15
St James' End. *Nptn* 4E 63
St James South Elmham. *Suff* 2F 67
St Jidgey. *Corn* 2D 6
St John. *Corn* 3A 8
St John's. *IOM* 3B 108
St John's. *Worc* 5C 60
St John's Chapel. *Devn* 4F 19
St John's Chapel. *Dur* 1B 104
St John's Fen End. *Norf* 4E 77
St John's Town of Dalry.
  Dum 1D 110

St Judes. *IOM* 2C 108
St Just. *Corn* 3A 4
St Just in Roseland. *Corn* 5C 6
St Katherines. *Abers* 5E 161
St Keverne. *Corn* 4E 5
St Kew. *Corn* 5A 10
St Kew Highway. *Corn* 5A 10
St Keyne. *Corn* 2G 7
St Lawrence. *Corn* 2E 7
St Lawrence. *Essx* 5C 54
St Lawrence. *IOW* 5D 16
St Leonards. *Buck* 5H 51
St Leonards. *Dors* 2G 15
St Leonards. *E Sus* 5B 28
St Levan. *Corn* 4A 4
St Lythans. *V Glam* 4E 32
St Mabyn. *Corn* 5A 10
St Madoes. *Per* 1D 136
St Margarets. *Here* 2G 47
St Margaret's. *Herts* 4A 52
St Margarets. *Herts* 4D 53
St Margaret's. *Wilts* 5H 35
St Margaret's at Cliffe. *Kent* 1H 29
St Margaret's Hope. *Orkn* 8D 172
St Margaret South Elmham.
  Suff 2F 67
St Mark's. *IOM* 4B 108
St Martin. *Corn*
  nr. Helston 4E 5
  nr. Looe 3G 7
St Martins. *Per* 5A 144
St Martin's. *Shrp* 2F 71
St Mary Bourne. *Hants* 1C 24
St Marychurch. *Torb* 2F 9
St Mary Church. *V Glam* 4D 32
St Mary Cray. *G Lon* 4F 39
St Mary Hill. *V Glam* 4C 32
St Mary Hoo. *Medw* 3C 40
St Mary in the Marsh. *Kent* 3E 29
St Mary's. *Orkn* 7D 172
St Mary's Bay. *Kent* 3E 29
St Marys Platt. *Kent* 5H 39
St Maughan's Green. *Mon* 4H 47
St Mawes. *Corn* 5C 6
St Mawgan. *Corn* 2C 6
St Mellion. *Corn* 2H 7
St Mellons. *Card* 3F 33
St Merryn. *Corn* 1C 6
St Mewan. *Corn* 3D 6
St Michael Caerhays. *Corn* 4D 6
St Michael Penkevil. *Corn* 4C 6
St Michaels. *Kent* 2C 28
St Michaels. *Torb* 3E 9
St Michaels. *Worc* 4H 59
St Michael's on Wyre. *Lanc* 5D 96
St Michael South Elmham. *Suff* 2F 67
St Minver. *Corn* 1D 6
St Monans. *Fife* 3H 137
St Neot. *Corn* 2F 7
St Neots. *Cambs* 4A 64
St Newlyn East. *Corn* 3C 6
St Nicholas. *Pemb* 1C 42
St Nicholas. *V Glam* 4D 32
St Nicholas at Wade. *Kent* 4G 41
St Nicholas South Elmham.
  Suff 2F 67
St Ninians. *Stir* 4G 135
St Olaves. *Norf* 1G 67
St Osyth. *Essx* 4E 54
St Osyth Heath. *Essx* 4E 55
St Owen's Cross. *Here* 3A 48
St Paul's Cray. *G Lon* 4F 39
St Paul's Walden. *Herts* 3B 52
St Peter's. *Kent* 4H 41
St Peter The Great. *Worc* 5C 60
St Petrox. *Pemb* 5D 42
St Pinnock. *Corn* 2G 7
St Quivox. *S Ayr* 2C 116
St Ruan. *Corn* 5E 5
St Stephen. *Corn* 3D 6
St Stephens. *Corn*
  nr. Launceston 4D 10
  nr. Saltash 3A 8
St Teath. *Corn* 4A 10
St Thomas. *Devn* 3C 12
St Thomas. *Swan* 3F 31
St Tudy. *Corn* 5A 10
St Twynnells. *Pemb* 5D 42
St Veep. *Corn* 3F 7
St Vigeans. *Ang* 4F 145
St Wenn. *Corn* 2D 6
St Weonards. *Here* 3H 47
St Winnolls. *Corn* 3H 7
St Winnow. *Corn* 3F 7
Salcombe. *Devn* 5D 8
Salcombe Regis. *Devn* 4E 13
Salcott. *Essx* 4C 54
Sale. *G Man* 1B 84
Saleby. *Linc* 3D 88
Sale Green. *Worc* 5D 60
Salehurst. *E Sus* 3B 28
Salem. *Carm* 3G 45
Salem. *Cdgn* 2F 57
Salen. *Arg* 4G 139
Salen. *High* 2A 140
Salesbury. *Lanc* 1E 91
Salford. *C Beds* 2H 51
Salford. *G Man* **201** (1C 84)
Salford. *Oxon* 3A 50
Salford Priors. *Warw* 5F 61
Salfords. *Surr* 1D 27
Salhouse. *Norf* 4F 79
Saligo. *Arg* 3A 124
Saline. *Fife* 4C 136
Salisbury. *Wilts* **210** (3G 23)
Salkeld Dykes. *Cumb* 1G 103
Sallachan. *High* 2D 141
Sallachy. *High*
  nr. Lairg 3C 164
  nr. Stromeferry 5B 156

Salle. *Norf* 3D 78
Salmonby. *Linc* 3C 88
Salmond's Muir. *Ang* 5E 145
Salperton. *Glos* 3F 49
Salph End. *Bed* 5H 63
Salsburgh. *N Lan* 3B 128
Salt. *Staf* 3D 72
Salta. *Cumb* 5B 112
Saltaire. *W Yor* 1B 92
Saltash. *Corn* 3A 8
Saltburn. *High* 2B 158
Saltburn-by-the-Sea. *Red C* 2D 106
Saltby. *Leics* 3F 75
Saltcoats. *Cumb* 5B 102
Saltcoats. *N Ayr* 5D 126
Saltdean. *Brig* 5E 27
Salt End. *E Yor* 2E 95
Salter. *Lanc* 3F 97
Salterforth. *Lanc* 5A 98
Salters Lode. *Norf* 5E 77
Salterswall. *Ches W* 4A 84
Salterton. *Wilts* 3G 23
Saltfleet. *Linc* 1D 88
Saltfleetby All Saints. *Linc* 1D 88
Saltfleetby St Clements. *Linc* 1D 88
Saltfleetby St Peter. *Linc* 2D 88
Saltford. *Bath* 5B 34
Salthouse. *Norf* 1C 78
Saltmarshe. *E Yor* 2A 94
Saltness. *Orkn* 9B 172
Saltness. *Shet* 7D 173
Saltney. *Flin* 4F 83
Salton. *N Yor* 2B 100
Saltrens. *Devn* 4E 19
Saltwick. *Nmbd* 2E 115
Saltwood. *Kent* 2F 29
Salum. *Arg* 4B 138
Salwarpe. *Worc* 4C 60
Salwayash. *Dors* 3H 13
Samalaman. *High* 1A 140
Sambourne. *Warw* 4E 61
Sambourne. *Wilts* 3D 22
Sambrook. *Telf* 3B 72
Samhla. *W Isl* 2C 170
Samlesbury. *Lanc* 1D 90
Samlesbury Bottoms. *Lanc* 2E 90
Sampford Arundel. *Som* 1E 12
Sampford Brett. *Som* 2D 20
Sampford Courtenay. *Devn* 2G 11
Sampford Peverell. *Devn* 1D 12
Sampford Spiney. *Devn* 5F 11
Samsonslane. *Orkn* 5F 172
Samuelston. *E Lot* 2A 130
Sanaigmore. *Arg* 2A 124
Sancreed. *Corn* 4B 4
Sancton. *E Yor* 1C 94
Sand. *High* 4D 162
Sand. *Shet* 7E 173
Sand. *Som* 2H 21
Sandaig. *Arg* 4A 138
Sandaig. *High* 3F 147
Sandale. *Cumb* 5D 112
Sandal Magna. *W Yor* 3D 92
Sandavore. *High* 5C 146
Sandbach. *Ches E* 4B 84
Sandbank. *Arg* 1C 126
Sandbanks. *Pool* 4F 15
Sandend. *Abers* 2C 160
Sanderstead. *G Lon* 4E 39
Sandfields. *Neat* 3G 31
Sandford. *Cumb* 3A 104
Sandford. *Devn* 2B 12
Sandford. *Dors* 4E 15
Sandford. *Hants* 2G 15
Sandford. *IOW* 4D 16
Sandford. *N Som* 1H 21
Sandford. *Shrp*
  nr. Oswestry 3F 71
  nr. Whitchurch 2H 71
Sandford. *S Lan* 5A 128
Sandfordhill. *Abers* 4H 161
Sandford-on-Thames. *Oxon* 5D 50
Sandford Orcas. *Dors* 4B 22
Sandford St Martin. *Oxon* 3C 50
Sandgate. *Kent* 2F 29
Sandgreen. *Dum* 4C 110
Sandhaven. *Abers* 2G 161
Sandhead. *Dum* 4F 109
Sandhill. *Cambs* 2E 65
Sandhills. *Dors* 1B 14
Sandhills. *Oxon* 5D 50
Sandhills. *Surr* 2A 26
Sandhoe. *Nmbd* 3C 114
Sand Hole. *E Yor* 1B 94
Sandholme. *E Yor* 1B 94
Sandholme. *Linc* 2C 76
Sandhurst. *Brac* 5G 37
Sandhurst. *Glos* 3D 48
Sandhurst. *Kent* 3B 28
Sandhurst Cross. *Kent* 3B 28
Sand Hutton. *N Yor* 4A 100
Sandhutton. *N Yor* 1F 99
Sandiacre. *Derbs* 2B 74
Sandilands. *Linc* 2E 89
Sandiway. *Ches W* 3A 84
Sandleheath. *Hants* 1G 15
Sandling. *Kent* 5B 40
Sandlow Green. *Ches E* 4B 84
Sandness. *Shet* 6C 173
Sandon. *Essx* 5H 53
Sandon. *Herts* 2D 52
Sandon. *Staf* 3D 72
Sandonbank. *Staf* 3D 72
Sandown. *IOW* 4D 16
Sandplace. *Corn* 3G 7
Sandridge. *Herts* 4B 52
Sandringham. *Norf* 3F 77
Sands, The. *Surr* 2G 25
Sandsend. *N Yor* 3F 107
Sandside. *Cumb* 2C 96

Sandsound. *Shet* 7E 173
Sandtoft. *N Lin* 4H 93
Sandvoe. *Shet* 2E 173
Sandway. *Kent* 5C 40
Sandwich. *Kent* 5H 41
Sandwick. *Cumb* 3F 103
Sandwick. *Orkn*
  on Mainland 6B 172
  on South Ronaldsay 9D 172
Sandwick. *Shet*
  on Mainland 9F 173
  on Whalsay 5G 173
Sandwith. *Cumb* 3A 102
Sandy. *Carm* 5E 45
Sandy. *C Beds* 1B 52
Sandy Bank. *Linc* 5B 88
Sandycroft. *Flin* 4F 83
Sandy Cross. *Here* 5A 60
Sandygate. *Devn* 5B 12
Sandygate. *IOM* 2C 108
Sandyhills. *Dum* 4F 111
Sandylands. *Lanc* 3D 96
Sandylane. *Swan* 4E 31
Sandy Lane. *Wilts* 5E 35
Sandystones. *Bord* 2H 119
Sandyway. *Here* 3H 47
Sangobeg. *High* 2E 167
Sangomore. *High* 2E 166
Sankyn's Green. *Worc* 4B 60
Sanna. *High* 2F 139
Sanndabhaig. *W Isl*
  on Isle of Lewis 4G 171
  on South Uist 4D 170
Sannox. *N Ayr* 5B 126
Sanquhar. *Dum* 3G 117
Santon. *Cumb* 4B 102
Santon Bridge. *Cumb* 4C 102
Santon Downham. *Suff* 2H 65
Sapcote. *Leics* 1B 62
Sapey Common. *Here* 4B 60
Sapiston. *Suff* 3B 66
Sapley. *Cambs* 3B 64
Sapperton. *Derbs* 2F 73
Sapperton. *Glos* 5E 49
Sapperton. *Linc* 2H 75
Saracen's Head. *Linc* 3C 76
Sarclet. *High* 4F 169
Sardis. *Carm* 5F 45
Sardis. *Pemb*
  nr. Milford Haven 4D 42
  nr. Tenby 4F 43
Sarisbury Green. *Hants* 2D 16
Sarn. *B'end* 3C 32
Sarn. *Powy* 1E 58
Sarnau. *Carm* 3E 45
Sarnau. *Cdgn* 5C 56
Sarnau. *Gwyn* 2B 70
Sarnau. *Powy*
  nr. Brecon 2D 46
  nr. Welshpool 4E 71
Sarn Bach. *Gwyn* 3C 68
Sarnesfield. *Here* 5F 59
Sarn Meyllteyrn. *Gwyn* 2B 68
Saron. *Carm*
  nr. Ammanford 4G 45
  nr. Newcastle Emlyn 2D 45
Saron. *Gwyn*
  nr. Bethel 4E 81
  nr. Bontnewydd 5D 80
Sarratt. *Herts* 1B 38
Sarre. *Kent* 4G 41
Sarsden. *Oxon* 3A 50
Satley. *Dur* 5E 115
Satron. *N Yor* 5C 104
Satterleigh. *Devn* 4G 19
Satterthwaite. *Cumb* 5E 103
Satwell. *Oxon* 3F 37
Sauchen. *Abers* 2D 152
Saucher. *Per* 5A 144
Saughall. *Ches W* 3F 83
Saughtree. *Bord* 5H 119
Saul. *Glos* 5C 48
Saundby. *Notts* 2E 87
Saundersfoot. *Pemb* 4F 43
Saunderton. *Buck* 5F 51
Saunderton Lee. *Buck* 2G 37
Saunton. *Devn* 3E 19
Sausthorpe. *Linc* 4C 88
Saval. *High* 3C 164
Saverley Green. *Staf* 2D 72
Sawbridge. *Warw* 4C 62
Sawbridgeworth. *Herts* 4E 53
Sawdon. *N Yor* 1D 100
Sawley. *Derbs* 2B 74
Sawley. *Lanc* 5G 97
Sawley. *N Yor* 3E 99
Sawston. *Cambs* 1E 53
Sawtry. *Cambs* 2A 64
Saxby. *Leics* 3F 75
Saxby. *Linc* 2H 87
Saxby All Saints. *N Lin* 3C 94
Saxelby. *Leics* 3D 74
Saxelbye. *Leics* 3D 74
Saxham Street. *Suff* 4C 66
Saxilby. *Linc* 3F 87
Saxlingham. *Norf* 2C 78
Saxlingham Green. *Norf* 1E 67
Saxlingham Nethergate.
  Norf 1E 67
Saxlingham Thorpe. *Norf* 1E 66
Saxmundham. *Suff* 4F 67
Saxondale. *Notts* 1D 74
Saxon Street. *Cambs* 5F 65
Saxtead. *Suff* 4E 67
Saxtead Green. *Suff* 4E 67
Saxthorpe. *Norf* 2D 78
Saxton. *N Yor* 1E 93
Sayers Common. *W Sus* 4D 26
Scackleton. *N Yor* 2A 100
Scadabhagh. *W Isl* 8D 171

Scaftworth—Shortstown

Scaftworth. *Notts* 1D 86
Scagglethorpe. *N Yor* 2C 100
Scaitcliffe. *Lanc* 2F 91
Scaladal. *W Isl* 6D 171
Scalasaig. *Arg* 4A 132
Scalby. *E Yor* 2B 94
Scalby. *N Yor* 5H 107
Scalby Mills. *N Yor* 5H 107
Scaldwell. *Nptn* 3E 63
Scaleby. *Cumb* 3F 113
Scaleby Hill. *Cumb* 3F 113
Scale Houses. *Cumb* 5G 113
Scales. *Cumb*
nr. Barrow-in-Furness 2B 96
nr. Keswick 2E 103
Scalford. *Leics* 3E 75
Scaling. *N Yor* 3E 107
Scaling Dam. *Red C* 3E 107
Scalloway. *Shet* 8F 173
Scalpaigh. *W Isl* 8E 171
Scalpay House. *High* 1E 147
Scamblesby. *Linc* 3B 88
Scamodale. *High* 1C 140
Scampston. *N Yor* 2C 100
Scampton. *Linc* 3G 87
Scaniport. *High* 5A 158
Scapa. *Orkn* 7D 172
Scapegoat Hill. *W Yor* 3A 92
Scar. *Orkn* 3F 172
Scarasta. *W Isl* 8C 171
Scarborough. *N Yor* 1E 101
Scarcliffe. *Derbs* 4B 86
Scarcroft. *W Yor* 5F 99
Scardroy. *High* 3E 156
Scarfskerry. *High* 1E 169
Scargill. *Dur* 3D 104
Scarinish. *Arg* 4B 138
Scarisbrick. *Lanc* 3B 90
Scarning. *Norf* 4B 78
Scarrington. *Notts* 1E 75
Scarth Hill. *Lanc* 4C 90
Scartho. *NE Lin* 4F 95
Scarvister. *Shet* 7E 173
Scatness. *Shet* 10E 173
Scatwell. *High* 3F 157
Scaur. *Dum* 4F 111
Scawby. *N Lin* 4C 94
Scawby Brook. *N Lin* 4C 94
Scawsby. *S Yor* 4F 93
Scawton. *N Yor* 1H 99
Scaynes Hill. *W Sus* 3E 27
Scethrog. *Powy* 3E 46
Scholar Green. *Ches E* 5C 84
Scholes. *G Man* 4D 90
Scholes. *W Yor*
nr. Bradford 2B 92
nr. Holmfirth 4B 92
nr. Leeds 1D 93
Scholey Hill. *W Yor* 2D 93
School Aycliffe. *Darl* 2F 105
School Green. *Ches W* 4A 84
School Green. *Essx* 2H 53
Scissett. *W Yor* 3C 92
Scleddau. *Pemb* 1D 42
Scofton. *Notts* 2D 86
Scole. *Norf* 3D 66
Scolpaig. *W Isl* 1C 170
Scolton. *Pemb* 2D 43
Scone. *Per* 1D 136
Sconser. *High* 5E 155
Scoonie. *Fife* 3F 137
Scopwick. *Linc* 5H 87
Scoraig. *High* 4E 163
Scorborough. *E Yor* 5E 101
Scorrier. *Corn* 4B 6
Scorriton. *Devn* 2D 8
Scorton. *Lanc* 5E 97
Scorton. *N Yor* 4F 105
Sco Ruston. *Norf* 3E 79
Scotbheinn. *W Isl* 3D 170
Scotby. *Cumb* 4F 113
Scotch Corner. *N Yor* 4F 105
Scotforth. *Lanc* 3D 97
Scot Hay. *Staf* 1C 72
Scothern. *Linc* 3H 87
Scotland End. *Oxon* 2B 50
Scotlandwell. *Per* 3D 136
Scot Lane End. *G Man* 4E 91
Scotsburn. *High* 1B 158
Scotsburn. *Mor* 2G 159
Scotsdike. *Cumb* 2E 113
Scot's Gap. *Nmbd* 1D 114
Scotstoun. *Glas* 3G 127
Scotstown. *High* 2C 140
Scotswood. *Tyne* 3F 115
Scottas. *High* 3F 147
Scotter. *Linc* 4B 94
Scotterthorpe. *Linc* 4B 94
Scottlethorpe. *Linc* 3H 75
Scotton. *Linc* 1F 87
Scotton. *N Yor*
nr. Catterick Garrison 5E 105
nr. Harrogate 4F 99
Scottow. *Norf* 3E 79
Scoulton. *Norf* 5B 78
Scounslow Green. *Staf* 3E 73
Scourie. *High* 4B 166
Scourie More. *High* 4B 166
Scousburgh. *Shet* 10E 173
Scout Green. *Cumb* 4G 103
Scouthead. *G Man* 4H 91
Scrabster. *High* 1C 168
Scrafield. *Linc* 4C 88
Scrainwood. *Nmbd* 4D 121
Scrane End. *Linc* 1C 76
Scraptoft. *Leics* 5D 74
Scratby. *Norf* 4H 79
Scrayingham. *N Yor* 3B 100
Scredington. *Linc* 1H 75
Scremby. *Linc* 4D 88
Scremerston. *Nmbd* 5G 131
Screveton. *Notts* 1E 75
Scrivelsby. *Linc* 4B 88
Scriven. *N Yor* 4F 99
Scronkey. *Lanc* 5D 96
Scrooby. *Notts* 1D 86
Scropton. *Derbs* 2F 73
Scrub Hill. *Linc* 5B 88
Scruton. *N Yor* 5F 105
Scuggate. *Cumb* 2F 113
Sculamus. *High* 1E 147
Sculcoates. *Hull* 1D 94
Sculthorpe. *Norf* 2B 78
Scunthorpe. *N Lin* 3B 94
Scurlage. *Swan* 4D 30
Sea. *Som* 1G 13
Seaborough. *Dors* 2H 13
Seabridge. *Staf* 1C 72
Seabrook. *Kent* 2F 29
Seaburn. *Tyne* 3H 115
Seacombe. *Mers* 1F 83
Seacroft. *Linc* 4E 89
Seacroft. *W Yor* 1D 92
Seadyke. *Linc* 2C 76
Seafield. *High* 5G 165
Seafield. *Midl* 3F 129
Seafield. *S Ayr* 2C 116
Seafield. *W Lot* 3D 128
Seaford. *E Sus* 5F 27
Seaforth. *Mers* 1F 83
Seagrave. *Leics* 4D 74
Seaham. *Dur* 5H 115
Seahouses. *Nmbd* 1G 121
Seal. *Kent* 5G 39
Sealand. *Flin* 4F 83
Seale. *Surr* 2G 25
Seamer. *N Yor*
nr. Scarborough 1E 101
nr. Stokesley 3B 106
Seamill. *N Ayr* 5D 126
Sea Mills. *Bris* 4A 34
Sea Palling. *Norf* 3G 79
Searby. *Linc* 4D 94
Seasalter. *Kent* 4E 41
Seascale. *Cumb* 4B 102
Seaside. *Per* 1E 137
Seater. *High* 1F 169
Seathorne. *Linc* 4E 89
Seathwaite. *Cumb*
nr. Buttermere 3D 102
nr. Ulpha 5D 102
Seatle. *Cumb* 1C 96
Seatoller. *Cumb* 3D 102
Seaton. *Corn* 3H 7
Seaton. *Cumb* 1B 102
Seaton. *Devn* 3F 13
Seaton. *Dur* 4G 115
Seaton. *E Yor* 5F 101
Seaton. *Nmbd* 2G 115
Seaton. *Rut* 1G 63
Seaton Burn. *Tyne* 2F 115
Seaton Carew. *Hart* 2C 106
Seaton Delaval. *Nmbd* 2G 115
Seaton Junction. *Devn* 3F 13
Seaton Ross. *E Yor* 5B 100
Seaton Sluice. *Nmbd* 2G 115
Seatown. *Abers* 2C 160
Seatown. *Dors* 3H 13
Seatown. *Mor*
nr. Cullen 2C 160
nr. Lossiemouth 1G 159
Seave Green. *N Yor* 4C 106
Seaview. *IOW* 3E 17
Seaville. *Cumb* 4C 112
Seavington St Mary. *Som* 1H 13
Seavington St Michael. *Som* 1H 13
Seawick. *Essx* 4E 55
Sebastopol. *Torf* 2F 33
Sebergham. *Cumb* 5E 113
Seckington. *Warw* 5G 73
Second Coast. *High* 4D 162
Sedbergh. *Cumb* 5H 103
Sedbury. *Glos* 2A 34
Sedbusk. *N Yor* 5B 104
Sedgeberrow. *Worc* 2F 49
Sedgebrook. *Linc* 2F 75
Sedgefield. *Dur* 2A 106
Sedgeford. *Norf* 2G 77
Sedgehill. *Wilts* 4D 22
Sedgley. *W Mid* 1D 60
Sedgwick. *Cumb* 1E 97
Sedlescombe. *E Sus* 4B 28
Seend. *Wilts* 5E 35
Seend Cleeve. *Wilts* 5E 35
Seer Green. *Buck* 1A 38
Seething. *Norf* 1F 67
Sefster. *Shet* 6E 173
Sefton. *Mers* 4B 90
Sefton Park. *Mers* 2F 83
Segensworth. *Hants* 2D 16
Seggat. *Abers* 4E 161
Seghill. *Nmbd* 2F 115
Seifton. *Shrp* 2G 59
Seighford. *Staf* 3C 72
Seilebost. *W Isl* 8C 171
Seisdon. *Staf* 1C 60
Seisiadar. *W Isl* 4H 171
Selattyn. *Shrp* 2E 71
Selborne. *Hants* 3F 25
Selby. *N Yor* 1G 93
Selham. *W Sus* 3A 26
Selkirk. *Bord* 2G 119
Sellack. *Here* 3A 48
Sellafirth. *Shet* 2G 173
Sellick's Green. *Som* 1F 13
Sellindge. *Kent* 2F 29
Selling. *Kent* 5E 41
Sells Green. *Wilts* 5E 35
Selly Oak. *W Mid* 2E 61
Selmeston. *E Sus* 5G 27
Selsdon. *G Lon* 4E 39
Selsey. *W Sus* 3G 17
Selsfield Common. *W Sus* 2E 27
Selside. *Cumb* 5G 103
Selside. *N Yor* 2G 97
Selsley. *Glos* 5D 48
Selsted. *Kent* 1G 29
Selston. *Notts* 5B 86
Selworthy. *Som* 2C 20
Semblister. *Shet* 6E 173
Semer. *Suff* 1D 54
Semington. *Wilts* 5D 35
Semley. *Wilts* 4D 23
Sempringham. *Linc* 2A 76
Send. *Surr* 5B 38
Send Marsh. *Surr* 5B 38
Senghenydd. *Cphy* 2E 32
Sennen. *Corn* 4A 4
Sennen Cove. *Corn* 4A 4
Sennybridge. *Powy* 3C 46
Serlby. *Notts* 2D 86
Sessay. *N Yor* 2G 99
Setchey. *Norf* 4F 77
Setley. *Hants* 2B 16
Setter. *Shet* 3F 173
Settiscarth. *Orkn* 6C 172
Settle. *N Yor* 3H 97
Settrington. *N Yor* 2C 100
Seven Ash. *Som* 3E 21
Sevenhampton. *Glos* 3F 49
Sevenhampton. *Swin* 2H 35
Sevenoaks. *Kent* 5G 39
Sevenoaks Weald. *Kent* 5G 39
Seven Sisters. *Neat* 5B 46
Seven Springs. *Glos* 4E 49
Severn Beach. *S Glo* 3A 34
Severn Stoke. *Worc* 1D 48
Sevington. *Kent* 1E 29
Sewards End. *Essx* 2F 53
Sewardstone. *Essx* 1E 39
Sewell. *C Beds* 3H 51
Sewerby. *E Yor* 3G 101
Seworgan. *Corn* 5B 6
Sewstern. *Leics* 3F 75
Sgallairidh. *W Isl* 9B 170
Sgarasta Mhor. *W Isl* 8C 171
Sgiogarstaigh. *W Isl* 1H 171
Sgreadan. *Arg* 4A 132
Shabbington. *Buck* 5E 51
Shackerley. *Shrp* 5C 72
Shackerstone. *Leics* 5A 74
Shackleford. *Surr* 1A 26
Shadforth. *Dur* 5G 115
Shadingfield. *Suff* 2G 67
Shadoxhurst. *Kent* 2D 28
Shadsworth. *Bkbn* 2F 91
Shadwell. *Norf* 2B 66
Shadwell. *W Yor* 1D 92
Shaftesbury. *Dors* 4D 22
Shafton. *S Yor* 3D 93
Shafton Two Gates. *S Yor* 3D 93
Shaggs. *Dors* 4D 14
Shakesfield. *Glos* 2B 48
Shalbourne. *Wilts* 5B 36
Shalcombe. *IOW* 4B 16
Shalden. *Hants* 2E 25
Shaldon. *Devn* 5C 12
Shalfleet. *IOW* 4C 16
Shalford. *Essx* 3H 53
Shalford. *Surr* 1B 26
Shalford Green. *Essx* 3H 53
Shallowford. *Devn* 2H 19
Shallowford. *Staf* 3C 72
Shalmsford Street. *Kent* 5E 41
Shalstone. *Buck* 2E 51
Shamley Green. *Surr* 1B 26
Shandon. *Arg* 1D 126
Shandwick. *High* 1C 158
Shangton. *Leics* 1E 62
Shankhouse. *Nmbd* 2F 115
Shanklin. *IOW* 4D 16
Shannochie. *N Ayr* 3D 123
Shap. *Cumb* 3G 103
Shapwick. *Dors* 2E 15
Shapwick. *Som* 3H 21
Sharcott. *Wilts* 1G 23
Shardlow. *Derbs* 2B 74
Shareshill. *Staf* 5D 72
Sharlston. *W Yor* 3D 93
Sharlston Common. *W Yor* 3D 93
Sharnal Street. *Medw* 3B 40
Sharnbrook. *Bed* 5G 63
Sharneyford. *Lanc* 2G 91
Sharnford. *Leics* 1B 62
Sharnhill Green. *Dors* 2C 14
Sharoe Green. *Lanc* 1D 90
Sharow. *N Yor* 2F 99
Sharpenhoe. *C Beds* 2A 52
Sharperton. *Nmbd* 4D 120
Sharpness. *Glos* 5B 48
Sharp Street. *Norf* 3F 79
Sharpthorne. *W Sus* 2E 27
Sharrington. *Norf* 2C 78
Shatterford. *Worc* 2B 60
Shatton. *Derbs* 2F 85
Shaugh Prior. *Devn* 2B 8
Shavington. *Ches E* 5B 84
Shaw. *G Man* 4H 91
Shaw. *W Ber* 5C 36
Shaw. *Wilts* 5D 35
Shawbirch. *Telf* 4A 72
Shawbury. *Shrp* 3H 71
Shawell. *Leics* 2C 62
Shawford. *Hants* 4C 24
Shawforth. *Lanc* 2G 91
Shaw Green. *Lanc* 3D 90
Shawhead. *Dum* 2F 111
Shaw Mills. *N Yor* 3E 99
Shawwood. *E Ayr* 2E 117
Shearington. *Dum* 3B 112
Shearsby. *Leics* 1D 62
Shearston. *Som* 3F 21
Shebbear. *Devn* 2E 11
Shebdon. *Staf* 3B 72
Shebster. *High* 2C 168
Sheddocksley. *Aber* 3F 153
Shedfield. *Hants* 1D 16
Shedog. *N Ayr* 2D 122
Sheen. *Staf* 4F 85
Sheepbridge. *Derbs* 3A 86
Sheep Hill. *Dur* 4E 115
Sheepscar. *W Yor* 1D 92
Sheepscombe. *Glos* 4D 49
Sheepstor. *Devn* 2B 8
Sheepwash. *Devn* 2E 11
Sheepwash. *Nmbd* 1F 115
Sheepway. *N Som* 4H 33
Sheepy Magna. *Leics* 5H 73
Sheepy Parva. *Leics* 5H 73
Sheering. *Essx* 4F 53
Sheerness. *Kent* 3D 40
Sheerwater. *Surr* 4B 38
Sheet. *Hants* 4F 25
Sheffield. *S Yor* 210 (2A 86)
Sheffield Bottom. *W Ber* 5E 37
Sheffield Green. *E Sus* 3F 27
Shefford. *C Beds* 2B 52
Shefford Woodlands. *W Ber* 4B 36
Sheigra. *High* 2B 166
Sheinton. *Shrp* 5A 72
Shelderton. *Shrp* 3G 59
Sheldon. *Derbs* 4F 85
Sheldon. *Devn* 2E 12
Sheldon. *W Mid* 2F 61
Sheldwich. *Kent* 5E 40
Sheldwich Lees. *Kent* 5E 40
Shelf. *W Yor* 2B 92
Shelfanger. *Norf* 2D 66
Shelfield. *Warw* 4F 61
Shelfield. *W Mid* 5E 73
Shelford. *Notts* 1D 74
Shelford. *Warw* 2B 62
Shell. *Worc* 5D 60
Shelley. *Suff* 2D 54
Shelley. *W Yor* 3C 92
Shell Green. *Hal* 2H 83
Shellingford. *Oxon* 2B 36
Shellow Bowells. *Essx* 5G 53
Shelsley Beauchamp. *Worc* 4B 60
Shelsley Walsh. *Worc* 4B 60
Shelthorpe. *Leics* 4C 74
Shelton. *Bed* 4H 63
Shelton. *Norf* 1E 67
Shelton. *Notts* 1E 75
Shelton. *Shrp* 4G 71
Shelton Green. *Norf* 1E 67
Shelton Lock. *Derb* 2A 74
Shelve. *Shrp* 1F 59
Shelwick. *Here* 1A 48
Shelwick Green. *Here* 1A 48
Shenfield. *Essx* 1H 39
Shenington. *Oxon* 1B 50
Shenley. *Herts* 5B 52
Shenley Brook End. *Mil* 2G 51
Shenleybury. *Herts* 5B 52
Shenley Church End. *Mil* 2G 51
Shenmore. *Here* 2G 47
Shennanton. *Dum* 3A 110
Shenstone. *Staf* 5F 73
Shenstone. *Worc* 3C 60
Shenstone Woodend. *Staf* 5F 73
Shenton. *Leics* 5A 74
Shenval. *Mor* 1G 151
Shepeau Stow. *Linc* 4C 76
Shephall. *Herts* 3C 52
Shepherd's Bush. *G Lon* 2D 38
Shepherd's Gate. *Norf* 4E 77
Shepherd's Green. *Oxon* 3F 37
Shepherd's Port. *Norf* 2F 77
Shepherdswell. *Kent* 1G 29
Shepley. *W Yor* 4B 92
Sheppardstown. *High* 4D 169
Shepperdine. *S Glo* 2B 34
Shepperton. *Surr* 4B 38
Shepreth. *Cambs* 1D 53
Shepshed. *Leics* 4B 74
Shepton Beauchamp. *Som* 1H 13
Shepton Mallet. *Som* 2B 22
Shepton Montague. *Som* 3B 22
Shepway. *Kent* 5B 40
Sheraton. *Dur* 1B 106
Sherborne. *Dors* 1B 14
Sherborne. *Glos* 4G 49
Sherborne. *Som* 1A 22
Sherborne Causeway. *Dors* 4D 22
Sherborne St John. *Hants* 1E 24
Sherbourne. *Warw* 4G 61
Sherburn. *Dur* 5G 115
Sherburn. *N Yor* 2D 100
Sherburn Hill. *Dur* 5G 115
Sherburn in Elmet. *N Yor* 1E 93
Shere. *Surr* 1B 26
Shereford. *Norf* 3A 78
Sherfield English. *Hants* 4A 24
Sherfield on Loddon. *Hants* 1E 25
Sherford. *Devn* 4D 9
Sherford. *Dors* 3E 15
Sheriffhales. *Shrp* 4B 72
Sheriff Hutton. *N Yor* 3A 100
Sheriffston. *Mor* 2G 159
Sheringham. *Norf* 1D 78
Sherington. *Mil* 1G 51
Shermanbury. *W Sus* 4D 26
Shernal Green. *Worc* 4D 60
Shernborne. *Norf* 2G 77
Sherrington. *Wilts* 3E 23
Sherston. *Wilts* 3D 34
Sherwood. *Nott* 1C 74
Sherwood Green. *Devn* 4F 19
Shettleston. *Glas* 3H 127
Shevington. *G Man* 4D 90
Shevington Moor. *G Man* 3D 90
Shevington Vale. *G Man* 4D 90
Sheviock. *Corn* 3H 7
Shide. *IOW* 4C 16
Shiel Bridge. *High* 2B 148
Shieldaig. *High*
nr. Charlestown 1H 155
nr. Torridon 3H 155
Shieldhill. *Dum* 1B 112
Shieldhill. *Falk* 2B 128
Shieldhill. *S Lan* 5D 128
Shieldmuir. *N Lan* 4A 128
Shielfoot. *High* 1A 140
Shielhill. *Abers* 3H 161
Shielhill. *Ang* 3D 144
Shifnal. *Shrp* 5B 72
Shilbottle. *Nmbd* 4F 121
Shilbottle Grange. *Nmbd* 4G 121
Shildon. *Dur* 2F 105
Shillford. *E Ren* 4F 127
Shillingford. *Devn* 4C 20
Shillingford. *Oxon* 2D 36
Shillingford St George. *Devn* 4C 12
Shillingstone. *Dors* 1D 14
Shillington. *C Beds* 2B 52
Shillmoor. *Nmbd* 4C 120
Shilton. *Oxon* 5A 50
Shilton. *Warw* 2B 62
Shilvinghampton. *Dors* 4B 14
Shilvington. *Nmbd* 1E 115
Shimpling. *Norf* 2D 66
Shimpling. *Suff* 5A 66
Shimpling Street. *Suff* 5A 66
Shincliffe. *Dur* 5F 115
Shiney Row. *Tyne* 4G 115
Shinfield. *Wok* 5F 37
Shingay. *Cambs* 1D 52
Shingham. *Norf* 5G 77
Shingle Street. *Suff* 1G 55
Shinner's Bridge. *Devn* 2D 9
Shinness. *High* 2C 164
Shipbourne. *Kent* 5G 39
Shipdham. *Norf* 5B 78
Shipham. *Som* 1H 21
Shiphay. *Torb* 2E 9
Shiplake. *Oxon* 4F 37
Shipley. *Derbs* 1B 74
Shipley. *Nmbd* 3F 121
Shipley. *Shrp* 1C 60
Shipley. *W Sus* 3C 26
Shipley. *W Yor* 1B 92
Shipley Bridge. *Surr* 1E 27
Shipmeadow. *Suff* 2F 67
Shippon. *Oxon* 2C 36
Shipston-on-Stour. *Warw* 1A 50
Shipton. *Buck* 3F 51
Shipton. *Glos* 4F 49
Shipton. *N Yor* 4H 99
Shipton. *Shrp* 1H 59
Shipton Bellinger. *Hants* 2H 23
Shipton Gorge. *Dors* 3H 13
Shipton Green. *W Sus* 3G 17
Shipton Moyne. *Glos* 3D 35
Shipton-on-Cherwell. *Oxon* 4C 50
Shiptonthorpe. *E Yor* 5C 100
Shipton-under-Wychwood.
Oxon 4A 50
Shirburn. *Oxon* 2E 37
Shirdley Hill. *Lanc* 3B 90
Shire. *Cumb* 1H 103
Shirebrook. *Derbs* 4C 86
Shiregreen. *S Yor* 1A 86
Shirehampton. *Bris* 4A 34
Shiremoor. *Tyne* 2G 115
Shirenewton. *Mon* 2H 33
Shireoaks. *Notts* 2C 86
Shires Mill. *Fife* 1D 128
Shirkoak. *Kent* 2D 28
Shirland. *Derbs* 5A 86
Shirley. *Derbs* 1G 73
Shirley. *Sotn* 1B 16
Shirley. *W Mid* 3F 61
Shirleywich. *Staf* 3D 73
Shirl Heath. *Here* 5G 59
Shirrell Heath. *Hants* 1D 16
Shirwell. *Devn* 3F 19
Shiskine. *N Ayr* 3D 122
Shobdon. *Here* 4F 59
Shobnall. *Staf* 3G 73
Shobrooke. *Devn* 2B 12
Shoby. *Leics* 3D 74
Shocklach. *Ches W* 1G 71
Shoeburyness. *S'end* 2D 40
Sholden. *Kent* 5H 41
Sholing. *Sotn* 1C 16
Sholver. *G Man* 4H 91
Shoot Hill. *Shrp* 4G 71
Shop. *Corn*
nr. Bude 1C 10
nr. Padstow 1C 6
Shop. *Devn* 1D 11
Shopford. *Cumb* 2G 113
Shoreditch. *G Lon* 2E 39
Shoreditch. *Som* 4F 21
Shoregill. *Cumb* 4A 104
Shoreham. *Kent* 4G 39
Shoreham-by-Sea. *W Sus* 5D 26
Shoresdean. *Nmbd* 5F 131
Shoreswood. *Nmbd* 5F 131
Shorncote. *Glos* 2F 35
Shorne. *Kent* 3A 40
Shorne Ridgeway. *Kent* 3A 40
Shortacombe. *Devn* 4F 11
Shortbridge. *E Sus* 3F 27
Shortgate. *E Sus* 4F 27
Short Green. *Norf* 2C 66
Shorthampton. *Oxon* 3B 50
Short Heath. *Derbs* 4H 73
Short Heath. *W Mid*
nr. Erdington 1E 61
nr. Wednesfield 5D 73
Shortlanesend. *Corn* 4C 6
Shorton. *Torb* 2E 9
Shortstown. *Bed* 1A 52

Shortwood—Southill

Shortwood. S Glo 4B 34
Shorwell. IOW 4C 16
Shoscombe. Bath 1C 22
Shotesham. Norf 1E 67
Shotgate. Essx 1B 40
Shotley. Suff 2F 55
Shotley Bridge. Dur 4D 115
Shotleyfield. Nmbd 4D 114
Shotley Gate. Suff 2F 55
Shottenden. Kent 5E 41
Shottermill. Surr 3G 25
Shottery. Warw 5F 61
Shotteswell. Warw 1C 50
Shottisham. Suff 1G 55
Shottle. Derbs 1H 73
Shotton. Dur
nr. Peterlee 1B 106
nr. Sedgefield 2A 106
Shotton. Flin 4F 83
Shotton. Nmbd
nr. Morpeth 2F 115
nr. Town Yetholm 1C 120
Shotton Colliery. Dur 5G 115
Shotts. N Lan 3B 128
Shotwick. Ches W 3F 83
Shouldham. Norf 5F 77
Shouldham Thorpe. Norf 5F 77
Shoulton. Worc 5C 60
Shrawardine. Shrp 4G 71
Shrawley. Worc 4C 60
Shreding Green. Buck 2B 38
Shrewley. Warw 4G 61
Shrewsbury. Shrp 210 (4G 71)
Shrewton. Wilts 2F 23
Shripney. W Sus 5A 26
Shrivenham. Oxon 3H 35
Shropham. Norf 1B 66
Shroton. Dors 1D 14
Shrub End. Essx 3C 54
Shucknall. Here 1A 48
Shudy Camps. Cambs 1G 53
Shulishadermor. High 4D 155
Shulista. High 1D 154
Shurdington. Glos 4E 49
Shurlock Row. Wind 4G 37
Shurrery. High 3C 168
Shurton. Som 2F 21
Shustoke. Warw 1G 61
Shute. Devn
nr. Axminster 3F 13
nr. Crediton 2B 12
Shutford. Oxon 1B 50
Shut Heath. Staf 3C 72
Shuthonger. Glos 2D 49
Shutlanehead. Staf 1C 72
Shutlanger. Nptn 1F 51
Shutt Green. Staf 5C 72
Shuttington. Warw 5G 73
Shuttlewood. Derbs 3B 86
Shuttleworth. G Man 3G 91
Siabost. W Isl 3E 171
Siabost bho Dheas. W Isl 3E 171
Siabost bho Thuath. W Isl 3E 171
Siadar. W Isl 2F 171
Siadar Uarach. W Isl 2F 171
Sibbaldbie. Dum 1C 112
Sibbertoft. Nptn 2D 62
Sibdon Carwood. Shrp 2G 59
Sibertswold. Kent 1G 29
Sibford Ferris. Oxon 2B 50
Sibford Gower. Oxon 2B 50
Sible Hedingham. Essx 2A 54
Sibsey. Linc 5C 88
Sibsey Fen Side. Linc 5C 88
Sibson. Cambs 1H 63
Sibson. Leics 5A 74
Sibster. High 3F 169
Sibthorpe. Notts 1E 75
Sibton. Suff 4F 67
Sicklesmere. Suff 4A 66
Sicklinghall. N Yor 5F 99
Sid. Devn 4E 13
Sidbury. Devn 3E 13
Sidbury. Shrp 2A 60
Sidcot. N Som 1H 21
Sidcup. G Lon 3F 39
Siddick. Cumb 1B 102
Siddington. Ches E 3C 84
Siddington. Glos 2F 35
Side of the Moor. G Man 3F 91
Sidestrand. Norf 2E 79
Sidford. Devn 3E 13
Sidlesham. W Sus 3G 17
Sidley. E Sus 5B 28
Sidlow. Surr 1D 26
Sidmouth. Devn 4E 13
Sigford. Devn 5A 12
Sigglesthorne. E Yor 5F 101
Sighthill. Edin 2E 129
Sigingstone. V Glam 4C 32
Signet. Oxon 4H 49
Silchester. Hants 5E 37
Sildinis. W Isl 6E 171
Sileby. Leics 4D 74
Silecroft. Cumb 1A 96
Silfield. Norf 1D 66
Silian. Cdgn 5E 57
Silkstone. S Yor 4C 92
Silkstone Common. S Yor 4C 92
Silksworth. Tyne 4G 115
Silk Willoughby. Linc 1H 75
Silloth. Cumb 4C 112
Sills. Nmbd 4C 120
Sillyearn. Mor 3C 160
Silpho. N Yor 5G 107
Silsden. W Yor 5C 98
Silsoe. C Beds 2A 52
Silverbank. Abers 4E 152
Silverburn. Midl 3F 129
Silverdale. Lanc 2D 96
Silverdale. Staf 1C 72
Silverdale Green. Lanc 2D 96
Silver End. Essx 4B 54
Silver End. W Mid 2D 60
Silvergate. Norf 3D 78
Silver Green. Norf 1E 67
Silverhillocks. Abers 2E 161
Silverley's Green. Suff 3E 67
Silverstone. Nptn 1E 51
Silverton. Devn 2C 12
Silverton. W Dun 2F 127
Silvington. Shrp 3A 60
Simm's Cross. Hal 2H 83
Simm's Lane End. Mers 4D 90
Simonburn. Nmbd 2B 114
Simonsbath. Som 3A 20
Simonstone. Lanc 1F 91
Simprim. Bord 5E 131
Simpson. Pemb 3C 42
Simpson Cross. Pemb 3C 42
Sinclairston. E Ayr 3D 116
Sinclairtown. Fife 4E 137
Sinderby. N Yor 1F 99
Sinderhope. Nmbd 4B 114
Sindlesham. Wok 5F 37
Sinfin. Derb 2H 73
Singleborough. Buck 2F 51
Singleton. Kent 1D 28
Singleton. Lanc 1B 90
Singleton. W Sus 1G 17
Singlewell. Kent 3A 40
Sinkhurst Green. Kent 1C 28
Sinnahard. Abers 2B 152
Sinnington. N Yor 1B 100
Sinton Green. Worc 4C 60
Sipson. G Lon 3B 38
Sirhowy. Blae 4E 47
Sisland. Norf 1F 67
Sissinghurst. Kent 2B 28
Siston. S Glo 4B 34
Sithney. Corn 4D 4
Sittingbourne. Kent 4D 40
Six Ashes. Staf 2B 60
Six Bells. Blae 5F 47
Six Hills. Leics 3D 74
Sixhills. Linc 2A 88
Six Mile Bottom. Cambs 5E 65
Sixpenny Handley. Dors 1E 15
Sizewell. Suff 4G 67
Skail. High 4H 167
Skaill. Orkn 6B 172
Skaills. Orkn 7E 172
Skares. E Ayr 3E 117
Skateraw. E Lot 2D 130
Skaw. Shet 5G 173
Skeabost. High 4D 154
Skeabrae. Orkn 5B 172
Skeeby. N Yor 4E 105
Skeffington. Leics 5E 75
Skeffling. E Yor 3G 95
Skegby. Notts
nr. Mansfield 4B 86
nr. Tuxford 3E 87
Skegness. Linc 4E 89
Skelberry. Shet
nr. Boddam 10E 173
nr. Housetter 3E 173
Skelbo. High 4E 165
Skelbo Street. High 4E 165
Skelbrooke. S Yor 3F 93
Skeldyke. Linc 2C 76
Skelfhill. Bord 4G 119
Skellingthorpe. Linc 3G 87
Skellister. Shet 6F 173
Skellorn Green. Ches E 2D 84
Skellow. S Yor 3F 93
Skelmanthorpe. W Yor 3C 92
Skelmersdale. Lanc 4C 90
Skelmorlie. N Ayr 3C 126
Skelpick. High 3H 167
Skelton. Cumb 1F 103
Skelton. E Yor 2A 94
Skelton. N Yor
nr. Richmond 4D 105
nr. Ripon 3F 99
Skelton. Red C 3D 106
Skelton. York 4H 99
Skelton Green. Red C 3D 106
Skelwick. Orkn 3D 172
Skelwith Bridge. Cumb 4E 103
Skendleby. Linc 4D 88
Skendleby Psalter. Linc 3D 88
Skenfrith. Mon 3H 47
Skerne. E Yor 4E 101
Skeroblingarry. Arg 3B 122
Skerray. High 2G 167
Skerricha. High 3C 166
Skerries Airport. Shet 4H 173
Skerton. Lanc 3D 97
Sketchley. Leics 1B 62
Sketty. Swan 3F 31
Skewen. Neat 3G 31
Skewsby. N Yor 2A 100
Skeyton. Norf 3E 79
Skeyton Corner. Norf 3E 79
Skiall. High 2C 168
Skidbrooke. Linc 1D 88
Skidbrooke North End. Linc 1D 88
Skidby. E Yor 1D 94
Skilgate. Som 4C 20
Skillington. Linc 3F 75
Skinburness. Cumb 4C 112
Skinflats. Falk 1C 128
Skinidin. High 4B 154
Skinnet. High 2F 167
Skinningrove. Red C 3E 107
Skipness. Arg 4G 125
Skippool. Lanc 5C 96
Skiprigg. Cumb 5E 113
Skipsea. E Yor 4F 101
Skipsea Brough. E Yor 4F 101
Skipton. N Yor 4B 98
Skipton-on-Swale. N Yor 2F 99
Skipwith. N Yor 1G 93
Skirbeck. Linc 1C 76
Skirbeck Quarter. Linc 1C 76
Skirlaugh. E Yor 1E 95
Skirling. Bord 1C 118
Skirmett. Buck 2F 37
Skirpenbeck. E Yor 4B 100
Skirwith. Cumb 1H 103
Skirwith. N Yor 2G 97
Skirza. High 2F 169
Skitby. Cumb 3F 113
Skitham. Lanc 5D 96
Skittle Green. Buck 5F 51
Skroo. Shet 1B 172
Skulamus. High 1E 147
Skullomie. High 2G 167
Skyborry Green. Shrp 3E 59
Skye Green. Essx 3B 54
Skye of Curr. High 1D 151
Slack, The. Dur 2E 105
Slack. W Yor 2H 91
Slackhall. Derbs 2E 85
Slack Head. Cumb 2D 97
Slackhead. Mor 2B 160
Slackholme End. Linc 3E 89
Slacks of Cairnbanno. Abers 4F 161
Slad. Glos 5D 48
Slade. Swan 4D 31
Slade, The. W Ber 5D 36
Slade End. Oxon 2D 36
Slade Field. Cambs 2C 64
Slade Green. G Lon 3G 39
Slade Heath. Staf 5D 72
Slade Hooton. S Yor 2C 86
Sladesbridge. Corn 5A 10
Slaggyford. Nmbd 4H 113
Slaidburn. Lanc 4G 97
Slaid Hill. W Yor 5F 99
Slaithwaite. W Yor 3A 92
Slaley. Derbs 5G 85
Slaley. Nmbd 4C 114
Slamannan. Falk 2B 128
Slapton. Buck 3H 51
Slapton. Devn 4E 9
Slapton. Nptn 1E 51
Slattocks. G Man 4G 91
Slaugham. W Sus 3D 26
Slaughterbridge. Corn 4B 10
Slaughterford. Wilts 4D 34
Slawston. Leics 1E 63
Sleaford. Hants 3G 25
Sleaford. Linc 1H 75
Sleagill. Cumb 3G 103
Sleap. Shrp 3G 71
Sledmere. E Yor 3D 100
Sleightholme. Dur 3C 104
Sleights. N Yor 4F 107
Slepe. Dors 3E 15
Slickly. High 2E 169
Sliddery. N Ayr 3D 122
Sligachan. High 1C 146
Slimbridge. Glos 5C 48
Slindon. Staf 2C 72
Slindon. W Sus 5A 26
Slinfold. W Sus 2C 26
Slingsby. N Yor 2A 100
Slip End. C Beds 4A 52
Slipton. Nptn 3G 63
Slitting Mill. Staf 4E 73
Slochd. High 1C 150
Slockavullin. Arg 4F 133
Sloley. Norf 3E 79
Sloncombe. Devn 4H 11
Sloothby. Linc 3D 89
Slough. Slo 3A 38
Slough Green. Som 4F 21
Slough Green. W Sus 3D 27
Sluggan. High 1C 150
Slyne. Lanc 3D 97
Smailholm. Bord 1A 120
Smallbridge. G Man 3H 91
Smallbrook. Devn 3B 12
Smallburgh. Norf 3F 79
Smallburn. E Ayr 2F 117
Smalldale. Derbs 3E 85
Small Dole. W Sus 4D 26
Smalley. Derbs 1B 74
Smallfield. Surr 1E 27
Small Heath. W Mid 2E 61
Smallholm. Dum 2C 112
Small Hythe. Kent 2C 28
Smallrice. Staf 2D 72
Smallridge. Devn 2G 13
Smallwood Hey. Lanc 5C 96
Smallworth. Norf 2C 66
Smannell. Hants 2B 24
Smardale. Cumb 4A 104
Smarden. Kent 1C 28
Smarden Bell. Kent 1C 28
Smart's Hill. Kent 1G 27
Smeatharpe. Devn 1F 13
Smeeth. Kent 2E 29
Smeeth, The. Norf 4E 77
Smeeton Westerby. Leics 1D 62
Smeircleit. W Isl 7C 170
Smerral. High 5D 168
Smestow. Staf 1C 60
Smethwick. W Mid 2E 61
Smirisary. High 1A 140
Smisby. Derbs 4H 73
Smitham Hill. Bath 1A 22
Smith End Green. Worc 5B 60
Smithfield. Cumb 3F 113
Smith Green. Lanc 4D 97
Smithies, The. Shrp 1A 60
Smithincott. Devn 1D 12
Smith's Green. Essx 3F 53
Smithstown. High 1G 155
Smithton. High 4B 158
Smithwood Green. Suff 5B 66
Smithy Bridge. G Man 3H 91
Smithy Green. Ches E 3B 84
Smithy Lane Ends. Lanc 3C 90
Smockington. Leics 2B 62
Smoogro. Orkn 7C 172
Smythe's Green. Essx 4C 54
Snaigow House. Per 4H 143
Snailbeach. Shrp 5F 71
Snailwell. Cambs 4F 65
Snainton. N Yor 1D 100
Snaith. E Yor 2G 93
Snape. N Yor 1E 99
Snape. Suff 5F 67
Snape Green. Lanc 3B 90
Snapper. Devn 3F 19
Snarestone. Leics 5H 73
Snarford. Linc 2H 87
Snargate. Kent 3D 28
Snave. Kent 3E 28
Sneachill. Worc 5D 60
Snead. Powy 1F 59
Snead Common. Worc 4B 60
Sneaton. N Yor 4F 107
Sneatonthorpe. N Yor 4G 107
Snelland. Linc 2H 87
Snelston. Derbs 1F 73
Snetterton. Norf 1B 66
Snettisham. Norf 2F 77
Snibston. Leics 4B 74
Sniseabhal. W Isl 5C 170
Snitter. Nmbd 4E 121
Snitterby. Linc 1G 87
Snitterfield. Warw 5G 61
Snitton. Shrp 3H 59
Snodhill. Here 1G 47
Snodland. Kent 4B 40
Snods Edge. Nmbd 4D 114
Snowshill. Glos 2F 49
Snow Street. Norf 2C 66
Snydale. W Yor 2E 93
Soake. Hants 1E 17
Soar. Carm 3G 45
Soar. Gwyn 2F 69
Soar. IOA 3C 80
Soar. Powy 2C 46
Soberton. Hants 1E 16
Soberton Heath. Hants 1E 16
Sockbridge. Cumb 2G 103
Sockburn. Darl 4A 106
Sodom. Den 3C 82
Sodom. Shet 5G 173
Soham. Cambs 3E 65
Soham Cotes. Cambs 3E 65
Solas. W Isl 1D 170
Soldon Cross. Devn 1D 10
Soldridge. Hants 3E 25
Solent Breezes. Hants 2D 16
Sole Street. Kent
nr. Meopham 4A 40
nr. Waltham 1E 29
Solihull. W Mid 2F 61
Sollers Dilwyn. Here 5G 59
Sollers Hope. Here 2B 48
Sollom. Lanc 3C 90
Solva. Pemb 2B 42
Somerby. Leics 4E 75
Somerby. Linc 4D 94
Somercotes. Derbs 5B 86
Somerford. Dors 3G 15
Somerford. Staf 5C 72
Somerford Keynes. Glos 2F 35
Somerley. W Sus 3G 17
Somerleyton. Suff 1G 67
Somersal Herbert. Derbs 2F 73
Somersby. Linc 3C 88
Somersham. Cambs 3C 64
Somersham. Suff 1D 54
Somerton. Oxon 3C 50
Somerton. Som 4H 21
Somerton. Suff 5H 65
Sompting. W Sus 5C 26
Sonning. Wok 4F 37
Sonning Common. Oxon 3F 37
Sonning Eye. Oxon 4F 37
Sookholme. Notts 4C 86
Sopley. Hants 3G 15
Sopworth. Wilts 3D 34
Sorbie. Dum 5B 110
Sordale. High 2D 168
Sorisdale. Arg 2D 138
Sorn. E Ayr 2E 117
Sornhill. E Ayr 1E 117
Sortat. High 2E 169
Sotby. Linc 3B 88
Sots Hole. Linc 4A 88
Sotterley. Suff 2G 67
Soudley. Shrp
nr. Church Stretton 1G 59
nr. Market Drayton 3B 72
Soughton. Flin 4E 83
Soulbury. Buck 3G 51
Soulby. Cumb
nr. Appleby 3A 104
nr. Penrith 2F 103
Souldern. Oxon 2D 50
Souldrop. Bed 4G 63
Sound. Ches E 1A 72
Sound. Shet
nr. Lerwick 7F 173
nr. Tresta 6E 173
Soundwell. S Glo 4B 34
Sourhope. Bord 2C 120
Sourin. Orkn 4D 172
Sour Nook. Cumb 5E 113
Sourton. Devn 3F 11
Soutergate. Cumb 1B 96
South Acre. Norf 4H 77
Southall. G Lon 3C 38
South Allington. Devn 5D 9
South Alloa. Falk 4A 136
Southam. Glos 3E 49
Southam. Warw 4B 62
South Ambersham. W Sus 3A 26
Southampton. Sotn 211 (1C 16)
Southampton Airport. Hants 1C 16
Southannan. N Ayr 4D 126
South Anston. S Yor 2C 86
South Ascot. Wind 4A 38
South Baddesley. Hants 3B 16
South Balfern. Dum 4B 110
South Ballachulish. High 3E 141
South Bank. Red C 2C 106
South Barrow. Som 4B 22
South Benfleet. Essx 2B 40
South Bents. Tyne 3H 115
South Bersted. W Sus 5A 26
Southborough. Kent 1G 27
Southbourne. Bour 3G 15
Southbourne. W Sus 2F 17
South Bowood. Dors 3H 13
South Brent. Devn 3C 8
South Brewham. Som 3C 22
South Broomage. Falk 1B 128
South Broomhill. Nmbd 5G 121
Southburgh. Norf 5B 78
South Burlingham. Norf 5F 79
Southburn. E Yor 4D 101
South Cadbury. Som 4B 22
South Carlton. Linc 3G 87
South Cave. E Yor 1C 94
South Cerney. Glos 2F 35
South Chailey. E Sus 4E 27
South Chard. Som 2G 13
South Charlton. Nmbd 2F 121
South Cheriton. Som 4B 22
South Church. Dur 2F 105
Southchurch. S'end 2D 40
South Cleatlam. Dur 3E 105
South Cliffe. E Yor 1B 94
South Clifton. Notts 3F 87
South Clunes. High 4H 157
South Cockerington. Linc 2C 88
South Common. Devn 2G 13
South Cornelly. B'end 3B 32
Southcott. Devn
nr. Great Torrington 1E 11
nr. Okehampton 3F 11
Southcott. Wilts 1G 23
Southcourt. Buck 4G 51
South Cove. Suff 2G 67
South Creagan. Arg 4D 141
South Creake. Norf 2A 78
South Crosland. W Yor 3B 92
South Croxton. Leics 4D 74
South Dalton. E Yor 5D 100
South Darenth. Kent 4G 39
Southdean. Bord 4A 120
Southdown. Bath 5C 34
South Duffield. N Yor 1G 93
Southease. E Sus 5F 27
South Elkington. Linc 2B 88
South Elmsall. W Yor 3E 93
Southend. Arg 5A 122
South End. Cumb 3B 96
Southend. Glos 2C 34
South End. N Lin 2E 94
Southend. W Ber 4D 36
Southend Airport. Essx 2C 40
Southend-on-Sea. S'end 2C 40
Southerfield. Cumb 5C 112
Southerhouse. Shet 8E 173
Southerly. Devn 4F 11
Southernden. Kent 1C 28
Southerndown. V Glam 4B 32
Southerness. Dum 4A 112
South Erradale. High 1G 155
Southerton. Devn 3D 12
Southery. Norf 1F 65
Southey Green. Essx 2A 54
South Fambridge. Essx 1C 40
South Fawley. W Ber 3B 36
South Feorline. N Ayr 3D 122
South Ferriby. N Lin 2C 94
South Field. E Yor 2D 94
Southfleet. Kent 3H 39
South Garvan. High 1D 141
Southgate. Cdgn 2E 57
Southgate. G Lon 1E 39
Southgate. Norf
nr. Aylsham 3D 78
nr. Fakenham 2A 78
Southgate. Swan 4E 31
South Gluss. Shet 4E 173
South Godstone. Surr 1E 27
South Gorley. Hants 1G 15
South Green. Essx
nr. Billericay 1A 40
nr. Colchester 4D 54
South Green. Kent 4C 40
South Hanningfield. Essx 1B 40
South Harting. W Sus 1F 17
South Hayling. Hants 3F 17
South Hazelrigg. Nmbd 1E 121
South Heath. Buck 5H 51
South Heath. Essx 4E 54
South Heighton. E Sus 5F 27
South Hetton. Dur 5G 115
South Hiendley. W Yor 3D 93
South Hill. Corn 5D 10
South Hill. Som 4H 21
South Hinksey. Oxon 5D 50
South Hole. Devn 4C 18
South Holme. N Yor 2B 100
South Holmwood. Surr 1C 26
South Hornchurch. G Lon 2G 39
South Huish. Devn 4C 8
South Hykeham. Linc 4G 87
South Hylton. Tyne 4G 115
Southill. C Beds 1B 52

Southington—Stocking

Southington. Hants 2D 24
South Kelsey. Linc 1H 87
South Kessock. High 4A 158
South Killingholme. N Lin 3E 95
South Kilvington. N Yor 1G 99
South Kilworth. Leics 2D 62
South Kirkby. W Yor 3E 93
South Kirkton. Abers 3E 153
South Knighton. Devn 5B 12
South Kyme. Linc 1A 76
South Lancing. W Sus 5C 26
South Ledaig. Arg 5D 140
Southleigh. Devn 3F 13
South Leigh. Oxon 5B 50
South Leverton. Notts 2E 87
South Littleton. Worc 1F 49
South Lopham. Norf 2C 66
South Luffenham. Rut 5G 75
South Malling. E Sus 4F 27
South Marston. Swin 3G 35
South Middleton. Nmbd 2D 121
South Milford. N Yor 1E 93
South Milton. Devn 4D 8
South Mimms. Herts 5C 52
Southminster. Essx 1D 40
South Molton. Devn 4H 19
South Moor. Dur 4E 115
Southmoor. Oxon 2B 36
South Moreton. Oxon 3D 36
South Mundham. W Sus 2G 17
South Muskham. Notts 5E 87
South Newbald. E Yor 1C 94
South Newington. Oxon 2C 50
South Newsham. Nmbd 2G 115
South Newton. N Ayr 4H 125
South Newton. Wilts 3F 23
South Normanton. Derbs 5B 86
South Norwood. G Lon 4E 39
South Nutfield. Surr 1E 27
South Ockendon. Thur 2G 39
Southoe. Cambs 4A 64
Southolt. Suff 4D 66
South Ormsby. Linc 3C 88
Southorpe. Pet 5H 75
South Otterington. N Yor 1F 99
South Owersby. Linc 1H 87
Southowram. W Yor 2B 92
South Oxhey. Herts 1C 38
South Perrott. Dors 2H 13
South Petherton. Som 1H 13
South Petherwin. Corn 4D 10
South Pickenham. Norf 5A 78
South Pool. Devn 4D 9
South Poorton. Dors 3A 14
South Port. Arg 1H 133
Southport. Mers 3B 90
Southpunds. Shet 10F 173
South Queensferry. Edin 2E 129
South Radworthy. Devn 3A 20
South Rauceby. Linc 1H 75
South Raynham. Norf 3A 78
Southrepps. Norf 2E 79
South Reston. Linc 2D 88
Southrey. Linc 4A 88
Southrop. Glos 5G 49
Southrope. Hants 2E 25
South Runcton. Norf 5F 77
South Scarle. Notts 4F 87
Southsea. Port 3E 17
South Shields. Tyne 3G 115
South Shore. Bkpl 1B 90
Southside. Orkn 5E 172
South Somercotes. Linc 1D 88
South Stainley. N Yor 3F 99
South Stainmore. Cumb 3B 104
South Stifford. Thur 3G 39
South Stoke. Bath 5C 34
South Stoke. Oxon 3D 36
South Stoke. W Sus 5B 26
South Street. E Sus 4E 27
South Street. Kent
nr. Faversham 5E 41
nr. Whitstable 4F 41
South Tawton. Devn 3G 11
South Thoresby. Linc 3D 88
South Tidworth. Wilts 2H 23
South Town. Devn 4C 12
South Town. Hants 3E 25
Southtown. Norf 5H 79
Southtown. Orkn 8D 172
South View. Shet 7E 173
Southwaite. Cumb 5F 113
South Walsham. Norf 4F 79
South Warnborough. Hants 2F 25
Southwater. W Sus 3C 26
Southwater Street. W Sus 3C 26
Southway. Som 2A 22
South Weald. Essx 1G 39
South Weirs. Hants 2A 16
Southwell. Dors 5B 14
Southwell. Notts 5E 86
South Weston. Oxon 2F 37
South Wheatley. Corn 3C 10
South Wheatley. Notts 2E 87
Southwick. Hants 2E 17
Southwick. Nptn 1H 63
Southwick. Tyne 4G 115
Southwick. W Sus 5D 26
Southwick. Wilts 1D 22
South Widcombe. Bath 1A 22
South Wigston. Leics 1C 62
South Willingham. Linc 2A 88
South Wingfield. Derbs 5A 86
South Witham. Linc 4G 75
Southwold. Suff 3H 67
South Wonston. Hants 3C 24
Southwood. Norf 5F 79
Southwood. Som 3A 22
South Woodham Ferrers.
Essx 1C 40
South Wootton. Norf 3F 77
South Wraxall. Wilts 5D 34
South Zeal. Devn 3G 11
Soval Lodge. W Isl 5F 171
Sowerby. N Yor 1G 99
Sowerby. W Yor 2A 92
Sowerby Bridge. W Yor 2A 92
Sowerby Row. Cumb 5E 113
Sower Carr. Lanc 5C 96
Sowley Green. Suff 5G 65
Sowood. W Yor 3A 92
Sowton. Devn 3C 12
Soyal. High 4C 164
Soyland Town. W Yor 2A 92
Spacey Houses. N Yor 4F 99
Spa Common. Norf 2E 79
Spalding. Linc 3B 76
Spaldington. E Yor 1A 94
Spaldwick. Cambs 3A 64
Spalford. Notts 4F 87
Spanby. Linc 2H 75
Sparham. Norf 4C 78
Sparhamhill. Norf 4C 78
Spark Bridge. Cumb 1C 96
Sparket. Cumb 2F 103
Sparkford. Som 4B 22
Sparkwell. Devn 3B 8
Sparrow Green. Norf 4B 78
Sparrowpit. Derbs 2E 85
Sparrow's Green. E Sus 2H 27
Sparsholt. Hants 3C 24
Sparsholt. Oxon 3B 36
Spartylea. Nmbd 5B 114
Spath. Staf 2E 73
Spaunton. N Yor 1B 100
Spaxton. Som 3F 21
Spean Bridge. High 5E 149
Spear Hill. W Sus 4C 26
Speen. Buck 2G 37
Speen. W Ber 5C 36
Speeton. N Yor 2F 101
Speke. Mers 2G 83
Speldhurst. Kent 1G 27
Spellbrook. Herts 4E 53
Spelsbury. Oxon 3B 50
Spencers Wood. Wok 5F 37
Spennithorne. N Yor 1D 98
Spennymoor. Dur 1F 105
Spernall. Warw 4E 61
Spetchley. Worc 5C 60
Spetisbury. Dors 2E 15
Spexhall. Suff 2F 67
Speybank. High 3C 150
Spey Bay. Mor 2A 160
Speybridge. High 1E 151
Speyview. Mor 4G 159
Spilsby. Linc 4D 88
Spindlestone. Nmbd 1F 121
Spinkhill. Derbs 3B 86
Spinney Hills. Leic 5D 74
Spinningdale. High 5D 164
Spital. Mers 2F 83
Spitalhill. Derbs 1F 73
Spital in the Street. Linc 1G 87
Spithurst. E Sus 4F 27
Spittal. Dum 4A 110
Spittal. E Lot 2A 130
Spittal. High 3D 168
Spittal. Nmbd 4G 131
Spittal. Pemb 2D 43
Spittalfield. Per 4A 144
Spittal of Glenmuick. Abers 5H 151
Spittal of Glenshee. Per 1A 144
Spittal-on-Rule. Bord 2H 119
Spixworth. Norf 4E 79
Splatt. Corn 4C 10
Spofforth. N Yor 4F 99
Spondon. Derb 2B 74
Spon End. W Mid 3H 61
Spooner Row. Norf 1C 66
Sporle. Norf 4H 77
Spott. E Lot 2C 130
Spratton. Nptn 3E 62
Spreakley. Surr 2G 25
Spreyton. Devn 3H 11
Spridlington. Linc 2H 87
Springburn. Glas 3H 127
Springfield. Dum 3E 113
Springfield. Fife 2F 137
Springfield. High 2A 158
Springfield. W Mid 2E 61
Springhill. Staf 5D 73
Spring Hill. W Mid 1C 60
Springholm. Dum 3F 111
Springside. N Ayr 1C 116
Springthorpe. Linc 2F 87
Spring Vale. IOW 3E 16
Spring Valley. IOM 4C 108
Springwell. Tyne 4F 115
Sproatley. E Yor 1E 95
Sproston Green. Ches W 4B 84
Sprotbrough. S Yor 4F 93
Sproughton. Suff 1E 54
Sprouston. Bord 1B 120
Sprowston. Norf 4E 79
Sproxton. Leics 3F 75
Sproxton. N Yor 1A 100
Sprunston. Cumb 5E 113
Spurstow. Ches E 5H 83
Squires Gate. Bkpl 1B 90
Sraid Ruadh. Arg 4A 138
Srannda. W Isl 9C 171
Sron an t-Sithein. High 2C 140
Sronphadruig Lodge. Per 1E 142
Sruth Mor. W Isl 2E 170
Stableford. Shrp 1B 60
Stackhouse. N Yor 3H 97
Stackpole. Pemb 5D 43
Stackpole Elidor. Pemb 5D 43
Stacksford. Norf 1C 66
Stacksteads. Lanc 2G 91
Staddiscombe. Plym 3B 8
Staddlethorpe. E Yor 2B 94
Staddon. Devn 2D 10
Stadhampton. Oxon 2E 36
Stadhlaigearraidh. W Isl 5C 170
Stafainn. High 2D 155
Staffield. Cumb 5G 113
Staffin. High 2D 155
Stafford. Staf 3D 72
Stafford Park. Telf 5B 72
Stagden Cross. Essx 4G 53
Stagsden. Bed 1H 51
Stag's Head. Devn 4G 19
Stainburn. Cumb 2B 102
Stainburn. N Yor 5E 99
Stainby. Linc 3G 75
Staincliffe. W Yor 2C 92
Staincross. S Yor 3D 92
Staindrop. Dur 2E 105
Staines-upon-Thames. Surr 3B 38
Stainfield. Linc
nr. Bourne 3H 75
nr. Lincoln 3A 88
Stainforth. N Yor 3H 97
Stainforth. S Yor 3G 93
Staining. Lanc 1B 90
Stainland. W Yor 3A 92
Stainsacre. N Yor 4G 107
Stainton. Cumb
nr. Carlisle 4E 113
nr. Kendal 1E 97
nr. Penrith 2F 103
Stainton. Dur 3D 104
Stainton. Midd 3B 106
Stainton. N Yor 5E 105
Stainton. S Yor 1C 86
Stainton by Langworth. Linc 3H 87
Staintondale. N Yor 5G 107
Stainton le Vale. Linc 1A 88
Stainton with Adgarley. Cumb 2B 96
Stair. Cumb 2D 102
Stair. E Ayr 2D 116
Stairhaven. Dum 4H 109
Staithes. N Yor 3E 107
Stakeford. Nmbd 1F 115
Stake Pool. Lanc 5D 96
Stakes. Hants 2E 17
Stalbridge. Dors 1C 14
Stalbridge Weston. Dors 1C 14
Stalham. Norf 3F 79
Stalham Green. Norf 3F 79
Stalisfield Green. Kent 5D 40
Stallen. Dors 1B 14
Stallingborough. NE Lin 3F 95
Stalling Busk. N Yor 1B 98
Stallington. Staf 2D 72
Stalmine. Lanc 5C 96
Stalybridge. G Man 1D 84
Stambourne. Essx 2H 53
Stamford. Linc 5H 75
Stamford. Nmbd 3G 121
Stamford Bridge. Ches W 4G 83
Stamford Bridge. E Yor 4B 100
Stamfordham. Nmbd 2D 115
Stamperland. E Ren 4G 127
Stanah. Lanc 5C 96
Stanborough. Herts 4C 52
Stanbridge. C Beds 3H 51
Stanbridge. Dors 2F 15
Stanbury. W Yor 1A 92
Stand. N Lan 3A 128
Standburn. Falk 2C 128
Standeford. Staf 5D 72
Standen. Kent 1C 28
Standen Street. Kent 2C 28
Standerwick. Som 1D 22
Standford. Hants 3G 25
Standford Bridge. Telf 3B 72
Standingstone. Cumb 5D 112
Standish. Glos 5D 48
Standish. G Man 3D 90
Standish Lower Ground.
G Man 4D 90
Standlake. Oxon 5B 50
Standon. Hants 4C 24
Standon. Herts 3D 53
Standon. Staf 2C 72
Standon Green End. Herts 4D 52
Stane. N Lan 4B 128
Stanecastle. N Ayr 1C 116
Stanfield. Norf 3B 78
Stanfield. Suff 5G 65
Stanford. C Beds 1B 52
Stanford. Kent 2F 29
Stanford Bishop. Here 5A 60
Stanford Bridge. Worc 4B 60
Stanford Dingley. W Ber 4D 36
Stanford in the Vale. Oxon 2B 36
Stanford-le-Hope. Thur 2A 40
Stanford on Avon. Nptn 3C 62
Stanford on Soar. Notts 3C 74
Stanford on Teme. Worc 4B 60
Stanford Rivers. Essx 5F 53
Stanfree. Derbs 3B 86
Stanghow. Red C 3D 107
Stanground. Pet 1B 64
Stanhoe. Norf 2H 77
Stanhope. Dur 1C 104
Stanhope. Bord 2D 118
Stanion. Nptn 2G 63
Stanley. Derbs 1B 74
Stanley. Dur 4E 115
Stanley. Per 5A 144
Stanley. Shrp 2B 60
Stanley. Staf 5D 84
Stanley. W Yor 2D 92
Stanley Common. Derbs 1B 74
Stanley Crook. Dur 1E 105
Stanley Hill. Here 1B 48
Stanlow. Ches W 3G 83
Stanmer. Brig 5E 27
Stanmore. G Lon 1C 38
Stanmore. Hants 4C 24
Stanmore. W Ber 4C 36
Stannersburn. Nmbd 1A 114
Stanningfield. Suff 5A 66
Stannington. Nmbd 2F 115
Stannington. S Yor 2H 85
Stansbatch. Here 4F 59
Stanshope. Staf 5F 85
Stanstead. Suff 1B 54
Stanstead Abbotts. Herts 4D 53
Stansted. Kent 4H 39
Stansted Airport. Essx 3F 53
Stansted Mountfitchet. Essx 3F 53
Stanthorne. Ches W 4A 84
Stanton. Derbs 4G 73
Stanton. Glos 2F 49
Stanton. Nmbd 5F 121
Stanton. Staf 1F 73
Stanton. Suff 3B 66
Stanton by Bridge. Derbs 3A 74
Stanton-by-Dale. Derbs 2B 74
Stanton Chare. Suff 3B 66
Stanton Drew. Bath 5A 34
Stanton Fitzwarren. Swin 2G 35
Stanton Harcourt. Oxon 5C 50
Stanton Hill. Notts 4B 86
Stanton in Peak. Derbs 4G 85
Stanton Lacy. Shrp 3G 59
Stanton Long. Shrp 1H 59
Stanton-on-the-Wolds. Notts 2D 74
Stanton Prior. Bath 5B 34
Stanton St Bernard. Wilts 5F 35
Stanton St John. Oxon 5D 50
Stanton St Quintin. Wilts 4E 35
Stanton Street. Suff 4B 66
Stanton under Bardon. Leics 4B 74
Stanton upon Hine Heath.
Shrp 3H 71
Stanton Wick. Bath 5B 34
Stanwardine in the Fields.
Shrp 3G 71
Stanwardine in the Wood.
Shrp 3G 71
Stanway. Essx 3C 54
Stanway. Glos 2F 49
Stanwell. Surr 3B 38
Stanwell Green. Suff 3D 66
Stanwell Moor. Surr 3B 38
Stanwick. Nptn 3G 63
Stanydale. Shet 6D 173
Staoinebrig. W Isl 5C 170
Stape. N Yor 5E 107
Stapehill. Dors 2F 15
Stapeley. Ches E 1A 72
Stapenhill. Staf 3G 73
Staple. Kent 5G 41
Staple Cross. Devn 4D 20
Staplecross. E Sus 3B 28
Staplefield. W Sus 3D 27
Staple Fitzpaine. Som 1F 13
Stapleford. Cambs 5D 64
Stapleford. Herts 4D 52
Stapleford. Leics 4F 75
Stapleford. Linc 5F 87
Stapleford. Notts 2B 74
Stapleford. Wilts 3F 23
Stapleford Abbotts. Essx 1G 39
Stapleford Tawney. Essx 1G 39
Staplegrove. Som 4F 21
Staplehay. Som 4F 21
Staple Hill. S Glo 4B 34
Staplehurst. Kent 1B 28
Staplers. IOW 4D 16
Stapleton. Bris 4B 34
Stapleton. Cumb 2G 113
Stapleton. Here 4F 59
Stapleton. Leics 1B 62
Stapleton. N Yor 3F 105
Stapleton. Shrp 5G 71
Stapleton. Som 4H 21
Stapley. Som 1E 13
Staploe. Bed 4A 64
Staplow. Here 1B 48
Star. Fife 3F 137
Star. Pemb 1G 43
Starbeck. N Yor 4F 99
Starbotton. N Yor 2B 98
Starcross. Devn 4C 12
Stareton. Warw 3H 61
Starkholmes. Derbs 5H 85
Starling. G Man 3F 91
Starling's Green. Essx 2E 53
Starston. Norf 2E 67
Start. Devn 4E 9
Startforth. Dur 3D 104
Start Hill. Essx 3F 53
Startley. Wilts 3E 35
Stathe. Som 4G 21
Stathern. Leics 2E 75
Station Town. Dur 1B 106
Staughton Green. Cambs 4A 64
Staughton Highway. Cambs 4A 64
Staunton. Glos
nr. Cheltenham 3C 48
nr. Monmouth 4A 48
Staunton in the Vale. Notts 1F 75
Staunton on Arrow. Here 4F 59
Staunton on Wye. Here 1G 47
Staveley. Cumb 5F 103
Staveley. Derbs 3B 86
Staveley. N Yor 3F 99
Staveley-in-Cartmel. Cumb 1C 96
Staverton. Devn 2D 9
Staverton. Glos 3D 49
Staverton. Nptn 4C 62
Staverton. Wilts 5D 34
Stawell. Som 3G 21
Stawley. Som 4D 20
Staxigoe. High 3F 169
Staxton. N Yor 2E 101
Staylittle. Powy 1A 58
Staynall. Lanc 5C 96
Staythorpe. Notts 5E 87
Stean. N Yor 2C 98
Stearsby. N Yor 2A 100
Steart. Som 2F 21
Stebbing. Essx 3G 53
Stebbing Green. Essx 3G 53
Stedham. W Sus 4G 25
Steel. Nmbd 4C 114
Steel Cross. E Sus 2G 27
Steelend. Fife 4C 136
Steele Road. Bord 5H 119
Steel Heath. Shrp 2H 71
Steen's Bridge. Here 5H 59
Steep. Hants 4F 25
Steep Lane. W Yor 2A 92
Steeple. Dors 4E 15
Steeple. Essx 5C 54
Steeple Ashton. Wilts 1E 23
Steeple Aston. Oxon 3C 50
Steeple Barton. Oxon 3C 50
Steeple Bumpstead. Essx 1G 53
Steeple Claydon. Buck 3E 51
Steeple Gidding. Cambs 2A 64
Steeple Langford. Wilts 3F 23
Steeple Morden. Cambs 1C 52
Steeton. W Yor 5C 98
Stein. High 3B 154
Steinmanhill. Abers 4E 161
Stelling Minnis. Kent 1F 29
Stembridge. Som 4H 21
Stemster. High
nr. Halkirk 2D 169
nr. Westfield 2C 168
Stenalees. Corn 3E 6
Stenhill. Devn 1D 12
Stenhouse. Edin 2F 129
Stenhousemuir. Falk 1B 128
Stenigot. Linc 2B 88
Stenscholl. High 2D 155
Stenso. Orkn 5C 172
Stenson. Derbs 3H 73
Stenson Fields. Derbs 2H 73
Stenton. E Lot 2C 130
Stenwith. Linc 2F 75
Steòrnabhagh. W Isl 4G 171
Stepaside. Pemb 4F 43
Stepford. Dum 1F 111
Stepney. G Lon 2E 39
Steppingley. C Beds 2A 52
Stepps. N Lan 3H 127
Sterndale Moor. Derbs 4F 85
Sternfield. Suff 4F 67
Stert. Wilts 1F 23
Stetchworth. Cambs 5F 65
Stevenage. Herts 3C 52
Stevenston. N Ayr 5D 126
Stevenstone. Devn 1F 11
Steventon. Hants 2D 24
Steventon. Oxon 2C 36
Steventon End. Essx 1F 53
Stevington. Bed 5G 63
Stewartby. Bed 1A 52
Stewarton. Arg 4A 122
Stewarton. E Ayr 5F 127
Stewkley. Buck 3G 51
Stewkley Dean. Buck 3G 51
Stewley. Som 1G 13
Stewton. Linc 2C 88
Steyning. W Sus 4C 26
Steynton. Pemb 4D 42
Stibb. Corn 1C 10
Stibbard. Norf 3B 78
Stibb Cross. Devn 1E 11
Stibb Green. Wilts 5H 35
Stibbington. Cambs 1H 63
Stichill. Bord 1B 120
Sticker. Corn 3D 6
Stickford. Linc 4C 88
Sticklepath. Devn 3G 11
Sticklinch. Som 3A 22
Stickling Green. Essx 2E 53
Stickney. Linc 5C 88
Stiffkey. Norf 1B 78
Stifford's Bridge. Here 1C 48
Stileway. Som 2H 21
Stillingfleet. N Yor 5H 99
Stillington. N Yor 3H 99
Stillington. Stoc T 2A 106
Stilton. Cambs 2A 64
Stinchcombe. Glos 2C 34
Stinsford. Dors 3C 14
Stiperstones. Shrp 5F 71
Stirchley. Telf 5B 72
Stirchley. W Mid 2E 61
Stirling. Abers 4H 161
Stirling. Stir 211 (4G 135)
Stirton. N Yor 4B 98
Stisted. Essx 3A 54
Stitchcombe. Wilts 5H 35
Stithians. Corn 5B 6
Stittenham. High 1A 158
Stivichall. W Mid 3H 61
Stixwould. Linc 4A 88
Stoak. Ches W 3G 83
Stobo. Bord 1D 118
Stobo Castle. Bord 1D 118
Stoborough. Dors 4E 15
Stoborough Green. Dors 4E 15
Stobs Castle. Bord 4H 119
Stobswood. Nmbd 5G 121
Stock. Essx 1A 40
Stockbridge. Hants 3B 24
Stockbridge. W Yor 5C 98
Stockbury. Kent 4C 40
Stockcross. W Ber 5C 36
Stockdalewath. Cumb 5E 113
Stocker's Head. Kent 5D 40
Stockerston. Leics 1F 63
Stock Green. Worc 5D 61
Stocking. Here 2B 48

Stockingford—Swanton Abbott

Stockingford. *Warw* 1H 61
Stocking Green. *Essx* 2F 53
Stocking Pelham. *Herts* 3E 53
Stockland. *Devn* 2F 13
Stockland Bristol. *Som* 2F 21
Stockleigh English. *Devn* 2B 12
Stockleigh Pomeroy. *Devn* 2B 12
Stockley. *Wilts* 5F 35
Stocklinch. *Som* 1G 13
Stockport. *G Man* 2C 84
Stocks, The. *Kent* 3D 28
Stocksbridge. *S Yor* 1G 85
Stocksfield. *Nmbd* 3D 114
Stockstreet. *Essx* 3B 54
Stockton. *Here* 4H 59
Stockton. *Norf* 1F 67
Stockton. *Shrp*
nr. Bridgnorth 1B 60
nr. Chirbury 5E 71
Stockton. *Telf* 4B 72
Stockton. *Warw* 4B 62
Stockton. *Wilts* 3E 23
Stockton Brook. *Staf* 5D 84
Stockton Cross. *Here* 4H 59
Stockton Heath. *Warr* 2A 84
Stockton-on-Tees. *Stoc T* 3B 106
Stockton on Teme. *Worc* 4B 60
Stockton-on-the-Forest. *York* 4A 100
Stockwell Heath. *Staf* 3E 73
Stockwood. *Bris* 5B 34
Stock Wood. *Worc* 5E 61
Stodmarsh. *Kent* 4G 41
Stody. *Norf* 2C 78
Stoer. *High* 1E 163
Stoford. *Som* 1A 14
Stoford. *Wilts* 3F 23
Stogumber. *Som* 3D 20
Stogursey. *Som* 2F 21
Stoke. *Devn* 4C 18
Stoke. *Hants*
nr. Andover 1C 24
nr. South Hayling 2F 17
Stoke. *Medw* 3C 40
Stoke. *W Mid* 3A 62
Stoke Abbott. *Dors* 2H 13
Stoke Albany. *Nptn* 2F 63
Stoke Ash. *Suff* 3D 66
Stoke Bardolph. *Notts* 1D 74
Stoke Bliss. *Worc* 4A 60
Stoke Bruerne. *Nptn* 1F 51
Stoke by Clare. *Suff* 1H 53
Stoke-by-Nayland. *Suff* 2C 54
Stoke Canon. *Devn* 3C 12
Stoke Charity. *Hants* 3C 24
Stoke Climsland. *Corn* 5D 10
Stoke Cross. *Here* 5A 60
Stoke D'Abernon. *Surr* 5C 38
Stoke Doyle. *Nptn* 2H 63
Stoke Dry. *Rut* 1F 63
Stoke Edith. *Here* 1B 48
Stoke Farthing. *Wilts* 4F 23
Stoke Ferry. *Norf* 5G 77
Stoke Fleming. *Devn* 4E 9
Stokeford. *Dors* 4D 14
Stoke Gabriel. *Devn* 3E 9
Stoke Gifford. *S Glo* 4B 34
Stoke Golding. *Leics* 1A 62
Stoke Goldington. *Mil* 1G 51
Stokeham. *Notts* 3E 87
Stoke Hammond. *Buck* 3G 51
Stoke Heath. *Shrp* 3A 72
Stoke Holy Cross. *Norf* 5E 79
Stokeinteignhead. *Devn* 5C 12
Stoke Lacy. *Here* 1B 48
Stoke Lyne. *Oxon* 3D 50
Stoke Mandeville. *Buck* 4G 51
Stokenchurch. *Buck* 2F 37
Stoke Newington. *G Lon* 2E 39
Stokenham. *Devn* 4E 9
Stoke on Tern. *Shrp* 3A 72
Stoke-on-Trent. *Stoke* 211 (1C 72)
Stoke Orchard. *Glos* 3E 49
Stoke Pero. *Som* 2B 20
Stoke Poges. *Buck* 2A 38
Stoke Prior. *Here* 5H 59
Stoke Prior. *Worc* 4D 60
Stoke Rivers. *Devn* 3G 19
Stoke Rochford. *Linc* 3G 75
Stoke Row. *Oxon* 3E 37
Stoke St Gregory. *Som* 4G 21
Stoke St Mary. *Som* 4F 21
Stoke St Michael. *Som* 2B 22
Stoke St Milborough. *Shrp* 2H 59
Stokesay. *Shrp* 2G 59
Stokesby. *Norf* 4G 79
Stokesley. *N Yor* 4C 106
Stoke sub Hamdon. *Som* 1H 13
Stoke Talmage. *Oxon* 2E 37
Stoke Town. *Stoke* 211 (1C 72)
Stoke Trister. *Som* 4C 22
Stoke Wake. *Dors* 2C 14
Stolford. *Som* 2F 21
Stondon Massey. *Essx* 5F 53
Stone. *Buck* 4F 51
Stone. *Glos* 2B 34
Stone. *Kent* 3G 39
Stone. *Som* 3A 22
Stone. *Staf* 2D 72
Stone. *Worc* 3C 60
Stonea. *Cambs* 1D 64
Stoneacton. *Shrp* 1H 59
Stone Allerton. *Som* 1H 21
Ston Easton. *Som* 1B 22
Stonebridge. *N Som* 1G 21
Stonebridge. *Surr* 1C 26
Stone Bridge Corner. *Pet* 5B 76
Stonebroom. *Derbs* 5B 86
Stonebyres Holdings. *S Lan* 5B 128
Stone Chair. *W Yor* 2B 92
Stone Cross. *E Sus* 5H 27
Stone Cross. *Kent* 2G 27
Stone-edge Batch. *N Som* 4H 33
Stoneferry. *Hull* 1D 94
Stonefield. *Arg* 5D 140
Stonefield. *S Lan* 4H 127
Stonegate. *E Sus* 3A 28
Stonegate. *N Yor* 4E 107
Stonegrave. *N Yor* 2A 100
Stonehall. *Worc* 1D 49
Stonehaugh. *Nmbd* 2A 114
Stonehaven. *Abers* 5F 153
Stone Heath. *Staf* 2D 72
Stone Hill. *Kent* 2E 29
Stone House. *Cumb* 1G 97
Stonehouse. *Glos* 5D 48
Stonehouse. *Nmbd* 4H 113
Stonehouse. *S Lan* 5A 128
Stone in Oxney. *Kent* 3D 28
Stoneleigh. *Warw* 3H 61
Stoneley Green. *Ches E* 5A 84
Stonely. *Cambs* 4A 64
Stonepits. *Worc* 5E 61
Stoner Hill. *Hants* 4F 25
Stonesby. *Leics* 3F 75
Stonesfield. *Oxon* 4B 50
Stones Green. *Essx* 3E 55
Stone Street. *Kent* 5G 39
Stone Street. *Suff*
nr. Boxford 2C 54
nr. Halesworth 2F 67
Stonethwaite. *Cumb* 3D 102
Stoneyburn. *W Lot* 3C 128
Stoney Cross. *Hants* 1A 16
Stoneyford. *Devn* 2D 12
Stoneygate. *Leic* 5D 74
Stoneyhills. *Essx* 1D 40
Stoneykirk. *Dum* 4F 109
Stoney Middleton. *Derbs* 3G 85
Stoney Stanton. *Leics* 1B 62
Stoney Stoke. *Som* 3C 22
Stoney Stratton. *Som* 3B 22
Stoney Stretton. *Shrp* 5F 71
Stoneywood. *Aber* 2F 153
Stonham Aspal. *Suff* 5D 66
Stonnall. *Staf* 5E 73
Stonor. *Oxon* 3F 37
Stonton Wyville. *Leics* 1E 63
Stonybreck. *Shet* 1B 172
Stony Cross. *Devn* 4F 19
Stony Cross. *Here*
nr. Great Malvern 1C 48
nr. Leominster 4H 59
Stony Houghton. *Derbs* 4B 86
Stony Stratford. *Mil* 1F 51
Stoodleigh. *Devn*
nr. Barnstaple 3G 19
nr. Tiverton 1C 12
Stopham. *W Sus* 4B 26
Stopsley. *Lutn* 3B 52
Stoptide. *Corn* 1D 6
Storeton. *Mers* 2F 83
Stormontfield. *Per* 1D 136
Stornoway. *W Isl* 4G 171
Stornoway Airport. *W Isl* 4G 171
Storridge. *Here* 1C 48
Storrington. *W Sus* 4B 26
Storrs. *Cumb* 5E 103
Storth. *Cumb* 1D 97
Storwood. *E Yor* 5B 100
Stotfield. *Mor* 1G 159
Stotfold. *C Beds* 2C 52
Stottesdon. *Shrp* 2A 60
Stoughton. *Leics* 5D 74
Stoughton. *Surr* 5A 38
Stoughton. *W Sus* 1G 17
Stoul. *High* 4F 147
Stoulton. *Worc* 1E 49
Stourbridge. *W Mid* 2C 60
Stourpaine. *Dors* 2D 14
Stourport-on-Severn. *Worc* 3C 60
Stour Provost. *Dors* 4C 22
Stour Row. *Dors* 4D 22
Stourton. *Staf* 2C 60
Stourton. *Warw* 2A 50
Stourton. *W Yor* 1D 92
Stourton. *Wilts* 3C 22
Stourton Caundle. *Dors* 1C 14
Stove. *Orkn* 4F 172
Stove. *Shet* 9F 173
Stoven. *Suff* 2G 67
Stow. *Linc*
nr. Billingborough 2H 75
nr. Gainsborough 2F 87
Stow. *Bord* 5A 130
Stow Bardolph. *Norf* 5F 77
Stow Bedon. *Norf* 1B 66
Stowbridge. *Norf* 5F 77
Stow cum Quy. *Cambs* 4E 65
Stowe. *Glos* 5A 48
Stowe. *Shrp* 3F 59
Stowe. *Staf* 4F 73
Stowe-by-Chartley. *Staf* 3E 73
Stowell. *Som* 4B 22
Stowey. *Bath* 1A 22
Stowford. *Devn*
nr. Colaton Raleigh 4D 12
nr. Combe Martin 2G 19
nr. Tavistock 4E 11
Stowlangtoft. *Suff* 4B 66
Stow Longa. *Cambs* 3A 64
Stow Maries. *Essx* 1C 40
Stowmarket. *Suff* 5C 66
Stow-on-the-Wold. *Glos* 3G 49
Stowting. *Kent* 1F 29
Stowupland. *Suff* 5C 66
Straad. *Arg* 3B 126
Strachan. *Abers* 4D 152
Stradbroke. *Suff* 3E 67
Stradishall. *Suff* 5G 65
Stradsett. *Norf* 5F 77
Stragglethorpe. *Linc* 5G 87
Stragglethorpe. *Notts* 2D 74
Straid. *S Ayr* 5A 116
Straight Soley. *Wilts* 4B 36
Straiton. *Midl* 3F 129
Straiton. *S Ayr* 4C 116
Straloch. *Per* 2H 143
Stramshall. *Staf* 2E 73
Strang. *IOM* 4C 108
Strangford. *Here* 3A 48
Stranraer. *Dum* 3F 109
Strata Florida. *Cdgn* 4G 57
Stratfield Mortimer. *W Ber* 5E 37
Stratfield Saye. *Hants* 5E 37
Stratfield Turgis. *Hants* 1E 25
Stratford. *G Lon* 2E 39
Stratford. *Worc* 2D 49
Stratford St Andrew. *Suff* 4F 67
Stratford St Mary. *Suff* 2D 54
Stratford sub Castle. *Wilts* 3G 23
Stratford Tony. *Wilts* 4F 23
Stratford-upon-Avon.
Warw 212 (5G 61)
Strath. *High*
nr. Gairloch 1G 155
nr. Wick 3E 169
Strathan. *High*
nr. Fort William 4B 148
nr. Lochinver 1E 163
nr. Tongue 2F 167
Strathan Skerray. *High* 2G 167
Strathaven. *S Lan* 5A 128
Strathblane. *Stir* 2G 127
Strathcanaird. *High* 3F 163
Strathcarron. *High* 4B 156
Strathcoil. *Arg* 5A 140
Strathdon. *Abers* 2A 152
Strathkinness. *Fife* 2G 137
Strathmashie House. *High* 4H 149
Strathmiglo. *Fife* 2E 136
Strathmore Lodge. *High* 4D 168
Strathpeffer. *High* 3G 157
Strathrannoch. *High* 1F 157
Strathtay. *Per* 3G 143
Strathvaich Lodge. *High* 1F 157
Strathwhillan. *N Ayr* 2E 123
Strathy. *High*
nr. Invergordon 1A 158
nr. Melvich 2A 168
Strathyre. *Stir* 2E 135
Stratton. *Corn* 2C 10
Stratton. *Dors* 3B 14
Stratton. *Glos* 5F 49
Stratton Audley. *Oxon* 3E 50
Stratton-on-the-Fosse.
Som 1B 22
Stratton St Margaret. *Swin* 3G 35
Stratton St Michael. *Norf* 1E 66
Stratton Strawless. *Norf* 3E 78
Stravithie. *Fife* 2H 137
Stream. *Som* 3D 20
Streat. *E Sus* 4E 27
Streatham. *G Lon* 3E 39
Streatley. *C Beds* 3A 52
Streatley. *W Ber* 3D 36
Street. *Corn* 3C 10
Street. *Lanc* 4E 97
Street. *N Yor* 4E 107
Street. *Som*
nr. Chard 2G 13
Street. *Som*
nr. Glastonbury 3H 21
Street Ash. *Som* 1F 13
Street Dinas. *Shrp* 2F 71
Street End. *Kent* 5F 41
Street End. *W Sus* 3G 17
Streetgate. *Tyne* 4F 115
Streethay. *Staf* 4F 73
Streethouse. *W Yor* 2D 93
Streetlam. *N Yor* 5A 106
Street Lane. *Derbs* 1A 74
Streetly. *W Mid* 1E 61
Streetly End. *Cambs* 1G 53
Street on the Fosse. *Som* 3B 22
Strefford. *Shrp* 2G 59
Strelley. *Notts* 1C 74
Strensall. *York* 3A 100
Strensall Camp. *York* 4A 100
Stretcholt. *Som* 2F 21
Strete. *Devn* 4E 9
Stretford. *G Man* 1C 84
Stretford. *Here* 5H 59
Strethall. *Essx* 2E 53
Stretham. *Cambs* 3E 65
Stretton. *Ches W* 5G 83
Stretton. *Derbs* 4A 86
Stretton. *Rut* 4G 75
Stretton. *Staf*
nr. Brewood 4C 72
nr. Burton upon Trent 3G 73
Stretton. *Warr* 2A 84
Stretton en le Field. *Leics* 4H 73
Stretton Grandison. *Here* 1B 48
Stretton Heath. *Shrp* 4F 71
Stretton-on-Dunsmore.
Warw 3B 62
Stretton-on-Fosse. *Warw* 2H 49
Stretton Sugwas. *Here* 1H 47
Stretton under Fosse.
Warw 2B 62
Stretton Westwood. *Shrp* 1H 59
Strichen. *Abers* 3G 161
Strines. *G Man* 2D 84
Stringston. *Som* 2E 21
Strixton. *Nptn* 4G 63
Stroanfreggan. *Dum* 5F 117
Stroat. *Glos* 2A 34
Stromeferry. *High* 5A 156
Stromemore. *High* 5A 156
Stromness. *Orkn* 7B 172
Stronachie. *Per* 3C 136
Stronachlachar. *Stir* 2D 134
Stronchreggan. *High* 1E 141
Strone. *Arg* 1C 126
Strone. *High*
nr. Drumnadrochit 1H 149
nr. Kingussie 3B 150
Stronenaba. *High* 5E 148
Stronganess. *Shet* 1G 173
Stronmilchan. *Arg* 1A 134
Stronsay Airport. *Orkn* 5F 172
Strontian. *High* 2C 140
Strood. *Kent* 2C 28
Strood. *Medw* 4B 40
Strood Green. *Surr* 1D 26
Strood Green. *W Sus*
nr. Billingshurst 3B 26
nr. Horsham 2C 26
Strothers Dale. *Nmbd* 4C 114
Stroud. *Glos* 5D 48
Stroud. *Hants* 4F 25
Stroud Green. *Essx* 1C 40
Stroxton. *Linc* 2G 75
Struan. *High* 5C 154
Struan. *Per* 2F 143
Struanmore. *High* 5C 154
Strubby. *Linc* 2D 88
Strugg's Hill. *Linc* 2B 76
Strumpshaw. *Norf* 5F 79
Strutherhill. *S Lan* 4A 128
Struy. *High* 5G 157
Stryd. *IOA* 2B 80
Stryt-issa. *Wrex* 1E 71
Stuartfield. *Abers* 4G 161
Stubbington. *Hants* 2D 16
Stubbins. *Lanc* 3F 91
Stubble Green. *Cumb* 5B 102
Stubb's Cross. *Kent* 2D 28
Stubbs Green. *Norf* 1F 67
Stubhampton. *Dors* 1E 15
Stubton. *Linc* 1F 75
Stubwood. *Staf* 2E 73
Stuckton. *Hants* 1G 15
Studham. *C Beds* 4A 52
Studland. *Dors* 4F 15
Studley. *Warw* 4E 61
Studley. *Wilts* 4E 35
Studley Roger. *N Yor* 2E 99
Stuntney. *Cambs* 3E 65
Stunts Green. *E Sus* 4H 27
Sturbridge. *Staf* 2C 72
Sturgate. *Linc* 2F 87
Sturmer. *Essx* 1G 53
Sturminster Marshall. *Dors* 2E 15
Sturminster Newton. *Dors* 1C 14
Sturry. *Kent* 4F 41
Sturton. *N Lin* 4C 94
Sturton by Stow. *Linc* 2F 87
Sturton le Steeple. *Notts* 2E 87
Stuston. *Suff* 3D 66
Stutton. *N Yor* 5G 99
Stutton. *Suff* 2E 55
Styal. *Ches E* 2C 84
Stydd. *Lanc* 1E 91
Styrrup. *Notts* 1D 86
Suainebost. *W Isl* 1H 171
Suardail. *W Isl* 4G 171
Succoth. *Abers* 5B 160
Succoth. *Arg* 3B 134
Suckley. *Worc* 5B 60
Suckley Knowl. *Worc* 5B 60
Sudborough. *Nptn* 2G 63
Sudbourne. *Suff* 5G 67
Sudbrook. *Linc* 1G 75
Sudbrook. *Mon* 3A 34
Sudbrooke. *Linc* 3H 87
Sudbury. *Derbs* 2F 73
Sudbury. *Suff* 1B 54
Sudgrove. *Glos* 5E 49
Suffield. *Norf* 2E 79
Suffield. *N Yor* 5G 107
Sugnall. *Staf* 2B 72
Sugwas Pool. *Here* 1H 47
Suisnish. *High* 5E 155
Sulaisiadar. *W Isl* 4H 171
Sùlaisiadar Mòr. *High* 4D 155
Sulby. *IOM* 2C 108
Sulgrave. *Nptn* 1D 50
Sulham. *W Ber* 4E 37
Sulhamstead. *W Ber* 5E 37
Sullington. *W Sus* 4B 26
Sullom. *Shet* 4E 173
Sully. *V Glam* 5E 33
Sumburgh. *Shet* 10F 173
Sumburgh Airport. *Shet* 10E 173
Summer Bridge. *N Yor* 3E 98
Summercourt. *Corn* 3C 6
Summergangs. *Hull* 1E 94
Summerhill. *Aber* 3G 153
Summerhill. *Pemb* 4F 43
Summer Hill. *W Mid* 1D 60
Summerhouse. *Darl* 3F 105
Summersdale. *W Sus* 2G 17
Summerseat. *G Man* 3F 91
Summit. *G Man* 3H 91
Sunbury. *Surr* 4C 38
Sunderland. *Cumb* 1C 102
Sunderland. *Lanc* 4D 96
Sunderland. *Tyne* 212 (4G 115)
Sunderland Bridge. *Dur* 1F 105
Sundon Park. *Lutn* 3A 52
Sundridge. *Kent* 5F 39
Sunk Island. *E Yor* 3F 95
Sunningdale. *Wind* 4A 38
Sunninghill. *Wind* 4A 38
Sunningwell. *Oxon* 5C 50
Sunniside. *Dur* 1E 105
Sunniside. *Tyne* 4F 115
Sunny Bank. *Cumb* 5D 102
Sunny Hill. *Derb* 2H 73
Sunnyhurst. *Bkbn* 2E 91
Sunnylaw. *Stir* 4G 135
Sunnymead. *Oxon* 5D 50
Sunnyside. *S Yor* 1B 86
Sunnyside. *W Sus* 2E 27
Sunton. *Wilts* 1H 23
Surbiton. *G Lon* 4C 38
Surby. *IOM* 4B 108
Surfleet. *Linc* 3B 76
Surfleet Seas End. *Linc* 3B 76
Surlingham. *Norf* 5F 79
Surrex. *Essx* 3B 54
Sustead. *Norf* 2D 78
Susworth. *Linc* 4B 94
Sutcombe. *Devn* 1D 10
Suton. *Norf* 1C 66
Sutors of Cromarty. *High* 2C 158
Sutterby. *Linc* 3C 88
Sutterton. *Linc* 2B 76
Sutterton Dowdyke. *Linc* 2B 76
Sutton. *Buck* 3B 38
Sutton. *Cambs* 3D 64
Sutton. *C Beds* 1C 52
Sutton. *E Sus* 5F 27
Sutton. *G Lon* 4D 38
Sutton. *Kent* 1H 29
Sutton. *Norf* 3F 79
Sutton. *Notts* 2E 75
Sutton. *Oxon* 5C 50
Sutton. *Pemb* 3D 42
Sutton. *Pet* 1H 63
Sutton. *Shrp*
nr. Bridgnorth 2B 60
nr. Market Drayton 2A 72
nr. Oswestry 3F 71
nr. Shrewsbury 4H 71
Sutton. *Som* 3B 22
Sutton. *S Yor* 3F 93
Sutton. *Staf* 3B 72
Sutton. *Suff* 1G 55
Sutton. *W Sus* 4A 26
Sutton. *Worc* 4A 60
Sutton Abinger. *Surr* 1C 26
Sutton at Hone. *Kent* 3G 39
Sutton Bassett. *Nptn* 1E 63
Sutton Benger. *Wilts* 4E 35
Sutton Bingham. *Som* 1A 14
Sutton Bonington. *Notts* 3C 74
Sutton Bridge. *Linc* 3D 76
Sutton Cheney. *Leics* 5B 74
Sutton Coldfield, Royal.
W Mid 1F 61
Sutton Corner. *Linc* 3D 76
Sutton Courtenay. *Oxon* 2D 36
Sutton Crosses. *Linc* 3D 76
Sutton cum Lound. *Notts* 2D 86
Sutton Gault. *Cambs* 3D 64
Sutton Grange. *N Yor* 2E 99
Sutton Green. *Surr* 5B 38
Sutton Howgrave. *N Yor* 2F 99
Sutton in Ashfield. *Notts* 5B 86
Sutton-in-Craven. *N Yor* 5C 98
Sutton Ings. *Hull* 1E 94
Sutton in the Elms. *Leics* 1C 62
Sutton Lane Ends. *Ches E* 3D 84
Sutton Leach. *Mers* 1H 83
Sutton Maddock. *Shrp* 5B 72
Sutton Mallet. *Som* 3G 21
Sutton Mandeville. *Wilts* 4E 23
Sutton Montis. *Som* 4B 22
Sutton on Hull. *Hull* 1E 94
Sutton on Sea. *Linc* 2E 89
Sutton-on-the-Forest. *N Yor* 3H 99
Sutton on the Hill. *Derbs* 2G 73
Sutton on Trent. *Notts* 4E 87
Sutton Poyntz. *Dors* 4C 14
Sutton St Edmund. *Linc* 4C 76
Sutton St Edmund's Common.
Linc 5C 76
Sutton St James. *Linc* 4C 76
Sutton St Michael. *Here* 1A 48
Sutton St Nicholas. *Here* 1A 48
Sutton Scarsdale. *Derbs* 4B 86
Sutton Scotney. *Hants* 3C 24
Sutton-under-Brailes. *Warw* 2B 50
Sutton-under-Whitestonecliffe.
N Yor 1G 99
Sutton upon Derwent. *E Yor* 5B 100
Sutton Valence. *Kent* 1C 28
Sutton Veny. *Wilts* 2E 23
Sutton Waldron. *Dors* 1D 14
Sutton Weaver. *Ches W* 3H 83
Swaby. *Linc* 3C 88
Swadlincote. *Derbs* 4G 73
Swaffham. *Norf* 5H 77
Swaffham Bulbeck. *Cambs* 4E 65
Swaffham Prior. *Cambs* 4E 65
Swafield. *Norf* 2E 79
Swainby. *N Yor* 4B 106
Swainshill. *Here* 1H 47
Swainsthorpe. *Norf* 5E 78
Swainswick. *Bath* 5C 34
Swalcliffe. *Oxon* 2B 50
Swalecliffe. *Kent* 4F 41
Swallow. *Linc* 4E 95
Swallow Beck. *Linc* 4G 87
Swallowcliffe. *Wilts* 4E 23
Swallowfield. *Wok* 5F 37
Swallownest. *S Yor* 2B 86
Swampton. *Hants* 1C 24
Swanage. *Dors* 5F 15
Swanbister. *Orkn* 7C 172
Swanbourne. *Buck* 3G 51
Swanbridge. *V Glam* 5E 33
Swan Green. *Ches W* 3B 84
Swanland. *E Yor* 2C 94
Swanley. *Kent* 4G 39
Swanmore. *Hants* 1D 16
Swannington. *Leics* 4B 74
Swannington. *Norf* 4D 78
Swanpool. *Linc* 4G 87
Swanscombe. *Kent* 3H 39
Swansea. *Swan* 212 (3F 31)
Swan Street. *Essx* 3B 54
Swanton Abbott. *Norf* 3E 79

Swanton Morley. *Norf* 4C 78
Swanton Novers. *Norf* 2C 78
Swanton Street. *Kent* 5C 40
Swanwick. *Derbs* 5B 86
Swanwick. *Hants* 2D 16
Swanwick Green. *Ches E* 1H 71
Swarby. *Linc* 1H 75
Swardeston. *Norf* 5E 78
Swarister. *Shet* 3G 173
Swarkestone. *Derbs* 3A 74
Swarland. *Nmbd* 4F 121
Swarraton. *Hants* 3D 24
Swartha. *W Yor* 5C 98
Swarthmoor. *Cumb* 2B 96
Swaton. *Linc* 2A 76
Swavesey. *Cambs* 4C 64
Sway. *Hants* 3A 16
Swayfield. *Linc* 3G 75
Swaythling. *Sotn* 1C 16
Sweet Green. *Worc* 4A 60
Sweetham. *Devn* 3B 12
Sweetholme. *Cumb* 3G 103
Sweets. *Corn* 3B 10
Sweetshouse. *Corn* 2E 7
Swefling. *Suff* 4F 67
Swell. *Som* 4G 21
Swepstone. *Leics* 4A 74
Swerford. *Oxon* 2B 50
Swettenham. *Ches E* 4C 84
Swetton. *N Yor* 2D 98
Swffryd. *Blae* 2F 33
Swiftsden. *E Sus* 3B 28
Swilland. *Suff* 5D 66
Swillington. *W Yor* 1D 93
Swimbridge. *Devn* 4G 19
Swimbridge Newland. *Devn* 3G 19
Swinbrook. *Oxon* 4A 50
Swincliffe. *N Yor* 4E 99
Swincliffe. *W Yor* 2C 92
Swinderby. *Linc* 4F 87
Swindon. *Glos* 3E 49
Swindon. *Nmbd* 5D 121
Swindon. *Staf* 1C 60
Swindon. *Swin* . . . . . **212 (3G 35)**
Swine. *E Yor* 1E 95
Swinefleet. *E Yor* 2A 94
Swineford. *S Glo* 5B 34
Swineshead. *Bed* 4H 63
Swineshead. *Linc* 1B 76
Swineshead Bridge. *Linc* 1B 76
Swiney. *High* 5E 169
Swinford. *Leics* 3C 62
Swinford. *Oxon* 5C 50
Swingate. *Notts* 1C 74
Swingbrow. *Cambs* 2C 64
Swingfield Minnis. *Kent* 1G 29
Swingfield Street. *Kent* 1G 29
Swingleton Green. *Suff* 1C 54
Swinhill. *S Lan* 5A 128
Swinhoe. *Nmbd* 2G 121
Swinhope. *Linc* 1B 88
Swinister. *Shet* 3E 173
Swinithwaite. *N Yor* 1C 98
Swinmore Common. *Here* 1B 48
Swinscoe. *Staf* 1F 73
Swinside Hall. *Bord* 3B 120
Swinstead. *Linc* 3H 75
Swinton. *G Man* 4F 91
Swinton. *N Yor*
 nr. Malton 2B 100
 nr. Masham 2E 98
Swinton. *Bord* 5E 131
Swinton. *S Yor* 1B 86
Swithland. *Leics* 4C 74
Swordale. *High* 2H 157
Swordly. *High* 2H 167
Sworton Heath. *Ches E* 2A 84
Swyddffynnon. *Cdgn* 4F 57
Swyre. *Dors* 4A 14
Sycharth. *Powy* 3E 70
Sychdyn. *Flin* 4E 83
Sychnant. *Powy* 3B 58
Sychtyn. *Powy* 5B 70
Syde. *Glos* 4E 49
Sydenham. *G Lon* 3E 39
Sydenham. *Oxon* 5F 51
Sydenham. *Som* 3G 21
Sydenham Damerel. *Devn* 5E 11
Syderstone. *Norf* 2H 77
Sydling St Nicholas. *Dors* 3B 14
Sydmonton. *Hants* 1C 24
Sydney. *Ches E* 5B 84
Syerston. *Notts* 1E 75
Syke. *G Man* 3G 91
Sykehouse. *S Yor* 3G 93
Sykes. *Lanc* 4F 97
Syleham. *Suff* 3E 66
Sylen. *Carm* 5F 45
Sylfaen. *Powy* 5D 70
Symbister. *Shet* 5G 173
Symington. *S Ayr* 1C 116
Symington. *S Lan* 1B 118
Symondsbury. *Dors* 3H 13
Symonds Yat. *Here* 4A 48
Synod Inn. *Cdgn* 5D 56
Syre. *High* 4G 167
Syreford. *Glos* 3F 49
Syresham. *Nptn* 1E 51
Syston. *Leics* 4D 74
Syston. *Linc* 1G 75
Sytchampton. *Worc* 4C 60
Sywell. *Nptn* 4F 63

T

Tabost. *W Isl*
 nr. Cearsiadar 6F 171
 nr. Suainebost 1H 171
Tachbrook Mallory. *Warw* 4H 61

Tackley. *Oxon* 3C 50
Tacleit. *W Isl* 4D 171
Tacolneston. *Norf* 1D 66
Tadcaster. *N Yor* 5G 99
Taddington. *Derbs* 3F 85
Taddington. *Glos* 2F 49
Taddiport. *Devn* 1E 11
Tadley. *Hants* 5E 36
Tadlow. *Cambs* 1C 52
Tadmarton. *Oxon* 2B 50
Tadwick. *Bath* 4C 34
Tadworth. *Surr* 5D 38
Tafarnaubach. *Blae* 4E 46
Tafarn-y-bwlch. *Pemb* 1E 43
Tafarn-y-Gelyn. *Den* 4D 82
Taff's Well. *Rhon* 3E 33
Tafolwern. *Powy* 5A 70
Taibach. *Neat* 3A 32
Tai-bach. *Powy* 3D 70
Taigh a Ghearraidh.
 W Isl 1C 170
Taigh Bhuirgh. *W Isl* 8C 171
Tain. *High*
 nr. Invergordon 5E 165
 nr. Thurso 2E 169
Tai-Nant. *Wrex* 1E 71
Tai'n Lon. *Gwyn* 5D 80
Tairbeart. *W Isl* 8D 171
Tairgwaith. *Neat* 4H 45
Takeley. *Essx* 3F 53
Takeley Street. *Essx* 3F 53
Talachddu. *Powy* 2D 46
Talacre. *Flin* 2D 82
Talardd. *Gwyn* 3A 70
Talaton. *Devn* 3D 12
Talbenny. *Pemb* 3C 42
Talbot Green. *Rhon* 3D 32
Taleford. *Devn* 3D 12
Talerddig. *Powy* 5B 70
Talgarreg. *Cdgn* 5D 56
Talgarth. *Powy* 2E 47
Talisker. *High* 5C 154
Talke. *Staf* 5C 84
Talkin. *Cumb* 4G 113
Talladale. *High* 1B 156
Talla Linnfoots. *Bord* 2D 118
Tallaminnock. *S Ayr* 5C 116
Tallarn Green. *Wrex* 1G 71
Tallentire. *Cumb* 1C 102
Talley. *Carm* 2G 45
Tallington. *Linc* 5H 75
Talmine. *High* 2F 167
Talog. *Carm* 2H 43
Talsarn. *Carm* 3A 46
Talsarn. *Cdgn* 5E 57
Talsarnau. *Gwyn* 2F 69
Talskiddy. *Corn* 2D 6
Talwrn. *IOA* 3D 81
Talwrn. *Wrex* 1E 71
Tal-y-bont. *Cdgn* 2F 57
Tal-y-bont. *Cnwy* 4G 81
Tal-y-bont. *Gwyn*
 nr. Bangor 3F 81
 nr. Barmouth 3E 69
Talybont-on-Usk. *Powy* 3E 46
Tal-y-cafn. *Cnwy* 3G 81
Tal-y-coed. *Mon* 4H 47
Tal-y-llyn. *Gwyn* 5G 69
Talyllyn. *Powy* 3E 46
Talysarn. *Gwyn* 5D 81
Tal-y-waenydd. *Gwyn* 1F 69
Talywain. *Torf* 5F 47
Tal-y-Wern. *Powy* 5H 69
Tamerton Foliot. *Plym* 2A 8
Tamworth. *Staf* 5G 73
Tamworth Green. *Linc* 1C 76
Tandlehill. *Ren* 3F 127
Tandridge. *Surr* 5E 39
Tanerdy. *Carm* 3E 45
Tanfield. *Dur* 4E 115
Tanfield Lea. *Dur* 4E 115
Tangasdal. *W Isl* 8B 170
Tang Hall. *York* 4A 100
Tangiers. *Pemb* 3D 42
Tangley. *Hants* 1B 24
Tangmere. *W Sus* 5A 26
Tangwick. *Shet* 4D 173
Tankerness. *Orkn* 7E 172
Tankersley. *S Yor* 1H 85
Tankerton. *Kent* 4F 41
Tan-lan. *Cnwy* 4G 81
Tan-lan. *Gwyn* 1F 69
Tannach. *High* 4F 169
Tannadice. *Ang* 3D 145
Tanner's Green. *Worc* 3E 61
Tannington. *Suff* 4E 67
Tannochside. *N Lan* 3A 128
Tan Office Green. *Suff* 5G 65
Tansley. *Derbs* 5H 85
Tansley Knoll. *Derbs* 4H 85
Tansor. *Nptn* 1H 63
Tantobie. *Dur* 4E 115
Tanton. *N Yor* 3C 106
Tanvats. *Linc* 4A 88
Tanworth-in-Arden.
 Warw 3F 61
Tan-y-bwlch. *Gwyn* 1F 69
Tan-y-fron. *Cnwy* 4B 82
Tanyfron. *Wrex* 5E 83
Tanygrisiau. *Gwyn* 1F 69
Tan-y-groes. *Cdgn* 1C 44
Tan-y-pistyll. *Powy* 3C 70
Tan-yr-allt. *Den* 2C 82
Taobh a Chaolais. *W Isl* 7C 170
Taobh a Deas Loch Aineort.
 W Isl 6C 170
Taobh a Ghlinne. *W Isl* 6F 171
Taobh a Tuath Loch Aineort.
 W Isl 6C 170
Taplow. *Buck* 2A 38
Tapton. *Derbs* 3A 86

Tarbert. *Arg*
 on Jura 1E 125
 on Kintyre 3G 125
Tarbert. *W Isl* 8D 171
Tarbet. *Arg* 3C 134
Tarbet. *High*
 nr. Mallaig 4F 147
 nr. Scourie 4B 166
Tarbock Green. *Mers* 2G 83
Tarbolton. *S Ayr* 2D 116
Tarbrax. *S Lan* 4D 128
Tardebigge. *Worc* 4D 61
Tarfside. *Ang* 1D 145
Tarland. *Abers* 3B 152
Tarleton. *Lanc* 2C 90
Tarlogie. *High* 5E 165
Tarlscough. *Lanc* 3C 90
Tarlton. *Glos* 2E 35
Tarnbrook. *Lanc* 4E 97
Tarnock. *Som* 1G 21
Tarns. *Cumb* 5C 112
Tarporley. *Ches W* 4H 83
Tarpots. *Essx* 2B 40
Tarr. *Som* 3E 20
Tarrant Crawford. *Dors* 2E 15
Tarrant Gunville. *Dors* 1E 15
Tarrant Hinton. *Dors* 1E 15
Tarrant Keyneston. *Dors* 2E 15
Tarrant Launceston. *Dors* 2E 15
Tarrant Monkton. *Dors* 2E 15
Tarrant Rawston. *Dors* 2E 15
Tarrant Rushton. *Dors* 2E 15
Tarrel. *High* 5F 165
Tarring Neville. *E Sus* 5F 27
Tarrington. *Here* 1B 48
Tarsappie. *Per* 1D 136
Tarscabhaig. *High* 3D 147
Tarskavaig. *High* 3D 147
Tarves. *Abers* 5F 161
Tarvie. *High* 3G 157
Tarvin. *Ches W* 4G 83
Tasburgh. *Norf* 1E 66
Tasley. *Shrp* 1A 60
Taston. *Oxon* 3B 50
Tatenhill. *Staf* 3G 73
Tathall End. *Mil* 1G 51
Tatham. *Lanc* 3F 97
Tathwell. *Linc* 2C 88
Tatling End. *Buck* 2B 38
Tatsfield. *Surr* 5F 39
Tattenhall. *Ches W* 5G 83
Tatterford. *Norf* 3A 78
Tattersett. *Norf* 2H 77
Tattershall. *Linc* 5B 88
Tattershall Bridge. *Linc* 5A 88
Tattershall Thorpe. *Linc* 5B 88
Tattingstone. *Suff* 2E 55
Tattingstone White Horse. *Suff* . .2E 55
Tattle Bank. *Warw* 4F 61
Tatworth. *Som* 2G 13
Taunton. *Som* . . . .**213 (4F 21)**
Taverham. *Norf* 4D 78
Taverners Green. *Essx* 4F 53
Tavernspite. *Pemb* 3F 43
Tavistock. *Devn* 5E 11
Tavool House. *Arg* 1B 132
Taw Green. *Devn* 3G 11
Tawstock. *Devn* 4F 19
Taxal. *Derbs* 2E 85
Tayinloan. *Arg* 5E 125
Taynish. *Arg* 1F 125
Taynton. *Glos* 3C 48
Taynton. *Oxon* 4H 49
Taynuilt. *Arg* 5E 141
Tayport. *Fife* 1G 137
Tay Road Bridge. *D'dee* 1G 137
Tayvallich. *Arg* 1F 125
Tealby. *Linc* 1A 88
Tealing. *Ang* 5D 144
Teams. *Tyne* 3F 115
Teangue. *High* 3E 147
Teanna Mhachair. *W Isl* 2C 170
Tebay. *Cumb* 4H 103
Tebworth. *C Beds* 3H 51
Tedburn St Mary. *Devn* 3B 12
Teddington. *Glos* 2E 49
Teddington. *G Lon* 3C 38
Tedsmore. *Shrp* 3F 71
Tedstone Delamere. *Here* 5A 60
Tedstone Wafer. *Here* 5A 60
Teesport. *Red C* 2C 106
Teesside. *Stoc T* 2C 106
Teeton. *Nptn* 3D 62
Teffont Evias. *Wilts* 3E 23
Teffont Magna. *Wilts* 3E 23
Tegryn. *Pemb* 1G 43
Teigh. *Rut* 4F 75
Teigncombe. *Devn* 4G 11
Teigngrace. *Devn* 5B 12
Teignmouth. *Devn* 5C 12
Telford. *Telf* 4A 72
Telham. *E Sus* 4B 28
Tellisford. *Som* 1D 22
Telscombe. *E Sus* 5F 27
Telscombe Cliffs. *E Sus* 5F 27
Tempar. *Per* 3D 142
Templand. *Dum* 1B 112
Temple. *Corn* 5B 10
Temple. *Glas* 3G 127
Temple. *Midl* 4G 129
Temple Balsall. *W Mid* 3G 61
Temple Bar. *Carm* 4F 45
Temple Bar. *Cdgn* 5E 57
Temple Cloud. *Bath* 1B 22
Templecombe. *Som* 4C 22
Temple Ewell. *Kent* 1G 29
Temple Grafton. *Warw* 5F 61
Temple Guiting. *Glos* 3F 49
Templehall. *Fife* 4E 137
Temple Hirst. *N Yor* 2G 93
Temple Normanton. *Derbs* 4B 86

Tarbert. *Arg* 1E 125
Temple Sowerby. *Cumb* 2H 103
Templeton. *Devn* 1B 12
Templeton. *Pemb* 3F 43
Templeton. *W Ber* 5B 36
Templetown. *Dur* 5E 115
Tempsford. *C Beds* 5A 64
Tenandry. *Per* 2G 143
Tenbury Wells. *Worc* 4H 59
Tenby. *Pemb* 4F 43
Tendring. *Essx* 3E 55
Tendring Green. *Essx* 3E 55
Tenga. *Arg* 4G 139
Ten Mile Bank. *Norf* 1F 65
Tenterden. *Kent* 2C 28
Terfyn. *Cnwy* 3B 82
Terhill. *Som* 3E 21
Terling. *Essx* 4A 54
Ternhill. *Shrp* 2A 72
Terregles. *Dum* 2G 111
Terrick. *Buck* 5G 51
Terrington. *N Yor* 2A 100
Terrington St Clement. *Norf* 3E 77
Terrington St John. *Norf* 4E 77
Terry's Green. *Warw* 3F 61
Teston. *Kent* 5B 40
Testwood. *Hants* 1B 16
Tetbury. *Glos* 2D 35
Tetbury Upton. *Glos* 2D 35
Tetchill. *Shrp* 2F 71
Tetcott. *Devn* 3D 10
Tetford. *Linc* 3C 88
Tetney. *Linc* 4G 95
Tetney Lock. *Linc* 4G 95
Tetsworth. *Oxon* 5E 51
Tettenhall. *W Mid* 5C 72
Teversal. *Notts* 4B 86
Teversham. *Cambs* 5D 65
Teviothead. *Bord* 4G 119
Tewel. *Abers* 5F 153
Tewin. *Herts* 4C 52
Tewkesbury. *Glos* 2D 49
Teynham. *Kent* 4D 40
Teynham Street. *Kent* 4D 40
Thackthwaite. *Cumb* 2F 103
Thakeham. *W Sus* 4C 26
Thame. *Oxon* 5F 51
Thames Ditton. *Surr* 4C 38
Thames Haven. *Thur* 2B 40
Thamesmead. *G Lon* 2F 39
Thamesport. *Medw* 3C 40
Thanington Without. *Kent* 5F 41
Thankerton. *S Lan* 1B 118
Tharston. *Norf* 1D 66
Thatcham. *W Ber* 5D 36
Thatto Heath. *Mers* 1H 83
Thaxted. *Essx* 2G 53
The . . . .
 Names prefixed with 'The' for
 example 'The Aird' are indexed
 under the main name such as 'Aird,
 The'
Theakston. *N Yor* 1F 99
Thealby. *N Lin* 3B 94
Theale. *Som* 2H 21
Theale. *W Ber* 4E 37
Thearne. *E Yor* 1D 94
Theberton. *Suff* 4G 67
Theddingworth. *Leics* 2D 62
Theddlethorpe All Saints.
 Linc 2D 88
Theddlethorpe St Helen. *Linc* . . .2D 89
Thelbridge Barton. *Devn* 1A 12
Thelnetham. *Suff* 3C 66
Thelveton. *Norf* 2D 66
Thelwall. *Warr* 2A 84
Themelthorpe. *Norf* 3C 78
Thenford. *Nptn* 1D 50
Therfield. *Herts* 2D 52
Thetford. *Linc* 4A 76
Thetford. *Norf* 2A 66
Thethwaite. *Cumb* 5E 113
Theydon Bois. *Essx* 1F 39
Thick Hollins. *W Yor* 3B 92
Thickwood. *Wilts* 4D 34
Thimbleby. *Linc* 4B 88
Thimbleby. *N Yor* 5B 106
Thingwall. *Mers* 2E 83
Thirlby. *N Yor* 1G 99
Thirlestane. *Bord* 5B 130
Thirn. *N Yor* 1E 98
Thirsk. *N Yor* 1G 99
Thirtleby. *E Yor* 1E 95
Thistleton. *Lanc* 1C 90
Thistleton. *Rut* 4G 75
Thistley Green. *Suff* 3F 65
Thixendale. *N Yor* 3C 100
Thockrington. *Nmbd* 2C 114
Tholomas Drove. *Cambs* 5D 76
Tholthorpe. *N Yor* 3G 99
Thomas Chapel. *Pemb* 4F 43
Thomas Close. *Cumb* 5F 113
Thomastown. *Abers* 4E 160
Thomastown. *Rhon* 3D 32
Thompson. *Norf* 1B 66
Thomshill. *Mor* 3G 159
Thong. *Kent* 3A 40
Thongsbridge. *W Yor* 4B 92
Thoralby. *N Yor* 1C 98
Thoresby. *Notts* 3D 86
Thoresway. *Linc* 1A 88
Thorganby. *Linc* 1B 88
Thorganby. *N Yor* 5A 100
Thorgill. *N Yor* 5E 107
Thorington. *Suff* 3G 67
Thorington Street. *Suff* 2D 54
Thorlby. *N Yor* 4B 98
Thorley. *Herts* 4E 53
Thorley Street. *Herts* 4E 53
Thorley Street. *IOW* 4B 16
Thormanby. *N Yor* 2G 99
Thorn. *Powy* 4E 59

Thornaby-on-Tees. *Stoc T* 3B 106
Thornage. *Norf* 2C 78
Thornborough. *Buck* 2F 51
Thornborough. *N Yor* 2E 99
Thornbury. *Devn* 2E 11
Thornbury. *Here* 5A 60
Thornbury. *S Glo* 2B 34
Thornby. *Cumb* 4D 112
Thornby. *Nptn* 3D 62
Thorncliffe. *Staf* 5E 85
Thorncombe. *Dors* 2G 13
Thorncombe Street. *Surr* 1A 26
Thorncote Green. *C Beds* 1B 52
Thorndon. *Suff* 4D 66
Thorndon Cross. *Devn* 3F 11
Thorne. *S Yor* 3G 93
Thornehillhead. *Devn* 1E 11
Thorner. *W Yor* 5F 99
Thorne St Margaret. *Som* 4D 20
Thorney. *Notts* 3F 87
Thorney. *Pet* 5B 76
Thorney. *Som* 4H 21
Thorney Hill. *Hants* 3G 15
Thorney Toll. *Cambs* 5C 76
Thornfalcon. *Som* 4F 21
Thornford. *Dors* 1B 14
Thorngrafton. *Nmbd* 3A 114
Thorngrove. *Som* 3G 21
Thorngumbald. *E Yor* 2F 95
Thornham. *Norf* 1G 77
Thornham Magna. *Suff* 3D 66
Thornham Parva. *Suff* 3D 66
Thornhaugh. *Pet* 5H 75
Thornhill. *Cphy* 3E 33
Thornhill. *Cumb* 4B 102
Thornhill. *Derbs* 2F 85
Thornhill. *Dum* 5A 118
Thornhill. *Sotn* 1C 16
Thornhill. *Stir* 4F 135
Thornhill. *W Yor* 3C 92
Thornhill Lees. *W Yor* 3C 92
Thornhills. *W Yor* 2B 92
Thornholme. *E Yor* 3F 101
Thornicombe. *Dors* 2D 14
Thornington. *Nmbd* 1C 120
Thornley. *Dur*
 nr. Durham 1A 106
 nr. Tow Law 1E 105
Thornley Gate. *Nmbd* 4B 114
Thornliebank. *E Ren* 3G 127
Thornroan. *Abers* 5F 161
Thorns. *Suff* 5G 65
Thornsett. *Derbs* 2E 85
Thornthwaite. *Cumb* 2D 102
Thornthwaite. *N Yor* 4D 98
Thornton. *Ang* 4C 144
Thornton. *Buck* 2F 51
Thornton. *E Yor* 5B 100
Thornton. *Fife* 4E 137
Thornton. *Lanc* 5C 96
Thornton. *Leics* 5B 74
Thornton. *Linc* 4B 88
Thornton. *Mers* 4B 90
Thornton. *Midd* 3B 106
Thornton. *Nmbd* 5F 131
Thornton. *Pemb* 4D 42
Thornton. *W Yor* 1A 92
Thornton Curtis. *N Lin* 3D 94
Thornton Hall. *N Yor* 2H 99
Thornton Heath. *G Lon* 4E 39
Thornton Hough. *Mers* 2F 83
Thornton-in-Craven. *N Yor* 5B 98
Thornton in Lonsdale. *N Yor* 2F 97
Thornton-le-Beans. *N Yor* 5A 106
Thornton-le-Clay. *N Yor* 3A 100
Thornton-le-Dale. *N Yor* 1C 100
Thornton le Moor. *Linc* 1H 87
Thornton-le-Moor. *N Yor* 1F 99
Thornton-le-Moors. *Ches W* 3G 83
Thornton-le-Street. *N Yor* 1G 99
Thorntonloch. *E Lot* 2D 130
Thornton Rust. *N Yor* 1B 98
Thornton Steward. *N Yor* 1D 98
Thornton Watlass. *N Yor* 1E 98
Thornwood Common. *Essx* 5E 53
Thornythwaite. *Cumb* 2E 103
Thoroton. *Notts* 1E 75
Thorp Arch. *W Yor* 5G 99
Thorpe. *Derbs* 5F 85
Thorpe. *E Yor* 5D 101
Thorpe. *Linc* 2D 89
Thorpe. *Norf* 1G 67
Thorpe. *N Yor* 3C 98
Thorpe. *Notts* 1E 75
Thorpe. *Surr* 4B 38
Thorpe Abbotts. *Norf* 3D 66
Thorpe Acre. *Leics* 3C 74
Thorpe Arnold. *Leics* 3E 75
Thorpe Audlin. *W Yor* 3E 93
Thorpe Bassett. *N Yor* 2C 100
Thorpe Bay. *S'end* 2D 40
Thorpe by Water. *Rut* 1F 63
Thorpe Common. *S Yor* 1A 86
Thorpe Common. *Suff* 2F 55
Thorpe Constantine. *Staf* 5G 73
Thorpe End. *Norf* 4E 79
Thorpe Fendike. *Linc* 4D 88
Thorpe Green. *Essx* 3E 55
Thorpe Green. *Suff* 5B 66
Thorpe Hall. *N Yor* 2H 99
Thorpe Hamlet. *Norf* 5E 79
Thorpe Hesley. *S Yor* 1A 86
Thorpe in Balne. *S Yor* 3F 93
Thorpe in the Fallows. *Linc* 2G 87
Thorpe Langton. *Leics* 1E 63
Thorpe Larches. *Dur* 2A 106
Thorpe Latimer. *Linc* 1A 76
Thorpe-le-Soken. *Essx* 3E 55
Thorpe le Street. *E Yor* 5C 100
Thorpe Malsor. *Nptn* 3F 63
Thorpe Mandeville. *Nptn* 1D 50

Thorpe Market—Trekenner

Thorpe Market. *Norf* 2E **79**
Thorpe Marriott. *Norf* 4D **78**
Thorpe Morieux. *Suff* 5B **66**
Thorpeness. *Suff* 5G **67**
Thorpe on the Hill. *Linc* 4G **87**
Thorpe on the Hill. *W Yor* 2D **92**
Thorpe St Andrew. *Norf* 5E **79**
Thorpe St Peter. *Linc* 4D **89**
Thorpe Salvin. *S Yor* 2C **86**
Thorpe Satchville. *Leics* 4E **75**
Thorpe Thewles. *Stoc T* 2A **106**
Thorpe Tilney. *Linc* 5A **88**
Thorpe Underwood. *N Yor* 4G **99**
Thorpe Waterville. *Nptn* 2H **63**
Thorpe Willoughby. *N Yor* 1F **93**
Thorpland. *Norf* 5F **77**
Thorrington. *Essx* 3D **54**
Thorverton. *Devn* 2C **12**
Thrandeston. *Suff* 3D **66**
Thrapston. *Nptn* 3G **63**
Thrashbush. *N Lan* 3A **128**
Threapland. *Cumb* 1C **102**
Threapland. *N Yor* 3B **98**
Threapwood. *Ches W* 1G **71**
Threapwood. *Staf* 1E **73**
Three Ashes. *Here* 3A **48**
Three Bridges. *Linc* 2D **88**
Three Bridges. *W Sus* 2D **27**
Three Burrows. *Corn* 4B **6**
Three Chimneys. *Kent* 2C **28**
Three Cocks. *Powy* 2E **47**
Three Crosses. *Swan* 3E **31**
Three Cups Corner. *E Sus* 3H **27**
Threehammer Common. *Norf* 3F **79**
Three Holes. *Norf* 5E **77**
Threekingham. *Linc* 2H **75**
Three Leg Cross. *E Sus* 2A **28**
Three Legged Cross. *Dors* 2F **15**
Three Mile Cross. *Wok* 5F **37**
Threemilestone. *Corn* 4B **6**
Three Oaks. *E Sus* 4C **28**
Threlkeld. *Cumb* 2E **102**
Threshfield. *N Yor* 3B **98**
Thrigby. *Norf* 4G **79**
Thringarth. *Dur* 2C **104**
Thringstone. *Leics* 4B **74**
Thrintoft. *N Yor* 5A **106**
Thriplow. *Cambs* 1E **53**
Throckenholt. *Linc* 5C **76**
Throcking. *Herts* 2D **52**
Throckley. *Tyne* 3E **115**
Throckmorton. *Worc* 1E **49**
Throop. *Bour* 3G **15**
Throphill. *Nmbd* 1E **115**
Thropton. *Nmbd* 4E **121**
Throsk. *Stir* 4A **136**
Througham. *Glos* 5E **49**
Throughgate. *Dum* 1F **111**
Throwleigh. *Devn* 3G **11**
Throwley. *Kent* 5D **40**
Throwley Forstal. *Kent* 5D **40**
Throxenby. *N Yor* 1E **101**
Thrumpton. *Notts* 2C **74**
Thrumster. *High* 4F **169**
Thrunton. *Nmbd* 3E **121**
Thrupp. *Glos* 5D **48**
Thrupp. *Oxon* 4C **50**
Thrushelton. *Devn* 4E **11**
Thrushgill. *Lanc* 3F **97**
Thrussington. *Leics* 4D **74**
Thruxton. *Hants* 2A **24**
Thruxton. *Here* 2H **47**
Thrybergh. *S Yor* 1B **86**
Thulston. *Derbs* 2B **74**
Thundergay. *N Ayr* 5G **125**
Thundersley. *Essx* 2B **40**
Thundridge. *Herts* 4D **52**
Thurcaston. *Leics* 4C **74**
Thurcroft. *S Yor* 2B **86**
Thurdon. *Corn* 1C **10**
Thurgarton. *Norf* 2D **78**
Thurgarton. *Notts* 1D **74**
Thurgoland. *S Yor* 4C **92**
Thurlaston. *Leics* 1C **62**
Thurlaston. *Warw* 3B **62**
Thurlbear. *Som* 4F **21**
Thurlby. *Linc*
nr. Alford 3D **89**
nr. Baston 4A **76**
nr. Lincoln 4G **87**
Thurleigh. *Bed* 5H **63**
Thurlestone. *Devn* 4C **8**
Thurloxton. *Som* 3F **21**
Thurlstone. *S Yor* 4C **92**
Thurlton. *Norf* 1G **67**
Thurmaston. *Leics* 5D **74**
Thurnby. *Leics* 5D **74**
Thurne. *Norf* 4G **79**
Thurnham. *Kent* 5C **40**
Thurning. *Norf* 3C **78**
Thurning. *Nptn* 2H **63**
Thurnscoe. *S Yor* 4E **93**
Thursby. *Cumb* 4E **113**
Thursford. *Norf* 2B **78**
Thursford Green. *Norf* 2B **78**
Thursley. *Surr* 2A **26**
Thurso. *High* 2D **168**
Thurso East. *High* 2D **168**
Thurstaston. *Mers* 2E **83**
Thurston. *Suff* 4B **66**
Thurston End. *Suff* 5G **65**
Thurstonfield. *Cumb* 4E **112**
Thurstonland. *W Yor* 3B **92**
Thurton. *Norf* 5F **79**
Thurvaston. *Derbs*
nr. Ashbourne 2F **73**
nr. Derby 2G **73**
Thuxton. *Norf* 5C **78**
Thwaite. *Dur* 3D **104**
Thwaite. *N Yor* 5B **104**
Thwaite. *Suff* 4D **66**
Thwaite Head. *Cumb* 5E **103**
Thwaites. *W Yor* 5C **98**
Thwaite St Mary. *Norf* 1F **67**
Thwing. *E Yor* 2E **101**
Tibbermore. *Per* 1C **136**
Tibberton. *Glos* 3C **48**
Tibberton. *Telf* 3A **72**
Tibberton. *Worc* 5D **60**
Tibenham. *Norf* 2D **66**
Tibshelf. *Derbs* 4B **86**
Tibthorpe. *E Yor* 4D **100**
Ticehurst. *E Sus* 2A **28**
Tichborne. *Hants* 3D **24**
Tickencote. *Rut* 5G **75**
Tickenham. *N Som* 4H **33**
Tickhill. *S Yor* 1C **86**
Ticklerton. *Shrp* 1G **59**
Ticknall. *Derbs* 3A **74**
Tickton. *E Yor* 5E **101**
Tidbury Green. *W Mid* 3F **61**
Tidcombe. *Wilts* 1A **24**
Tiddington. *Oxon* 5E **51**
Tiddington. *Warw* 5G **61**
Tiddleywink. *Wilts* 4D **34**
Tidebrook. *E Sus* 3H **27**
Tideford. *Corn* 3H **7**
Tideford Cross. *Corn* 2H **7**
Tidenham. *Glos* 2A **34**
Tideswell. *Derbs* 3F **85**
Tidmarsh. *W Ber* 4E **37**
Tidmington. *Warw* 2A **50**
Tidpit. *Hants* 1F **15**
Tidworth. *Wilts* 2H **23**
Tidworth Camp. *Wilts* 2H **23**
Tiers Cross. *Pemb* 3D **42**
Tiffield. *Nptn* 5D **62**
Tifty. *Abers* 4E **161**
Tigerton. *Ang* 2E **145**
Tighnabruaich. *Arg* 2A **126**
Tigley. *Devn* 2D **8**
Tilbrook. *Cambs* 4H **63**
Tilbury. *Thur* 3H **39**
Tilbury Green. *Essx* 1H **53**
Tilbury Juxta Clare. *Essx* 1A **54**
Tile Hill. *W Mid* 3G **61**
Tilehurst. *Read* 4E **37**
Tilford. *Surr* 2G **25**
Tilgate Forest Row. *W Sus* 2D **26**
Tillathrowie. *Abers* 5B **160**
Tillers Green. *Glos* 2B **48**
Tillery. *Abers* 1G **153**
Tilley. *Shrp* 3H **71**
Tillicoultry. *Clac* 4B **136**
Tillingham. *Essx* 5C **54**
Tillington. *Here* 1H **47**
Tillington. *W Sus* 3A **26**
Tillington Common. *Here* 1H **47**
Tillybirloch. *Abers* 3D **152**
Tillyfourie. *Abers* 2D **152**
Tilmanstone. *Kent* 5H **41**
Tilney All Saints. *Norf* 4E **77**
Tilney Fen End. *Norf* 4E **77**
Tilney High End. *Norf* 4E **77**
Tilney St Lawrence. *Norf* 4E **77**
Tilshead. *Wilts* 2F **23**
Tilstock. *Shrp* 2H **71**
Tilston. *Ches W* 5G **83**
Tilstone Fearnall. *Ches W* 4H **83**
Tilsworth. *C Beds* 3H **51**
Tilton on the Hill. *Leics* 5E **75**
Tiltups End. *Glos* 2D **34**
Timberland. *Linc* 5A **88**
Timbersbrook. *Ches E* 4C **84**
Timberscombe. *Som* 2C **20**
Timble. *N Yor* 4D **98**
Timperley. *G Man* 2B **84**
Timsbury. *Bath* 1B **22**
Timsbury. *Hants* 4B **24**
Timsgearraidh. *W Isl* 4C **171**
Timworth Green. *Suff* 4A **66**
Tincleton. *Dors* 3C **14**
Tindale. *Cumb* 4H **113**
Tindale Crescent. *Dur* 2F **105**
Tingewick. *Buck* 2E **51**
Tingrith. *C Beds* 2A **52**
Tingwall. *Orkn* 5D **172**
Tinhay. *Devn* 4D **11**
Tinshill. *W Yor* 1C **92**
Tinsley. *S Yor* 1B **86**
Tinsley Green. *W Sus* 2D **27**
Tintagel. *Corn* 4A **10**
Tintern. *Mon* 5A **48**
Tintinhull. *Som* 1H **13**
Tintwistle. *Derbs* 1E **85**
Tinwald. *Dum* 1B **112**
Tinwell. *Rut* 5H **75**
Tippacott. *Devn* 2A **20**
Tipperty. *Abers* 1G **153**
Tipps End. *Cambs* 1E **65**
Tiptoe. *Hants* 3A **16**
Tipton. *W Mid* 1D **60**
Tipton St John. *Devn* 3D **12**
Tiptree. *Essx* 4B **54**
Tiptree Heath. *Essx* 4B **54**
Tirabad. *Powy* 1B **46**
Tircoed Forest Village.
Swan 5G **45**
Tiree Airport. *Arg* 4B **138**
Tirinie. *Per* 2F **143**
Tirley. *Glos* 3D **48**
Tiroran. *Arg* 1B **132**
Tir-Phil. *Cphy* 5E **47**
Tirril. *Cumb* 2G **103**
Tirryside. *High* 2C **164**
Tir-y-dail. *Carm* 4G **45**
Tisbury. *Wilts* 4E **23**
Tisman's Common. *W Sus* 2B **26**
Tissington. *Derbs* 5F **85**
Titchberry. *Devn* 4C **18**
Titchfield. *Hants* 2D **16**
Titchmarsh. *Nptn* 3H **63**
Titchwell. *Norf* 1G **77**
Tithby. *Notts* 2D **74**
Titley. *Here* 5F **59**
Titlington. *Nmbd* 3E **121**
Titsey. *Surr* 5F **39**
Titson. *Corn* 2C **10**
Tittensor. *Staf* 2C **72**
Tittleshall. *Norf* 3A **78**
Titton. *Worc* 4C **60**
Tiverton. *Ches W* 4H **83**
Tiverton. *Devn* 1C **12**
Tivetshall St Margaret. *Norf* 2D **66**
Tivetshall St Mary. *Norf* 2D **66**
Tivington. *Som* 2C **20**
Tixall. *Staf* 3D **73**
Tixover. *Rut* 5G **75**
Toab. *Orkn* 7E **172**
Toab. *Shet* 10E **173**
Toadmoor. *Derbs* 5A **86**
Tobermory. *Arg* 3G **139**
Toberonochy. *Arg* 3E **133**
Tobha Beag. *W Isl* 5C **170**
Tobha-Beag. *W Isl* 1E **170**
Tobha Mor. *W Isl* 5C **170**
Tobhtarol. *W Isl* 4D **171**
Tobson. *W Isl* 4D **171**
Tocabhaig. *High* 2E **147**
Tocher. *Abers* 5D **160**
Tockenham. *Wilts* 4F **35**
Tockenham Wick. *Wilts* 3F **35**
Tockholes. *Bkbn* 2E **91**
Tockington. *S Glo* 3B **34**
Tockwith. *N Yor* 4G **99**
Todber. *Dors* 4D **22**
Todding. *Here* 3G **59**
Toddington. *C Beds* 3A **52**
Toddington. *Glos* 2F **49**
Todenham. *Glos* 2H **49**
Todhills. *Cumb* 3E **113**
Todmorden. *W Yor* 2H **91**
Todwick. *S Yor* 2B **86**
Toft. *Cambs* 5C **64**
Toft. *Linc* 4H **75**
Toft Hill. *Dur* 2E **105**
Toft Monks. *Norf* 1G **67**
Toft next Newton. *Linc* 2H **87**
Toftrees. *Norf* 3A **78**
Tofts. *High* 2F **169**
Toftwood. *Norf* 4B **78**
Togston. *Nmbd* 4G **121**
Tokavaig. *High* 2E **147**
Tokers Green. *Oxon* 4F **37**
Tolastadh a Chaolais. *W Isl* 4D **171**
Tolladine. *Worc* 5C **60**
Tolland. *Som* 3E **20**
Tollard Farnham. *Dors* 1E **15**
Tollard Royal. *Wilts* 1E **15**
Toll Bar. *S Yor* 4F **93**
Toller Fratrum. *Dors* 3A **14**
Toller Porcorum. *Dors* 3A **14**
Tollerton. *N Yor* 3H **99**
Tollerton. *Notts* 2D **74**
Toller Whelme. *Dors* 2A **14**
Tollesbury. *Essx* 4C **54**
Tolleshunt D'Arcy. *Essx* 4C **54**
Tolleshunt Knights. *Essx* 4C **54**
Tolleshunt Major. *Essx* 4C **54**
Tollie. *High* 3H **157**
Tollie Farm. *High* 1A **156**
Tolm. *W Isl* 4G **171**
Tolpuddle. *Dors* 3C **14**
Tolstadh bho Thuath.
W Isl 3H **171**
Tolworth. *G Lon* 4C **38**
Tomachlaggan. *Mor* 1F **151**
Tomaknock. *Per* 1A **136**
Tomatin. *High* 1C **150**
Tombuidhe. *Arg* 3H **133**
Tomdoun. *High* 3D **148**
Tomich. *High*
nr. Cannich 1F **149**
nr. Invergordon 1B **158**
nr. Lairg 3D **164**
Tomintoul. *Mor* 2F **151**
Tomnavoulin. *Mor* 1G **151**
Tomsléibhe. *Arg* 5A **140**
Ton. *Mon* 2G **33**
Tonbridge. *Kent* 1G **27**
Tondu. *B'end* 3B **32**
Tonedale. *Som* 4E **21**
Tonfanau. *Gwyn* 5E **69**
Tong. *Shrp* 5B **72**
Tonge. *Leics* 3B **74**
Tong Forge. *Shrp* 5B **72**
Tongham. *Surr* 2G **25**
Tongland. *Dum* 4D **111**
Tong Norton. *Shrp* 5B **72**
Tongue. *High* 3F **167**
Tongue End. *Linc* 4A **76**
Tongwynlais. *Card* 3E **33**
Tonmawr. *Neat* 2B **32**
Tonna. *Neat* 2A **32**
Tonnau. *Neat* 2A **32**
Ton Pentre. *Rhon* 2C **32**
Ton-Teg. *Rhon* 3D **32**
Tonwell. *Herts* 4D **52**
Tonypandy. *Rhon* 2C **32**
Tonyrefail. *Rhon* 3D **32**
Toot Baldon. *Oxon* 5D **50**
Toot Hill. *Essx* 5F **53**
Toothill. *Hants* 1B **16**
Topcliffe. *N Yor* 2G **99**
Topcliffe. *W Yor* 2C **92**
Topcroft. *Norf* 1E **67**
Topcroft Street. *Norf* 1E **67**
Toppesfield. *Essx* 2H **53**
Toppings. *G Man* 3F **91**
Toprow. *Norf* 1D **66**
Topsham. *Devn* 4C **12**
Torbay. *Torb* 2F **9**
Torbeg. *N Ayr* 3C **122**
Torbothie. *N Lan* 4B **128**
Torbryan. *Devn* 2E **9**
Torcross. *Devn* 4E **9**
Tore. *High* 3A **158**
Torgyle. *High* 2F **149**
Torinturk. *Arg* 3G **125**
Torksey. *Linc* 3F **87**
Torlum. *W Isl* 3C **170**
Torlundy. *High* 1F **141**
Tormarton. *S Glo* 4C **34**
Tormitchell. *S Ayr* 5B **116**
Tormore. *High* 3E **147**
Tormore. *N Ayr* 2C **122**
Tornagrain. *High* 4B **158**
Tornaveen. *Abers* 3D **152**
Torness. *High* 1H **149**
Toronto. *Dur* 1E **105**
Torpenhow. *Cumb* 1D **102**
Torphichen. *W Lot* 2C **128**
Torphins. *Abers* 3D **152**
Torpoint. *Corn* 3A **8**
Torquay. *Torb* 2F **9**
Torr. *Devn* 3B **8**
Torra. *Arg* 4B **124**
Torran. *High* 4E **155**
Torrance. *E Dun* 2H **127**
Torrans. *Arg* 1B **132**
Torranyard. *N Ayr* 5E **127**
Torre. *Som* 3D **20**
Torre. *Torb* 2F **9**
Torridon. *High* 3B **156**
Torrin. *High* 1D **147**
Torrisdale. *Arg* 2B **122**
Torrisdale. *High* 2G **167**
Torrish. *High* 2G **165**
Torrisholme. *Lanc* 3D **96**
Torroble. *High* 3C **164**
Torroy. *High* 4C **164**
Torry. *Aber* 3G **153**
Torryburn. *Fife* 1D **128**
Torthorwald. *Dum* 2B **112**
Tortington. *W Sus* 5B **26**
Tortworth. *S Glo* 2C **34**
Torvaig. *High* 4D **155**
Torver. *Cumb* 5D **102**
Torwood. *Falk* 1B **128**
Torworth. *Notts* 2D **86**
Toscaig. *High* 5G **155**
Toseland. *Cambs* 4B **64**
Tosside. *N Yor* 4G **97**
Tostock. *Suff* 4B **66**
Totaig. *High* 3A **154**
Totardor. *High* 5C **154**
Tote. *High* 4D **154**
Totegan. *High* 2A **168**
Tothill. *Linc* 2D **88**
Totland. *IOW* 4B **16**
Totley. *S Yor* 3H **85**
Totnell. *Dors* 2B **14**
Totnes. *Devn* 2E **9**
Toton. *Notts* 2B **74**
Totronald. *Arg* 3C **138**
Totscore. *High* 2C **154**
Tottenham. *G Lon* 1E **39**
Tottenhill. *Norf* 4F **77**
Tottenhill Row. *Norf* 4F **77**
Totteridge. *G Lon* 1D **38**
Totternhoe. *C Beds* 3H **51**
Tottington. *G Man* 3F **91**
Totton. *Hants* 1B **16**
Touchen-end. *Wind* 4G **37**
Toulvaddie. *High* 5F **165**
Towans, The. *Corn* 3C **4**
Toward. *Arg* 3C **126**
Towcester. *Nptn* 1E **51**
Towednack. *Corn* 3B **4**
Tower End. *Norf* 4F **77**
Tower Hill. *Mers* 4C **90**
Tower Hill. *W Sus* 3C **26**
Towersey. *Oxon* 5F **51**
Towie. *Abers* 2B **152**
Towiemore. *Mor* 4A **160**
Tow Law. *Dur* 1E **105**
Town, The. *IOS* 1A **4**
Town End. *Cambs* 1D **64**
Town End. *Cumb*
nr. Ambleside 4F **103**
nr. Kirkby Thore 2H **103**
nr. Lindale 1D **96**
nr. Newby Bridge 1C **96**
Town End. *Mers* 2G **83**
Townend. *W Dun* 2F **127**
Townfield. *Dur* 5C **114**
Towngate. *Cumb* 5G **113**
Towngate. *Linc* 4A **76**
Town Green. *Lanc* 4C **90**
Town Head. *Cumb*
nr. Grasmere 4E **103**
nr. Great Asby 3H **103**
Townhead. *Cumb*
nr. Lazonby 1G **103**
nr. Maryport 1B **102**
nr. Ousby 1H **103**
Townhead. *Dum* 5D **111**
Townhead of Greenlaw.
Dum 3E **111**
Townhill. *Fife* 1E **129**
Townhill. *Swan* 3F **31**
Town Kelloe. *Dur* 1A **106**
Town Littleworth. *E Sus* 4F **27**
Town Row. *E Sus* 2G **27**
Towns End. *Hants* 1D **24**
Townsend. *Herts* 5B **52**
Townshend. *Corn* 3C **4**
Town Street. *Suff* 2G **65**
Town Yetholm. *Bord* 2C **120**
Towthorpe. *E Yor* 3D **100**
Towthorpe. *York* 4A **100**
Towton. *N Yor* 1E **93**
Towyn. *Cnwy* 3B **82**
Toxteth. *Mers* 2F **83**
Toynton All Saints. *Linc* 4C **88**
Toynton Fen Side. *Linc* 4C **88**
Toynton St Peter. *Linc* 4D **88**
Toy's Hill. *Kent* 5F **39**
Trabboch. *E Ayr* 2D **116**
Traboe. *Corn* 4E **5**
Tradespark. *High* 3C **158**
Tradespark. *Orkn* 7D **172**
Trafford Park. *G Man* 1B **84**
Trallong. *Powy* 3C **46**
Y Trallwng. *Powy* 5E **70**
Tranent. *E Lot* 2H **129**
Tranmere. *Mers* 2F **83**
Trantlebeg. *High* 3A **168**
Trantlemore. *High* 3A **168**
Tranwell. *Nmbd* 1E **115**
Trapp. *Carm* 4G **45**
Traquair. *Bord* 1F **119**
Trash Green. *W Ber* 5E **37**
Trawden. *Lanc* 1H **91**
Trawscoed. *Powy* 2D **46**
Trawsfynydd. *Gwyn* 2G **69**
Trawsgoed. *Cdgn* 3F **57**
Treaddow. *Here* 3A **48**
Trealaw. *Rhon* 2D **32**
Treales. *Lanc* 1C **90**
Trearddur. *IOA* 3B **80**
Treaslane. *High* 3C **154**
Treator. *Corn* 1D **6**
Trebanog. *Rhon* 2D **32**
Trebanos. *Neat* 5H **45**
Trebarber. *Corn* 2C **6**
Trebartha. *Corn* 5C **10**
Trebarwith. *Corn* 4A **10**
Trebetherick. *Corn* 1D **6**
Treborough. *Som* 3D **20**
Trebudannon. *Corn* 2C **6**
Trebullett. *Corn* 5D **10**
Treburley. *Corn* 5D **10**
Treburrick. *Corn* 1C **6**
Trebyan. *Corn* 2E **7**
Trecastle. *Powy* 3B **46**
Trecenydd. *Cphy* 3E **33**
Trecott. *Devn* 2G **11**
Trecwn. *Pemb* 1D **42**
Trecynon. *Rhon* 5C **46**
Tredaule. *Corn* 4C **10**
Tredavoe. *Corn* 4B **4**
Tredegar. *Blae* 5E **47**
Trederwen. *Powy* 4E **71**
Tredington. *Glos* 3E **49**
Tredington. *Warw* 1A **50**
Tredinnick. *Corn*
nr. Bodmin 2F **7**
nr. Looe 3G **7**
nr. Padstow 1D **6**
Tredogan. *V Glam* 5D **32**
Tredomen. *Powy* 2E **46**
Tredunnock. *Mon* 2G **33**
Tredustan. *Powy* 2E **47**
Treen. *Corn*
nr. Land's End 4A **4**
nr. St Ives 3B **4**
Treeton. *S Yor* 2B **86**
Trefaldwyn. *Powy* 1E **58**
Trefasser. *Pemb* 1C **42**
Trefdraeth. *IOA* 3D **80**
Trefdraeth. *Pemb* 1E **43**
Trefecca. *Powy* 2E **47**
Trefechan. *Mer T* 5D **46**
Trefeglwys. *Powy* 1B **58**
Trefenter. *Cdgn* 4F **57**
Treffgarne. *Pemb* 2D **42**
Treffynnon. *Flin* 3D **82**
Treffynnon. *Pemb* 2C **42**
Trefil. *Blae* 4E **46**
Trefilan. *Cdgn* 5E **57**
Trefin. *Pemb* 1C **42**
Treflach. *Shrp* 3E **71**
Trefnant. *Den* 3C **82**
Trefonen. *Shrp* 3E **71**
Trefor. *Gwyn* 1C **68**
Trefor. *IOA* 2C **80**
Treforest. *Rhon* 3D **32**
Trefrew. *Corn* 4B **10**
Trefriw. *Cnwy* 4G **81**
Tref-y-Clawdd. *Powy* 3E **59**
Trefynwy. *Mon* 4A **48**
Tregada. *Corn* 4D **10**
Tregadillett. *Corn* 4C **10**
Tregare. *Mon* 4H **47**
Tregarne. *Corn* 4E **5**
Tregaron. *Cdgn* 5F **57**
Tregarth. *Gwyn* 4F **81**
Tregear. *Corn* 3C **6**
Tregeare. *Corn* 4C **10**
Tregeiriog. *Wrex* 2D **70**
Tregele. *IOA* 1C **80**
Tregeseal. *Corn* 3A **4**
Tregiskey. *Corn* 4E **6**
Tregole. *Corn* 3B **10**
Tregolwyn. *V Glam* 4C **32**
Tregonetha. *Corn* 2D **6**
Tregonhawke. *Corn* 3A **8**
Tregony. *Corn* 4D **6**
Tregoodwell. *Corn* 4B **10**
Tregorrick. *Corn* 3E **6**
Tregoss. *Corn* 2D **6**
Tregowris. *Corn* 4E **5**
Tregoyd. *Powy* 2E **47**
Tregrehan Mills. *Corn* 3E **7**
Tre-groes. *Cdgn* 1E **45**
Tregullon. *Corn* 2E **7**
Tregurrian. *Corn* 2C **6**
Tregynon. *Powy* 1C **58**
Trehafod. *Rhon* 2D **32**
Trehan. *Corn* 3A **8**
Treharris. *Mer T* 2D **32**
Treherbert. *Rhon* 2C **32**
Trehunist. *Corn* 2H **7**
Trekenner. *Corn* 5D **10**

Trekenning. *Corn* 2D **6**
Treknow. *Corn* 4A **10**
Trelales. *B'end* 3B **32**
Trelan. *Corn* 5E **5**
Trelash. *Corn* 3B **10**
Trelassick. *Corn* 3C **6**
Trelawnyd. *Flin* 3C **82**
Trelech. *Carm* 1G **43**
Treleddyd-fawr. *Pemb* 2B **42**
Trelewis. *Mer T* 2E **32**
Treligga. *Corn* 4A **10**
Trelights. *Corn* 1D **6**
Trelill. *Corn* 5A **10**
Trelissick. *Corn* 5C **6**
Trellech. *Mon* 5A **48**
Trelleck Grange. *Mon* 5H **47**
Trelogan. *Flin* 2D **82**
Trelystan. *Powy* 5E **71**
Tremadog. *Gwyn* 1E **69**
Tremail. *Corn* 4B **10**
Tremain. *Cdgn* 1C **44**
Tremaine. *Corn* 4C **10**
Tremar. *Corn* 2G **7**
Trematon. *Corn* 3H **7**
Tremeirchion. *Den* 3C **82**
Tremore. *Corn* 2E **6**
Tremorfa. *Card* 4F **33**
Trenance. *Corn*
  nr. Newquay 2C **6**
  nr. Padstow 1D **6**
Trenarren. *Corn* 4E **7**
Trench. *Telf* 4A **72**
Trencreek. *Corn* 2C **6**
Trendeal. *Corn* 3C **6**
Trenear. *Corn* 5A **6**
Treneglos. *Corn* 4C **10**
Trenewan. *Corn* 3F **7**
Trengune. *Corn* 3B **10**
Trent. *Dors* 1A **14**
Trentham. *Stoke* 1C **72**
Trentishoe. *Devn* 2G **19**
Trentlock. *Derbs* 2B **74**
Treoes. *V Glam* 4C **32**
Treorchy. *Rhon* 2C **32**
Treorci. *Rhon* 2C **32**
Tre'r-ddol. *Cdgn* 1F **57**
Tre'r Llai. *Powy* 5E **71**
Trerulefoot. *Corn* 3H **7**
Tresaith. *Cdgn* 5B **56**
Trescott. *Staf* 1C **60**
Trescowe. *Corn* 3C **4**
Tresham. *Glos* 2C **34**
Tresigin. *V Glam* 4C **32**
Tresillian. *Corn* 4C **6**
Tresimwn. *V Glam* 4D **32**
Tresinney. *Corn* 4B **10**
Treskillard. *Corn* 5A **6**
Treskinnick Cross. *Corn* 3C **10**
Tresmeer. *Corn* 4C **10**
Tresparrett. *Corn* 3B **10**
Tresparrett Posts. *Corn* 3B **10**
Tressady. *High* 3D **164**
Tressait. *Per* 2F **143**
Tresta. *Shet*
  on Fetlar 2H **173**
  on Mainland 6E **173**
Treswell. *Notts* 3E **87**
Treswithian. *Corn* 3D **4**
Tre Taliesin. *Cdgn* 1F **57**
Trethomas. *Cphy* 3E **33**
Trethosa. *Corn* 3D **6**
Trethurgy. *Corn* 3E **7**
Tretio. *Pemb* 2B **42**
Tretire. *Here* 3A **48**
Tretower. *Powy* 3E **47**
Treuddyn. *Flin* 5E **83**
Trevadlock. *Corn* 5C **10**
Trevalga. *Corn* 4A **10**
Trevalyn. *Wrex* 5F **83**
Trevance. *Corn* 1D **6**
Trevanger. *Corn* 1D **6**
Trevanson. *Corn* 1D **6**
Trevarrack. *Corn* 3B **4**
Trevarren. *Corn* 2D **6**
Trevarrian. *Corn* 2C **6**
Trevarrick. *Corn* 4D **6**
Trevaughan. *Carm*
  nr. Carmarthen 3E **45**
  nr. Whitland 3F **43**
Treveighan. *Corn* 5A **10**
Trevellas. *Corn* 3B **6**
Trevelmond. *Corn* 2G **7**
Treverva. *Corn* 5B **6**
Trevescan. *Corn* 4A **4**
Trevethin. *Torf* 5F **47**
Trevia. *Corn* 4A **10**
Trevigro. *Corn* 2H **7**
Trevilley. *Corn* 4A **4**
Treviscoe. *Corn* 3D **6**
Trevivian. *Corn* 4B **10**
Trevone. *Corn* 1C **6**
Trevor. *Wrex* 1E **71**
Trevor Uchaf. *Den* 1E **71**
Trew. *Corn* 4D **4**
Trewalder. *Corn* 4A **10**
Trewarlett. *Corn* 4D **10**
Trewarmett. *Corn* 4A **10**
Trewassa. *Corn* 4B **10**
Treween. *Corn* 4C **10**
Trewellard. *Corn* 3A **4**
Trewen. *Corn* 4C **10**
Trewennack. *Corn* 4D **5**
Trewern. *Powy* 4E **71**
Trewetha. *Corn* 5A **10**
Trewidland. *Corn* 3G **7**

Trewint. *Corn* 3B **10**
Trewithian. *Corn* 5C **6**
Trewoofe. *Corn* 4B **4**
Trewoon. *Corn* 3D **6**
Treworthal. *Corn* 5C **6**
Treyarnon. *Pemb* 1B **44**
Treyarnon. *Corn* 1C **6**
Treyford. *W Sus* 1G **17**
Triangle. *Staf* 5E **73**
Triangle. *W Yor* 2A **92**
Trickett's Cross. *Dors* 2F **15**
Trimdon. *Dur* 1A **106**
Trimdon Colliery. *Dur* 1A **106**
Trimdon Grange. *Dur* 1A **106**
Trimingham. *Norf* 2E **79**
Trimley Lower Street. *Suff* 2F **55**
Trimley St Martin. *Suff* 2F **55**
Trimley St Mary. *Suff* 2F **55**
Trimpley. *Worc* 3B **60**
Trimsaran. *Carm* 5E **45**
Trimstone. *Devn* 2F **19**
Trinafour. *Per* 2E **143**
Trinant. *Cphy* 2F **33**
Tring. *Herts* 4H **51**
Trinity. *Ang* 2F **145**
Trinity. *Edin* 2F **129**
Trisant. *Cdgn* 3G **57**
Triscombe. *Som* 3E **21**
Trislaig. *High* 1E **141**
Trispen. *Corn* 3C **6**
Tritlington. *Nmbd* 5G **121**
Trochry. *Per* 4G **143**
Troedrhiwdalar. *Powy* 5B **58**
Troedrhiwfuwch. *Cphy* 5E **47**
Troedrhiw-gwair. *Blae* 5E **47**
Troedyraur. *Cdgn* 1D **44**
Troedyrhiw. *Mer T* 5D **46**
Trondavoe. *Shet* 4E **173**
Troon. *Corn* 5A **6**
Troon. *S Ayr* 1C **116**
Troqueer. *Dum* 2A **112**
Troston. *Suff* 3A **66**
Trostiscliffe. *Kent* 4H **39**
Trotton. *W Sus* 4G **25**
Troutbeck. *Cumb*
  nr. Ambleside 4F **103**
  nr. Penrith 2E **103**
Troutbeck Bridge. *Cumb* 4F **103**
Troway. *Derbs* 3A **86**
Trowbridge. *Wilts* 1D **22**
Trowell. *Notts* 2B **74**
Trowle Common. *Wilts* 1D **22**
Trowley Bottom. *Herts* 4A **52**
Trowse Newton. *Norf* 5E **79**
Trudoxhill. *Som* 2C **22**
Trull. *Som* 4F **21**
Trumaisgearraidh. *W Isl* 1D **170**
Trumpan. *High* 2B **154**
Trumpet. *Here* 2B **48**
Trumpington. *Cambs* 5D **64**
Trumps Green. *Surr* 4A **38**
Trunch. *Norf* 2E **79**
Trunnah. *Lanc* 5C **96**
Truro. *Corn* 4C **6**
Trusham. *Devn* 4B **12**
Trusley. *Derbs* 2G **73**
Trusthorpe. *Linc* 2E **89**
Tryfil. *IOA* 2D **80**
Trysull. *Staf* 1C **60**
Tubney. *Oxon* 2C **36**
Tuckenhay. *Devn* 3E **9**
Tuckhill. *Shrp* 2B **60**
Tuckingmill. *Corn* 4A **6**
Tuckton. *Bour* 3G **15**
Tuddenham. *Suff* 3G **65**
Tuddenham St Martin. *Suff* 1E **55**
Tudeley. *Kent* 1H **27**
Tudhoe. *Dur* 1F **105**
Tudhoe Grange. *Dur* 1F **105**
Tudorville. *Here* 3A **48**
Tudweiliog. *Gwyn* 2B **68**
Tuesley. *Surr* 1A **26**
Tufton. *Hants* 2C **24**
Tufton. *Pemb* 2E **43**
Tugby. *Leics* 5E **75**
Tugford. *Shrp* 2H **59**
Tughall. *Nmbd* 2G **121**
Tulchan. *Per* 1B **136**
Tullibardine. *Per* 2B **136**
Tullibody. *Clac* 4A **136**
Tullich. *Arg* 2H **133**
Tullich. *High*
  nr. Lochcarron 4B **156**
  nr. Tain 1C **158**
Tullich. *Mor* 4H **159**
Tullich Muir. *High* 1B **158**
Tulliemet. *Per* 3G **143**
Tulloch. *Abers* 5F **161**
Tulloch. *High*
  nr. Bonar Bridge 4D **164**
  nr. Fort William 5F **149**
  nr. Grantown-on-Spey 2D **151**
Tulloch. *Per* 1C **136**
Tullochgorm. *Arg* 4G **133**
Tullybeagles Lodge. *Per* 5H **143**
Tullymurdoch. *Per* 3B **144**
Tullynessle. *Abers* 2C **152**
Tumble. *Carm* 4F **45**
Tumbler's Green. *Essx* 3B **54**
Tumby. *Linc* 4B **88**
Tumby Woodside. *Linc* 5B **88**
Tummel Bridge. *Per* 3E **143**
Tunbridge Wells, Royal.
  Kent 2G **27**
Tunga. *W Isl* 4G **171**

Tungate. *Norf* 3E **79**
Tunley. *Bath* 1B **22**
Tunstall. *E Yor* 1G **95**
Tunstall. *Kent* 4C **40**
Tunstall. *Lanc* 2F **97**
Tunstall. *Norf* 5G **79**
Tunstall. *N Yor* 5F **105**
Tunstall. *Staf* 3B **72**
Tunstall. *Stoke* 5C **84**
Tunstall. *Suff* 5F **67**
Tunstall. *Tyne* 4G **115**
Tunstead. *Derbs* 3F **85**
Tunstead. *Norf* 3E **79**
Tunstead Milton. *Derbs* 2E **85**
Tunworth. *Hants* 2E **25**
Tupsley. *Here* 1A **48**
Tupton. *Derbs* 4A **86**
Turfholm. *S Lan* 1H **117**
Turfmoor. *Devn* 2F **13**
Turgis Green. *Hants* 1E **25**
Turkdean. *Glos* 4G **49**
Turkey Island. *Hants* 1D **16**
Tur Langton. *Leics* 1E **62**
Turleigh. *Wilts* 5D **34**
Turlin Moor. *Pool* 3E **15**
Turnastone. *Here* 2G **47**
Turnberry. *S Ayr* 4B **116**
Turnchapel. *Plym* 3A **8**
Turnditch. *Derbs* 1G **73**
Turners Hill. *W Sus* 2E **27**
Turners Puddle. *Dors* 3D **14**
Turnford. *Herts* 5D **52**
Turnhouse. *Edin* 2E **129**
Turton Bottoms. *Bkbn* 3F **91**
Turtory. *Mor* 4C **160**
Turves Green. *W Mid* 3E **61**
Turvey. *Bed* 5G **63**
Turville. *Buck* 2F **37**
Turville Heath. *Buck* 2F **37**
Turweston. *Buck* 2E **50**
Tushielaw. *Bord* 3F **119**
Tutbury. *Staf* 3G **73**
Tutnall. *Worc* 3D **61**
Tutshill. *Glos* 2A **34**
Tuttington. *Norf* 3E **79**
Tutts Clump. *W Ber* 4D **36**
Tutwell. *Corn* 5D **11**
Tuxford. *Notts* 3E **87**
Twatt. *Orkn* 5B **172**
Twatt. *Shet* 6E **173**
Twechar. *E Dun* 2H **127**
Tweedale. *Telf* 5B **72**
Tweedbank. *Bord* 1H **119**
Tweedmouth. *Nmbd* 4F **131**
Tweedsmuir. *Bord* 2C **118**
Twelveheads. *Corn* 4B **6**
Twemlow Green. *Ches E* 4B **84**
Twenty. *Linc* 3A **76**
Twerton. *Bath* 5C **34**
Twickenham. *G Lon* 3C **38**
Twigworth. *Glos* 3D **48**
Twineham. *W Sus* 4D **26**
Twinhoe. *Bath* 1C **22**
Twinstead. *Essx* 2B **54**
Twinstead Green. *Essx* 2B **54**
Twiss Green. *Warr* 1A **84**
Twiston. *Lanc* 5H **97**
Twitchen. *Devn* 3A **20**
Twitchen. *Shrp* 3F **59**
Two Bridges. *Devn* 5G **11**
Two Bridges. *Glos* 5B **48**
Two Dales. *Derbs* 4G **85**
Two Gates. *Staf* 5G **73**
Two Mile Oak. *Devn* 2E **9**
Twycross. *Leics* 5H **73**
Twyford. *Buck* 3E **51**
Twyford. *Derbs* 3H **73**
Twyford. *Dors* 1D **14**
Twyford. *Hants* 4C **24**
Twyford. *Leics* 4E **75**
Twyford. *Norf* 3C **78**
Twyford. *Wok* 4F **37**
Twyford Common. *Here* 2A **48**
Twynholm. *Dum* 4D **110**
Twyning. *Glos* 2D **49**
Twyning Green. *Glos* 2E **49**
Twynllanan. *Carm* 3A **46**
Twyn-y-Sheriff. *Mon* 5H **47**
Twywell. *Nptn* 3G **63**
Tyberton. *Here* 2G **47**
Tyburn. *W Mid* 1F **61**
Tycroes. *Carm* 4G **45**
Tycrwyn. *Powy* 4D **70**
Tydd Gote. *Linc* 4D **76**
Tydd St Giles. *Cambs* 4D **76**
Tydd St Mary. *Linc* 4D **76**
Tye. *Hants* 2F **17**
Tye Green. *Essx*
  nr. Bishop's Stortford 3F **53**
  nr. Braintree 3A **54**
  nr. Saffron Walden 2F **53**
Tyersal. *W Yor* 1B **92**
Ty Issa. *Powy* 2D **70**
Tyldesley. *G Man* 4E **91**
Tyler Hill. *Kent* 4F **41**
Tylers Green. *Buck* 2G **37**
Tyler's Green. *Essx* 5F **53**
Tylorstown. *Rhon* 2D **32**
Tylwch. *Powy* 2B **58**
Y Tymbl. *Carm* 4F **45**

Ty-nant. *Cnwy* 1B **70**
Tyndrum. *Stir* 5H **141**
Tyneham. *Dors* 4D **15**
Tynehead. *Midl* 4G **129**
Tynemouth. *Tyne* 3G **115**
Tyneside. *Tyne* 3F **115**
Tyne Tunnel. *Tyne* 3G **115**
Tynewydd. *Rhon* 2C **32**
Tyninghame. *E Lot* 2C **130**
Tynron. *Dum* 5H **117**
Ty'n-y-bryn. *Rhon* 3D **32**
Tyn-y-celyn. *Wrex* 2D **70**
Tyn-y-cwm. *Swan* 5G **45**
Tyn-y-ffridd. *Powy* 2D **70**
Tynygongl. *IOA* 2E **81**
Tynygraig. *Cdgn* 4F **57**
Ty'n-y-groes. *Cnwy* 3G **81**
Ty'n-yr-eithin. *Cdgn* 4F **57**
Tyn-y-rhyd. *Powy* 4C **70**
Tyn-y-wern. *Powy* 2C **70**
Tyrie. *Abers* 2G **161**
Tyringham. *Mil* 1G **51**
Tythecott. *Devn* 1E **11**
Tythegston. *B'end* 4B **32**
Tytherington. *Ches E* 3D **84**
Tytherington. *Som* 2C **22**
Tytherington. *S Glo* 3B **34**
Tytherington. *Wilts* 2E **23**
Tytherleigh. *Devn* 2G **13**
Tywardreath. *Corn* 3E **7**
Tywardreath Highway. *Corn* 3E **7**
Tywyn. *Cnwy* 3G **81**
Tywyn. *Gwyn* 5E **69**

U

Uachdar. *W Isl* 3D **170**
Uags. *High* 5G **155**
Ubbeston Green. *Suff* 3F **67**
Ubley. *Bath* 1A **22**
Uckerby. *N Yor* 4F **105**
Uckfield. *E Sus* 3F **27**
Uckinghall. *Worc* 2D **48**
Uckington. *Glos* 3E **49**
Uckington. *Shrp* 5H **71**
Uddingston. *S Lan* 3H **127**
Uddington. *S Lan* 1A **118**
Udimore. *E Sus* 4C **28**
Udny Green. *Abers* 1F **153**
Udny Station. *Abers* 1G **153**
Udston. *S Lan* 4H **127**
Udstonhead. *S Lan* 5A **128**
Uffcott. *Wilts* 4G **35**
Uffculme. *Devn* 1D **12**
Uffington. *Linc* 5H **75**
Uffington. *Oxon* 3B **36**
Uffington. *Shrp* 4H **71**
Ufford. *Pet* 5H **75**
Ufford. *Suff* 5E **67**
Ufton. *Warw* 4A **62**
Ufton Nervet. *W Ber* 5E **37**
Ugadale. *Arg* 3B **122**
Ugborough. *Devn* 3C **8**
Ugford. *Wilts* 3F **23**
Uggeshall. *Suff* 2G **67**
Ugglebarnby. *N Yor* 4F **107**
Ugley. *Essx* 3F **53**
Ugley Green. *Essx* 3F **53**
Ugthorpe. *N Yor* 3E **107**
Uidh. *W Isl* 9B **170**
Uig. *Arg* 3C **138**
Uig. *High*
  nr. Balgown 2C **154**
  nr. Dunvegan 3A **154**
Uigshader. *High* 4D **154**
Uisken. *Arg* 2A **132**
Ulbster. *High* 4F **169**
Ulcat Row. *Cumb* 2F **103**
Ulceby. *Linc* 3D **88**
Ulceby. *N Lin* 3E **94**
Ulceby Skitter. *N Lin* 3E **94**
Ulcombe. *Kent* 1C **28**
Uldale. *Cumb* 1D **102**
Uley. *Glos* 2C **34**
Ulgham. *Nmbd* 5G **121**
Ullapool. *High* 4F **163**
Ullenhall. *Warw* 4F **61**
Ulleskelf. *N Yor* 1F **93**
Ullesthorpe. *Leics* 2C **62**
Ulley. *S Yor* 2B **86**
Ullingswick. *Here* 5H **59**
Ullinish. *High* 5C **154**
Ullock. *Cumb* 2B **102**
Ulpha. *Cumb* 5C **102**
Ulrome. *E Yor* 4F **101**
Ulsta. *Shet* 3F **173**
Ulting. *Essx* 5B **54**
Ulva House. *Arg* 5F **139**
Ulverston. *Cumb* 2B **96**
Ulwell. *Dors* 4F **15**
Umberleigh. *Devn* 4G **19**
Unapool. *High* 5C **166**
Underbarrow. *Cumb* 5F **103**
Undercliffe. *W Yor* 1B **92**
Underdale. *Shrp* 4H **71**
Underhoull. *Shet* 1G **173**
Underriver. *Kent* 5G **39**
Under Tofts. *S Yor* 2H **85**
Underton. *Shrp* 1A **60**
Underwood. *Newp* 3G **33**
Underwood. *Notts* 5B **86**
Underwood. *Plym* 3B **8**
Undley. *Suff* 2F **65**
Undy. *Mon* 3H **33**

Union Mills. *IOM* 4C **108**
Union Street. *E Sus* 2B **28**
Unstone. *Derbs* 3A **86**
Unstone Green. *Derbs* 3A **86**
Unthank. *Cumb*
  nr. Carlisle 5E **113**
  nr. Gamblesby 5H **113**
  nr. Penrith 1F **103**
Unthank End. *Cumb* 1F **103**
Upavon. *Wilts* 1G **23**
Up Cerne. *Dors* 2B **14**
Upchurch. *Kent* 4C **40**
Upcott. *Devn* 2F **11**
Upcott. *Here* 5F **59**
Upend. *Cambs* 5F **65**
Up Exe. *Devn* 2C **12**
Upgate. *Norf* 4D **78**
Upgate Street. *Norf* 1C **66**
Uphall. *Dors* 2A **14**
Uphall. *W Lot* 2D **128**
Uphall Station. *W Lot* 2D **128**
Upham. *Devn* 2B **12**
Upham. *Hants* 4D **24**
Uphampton. *Here* 4F **59**
Uphampton. *Worc* 4C **60**
Up Hatherley. *Glos* 3E **49**
Uphill. *N Som* 1G **21**
Up Holland. *Lanc* 4D **90**
Uplawmoor. *E Ren* 4F **127**
Upleadon. *Glos* 3C **48**
Upleatham. *Red C* 3D **106**
Uplees. *Kent* 4D **40**
Uploders. *Dors* 3A **14**
Uplowman. *Devn* 1D **12**
Uplyme. *Devn* 3G **13**
Up Marden. *W Sus* 1F **17**
Upminster. *G Lon* 2G **39**
Up Nately. *Hants* 1E **25**
Upottery. *Devn* 2F **13**
Uppat. *High* 3F **165**
Upper Affcot. *Shrp* 2G **59**
Upper Arley. *Worc* 2B **60**
Upper Armley. *W Yor* 1C **92**
Upper Arncott. *Oxon* 4E **50**
Upper Astrop. *Nptn* 2D **50**
Upper Badcall. *High* 4B **166**
Upper Bangor. *Gwyn* 3E **81**
Upper Basildon. *W Ber* 4D **36**
Upper Batley. *W Yor* 2C **92**
Upper Beeding. *W Sus* 4C **26**
Upper Benefield. *Nptn* 2G **63**
Upper Bentley. *Worc* 4D **61**
Upper Bighouse. *High* 3A **168**
Upper Boddam. *Abers* 5D **160**
Upper Boddington. *Nptn* 5B **62**
Upper Bogside. *Mor* 3G **159**
Upper Booth. *Derbs* 2F **85**
Upper Borth. *Cdgn* 2F **57**
Upper Boyndlie. *Abers* 2G **161**
Upper Brailes. *Warw* 1B **50**
Upper Breinton. *Here* 1H **47**
Upper Broughton. *Notts* 3D **74**
Upper Brynamman. *Carm* 4H **45**
Upper Bucklebury. *W Ber* 5D **36**
Upper Bullington. *Hants* 2C **24**
Upper Burgate. *Hants* 1G **15**
Upper Caldecote. *C Beds* 1B **52**
Upper Canterton. *Hants* 1A **16**
Upper Catesby. *Nptn* 5C **62**
Upper Chapel. *Powy* 1D **46**
Upper Cheddon. *Som* 4F **21**
Upper Chicksgrove. *Wilts* 4E **23**
Upper Church Village. *Rhon* 3D **32**
Upper Chute. *Wilts* 1A **24**
Upper Clatford. *Hants* 2B **24**
Upper Coberley. *Glos* 4E **49**
Upper Coedcae. *Torf* 5F **47**
Upper Cound. *Shrp* 5H **71**
Upper Cudworth. *S Yor* 4D **93**
Upper Cumberworth. *W Yor* 4C **92**
Upper Cuttlehill. *Abers* 4B **160**
Upper Cwmbran. *Torf* 2F **33**
Upper Dallachy. *Mor* 2A **160**
Upper Dean. *Bed* 4H **63**
Upper Denby. *W Yor* 4C **92**
Upper Derraid. *High* 5E **159**
Upper Diabaig. *High* 2H **155**
Upper Dicker. *E Sus* 5G **27**
Upper Dinchope. *Shrp* 2G **59**
Upper Dochcarty. *High* 2H **157**
Upper Dounreay. *High* 2B **168**
Upper Dovercourt. *Essx* 2F **55**
Upper Dunsforth. *N Yor* 3G **99**
Upper Dunsley. *Herts* 4H **51**
Upper Eastern Green.
  W Mid 2G **61**
Upper Elkstone. *Staf* 5E **85**
Upper Ellastone. *Staf* 1F **73**
Upper End. *Derbs* 3E **85**
Upper Enham. *Hants* 2B **24**
Upper Farmcote. *Shrp* 1B **60**
Upper Farringdon. *Hants* 3F **25**
Upper Framilode. *Glos* 4C **48**
Upper Froyle. *Hants* 2F **25**
Upper Gills. *High* 1F **169**
Upper Glenfintaig. *High* 5E **149**
Upper Godney. *Som* 2H **21**
Upper Gravenhurst. *C Beds* 2B **52**
Upper Green. *Essx* 2E **53**
Upper Green. *W Ber* 5B **36**
Upper Green. *W Yor* 2C **92**
Upper Grove Common.
  Here 3A **48**
Upper Hackney. *Derbs* 4G **85**
Upper Hale. *Surr* 2G **25**

Upper Halliford—Warthill

Upper Halliford. *Surr* 4B 38
Upper Halling. *Medw* 4A 40
Upper Hambleton. *Rut* 5G 75
Upper Hardres Court. *Kent* 5F 41
Upper Hardwick. *Here* 5G 59
Upper Hartfield. *E Sus* 2F 27
Upper Haugh. *S Yor* 1B 86
Upper Hayton. *Shrp* 2H 59
Upper Heath. *Shrp* 2H 59
Upper Hellesdon. *Norf* 4E 78
Upper Helmsley. *N Yor* 4A 100
Upper Hengoed. *Shrp* 2E 71
Upper Hergest. *Here* 5E 59
Upper Heyford. *Nptn* 5D 62
Upper Heyford. *Oxon* 3C 50
Upper Hill. *Here* 5G 59
Upper Hindhope. *Bord* 4B 120
Upper Hopton. *W Yor* 3B 92
Upper Howsell. *Worc* 1C 48
Upper Hulme. *Staf* 4E 85
Upper Inglesham. *Swin* 2H 35
Upper Kilcott. *S Glo* 3C 34
Upper Killay. *Swan* 3E 31
Upper Kirkton. *Abers* 5E 161
Upper Kirkton. *N Ayr* 4C 126
Upper Knockando. *Mor* 4F 159
Upper Knockchoilum. *High* 2G 149
Upper Lambourn. *W Ber* 3B 36
Upper Langford. *N Som* 1H 21
Upper Langwith. *Derbs* 4C 86
Upper Largo. *Fife* 3G 137
Upper Latheron. *High* 5D 169
Upper Layham. *Suff* 1D 54
Upper Leigh. *Staf* 2E 73
Upper Lenie. *High* 1H 149
Upper Lochton. *Abers* 4D 152
Upper Longdon. *Staf* 4E 73
Upper Longwood. *Shrp* 5A 72
Upper Lybster. *High* 5E 169
Upper Lydbrook. *Glos* 4B 48
Upper Lye. *Here* 4F 59
Upper Maes-coed. *Here* 2G 47
Upper Midway. *Derbs* 3G 73
Uppermill. *G Man* 4H 91
Upper Millichope. *Shrp* 2H 59
Upper Milovaig. *High* 4A 154
Upper Minety. *Wilts* 2F 35
Upper Mitton. *Worc* 3C 60
Upper Nash. *Pemb* 4E 43
Upper Neepaback. *Shet* 3G 173
Upper Netchwood. *Shrp* 1A 60
Upper Nobut. *Staf* 2E 73
Upper North Dean. *Buck* 2G 37
Upper Norwood. *W Sus* 4A 26
Upper Nyland. *Dors* 4C 22
Upper Oddington. *Glos* 3H 49
Upper Ollach. *High* 5E 155
Upper Outwoods. *Staf* 3G 73
Upper Padley. *Derbs* 3G 85
Upper Pennington. *Hants* 3B 16
Upper Poppleton. *York* 4H 99
Upper Quinton. *Warw* 1G 49
Upper Rissington. *Glos* 4H 49
Upper Rochford. *Worc* 4A 60
Upper Rusko. *Dum* 3C 110
Upper Sandaig. *High* 2F 147
Upper Sanday. *Orkn* 7E 172
Upper Sapey. *Here* 4A 60
Upper Seagry. *Wilts* 3E 35
Upper Shelton. *C Beds* 1H 51
Upper Sheringham. *Norf* 1D 78
Upper Skelmorlie. *N Ayr* 3C 126
Upper Slaughter. *Glos* 3G 49
Upper Sonachan. *Arg* 1H 133
Upper Soudley. *Glos* 4B 48
Upper Staploe. *Bed* 5A 64
Upper Stoke. *Norf* 5E 79
Upper Stondon. *C Beds* 2B 52
Upper Stowe. *Nptn* 5D 62
Upper Street. *Hants* 1G 15
Upper Street. *Norf*
nr. Horning 4F 79
nr. Hoveton 4F 79
Upper Street. *Suff* 2E 55
Upper Strensham. *Worc* 2E 49
Upper Studley. *Wilts* 1D 22
Upper Sundon. *C Beds* 3A 52
Upper Swell. *Glos* 3G 49
Upper Tankersley. *S Yor* 1H 85
Upper Tean. *Staf* 2E 73
Upperthong. *W Yor* 4B 92
Upperthorpe. *N Lin* 4A 94
Upper Thurnham. *Lanc* 4D 96
Upper Tillyrie. *Per* 3D 136
Upperton. *W Sus* 3A 26
Upper Tooting. *G Lon* 3D 39
Upper Town. *Derbs*
nr. Bonsall 5G 85
nr. Hognaston 5G 85
Uppertown. *Derbs* 4H 85
Upper Town. *Here* 1A 48
Uppertown. *High* 1F 169
Upper Town. *N Som* 5A 34
Uppertown. *Nmbd* 2B 114
Uppertown. *Orkn* 8D 172
Upper Tysoe. *Warw* 1B 50
Upper Upham. *Wilts* 4H 35
Upper Upnor. *Medw* 3B 40
Upper Urquhart. *Fife* 3D 136
Upper Wardington. *Oxon* 1C 50
Upper Weald. *Mil* 2F 51
Upper Weedon. *Nptn* 5D 62
Upper Wellingham. *E Sus* 4F 27
Upper Whiston. *S Yor* 2B 86
Upper Wield. *Hants* 3E 25
Upper Winchendon. *Buck* 4F 51
Upperwood. *Derbs* 5G 85
Upper Woodford. *Wilts* 3G 23
Upper Wootton. *Hants* 1D 24
Upper Wraxall. *Wilts* 4D 34
Upper Wyche. *Worc* 1C 48
Uppincott. *Devn* 2B 12
Uppingham. *Rut* 1F 63
Uppington. *Shrp* 5A 72
Upsall. *N Yor* 1G 99
Upsettlington. *Bord* 5E 131
Upshire. *Essx* 5E 53
Up Somborne. *Hants* 3B 24
Upstreet. *Kent* 4G 41
Up Sydling. *Dors* 2B 14
Upthorpe. *Suff* 3B 66
Upton. *Buck* 4F 51
Upton. *Cambs* 3A 64
Upton. *Ches W* 4G 83
Upton. *Corn*
nr. Bude 2C 10
nr. Liskeard 5C 10
Upton. *Cumb* 1E 102
Upton. *Devn*
nr. Honiton 2D 12
nr. Kingsbridge 4D 8
Upton. *Dors*
nr. Poole 3E 15
nr. Weymouth 4C 14
Upton. *E Yor* 4F 101
Upton. *Hants*
nr. Andover 1B 24
nr. Southampton 1B 16
Upton. *IOW* 3D 16
Upton. *Leics* 1A 62
Upton. *Linc* 2F 87
Upton. *Mers* 2E 83
Upton. *Norf* 4F 79
Upton. *Nptn* 4E 62
Upton. *Notts*
nr. Retford 3E 87
nr. Southwell 5E 87
Upton. *Oxon* 3D 36
Upton. *Pemb* 4E 43
Upton. *Pet* 5A 76
Upton. *Slo* 3A 38
Upton. *Som*
nr. Somerton 4H 21
nr. Wiveliscombe 4C 20
Upton. *Warw* 5F 61
Upton. *W Yor* 3E 93
Upton. *Wilts* 3D 22
Upton Bishop. *Here* 3B 48
Upton Cheyney. *S Glo* 5B 34
Upton Cressett. *Shrp* 1A 60
Upton Crews. *Here* 3B 48
Upton Cross. *Corn* 5C 10
Upton End. *C Beds* 2B 52
Upton Grey. *Hants* 2E 25
Upton Heath. *Ches W* 4G 83
Upton Hellions. *Devn* 2B 12
Upton Lovell. *Wilts* 2E 23
Upton Magna. *Shrp* 4H 71
Upton Noble. *Som* 3C 22
Upton Pyne. *Devn* 3C 12
Upton St Leonards. *Glos* 4D 48
Upton Scudamore. *Wilts* 2D 22
Upton Snodsbury. *Worc* 5D 60
Upton upon Severn. *Worc* 1D 48
Upton Warren. *Worc* 4D 60
Upwaltham. *W Sus* 4A 26
Upware. *Cambs* 3E 65
Upwell. *Norf* 5E 77
Upwey. *Dors* 4B 14
Upwick Green. *Herts* 3E 53
Upwood. *Cambs* 2B 64
Urafirth. *Shet* 4E 173
Uragaig. *Arg* 4A 132
Urchany. *High* 4C 158
Urchfont. *Wilts* 1F 23
Urdimarsh. *Here* 1A 48
Ure. *Shet* 4D 173
Ure Bank. *N Yor* 2F 99
Urgha. *W Isl* 8D 171
Urlay Nook. *Stoc T* 3B 106
Urmston. *G Man* 1B 84
Urquhart. *Mor* 2G 159
Urra. *N Yor* 4C 106
Urray. *High* 3H 157
Usan. *Ang* 3G 145
Ushaw Moor. *Dur* 5F 115
Usk. *Mon* 5G 47
Usselby. *Linc* 1H 87
Usworth. *Tyne* 4G 115
Utkinton. *Ches W* 4H 83
Uton. *Devn* 3B 12
Utterby. *Linc* 1C 88
Uttoxeter. *Staf* 2E 73
Uwchmynydd. *Gwyn* 3A 68
Uxbridge. *G Lon* 2B 38
Uyeasound. *Shet* 1G 173
Uzmaston. *Pemb* 3D 42

V

Valley. *IOA* 3B 80
Valley End. *Surr* 4A 38
Valley Truckle. *Corn* 4B 10
Valsgarth. *Shet* 1H 173
Valtos. *High* 2E 155
Van. *Powy* 2B 58
Vange. *Essx* 2B 40
Varteg. *Torf* 5F 47
Vatsetter. *Shet* 3G 173
Vatten. *High* 4B 154
Vaul. *Arg* 4B 138
Vauld, The. *Here* 1A 48
Vaynor. *Mer T* 4D 46
Veensgarth. *Shet* 7F 173
Velindre. *Powy* 2E 47
Vellow. *Som* 3D 20
Velly. *Devn* 4C 18
Veness. *Orkn* 5E 172
Venhay. *Devn* 1A 12
Venn. *Devn* 4D 8
Venngreen. *Devn* 1D 11
Vennington. *Shrp* 5F 71
Venn Ottery. *Devn* 3D 12
Venn's Green. *Here* 1A 48
Venny Tedburn. *Devn* 3B 12
Venterdon. *Corn* 5D 10
Ventnor. *IOW* 5D 16
Vernham Dean. *Hants* 1B 24
Vernham Street. *Hants* 1B 24
Vernolds Common. *Shrp* 2G 59
Verwood. *Dors* 2F 15
Veryan. *Corn* 5D 6
Veryan Green. *Corn* 5D 6
Vicarage. *Devn* 4F 13
Vickerstown. *Cumb* 3A 96
Victoria. *Corn* 2D 6
Vidlin. *Shet* 5F 173
Viewpark. *N Lan* 3A 128
Vigo. *W Mid* 5E 73
Vigo Village. *Kent* 4H 39
Vinehall Street. *E Sus* 3B 28
Vine's Cross. *E Sus* 4G 27
Viney Hill. *Glos* 5B 48
Virginia Water. *Surr* 4A 38
Virginstow. *Devn* 3D 11
Vobster. *Som* 2C 22
Voe. *Shet*
nr. Hillside 5F 173
nr. Swinister 3E 173
Vole. *Som* 2G 21
Vowchurch. *Here* 2G 47
Voxter. *Shet* 4E 173
Voy. *Orkn* 6B 172
Vulcan Village. *Mers* 1H 83

W

Waberthwaite. *Cumb* 5C 102
Wackerfield. *Dur* 2E 105
Wacton. *Norf* 1D 66
Wadbister. *Shet* 7F 173
Wadborough. *Worc* 1E 49
Wadbrook. *Devn* 2G 13
Waddesdon. *Buck* 4F 51
Waddeton. *Devn* 3E 9
Waddicar. *Mers* 1F 83
Waddingham. *Linc* 1G 87
Waddington. *Lanc* 5G 97
Waddington. *Linc* 4G 87
Waddon. *Devn* 5B 12
Wadebridge. *Corn* 1D 6
Wadeford. *Som* 1G 13
Wadenhoe. *Nptn* 2H 63
Wadesmill. *Herts* 4D 52
Wadhurst. *E Sus* 2H 27
Wadshelf. *Derbs* 3H 85
Wadsley. *S Yor* 1H 85
Wadsley Bridge. *S Yor* 1H 85
Wadswick. *Wilts* 5D 34
Wadwick. *Hants* 1C 24
Wadworth. *S Yor* 1C 86
Waen. *Den*
nr. Llandymog 4D 82
nr. Nantglyn 4B 82
Waen. *Powy* 1B 58
Waen Fach. *Powy* 4E 70
Waen Goleugoed. *Den* 3C 82
Wag. *High* 1H 165
Wainfleet All Saints. *Linc* 5D 89
Wainfleet Bank. *Linc* 5D 88
Wainfleet St Mary. *Linc* 5D 89
Wainhouse Corner. *Corn* 3B 10
Wainscott. *Medw* 3B 40
Wainstalls. *W Yor* 2A 92
Waitby. *Cumb* 4A 104
Waithe. *Linc* 4F 95
Wakefield. *W Yor* 2D 92
Wakerley. *Nptn* 1G 63
Wakes Colne. *Essx* 3B 54
Walberswick. *Suff* 3G 67
Walberton. *W Sus* 5A 26
Walbottle. *Tyne* 3E 115
Walby. *Cumb* 3F 113
Walcombe. *Som* 2A 22
Walcot. *Linc* 2H 75
Walcot. *N Lin* 2B 94
Walcot. *Swin* 3G 35
Walcot. *Telf* 4H 71
Walcot. *Warw* 5F 61
Walcote. *Leics* 2C 62
Walcot Green. *Norf* 2D 66
Walcott. *Linc* 5A 88
Walcott. *Norf* 2F 79
Walden. *N Yor* 1C 98
Walden Head. *N Yor* 1B 98
Walden Stubbs. *N Yor* 3F 93
Walderslade. *Medw* 4B 40
Walderton. *W Sus* 1F 17
Walditch. *Dors* 3H 13
Waldley. *Derbs* 2F 73
Waldridge. *Dur* 4F 115
Waldringfield. *Suff* 1F 55
Waldron. *E Sus* 4G 27
Wales. *S Yor* 2B 86
Walesby. *Linc* 1A 88
Walesby. *Notts* 3D 86
Walford. *Here*
nr. Leintwardine 3F 59
nr. Ross-on-Wye 3A 48
Walford. *Shrp* 3G 71
Walford. *Staf* 2C 72
Walford Heath. *Shrp* 4G 71
Walgherton. *Ches E* 1A 72
Walgrave. *Nptn* 3F 63
Walhampton. *Hants* 3B 16
Walkden. *G Man* 4F 91
Walker. *Tyne* 3F 115
Walkerburn. *Bord* 1F 119
Walker Fold. *Lanc* 5F 97
Walkeringham. *Notts* 1E 87
Walkerith. *Linc* 1E 87
Walkern. *Herts* 3C 52
Walker's Green. *Here* 1A 48
Walkerton. *Fife* 3E 137
Walkerville. *N Yor* 5F 105
Walkford. *Dors* 3H 15
Walkhampton. *Devn* 2B 8
Walkington. *E Yor* 1C 94
Walkley. *S Yor* 2H 85
Walk Mill. *Lanc* 1G 91
Wall. *Corn* 3D 4
Wall. *Nmbd* 3C 114
Wall. *Staf* 5F 73
Wallaceton. *Dum* 1F 111
Wallacetown. *Shet* 6E 173
Wallacetown. *S Ayr*
nr. Ayr 2C 116
nr. Dailly 4B 116
Wallands Park. *E Sus* 4F 27
Wallasey. *Mers* 1E 83
Wallaston Green. *Pemb* 4D 42
Wallbrook. *W Mid* 1D 60
Wallcrouch. *E Sus* 2A 28
Wall End. *Cumb* 1B 96
Wallend. *Medw* 3C 40
Wall Heath. *W Mid* 2C 60
Wallingford. *Oxon* 3E 36
Wallington. *G Lon* 4D 39
Wallington. *Hants* 2D 16
Wallington. *Herts* 2C 52
Wallis. *Pemb* 2E 43
Wallisdown. *Bour* 3F 15
Walliswood. *Surr* 2C 26
Wall Nook. *Dur* 5F 115
Walls. *Shet* 7D 173
Wallsend. *Tyne* 3G 115
Wallsworth. *Glos* 3D 48
Wall under Heywood. *Shrp* 1H 59
Wallyford. *E Lot* 2G 129
Walmer. *Kent* 5H 41
Walmer Bridge. *Lanc* 2C 90
Walmersley. *G Man* 3G 91
Walmley. *W Mid* 1F 61
Walnut Grove. *Per* 1D 136
Walpole. *Suff* 3F 67
Walpole Cross Keys. *Norf* 4E 77
Walpole Gate. *Norf* 4E 77
Walpole Highway. *Norf* 4E 77
Walpole Marsh. *Norf* 4D 77
Walpole St Andrew. *Norf* 4E 77
Walpole St Peter. *Norf* 4E 77
Walsall. *W Mid* 1E 61
Walsall Wood. *W Mid* 5E 73
Walsden. *W Yor* 2H 91
Walsgrave on Sowe. *W Mid* 2A 62
Walsham le Willows. *Suff* 3C 66
Walshaw. *G Man* 3F 91
Walshford. *N Yor* 4G 99
Walsoken. *Norf* 4D 76
Walston. *S Lan* 5D 128
Walsworth. *Herts* 2B 52
Walter's Ash. *Buck* 2G 37
Walterston. *V Glam* 4D 32
Walterstone. *Here* 3G 47
Waltham. *Kent* 1F 29
Waltham. *NE Lin* 4F 95
Waltham Abbey. *Essx* 5D 53
Waltham Chase. *Hants* 1D 16
Waltham Cross. *Herts* 5D 52
Waltham on the Wolds.
Leics 3F 75
Waltham St Lawrence. *Wind* 4G 37
Waltham's Cross. *Essx* 2G 53
Walthamstow. *G Lon* 2E 39
Walton. *Cumb* 3G 113
Walton. *Derbs* 4A 86
Walton. *Leics* 2C 62
Walton. *Mers* 1F 83
Walton. *Mil* 2G 51
Walton. *Pet* 5A 76
Walton. *Powy* 5E 59
Walton. *Som* 3H 21
Walton. *Staf*
nr. Eccleshall 3C 72
nr. Stone 2C 72
Walton. *Suff* 2F 55
Walton. *Telf* 4H 71
Walton. *Warw* 5G 61
Walton. *W Yor*
nr. Wakefield 3D 92
nr. Wetherby 5G 99
Walton Cardiff. *Glos* 2E 49
Walton East. *Pemb* 2E 43
Walton Elm. *Dors* 1C 14
Walton Highway. *Norf* 4D 77
Walton in Gordano. *N Som* 4H 33
Walton-le-Dale. *Lanc* 2D 90
Walton-on-Thames. *Surr* 4C 38
Walton-on-the-Hill. *Staf* 3D 72
Walton on the Hill. *Surr* 5D 38
Walton-on-the-Naze. *Essx* 3F 55
Walton on the Wolds. *Leics* 4C 74
Walton-on-Trent. *Derbs* 4G 73
Walton West. *Pemb* 3C 42
Walwick. *Nmbd* 2C 114
Walworth. *Darl* 3F 105
Walworth Gate. *Darl* 2F 105
Walwyn's Castle. *Pemb* 3C 42
Wambrook. *Som* 2F 13
Wampool. *Cumb* 4D 112
Wanborough. *Surr* 1A 26
Wanborough. *Swin* 3H 35
Wandel. *S Lan* 2B 118
Wandsworth. *G Lon* 3D 38
Wangford. *Suff*
nr. Lakenheath 2G 65
nr. Southwold 3G 67
Wanlip. *Leics* 4C 74
Wanlockhead. *Dum* 3A 118
Wannock. *E Sus* 5G 27
Wansford. *E Yor* 4E 101
Wansford. *Pet* 1H 63
Wanshurst Green. *Kent* 1B 28
Wanstead. *G Lon* 2F 39
Wanstrow. *Som* 2C 22
Wanswell. *Glos* 5B 48
Wantage. *Oxon* 3C 36
Wapley. *S Glo* 4C 34
Wappenbury. *Warw* 4A 62
Wappenham. *Nptn* 1E 51
Warbleton. *E Sus* 4H 27
Warblington. *Hants* 2F 17
Warborough. *Oxon* 2D 36
Warboys. *Cambs* 2C 64
Warbreck. *Bkpl* 1B 90
Warbstow. *Corn* 3C 10
Warburton. *G Man* 2B 84
Warcop. *Cumb* 3A 104
Warden. *Kent* 3E 40
Warden. *Nmbd* 3C 114
Ward End. *W Mid* 2F 61
Ward Green. *Suff* 4C 66
Ward Green Cross. *Lanc* 1E 91
Wardhedges. *C Beds* 2A 52
Wardhouse. *Abers* 5C 160
Wardington. *Oxon* 1C 50
Wardle. *Ches E* 5A 84
Wardle. *G Man* 3H 91
Wardley. *Rut* 5F 75
Wardley. *W Sus* 4G 25
Wardlow. *Derbs* 3F 85
Wardsend. *Ches E* 2D 84
Wardy Hill. *Cambs* 2D 64
Ware. *Herts* 4D 52
Ware. *Kent* 4G 41
Wareham. *Dors* 4E 15
Warehorne. *Kent* 2D 28
Warenford. *Nmbd* 2F 121
Waren Mill. *Nmbd* 1F 121
Warenton. *Nmbd* 1F 121
Wareside. *Herts* 4D 53
Waresley. *Cambs* 5B 64
Waresley. *Worc* 4C 60
Warfield. *Brac* 4G 37
Warfleet. *Devn* 3E 9
Wargate. *Linc* 2B 76
Wargrave. *Wok* 4F 37
Warham. *Norf* 1B 78
Wark. *Nmbd*
nr. Coldstream 1C 120
nr. Hexham 2B 114
Warkleigh. *Devn* 4G 19
Warkton. *Nptn* 3F 63
Warkworth. *Nptn* 1C 50
Warkworth. *Nmbd* 4G 121
Warlaby. *N Yor* 5A 106
Warland. *W Yor* 2H 91
Warleggan. *Corn* 2F 7
Warlingham. *Surr* 5E 39
Warmanbie. *Dum* 3C 112
Warmfield. *W Yor* 2D 93
Warmingham. *Ches E* 4B 84
Warminghurst. *W Sus* 4C 26
Warmington. *Nptn* 1H 63
Warmington. *Warw* 1C 50
Warminster. *Wilts* 2D 23
Warmley. *S Glo* 4B 34
Warmsworth. *S Yor* 4F 93
Warmwell. *Dors* 4C 14
Warndon. *Worc* 5C 60
Warners End. *Herts* 5A 52
Warnford. *Hants* 4E 24
Warnham. *W Sus* 2C 26
Warningcamp. *W Sus* 5B 26
Warninglid. *W Sus* 3D 26
Warren. *Ches E* 3C 84
Warren. *Pemb* 5D 42
Warrenby. *Red C* 2C 106
Warren Corner. *Hants*
nr. Aldershot 2G 25
nr. Petersfield 4F 25
Warren Row. *Wind* 3G 37
Warren Street. *Kent* 5D 40
Warrington. *Mil* 5F 63
Warrington. *Warr* 2A 84
Warsash. *Hants* 2C 16
Warse. *High* 1F 169
Warslow. *Staf* 5E 85
Warsop. *Notts* 4C 86
Warsop Vale. *Notts* 4C 86
Warter. *E Yor* 4C 100
Warthermarske. *N Yor* 2E 98
Warthill. *N Yor* 4A 100

Wartling. E Sus ...5A 28
Wartnaby. Leics ...3E 74
Warton. Lanc
  nr. Carnforth ...2D 97
  nr. Freckleton ...2C 90
Warton. Nmbd ...4E 121
Warton. Warw ...5G 73
Warwick. Warw ...4G 61
Warwick Bridge. Cumb ...4F 113
Warwick-on-Eden. Cumb ...4F 113
Warwick Wold. Surr ...5E 39
Wasbister. Orkn ...4C 172
Wasdale Head. Cumb ...4C 102
Wash. Derbs ...2E 85
Washaway. Corn ...2E 7
Washbourne. Devn ...3D 9
Washbrook. Suff ...1E 54
Wash Common. W Ber ...5C 36
Washerwall. Staf ...1D 72
Washfield. Devn ...1C 12
Washfold. N Yor ...4D 104
Washford. Som ...2D 20
Washford Pyne. Devn ...1B 12
Washingborough. Linc ...3H 87
Washington. Tyne ...4G 115
Washington. W Sus ...4C 26
Washington Village. Tyne ...4G 115
Waskerley. Dur ...5D 114
Wasperton. Warw ...5G 61
Wasp Green. Surr ...1E 27
Wasps Nest. Linc ...4H 87
Wass. N Yor ...2H 99
Watchet. Som ...2D 20
Watchfield. Oxon ...2H 35
Watchgate. Cumb ...5G 103
Watchhill. Cumb ...5C 112
Watcombe. Torb ...2F 9
Watendlath. Cumb ...3D 102
Water. Devn ...4A 12
Water. Lanc ...2G 91
Waterbeach. Cambs ...4D 65
Waterbeach. W Sus ...2G 17
Waterbeck. Dum ...2D 112
Waterditch. Hants ...3G 15
Water End. C Beds ...2A 52
Water End. E Yor ...1A 94
Water End. Essx ...1F 53
Water End. Herts
  nr. Hatfield ...5C 52
  nr. Hemel Hempstead ...4A 52
Waterfall. Staf ...5E 85
Waterfoot. E Ren ...4G 127
Waterfoot. Lanc ...2G 91
Waterford. Herts ...4D 52
Water Fryston. W Yor ...2E 93
Waterhead. Cumb ...4E 103
Waterhead. E Ayr ...3E 117
Waterhead. S Ayr ...5C 116
Waterheads. Bord ...4F 129
Waterhouses. Dur ...5E 115
Waterhouses. Staf ...5E 85
Wateringbury. Kent ...5A 40
Waterlane. Glos ...5E 49
Waterlip. Som ...2B 22
Waterloo. Cphy ...3E 33
Waterloo. Corn ...5B 10
Waterloo. Here ...1G 47
Waterloo. High ...1E 147
Waterloo. Mers ...1F 83
Waterloo. Norf ...4E 78
Waterloo. N Lan ...4B 128
Waterloo. Pemb ...4D 42
Waterloo. Per ...5H 143
Waterloo. Pool ...3F 15
Waterloo. Shrp ...2G 71
Waterlooville. Hants ...2E 17
Watermead. Buck ...4G 51
Watermillock. Cumb ...2F 103
Water Newton. Cambs ...1A 64
Water Orton. Warw ...1F 61
Waterperry. Oxon ...5E 51
Waterrow. Som ...4D 20
Watersfield. W Sus ...4B 26
Waterside. Buck ...5H 51
Waterside. Cambs ...3E 65
Waterside. Cumb ...5D 112
Waterside. E Ayr
  nr. Ayr ...4D 116
  nr. Kilmarnock ...5F 127
Waterside. E Dun ...2H 127
Waterstein. High ...4A 154
Waterstock. Oxon ...5E 51
Waterston. Pemb ...4D 42
Water Stratford. Buck ...2E 51
Waters Upton. Telf ...4A 72
Water Yeat. Cumb ...1B 96
Watford. Herts ...1C 38
Watford. Nptn ...4D 62
Wath. Cumb ...4H 103
Wath. N Yor
  nr. Pateley Bridge ...3D 98
  nr. Ripon ...2F 99
Wath Brow. Cumb ...3B 102
Wath upon Dearne. S Yor ...4E 93
Watlington. Norf ...4F 77
Watlington. Oxon ...2E 37
Watten. High ...3E 169
Wattisfield. Suff ...3C 66
Wattisham. Suff ...5C 66
Wattlesborough Heath. Shrp ...4F 71
Watton. Dors ...3H 13
Watton. E Yor ...4E 101
Watton. Norf ...5B 78
Watton at Stone. Herts ...4C 52
Wattston. N Lan ...2A 128

Wattstown. Rhon ...2D 32
Wattsville. Cphy ...2F 33
Wauldby. E Yor ...2C 94
Waulkmill. Abers ...4D 152
Waun. Powy ...4E 71
Y Waun. Wrex ...2E 71
Waunarlwydd. Swan ...3F 31
Waun Fawr. Cdgn ...2F 57
Waunfawr. Gwyn ...5E 81
Waungilwen. Carm ...1H 43
Waun-Lwyd. Blae ...5E 47
Waun y Clyn. Carm ...5E 45
Wavendon. Mil ...2H 51
Waverbridge. Cumb ...5D 112
Waverley. Surr ...2G 25
Waverton. Ches W ...4G 83
Waverton. Cumb ...5D 112
Wavertree. Mers ...2F 83
Wawne. E Yor ...1D 94
Waxham. Norf ...3G 79
Waxholme. E Yor ...2G 95
Wayford. Som ...2H 13
Way Head. Cambs ...2D 65
Waytown. Dors ...3H 13
Way Village. Devn ...1B 12
Wdig. Pemb ...1D 42
Wealdstone. G Lon ...2C 38
Weardley. W Yor ...5E 99
Weare. Som ...1H 21
Weare Giffard. Devn ...4E 19
Wearhead. Dur ...1B 104
Wearne. Som ...4H 21
Weasdale. Cumb ...4H 103
Weasenham All Saints. Norf ...3H 77
Weasenham St Peter. Norf ...3A 78
Weaverham. Ches W ...3A 84
Weaverthorpe. N Yor ...2D 100
Webheath. Worc ...4E 61
Webton. Here ...2H 47
Wedderlairs. Abers ...5F 161
Weddington. Warw ...1A 62
Wedhampton. Wilts ...1F 23
Wedmore. Som ...2H 21
Wednesbury. W Mid ...1D 61
Wednesfield. W Mid ...5D 72
Weecar. Notts ...4F 87
Weedon. Buck ...4G 51
Weedon Bec. Nptn ...5D 62
Weedon Lois. Nptn ...1E 50
Weeford. Staf ...5F 73
Week. Devn
  nr. Barnstaple ...4F 19
  nr. Okehampton ...2G 11
  nr. South Molton ...1H 11
  nr. Totnes ...2D 9
Week. Som ...3C 20
Weeke. Devn ...2A 12
Weeke. Hants ...3C 24
Week Green. Corn ...3C 10
Weekley. Nptn ...2F 63
Week St Mary. Corn ...3C 10
Weel. E Yor ...1D 94
Weeley. Essx ...3E 55
Weeley Heath. Essx ...3E 55
Weem. Per ...4F 143
Weeping Cross. Staf ...3D 72
Weethly. Warw ...5E 61
Weeting. Norf ...2G 65
Weeton. E Yor ...2G 95
Weeton. Lanc ...1B 90
Weeton. N Yor ...5E 99
Weetwood Hall. Nmbd ...2E 121
Weir. Lanc ...2G 91
Welborne. Norf ...4C 78
Welbourn. Linc ...5G 87
Welburn. N Yor
  nr. Kirkbymoorside ...1A 100
  nr. Malton ...3B 100
Welbury. N Yor ...4A 106
Welby. Linc ...2G 75
Welches Dam. Cambs ...2D 64
Welcombe. Devn ...1C 10
Weld Bank. Lanc ...3D 90
Weldon. Nptn ...2G 63
Weldon. Nmbd ...5F 121
Welford. Nptn ...2D 62
Welford. W Ber ...4C 36
Welford-on-Avon. Warw ...5F 61
Welham. Leics ...1E 63
Welham. Notts ...2E 87
Welham Green. Herts ...5C 52
Well. Hants ...2F 25
Well. Linc ...3D 88
Well. N Yor ...1E 99
Welland. Worc ...1C 48
Wellbank. Ang ...5D 144
Well Bottom. Dors ...1E 15
Welldale. Dum ...3C 112
Wellesbourne. Warw ...5G 61
Well Hill. Kent ...4F 39
Wellhouse. W Ber ...4D 36
Welling. G Lon ...3F 39
Wellingborough. Nptn ...4F 63
Wellingham. Norf ...3A 78
Wellingore. Linc ...5G 87
Wellington. Cumb ...4B 102
Wellington. Here ...1H 47
Wellington. Som ...4E 21
Wellington. Telf ...4A 72
Wellington Heath. Here ...1C 48
Wellow. Bath ...1C 22
Wellow. IOW ...4B 16
Wellow. Notts ...4D 86
Wellpond Green. Herts ...3E 53
Wells. Som ...2A 22

Wellsborough. Leics ...5A 74
Wells Green. Ches E ...5A 84
Wells-next-the-Sea. Norf ...1B 78
Wellswood. Torb ...2F 9
Wellwood. Fife ...1D 129
Welney. Norf ...1E 65
Welsford. Devn ...4C 18
Welshampton. Shrp ...2G 71
Welsh End. Shrp ...2H 71
Welsh Frankton. Shrp ...2F 71
Welsh Hook. Pemb ...2D 42
Welsh Newton. Here ...4H 47
Welsh Newton Common.
  Here ...4A 48
Welshpool. Powy ...5E 70
Welsh St Donats. V Glam ...4D 32
Welton. Bath ...1B 22
Welton. Cumb ...5E 113
Welton. E Yor ...2C 94
Welton. Linc ...2H 87
Welton. Nptn ...4C 62
Welton le Marsh. Linc ...4D 88
Welton le Wold. Linc ...2B 88
Welwick. E Yor ...2G 95
Welwyn. Herts ...4C 52
Welwyn Garden City. Herts ...4C 52
Wem. Shrp ...3H 71
Wembdon. Som ...3F 21
Wembley. G Lon ...2C 38
Wembury. Devn ...4B 8
Wembworthy. Devn ...2G 11
Wemyss Bay. Inv ...2C 126
Wenallt. Cdgn ...3F 57
Wenallt. Gwyn ...1B 70
Wendens Ambo. Essx ...2F 53
Wendlebury. Oxon ...4D 50
Wendling. Norf ...4B 78
Wendover. Buck ...5G 51
Wendron. Corn ...5A 6
Wendy. Cambs ...1D 52
Wenfordbridge. Corn ...5A 10
Wenhaston. Suff ...3G 67
Wennington. Cambs ...3B 64
Wennington. G Lon ...2G 39
Wennington. Lanc ...2F 97
Wensley. Derbs ...4G 85
Wensley. N Yor ...1C 98
Wentbridge. W Yor ...3E 93
Wentnor. Shrp ...1F 59
Wentworth. Cambs ...3D 65
Wentworth. S Yor ...1A 86
Wenvoe. V Glam ...4E 32
Weobley. Here ...5G 59
Weobley Marsh. Here ...5G 59
Wepham. W Sus ...5B 26
Wereham. Norf ...5F 77
Wergs. W Mid ...5C 72
Wern. Gwyn ...1E 69
Wern. Powy
  nr. Brecon ...4E 46
  nr. Guilsfield ...4E 71
  nr. Llangadfan ...4B 70
  nr. Llanymynech ...3E 71
Wernffrwd. Swan ...3E 31
Wernyrheolydd. Mon ...4G 47
Werrington. Corn ...4D 10
Werrington. Pet ...5A 76
Werrington. Staf ...1D 72
Wervin. Ches W ...3G 83
Wesham. Lanc ...1C 90
Wessington. Derbs ...5A 86
West Aberthaw. V Glam ...5D 32
West Acre. Norf ...4G 77
West Allerdean. Nmbd ...5F 131
West Alvington. Devn ...4D 8
West Amesbury. Wilts ...2G 23
West Anstey. Devn ...4B 20
West Appleton. N Yor ...5F 105
West Ardsley. W Yor ...2C 92
West Arthurlie. E Ren ...4F 127
West Ashby. Linc ...3B 88
West Ashling. W Sus ...2G 17
West Ashton. Wilts ...1D 23
West Auckland. Dur ...2E 105
West Ayton. N Yor ...1D 101
West Bagborough. Som ...3E 21
West Bank. Hal ...2H 83
West Barkwith. Linc ...2A 88
West Barnby. N Yor ...3F 107
West Barns. E Lot ...2C 130
West Barsham. Norf ...2B 78
West Bay. Dors ...3H 13
West Beckham. Norf ...2D 78
West Bennan. N Ayr ...3D 123
Westbere. Kent ...4F 41
West Bergholt. Essx ...3C 54
West Bexington. Dors ...4A 14
West Bilney. Norf ...4G 77
West Blackdene. Dur ...1B 104
West Blatchington. Brig ...5D 27
Westborough. Linc ...1F 75
Westbourne. Bour ...3F 15
Westbourne. W Sus ...2F 17
West Bowling. W Yor ...1B 92
West Brabourne. Kent ...1E 29
West Bradford. Lanc ...5G 97
West Bradley. Som ...3A 22
West Bretton. W Yor ...3C 92
West Bridgford. Notts ...2C 74
West Briggs. Norf ...4F 77
West Bromwich. W Mid ...1E 61
Westbrook. Here ...1G 47
Westbrook. Kent ...3H 41
Westbrook. Wilts ...5E 35

West Buckland. Devn
  nr. Barnstaple ...3G 19
  nr. Thurlestone ...4C 8
West Buckland. Som ...4E 21
West Burnside. Abers ...1G 145
West Burrafirth. Shet ...6D 173
West Burton. N Yor ...1C 98
West Burton. W Sus ...4B 26
Westbury. Buck ...2E 50
Westbury. Shrp ...5F 71
Westbury. Wilts ...1D 22
Westbury Leigh. Wilts ...1D 22
Westbury-on-Severn. Glos ...4C 48
Westbury on Trym. Bris ...4A 34
Westbury-sub-Mendip.
  Som ...2A 22
West Butsfield. Dur ...5E 115
West Butterwick. N Lin ...4B 94
Westby. Linc ...3G 75
West Byfleet. Surr ...4B 38
West Caister. Norf ...4H 79
West Calder. W Lot ...3D 128
West Camel. Som ...4A 22
West Carr. N Lin ...4H 93
West Chaldon. Dors ...4C 14
West Challow. Oxon ...3B 36
West Charleton. Devn ...4D 8
West Chelborough. Dors ...2A 14
West Chevington. Nmbd ...5G 121
West Chiltington. W Sus ...4B 26
West Chiltington Common.
  W Sus ...4B 26
West Chinnock. Som ...1H 13
West Chisenbury. Wilts ...1G 23
West Clandon. Surr ...5B 38
West Cliffe. Kent ...1H 29
West Clyne. High ...3F 165
West Coker. Som ...1A 14
Westcombe. Som
  nr. Evercreech ...3B 22
  nr. Somerton ...4H 21
West Compton. Dors ...3A 14
West Compton. Som ...2A 22
West Cornforth. Dur ...1A 106
Westcot. Oxon ...3B 36
Westcott. Buck ...4F 51
Westcott. Devn ...2D 12
Westcott. Surr ...1C 26
Westcott Barton. Oxon ...3C 50
West Cowick. E Yor ...2G 93
West Cranmore. Som ...2B 22
West Croftmore. High ...2D 150
West Cross. Swan ...4F 31
West Cullerlie. Abers ...3E 153
West Culvennan. Dum ...3H 109
West Curry. Corn ...3C 10
West Curthwaite. Cumb ...5E 113
Westdean. E Sus ...5G 27
West Dean. W Sus ...1G 17
West Dean. Wilts ...4A 24
West Deeping. Linc ...5A 76
West Derby. Mers ...1F 83
West Dereham. Norf ...5F 77
West Down. Devn ...2F 19
Westdowns. Corn ...4A 10
West Drayton. G Lon ...3B 38
West Drayton. Notts ...3E 86
West Dunnet. High ...1E 169
West Ella. E Yor ...2D 94
West End. Bed ...5G 63
West End. Cambs ...1D 64
West End. Dors ...2E 15
West End. E Yor
  nr. Kilham ...3E 101
  nr. Preston ...1E 95
  nr. South Cove ...1C 94
  nr. Ulrome ...4F 101
West End. G Lon ...2D 39
West End. Hants ...1C 16
West End. Herts ...5C 52
West End. Kent ...4F 41
West End. Linc ...1C 76
West End. Norf ...4H 79
West End. N Som ...5H 33
West End. N Yor ...4D 98
West End. S Glo ...3C 34
West End. S Lan ...5C 128
West End. Surr ...4A 38
West End. Wilts ...4E 23
West End. Wind ...4G 37
West End Green. Hants ...5E 37
Westenhanger. Kent ...2F 29
Wester Aberchalder. High ...2H 149
Wester Balgedie. Per ...3D 136
Wester Brae. High ...2A 158
Wester Culbeuchly. Abers ...2D 160
Westerdale. High ...3D 168
Westerdale. N Yor ...4D 106
Wester Dechmont. W Lot ...2D 128
Wester Fearn. High ...5D 164
Westerfield. Suff ...1E 55
Wester Galcantray. High ...4C 158
Westergate. W Sus ...5A 26
Wester Gruinards. High ...4C 164
Westerham. Kent ...5F 39
Wester Leirgs. S Glo ...4C 34
Westerloch. High ...3E 169
Wester Mandally. High ...3E 149
Wester Quarff. Shet ...8F 173
Wester Rarichie. High ...1C 158
Wester Shian. Per ...5F 143
Wester Skeld. Shet ...7D 173
Westerton. Ang ...3F 145

Westerton. Dur ...1F 105
Westerton. W Sus ...2G 17
Westerwick. Shet ...7D 173
West Farleigh. Kent ...5B 40
West Farndon. Nptn ...5C 62
West Felton. Shrp ...3F 71
Westfield. Cumb ...2A 102
Westfield. E Sus ...4C 28
Westfield. High ...2C 168
Westfield. Norf ...5B 78
Westfield. N Lan ...2A 128
Westfield. W Lot ...2C 128
Westfields. Dors ...2C 14
Westfields of Rattray. Per ...4A 144
West Fleetham. Nmbd ...2F 121
Westford. Som ...4E 20
West Garforth. W Yor ...1D 93
Westgate. Dur ...1C 104
Westgate. Norf ...1B 78
Westgate. N Lin ...4A 94
Westgate on Sea. Kent ...3H 41
West Ginge. Oxon ...3C 36
West Grafton. Wilts ...5H 35
West Green. Hants ...1F 25
West Grimstead. Wilts ...4H 23
West Grinstead. W Sus ...3C 26
West Haddlesey. N Yor ...2F 93
West Haddon. Nptn ...3D 62
West Hagbourne. Oxon ...3D 36
West Hagley. Worc ...2D 60
West Hall. Cumb ...3G 113
Westhall. Suff ...2G 67
West Hallam. Derbs ...1B 74
Westhall Terrace. Ang ...5D 144
West Halton. N Lin ...2C 94
Westham. Dors ...5B 14
Westham. E Sus ...5H 27
West Ham. G Lon ...2E 39
Westham. Som ...2H 21
Westhampnett. W Sus ...2G 17
West Handley. Derbs ...3A 86
West Hanney. Oxon ...2C 36
West Hanningfield. Essx ...1B 40
West Hardwick. W Yor ...3E 93
West Harptree. Bath ...1A 22
West Harting. W Sus ...4F 25
West Harton. Tyne ...3G 115
West Hatch. Som ...4F 21
Westhay. Som ...2H 21
Westhead. Lanc ...4C 90
West Head. Norf ...5E 77
West Heath. Hants
  nr. Basingstoke ...1D 24
  nr. Farnborough ...1G 25
West Helmsdale. High ...2H 165
West Hendred. Oxon ...3C 36
West Heogaland. Shet ...4D 173
West Heslerton. N Yor ...2D 100
West Hewish. N Som ...5G 33
Westhide. Here ...1A 48
Westhill. Abers ...3F 153
West Hill. Devn ...3D 12
West Hill. E Yor ...3F 101
Westhill. High ...4B 158
West Hill. N Som ...4H 33
West Hill. W Sus ...2E 27
West Hoathly. W Sus ...2E 27
West Holme. Dors ...4D 15
Westhope. Here ...5G 59
Westhope. Shrp ...2G 59
West Horndon. Essx ...2H 39
Westhorp. Nptn ...5C 62
Westhorpe. Linc ...2B 76
Westhorpe. Suff ...4C 66
West Horrington. Som ...2A 22
West Horsley. Surr ...5B 38
West Horton. Nmbd ...1E 121
West Hougham. Kent ...1G 29
Westhoughton. G Man ...4E 91
West Houlland. Shet ...6D 173
Westhouse. N Yor ...2F 97
Westhouses. Derbs ...5B 86
West Howe. Bour ...3F 15
Westhumble. Surr ...5C 38
West Huntspill. Som ...2G 21
West Hyde. Herts ...1B 38
West Hynish. Arg ...5A 138
West Hythe. Kent ...2F 29
West Ilsley. W Ber ...3C 36
Westing. Shet ...1G 173
West Keal. Linc ...4C 88
West Kennett. Wilts ...5G 35
West Kilbride. N Ayr ...5D 126
West Kingsdown. Kent ...4G 39
West Kington. Wilts ...4D 34
West Kirby. Mers ...2E 82
West Knapton. N Yor ...2C 100
West Knighton. Dors ...4C 14
West Knoyle. Wilts ...3D 22
West Kyloe. Nmbd ...5G 131
Westlake. Devn ...3C 8
West Lambrook. Som ...1H 13
West Langdon. Kent ...1H 29
West Langwell. High ...3D 164
West Lavington. W Sus ...4G 25
West Lavington. Wilts ...1F 23
West Layton. N Yor ...4E 105
West Leake. Notts ...3C 74
West Learmouth. Nmbd ...1C 120
West Leigh. Devn ...2G 11
Westleigh. Devn
  nr. Bideford ...4E 19
  nr. Tiverton ...1D 12
Westleigh. G Man ...4E 91
West Leith. Herts ...4H 51

Westleton—Widdrington Station

Westleton. *Suff* 4G **67**
West Lexham. *Norf* 4H **77**
Westley. *Shrp* 5F **71**
Westley. *Suff* 4H **65**
Westley Waterless. *Cambs* 5F **65**
West Lilling. *N Yor* 3A **100**
West Lingo. *Fife* 3G **137**
Westlington. *Buck* 4F **51**
Westlinton. *Cumb* 3E **113**
West Linton. *Bord* 4E **129**
West Littleton. *S Glo* 4C **34**
West Looe. *Corn* 3G **7**
West Lulworth. *Dors* 4D **14**
West Lutton. *N Yor* 3D **100**
West Lydford. *Som* 3A **22**
West Lyng. *Som* 4G **21**
West Lynn. *Norf* 4F **77**
West Mains. *Per* 2B **136**
West Malling. *Kent* 5A **40**
West Malvern. *Worc* 1C **48**
Westmancote. *Worc* 2E **49**
West Marden. *W Sus* 1F **17**
West Markham. *Notts* 3E **86**
Westmarsh. *Kent* 4G **41**
West Marsh. *NE Lin* 4F **95**
West Marton. *N Yor* 4A **98**
West Meon. *Hants* 4E **25**
West Mersea. *Essx* 4D **54**
Westmeston. *E Sus* 4E **27**
Westmill. *Herts*
nr. Buntingford 3D **52**
nr. Hitchin 2B **52**
West Milton. *Dors* 3A **14**
Westminster. *G Lon* 3D **39**
West Molesey. *Surr* 4C **38**
West Monkton. *Som* 4F **21**
Westmoor End. *Cumb* 1B **102**
West Moors. *Dors* 2F **15**
West Morden. *Dors* 3E **15**
West Muir. *Ang* 2E **145**
Westmuir. *Ang* 3C **144**
West Murkle. *High* 2D **168**
West Ness. *N Yor* 2A **100**
Westness. *Orkn* 5C **172**
Westnewton. *Cumb* 5C **112**
West Newton. *E Yor* 1E **95**
West Newton. *Norf* 3F **77**
Westnewton. *Nmbd* 1D **120**
West Newton. *Som* 4F **21**
West Norwood. *G Lon* 3E **39**
Westoe. *Tyne* 3G **115**
West Ogwell. *Devn* 2E **9**
Weston. *Bath* 5C **34**
Weston. *Ches E*
nr. Crewe 5B **84**
nr. Macclesfield 3C **84**
Weston. *Devn*
nr. Honiton 2E **13**
nr. Sidmouth 4E **13**
Weston. *Dors*
nr. Weymouth 5B **14**
nr. Yeovil 2A **14**
Weston. *Hal* 2H **83**
Weston. *Hants* 4F **25**
Weston. *Here* 5F **59**
Weston. *Herts* 2C **52**
Weston. *Linc* 3B **76**
Weston. *Nptn* 1D **50**
Weston. *Notts* 4E **87**
Weston. *Shrp*
nr. Bridgnorth 1H **59**
nr. Knighton 3F **59**
nr. Wem 3H **71**
Weston. *S Lan* 5D **128**
Weston. *Staf* 3D **73**
Weston. *Suff* 2G **67**
Weston. *W Ber* 4B **36**
Weston Bampfylde. *Som* 4B **22**
Weston Beggard. *Here* 1A **48**
Westonbirt. *Glos* 3D **34**
Weston by Welland. *Nptn* 1E **63**
Weston Colville. *Cambs* 5F **65**
Westoncommon. *Shrp* 3G **71**
Weston Coyney. *Stoke* 1D **72**
Weston Ditch. *Suff* 3F **65**
Weston Favell. *Nptn* 4E **63**
Weston Green. *Cambs* 5F **65**
Weston Green. *Norf* 4D **78**
Weston Heath. *Shrp* 4B **72**
Weston Hills. *Linc* 4B **76**
Weston in Arden. *Warw* 2A **62**
Westoning. *C Beds* 2A **52**
Weston in Gordano. *N Som* 4H **33**
Weston Jones. *Staf* 3B **72**
Weston Longville. *Norf* 4D **78**
Weston Lullingfields. *Shrp* 3G **71**
Weston-on-Avon. *Warw* 5F **61**
Weston-on-the-Green. *Oxon* 4D **50**
Weston-on-Trent. *Derbs* 3B **74**
Weston Patrick. *Hants* 2E **25**
Weston Rhyn. *Shrp* 2E **71**
Weston-sub-Edge. *Glos* 1G **49**
Weston-super-Mare. *N Som* 5G **33**
Weston Town. *Som* 2C **22**
Weston Turville. *Buck* 4G **51**
Weston under Lizard. *Staf* 4C **72**
Weston under Penyard. *Here* 3B **48**
Weston under Wetherley.
Warw 4A **62**
Weston Underwood. *Derbs* 1G **73**
Weston Underwood. *Mil* 5F **63**
Westonzoyland. *Som* 3G **21**
West Orchard. *Dors* 1D **14**
West Overton. *Wilts* 5G **35**
Westow. *N Yor* 3B **100**
Westown. *Per* 1E **137**
West Panson. *Devn* 3D **10**
West Park. *Hart* 1B **106**
West Parley. *Dors* 3F **15**
West Peckham. *Kent* 5H **39**
West Pelton. *Dur* 4F **115**
West Pennard. *Som* 3A **22**
West Pentire. *Corn* 2B **6**
West Perry. *Cambs* 4A **64**
West Pitcorthie. *Fife* 3H **137**
West Plean. *Stir* 1B **128**
West Poringland. *Norf* 5E **79**
West Porlock. *Som* 2B **20**
Westport. *Som* 1G **13**
West Putford. *Devn* 1D **10**
West Quantoxhead. *Som* 2E **20**
Westra. *V Glam* 4E **33**
West Rainton. *Dur* 5G **115**
West Rasen. *Linc* 2H **87**
West Ravendale. *NE Lin* 1B **88**
Westray Airport. *Orkn* 2D **172**
West Raynham. *Norf* 3A **78**
Westrigg. *W Lot* 3C **128**
West Rounton. *N Yor* 4B **106**
West Row. *Suff* 3F **65**
West Rudham. *Norf* 3H **77**
West Runton. *Norf* 1D **78**
Westruther. *Bord* 4C **130**
Westry. *Cambs* 1C **64**
West Saltoun. *E Lot* 3A **130**
West Sandford. *Devn* 2B **12**
West Sandwick. *Shet* 3F **173**
West Scrafton. *N Yor* 1C **98**
Westside. *Orkn* 5C **172**
West Sleekburn. *Nmbd* 1F **115**
West Somerton. *Norf* 4G **79**
West Stafford. *Dors* 4C **14**
West Stockwith. *Notts* 1E **87**
West Stoke. *W Sus* 2G **17**
West Stonesdale. *N Yor* 4B **104**
West Stoughton. *Som* 2H **21**
West Stour. *Dors* 4C **22**
West Stourmouth. *Kent* 4G **41**
West Stow. *Suff* 3H **65**
West Stowell. *Wilts* 5G **35**
West Strathan. *High* 2F **167**
West Stratton. *Hants* 2D **24**
West Street. *Kent* 5D **40**
West Tanfield. *N Yor* 2E **99**
West Taphouse. *Corn* 2F **7**
West Tarbert. *Arg* 3G **125**
West Thirston. *Nmbd* 4F **121**
West Thorney. *W Sus* 2F **17**
West Thurrock. *Thur* 3G **39**
West Tilbury. *Thur* 3A **40**
West Tisted. *Hants* 4E **25**
West Tofts. *Norf* 1H **65**
West Torrington. *Linc* 2A **88**
West Town. *Bath* 5A **34**
West Town. *Hants* 3F **17**
West Town. *N Som* 5H **33**
West Tytherley. *Hants* 4A **24**
West Tytherton. *Wilts* 4E **35**
West View. *Hart* 1B **106**
Westville. *Notts* 1C **74**
West Walton. *Norf* 4D **76**
Westward. *Cumb* 5D **112**
Westward Ho!. *Devn* 4E **19**
Westwell. *Kent* 1D **28**
Westwell. *Oxon* 5H **49**
Westwell Leacon. *Kent* 1D **28**
West Wellow. *Hants* 1A **16**
West Wemyss. *Fife* 4F **137**
Westwick. *Cambs* 4D **64**
Westwick. *Dur* 3D **104**
Westwick. *Norf* 3E **79**
West Wick. *N Som* 5G **33**
West Wickham. *Cambs* 1G **53**
West Wickham. *G Lon* 4E **39**
West Williamston. *Pemb* 4E **43**
West Willoughby. *Linc* 1G **75**
West Winch. *Norf* 4F **77**
West Winterslow. *Wilts* 3H **23**
West Wittering. *W Sus* 3F **17**
West Witton. *N Yor* 1C **98**
Westwood. *Devn* 3D **12**
Westwood. *Kent* 4H **41**
Westwood. *Pet* 5A **76**
Westwood. *S Lan* 4H **127**
Westwood. *Wilts* 1D **22**
West Woodburn. *Nmbd* 1B **114**
West Woodhay. *W Ber* 5B **36**
West Woodlands. *Som* 2C **22**
West Woodside. *Cumb* 5E **112**
Westwoodside. *N Lin* 1E **87**
West Worldham. *Hants* 3F **25**
West Worlington. *Devn* 1A **12**
West Worthing. *W Sus* 5C **26**
West Wratting. *Cambs* 5F **65**
West Wycombe. *Buck* 2G **37**
West Wylam. *Nmbd* 3E **115**
West Yatton. *Wilts* 4D **34**
West Yell. *Shet* 3F **173**
West Youlstone. *Corn* 1C **10**
Wetheral. *Cumb* 4F **113**
Wetherby. *W Yor* 5G **99**
Wetherden. *Suff* 4C **66**
Wetheringsett. *Suff* 4D **66**
Wethersfield. *Essx* 2H **53**
Wethersta. *Shet* 5E **173**
Wetherup Street. *Suff* 4D **66**
Wetley Rocks. *Staf* 1D **72**
Wettenhall. *Ches E* 4A **84**
Wetton. *Staf* 5F **85**
Wetwang. *E Yor* 4D **100**
Wetwood. *Staf* 2B **72**
Wexcombe. *Wilts* 1A **24**
Wexham Street. *Buck* 2A **38**
Weybourne. *Norf* 1D **78**
Weybourne. *Surr* 2G **25**
Weybread. *Suff* 2E **67**
Weybridge. *Surr* 4B **38**
Weycroft. *Devn* 3G **13**
Weydale. *High* 2D **168**
Weyhill. *Hants* 2B **24**
Weymouth. *Dors* **215** (5B **14**)
Weythel. *Powy* 5E **59**
Whaddon. *Buck* 2G **51**
Whaddon. *Cambs* 1D **52**
Whaddon. *Glos* 4D **48**
Whaddon. *Wilts* 4G **23**
Whale. *Cumb* 2G **103**
Whaley. *Derbs* 3C **86**
Whaley Bridge. *Derbs* 2E **85**
Whaley Thorns. *Derbs* 3C **86**
Whalley. *Lanc* 1F **91**
Whalton. *Nmbd* 1E **115**
Whaplode. *Linc* 3C **76**
Whaplode Drove. *Linc* 4C **76**
Whaplode St Catherine. *Linc* 3C **76**
Wharfe. *N Yor* 3G **97**
Wharles. *Lanc* 1C **90**
Wharley End. *C Beds* 1H **51**
Wharncliffe Side. *S Yor* 1G **85**
Wharram-le-Street. *N Yor* 3C **100**
Wharton. *Ches W* 4A **84**
Wharton. *Here* 5H **59**
Whashton. *N Yor* 4E **105**
Whasset. *Cumb* 1E **97**
Whatcote. *Warw* 1B **50**
Whateley. *Warw* 1G **61**
Whatfield. *Suff* 1D **54**
Whatley. *Som*
nr. Chard 2G **13**
nr. Frome 2C **22**
Whatlington. *E Sus* 4B **28**
Whatmore. *Shrp* 3A **60**
Whatstandwell. *Derbs* 5H **85**
Whatton. *Notts* 2E **75**
Whauphill. *Dum* 5B **110**
Whaw. *N Yor* 4C **104**
Wheatacre. *Norf* 1G **67**
Wheatcroft. *Derbs* 5A **86**
Wheathampstead. *Herts* 4B **52**
Wheathill. *Shrp* 2A **60**
Wheatley. *Devn* 3B **12**
Wheatley. *Hants* 2F **25**
Wheatley. *Oxon* 5E **50**
Wheatley. *S Yor* 4F **93**
Wheatley. *W Yor* 2A **92**
Wheatley Hill. *Dur* 1A **106**
Wheatley Lane. *Lanc* 1G **91**
Wheatley Park. *S Yor* 4F **93**
Wheaton Aston. *Staf* 4C **72**
Wheatstone Park. *Staf* 5C **72**
Wheddon Cross. *Som* 3C **20**
Wheelerstreet. *Surr* 1A **26**
Wheelock. *Ches E* 5B **84**
Wheelock Heath. *Ches E* 5B **84**
Wheelton. *Lanc* 2E **90**
Wheldrake. *York* 5A **100**
Whelford. *Glos* 2G **35**
Whelpley Hill. *Buck* 5H **51**
Whelpo. *Cumb* 1E **102**
Whelston. *Flin* 3E **82**
Whenby. *N Yor* 3A **100**
Whepstead. *Suff* 5H **65**
Wherstead. *Suff* 1E **55**
Wherwell. *Hants* 2B **24**
Wheston. *Derbs* 3F **85**
Whetsted. *Kent* 1A **28**
Whetstone. *G Lon* 1D **38**
Whetstone. *Leics* 1C **62**
Whicham. *Cumb* 1A **96**
Whichford. *Warw* 2B **50**
Whickham. *Tyne* 3F **115**
Whiddon. *Devn* 2E **11**
Whiddon Down. *Devn* 3G **11**
Whigstreet. *Ang* 4D **145**
Whilton. *Nptn* 4D **62**
Whimble. *Devn* 2D **10**
Whimple. *Devn* 3D **12**
Whimpwell Green. *Norf* 3F **79**
Whinburgh. *Norf* 5C **78**
Whin Lane End. *Lanc* 5C **96**
Whinney Hill. *Stoc T* 3A **106**
Whinnyfold. *Abers* 5H **161**
Whippingham. *IOW* 3D **16**
Whipsnade. *C Beds* 4A **52**
Whipton. *Devn* 3C **12**
Whirlow. *S Yor* 2H **85**
Whisby. *Linc* 4G **87**
Whissendine. *Rut* 4F **75**
Whissonsett. *Norf* 3B **78**
Whisterfield. *Ches E* 3C **84**
Whistley Green. *Wok* 4F **37**
Whiston. *Mers* 1G **83**
Whiston. *Nptn* 4F **63**
Whiston. *S Yor* 1B **86**
Whiston. *Staf*
nr. Cheadle 1E **73**
nr. Penkridge 4C **72**
Whiston Cross. *Shrp* 5B **72**
Whiston Eaves. *Staf* 1E **73**
Whitacre Heath. *Warw* 1G **61**
Whitbeck. *Cumb* 1A **96**
Whitbourne. *Here* 5B **60**
Whitburn. *Tyne* 3H **115**
Whitburn. *W Lot* 3C **128**
Whitburn Colliery. *Tyne* 3H **115**
Whitby. *Ches W* 3F **83**
Whitby. *N Yor* 3F **107**
Whitbyheath. *Ches W* 3F **83**
Whitchester. *Bord* 4D **130**
Whitchurch. *Bath* 5B **34**
Whitchurch. *Buck* 3F **51**
Whitchurch. *Card* 4E **33**
Whitchurch. *Devn* 5E **11**
Whitchurch. *Hants* 2C **24**
Whitchurch. *Here* 4A **48**
Whitchurch. *Pemb* 2B **42**
Whitchurch. *Shrp* 1H **71**
Whitchurch Canonicorum.
Dors 3G **13**
Whitchurch Hill. *Oxon* 4E **37**
Whitchurch-on-Thames. *Oxon* 4E **37**
Whitcombe. *Dors* 4C **14**
Whitcot. *Shrp* 1F **59**
Whitcott Keysett. *Shrp* 2E **59**
Whiteash Green. *Essx* 2A **54**
Whitebog. *High* 2B **158**
Whitebridge. *High* 2G **149**
Whitebrook. *Mon* 5A **48**
Whitecairns. *Abers* 2G **153**
Whitechapel. *Lanc* 5E **97**
Whitechurch. *Pemb* 1F **43**
White Colne. *Essx* 3B **54**
White Coppice. *Lanc* 3E **90**
White Corries. *High* 3G **141**
Whitecraig. *E Lot* 2G **129**
Whitecroft. *Glos* 5B **48**
White Cross. *Corn* 4D **5**
Whitecross. *Corn* 1D **6**
Whitecross. *Falk* 2C **128**
White End. *Worc* 2C **48**
Whiteface. *High* 5E **164**
Whitefarland. *N Ayr* 5G **125**
Whitefaulds. *S Ayr* 4B **116**
Whitefield. *Dors* 3E **15**
Whitefield. *G Man* 4G **91**
Whitefield. *Som* 4D **20**
Whiteford. *Abers* 1E **152**
Whitegate. *Ches W* 4A **84**
Whitehall. *Devn* 1E **12**
Whitehall. *Hants* 1F **25**
Whitehall. *Orkn* 5F **172**
Whitehall. *W Sus* 3C **26**
Whitehaven. *Cumb* 3A **102**
Whitehaven. *Shrp* 3E **71**
Whitehill. *Hants* 3F **25**
Whitehill. *N Ayr* 4D **126**
Whitehills. *Abers* 2D **160**
Whitehills. *Ang* 3D **144**
White Horse Common. *Norf* 3F **79**
Whitehough. *Derbs* 2E **85**
Whitehouse. *Abers* 2D **152**
Whitehouse. *Arg* 3G **125**
Whiteinch. *Glas* 3G **127**
Whitekirk. *E Lot* 1B **130**
White Kirkley. *Dur* 1D **104**
White Lackington. *Dors* 3C **14**
Whitelackington. *Som* 1G **13**
White Ladies Aston. *Worc* 5D **60**
White Lee. *W Yor* 2C **92**
Whiteley. *Hants* 2D **16**
Whiteley Bank. *IOW* 4D **16**
Whiteley Village. *Surr* 4B **38**
Whitemans Green. *W Sus* 3E **27**
White Mill. *Carm* 3E **45**
Whitemire. *Mor* 3D **159**
Whitemoor. *Corn* 3D **6**
Whitenap. *Hants* 4B **24**
Whiteness. *Shet* 7F **173**
White Notley. *Essx* 4A **54**
Whiteoak Green. *Oxon* 4B **50**
Whiteparish. *Wilts* 4H **23**
White Pit. *Linc* 3C **88**
Whiterashes. *Abers* 1F **153**
White Rocks. *Here* 3H **47**
White Roding. *Essx* 4F **53**
Whiterow. *High* 4F **169**
Whiterow. *Mor* 3E **159**
Whiteshill. *Glos* 5D **48**
Whiteside. *Nmbd* 3A **114**
Whiteside. *W Lot* 3C **128**
Whitesmith. *E Sus* 4G **27**
Whitestaunton. *Som* 1F **13**
Whitestone. *Abers* 4D **152**
Whitestone. *Devn* 3B **12**
White Stone. *Here* 1A **48**
Whitestones. *Abers* 3F **161**
Whitestreet Green. *Suff* 2C **54**
Whitewall Corner. *N Yor* 2B **100**
White Waltham. *Wind* 4G **37**
Whiteway. *Glos* 4E **49**
Whitewell. *Lanc* 5F **97**
Whitewell Bottom. *Lanc* 2G **91**
Whiteworks. *Devn* 5G **11**
Whitewreath. *Mor* 3G **159**
Whitfield. *D'dee* 5D **144**
Whitfield. *Kent* 1H **29**
Whitfield. *Nptn* 2E **50**
Whitfield. *Nmbd* 4A **114**
Whitfield. *S Glo* 2B **34**
Whitford. *Devn* 3F **13**
Whitford. *Flin* 3D **82**
Whitgift. *E Yor* 2B **94**
Whitgreave. *Staf* 3C **72**
Whithorn. *Dum* 5B **110**
Whiting Bay. *N Ayr* 3E **123**
Whitkirk. *W Yor* 1D **92**
Whitland. *Carm* 3G **43**
Whitleigh. *Plym* 3A **8**
Whitletts. *S Ayr* 2C **116**
Whitley. *N Yor* 2F **93**
Whitley. *Wilts* 5D **35**
Whitley Bay. *Tyne* 2G **115**
Whitley Chapel. *Nmbd* 4C **114**
Whitley Heath. *Staf* 3C **72**
Whitley Lower. *W Yor* 3C **92**
Whitley Thorpe. *N Yor* 2F **93**
Whitlock's End. *W Mid* 3F **61**
Whitminster. *Glos* 5C **48**
Whitmore. *Dors* 2F **15**
Whitmore. *Staf* 1C **72**
Whitnage. *Devn* 1D **12**
Whitnash. *Warw* 4H **61**
Whitney. *Here* 1F **47**
Whitrigg. *Cumb*
nr. Kirkbride 4D **112**
nr. Torpenhow 1D **102**
Whitsbury. *Hants* 1G **15**
Whitsome. *Bord* 4E **131**
Whitson. *Newp* 3G **33**
Whitstable. *Kent* 4F **41**
Whitstone. *Corn* 3C **10**
Whittingham. *Nmbd* 3E **121**
Whittingslow. *Shrp* 2G **59**
Whittington. *Derbs* 3B **86**
Whittington. *Glos* 3F **49**
Whittington. *Lanc* 2F **97**
Whittington. *Norf* 1G **65**
Whittington. *Shrp* 2F **71**
Whittington. *Staf*
nr. Kinver 2C **60**
nr. Lichfield 5F **73**
Whittington. *Warw* 1G **61**
Whittington. *Worc* 5C **60**
Whittington Barracks. *Staf* 5F **73**
Whittlebury. *Nptn* 1E **51**
Whittleford. *Warw* 1H **61**
Whittle-le-Woods. *Lanc* 2D **90**
Whittlesey. *Cambs* 1B **64**
Whittlesford. *Cambs* 1E **53**
Whittlestone Head. *Bkbn* 3F **91**
Whitton. *N Lin* 2C **94**
Whitton. *Nmbd* 4E **121**
Whitton. *Powy* 4E **59**
Whitton. *Bord* 2B **120**
Whitton. *Shrp* 3H **59**
Whitton. *Stoc T* 2A **106**
Whittonditch. *Wilts* 4A **36**
Whittonstall. *Nmbd* 4D **114**
Whitway. *Hants* 1C **24**
Whitwell. *Derbs* 3C **86**
Whitwell. *Herts* 3B **52**
Whitwell. *IOW* 5D **16**
Whitwell. *N Yor* 5F **105**
Whitwell. *Rut* 5G **75**
Whitwell-on-the-Hill. *N Yor* 3B **100**
Whitwick. *Leics* 4B **74**
Whitwood. *W Yor* 2E **93**
Whitworth. *Lanc* 3G **91**
Whixall. *Shrp* 2H **71**
Whixley. *N Yor* 4G **99**
Whoberley. *W Mid* 3H **61**
Whorlton. *Dur* 3E **105**
Whorlton. *N Yor* 4B **106**
Whygate. *Nmbd* 2A **114**
Whyle. *Here* 4H **59**
Whyteleafe. *Surr* 5E **39**
Wibdon. *Glos* 2A **34**
Wibtoft. *Warw* 2B **62**
Wichenford. *Worc* 4B **60**
Wichling. *Kent* 5D **40**
Wick. *Bour* 3G **15**
Wick. *Devn* 2E **13**
Wick. *High* 3F **169**
Wick. *Shet*
on Mainland 8F **173**
on Unst 1G **173**
Wick. *Som*
nr. Bridgwater 2F **21**
nr. Burnham-on-Sea 1G **21**
nr. Somerton 4H **21**
Wick. *S Glo* 4C **34**
Wick. *V Glam* 4C **32**
Wick. *W Sus* 5B **26**
Wick. *Wilts* 4G **23**
Wick. *Worc* 1E **49**
Wick Airport. *High* 3F **169**
Wicken. *Cambs* 3E **65**
Wicken. *Nptn* 2F **51**
Wicken Bonhunt. *Essx* 2E **53**
Wickenby. *Linc* 2H **87**
Wicken Green Village. *Norf* 2H **77**
Wickersley. *S Yor* 1B **86**
Wicker Street Green. *Suff* 1C **54**
Wickford. *Essx* 1B **40**
Wickham. *Hants* 1D **16**
Wickham. *W Ber* 4B **36**
Wickham Bishops. *Essx* 4B **54**
Wickhambreaux. *Kent* 5G **41**
Wickhambrook. *Suff* 5G **65**
Wickhamford. *Worc* 1F **49**
Wickham Green. *Suff* 4C **66**
Wickham Heath. *W Ber* 5C **36**
Wickham Market. *Suff* 5F **67**
Wickhampton. *Norf* 5G **79**
Wickham St Paul. *Essx* 2B **54**
Wickham Skeith. *Suff* 4C **66**
Wickham Street. *Suff* 4C **66**
Wick Hill. *Wok* 5F **37**
Wicklewood. *Norf* 5C **78**
Wickmere. *Norf* 2D **78**
Wick St Lawrence. *N Som* 5G **33**
Wickwar. *S Glo* 3C **34**
Widdington. *Essx* 2F **53**
Widdrington. *Nmbd* 5G **121**
Widdrington Station. *Nmbd* 5G **121**

Widecombe in the Moor—Wood Street Village

Widecombe in the Moor. Devn 5H 11
Widegates. Corn 3G 7
Widemouth Bay. Corn 2C 10
Wide Open. Tyne 2F 115
Widewall. Orkn 8D 172
Widford. Essx 5G 53
Widford. Herts 4E 53
Widham. Wilts 3F 35
Widmer End. Buck 2G 37
Widmerpool. Notts 3D 74
Widnes. Hal 2H 83
Widworthy. Devn 3F 13
Wigan. G Man 4D 90
Wigbeth. Dors 2F 15
Wigborough. Som 1H 13
Wiggaton. Devn 3E 12
Wiggenhall St Germans. Norf 4E 77
Wiggenhall St Mary Magdalen. Norf 4E 77
Wiggenhall St Mary the Virgin. Norf 4E 77
Wiggenhall St Peter. Norf 4F 77
Wiggens Green. Essx 1G 53
Wigginton. Herts 4H 51
Wigginton. Oxon 2B 50
Wigginton. Staf 5G 73
Wigginton. York 4H 99
Wigglesworth. N Yor 4H 97
Wiggonby. Cumb 4D 112
Wiggonholt. W Sus 4B 26
Wighill. N Yor 5G 99
Wighton. Norf 2B 78
Wightwick. W Mid 1C 60
Wigley. Hants 1B 16
Wigmore. Here 4G 59
Wigmore. Medw 4B 40
Wigsley. Notts 3F 87
Wigsthorpe. Nptn 2H 63
Wigston. Leics 1D 62
Wigtoft. Linc 2B 76
Wigton. Cumb 5D 112
Wigtown. Dum 4B 110
Wike. W Yor 5F 99
Wilbarston. Nptn 2F 63
Wilberfoss. E Yor 4B 100
Wilburton. Cambs 3D 65
Wilby. Norf 2C 66
Wilby. Nptn 4F 63
Wilby. Suff 3E 67
Wilcot. Wilts 5G 35
Wilcott. Shrp 4F 71
Wilcove. Corn 3A 8
Wildboarclough. Ches E 4D 85
Wilden. Bed 5H 63
Wilden. Worc 3C 60
Wildern. Hants 1C 16
Wilderspool. Warr 2A 84
Wilde Street. Suff 3G 65
Wildhern. Hants 1B 24
Wildmanbridge. S Lan 4B 128
Wildmoor. Worc 3D 60
Wildsworth. Linc 1F 87
Wildwood. Staf 3D 72
Wilford. Nott 2C 74
Wilkesley. Ches E 1A 72
Wilkhaven. High 5G 165
Wilkieston. W Lot 3E 129
Wilksby. Linc 4B 88
Willand. Devn 1D 12
Willaston. Ches E 5A 84
Willaston. Ches W 3F 83
Willaston. IOM 4C 108
Willen. Mil 1G 51
Willenhall. W Mid
nr. Coventry 3A 62
nr. Wolverhampton 1D 60
Willerby. E Yor 1D 94
Willerby. N Yor 2E 101
Willersey. Glos 2G 49
Willersley. Here 1G 47
Willesborough. Kent 1E 28
Willesborough Lees. Kent 1E 29
Willesden. G Lon 2D 38
Willesley. Wilts 3D 34
Willett. Som 3E 20
Willey. Shrp 1A 60
Willey. Warw 2B 62
Willey Green. Surr 5A 38
Williamscot. Oxon 1C 50
Williamsetter. Shet 9E 173
Willian. Herts 2C 52
Willingale. Essx 5F 53
Willingdon. E Sus 5G 27
Willingham. Cambs 3D 64
Willingham by Stow. Linc 2F 87
Willingham Green. Cambs 5F 65
Willington. Bed 1B 52
Willington. Derbs 3G 73
Willington. Dur 1E 105
Willington. Tyne 3G 115
Willington. Warw 2A 50
Willington Corner. Ches W 4H 83
Willisham Tye. Suff 5C 66
Willitoft. E Yor 1H 93
Williton. Som 2D 20
Willoughbridge. Staf 1B 72
Willoughby. Linc 3D 88
Willoughby. Warw 4C 62
Willoughby-on-the-Wolds. Notts 3D 74
Willoughby Waterleys. Leics 1C 62
Willoughton. Linc 1G 87
Willow Green. Worc 5B 60
Willows Green. Essx 4H 53
Willsbridge. S Glo 4B 34
Willslock. Staf 2E 73
Wilmcote. Warw 5F 61
Wilmington. Bath 5B 34
Wilmington. Devn 3F 13
Wilmington. E Sus 5G 27
Wilmington. Kent 3G 39
Wilmslow. Ches E 2C 84
Wilnecote. Staf 5G 73
Wilney Green. Norf 2C 66
Wilpshire. Lanc 1E 91
Wilsden. W Yor 1A 92
Wilsford. Linc 1H 75
Wilsford. Wilts
nr. Amesbury 3G 23
nr. Devizes 1F 23
Wilsill. N Yor 3D 98
Wilsley Green. Kent 2B 28
Wilson. Here 3A 48
Wilson. Leics 3B 74
Wilsontown. S Lan 4C 128
Wilstead. Bed 1A 52
Wilsthorpe. E Yor 3F 101
Wilsthorpe. Linc 4H 75
Wilstone. Herts 4H 51
Wilton. Cumb 3B 102
Wilton. N Yor 1C 100
Wilton. Red C 3C 106
Wilton. Bord 3H 119
Wilton. Wilts
nr. Marlborough 5A 36
nr. Salisbury 3F 23
Wimbish. Essx 2F 53
Wimbish Green. Essx 2G 53
Wimblebury. Staf 4E 73
Wimbledon. G Lon 3D 38
Wimblington. Cambs 1D 64
Wimboldsley. Ches W 4A 84
Wimborne Minster. Dors 2F 15
Wimborne St Giles. Dors 1F 15
Wimbotsham. Norf 5F 77
Wimpole. Cambs 1D 52
Wimpstone. Warw 1H 49
Wincanton. Som 4C 22
Winceby. Linc 4C 88
Wincham. Ches W 3A 84
Winchburgh. W Lot 2D 129
Winchcombe. Glos 3F 49
Winchelsea. E Sus 4D 28
Winchelsea Beach. E Sus 4D 28
Winchester. Hants 213 (4C 24)
Winchet Hill. Kent 1B 28
Winchfield. Hants 1F 25
Winchmore Hill. Buck 1A 38
Winchmore Hill. G Lon 1E 39
Wincle. Ches E 4D 84
Windermere. Cumb 5F 103
Winderton. Warw 1B 50
Windhill. High 4H 157
Windle Hill. Ches W 3F 83
Windlesham. Surr 4A 38
Windley. Derbs 1H 73
Windmill. Derbs 3F 85
Windmill Hill. E Sus 4H 27
Windmill Hill. Som 1G 13
Windrush. Glos 4G 49
Windsor. Wind 213 (3A 38)
Windsor Green. Suff 5A 66
Windyedge. Abers 4F 153
Windygates. Fife 3F 137
Windyharbour. Ches E 3C 84
Windyknowe. W Lot 3C 128
Wineham. W Sus 3D 26
Winestead. E Yor 2G 95
Winfarthing. Norf 2D 66
Winford. IOW 4D 16
Winford. N Som 5A 34
Winforton. Here 1F 47
Winfrith Newburgh. Dors 4D 14
Wing. Buck 3G 51
Wing. Rut 5F 75
Wingate. Dur 1B 106
Wingates. G Man 4E 91
Wingates. Nmbd 5F 121
Wingerworth. Derbs 4A 86
Wingfield. C Beds 3A 52
Wingfield. Suff 3E 67
Wingfield. Wilts 1D 22
Wingfield Park. Derbs 5A 86
Wingham. Kent 5G 41
Wingmore. Kent 1F 29
Wingrave. Buck 4G 51
Winkburn. Notts 5E 86
Winkfield. Brac 3A 38
Winkfield Row. Brac 4G 37
Winkhill. Staf 5E 85
Winklebury. Hants 1E 24
Winkleigh. Devn 2G 11
Winksley. N Yor 2E 99
Winkton. Dors 3G 15
Winlaton. Tyne 3E 115
Winlaton Mill. Tyne 3E 115
Winless. High 3F 169
Winmarleigh. Lanc 5D 96
Winnal Common. Here 2H 47
Winnard's Perch. Corn 2D 6
Winnersh. Wok 4F 37
Winnington. Ches W 3A 84
Winnington. Staf 2B 72
Winnothdale. Staf 1E 73
Winscales. Cumb 2B 102
Winscombe. N Som 1H 21
Winsford. Ches W 4A 84
Winsford. Som 3C 20
Winsham. Devn 3E 19
Winsham. Som 2G 13
Winshill. Staf 3G 73
Winsh-wen. Swan 3F 31
Winskill. Cumb 1G 103
Winslade. Hants 2E 25
Winsley. Wilts 5D 34
Winslow. Buck 3F 51
Winson. Glos 5F 49
Winson Green. W Mid 2E 61
Winsor. Hants 1B 16
Winster. Cumb 5F 103
Winster. Derbs 4G 85
Winston. Dur 3E 105
Winston. Suff 4D 66
Winstone. Glos 5E 49
Winswell. Devn 1E 11
Winterborne Clenston. Dors 2D 14
Winterborne Herringston. Dors 4B 14
Winterborne Houghton. Dors 2D 14
Winterborne Kingston. Dors 3D 14
Winterborne Monkton. Dors 4B 14
Winterborne St Martin. Dors 4B 14
Winterborne Stickland. Dors 2D 14
Winterborne Whitechurch. Dors 2D 14
Winterborne Zelston. Dors 3D 15
Winterbourne. S Glo 3B 34
Winterbourne. W Ber 4C 36
Winterbourne Abbas. Dors 3B 14
Winterbourne Bassett. Wilts 4G 35
Winterbourne Dauntsey. Wilts 3G 23
Winterbourne Earls. Wilts 3G 23
Winterbourne Gunner. Wilts 3G 23
Winterbourne Monkton. Wilts 4G 35
Winterbourne Steepleton. Dors 4B 14
Winterbourne Stoke. Wilts 2F 23
Winterbrook. Oxon 3E 36
Winterburn. N Yor 4B 98
Winter Gardens. Essx 2B 40
Winterhay Green. Som 1G 13
Winteringham. N Lin 2C 94
Winterley. Ches E 5B 84
Wintersett. W Yor 3D 93
Winterton. N Lin 3C 94
Winterton-on-Sea. Norf 4G 79
Winthorpe. Linc 4E 89
Winthorpe. Notts 5F 87
Winton. Bour 3F 15
Winton. Cumb 3A 104
Winton. E Sus 5G 27
Wintringham. N Yor 2C 100
Winwick. Cambs 2A 64
Winwick. Nptn 3D 62
Winwick. Warr 1A 84
Wirksworth. Derbs 5G 85
Wirswall. Ches E 1H 71
Wisbech. Cambs 4D 76
Wisbech St Mary. Cambs 5D 76
Wisborough Green. W Sus 3B 26
Wiseton. Notts 2E 86
Wishaw. N Lan 4A 128
Wishaw. Warw 1F 61
Wisley. Surr 5B 38
Wispington. Linc 3B 88
Wissenden. Kent 1D 28
Wissett. Suff 3F 67
Wistanstow. Shrp 2G 59
Wistanswick. Shrp 3A 72
Wistaston. Ches E 5A 84
Wiston. Pemb 3E 43
Wiston. S Lan 1B 118
Wiston. W Sus 4C 26
Wistow. Cambs 2B 64
Wistow. N Yor 1F 93
Wiswell. Lanc 1F 91
Witcham. Cambs 2D 64
Witchampton. Dors 2E 15
Witchford. Cambs 3E 65
Witham. Essx 4B 54
Witham Friary. Som 2C 22
Witham on the Hill. Linc 4H 75
Witham St Hughs. Linc 4F 87
Withcall. Linc 2B 88
Witherenden Hill. E Sus 3H 27
Withergate. Norf 3E 79
Witheridge. Devn 1B 12
Witheridge Hill. Oxon 3E 37
Witherley. Leics 1H 61
Withermarsh Green. Suff 2D 54
Withern. Linc 2D 88
Withernsea. E Yor 2G 95
Withernwick. E Yor 5F 101
Withersdale Street. Suff 2E 67
Withersfield. Suff 1G 53
Witherslack. Cumb 1D 96
Withiel. Corn 2D 6
Withiel Florey. Som 3C 20
Withington. Glos 4F 49
Withington. G Man 1C 84
Withington. Here 1A 48
Withington. Shrp 4H 71
Withington. Staf 2E 73
Withington Green. Ches E 3C 84
Withington Marsh. Here 1A 48
Withleigh. Devn 1C 12
Withnell. Lanc 2E 91
Withnell Fold. Lanc 2E 90
Withybrook. Warw 2B 62
Withycombe. Som 2D 20
Withycombe Raleigh. Devn 4D 12
Withyham. E Sus 2F 27
Withypool. Som 3B 20
Witley. Surr 1A 26
Witnesham. Suff 5D 66
Witney. Oxon 4B 50
Wittering. Pet 5H 75
Wittersham. Kent 3C 28
Witton. Norf 5F 79
Witton. Worc 4C 60
Witton Bridge. Norf 2F 79
Witton Gilbert. Dur 5F 115
Witton-le-Wear. Dur 1E 105
Witton Park. Dur 1E 105
Wiveliscombe. Som 4D 20
Wivelrod. Hants 3E 25
Wivelsfield. E Sus 3E 27
Wivelsfield Green. E Sus 4E 27
Wivenhoe. Essx 3D 54
Wiveton. Norf 1C 78
Wix. Essx 3E 55
Wixford. Warw 5E 61
Wixhill. Shrp 3H 71
Wixoe. Suff 1H 53
Woburn. C Beds 2H 51
Woburn Sands. Mil 2H 51
Woking. Surr 5B 38
Wokingham. Wok 5G 37
Wolborough. Devn 5B 12
Woldingham. Surr 5E 39
Wold Newton. E Yor 2E 101
Wold Newton. NE Lin 1B 88
Wolferlow. Here 4A 60
Wolferton. Norf 3F 77
Wolfhill. Per 5A 144
Wolf's Castle. Pemb 2D 42
Wolfsdale. Pemb 2D 42
Wolgarston. Staf 4D 72
Wollaston. Nptn 4G 63
Wollaston. Shrp 4F 71
Wollaston. W Mid 2C 60
Wollaton. Nott 1C 74
Wollerton. Shrp 2A 72
Wollescote. W Mid 2D 60
Wolseley Bridge. Staf 3E 73
Wolsingham. Dur 1D 105
Wolstanton. Staf 1C 72
Wolston. Warw 3B 62
Wolsty. Cumb 4C 112
Wolterton. Norf 2D 78
Wolvercote. Oxon 5C 50
Wolverhampton. W Mid 213 (1D 60)
Wolverley. Shrp 2G 71
Wolverley. Worc 3C 60
Wolverton. Hants 1D 24
Wolverton. Mil 1G 51
Wolverton. Warw 4G 61
Wolverton. Wilts 3C 22
Wolverton Common. Hants 1D 24
Wolvesnewton. Mon 2H 33
Wolvey. Warw 2B 62
Wolvey Heath. Warw 2B 62
Wolviston. Stoc T 2B 106
Womaston. Powy 4E 59
Wombleton. N Yor 1A 100
Wombourne. Staf 1C 60
Wombwell. S Yor 4D 93
Womenswold. Kent 5G 41
Womersley. N Yor 3F 93
Wonersh. Surr 1B 26
Wonson. Devn 4G 11
Wonston. Dors 2C 14
Wonston. Hants 3C 24
Wooburn. Buck 2A 38
Wooburn Green. Buck 2A 38
Wood. Pemb 2C 42
Woodacott. Devn 2D 11
Woodale. N Yor 2C 98
Woodall. S Yor 2B 86
Woodbank. Ches W 3F 83
Woodbastwick. Norf 4F 79
Woodbeck. Notts 3E 87
Woodborough. Notts 1D 74
Woodborough. Wilts 1G 23
Woodbridge. Devn 3E 13
Woodbridge. Dors 1C 14
Woodbridge. Suff 1F 55
Wood Burcote. Nptn 1E 51
Woodbury. Devn 4D 12
Woodbury Salterton. Devn 4D 12
Woodchester. Glos 5D 48
Woodchurch. Kent 2D 28
Woodchurch. Mers 2E 83
Woodcock Heath. Staf 3E 73
Woodcombe. Som 2C 20
Woodcote. Oxon 3E 37
Woodcote Green. Worc 3D 60
Woodcott. Hants 1C 24
Woodcroft. Glos 2A 34
Woodcutts. Dors 1E 15
Wood Dalling. Norf 3C 78
Woodditton. Cambs 5F 65
Woodeaton. Oxon 4D 50
Wood Eaton. Staf 4C 72
Wood End. Bed 4H 63
Woodend. Cumb 5C 102
Wood End. Herts 3D 52
Woodend. Nptn 1E 50
Woodend. Staf 3F 73
Wood End. Warw
nr. Bedworth 2G 61
nr. Dordon 1G 61
nr. Tanworth-in-Arden 3F 61
Woodend. W Sus 2G 17
Wood Enderby. Linc 4B 88
Woodend Green. Essx 3F 53
Woodfalls. Wilts 4G 23
Woodfield. Oxon 3D 50
Woodfields. Lanc 1E 91
Woodford. Corn 1C 10
Woodford. Devn 3D 9
Woodford. Glos 2B 34
Woodford. G Lon 1E 39
Woodford. G Man 2C 84
Woodford. Nptn 3G 63
Woodford. Plym 3B 8
Woodford Green. G Lon 1F 39
Woodford Halse. Nptn 5C 62
Woodgate. Norf 4C 78
Woodgate. W Mid 2D 61
Woodgate. W Sus 5A 26
Woodgate. Worc 4D 60
Wood Green. G Lon 1D 39
Woodgreen. Hants 1G 15
Woodgreen. Oxon 4B 50
Woodhall. Inv 2E 127
Woodhall. Linc 4B 88
Woodhall. N Yor 5C 104
Woodhall Spa. Linc 4A 88
Woodham. Surr 4B 38
Woodham Ferrers. Essx 1B 40
Woodham Mortimer. Essx 5B 54
Woodham Walter. Essx 5B 54
Woodhaven. Fife 1G 137
Wood Hayes. W Mid 5D 72
Woodhead. Abers
nr. Fraserburgh 2G 161
nr. Fyvie 5E 161
Woodhill. N Som 4H 33
Woodhill. Shrp 2B 60
Woodhill. Som 4G 21
Woodhorn. Nmbd 1F 115
Woodhouse. Leics 4C 74
Woodhouse. S Yor 2B 86
Woodhouse. W Yor
nr. Leeds 1C 92
nr. Normanton 2D 93
Woodhouse Eaves. Leics 4C 74
Woodhouses. Ches W 3H 83
Woodhouses. G Man
nr. Failsworth 4H 91
nr. Sale 1B 84
Woodhouses. Staf 4F 73
Woodhuish. Devn 3F 9
Woodhurst. Cambs 3C 64
Woodingdean. Brig 5E 27
Woodland. Devn 2D 9
Woodland. Dur 2D 104
Woodland Head. Devn 3A 12
Woodlands. Abers 4E 153
Woodlands. Dors 2F 15
Woodlands. Hants 1B 16
Woodlands. Kent 4G 39
Woodlands. N Yor 4F 99
Woodlands. S Yor 4F 93
Woodlands Park. Wind 4G 37
Woodlands St Mary. W Ber 4B 36
Woodlane. Shrp 3A 72
Woodlane. Staf 3F 73
Woodleigh. Devn 4D 8
Woodlesford. W Yor 2D 92
Woodley. G Man 1D 84
Woodley. Wok 4F 37
Woodmancote. Glos
nr. Cheltenham 3E 49
nr. Cirencester 5F 49
Woodmancote. W Sus
nr. Chichester 2F 17
nr. Henfield 4D 26
Woodmancote. Worc 1E 49
Woodmancott. Hants 2D 24
Woodmansey. E Yor 1D 94
Woodmansgreen. W Sus 4G 25
Woodmansterne. Surr 5D 38
Woodmanton. Devn 4D 12
Woodmill. Staf 3F 73
Woodminton. Wilts 4F 23
Woodnesborough. Kent 5H 41
Woodnewton. Nptn 1H 63
Woodnook. Linc 2G 75
Wood Norton. Norf 3C 78
Woodplumpton. Lanc 1D 90
Woodrising. Norf 5B 78
Woodrow. Cumb 5D 112
Woodrow. Dors
nr. Fifehead Neville 1C 14
nr. Hazelbury Bryan 2C 14
Wood Row. W Yor 2D 93
Woods Eaves. Here 1F 47
Woodseaves. Shrp 2A 72
Woodseaves. Staf 3C 72
Woodsend. Wilts 4H 35
Woodsetts. S Yor 2C 86
Woodsford. Dors 3C 14
Wood's Green. E Sus 2H 27
Woodshaw. Wilts 3F 35
Woodside. Aber 3G 153
Woodside. Brac 3A 38
Woodside. Derbs 1A 74
Woodside. Dum 2B 112
Woodside. Dur 2E 105
Woodside. Fife 3G 137
Woodside. Herts 5C 52
Woodside. Per 5B 144
Wood Stanway. Glos 2F 49
Woodstock. Oxon 4C 50
Woodstock Slop. Pemb 2E 43
Woodston. Pet 1A 64
Wood Street. Norf 3F 79
Wood Street Village. Surr 5A 38

Woodthorpe. *Derbs* 3B **86**
Woodthorpe. *Leics* 4C **74**
Woodthorpe. *Linc* 2D **88**
Woodthorpe. *Notts* 1C **74**
Woodthorpe. *York* 5H **99**
Woodton. *Norf* 1E **67**
Woodtown. *Devn*
   nr. Bideford 4E **19**
   nr. Littleham 4E **19**
Woodvale. *Mers* 3B **90**
Woodville. *Derbs* 4H **73**
Woodwalton. *Cambs* 2B **64**
Woodwick. *Orkn* 5C **172**
Woodyates. *Dors* 1F **15**
Woody Bay. *Devn* 2G **19**
Woofferton. *Shrp* 4H **59**
Wookey. *Som* 2A **22**
Wookey Hole. *Som* 2A **22**
Wool. *Dors* 4D **14**
Woolacombe. *Devn* 2E **19**
Woolage Green. *Kent* 1G **29**
Woolage Village. *Kent* 5G **41**
Woolaston. *Glos* 2A **34**
Woolavington. *Som* 2G **21**
Woolbeding. *W Sus* 4G **25**
Woolcotts. *Som* 3C **20**
Wooldale. *W Yor* 4B **92**
Wooler. *Nmbd* 2D **121**
Woolfardisworthy. *Devn*
   nr. Bideford 4D **18**
   nr. Crediton 2B **12**
Woolfords. *S Lan* 4D **128**
Woolgarston. *Dors* 4E **15**
Woolhampton. *W Ber* 5D **36**
Woolhope. *Here* 2B **48**
Woolland. *Dors* 2C **14**
Woollard. *Bath* 5B **34**
Woolley. *Bath* 5C **34**
Woolley. *Cambs* 3A **64**
Woolley. *Corn* 1C **10**
Woolley. *Derbs* 4A **86**
Woolley. *W Yor* 3D **92**
Woolley Green. *Wilts* 5D **34**
Woolmere Green. *Worc* 4D **60**
Woolmer Green. *Herts* 4C **52**
Woolminstone. *Som* 2H **13**
Woolpit. *Suff* 4B **66**
Woolridge. *Glos* 3D **48**
Woolscott. *Warw* 4B **62**
Woolsery. *Devn* 4D **18**
Woolsington. *Tyne* 3E **115**
Woolstaston. *Shrp* 1G **59**
Woolsthorpe By Belvoir. *Linc* 2F **75**
Woolsthorpe-by-Colsterworth.
   Linc 3G **75**
Woolston. *Devn* 4D **8**
Woolston. *Shrp*
   nr. Church Stretton 2G **59**
   nr. Oswestry 3F **71**
Woolston. *Som* 4B **22**
Woolston. *Sotn* 1C **16**
Woolston. *Warr* 2A **84**
Woolstone. *Glos* 2E **49**
Woolstone. *Oxon* 3A **36**
Woolston Green. *Devn* 2D **9**
Woolton. *Mers* 2G **83**
Woolton Hill. *Hants* 5C **36**
Woolverstone. *Suff* 2E **55**
Woolverton. *Som* 1C **22**
Woolwell. *Devn* 2B **8**
Woolwich. *G Lon* 3F **39**
Woonton. *Here*
   nr. Kington 5F **59**
   nr. Leominster 4H **59**
Wooperton. *Nmbd* 2E **121**
Woore. *Shrp* 1B **72**
Wooth. *Dors* 3H **13**
Wooton. *Shrp* 2B **60**
Wootton. *Bed* 1A **52**
Wootton. *Hants* 3H **15**
Wootton. *IOW* 3D **16**
Wootton. *Kent* 1G **29**
Wootton. *Nptn* 5E **63**
Wootton. *N Lin* 3D **94**
Wootton. *Oxon*
   nr. Abingdon 5C **50**
   nr. Woodstock 4C **50**

Wootton. *Shrp*
   nr. Ludlow 3G **59**
   nr. Oswestry 3F **71**
Wootton. *Staf*
   nr. Eccleshall 3C **72**
   nr. Ellastone 1F **73**
Wootton Bassett, Royal.
   Wilts 3F **35**
Wootton Bridge. *IOW* 3D **16**
Wootton Common. *IOW* 3D **16**
Wootton Courtenay. *Som* 2C **20**
Wootton Fitzpaine. *Dors* 3G **13**
Wootton Rivers. *Wilts* 5G **35**
Wootton St Lawrence.
   Hants 1D **24**
Wootton Wawen. *Warw* 4F **61**
Worcester. *Worc* **214** (5C **60**)
Worcester Park. *G Lon* 4D **38**
Wordsley. *W Mid* 2C **60**
Worfield. *Shrp* 1B **60**
Work. *Orkn* 6D **172**
Workhouse Green. *Suff* 2C **54**
Workington. *Cumb* 2A **102**
Worksop. *Notts* 3C **86**
Worlaby. *N Lin* 3D **94**
Worlds End. *Hants* 1E **17**
Worlds End. *Surr* 1G **59**
World's End. *W Ber* 4C **36**
World's End. *W Mid* 2F **61**
World's End. *W Sus* 4E **27**
Worle. *N Som* 5G **33**
Worleston. *Ches E* 5A **84**
Worlingham. *Suff* 2G **67**
Worlington. *Suff* 3F **65**
Worlingworth. *Suff* 4E **67**
Wormbridge. *Here* 2H **47**
Wormegay. *Norf* 4F **77**
Wormelow Tump. *Here* 2H **47**
Wormhill. *Derbs* 3F **85**
Wormingford. *Essx* 2C **54**
Worminghall. *Buck* 5E **51**
Wormington. *Glos* 2F **49**
Worminster. *Som* 2A **22**
Wormit. *Fife* 1F **137**
Wormleighton. *Warw* 5B **62**
Wormley. *Herts* 5D **52**
Wormley. *Surr* 2A **26**
Wormshill. *Kent* 5C **40**
Wormsley. *Here* 1H **47**
Worplesdon. *Surr* 5A **38**
Worrall. *S Yor* 1H **85**
Worsbrough. *S Yor* 4D **92**
Worsley. *G Man* 4F **91**
Worstead. *Norf* 3F **79**
Worsthorne. *Lanc* 1G **91**
Worston. *Lanc* 5G **97**
Worth. *Kent* 5H **41**
Worth. *W Sus* 2D **27**
Wortham. *Suff* 3C **66**
Worthen. *Shrp* 5F **71**
Worthenbury. *Wrex* 1G **71**
Worthing. *Norf* 4B **78**
Worthing. *W Sus* 5C **26**
Worthington. *Leics* 3B **74**
Worth Matravers. *Dors* 5E **15**
Worting. *Hants* 1E **24**
Wortley. *Glos* 2C **34**
Wortley. *S Yor* 1H **85**
Wortley. *W Yor* 1C **92**
Worton. *N Yor* 1B **98**
Worton. *Wilts* 1E **23**
Wortwell. *Norf* 2E **67**
Wotherton. *Shrp* 5E **71**
Wothorpe. *Pet* 5H **75**
Wotter. *Devn* 2B **8**
Wotton. *Glos* 4D **48**
Wotton. *Surr* 1C **26**
Wotton-under-Edge. *Glos* 2C **34**
Wotton Underwood. *Buck* 4E **51**
Wouldham. *Kent* 4B **40**
Wrabness. *Essx* 2E **55**
Wrafton. *Devn* 3E **19**
Wragby. *Linc* 3A **88**
Wragby. *W Yor* 3E **93**
Wramplingham. *Norf* 5D **78**
Wrangbrook. *W Yor* 3E **93**
Wrangle. *Linc* 5D **88**

Wrangle Lowgate. *Linc* 5D **88**
Wrangway. *Som* 1E **13**
Wrantage. *Som* 4G **21**
Wrawby. *N Lin* 4D **94**
Wraxall. *N Som* 4H **33**
Wraxall. *Som* 3B **22**
Wray. *Lanc* 3F **97**
Wraysbury. *Wind* 3B **38**
Wrayton. *Lanc* 2F **97**
Wrea Green. *Lanc* 1B **90**
Wreay. *Cumb*
   nr. Carlisle 5F **113**
   nr. Penrith 2F **103**
Wrecclesham. *Surr* 2G **25**
Wrecsam. *Wrex* **214** (5F **83**)
Wrekenton. *Tyne* 4F **115**
Wrelton. *N Yor* 1B **100**
Wrenbury. *Ches E* 1H **71**
Wreningham. *Norf* 1D **66**
Wrentham. *Suff* 2G **67**
Wrenthorpe. *W Yor* 2D **92**
Wrentnall. *Shrp* 5G **71**
Wressle. *E Yor* 1H **93**
Wressle. *N Lin* 4C **94**
Wrestlingworth. *C Beds* 1C **52**
Wretton. *Norf* 1F **65**
Wrexham. *Wrex* **214** (5F **83**)
Wreyland. *Devn* 4A **12**
Wrickton. *Shrp* 2A **60**
Wrightington Bar. *Lanc* 3D **90**
Wright's Green. *Essx* 4F **53**
Wrinehill. *Staf* 1B **72**
Wrington. *N Som* 5H **33**
Writtle. *Essx* 5G **53**
Wrockwardine. *Telf* 4A **72**
Wroot. *N Lin* 4H **93**
Wrotham. *Kent* 5H **39**
Wrotham Heath. *Kent* 5H **39**
Wroughton. *Swin* 3G **35**
Wroxall. *IOW* 4D **16**
Wroxall. *Warw* 3G **61**
Wroxeter. *Shrp* 5H **71**
Wroxham. *Norf* 4F **79**
Wroxton. *Oxon* 1C **50**
Wyaston. *Derbs* 1F **73**
Wyatt's Green. *Essx* 1G **39**
Wybers Wood. *NE Lin* 4F **95**
Wyberton. *Linc* 1C **76**
Wyboston. *Bed* 5A **64**
Wybunbury. *Ches E* 1A **72**
Wychbold. *Worc* 4D **60**
Wych Cross. *E Sus* 2F **27**
Wychnor. *Staf* 4F **73**
Wychnor Bridges. *Staf* 4F **73**
Wyck. *Hants* 3F **25**
Wyck Hill. *Glos* 3G **49**
Wyck Rissington. *Glos* 3G **49**
Wycliffe. *Dur* 3E **105**
Wycombe Marsh. *Buck* 2G **37**
Yr Wyddgrug. *Flin* 4E **83**
Wyddial. *Herts* 2D **52**
Wye. *Kent* 1E **29**
Wyesham. *Mon* 4A **48**
Wyfold. *Oxon* 3E **37**
Wyfordby. *Leics* 4E **75**
Wyke. *Devn* 3B **12**
Wyke. *Dors* 4C **22**
Wyke. *Shrp* 5A **72**
Wyke, The. *Shrp* 5B **72**
Wyke. *Surr* 5A **38**
Wyke. *W Yor* 2B **92**
Wyke Champflower.
   Som 3B **22**
Wykeham. *Linc* 3B **76**
Wykeham. *N Yor*
   nr. Malton 2C **100**
   nr. Scarborough 1D **100**
Wyken. *Shrp* 1B **60**
Wyken. *W Mid* 2A **62**
Wyke Regis. *Dors* 5B **14**
Wykey. *Shrp* 3F **71**
Wykin. *Leics* 1B **62**
Wylam. *Nmbd* 3E **115**
Wylde Green. *W Mid* 1F **61**
Wylye. *Wilts* 3F **23**
Wymering. *Port* 2E **17**
Wymeswold. *Leics* 3D **74**

Wymington. *Bed* 4G **63**
Wymondham. *Leics* 4F **75**
Wymondham. *Norf* 5D **78**
Wyndham. *B'end* 2C **32**
Wynford Eagle. *Dors* 3A **14**
Wyng. *Orkn* 8C **172**
Wynyard Village. *Stoc T* 2B **106**
Wyre Piddle. *Worc* 1E **49**
Wysall. *Notts* 3D **74**
Wyson. *Here* 4H **59**
Wythall. *Worc* 3E **61**
Wytham. *Oxon* 5C **50**
Wythenshawe. *G Man* 2C **84**
Wythop Mill. *Cumb* 2C **102**
Wyton. *Cambs* 3B **64**
Wyton. *E Yor* 1E **95**
Wyverstone. *Suff* 4C **66**
Wyverstone Street. *Suff* 4C **66**
Wyville. *Linc* 3F **75**
Wyvis Lodge. *High* 1G **157**

Y

Yaddlethorpe. *N Lin* 4B **94**
Yafford. *IOW* 4C **16**
Yafforth. *N Yor* 5A **106**
Yalding. *Kent* 5A **40**
Yanley. *N Som* 5A **34**
Yanwath. *Cumb* 2G **103**
Yanworth. *Glos* 4F **49**
Yapham. *E Yor* 4B **100**
Yapton. *W Sus* 5A **26**
Yarburgh. *Linc* 1C **88**
Yarcombe. *Devn* 2F **13**
Yarde. *Som* 3D **20**
Yardley. *W Mid* 2F **61**
Yardley Gobion. *Nptn* 1F **51**
Yardley Hastings. *Nptn* 5F **63**
Yardley Wood. *W Mid* 2F **61**
Yardro. *Powy* 5E **59**
Yarhampton. *Worc* 4B **60**
Yarkhill. *Here* 1B **48**
Yarlet. *Staf* 3D **72**
Yarley. *Som* 2A **22**
Yarlington. *Som* 4B **22**
Yarm. *Stoc T* 3B **106**
Yarmouth. *IOW* 4B **16**
Yarnbrook. *Wilts* 1D **22**
Yarnfield. *Staf* 2C **72**
Yarnscombe. *Devn* 4F **19**
Yarnton. *Oxon* 4C **50**
Yarpole. *Here* 4G **59**
Yarrow. *Nmbd* 1A **114**
Yarrow. *Bord* 2F **119**
Yarrow. *Som* 2G **21**
Yarrow Feus. *Bord* 2F **119**
Yarrow Ford. *Bord* 1G **119**
Yarsop. *Here* 1H **47**
Yarwell. *Nptn* 1H **63**
Yate. *S Glo* 3C **34**
Yateley. *Hants* 5G **37**
Yatesbury. *Wilts* 4F **35**
Yattendon. *W Ber* 4D **36**
Yatton. *Here*
   nr. Leominster 4G **59**
   nr. Ross-on-Wye 2B **48**
Yatton. *N Som* 5H **33**
Yatton Keynell. *Wilts* 4D **34**
Yaverland. *IOW* 4E **16**
Yawl. *Devn* 3G **13**
Yaxham. *Norf* 4C **78**
Yaxley. *Cambs* 1A **64**
Yaxley. *Suff* 3D **66**
Yazor. *Here* 1H **47**
Yeading. *G Lon* 2C **38**
Yeadon. *W Yor* 5E **98**
Yealand Conyers. *Lanc* 2E **97**
Yealand Redmayne. *Lanc* 2E **97**
Yealand Storrs. *Lanc* 2D **97**
Yealmpton. *Devn* 3B **8**
Yearby. *Red C* 2D **106**
Yearngill. *Cumb* 5C **112**
Yearsett. *Here* 5B **60**
Yearsley. *N Yor* 2H **99**
Yeaton. *Shrp* 4G **71**
Yeaveley. *Derbs* 1F **73**

Yeavering. *Nmbd* 1D **120**
Yedingham. *N Yor* 2C **100**
Yeldersley Hollies. *Derbs* 1G **73**
Yelford. *Oxon* 5B **50**
Yelland. *Devn* 3E **19**
Yelling. *Cambs* 4B **64**
Yelsted. *Kent* 4C **40**
Yelvertoft. *Nptn* 3C **62**
Yelverton. *Devn* 2B **8**
Yelverton. *Norf* 5E **79**
Yenston. *Som* 4C **22**
Yeoford. *Devn* 3A **12**
Yeolmbridge. *Corn* 4D **10**
Yeo Mill. *Devn* 4B **20**
Yeovil. *Som* 1A **14**
Yeovil Marsh. *Som* 1A **14**
Yeovilton. *Som* 4A **22**
Yerbeston. *Pemb* 4E **43**
Yesnaby. *Orkn* 6B **172**
Yetlington. *Nmbd* 4E **121**
Yetminster. *Dors* 1A **14**
Yett. *N Lan* 4A **128**
Yett. *S Ayr* 2D **116**
Yettington. *Devn* 4D **12**
Yetts o' Muckhart. *Clac* 3C **136**
Yielden. *Bed* 4H **63**
Yieldshields. *S Lan* 4B **128**
Yiewsley. *G Lon* 2B **38**
Yinstay. *Orkn* 6E **172**
Ynysboeth. *Rhon* 2D **32**
Ynysddu. *Cphy* 2E **33**
Ynysforgan. *Swan* 3F **31**
Ynyshir. *Rhon* 2D **32**
Ynyslas. *Cdgn* 1F **57**
Ynysmaerdy. *Rhon* 3D **32**
Ynysmeudwy. *Neat* 5H **45**
Ynystawe. *Swan* 5G **45**
Ynyswen. *Powy* 4B **46**
Ynys-wen. *Rhon* 2C **32**
Ynys y Barri. *V Glam* 5E **32**
Ynysybwl. *Rhon* 2D **32**
Ynysymaerdy. *Neat* 3G **31**
Yockenthwaite. *N Yor* 2B **98**
Yockleton. *Shrp* 4G **71**
Yokefleet. *E Yor* 2B **94**
Yoker. *Glas* 3G **127**
Yonder Bognie. *Abers* 4C **160**
Yonderton. *Abers* 5G **161**
York. *York* **214** (4A **100**)
Yorkletts. *Kent* 4E **41**
Yorkley. *Glos* 5B **48**
Yorton. *Shrp* 3H **71**
Yorton Heath. *Shrp* 3H **71**
Youlgreave. *Derbs* 4G **85**
Youlthorpe. *E Yor* 4B **100**
Youlton. *N Yor* 3G **99**
Young's End. *Essx* 4H **53**
Young Wood. *Linc* 3A **88**
Yoxall. *Staf* 4F **73**
Yoxford. *Suff* 4F **67**
Ysbyty Cynfyn. *Cdgn* 3G **57**
Ysbyty Ifan. *Cnwy* 1H **69**
Ysbyty Ystwyth. *Cdgn* 3G **57**
Ysceifiog. *Flin* 3D **82**
Yspitty. *Carm* 3E **31**
Ystalyfera. *Neat* 5A **46**
Ystrad. *Rhon* 2C **32**
Ystrad Aeron. *Cdgn* 5E **57**
Ystradfellte. *Powy* 4C **46**
Ystradffin. *Carm* 1A **46**
Ystradgynlais. *Powy* 4A **46**
Ystradmeurig. *Cdgn* 4G **57**
Ystrad Mynach. *Cphy* 2E **33**
Ystradowen. *Carm* 4A **46**
Ystradowen. *V Glam* 4D **32**
Ystumtuen. *Cdgn* 3G **57**
Ythanbank. *Abers* 5G **161**
Ythanwells. *Abers* 5D **160**

Z

Zeal Monachorum. *Devn* 2H **11**
Zeals. *Wilts* 3C **22**
Zelah. *Corn* 3C **6**
Zennor. *Corn* 3B **4**
Zouch. *Notts* 3C **74**

INDEX TO SELECTED PLACES OF INTEREST

(1) A strict alphabetical order is used e.g. Benmore Botanic Gdn. follows Ben Macdui but precedes Ben Nevis.

(2) Entries shown without a main map index reference have the name of the appropriate Town Plan and its page number; e.g. Ashmolean Mus. of Art & Archaeology (OX1 2PH) . . . . **Oxford 207**
The Town Plan title is not given when this is included in the name of the Place of Interest.

(3) Entries in italics are not named on the map but are shown with a symbol only.
Where this occurs the nearest town or village may also be given, unless that name is already included in the name of the Place of Interest.

SAT NAV POSTCODES

Postcodes (in brackets) are included as a navigation aid to assist Sat Nav users and are supplied on this basis. It should be noted that postcodes have been selected by their proximity to the Place of Interest and that they may not form part of the actual postal address.
Drivers should follow the Tourist Brown Signs when available.

ABBREVIATIONS USED IN THIS INDEX

Garden : Gdn.
Gardens : Gdns.
Museum : Mus.
National : Nat
Park : Pk.

A

Abbeydale Industrial Hamlet (S7 2QW) 2H **85**
Abbey House Mus. (LS5 3EH) 1C **92**
Abbot Hall Art Gallery, Kendal (LA9 5AL) 5G **103**
Abbotsbury Subtropical Gardens (DT3 4LA) 4A **14**
Abbotsbury Swannery (DT3 4JG) 4A **14**
Abbotsford (TD6 9BQ) .1H **119**
Aberdeen Maritime Mus. (AB11 5BY) **187**
Aberdour Castle (KY3 0XA) 1E **129**
Aberdulais Falls (SA10 8EU) 5A **46**
Aberglasney Gdns. (SA32 8QH) 3F **45**
Abernethy Round Tower (PH2 9RT) 2D **136**
Aberystwyth Castle (SY23 1DZ) **187**
Acorn Bank Gdn. & Watermill (CA10 1SP) 2H **103**
Acton Burnell Castle (SY5 7PF) 5H **71**
Acton Scott Historic Working Farm
(SY6 6QN) 2G **59**
Adlington Hall (SK10 4LF) 2D **84**
Africa Alive! (NR33 7TF) 2H **67**
Aintree Racecourse (L9 5AS) 1F **83**
Aira Force (CA11 0JX) .2F **103**
A la Ronde (EX8 5BD) .4D **12**
Alderley Edge (SK10 4UB) 3C **84**
Alfriston Clergy House (BN26 5TL) 5G **27**
Alloa Tower (FK10 1PP) 4A **136**
Alnwick Castle (NE66 1NQ) 3F **121**
Alnwick Gdn. (NE66 1YU) 3F **121**
Althorp (NN7 4HQ) 4D **62**
Alton Towers (ST10 4DB) 1E **73**
Amberley Mus. & Heritage Cen. (BN18 9LT) 4B **26**
American Mus. in Britain (BA2 7BD) 5C **34**
Angel of the North (NE9 6PG) 4F **115**
Anglesey Abbey & Lode Mill (CB25 9EJ) 4E **65**
Animalarium at Borth (SY24 5NA) 2F **57**
Anne Hathaway's Cottage (CV37 9HH) 5F **61**
Antonine Wall (FK4 2AA) 2B **128**
Antony (PL11 2QA) 3A **8**
Appuldurcombe House (PO38 3EW) 4D **16**
Arbeia Roman Fort & Mus. (NE33 2BB) 3G **115**
Arbroath Abbey (DD11 1JQ) 4F **145**
Arbury Hall (CV10 7PT) .2H **61**
Arbuthnott House Gdn. (AB30 1PA) 1G **145**
Ardkinglas Woodland Gdns. (PA26 8BG) 2A **134**
Ardnamurchan Point (PH36 4LN) 2E **139**
Arduaine Gdn. (PA34 4XQ) 2E **133**
Ardwell Gdns. (DG9 9LY) 5G **109**
Argyll's Lodging (FK8 1EG) . . . .**Stirling 211**
Arley Hall & Gdns. (CW9 6NA) 2A **84**
Arlington Court (EX31 4LP) 3G **19**
Arlington Row (GL7 5NJ) 5G **49**
Armadale Castle Gdns. (IV45 8RS) 3E **147**
Arniston House (EH23 4RY) 4G **129**
Arundel Castle (BN18 9AB) 5B **26**
Arundel Wetland Centre (BN18 9PB) 5B **26**
Ascot Racecourse (SL5 7JX) 4A **38**
Ascott (LU7 0PT) 3G **51**
Ashby-de-la-Zouch Castle (LE65 1BR) 4A **74**
Ashdown Forest (TN7 4EU) 2F **27**
Ashdown House (RG17 8RE) 3A **36**
Ashmolean Mus. of Art & Archaeology
(OX1 2PH) . . . .**Oxford 207**
Ashridge Estate (HP4 1LT) 4H **51**
Astley Hall Mus. & Art Gallery (PR7 1NP) 3D **90**
Athelhampton House (DT2 7LG) 3C **14**
Attingham Pk. (SY4 4TP) 5H **71**
Auchingarrich Wildlife Centre (PH6 2JE) 2G **135**
Auckland Castle, Bishop Auckland
(DL14 7NP) 1F **105**
Audley End House & Gdns. (CB11 4JF) 2F **53**
Avebury Stone Circle (SN8 1RE) 4G **35**
Avoncroft Mus. of Historic Buildings
(B60 4JR) 4D **60**
Avon Valley Adventure & Wildlife Pk.
(BS31 1TP) 5B **34**
Avon Valley Railway (BS30 6HD) 4B **34**
Aydon Castle (NE45 5PJ) 3C **114**
Ayr Racecourse (KA8 0JE) 2C **116**
Ayscoughfee Hall Mus. & Gdns. (PE11 2RA) 3B **76**
Aysgarth Falls (DL8 3SR) 1C **98**
Ayton Castle (Eyemouth) (TD14 5RD) 3F **131**

B

Bachelors' Club (KA5 5RB) 2D **116**
Baconsthorpe Castle (NR25 6PS) 2D **78**
Baddesley Clinton (B93 0DQ) 3F **61**
Bala Lake Railway (LL23 7DD) 2A **70**
Ballindalloch Castle (AB37 9AX) 5F **159**
Balmacara Estate (IV40 8DN) 1F **147**
Balmoral Castle (AB35 5TB) 4G **151**
Balvaird Castle (PH2 9PY) 2D **136**
Balvenie Castle (AB55 4DH) 4H **159**
Bamburgh Castle (NE69 7DF) 1F **121**
Bangor Cathedral (LL57 1DN) 3E **81**
Banham Zoo (NR16 2HE) 2C **66**
Bannockburn Battle Site (FK7 0PL) 4G **135**
Barbara Hepworth Mus. & Sculpture Gdn.
(TR26 1AD) 2C **4**
Barnard Castle (DL12 8PR) 3D **104**
Barnsdale Gdns. (LE15 8AH) 4G **75**
Barrington Court (TA19 0NQ) 1G **13**
Basildon Pk. (RG8 9NR) 4E **36**
Basing House (RG24 7HB) 1E **25**
Basingwerk Abbey (CH8 7GH) 3D **82**
Bateman's (TN19 7DS) .3A **28**
Bath Abbey (BA1 1LT) **187**
Bath Assembly Rooms (BA1 2QH) **187**
Bath Roman Baths & Pump Room (BA1 1LZ) **187**
Battle Abbey (TN33 0AD) 4B **28**
Battlefield Line Railway (CV13 0BS) 5A **74**
Battle of Britain Memorial (CT18 7JJ) 2G **29**
Battle of Britain Memorial Flight Visitors Centre,
RAF Coningsby (LN4 4SY) 5B **88**
Battle of Hastings Site (TN33 0AD) 4B **28**
Bayham Abbey (TN3 8BE) 2H **27**
Beachy Head (BN20 7YA) 5G **27**
Beamish (DH9 0RG) 4F **115**
Beatles Story (L3 4AD) . . . .**Liverpool 200**
Beatrix Potter's House, Hill Top (LA22 0LF) 5E **103**
Beaulieu Abbey (SO42 7ZN) 2B **16**
Beauly Priory (IV4 7BL) 4H **157**
Beaumaris Castle (LL58 8AP) 3F **81**
Beck Isle Museum of Rural Life
(YO18 8DU) 1B **100**
Bedgebury Nat. Pinetum (TN17 2SL) 2B **28**
Bedruthan Steps (PL27 7UW) 2C **6**
Beeston Castle & Woodland Pk. (CW6 9TX) 5H **83**
Bekonscot Model Village & Railway
(HP9 2PL) 1A **38**
Belgrave Hall Mus. & Gdns. (LE4 5PE) 5C **74**
Belmont House & Gdns. (ME13 0HH) 5D **40**
Belsay Hall, Castle & Gdns. (NE20 0DX) 2D **115**
Belton House (NG32 2LS) 2G **75**
Belvoir Castle (NG32 1PD) 2F **75**
Beningbrough Hall & Gardens (YO30 1DD) 4H **99**
Benington Lordship Gdns. (SG2 7BS) 3C **52**
Ben Lawers (PH15 2PA) 4D **142**
Ben Lomond (FK8 3TR) .3C **134**
Ben Macdui (PH22 1RB) 4D **151**
Benmore Botanic Gdn. (PA23 8QU) 1C **126**
Ben Nevis (PH33 6SY) .1F **141**
Benthall Hall (TF12 5RX) 5A **72**
Bentley Wildfowl & Motor Mus. (BN8 5AF) 4F **27**
Berkeley Castle (GL13 9BQ) 2B **34**
Berkhamsted Castle (HP4 1LJ) 5H **51**
Berney Arms Windmill (NR31 9HU) 5G **79**
Berrington Hall (HR6 0DW) 4H **59**
Berry Pomeroy Castle (TQ9 6LJ) 2E **9**
Bessie Surtees House
(NE1 3JF) . . . .**Newcastle upon Tyne 205**
Beverley Minster (HU17 0DP) 1D **94**
Bicton Pk. Botanical Gdns. (EX9 7BJ) 4D **12**
Biddulph Grange Gdn. (ST8 7SD) 5C **84**
Big Ben (SW1A 2PW) . . . .**London 203**
Bignor Roman Villa (RH20 1PH) 4A **26**
Big Pit: Nat. Coal Mus. (NP4 9XP) 5F **47**
Binham Priory (NR21 0DJ) 1B **78**
Birmingham Mus. & Art Gallery (B3 3DH) **188**
Bishop's Waltham Palace (SO32 1DP) 1D **16**
Black Country Living Mus., Dudley
(DY1 4SQ) 1D **60**
Blackgang Chine Theme Park (PO38 2HN) 5C **16**
Blackhouse (HS2 9DB) .3F **171**
Blackness Castle (EH49 7NH) 1D **128**
Blackpool Pleasure Beach (FY4 1EZ) 1B **90**
Blackpool Zoo (FY3 8PP) 1B **90**
Blackwell, The Arts & Crafts House
(LA23 3JR) 5F **103**
Blaenavon Ironworks (NP4 9RJ) 5F **47**
Blaenavon World Heritage Cen. (NP4 9AS) 5F **47**
Blair Castle (PH18 5TL) 2F **143**
Blair Drummond Safari & Adventure Pk.
(FK9 4UR) 4G **135**
Blairquhan Castle (KA19 7LZ) 4C **116**
Blakeney Point (NR25 7SA) 1C **78**
Blakesley Hall (B25 8RN) 2F **61**
Blenheim Palace (OX20 1PX) 4C **50**
Bletchley Pk. (MK3 6EB) 2G **51**
Blickling Estate (NR11 6NF) 3D **78**
Blists Hill Victorian Town, Telford (TF7 5DS) 5A **72**
Bluebell Railway (TN22 3QL) 3E **27**
Blue John Cavern (S33 8WP) 2F **85**
Blue Reef Aquarium, Hastings (TN34 3DW) 5C **28**
Blue Reef Aquarium, Newquay (TR7 1DU) 2C **6**
Blue Reef Aquarium, Portsmouth (PO5 3PB) **209**
Blue Reef Aquarium, Tynemouth
(NE30 4JF) 2G **115**
Boath Doocot (IV12 5TD) 3D **158**
Bodelwyddan Castle (LL18 5YA) 3B **82**
Bodiam Castle (TN32 5UA) 3B **28**
Bodleian Library (OX1 3BG) . . . .**Oxford 207**
Bodmin & Wenford Railway (PL31 1AQ) 2E **7**
Bodmin Moor (PL15 7TN) 5B **10**
Bodnant Gdn. (LL28 5RE) 3H **81**
Bodrhyddan Hall (LL18 5SB) 3C **82**
Bolingbroke Castle (PE23 4HH) 4C **88**
Bolsover Castle (S44 6PR) 3B **86**
Bolton Castle (DL8 4ET) 5D **104**
Bolton Priory (BD23 6AL) 4C **98**
Bonawe Historic Iron Furnace (PA35 1JQ) 5E **141**
Bo'ness & Kinneil Railway (EH51 9AQ) 1C **128**
Booth Mus. of Natural History
(BN1 5AA) . . . .**Brighton & Hove 189**
Borde Hill Gdn. (RH16 1XP) 3E **27**
Boscobel House (ST19 9AR) 5C **72**
Boston Stump (PE21 6NQ) 1C **76**
Bosworth Field Battle Site (CV13 0AB) 5A **74**
Bothwell Castle (G71 8BL) 4H **127**
Boughton (NN14 1BJ) .2G **63**
Bowes Castle (DL12 9LE) 3C **104**
Bowes Mus. (DL12 8NP) 3D **104**
Bowhill House & Country Estate (TD7 5ET) 2G **119**
Bowood House & Gdns. (SN11 0LZ) 5E **35**
Braemar Castle (AB35 5XR) 4F **151**
Bramall Hall, Bramhall (SK7 3NX) 2C **84**
Bramber Castle (BN44 3FJ) 4C **26**
Bramham Pk. (LS23 6ND) 5G **99**
Brands Hatch Motor Circuit (DA3 8NG) 4G **39**
Brantwood (LA21 8AD) .5E **102**
Breamore House (SP6 2DF) 1G **15**
Brean Down (TA8 2RS) .1F **21**
Brecon Beacons Nat. Pk. (CF44 9JG) 3C **46**
Brecon Mountain Railway (CF48 2UP) 4D **46**
Bressingham Steam & Gdns. (IP22 2AB) 2C **66**
Brimham Rocks (HG3 4DW) 3E **98**
Brindley Mill & Mus. (ST13 8FA) 5D **85**
Brinkburn Priory (NE65 8AR) 5F **121**
Bristol Aquarium (BS1 5TT) **189**
Bristol Cathedral (BS1 5TJ) **189**
Bristol Zoo Gdns. (BS8 3HA) **189**
Britannia Bridge (LL61 5BZ) 3E **81**
British Airways i360
(BN1 2LN) . . . .**Brighton & Hove 189**
British Golf Mus. (KY16 9AB) . . . .**St Andrews 209**
British in India Mus. (BB9 8AD) 1G **91**
British Library (NW1 2DB) . . . .**London 203**
British Motor Museum (CV35 0BJ) 5A **62**
British Mus. (WC1B 3DG) . . . .**London 203**
Broadlands (SO51 9ZD) 4B **24**
Broads Nat. Pk. (NR3 1BJ) 5G **79**
Broadway Tower (WR12 7LB) 2G **49**
Brobury House Gdns. (HR3 6BS) 1G **47**
Brockhampton Estate (WR6 5TB) 5A **60**
Brockhole, Lake District Visitor Centre
(LA23 1LJ) 4E **103**
Brodick Castle & Gardens (KA27 8HY) 2E **123**
Brodie Castle (IV36 2TE) 3D **159**
Brodsworth Hall & Gdns. (DN5 7XJ) 4F **93**
Brogdale (ME13 8XU) 5E **40**
Bronllys Castle (LD3 0HL) 2E **47**
Brontë Parsonage Mus. (BD22 8DR) 1A **92**
Broseley Pipe Works (TF12 5LX) 5A **72**
Brougham Castle (CA10 2AA) 2G **103**
Brough Castle (CA17 4EJ) 3A **104**
Broughton Castle (OX15 5EB) 2C **50**
Broughton House & Gdn. (DG6 4JX) 4D **111**
Brownsea Island (BH13 7EE) 4F **15**
Bruce's Stone (DG7 3SQ) 2C **110**
Brunel's SS Great Britain (BS1 6TY) . . . .**Bristol 189**
Bubble Car Mus. (PE22 7AW) 1B **76**
Buckfast Abbey (TQ11 0EE) 2D **8**
Buckingham Palace (SW1A 1AA) . . . .**London 202**
Buckland Abbey (PL20 6EY) 2A **8**
Buckler's Hard Maritime Museum
(SO42 7XB) 3C **16**
Buildwas Abbey (TF8 7BW) 5A **72**
Bungay Castle (NR35 1DD) 2F **67**
Bure Valley Railway (NR11 6BW) 3E **79**
Burford House Gdns. (WR15 8HQ) 4H **59**
Burghley (PE9 3JY) 5H **75**
Burleigh Castle (KY13 9TD) 3D **136**
Burnby Hall Gdns. & Mus. (YO42 2QF) 5C **100**
Burns House Mus. (KA5 5BZ) 2D **117**
Burton Agnes Hall (YO25 4ND) 3F **101**
Burton Constable Hall (HU11 4LN) 1E **95**
Bury St Edmunds Abbey (IP33 1RS) 4A **66**
Buscot Pk. (SN7 8BU) 2H **35**
Butser Ancient Farm (PO8 0QF) 1F **17**
Buttertubs, The (DL11 6DR) 5B **104**
Buxton Pavilion Gdns. (SK17 6XN) 3E **85**
Byland Abbey (YO61 4BD) 2H **99**

C

Cadair Idris (LL40 1TN) 4F **69**
Cadbury World (B30 1JR) 2E **61**
Caerlaverock Castle (DG1 4RU) 3B **112**
Caerleon Roman Fortress (NP18 1AY) 2G **33**
Caernarfon Castle (LL55 2AY) **190**
Caerphilly Castle (CF83 1JD) 3E **33**
Cairngorms Nat. Pk. (PH26 3HG) 3D **151**
Cairnpapple Hill (EH48 4NW) 2C **128**
Caister Castle, West Caister (NR30 5SN) 4H **79**
Calanais Standing Stones (HS2 9DY) 4E **171**
Caldey Island (SA70 7UH) 5F **43**
Caldicot Castle (NP26 5JB) 3H **33**
Caledonian Railway (DD9 7AF) 3F **145**
Calke Abbey (DE73 7LE) 3A **74**
Calshot Castle (SO45 1BR) 2C **16**
Camber Castle (TN31 7TB) 4D **28**
Cambo Gdns. (KY16 8QD) 2H **137**
Cambridge University Botanic Gdn.
(CB2 1JF) 5D **64**
Camperdown Wildlife Centre (DD2 4TF) 5C **144**
Canal Mus. (NN12 7SE) .5E **63**
Cannock Chase (WS12 4PW) 4D **73**
Cannon Hall Mus. (S75 4AT) 4C **92**
Canons Ashby House (NN11 3SD) 5C **62**
Canterbury Cathedral (CT1 2EH) **190**
Capesthorne Hall (SK11 9JY) 3C **84**
Cape Wrath (IV27 4QQ) 1C **166**
Captain Cook Schoolroom Mus.
(TS9 6NB) 3C **106**
Cardiff Castle (CF10 3RB) . . . .**Cardiff 191**
Cardoness Castle (DG7 2EH) 4C **110**
Carew Castle (SA70 8SL) 4E **43**
Carisbrooke Castle (PO30 1XY) 4C **16**
Carlisle Castle (CA3 8UR) **192**
Carlisle Cathedral (CA3 8TZ) **192**
Carlyle's Birthplace (DG11 3DG) 2C **112**
Carnasserie Castle (PA31 8RQ) 3F **133**
Carn Euny Ancient Village (TR20 8RB) 4B **4**
Carreg Cennen Castle & Farm (SA19 6UA) 4G **45**
Carsluith Castle (DG8 7DY) 4B **110**
Cartmel Priory Church (LA11 6QQ) 2C **96**
Castell Coch, Tongwynlais (CF15 7JS) 3E **33**
Castell Dinas Bran (LL20 8DY) 1E **70**
Castell y Bere (LL36 9TP) 5F **69**
Castle Acre Castle (PE32 2XB) 4H **77**
Castle Acre Priory (PE32 2AA) 4H **77**
Castle & Gdns. of Mey (KW14 8XH) 1E **169**
Castle Campbell & Gdn. (FK14 7PP) 4B **136**
Castle Drogo (EX6 6PB) 3H **11**
Castle Fraser (AB51 7LD) 2E **152**
Castle Howard (YO60 7DA) 2B **100**
Castle Kennedy Gdns. (DG9 8SJ) 3G **109**
Castle Leod (IV14 9AA) .3G **157**
Castle Menzies (PH15 2JD) 4F **143**
Castlerigg Stone Circle (CA12 4RN) 2D **102**
Castle Rising Castle (PE31 6AH) 3F **77**
Catalyst Science Discovery Centre
(WA8 0DF) 2H **83**
Cawdor Castle (IV12 5RD) 4C **158**
Cerne Giant (DT2 7TS) .2B **14**
Chanonry Point (IV10 8SD) 3B **158**
Charlecote Pk. (CV35 9ER) 5G **61**
Charleston (BN8 6LL) 5F **27**
Chartwell (TN16 1PS) 5F **39**
Chastleton House (GL56 0SU) 3H **49**
Chatsworth (DE45 1PP) 3G **85**
Chavenage House (GL8 8XP) 2D **34**
Cheddar Gorge (BS40 7XT) 1H **21**
Chedworth Roman Villa (GL54 3LJ) 4F **49**
Cheltenham Racecourse (GL50 4SH) 3E **49**
Chenies Manor House & Gdns. (WD3 6ER) 1B **38**
Chepstow Castle (NP16 5EZ) 2A **34**
Chepstow Racecourse (NP16 6EG) 2A **34**
Chesil Beach (DT3 4ED) 4B **14**
Chessington World of Adventures
(KT9 2NE) 4C **38**
Chester Cathedral (CH1 2HU) **192**
Chester Roman Amphitheatre (CH1 1RF) **192**
Chesters Roman Fort & Mus. (NE46 4ET) 2C **114**
Chester Zoo (CH2 1LH) 3G **83**
Chettle House (DT11 8DB) 1E **15**
Chichester Cathedral (PO19 1PX) 2G **17**
Chiddingstone Castle (TN8 7AD) 1F **27**
Chillingham Castle (NE66 5NJ) 2E **121**
Chillingham Wild Cattle (NE66 5NJ) 2E **121**
Chillington Hall (WV8 1RE) 5C **72**
Chiltern Hills (RG9 6DR) 3E **37**
Chiltern Open Air Mus. (HP8 4AB) 1B **38**
Chirk Castle (LL14 5AF) 2E **71**
Cholmondeley Castle Gdns. (SY14 8AH) 5H **83**
Christchurch Castle & Norman House
(BH23 1BW) 3G **15**
Christchurch Mansion (IP4 2BE) . . . .**Ipswich 198**
Churnet Valley Railway (ST13 7EE) 5D **85**
Chysauster Ancient Village (TR20 8XA) 3B **4**
Cilgerran Castle (SA43 2SF) 1B **44**
Cissbury Ring (BN14 0SQ) 5C **26**
Clandon Pk. (GU4 7RQ) 5B **38**
Claremont Landscape Gdn. (KT10 9JG) 4C **38**
Claydon (MK18 2EY) 3F **51**
Clearwell Caves (GL16 8JR) 5A **48**
Cleeve Abbey (TA23 0PS) 2D **20**
Clevedon Court (BS21 6QU) 4H **33**
Clifford's Tower (YO1 9SA) . . . .**York 214**
Clifton Suspension Bridge (BS8 3PA) . . . . .**Bristol 189**
Cliveden (SL6 0JA) 2A **38**
Clouds Hill (BH20 7NQ) 3D **14**
Clumber Pk. (S80 3BX) 3D **86**
Clun Castle (SY7 8JR) .2E **59**
Clyde Muirshiel Regional Pk. (PA10 2PZ) 3D **126**
Coalbrookdale Mus. of Iron (TF8 7DQ) 5A **72**
Coalport China Mus. (TF8 7HT) 5A **72**
Coca-Cola London Eye (SE1 7PB) **203**
Coed y Brenin Visitor Centre (LL40 2HZ) 3G **69**
Coggeshall Grange Barn (CO6 1RE) 3B **54**
Coity Castle (CF35 6AU) 3C **32**
Colby Woodland Gdn. (SA67 8PP) 4F **43**
Colchester Castle Mus. (CO1 1TJ) 3D **54**
Colchester Zoo (CO3 0SL) 3C **54**
Coleridge Cottage (TA5 1NQ) 3E **21**
Coleton Fishacre (TQ6 0EQ) 3F **9**
Colour Experience (BD1 2JB) . . . .**Bradford 190**
Colzium Walled Gdn. (G65 0PY) 2A **128**
Combe Martin Wildlife & Dinosaur Pk.
(EX34 0NG) 2F **19**
Compton Acres (BH13 7ES) 4F **15**
Compton Castle (TQ3 1TA) 2E **9**
Compton Verney (CV35 9HZ) 5H **61**
Conisbrough Castle (DN12 3BU) 1C **86**
Conishead Priory (LA12 9QQ) 2C **96**
Conkers (DE12 6GA) 4H **73**
Constable Burton Hall Gdns. (DL8 5LJ) 5E **105**
Conwy Castle (LL32 8LD) 3G **81**
Coombes & Churnet Nature Reserve, Basford
(ST13 7NN) 5E **85**
Corbridge Roman Town (NE45 5NT) 3C **114**
Corfe Castle (BH20 5EZ) 4E **15**
Corgarff Castle (AB36 8YP) 3G **151**
Corinium Mus. (GL7 2BX) 5F **49**
Cornish Seal Sanctuary (TR12 6UG) 4E **5**
Corrieshalloch Gorge (IV23 2PJ) 1E **156**
Corsham Court (SN13 0BZ) 4D **35**
Cotehele (PL12 6TA) 2A **8**
Coton Manor Gdn. (NN6 8RQ) 3D **62**
Cotswold Farm Pk. (GL54 5UG) 3G **49**
Cotswold Hills (GL8 8NU) 2E **35**
Cotswold Water Pk. (GL7 5TL) 2F **35**
Cottesbrooke Hall & Gdns. (NN6 8PF) 3E **62**
Cotton Mechanical Music Mus. (IP14 4QN) 4C **66**
Coughton Court (B49 5JA) 4E **61**
Courts Gdn., The (BA14 6RR) 5D **34**
Coventry Cathedral (CV1 5AB) **192**
Coventry Transport Mus. (CV1 1JD) **192**
Cowdray House (GU29 9AL) 4G **25**
Cragside (NE65 7PX) 4E **121**
Craigievar Castle (AB33 8JF) 3C **152**
Craigmillar Castle (EH16 4SY) 2F **129**
Craignethan Castle (ML11 9PL) 5B **128**
Craigston Castle (AB53 5PX) 3E **161**
Cranborne Manor Gardens (BH21 5PS) 1F **15**
Cranwell Aviation Heritage Centre
(NG34 8QR) 1H **75**
Crarae Gdn. (PA32 8YA) 4G **133**
Crathes Castle, Garden & Estate
(AB31 5QJ) 4E **153**
Creswell Crags (S80 3LH) 3C **86**
Crewe Heritage Centre (CW1 2DD) 5B **84**
Criccieth Castle (LL52 0DP) 2D **69**

Crichton Castle (EH37 5XA) 3G **129**
Crich Tramway Village (DE4 5DP) 5H **85**
Croft Castle (HR6 9PW) 4G **59**
Croft Motor Circuit (DL2 2PL) 4F **105**
Cromford Mill (DE4 3RQ) 5G **85**
Cromwell Mus. (PE29 3LF) 3B **64**
Crookston Castle (G53 5RR) 3G **127**
Croome (WR8 9JS) 1D **49**
Crossraguel Abbey (KA19 8HQ) 4B **116**
Croxden Abbey (ST14 5JG) 2E **73**
Croxteth Hall (L12 0HB) 1G **83**
Cruachan Power Station (PA33 1AN) 1H **133**
Culloden Battlefield Visitor Centre
  (IV2 5EU) 4B **158**
Culloden Battle Site (IV2 5EU) 4B **158**
Culross Palace (KY12 8JH) 1C **128**
Culzean Castle (KA19 8LE) 3B **116**
Curraghs Wildlife Pk. (IM7 5EA) 2C **108**
Cusworth Hall (DN5 7TU) 4F **93**
Cymer Abbey (LL40 2HE) 4G **69**

D

Dalemain (CA11 0HB) 2F **103**
Dales Countryside Mus. (DL8 3NT) 5B **104**
Dallas Dhu Historic Distillery (IV36 2RR) . .3E **159**
Dalmeny House (EH30 9TQ) 2E **129**
Darby Houses (TF8 7DQ) 5A **72**
Dartington Crystal (EX38 7AN) 1E **11**
Dartington Hall Gdns. (TQ9 6EL) 2E **9**
Dartmoor Nat. Pk. (TQ13 9JQ) 4F **11**
Dartmoor Zoo (PL7 5DG) 3B **8**
Dartmouth Castle (TQ6 0JN) 3E **9**
Dartmouth Steam Railway (TQ4 6AF) 3E **9**
Dawyck Botanic Gdn. (EH45 9JU) 1D **118**
Deal Castle (CT14 7BA) 5H **41**
Dean Castle (KA3 1XB) 1D **116**
Dean Forest Railway (GL15 4ET) 5B **48**
Deene Pk. (NN17 3EW) 1G **63**
Deep, The (HU1 4DP) . . . . .Kingston upon Hull **199**
Deep Sea World (KY11 1JR) 1E **129**
Delamere Forest Park (CW8 2JD) 3H **83**
Delgatie Castle (AB53 5TD) 3E **161**
The Den & the Glen (AB12 5FT) 4F **153**
Denbigh Castle (LL16 3NB) 4C **82**
Devil's Dyke (BN45 7DE) 4D **26**
Devil's Punch Bowl (GU26 6AB) 3G **25**
Dewa Roman Experience (CH1 1NL) . . . . .Chester **192**
DH Lawrence Birthplace Mus. (NG16 3AW) .1B **74**
Dickens House Mus. (WC1N 1QS) 4H **41**
Didcot Railway Centre (OX11 7NJ) 2D **36**
Dinefwr Castle (SA19 6PF) 3G **45**
Dinefwr Pk. (SA19 6RT) 3G **45**
Dinorwig Power Station (LL55 4UR) 5E **81**
Dinosaur Adventure (NR9 5JW) 4D **78**
Dinosaur Mus. (DT1 1EW) 3B **14**
Dirleton Castle & Gdn. (EH39 5ER) 1B **130**
Discovery Mus.
  (NE1 4JA) . . . . .Newcastle upon Tyne **205**
Discovery Point (DD1 4XA) . . . . .Dundee **194**
Dock Mus. (LA14 2PW) 3A **96**
Doddington Hall & Gdns. (LN6 4RU) 3F **87**
Doddington Place Gdns (ME9 0BB) 5D **40**
Dolaucothi Gold Mines (SA19 8RR) 2G **45**
Dolbadarn Castle (LL55 4SU) 5E **81**
Dolforwyn Castle (SY15 6JH) 1D **58**
Dolwyddelan Castle (LL25 0JD) 5G **81**
Domestic Fowl Trust and Honeybourne Rare Breeds
  (WR11 7QZ) 1G **49**
Doncaster Racecourse (DN2 6BB) 4G **93**
Donington Grand Prix Collection, Castle Donington
  (DE74 2RP) 3B **74**
Donington Pk. Motor Circuit (DE74 2RP) . . .3B **74**
Donnington Castle (RG14 2LE) 5C **36**
Dorfold Hall (CW5 8LD) 5A **84**
Dorothy Clive Gdn. (TF9 4EU) 2B **72**
Doune Castle (FK16 6EA) 3G **135**
Dove Cottage (Wordsworth Mus.)
  (LA22 9SH) 4E **103**
Dovedale (DE6 1NL) 5F **85**
Dover Castle (CT16 1HU) **193**
Down House (BR6 7JT) 4F **39**
Dozmary Pool (PL15 7TP) 5B **10**
Drayton Manor Theme Pk. (B78 3TW) 5F **73**
Drum Castle & Gdn. (AB31 5EY) 3E **153**
Drumlanrig Castle (DG3 4AQ) 5A **118**
Drummond Gdns. (PH5 2AA) 2H **135**
Drusillas (BN26 5QS) 5G **27**
Dryburgh Abbey (TD6 0RQ) 1H **119**
Dryslwyn Castle (SA32 8JQ) 3F **45**
Duart Castle (PA64 6AP) 5B **140**
Dudmaston Estate (WV15 6QN) 2B **60**
Duff House Country Gallery (AB45 3SX) 2D **160**
Duffus Castle (IV30 5RH) 2D **159**
Dukeries, The (S80 3BT) 3D **86**
Dumbarton Castle (G82 1JJ) 2F **127**
Dunblane Cathedral (FK15 0AQ) 3G **135**
Duncombe Park (YO62 5EB) 1A **100**
Dundonald Castle (KA2 9HD) 1C **116**
Dundrennan Abbey (DG6 4QH) 5E **111**
Dunfermline Abbey (KY12 7PE) 1D **129**
Dungeon Ghyll Force (LA22 9JY) 4D **102**
Dunge Valley Rhododendron Gdns.
  (SK23 7RF) 3D **85**
Dunham Massey (WA14 4SJ) 2B **84**
Dunkeld Cathedral (PH8 0AW) 4H **143**
Dunkery Beacon (TA24 7AT) 2B **20**
Dunnet Head (KW14 8XS) 1E **169**
Dunninald (DD10 9TD) 3G **145**
Dunnottar Castle (AB39 2TL) 5F **153**
Dunrobin Castle (KW10 6SF) 3F **165**
Dunstaffnage Castle (PA37 1PZ) 5C **140**
Dunstanburgh Castle (NE66 3TG) 2G **121**
Dunster Castle (TA24 6SL) 2C **20**
Durdle Door (BH20 5PU) 4D **14**
Durham Cathedral (DH1 3EH) **194**
Dyffryn Gdns. (CF5 6SU) 4D **32**
Dylan Thomas Boathouse (SA33 4SD) 3H **43**
Dyrham Pk. (SN14 8ER) 4C **34**

E

Eagle Heights Wildlife Pk. (DA4 0JB) 4G **39**
Easby Abbey (DL10 7JU) 4E **105**
East Anglian Railway Mus. (CO6 2DS) 3B **54**

East Bergholt Place Gdn. (CO7 6UP) 2D **54**
East Kent Railway (CT15 7PD) 1G **29**
East Lambrook Manor Gdns. (TA13 5HH) . . .1H **13**
East Lancashire Railway (BL9 0EY) 2G **91**
Eastnor Castle (HR8 1RD) 2C **48**
East Pool Mine (TR15 3NP) 4A **6**
East Riddlesden Hall (BD20 5EL) 5C **98**
East Somerset Railway (BA4 4QP) 2B **22**
Ebberston Hall (YO13 9RE) 5F **27**
Eden Project (PL24 2SG) 3E **7**
Edinburgh Castle (EH1 2NG) **194**
Edinburgh Zoo (EH12 6TS) 2F **129**
Edzell Castle & Gdn. (DD9 7UE) 2E **145**
Egglestone Abbey (DL12 9TN) 3D **104**
Eilean Donan Castle (IV40 8DX) 1A **148**
Elcho Castle (PH2 8QQ) 1D **136**
Electric Mountain (LL55 4UR) 4E **81**
Electric Railway Mus. (CV3 4LE) 3A **62**
Elgar Birthplace Mus. (WR2 6RH) 5C **60**
Elgin Cathedral (IV30 1EL) 2G **159**
Eltham Palace & Gdns. (SE9 5QE) 3F **39**
Elton Hall & Gdns. (PE8 6SH) 1H **63**
Ely Cathedral (CB7 4DL) 2E **65**
Embsay & Bolton Abbey Steam Railway
  (BD23 6AF) 4C **98**
Emmetts Gdn. (TN14 6BA) 5F **39**
Enginuity (TF8 7DQ) 5A **72**
Epping Ongar Railway (CM5 9BN) 5F **53**
Epsom Downs Racecourse (KT18 5LQ) 5D **38**
Erddig (LL13 0YT) .1F **71**
Escot (EX11 1LU) .3D **12**
Etal Castle (TD12 4TN) 1D **120**
Eureka! The Nat. Children's Mus., Halifax
  (HX1 2NE) 2A **92**
Euston Hall (IP24 2QW) 3A **66**
Ewloe Castle (CH5 3BZ) 4E **83**
Exbury Gdns. (SO45 1AZ) 2C **16**
Exeter Cathedral (EX1 1HS) **195**
Exmoor Nat. Pk. (TA22 9HL) 3B **20**
Eyam Hall (S32 5QW) 3G **85**
Eye Castle (IP23 7AP) 3D **66**
Eynsford Castle (DA4 0AA) 4G **39**

F

Fairbourne Steam Railway (LL38 2PZ) 4F **69**
Fairhaven Woodland & Water Gdn.
  (NR13 6DZ) 4F **79**
Falkirk Wheel (FK1 4RS) 1B **128**
Falkland Palace (KY15 7BU) 3E **137**
Falls of Glomach (IV40 8DS) 1C **148**
Falstaff Experience - Tudor World
  (CV37 6EE) . . . . .Stratford **212**
Farleigh Hungerford Castle (BA2 7RS) 1C **22**
Farmland Mus. & Denny Abbey
  (CB25 9PQ) 4D **65**
Farnborough Hall (OX17 1DU) 1C **50**
Farne Islands (NE68 7SY) 1G **121**
Farnham Castle Keep (GU9 0AE) 2G **25**
Felbrigg Hall (NR11 8PR) 2D **78**
Ferniehirst Castle (TD8 6NX) 3A **120**
Ffestiniog Railway (LL49 9NF) 1F **69**
Fiddleford Manor (DT10 2BU) 1D **14**
Finchale Priory (DH1 5SH) 5F **115**
Finch Foundry (EX20 2NW) 3G **11**
Fingal's Cave (PA73 6NA) 5E **138**
Finlaystone Country Estate (PA14 6TJ) 2E **127**
Fishbourne Roman Palace & Gdns.
  (PO19 3QR) 2G **17**
Fitzwilliam Mus. (CB2 1RB) . . . . .Cambridge **191**
Five Sisters of Kintail (IV40 8HQ) 2B **148**
Flambards (TR13 0QA) 4D **4**
Flamingo Land (YO17 6UX) 2B **100**
Fleet Air Arm Mus. (BA22 8HT) 4A **22**
Flint Castle (CH6 5PE) 3E **83**
Floors Castle & Gdns. (TD5 7SF) 1B **120**
Fonmon Castle (CF62 3ZN) 5D **32**
Forde Abbey & Gdns. (TA20 4LU) 2G **13**
Ford Green Hall (ST6 1NG) 5C **84**
Forest of Dean (GL15 4SL) 5B **48**
Forge Mill Mus. (B98 8HY) 4E **61**
Forth Bridge (EH30 9TB) 1E **129**
Fort Nelson (Royal Armouries)
  (PO17 6AN) 2E **16**
Fountains Abbey & Studley Royal
  (HG4 3DY) 3E **99**
Foxfield Steam Railway (ST11 9BG) 1D **72**
Foxton Locks (LE16 7RA) 2D **62**
Framlingham Castle (IP13 9BP) 4E **67**
Froghall Wharf (ST10 2HH) 1E **73**
Furness Abbey (LA13 0PG) 2B **96**
Furzey Gdns. (SO43 7GL) 1A **16**
Fyne Court (TA5 2EQ) 3F **21**
Fyvie Castle (AB53 8JS) 5E **161**

G

Gainsborough Old Hall (DN21 2NB) 1F **87**
Gainsborough's House (CO10 2EU) 1B **54**
Gallery of Modern Art (G1 3AH) . . . . . . .Glasgow **196**
Galloway Forest Pk. (DG8 6TA) 1B **110**
Galloway House Gdns. (DG8 8HF) 5B **110**
Galloway Wildlife Conservation Pk.
  (DG6 4XX) 4E **111**
Garden House, The (PL20 7LQ) 2A **8**
Gdns. of the Rose (AL2 3NR) 5B **52**
Gawsworth Hall (SK11 9RN) 4C **84**
Gawthorpe Hall (BB12 8UA) 1G **91**
Geevor Tin Mine Mus. (TR19 7EW) 3A **4**
George Stephenson's Birthplace
  (NE41 8BP) 3E **115**
Georgian House (EH2 4DR) . . . . .Edinburgh **194**
Gibside (NE16 6BG) 4E **115**
Gilbert White's House & Gdn. (GU34 3JH) . .3F **25**
Gladstone Pottery Mus. (ST3 1PQ) 1D **72**
Gladstone's Land (EH1 2NT) . . . . .Edinburgh **194**
Glamis Castle (DD8 1QJ) 4C **144**
Glastonbury Abbey (BA6 9EL) 3A **22**
Glastonbury Tor (BA6 8BG) 3A **22**
Glenarn (G84 8LL) .1D **126**
Glenbuchat Castle (AB36 8TN) 3A **152**
Glencoe Gorge (PH50 4SG) 3F **141**
Glendurgan Gdn. (TR11 5JZ) 4E **5**
Glenfinnan Monument (PH37 4LT) 5B **148**
Glenluce Abbey (DG8 0LW) 4G **109**

Glenmore Forest Pk. Visitor Centre, Aviemore
  (PH22 1QY) 3D **150**
Glenwhan Gdns. (DG9 8PH) 4G **109**
Gloucester Cathedral (GL1 2LR) **196**
Gloucestershire Warwickshire Railway
  (GL54 5DT) 2F **49**
Gloucester Waterways Mus. (GL1 2EH) **196**
Glynde Place (BN8 6SX) 5F **27**
Godinton House & Gdns. (TN23 3BP) 1D **28**
Godolphin (TR13 9RE) 3D **4**
Goodnestone Pk. Gdns. (CT3 1PL) 5G **41**
Goodrich Castle (HR9 6HY) 3A **48**
Goodwood House (PO18 0PX) 2G **17**
Goodwood Racecourse (PO18 0PS) 1G **17**
Gordale Scar (BD23 4DL) 3B **98**
Grange at Northington, The (SO24 9TG) 3D **24**
Grampian Transport Mus. (AB33 8AE) 2C **152**
Graves Gallery (S1 1XZ) . . . . .Sheffield **210**
Graythwaite Hall Gdns. (LA12 8BA) 5E **103**
Great Central Railway (LE11 1RW) 4C **74**
Great Central Railway (Nottingham)
  (NG11 6NX) 1C **74**
Great Chalfield Manor & Gdn. (SN12 8NH) . .5D **34**
Great Comp (TN15 8QS) 5G **39**
Great Dixter (TN31 6PH) 3C **28**
Great North Mus: Hancock
  (NE2 4PT) . . . . .Newcastle upon Tyne **205**
Greenbank House & Gdn. (G76 8RB) 4G **127**
Greenknowe Tower (TD3 6JL) 5C **130**
Greenway (TQ5 0ES) 3E **9**
Gretna Green Old Blacksmith's Shop
  (DG16 5EA) 3E **112**
Grey Mare's Tail Waterfall (DG10 9LH) 3D **118**
Greys Court (RG9 4PG) 3F **37**
Grimes Graves (IP26 5DE) 1H **65**
Grimsby Fishing Heritage Centre
  (DN31 1UZ) 4F **95**
Grimspound (PL20 6TB) 4H **11**
Grimsthorpe Castle (PE10 0LZ) 3H **75**
Grizedale Forest (LA22 0QJ) 5E **103**
Groombridge Place Gdns. (TN3 9QG) 2G **27**
Grove Mus. (IM8 3UA) 2D **108**
Gulliver's Matlock Bath (DE4 3PG) 5G **85**
Gulliver's Milton Keynes (MK15 0DT) **204**
Gulliver's Warrington (WA5 9YZ) 1A **84**
Gunby Hall (PE23 5SS) 4D **88**
Gwydir Castle (LL26 0PN) 4H **81**

H

Haddo House (AB41 7EQ) 5F **161**
Haddon Hall (DE45 1LA) 4G **85**
Hadleigh Castle (SS7 2AR) 2C **40**
Hadrian's Wall (NE47 7AW) 3A **114**
Hailes Abbey (GL54 5PB) 2F **49**
Hailes Castle (EH41 3SB) 2B **130**
Hall i' th' Wood Mus. (BL1 8UA) 3F **91**
Hall Place & Gdns. (DA5 1PQ) 3G **39**
Hamerton Zoo Park (PE28 5RE) 2A **64**
Ham House & Gdn. (TW10 7RS) 3C **38**
Hammerwood Pk. (RH19 3QE) 2F **27**
Hampden Pk. (G42 9AY) 3G **127**
Hampton Court Castle & Gdns.
  (HR6 0PN) 5H **59**
Hampton Court Palace (KT8 9AU) 4C **38**
Hanbury Hall (WR9 7EA) 4D **60**
Hardknott Roman Fort (LA20 6EQ) 4D **102**
Hardwick Hall (S44 5QJ) 3C **86**
Hardy Monument (DT2 9HY) 4B **14**
Hardy's Cottage (DT2 8QJ) 3C **14**
Hare Hill (SK10 4QA) 3C **84**
Harewood House (LS17 9LG) 5F **99**
Harlech Castle (LL46 2YH) 2E **69**
Harley Gallery (S80 3LW) 3C **86**
Hartland Abbey & Gdns. (EX39 6DT) 4C **18**
Harvington Hall (DY10 4LR) 3C **60**
Harwich Redoubt (CO12 3NL) 2F **55**
Hatchlands Pk. (GU4 7RT) 5B **38**
Hatfield House (AL9 5NQ) 5C **52**
Haughmond Abbey (SY4 4RW) 4H **59**
Haverfordwest Castle (SA61 2BW) 3D **42**
Haverfordwest Priory (SA61 1RN) 3D **42**
Hawk Conservancy Trust (SP11 8DY) 2B **24**
Haydock Pk. Racecourse (WA12 0HQ) 1H **83**
Head of Steam - Darlington Railway Mus.
  (DL3 6ST) 3F **105**
Heale Mus. (SP4 6NT) 3G **23**
Heaton Hall (M25 2SW) 4F **91**
Hedingham Castle (CO9 3DJ) 2A **54**
Heights of Abraham (DE4 3PB) 5G **85**
Hellens (HR8 2LY) .2B **48**
Helmingham Hall Gdns. (IP14 6EF) 5D **66**
Helmshore Mills Textile Museums
  (BB4 4NP) 2F **91**
Helmsley Castle (YO62 5AB) 1A **100**
Helvellyn (CA12 4TP) 3E **103**
Heptonstall Mus. (HX7 7PL) 2H **91**
Hereford Cathedral (HR1 2NG) **197**
Hereford Cider Mus. (HR4 0LW) **197**
Hergest Croft Gdns. (HR5 3EG) 5E **59**
Hermitage Castle (TD9 0LU) 5H **119**
Herstmonceux Castle & Gdn. (BN27 1RN) . .4H **27**
Herstmonceux (TA2 8LG) 4F **21**
Hever Castle & Gdns. (TN8 7NG) 1F **27**
Hexham Abbey (NE46 3NB) 3C **114**
Hidcote (GL55 6LR) 1G **49**
Higgins Art Gallery & Mus.
  (MK40 3RP) . . . . .Bedford **188**
High Beeches Gdns. (RH17 6HQ) 2D **27**
Highclere Castle (RG20 9RN) 1C **24**
Highland Folk Mus. (PH20 1AY) 4B **150**
Highland Wildlife Pk. (PH21 1NL) 3C **150**
Hill House (G84 9AJ) 1D **126**
Hill of Tarvit Mansionhouse & Gdns.
  (KY15 5PB) 2F **137**
Hinton Ampner (SO24 0LA) 4D **24**
Hirsel (TD12 4LP) 5D **130**
Historic Dockyard Chatham
  (ME4 4TZ) . . . . .Medway Towns **204**
HMS Victory (PO1 3LJ) . . . . .Portsmouth **209**
HMS Warrior 1860 (PO1 3QX) . . . . . .Portsmouth **209**
Hodnet Hall Gdns. (TF9 3NN) 3A **72**
Hoghton Tower (PR5 0SH) 2D **90**
Hog's Back (GU3 1AQ) 1A **26**
Holburne Mus. of Art (BA2 4DB) . . . . . . .Bath **187**
Holdenby House Gdns. & Falconry Centre
  (NN6 8DJ) 4D **63**
Holehird Gdns. (LA23 1NP) 4F **103**

Holker Hall & Gdns. (LA11 7PL) 2C **96**
Holkham (NR21 1AB) 1A **78**
Hollycombe (GU30 7LP) 4G **25**
Holst Birthplace Mus. (GL52 2AY) . . . . .Cheltenham **192**
Holy Jesus Hospital
  (NE1 2AS) . . . . .Newcastle upon Tyne **205**
Holyrood Palace (EH8 8DX) . . . . .Edinburgh **194**
Hopetoun (EH30 9SL) 2D **129**
Hop Farm Family Pk. (TN12 6PY) 1A **28**
Houghton Hall (PE31 6TZ) 3G **77**
Houghton House (MK45 2EZ) 2A **52**
Houghton Lodge Gdns. (SO20 6LQ) 3B **24**
House of Dun (DD10 9LQ) 3F **145**
House of Manannan Mus., Peel (IM5 1TA) . .3B **108**
House of the Binns (EH49 7NA) 1D **128**
Houses of Parliament (SW1A 0RS) . . . .London **203**
Housesteads Roman Fort & Mus.
  (NE47 6NN) 3A **114**
Hoveton Gdns. (NR12 8RJ) 3F **79**
Hovingham Hall (YO62 4LU) 2A **100**
Howick Hall Gdns. (NE66 3LB) 3G **121**
Howletts (Wild Animal Pk.) (CT4 5EL) 5F **41**
Hughenden Manor (HP14 4LA) 2G **37**
Hugh Miller Mus. & Birthplace Cottage
  (IV11 8XA) 2B **158**
Hunstanton Sea Life Sanctuary (PE36 5BH) . .1F **77**
Hunterian Mus. & Art Gallery (G12 8QQ) . .Glasgow **196**
Huntingtower Castle (PH1 3JL) 1C **136**
Huntly Castle (AB54 4SH) 4C **160**
Hurst Castle (SO41 0TP) 4B **16**
Hutton-in-the-Forest (CA11 9TH) 1F **103**
Hylands House & Gdns. (CM2 8WQ) 5G **53**

I

Ickworth (IP29 5QE) 4H **65**
Iford Manor (Peto Gdn.) (BA15 2BA) 1D **22**
Ightham Mote (TN15 0NT) 5G **39**
Ilam Pk. (DE6 2AZ) 5F **85**
Ilfracombe Aquarium (EX34 9EQ) 2F **19**
Imperial War Mus. Duxford (CB22 4QR) 1E **53**
Imperial War Mus. London (SE1 6HZ) **203**
Imperial War Mus. North, Trafford Park
  (M17 1TZ) 1C **84**
Inchcolm Abbey (KY3 0XR) 1E **129**
Inchmahome Priory (FK8 3RD) 3E **135**
Ingatestone Hall (CM4 9NS) 1A **40**
International Centre for Birds of Prey
  (GL18 1JJ) 3C **48**
Inveraray Castle (PA32 8XE) 3H **133**
Inveresk Lodge Gdn. (EH21 7TE) 2G **129**
Inverewe Gdn. (IV22 2LG) 5C **162**
Inverlochy Castle (PH33 6TQ) 1F **141**
Inverness Mus. & Art Gallery (IV2 3EB) **198**
Iona (PA76 6SP) 2A **132**
Iron Bridge, Ironbridge (TF8 7JP) 5A **72**
Isel Hall (CA13 0QG) 1C **102**
Isle of Man Steam Railway (IM1 4LL) 4C **108**
Isle of Wight Steam Railway (PO33 4DS) . . .4D **16**
Ivinghoe Beacon (LU6 2EG) 4H **51**
Izaak Walton's Cottage (ST15 0PA) 2C **72**

J

Jackfield Tile Mus. (TF8 7ND) 5A **72**
Jane Austen's House Mus. (GU34 1SD) 3F **25**
Jarlshof Prehistoric & Norse Settlement
  (ZE3 9JN) 10E **173**
Jedburgh Abbey (TD8 6JQ) 3A **120**
Jervaulx Abbey (HG4 4PH) 1D **98**
JM Barrie's Birthplace (DD8 4BX) 3C **144**
Jodrell Bank Discovery Centre (SK11 9DL) . .3B **84**
Jorvik Viking Centre (YO1 9WT) . . . . . . .York **214**

K

Kedleston Hall (DE22 5JH) 1H **73**
Keighley & Worth Valley Railway
  (BD22 8NJ) 1A **92**
Kelburn Castle & Country Centre
  (KA29 0BE) 4D **126**
Keld Chapel (CA10 3QF) 3G **103**
Kelham Island Mus. (S3 8RY) . . . . .Sheffield **210**
Kellie Castle & Gdn. (KY10 2RF) 3H **137**
Kelmarsh Hall & Gdns. (NN6 9LY) 3E **63**
Kelmscott Manor (GL7 3HJ) 2A **36**
Kelso Abbey (TD5 7BB) 1B **120**
Kelvingrove Art Gallery & Mus., Glasgow
  (G3 8AG) 3G **127**
Kempton Pk. Racecourse (TW16 5AE) 3C **38**
Kenilworth Castle (CV8 1NE) 3G **61**
Kent & East Sussex Railway (TN30 6HE) . . .3C **28**
Kentwell (CO10 9BA) 1B **54**
Kenwood House (NW3 7JR) 2D **38**
Keswick Mus. & Gallery (CA12 4NF) 2D **102**
Kettle's Yard (CB3 0AQ) . . . . .Cambridge **191**
Kew Gdns. (TW9 3AB) 3C **38**
Kidwelly Castle (SA17 5BQ) 5E **45**
Kielder Water & Forest Pk. (NE48 1QZ) 1H **113**
Kiftsgate Court Gdns. (GL55 6LN) 1G **49**
Kilchurn Castle (PA33 1AF) 1A **134**
Kildrummy Castle & Gdn. (AB33 8RA) 2B **152**
Killerton (EX5 3LE) .2C **12**
Kilmartin Glen Prehistoric Sites
  (PA31 8RQ) 4F **133**
Kilmartin House Mus. (PA31 8RQ) 4F **133**
Kinder Scout (S33 7ZJ) 2E **85**
King's College Chapel (CB2 1TN) . . . . .Cambridge **191**
Kingston Bagpuize House & Gdn.
  (OX13 5AX) 2C **36**
Kingston Lacy (BH21 4EA) 2E **15**
Kingston Maurward Animal Pk. & Gdns.
  (DT2 8PY) 3C **14**
Kinnersley Castle (HR3 6QF) 1G **47**
Kinver Edge (DY7 5NP) 2C **60**
Kiplin Hall (DL10 6AT) 5F **105**
Kirby Hall (NN17 3EN) 1G **63**
Kirkham Priory (YO60 7JS) 3B **100**
Kirklees Light Railway (HD8 9XJ) 3C **92**
Kirkstall Abbey (LS5 3EH) 1C **92**
Kirkwall Cathedral (KW15 1JF) 6D **172**
Knaresborough Castle (HG5 8BB) 4F **99**
Knebworth House (SG3 6PY) 3C **52**
Knightshayes Court (EX16 7RQ) 1C **12**
Knockhill Motor Circuit (KY12 9TF) 4C **136**

Knole (TN15 0RP) 5G **39**
Knoll Gdns. (BH21 7ND) 2F **15**
Knowsley Safari Pk. (L34 4AN) 1G **83**

L

Lacock Abbey (SN15 2LG) 5E **35**
Lady Lever Art Gallery (CH62 5EQ) . . .2F **83**
Lady of the North (NE23 8AU) 2F **115**
Laing Art Gallery
 (NE1 8AG) . . . .**Newcastle upon Tyne 205**
Lake District Nat. Pk. (LA9 7RL) 3E **103**
Lakeside & Haverthwaite Railway
 (LA12 8AL) 1C **96**
Lamb House (TN31 7ES) 3D **28**
Lamphey Bishop's Palace (SA71 5NT) . .4E **43**
Lamport Hall & Gdns. (NN6 9HD) 3E **63**
Lancaster Castle (LA1 1YJ) 3D **96**
Landmark Forest Adventure Pk. (PH23 3AJ) .1D **150**
Land's End (TR19 7AA) 4A **4**
Lanercost Priory (CA8 2HQ) 3G **113**
Langdale Pikes (LA22 9JY) 4D **102**
Langley Chapel (SY5 7HU) 1H **59**
Lanhydrock (PL30 5AD) 2E **7**
Lappa Valley Steam Railway (TR8 5LX) . .3C **6**
Larmer Tree Gdns. (SP5 5PZ) 1E **15**
Laugharne Castle (SA33 4SA) 3H **43**
Launceston Castle (PL15 7DR) 4D **10**
Launceston Steam Railway (PL15 8DA) . .4D **10**
Lauriston Castle (EH4 5QD) 2F **129**
Lavenham Guildhall (CO10 9QZ) 1C **54**
Laxey Wheel (IM4 7NL) 3D **108**
Layer Marney Tower (CO5 9US) 4C **54**
Leeds Castle (Kent) (ME17 1PL) 5C **40**
Leeds City Mus. (LS1 3AA) **199**
Legoland (SL4 4AY) 3A **38**
Leighton Buzzard Railway (LU7 4TN) . . .3H **51**
Leighton Hall (LA5 9ST) 2E **97**
Leiston Abbey (IP16 4TD) 4G **67**
Leith Hall (AB54 4NQ) 1C **152**
Leith Hill (RH5 6LX) 1C **26**
Lennoxlove House (EH41 4NZ) 2B **130**
Leonardslee Gdns. (RH13 6PP) 3D **26**
Levant Mine & Beam Engine (TR19 7SX) . .3A **4**
Levens Hall & Gdns. (LA8 0PD) 1D **97**
Lewes Castle (BN7 1YE) 4F **27**
Lichfield Cathedral (WS13 7LD) 4F **73**
Life (NE1 4EP) . . . . . . **Newcastle upon Tyne 205**
Lightwater Valley (HG4 3HT) 2E **99**
Lilleshall Abbey (TF10 9HW) 4B **72**
Lincoln Castle (LN1 3AA) **198**
Lincoln Cathedral (LN2 1PZ) **198**
Lincoln Medieval Bishops' Palace (LN2 1PU) . .198
Lincolnshire Road Transport Mus. (LN6 3QT) . .4G **87**
Lindisfarne (TD15 2SF) 5H **131**
Lindisfarne Castle (TD15 2SH) 5H **131**
Lindisfarne Priory (TD15 2RX) 5H **131**
Linlithgow Palace (EH49 7AL) 2D **128**
Linton Zoo (CB21 4XN) 1F **53**
Little Clarendon (SP3 5DZ) 3F **23**
Little Malvern Court (WR14 4JN) 1C **48**
Little Moreton Hall (CW12 4SD) 5C **84**
Liverpool Cathedral (L1 7AZ) 2F **83**
Liverpool Metropolitan RC Cathedral (L3 5TQ) . .200
Lizard Point (TR12 7NU) 5E **5**
Llanberis Lake Railway (LL55 3HB) 4E **81**
Llancarchaeron (SA48 8DG) 5D **57**
Llangollen Railway (LL20 7AJ) 1D **70**
Llansteffan Castle (SA33 5JX) 4D **44**
Llawhaden Castle (SA67 8HL) 3E **43**
Llechwedd Slate Caverns (LL41 3NB) . . .1G **69**
Llywernog Silver-Lead Mine (SY23 3AB) . .2G **57**
Lochalsh Woodland Gdn. (IV40 8DN) . . .1F **147**
Loch Doon Castle (KA6 7QE) 5D **117**
Lochleven Castle (KY13 8ET) 3D **136**
Loch Lomond (G83 8PA) 4C **134**
Loch Lomond and The Trossachs Nat. Pk.
 (FK8 3UA) 2D **134**
Lochmaben Castle (DG11 1JE) 1B **112**
Loch Ness Exhibition Centre (IV63 6TU) . .5H **157**
"Locomotion" Nat. Railway Mus. Shildon
 (DL4 1PQ) 1F **105**
Lodge Pk. (GL54 3PP) 4G **49**
Lodge RSPB Nature Reserve, The
 (SG19 2DL) 1B **52**
Logan Botanic Gdn. (DG9 9ND) 5F **109**
Logan Fish Pond & Marine Life Centre
 (DG9 9NF) 5F **109**
London Dungeon (SE1 2SZ) **203**
London Film Mus. (WC2E 7BN) **203**
London Zoo (NW1 4RY) **202**
Long Cross Victorian Gdns. (PL29 3TF) . . .1D **6**
Longleat Safari & Adventure Pk.
 (BA12 7NW) 2D **22**
Long Mynd (SY7 8BH) 1G **59**
Longthorpe Tower (PE3 6SU) 1A **64**
Longtown Castle (HR2 0LE) 3G **47**
Lord Leycester Hospital & The Master's Gdn.,
 Warwick (CV34 4BH) 4G **61**
Loseley Ho. (GU3 1HS) 1A **26**
Lost Gdns. of Heligan (PL26 6EN) 4D **6**
Lotherton Hall (LS25 3EB) 1E **93**
Loughwood Meeting House (EX13 7DU) . .3F **13**
Ludgershall Castle (SP11 9QS) 1A **24**
Ludlow Castle (SY8 1AY) 3H **59**
Lullingstone Castle & World Gdn. (DA4 0JA) . .4G **39**
Lullingstone Roman Villa (DA4 0JA) . . .4G **39**
Lulworth Castle (BH20 5QS) 4D **14**
Lundy Island (EX39 2LY) 2B **18**
Lyddington Bede House (LE15 9LZ) . . .1F **63**
Lydford Castle & Saxon Town (EX20 4BH) . .4F **11**
Lydford Gorge (EX20 4BH) 4F **11**
Lydiard House & Pk. (SN5 3PA) 3G **35**
Lydney Pk. Gdns. (GL15 6BU) 5B **48**
Lyme Pk. (SK12 2NX) 2D **84**
Lytes Cary Manor (TA11 7HU) 4A **22**
Lyveden New Bield (PE8 5AT) 2G **63**

M

Macclesfield Silk Museum, Park Lane Galleries
 (SK11 6PD) 3D **84**
Macduff Marine Aquarium (AB44 1SL) . . .2E **160**
MacLellan's Castle (DG6 4JD) 4D **111**
Madame Tussaud's (NW1 5LR) . . . . .**London 202**
Maeshowe Chambered Cairn (KW16 3HQ) . .6C **172**
MAGNA Science Adventure Centre (S60 1DX) . .1B **86**

Maiden Castle (DT2 9PP) 4B **14**
Major Oak (NG21 9HN) 4D **86**
Malham Cove (BD23 4DJ) 3A **98**
Malham Tarn (BD24 9PU) 3A **98**
Malleny Gdn. (EH14 7AF) 3E **129**
Malton Mus. (YO17 7LP) 2B **100**
Malvern Hills (HR8 1EN) 2C **48**
Manchester Art Gallery (M2 3JL) **201**
M & D's (Scotland's Theme Pk.), Motherwell
 (ML1 3RT) 4A **128**
Manderston (TD11 3PP) 4E **130**
Mannington Gdns. (NR11 7BB) 2D **78**
Manorbier Castle (SA70 7SY) 5E **43**
Manx Electric Railway (IM2 4NR) 2D **108**
Manx Mus. (IM1 3LY) 4C **108**
Mapledurham House (RG4 7TR) 4E **37**
Marble Hill House (TW1 2NL) 3C **38**
Markenfield Hall (HG4 3AD) 3E **99**
Mar Lodge Estate (AB35 5YJ) 5E **151**
Martin Mere Wetland Centre (L40 0TA) . .3C **90**
Marwell Wildlife (SO21 1JH) 4D **24**
Marwood Hill Gdns. (EX31 4EB) 3F **19**
Mary Arden's Farm (CV37 9UN) 5F **61**
Mary, Queen of Scots' House (TD8 6AS) . .3H **119**
Mary Rose Ship & Mus. (PO1 3LJ) . .**Portsmouth 209**
Max Gate (DT1 2AB) 3C **14**
Megginch Castle Gdns. (PH2 7SW) 1E **137**
Melbourne Hall & Gdns. (DE73 8EN) . . .3A **74**
Melford Hall (CO10 9AA) 1B **54**
Mellerstain House (TD3 6LG) 1A **120**
Melrose Abbey (TD6 9LG) 1H **119**
Menai Suspension Bridge (LL59 5HH) . . .3E **81**
Mendip Hills (BS40 7XS) 1H **21**
Merriments Gdns. (TN19 7RA) 3B **28**
Merseyside Maritime Mus. (L3 4AQ) . .**Liverpool 200**
Mertoun Gdns. (TD6 0EA) 1A **120**
Michelham Priory (BN27 3QS) 5G **27**
Middleham Castle (DL8 4QR) 1D **98**
Midland Railway Centre (DE5 3QZ) 5B **86**
Mid-Norfolk Railway (NR19 1DF) 5C **78**
Millennium Coastal Pk. (SA15 2LG) 3D **31**
Millennium Spinnaker Tower
 (PO1 3TN) . . . .**Portsmouth 209**
Millennium Stadium (CF10 1NS) . . . .**Cardiff 191**
Milton Manor House (OX14 4EN) 2C **36**
Milton's Cottage (HP8 4JH) 1A **38**
Minack Theatre (TR19 6JU) 4A **4**
Minsmere (IP17 3BY) 4G **67**
Minterne Gdns. (DT2 7AU) 2B **14**
Mirehouse (CA12 4QE) 2D **102**
Misarden Pk. Gdns. (GL6 7JA) 5E **49**
Mistley Towers (CO11 1ET) 2E **54**
Mompesson House (SP1 2EL) . . . . .**Salisbury 210**
Monk Bretton Priory (S71 5QE) 4D **93**
Monkey Forest at Trentham (ST4 8AY) . . .2C **72**
Monkey Sanctuary (PL13 1NZ) 3G **7**
Monkey World (BH20 6HH) 4D **14**
Monk's House (BN7 3HF) 5F **27**
Montacute House (TA15 6XP) 1H **13**
Monteviot House (TD8 6UH) 2A **120**
Montgomery Castle (SY15 6HN) 1E **58**
Moreton Corbet Castle, Shawbury
 (SY4 4DW) 3H **71**
Morwellham Quay (PL19 8JL) 2A **8**
Moseley Old Hall, Wolverhampton
 (WV10 7HY) 5D **72**
Mother Shipton's Cave & the Petrifying Well
 (HG5 8DD) 4F **99**
Mottisfont (SO51 0LP) 4B **24**
Mount Edgcumbe House (PL10 1HZ) . . .3A **8**
Mount Ephraim Gdns. (ME13 9TX) 4E **41**
Mountfitchet Castle (CM24 8SP) 3F **53**
Mount Grace Priory (DL6 3JG) 5B **106**
Mount Stuart (PA20 9LR) 4C **126**
Mr Straw's House (S81 0JG) 2C **86**
Muchelney Abbey (TA10 0DQ) 4H **21**
Muchelney Priest's House (TA10 0DQ) . .4H **21**
Mull of Kintyre (PA28 6RU) 5A **124**
Muncaster Castle & Gdns. (CA18 1RQ) . .5C **102**
Mus. of Army Flying (SO20 8DY) 3B **24**
Mus. of East Anglian Life (IP14 1DL) . . .5C **66**
Mus. of Lakeland Life & Industry, Kendal
 (LA9 5AL) 5G **103**
Mus. of Lincolnshire Life (LN1 3LY) **198**
Mus. of London (EC2Y 5HN) **203**
Museum of Royal Worcester (WR1 2NE) **214**
Mus. of Science & Industry
 (M3 4FP) . . . .**Manchester 201**
Mus. of Scottish Lighthouses (AB43 9DU) . .2G **161**
Mus. of the Gorge (TF8 7NH) 5A **72**
Mus. of the Isles (IV45 8RS) 3E **147**
Mus. of the Jewellery Quarter
 (B18 6HA) . . . .**Birmingham 188**

N

Nat. Botanic Gdn. of Wales (SA32 8HG) . .4F **45**
Nat. Coal Mining Mus. for England
 (WF4 4RH) 3C **92**
Nat. Coracle Centre (SA38 9JL) 1C **44**
Nat. Exhibition Centre (NEC) (B40 1NT) . . .2F **61**
Nat. Football Mus. (M4 3BG) . . . . .**Manchester 201**
Nat. Forest, The (DE12 6HZ) 4H **73**
Nat. Gallery (WC2N 5DN) . . . .**London 203**
Nat. Glass Centre (SR6 0GL) 4H **115**
Nat. Horseracing Mus. (CB8 8JL) 4F **65**
Nat. Marine Aquarium (PL4 0LF) . . .**Plymouth 208**
Nat. Maritime Mus., Greenwich (SE10 9NF) . .3E **39**
Nat. Maritime Mus. Cornwall, Falmouth
 (TR11 3QY) 5C **6**
Nat. Media Mus. (BD1 1NQ) . . . . . .**Bradford 190**
Nat. Memorial Arboretum (DE13 7AR) . . .4F **73**
National Mining Mus. Scotland (EH22 4QN) . .3G **129**
Nat. Motorcycle Mus. (B92 0EJ) 2G **61**
Nat. Motor Mus., (Beaulieu) (SO42 7ZN) . .1C **28**
Nat. Mus. Cardiff (CF10 3NP) . . . . . .**Cardiff 191**
Nat. Mus. of Flight (EH39 5LF) 2B **130**
Nat. Mus. of Rural Life Scotland
 (G76 9HR) 4H **127**
Nat. Mus. of Scotland (EH1 1JF) . . . .**Edinburgh 194**
Nat. Portrait Gallery (WC2H 0HE) . . .**London 203**
Nat. Railway Mus. (YO26 4XJ) . . . .**York 214**
Nat. Roman Legion Mus., Caerleon
 (NP18 1AE) 2G **33**
Nat. Sea Life Centre (B1 2HL) . . . . **Birmingham 188**
Nat. Showcaves Centre for Wales (SA9 1GJ) . .4B **46**
Nat. Slate Mus. (LL55 4TY) 4E **81**
Nat. Space Centre (LE4 5NS) 5C **74**

Nat. Waterfront Mus. (SA1 3RD) . . . . .**Swansea 212**
Nat. Waterways Mus. (CH65 4FW) 3G **83**
Nat. Wool Mus. (SA44 5UP) 2D **44**
Natural History Mus. (SW7 5BD) . . . .**London 202**
Natural History Mus. at Tring (HP23 6AP) . .4H **51**
Neath Abbey (SA10 7DW) 3G **31**
Needles, The (PO39 0JH) 4A **16**
Nene Valley Railway (PE8 6LR) 1A **64**
Ness Botanic Gdns. (CH64 4AY) 3F **83**
Nessieland (IV63 6TU) 5H **157**
Nether Winchendon House (HP18 0DY) . .4F **51**
Netley Abbey (SO31 5HB) 2C **16**
New Abbey Corn Mill (DG2 8DX) 3A **112**
New Air Mus. (NG24 2NY) 5F **87**
Newark Castle (Newark-on-Trent)
 (NG24 1BN) 5E **87**
Newark Castle (Port Glasgow)
 (PA14 5NG) 2E **127**
Newark Pk. (GL12 7PZ) 2C **34**
New Art Gallery Walsall (WS2 8LG) 1E **61**
Newburgh Priory (YO61 4AS) 2H **99**
Newburgh Racecourse (RG14 7NZ) 5C **36**
Newby Hall & Gdns. (HG4 5AE) 3E **99**
Newcastle Castle (Bridgend) (CF31 4JW) . .3B **32**
Newcastle Upon Tyne Castle Keep (NE1 1RQ) . .205
New Forest Nat. Pk. (SO43 7BD) 1H **15**
New Lanark World Heritage Site Visitor Centre
 (ML11 9DB) 5B **128**
Newmarket Racecourse (CB8 0TG) 4F **65**
Newquay Zoo (TR7 2LZ) 2C **6**
Newstead Abbey (NG15 8NA) 5C **86**
Nine Ladies Stone Circle (DE4 2LF) 4G **85**
Norfolk Broads Nat. Pk. (NR3 1BJ) 5G **79**
Norfolk Lavender (PE31 7JE) 2F **77**
Norham Castle (TD15 2LL) 5F **131**
Normanby Hall Mus. (DN15 9HU) 3B **94**
North Downs (GU10 5QE) 5C **38**
North Norfolk Railway (NR26 8RA) 1D **78**
Northumberland Nat. Pk. (NE46 1BS) . . .5C **120**
North York Moors Nat. Pk. (YO18 8RN) . .5D **107**
North Yorkshire Moors Railway (YO18 7AJ) . .1C **100**
Norton Conyers (HG4 5EQ) 2F **99**
Norton Priory Mus. & Gdns. (WA7 1SX) . .2H **83**
Norwich Castle Mus. & Art Gallery (NR1 3JU) . .205
Norwich Cathedral (NR1 4DH) **205**
Nostell Priory (WF4 1QE) 3E **93**
Nuffield Place (RG9 5RX) 3E **37**
Nunney Castle (BA11 4LN) 2C **22**
Nunnington Hall (YO62 5UY) 2A **100**
Nymans (RH17 6EB) 3D **26**

O

Oakham Castle (LE15 6DR) 5F **75**
Oakwell Hall, Birstall (WF17 9LG) 2C **92**
Oakwood Theme Pk. (SA67 8DE) 3E **43**
Observatory Science Centre (BN27 1RN) . .4A **28**
Oceanarium (BH2 5AA) . . . .**Bournemouth 190**
Offa's Dyke (NP16 7NQ) 5F **47**
Okehampton Castle (EX20 1JA) 3F **11**
Old Beaupre Castle (CF71 7LT) 4D **32**
Old Gorhambury House (AL3 6AH) 5B **52**
Old Oswestry Hill Fort (SY10 7AA) 2E **71**
Old Sarum (SP1 3SD) 3G **23**
Old Wardour Castle (SP3 6RR) 4E **23**
Old Winchester Hill Hill Fort (GU32 1HN) . .4E **25**
Orford Castle (IP12 2NF) 1H **55**
Orford Ness (IP12 2NU) 1H **55**
Ormesby Hall (TS7 9AS) 3C **106**
Osborne House (PO32 6JX) 3D **16**
Osterley Pk. & House (TW7 4RB) 3C **38**
Oulton Pk. Motor Circuit (CW6 9BW) . . .4H **83**
Our Dynamic Earth (EH8 8AS) . . . . .**Edinburgh 194**
Overbeck's (TQ8 8LW) 5D **8**
Owletts (DA12 3AP) 4A **40**
Oxburgh Hall (PE33 9PS) 5G **77**
Oxford Christ Church Cathedral (OX1 4JF) . .207
Oxwich Castle (SA3 1LU) 4D **31**
Oystermouth Castle (SA3 5TA) 4F **31**

P

Packwood House (B94 6AT) 3F **61**
Paignton Zoo (TQ4 7EU) 3E **9**
Painshill Pk. (KT11 1JE) 5B **38**
Painswick Rococo Gdn. (GL6 6TH) 4D **48**
Palace of Holyroodhouse
 (EH8 8DX) . . . .**Edinburgh 194**
Papplewick Pumping Station (NG15 9AJ) . .5C **86**
Paradise Pk. Wildlife Sanctuary (TR27 4HB) . .3C **4**
Paradise Wildlife Pk. (EN10 7QZ) 5D **52**
Parcevall Hall Gdns. (BD23 6DE) 3C **98**
Parham (RH20 4HS) 4B **26**
Pashley Manor Gdns. (TN5 7HE) 3B **28**
Paultons Family Theme Pk. (SO51 6AL) . .1B **16**
Paxton House (TD15 1SZ) 4F **131**
Paycocke's (CO6 1NS) 3B **54**
Peak Cavern (S33 8WS) 2F **85**
Peak District Nat. Pk. (DE45 1AE) 2F **85**
Peak Rail (DE4 3NA) 4G **85**
Peckover House & Gdn. (PE13 1JR) 5D **76**
Peel Castle (IM5 1AB) 4A **108**
Pembroke Castle (SA71 4LA) 4D **43**
Pembrokeshire Coast Nat. Pk. (SA41 3XD) . .4C **42**
Pencarrow (PL30 3AG) 5A **10**
Pendennis Castle (TR11 4LP) 5C **6**
Penhow Castle (NP26 3AD) 2H **33**
Penrhyn Castle (LL57 4HN) 3F **81**
Penrith Castle (CA11 7JB) 2G **103**
Penshurst Place & Gdns. (TN11 8DG) . . .1G **27**
Peover Hall (WA16 9HW) 3B **84**
Perth Mus. & Art Gallery (PH1 5LB) **207**
Peterborough Cathedral (PE1 1XZ) **208**
Petworth House & Pk. (GU28 0AE) 3A **26**
Pevensey Castle (BN24 5LE) 5H **27**
Peveril Castle (S33 8WQ) 2F **85**
Philipps House (SP3 5HH) 3F **23**
Pickering Castle (YO18 7AX) 1C **100**
Picton Castle (SA62 4AS) 3E **43**
Piel Castle (LA13 0QN) 3B **96**
Pistyll Rhaeadr (SY10 0BZ) 3C **70**
Pitmedden Gdn. (AB41 7PD) 1F **153**
Pitt Rivers Mus. (OX1 3PP) . . . .**Oxford 207**
Plantasia (SA1 2AL) . . . .**Swansea 212**
Plas Brondanw Gardens (LL48 6SW) . . .1F **69**
Plas Newydd (Llanfairpwllgwyngyll)
 (LL61 6DQ) 4E **81**

Plas Newydd (Llangollen) (LL20 8AW) . . .1E **70**
Plas yn Rhiw (LL53 8AB) 3B **68**
Pleasurewood Hills (NR32 5DZ) 1H **67**
Poldark Mine (TR13 0ES) 5A **6**
Polesden Lacey (RH5 6BD) 5C **38**
Pollok House, Glasgow (G43 1AT) 3G **127**
Pontcysyllte Aqueduct (LL20 7YS) 1E **71**
Porchester Castle (PO16 9QW) 2E **17**
Portland Castle (DT5 1AZ) 5B **14**
Port Lympne Reserve (CT21 4PD) 2F **29**
Portsmouth Historic Dockyard (PO1 3LJ) . .2E **17**
Potteries Mus. & Art Gallery (ST1 3DW) **211**
Powderham Castle (EX6 8JQ) 4C **12**
Powis Castle & Gdn. (SY21 8RF) 5E **70**
Prebendal Manor House (PE8 6QG) 1H **63**
Prestongrange Mus. (EH32 9RX) 2G **129**
Preston Manor (BN1 6SD) 5E **27**
Preston Mill & Phantassie Doocot
 (EH40 3DS) 2B **130**
Preston Tower (Northumberland)
 (NE67 5DH) 2F **121**
Preston Tower, Prestonpans (EH32 9NN) . .2G **129**
Prideaux Place (PL28 8RP) 1D **6**
Prior Pk. Landscape Gdn. (BA2 5AH) . . .5C **34**
Provan Hall (G34 9NJ) 3H **127**
Prudhoe Castle (NE42 6NA) 3D **115**

Q

Quantock Hills (TA4 4AP) 3E **21**
Quarry Bank Mill (SK9 4LA) 2C **84**
Quebec House (TN16 1TD) 5F **39**
Queen Elizabeth Country Pk. (PO8 0QE) . .1F **17**
Queen Elizabeth Forest Pk. (FK8 3UZ) . . .4D **134**
Queen Elizabeth Olympic Pk. (E20 2ST) . .2E **39**
Quex House & Gdns. (CT7 0BH) 4H **41**

R

Raby Castle (DL2 3AH) 2E **105**
RAF Holmpton (HU19 2RG) 2G **95**
RAF Mus. Cosford (TF11 8UP) 5B **72**
RAF Mus. London (NW9 5LL) 1D **38**
Raglan Castle (NP15 2BT) 5H **47**
Ragley (B49 5NJ) 5E **61**
Ramsey Island (SA62 6SA) 2A **42**
Ravenglass & Eskdale Railway (CA18 1SW) . .5C **102**
Raveningham Gdns. (NR14 6NS) 1F **67**
Ravenscraig Castle (KY1 2AZ) 4E **137**
Reculver Towers (CT6 6SX) 4G **41**
Red House, Bexleyheath (DA6 8JF) 3F **39**
Renishaw Hall & Gdns. (S21 3WB) 3B **86**
Restoration House (ME1 1HF) . . . .**Medway Towns 204**
Restormel Castle (PL22 0HN) 2F **7**
Revolution House (S41 9LA) 3A **86**
Rheged Centre (CA11 0DQ) 2F **103**
Rheidol Power Station & Vis. Cen.
 (SY23 3NF) 3G **57**
Rhossili Bay (SA3 1PR) 4D **31**
RHS Gdn. Harlow Carr (HG3 1QB) 4E **99**
RHS Gdn. Hyde Hall (CM3 8ET) 1B **40**
RHS Gdn. Rosemoor (EX38 8PH) 1F **11**
RHS Gdn. Wisley (GU23 6QB) 5B **38**
Rhuddlan Castle (LL18 5AD) 3C **82**
Ribchester Roman Mus. (PR3 3XS) 1E **91**
Richmond Castle (DL10 4QW) 4E **105**
Rievaulx Abbey (YO62 5LB) 1H **99**
Rievaulx Terrace (YO62 5LJ) 1H **99**
Ripley Castle (HG3 3AY) 3E **99**
Ripon Cathedral (HG4 1QT) 2F **99**
River & Rowing Mus. (RG9 1BF) 3F **37**
Riverside Mus., Glasgow (G3 8RS) 3G **127**
Robert Burns Birthplace Mus. (KA7 4PY) . .3C **116**
Robert Burns House (DG1 2PS) . . . .**Dumfries 193**
Roche Abbey (S66 8NW) 2C **86**
Rochester Castle (ME1 1SW) . . . .**Medway Towns 204**
Rochester Cathedral
 (ME1 1SX) . . . .**Medway Towns 204**
Rockbourne Roman Villa (SP6 3PG) 1G **15**
Rockingham Castle (LE16 8TH) 1F **63**
Rockingham Motor Speedway (NN17 5AF) . .1G **63**
Rocks by Rail (LE15 7BX) 4F **75**
Rode Hall (ST7 3QP) 5C **84**
Rodmarton Manor (GL7 6PF) 2E **35**
Rokeby Pk. (DL12 9RZ) 3D **105**
Rollright Stones (OX7 5QB) 2A **50**
Roman Army Mus. (CA8 7JB) 3H **113**
Roman Painted House (CT17 9AJ) . . .**Dover 193**
Roman Vindolanda (NE47 7JN) 3A **114**
Romney, Hythe & Dymchurch Railway
 (TN28 8PL) 2E **29**
Roseberry Topping (TS9 6QX) 3C **106**
Rothesay Castle (PA20 0DA) 3B **126**
Rothiemurchus Centre (PH22 1QH) 2D **150**
Rousham House & Gdns. (OX25 4QX) . . .3C **50**
Royal Academy of Arts (W1J 0BD) . . .**London 202**
Royal Albert Bridge, Plymouth (PL12 4GT) . .3A **8**
Royal Armouries Mus. (LS10 1LT) . . . .**Leeds 199**
Royal Botanic Gdn. Edinburgh (EH3 5LR) . .2F **129**
Royal Cornwall Mus. (TR1 2SJ) 4C **6**
Royal Crown Derby Mus. (DE23 8JZ) **193**
Royal Mint Mus. (CF72 8YT) 3D **32**
Royal Navy Submarine Mus. (PO12 2AS) . .3E **16**
Royal Pavilion (BN1 1EE) . . . .**Brighton & Hove 189**
Royal Pump Room Mus. (HG1 2RY) . .**Harrogate 197**
Royal Yacht Britannia (EH6 6JJ) 2F **129**
Ruddington Framework Knitters' Mus.
 (NG11 6HE) 2C **74**
Rufford Abbey (NG22 9DF) 4D **86**
Rufford Old Hall (L40 1SG) 3C **90**
Rufus Stone (SO43 7HN) 1A **16**
Runnymede (RG18 9NA) 3A **38**
Rushton Triangular Lodge (NN14 1RP) . . .2F **63**
Russell-Cotes Art Gallery & Mus.
 (BH1 3AA) . . . .**Bournemouth 190**
Rutland County Mus. (LE15 6HW) 5F **75**
Rydal Mount & Gdns. (LA22 9LU) 4E **103**
Ryedale Folk Mus. (YO62 6UA) 5E **107**
Ryton Gdns. (CV8 3LG) 3B **62**

S

Saatchi Gallery (SW3 4RY) . . . .**London 202**
Sainsbury Centre for Visual Arts (NR4 7TJ) . .5D **78**
St Abb's Head (TD14 5QF) 3F **131**
St Albans Cathedral (AL1 1BY) 5B **52**

St Andrews Aquarium (KY16 9AS) 209
St Andrews Cathedral (KY16 9QL) 209
St Augustine's Abbey (CT1 1PF) . . . . .**Canterbury 190**
St Davids Cathedral & Bishop's Palace
 (SA62 6RD) 2B 42
St Dogmaels Abbey (SA43 3JH) 1B 44
St Fagans: Nat. History Mus. (CF5 6XB) 4E 32
St Giles' Cathedral (EH1 1RE) . . . . **Edinburgh 194**
St John's Jerusalem (DA4 9HQ) 3G 39
St Mary's Cathedral, Glasgow (G4 9JB) **3G 127**
St Mary's House & Gdns. (BN44 3WE) 4C 26
St Mawes Castle (TR2 5DE) 5C 6
St Michael's Mount (TR17 0HS) 4C 4
St Paul's Cathedral (EC4M 8AE) . . . .**London 203**
Salford Mus. & Art Gallery
 (M5 4WU) . . . .**Manchester 201**
Salisbury Cathedral (SP1 2EG) 210
Saltaire World Heritage Village (BD18 4PL) 1B 92
Saltram (PL7 1UH) 3B 8
Samlesbury Hall (PR5 0UP) 1E 90
Sandford Orcas Manor House (DT9 4SB) 4B 22
Sandham Memorial Chapel (RG20 9JT) 5C 36
Sandown Pk. Racecourse (KT10 9AJ) 4C 38
Sandringham (PE35 6EP) 3F 77
Sarehole Mill (B13 0BD) 2E 61
Savill Gdn. (SL4 2HT) 3A 38
Sawley Abbey (BB7 4LE) 5G 97
Saxtead Green Post Mill (IP13 9QQ) 4E 67
Scafell Pike (CA20 1EX) 4D 102
Scampston Hall (YO17 8NG) 2C 100
Scarborough Castle (YO11 1HY) 1E 101
Science Mus. (SW7 2DD) . . . .**London 202**
Scone Palace (PH2 6BD) 1D 136
Scotch Whisky Experience
 (EH1 2NE) . . . .**Edinburgh 194**
Scotney Castle (TN3 8JN) 2A 28
Scotstarvit Tower (KY15 5PA) 2F 137
Scottish Deer Centre (KY15 4NQ) 2F 137
Scottish Fisheries Mus. (KY10 3AB) 3H 137
Scottish Industrial Railway Centre
 (KA6 7JF) 4D 116
Scottish Maritime Mus. (KA12 8QE) 1C 116
Scottish National Gallery (EH2 2EL) . . .**Edinburgh 194**
Scottish Nat. Gallery of Modern Art, Edinburgh
 (EH4 3DR) 2F 129
Scottish Nat. Portrait Gallery
 (EH2 1JD) . . . .**Edinburgh 194**
Scottish Parliament (EH99 1SP) . . . . . .**Edinburgh 194**
Scottish Sea Life Sanctuary (PA37 1SE) 4D 140
Sea Life Adventure (SS1 2ER) 2C 40
Sea Life Blackpool (FY1 5AA) 188
Sea Life Brighton (BN2 1TB) . . . . .**Brighton & Hove 189**
Sea Life Great Yarmouth (NR30 3AH) 196
Sea Life Loch Lomond (G83 8QL) 1E 127
Sea Life London Aquarium (SE1 7PB) 203
Sea Life Scarborough (YO12 6RP) 5H 107
Sea Life Weymouth (DT4 7SX) 4B 14
SeaQuarium, Rhyl (LL18 3AF) 2C 82
SeaQuarium, Weston-super-Mare (BS23 1BE) . . .5G 33
Seaton Delaval Hall (NE26 4QR) 2G 115
Seaton Tramway (EX12 2NQ) 3F 13
Selby Abbey (YO8 4PF) 1G 93
Selly Manor (B30 2AD) 2E 61
Severn Bridge (BS35 4BL) 2A 34
Severn Valley Railway (DY12 1BG) 2B 60
Sewerby Hall & Gdns. (YO15 1EA) 3G 101
Sezincote (GL56 9AW) 2G 49
Shaftesbury Abbey Mus. & Gdns. (SP7 8JR) . . .4D 22
Shakespeare's Birthplace
 (CV37 6QW) . . . .**Stratford 212**
Shandy Hall (YO61 4AD) 1H 99
Shap Abbey (CA10 3NB) 3G 103
Shaw's Corner (AL6 9BX) 4B 52
Sheffield Pk. & Gdn. (TN22 3QX) 3F 27
Sheffield Winter Gdn. (S1 2PP) 210
Shepreth Wildlife Pk. (SG8 6PZ) 1D 53
Sherborne Castle (DT9 3PY) 1B 14
Sherborne Old Castle (DT9 3SA) 1B 14
Sherwood Forest (NG21 9HN) 5C 86
Shibden Hall (HX3 6XG) 2B 92
Shipton Hall (TF13 6JZ) 1H 59
Shoe Mus. (BA16 0EQ) 3H 21
Shrewsbury Castle (SY1 2AT) 210
Shugborough (ST17 0XB) 3D 73
Shute Barton (EX13 7PT) 3F 13
Shuttleworth Collection (SG18 9EP) 1B 52
Silbury Hill (SN8 1QH) 5G 35
Silverstone Motor Circuit (NN12 8TN) 1E 51
Sir Harold Hillier Gdns. (SO51 0QA) 4B 24
Sir Walter Scott's Courtroom (TD7 4BT) 2G 119
Sissinghurst Castle Gdn. (TN17 2AB) 2C 28
Sizergh Castle & Gdn. (LA8 8AE) 1D 97
Skara Brae Prehistoric Village (KW16 3LR) 6B 172
Skenfrith Castle (NP7 8UH) 3H 47
Skiddaw (CA12 4QE) 2D 102
Skipness Castle (PA29 6XU) 4H 125
Skipton Castle (BD23 1AW) 4B 98
Skokholm Island (SA62 3BL) 4B 42
Skomer Island (SA62 3BL) 4B 42
Sledmere House (YO25 3XG) 3D 100

Slimbridge Wetland Centre (GL2 7BT) 5C 48
Smailholm Tower (TD5 7PG) 1A 120
Smallhythe Place (TN30 7NG) 3D 28
Snaefell Mountain Railway (IM4 7NL) 3D 108
Snowdon (LL55 4UL) 5F 81
Snowdonia Nat. Pk. (LL48 6LF) 2G 69
Snowdon Mountain Railway (LL55 4TY) 5F 81
Snowshill Manor & Gdn. (WR12 7JU) 2F 49
Somerleyton Estate (NR32 5QQ) 1G 67
Somerset Heritage Centre (TA2 6SF) 4F 21
Souter Lighthouse (SR6 7NH) 3H 115
South Devon Railway (TQ11 0DZ) 2D 8
South Downs Nat. Pk. (GU29 9SB) 5D 26
South Lakes Safari Zoo (LA15 8JR) 2B 96
South Tynedale Railway (CA9 3JB) 5A 114
Southwell Minster (NG25 0HD) 5E 86
Spa Valley Railway (TN2 5QY) 2G 27
Speedwell Cavern (S33 8WA) 2F 85
Speke Hall (L24 1XD) 2G 83
Spetchley Pk. Gdns. (WR5 1RR) 5C 60
Spinners Gdn. (SO41 5QE) 3B 16
Spofforth Castle (HG3 1HS) 4F 99
Sprivers Gdn. (TN12 8DR) 1A 28
Spurn Head (HU12 0UG) 3H 95
Spynie Palace (IV30 5QG) 2G 159
Squerryes (TN16 1SJ) 5F 39
Stafford Castle (ST16 1DJ) 3D 72
Stagshaw Gdn. (LA22 0HE) 4E 103
Stanage Edge (S33 0AD) 2G 85
Standen (RH19 4NE) 2E 27
Stanford Hall (LE17 6DH) 3C 62
Stansted Pk. (PO9 6DX) 2F 17
Stanway House & Fountain (GL54 5PQ) 2F 49
Staunton Harold Church (LE65 1RT) 3A 74
Steam - Mus. of the Great Western Railway
 (SN2 2EY) 3G 35
Stirling Castle (FK8 1EJ) 211
Stoke Pk. Pavilions (NN12 7RZ) 1F 51
Stokesay Castle (SY7 9AH) 2G 59
Stoke-sub-Hamdon Priory (TA14 6QP) 1H 13
Stoneacre (ME15 8RS) 5C 40
Stonehenge (SP4 7DE) 2G 23
Stoneleigh Abbey (CV8 2LF) 3H 61
Stonor (RG9 6HF) 3F 37
Stott Pk. Bobbin Mill (LA12 8AX) 1C 96
Stourhead (BA12 6QD) 3C 22
Stourton House Flower Gdn. (BA12 6QF) 3C 22
Stowe Landscape Gdns. (MK18 5EH) 2E 51
Stowe Landscape Gdns. (MK18 5EH) 2E 51
Strata Florida Abbey (SY25 6BJ) 4G 57
Stratfield Saye House (RG7 2BZ) 5E 37
Strathaven Castle (ML10 6QS) 5A 128
Strathspey Railway (PH22 1PY) 2D 150
Strawberry Hill, Twickenham (TW1 4ST) 3C 38
Strome Castle (IV54 8YJ) 5A 156
Sudbury Hall (DE6 5HT) 2F 73
Sudeley Castle (GL54 5JD) 3F 49
Sufton Court (HR1 4LU) 2A 48
Sulgrave Manor (OX17 2SD) 1D 50
Summerlee - Mus. of Scottish Industrial Life
 (ML5 1QD) 3A 128
Sundown Adventureland (DN22 0HX) 3E 87
Sutton Hoo (IP12 3DJ) 1F 55
Sutton Pk. (YO61 1DP) 3H 99
Sutton Scarsdale Hall (S44 5UT) 4B 86
Sutton Valence Castle (ME17 3DA) 1C 28
Swaledale Mus. (DL11 6QT) 5D 104
Swallow Falls (LL24 0DH) 5G 81
Swansea RC Cathedral (SA1 2BX) . . . .**Swansea 212**
Sweetheart Abbey (DG2 8BU) 3A 112
Swindon & Cricklade Railway (SN25 2DA) 2G 35
Swiss Gdn. (SG18 9ER) 1B 52
Syon Pk. (TW8 8JF) 3C 38

T

Tabley House (WA16 0HB) 3B 84
Talley Abbey (SA19 7AX) 2G 45
Talyllyn Railway (LL36 9EY) 5F 69
Tamworth Castle (B79 7NA) 5G 73
Tank Mus. (BH20 6JG) 4D 14
Tantallon Castle (EH39 5PN) 1B 130
Tarn Hows (LA22 0PR) 5E 103
Tar Tunnel (TF8 7HS) 5A 72
Tate Britain (SW1P 4RG) . . . .**London 203**
Tate Liverpool (L3 4BB) 200
Tate Modern (SE1 9TG) . . . .**London 203**
Tate St Ives (TR26 1TG) 2C 4
Tattershall Castle (LN4 4NR) 5B 88
Tatton Pk. (WA16 6QN) 2B 84
Tay Forest Pk. (PH17 2QG) 3C 142
Teifi Valley Railway (SA44 5TD) 1D 44
Temple Newsam (LS15 0AE) 1D 92
Tenby Castle (SA70 7BP) 4F 43
Thames Barrier (SE18 5NJ) 3F 39
The . . . .
 Names prefixed with 'The' for example 'The
 Buttertubs' are indexed under the main name
 such as 'Buttertubs, The'

Thetford Forest Pk. (IP26 5DB) 1A 66
Thetford Priory (IP24 1AZ) 2A 66
Thirlestane Castle (TD2 6RU) 5B 130
Thoresby Gallery (NG22 9EP) 3D 86
Thornham Walled Gdn. (IP23 8HH) 3D 66
Thornton Abbey & Gatehouse (DN39 6TU) 3E 94
Thorpe Pk. (KT16 8PN) 4B 38
Thorp Perrow Arboretum (DL8 2PR) 1E 99
Threave Castle (DG7 2AB) 3E 111
Threave Gdn. (DG7 1RX) 3E 111
Thrigby Hall Wildlife Gdns. (NR29 3DR) 4G 79
Thruxton Motor Circuit (SP11 8PW) 2A 24
Thursford Collection (NR21 0AS) 2B 78
Tilbury Fort (RM18 7NR) 3H 39
Tintagel Castle (PL34 0HE) 4A 10
Tintagel Visitor Information Centre
 (PL34 0AJ) 4A 10
Tintern Abbey (NP16 6SH) 4A 48
Tintinhull Garden (BA22 8QL) 4A 22
Titchfield Abbey (PO15 5RA) 2D 16
Tiverton Castle (EX16 6RP) 1C 12
Tolpuddle Martyrs Mus. (DT2 7EH) 3C 14
Tolquhon Castle (AB41 7LP) 1F 153
Torridon Countryside Centre (IV22 2EW) 3B 156
Totnes Castle (TQ9 5NU) 2E 9
Tower Bridge (SE1 2UP) . . . .**London 203**
Tower of London (EC3N 4AB) 203
Towneley Hall Art Gallery & Mus.
 (BB11 3RQ) 1G 91
Townend (LA23 1LB) 4F 103
Traquair House (EH44 6PW) 1F 119
Treasurer's House, Martock (TA12 6JL) 1H 13
Treasurer's House, York (YO1 7JL) 214
Trebah Gdn. (TR11 5JZ) 4E 5
Tredegar House (NP10 8YW) 3F 33
Tregrehan Gdn. (PL24 2SJ) 3E 7
Trelissick Garden (TR3 6QL) 5C 6
Trengwainton Gdn. (TR20 8RZ) 3B 4
Trentham Gdns. (ST4 8NF) 1C 72
Trerice (TR8 4PG) 3C 6
Tresco Abbey Gdns. (TR24 0QQ) 1A 4
Tretower Castle & Court (NP8 1RF) 3E 47
Trewithen (TR2 4DD) .4D 6
Tropical Birdland (LE9 9GN) 5B 74
Trossachs, The (FK17 8HZ) 3E 135
Tudor Merchant's House (SA70 7BX) 4F 43
Turner Contemporary (CT9 1HG) 3H 41
Turton Tower (BL7 0HG) 3F 91
Tutbury Castle (DE13 9JF) 3G 73
Twycross Zoo (CV9 3PX) 5H 73
Ty Mawr Wybrnant (LL25 0HJ) 5G 81
Tynemouth Castle (NE30 4BZ) 3G 115
Tyntesfield (BS48 1NT) 4A 34

U

Uffington White Horse (SN7 7QJ) 3B 36
Ugbrooke (TQ13 0AD) 5B 12
Upnor Castle (ME2 4XG) 4B 40
Uppark (GU31 5QR) .1F 17
Upton Castle Gdns. (SA72 4SE) 4E 43
Upton House & Gdns. (OX15 6HT) 1B 50
Urquhart Castle (IV63 6XJ) 1H 149
Usher Gallery (LN2 1NN) . . . .**Lincoln 198**
Usk Castle (NP15 1SD) 5G 47

V

Vale of Rheidol Railway (SY23 1PG) 3F 57
Valle Crucis Abbey (LL20 8DT) 1E 70
Valley Gdns. (SL4 2HT) 4A 38
V&A Museum of Design (DD1 4QB) . . . .**Dundee 194**
Veddw House Gdn. (NP16 6PH) 2H 33
Verulamium Mus., St Albans (AL3 4SW) 5B 52
Victoria & Albert Mus. (SW7 2RL) . . . .**London 202**
Vyne, The (RG24 9HL) 1E 25

W

Waddesdon Manor (HP18 0JH) 4F 51
Wakehurst Place (RH17 6TN) 2E 27
Walker Art Gallery (L3 8EL) . . . .**Liverpool 200**
Wallington (NE61 4AR) 1D 114
Walmer Castle & Gdns. (CT14 7LJ) 1H 29
Walsingham Abbey (NR22 6BL) 2B 78
Warkworth Castle & Hermitage (NE65 0UJ) 4G 121
Warwick Castle (CV34 4QX) 4G 61
Washington Old Hall (NE38 7LE) 4G 115
Watercress Line (SO24 9JG) 3E 25
Watermouth Castle (EX34 9SL) 2F 19
Waterperry Gdns. (OX33 1JZ) 5E 51
Watersmeet (EX35 6NT) 2H 19
Weald & Downland Open Air Mus.
 (PO18 0EU) 1G 17
Weaver Hall Mus. & Workhouse (CW9 8AB) 3A 84
Weaver's Cottage (PA10 2JG) 3E 127
Wedgwood Visitor Centre (ST12 9ER) 2C 72

Weir, The (HR4 7QF) .1H 47
Wells & Walsingham Light Railway
 (NR23 1QB) 1B 78
Wells Cathedral (BA5 2UE) 2A 22
Welney Wetland Centre & Visitor Centre
 (PE14 9TN) 1E 65
Welsh Highland Heritage Railway
 (LL49 9DY) 2E 69
Welsh Highland Railway
 (LL54 5UP) . . . .**Caernarfon 190**
Welsh Mountain Zoo, Colwyn Bay
 (LL28 5UY) 3H 81
Welshpool & Llanfair Light Railway
 (SY21 0SF) 5D 70
Wembley Stadium (HA9 0WS) 2C 38
Wenlock Edge (SY7 9JH) 2G 59
Wenlock Priory (TF13 6HS) 5A 72
Wentworth Castle Gdns. (S75 3ET) 4D 92
Weobley Castle (SA3 1HB) 3D 31
Weoley Castle (B29 5RX) 2E 61
Wesley Cottage (PL15 7TG) 4C 10
Westbury Court Gdn. (GL14 1PD) 4C 48
West Green House Gardens (RG27 8JB) 1F 25
West Highland Mus. (PH33 6AJ) 1F 141
West Midland Safari & Leisure Pk.
 (DY12 1LF) 3C 60
Westminster Abbey (SW1P 3PA) . . . .**London 203**
Westminster RC Cathedral
 (SW1P 1QH) . . . .**London 202**
Westonbirt Nat. Arboretum (GL8 8QS) 3D 34
Weston Pk. (TF11 8LE) 4C 72
West Somerset Railway (TA24 5BG) 4E 21
Westwood Manor (BA15 2AF) 1D 22
West Wycombe Pk. (HP14 3AJ) 2G 37
Wetlands Animal Pk. (DN22 0SB) 2D 86
Whalley Abbey (BB7 9TN) 1F 91
Wheal Martyn (PL26 8XG) 3E 6
Whipsnade Tree Cathedral (LU6 2LL) 4A 52
Whipsnade Zoo (LU6 2LF) 4A 52
Whitby Abbey (YO22 4JT) 3G 107
White Castle (NP7 8UD) 4G 47
Whitehorse Hill (DT2 7QJ) 3B 36
White Scar Cave (LA6 3AW) 2G 97
Whithorn Priory & Mus. (DG8 8PY) 5B 110
Whitmore Hall (ST5 5HW) 1C 72
Whitworth Art Gallery, Hulme (M15 6ER) 1C 84
Wicken Fen Nat. Nature Reserve (CB7 5YG) 3E 65
Wicksteed Pk. (NN15 6NJ) 3F 63
Wightwick Manor & Gdns. (WV6 8EE) 1C 60
Wigmore Castle (HR6 9UJ) 4G 59
Wilberforce House Mus.
 (HU1 1NE) . . . .**Kingston upon Hull 199**
Wilderhope Manor (TF13 6EG) 1H 59
Wilton House (SP2 0BJ) 3F 23
Wimbledon Lawn Tennis Mus. (SW19 5HP) 3D 38
Wimpole Hall & Gdns. (SG8 0BW) 5C 64
Winchester Cathedral (SO23 9LS) 213
Windmill Hill (SN4 9NW) 4F 35
Windsor Castle (SL4 1NJ) 213
Wingfield Manor (DE55 7NH) 5A 86
Winkworth Arboretum (GU8 4AD) 1A 26
Witley Court & Gdns. (WR6 6JT) 4B 60
Woburn Abbey (MK17 9WA) 2H 51
Woburn Safari Pk. (MK17 9QN) 2H 51
Wolds, The (Lincolnshire) (LN8 6BL) 1B 88
Wolds, The (Yorkshire) (YO25 9EN) 4D 100
Wolfeton House (DT2 9QN) 3B 14
Wollaton Hall (NG8 2AE) 2C 74
Wolseley Cen. (ST17 0WT) 3E 73
Wolvesey Castle (SO23 9NB) . . . .**Winchester 213**
Woodchester Mansion (GL10 3TS) 5D 48
Woodhenge (SP4 7AR) 2G 23
Wookey Hole (BA5 1BB) 2A 22
Woolsthorpe Manor (NG33 5PD) 3G 75
Worcester Cathedral (WR1 2LH) 214
Worcestershire County Mus. (DY11 7XZ) 3C 60
Wordsworth House (CA13 9RX) 1C 102
Wordsworth Mus. (Dove Cottage)
 (LA22 9SH) 4E 103
Wotton House Landscape Gdns. (HP18 0SB) . . .4E 51
Wrest Pk. (MK45 4HR) 2A 52
Wrexham RC Cathedral (LL11 1RB) . . . . . .**Wrexham 214**
Wroxeter Roman City (SY5 6PH) 5H 71
Wroxton Abbey Gdns. (OX15 6PX) 1C 50
Wylfa Visitor Centre (LL67 0DH) 1C 80
Wyre Forest (DY14 9UH) 3B 60
Wythenshawe Hall (M23 0AB) 2C 84

Y

Yarmouth Castle (PO41 0PB) 4B 16
York Art Gallery (YO1 7EW) 214
York Castle Mus. (YO1 9RY) 214
York Minster (YO1 7JN) 214
York Racecourse (YO23 1EX) 5H 99
Yorkshire Dales Nat. Pk. (BD23 5LB) 2H 97
Yorkshire Mus. (YO30 7DR) 214
Yorkshire Mus. of Farming (YO19 5GH) 4A 100
Yorkshire Sculpture Pk. (WF4 4LG) 3C 92

Limited Interchange Motorway Junctions are shown on the maps by RED junction indicators

M1

Junction 2
Northbound: No exit, access from A1 only
Southbound: No access, exit to A1 only

Junction 4
Northbound: No exit, access from A41 only
Southbound: No access, exit to A41 only

Junction 6a
Northbound: No exit, access from M25 only
Southbound: No access, exit to M25 only

Junction 17
Northbound: No access, exit to M45 only
Southbound: No exit, access from M45 only

Junction 19
Northbound: Exit to M6 only,
access from A14 only
Southbound: Access from M6 only,
exit to A14 only

Junction 21a
Northbound: No access, exit to A46 only
Southbound: No exit, access from A46 only

Junction 24a
Northbound: Access from A50 only
Southbound: Exit to A50 only

Junction 35a
Northbound: No access, exit to A616 only
Southbound: No exit, access from A616 only

Junction 43
Northbound: Exit to M621 only
Southbound: Access from M621 only

Junction 48
Eastbound: Exit to A1(M)
Northbound only
Westbound: Access from A1(M) Southbound
only

M2

Junction 1
Eastbound: Access from A2 Eastbound only
Westbound: Exit to A2 Westbound only

M3

Junction 8
Westbound: No access, exit to A303 only
Eastbound: No exit, access from A303 only

Junction 10
Northbound: No access from A31
Southbound: No exit to A31

Junction 13
Southbound: No access from A335 to M3
leading to M27 Eastbound

M4

Junction 1
Westbound: Access from A4 Westbound only
Eastbound: Exit to A4 Eastbound only

Junction 21
Westbound: No access from M48
Eastbound: No exit to M48

Junction 23
Westbound: No exit to M48
Eastbound: No access from M48

Junction 25
Westbound: No access
Eastbound: No exit

Junction 25a
Westbound: No access
Eastbound: No exit

Junction 29
Westbound: No access, exit to A48(M) only
Eastbound: No exit, access from A48(M) only

Junction 38
Westbound: No access, exit to A48 only

Junction 39
Westbound: No exit, access from A48 only
Eastbound: No access or exit

Junction 42
Westbound: No exit to A48
Eastbound: No access from A48

M5

Junction 10
Southbound: No access, exit to A4019 only
Northbound: No exit, access from A4019 only

Junction 11a
Southbound: No exit to A417 Westbound

Junction 18a
Southbound: No exit to M49
Northbound: No access from M49

M6

Junction 3a
Eastbound: No exit to M6 TOLL
Westbound: No access from M6 TOLL

Junction 4
Northbound: No exit to M42 Northbound
No access from M42 Southbound
Southbound: No exit to M42
No access from M42 Southbound

Junction 4a
Northbound: No exit, access from M42
Southbound only
Southbound: No access, exit to M42 only

Junction 5
Northbound: No access, exit to A452 only
Southbound: No exit, access from A452 only

Junction 10a
Northbound: No access, exit to M54 only
Southbound: No exit, access from M54 only

Junction 11a
Northbound: No exit to M6 TOLL
Southbound: No access from M6 TOLL

Junction 20
Northbound: No exit to M56 Eastbound
Southbound: No access from M56 Westbound

Junction 24
Northbound: No exit, access from A58 only
Southbound: No access, exit to A58 only

Junction 25
Northbound: No access, exit to A49 only
Southbound: No exit, access from A49 only

Junction 30
Northbound: No exit, access from M61
Northbound only
Southbound: No access, exit to M61
Southbound only

Junction 31a
Northbound: No access, exit to B6242 only
Southbound: No exit, access from B6242 only

Junction 45
Northbound: No access onto A74(M)
Southbound: No exit from A74(M)

M6 TOLL

Junction T1
Northbound: No exit
Southbound: No access

Junction T2
Northbound: No access or exit
Southbound: No access

Junction T5
Northbound: No exit
Southbound: No access

Junction T7
Northbound: No access from A5
Southbound: No exit

Junction T8
Northbound: No exit to A460 Northbound
Southbound: No exit

M8

Junction 6
Westbound: No access, exit only
Eastbound: No exit, access only

Junction 6a
Westbound: No exit, access only
Eastbound: No access, exit only

Junction 7
Westbound: No exit, access only
Eastbound: No access, exit only

Junction 7a
Westbound: No access,
Exit to A725 Southbound only
Eastbound: No exit,
Access from A725 Northbound only

Junction 8
Westbound: No access from M73 Southbound
Eastbound: No exit to M73 Northbound

Junction 9
Westbound: No exit, access only
Eastbound: No access, exit only

Junction 13
Westbound: No exit to M80 Northbound
Eastbound: No access from M80 Southbound

Junction 14
Westbound: No exit, access only
Eastbound: No access, exit only

Junction 16
Westbound: No access, exit only
Eastbound: No exit, access only

Junction 17
Westbound: No access, exit to A82 only
Eastbound: No exit, access from A82 only

M8 CONTINUED

Junction 18
Westbound: No exit, access only

Junction 19
Westbound: No access from A814 Westbound
Eastbound: No exit to A814 Eastbound

Junction 20
Westbound: No access, exit only
Eastbound: No exit, access only

Junction 21
Westbound: No exit, access only
Eastbound: No access, exit only

Junction 22
Westbound: No access, exit to M77 only
Eastbound: No exit, access from M77 only

Junction 23
Westbound: No access, exit to B768 only
Eastbound: No exit, access from B768 only

Junction 25
Westbound and Eastbound:
Exit to A739 Northbound only
Access from A739 Southbound only

Junction 25a
Eastbound: Access only
Westbound: Exit only

Junction 28
Westbound: No access, exit to airport only
Eastbound: no exit, access from airport only

M9

Junction 2
Northbound: No exit, access from B8046 only
Southbound: No access, exit to B8046 only

Junction 3
Northbound: No access, exit to A803 only
Southbound: No exit, access from A803 only

Junction 6
Northbound: No exit, access only
Southbound: No access, exit to A905 only

Junction 8
Northbound: No access, exit to M876 only
Southbound: No exit, access from M876 only

M11

Junction 4
Northbound: No exit, access from A406
Eastbound only
Southbound: No access, exit to A406
Westbound only

Junction 5
Northbound: No access, exit to A1168 only
Southbound: No exit, access from A1168 only

Junction 8a
Northbound: No exit, access only
Southbound: No exit, access only

Junction 9
Northbound: No exit, access only
Southbound: No access, exit only

Junction 13
Northbound: No exit, access only
Southbound: No access, exit only

Junction 14
Northbound: No access from A428 Eastbound
No exit to A428 Westbound
Southbound: No exit, access from A428
Eastbound only

M20

Junction 2
Eastbound: No access, exit to A20 only
(access via M26 Junction 2a)
Westbound: No exit, access only
(exit via M26 Junction 2a)

Junction 3
Eastbound: No exit, access from M26
Eastbound only
Westbound: No access, exit to M26
Westbound only

Junction 11a
Westbound: No exit to Channel Tunnel
Eastbound: No access from Channel Tunnel

M23

Junction 7
Southbound: No access from A23 Northbound
Northbound: No exit to A23 Southbound

Junction 10a
Northbound: No access, exit only
Southbound: No access, exit only

M25

Junction 5
Clockwise: No exit to M26 Eastbound
Anti-clockwise: No access from M26 Westbound

Spur to A21
Southbound: No access from M26 Westbound
Northbound: No exit to M26 Eastbound

Junction 19
Clockwise: No access exit only
Anti-clockwise: No exit access only

Junction 21
Clockwise and Anti-clockwise:
No exit to M1 Southbound
No access from M1 Northbound

Junction 31
Southbound: No exit access only
(exit via Junction 30)
Northbound: No access exit only
(access via Junction 30)

M26

Junction with M25 (M25 Junc. 5)
Westbound: No exit to M25 anti-clockwise
or spur to A21 Southbound
Eastbound: No access from M25 clockwise
or spur from A21 Northbound

Junction with M20 (M20 Junc. 3)
Eastbound: No exit to M20 Westbound
Westbound: No access from M20 Eastbound

M27

Junction 4
Eastbound and Westbound: No exit to A33
Southbound (Southampton)
No access from A33 Northbound

Junction 10
Eastbound: No exit, access from A32 only
Westbound: No access, exit to A32 only

M40

Junction 3
North-Westbound: No access,
exit to A40 only
South-Eastbound: No exit,
access from A40 only

Junction 7
South-Eastbound: No exit, access only
North-Westbound: No access, exit only

Junction 13
South-Eastbound: No exit, access only
North-Westbound: No access, exit only

Junction 14
South-Eastbound: No access, exit only
North-Westbound: No exit, access only

Junction 16
South-Eastbound: No access, exit only
North-Westbound: No exit, access only

M42

Junction 1
Eastbound: No exit
Westbound: No access

Junction 7
Northbound: No access, exit to M6 only
Southbound: No exit, access from M6
Northbound only

Junction 8
Northbound: No exit, access from M6
Southbound only
Southbound: Exit to M6 Northbound only
Access from M6 Southbound only

M45

Junction with M1 (M1 Junc. 17)
Eastbound: No exit to M1 Northbound
Westbound: No access from M1 Southbound

**Junction with A45 east
of Dunchurch**
Eastbound: No access, exit to A45 only
Westbound: No exit, access from A45
Northbound only

M48

Junction with M4 (M4 Junc. 21)
Westbound: No access from M4 Eastbound

Junction with M4 (M4 Junc. 23)
Westbound: No exit to M4 Eastbound
Eastbound: No access from M4 Westbound

M53

Junction 11
Southbound and Northbound: No access from
M56 Eastbound, no exit to M56 Westbound

M56

Junction 1
Westbound: No access from M60
South-Eastbound
    No access from A34 Northbound
Eastbound: No exit to M60 North-Westbound
    No exit to A34 Southbound
Junction 2
Westbound: No access, exit to A560 only
Eastbound: No exit, access from A560 only
Junction 3
Westbound: No exit, access only
Eastbound: No access, exit only
Junction 4
Westbound: No exit, access only
Eastbound: No exit, access only
Junction 7
Westbound: No access, exit only
Junction 8
Westbound: No exit, access from A556 only
Eastbound: No access or exit
Junction 9
Westbound: No exit to M6 Southbound
Eastbound: No access from M6 Northbound
Junction 15
Westbound: No access from M53
Eastbound: No exit to M53

M57

Junction 3
Northbound: No exit, access only
Southbound: No access, exit only
Junction 5
Northbound: No exit, access from A580
Westbound only
Southbound: No access, exit to A580
Eastbound only

M58

Junction 1
Eastbound: No exit, access from A506 only
Westbound: No access, exit to A506 only

M60

Junction 2
Nth.-Eastbound: No access, exit to A560 only
Sth.-Westbound: No exit,
    access from A560 only
Junction 3
Westbound: No exit to A34 Northbound
Eastbound: No access from A34 Southbound
Junction 4
Westbound: No access from A34 Southbound
    No access from M56 Eastbound
Eastbound: No exit to M56 South-Westbound
    No exit to A34 Northbound
Junction 5
South-Eastbound: No access from or exit to
A5103 Northbound
North-Westbound: No access from or exit to
A5103 Southbound
Junction 14
Eastbound: No exit to A580
    No access from A580 Westbound
Westbound: No exit to A580 Eastbound
    No access from A580
Junction 16
Eastbound: No exit, access from A666 only
Westbound: No access, exit to A666 only
Junction 20
Eastbound: No access from A664
Westbound: No exit to A664
Junction 22
Westbound: No access from A62
Junction 25
South-Westbound:
    No access from A560/A6017
Junction 26
North-Eastbound: No access or exit
Junction 27
North-Eastbound: No exit, access only
South-Westbound: No exit, access only

M61

Junctions 2 and 3
North-Westbound:
    No access from A580 Eastbound
Sth.-Eastbound: No exit to A580 Westbound

M61 CONTINUED

Junction with M6 (M6 Junc. 30)
North-Westbound:
    No exit to M6 Southbound
South-Eastbound:
    No access from M6 Northbound

M62

Junction 23
Eastbound: No access, exit to A640 only
Westbound: No exit, access from A640 only

M65

Junction 9
Nth.-Eastbound: No access, exit to A679 only
Sth.-Westbound:
    No exit, access from A679 only
Junction 11
North-Eastbound: No exit, access only
South-Westbound: No access, exit only

M66

Junction 1
Southbound: No exit, access from A56 only
Northbound: No access, exit to A56 only

M67

Junction 1
Eastbound: Access from A57 Eastbound only
Westbound: Exit to A57 Westbound only
Junction 1a
Eastbound: No access, exit to A6017 only
Westbound: No exit, access from A6017 only
Junction 2
Eastbound: No access, exit to A57 only
Westbound: No access, exit to A57 only

M69

Junction 2
North-Eastbound:
    No exit, access from B4669 only
South-Westbound:
    No access, exit to B4669 only

M73

Junction 1
Southbound: No exit to A74 Eastbound
Junction 2
Northbound: No access from M8 Eastbound
    No exit to A89 Eastbound
Southbound: No exit to M8 Westbound
    No access from A89 Westbound
Junction 3
Northbound: No exit to A80 South-Westbound
Southbound:
    No access from A80 North-Eastbound

M74

Junction 1
Eastbound: No access from M8 Westbound
Westbound: No exit to M8 Westbound
Junction 3
Eastbound: No exit
Westbound: No access
Junction 7
Southbound: No access, exit to A72 only
Northbound: No exit, access from A72 only
Junction 9
Southbound: No access, exit to B7078 only
Northbound: No access or exit
Junction 10
Southbound: No exit, access from B7078 only
Junction 11
Southbound: No access, exit to B7078 only
Northbound: No exit, access from B7078 only
Junction 12
Southbound: No exit, access from A70 only
Northbound: No access, exit to A70 only

M77

Junction with M8 (M8 Junc. 22)
Southbound: No access from M8 Eastbound
Northbound: No exit to M8 Westbound
Junction 4
Southbound: No access
Northbound: No exit
Junction 6
Southbound: No access from A77
Northbound: No exit to A77
Junction 7
Northbound: No access from A77
    No exit to A77

M80

Junction 1
Northbound: No access from M8 Westbound
Southbound: No exit to M8 Eastbound
Junction 4a
Northbound: No access
Southbound: No exit
Junction 6a
Northbound: No exit
Southbound: No access
Junction 8
Northbound: No access from M876
Southbound: No exit to M876

M90

Junction 1
Northbound: No exit to A90
Southbound: No access from A90
Junction 2a
Northbound: No access, exit to A92 only
Southbound: No exit, access from A92 only
Junction 7
Northbound: No exit, access from A91 only
Southbound: No access, exit to A91 only
Junction 8
Northbound: No access, exit to A91 only
Southbound: No exit, access from A91 only
Junction 10
Northbound: No access from A912
    Exit to A912 Northbound only
Southbound: No exit to A912
    Access from A912 Southbound only

M180

Junction 1
Eastbound: No access, exit only
Westbound: No access, access from A18 only

M606

Junction 2
Northbound: No access, exit only

M621

Junction 2a
Eastbound: No exit, access only
Westbound: No access, exit only
Junction 4
Southbound: No exit
Junction 5
Northbound: No access, exit to A61 only
Southbound: No exit, access from A61 only
Junction 6
Northbound: No exit, access only
Southbound: No access, exit only
Junction 7
Westbound: No exit, access only
Eastbound: No access, exit only
Junction 8
Northbound: No access, exit only
Southbound: No exit, access only

M876

Junction with M80 (M80 Junc. 5)
North-Eastbound:
    No access from M80 Southbound
South-Westbound: No exit to M80 Northbound
Junction with M9 (M9 Junc. 8)
North-Eastbound: No exit to M9 Northbound
South-Westbound:
    No access from M9 Southbound

A1(M) (Hertfordshire Section)

Junction 2
Southbound: No exit, access from A1001 only
Northbound: No access, exit only
Junction 3
Southbound: No access, exit only
Junction 5
Northbound: No access, exit only
Southbound: No access or exit

A1(M) (Cambridgeshire Section)

Junction 14
Northbound: No exit, access only
Southbound: No access, exit only

A1(M) (Leeds Section)

Junction 40
Southbound: Exit to A1 Southbound only
Junction 43
Northbound: Access from M1 Eastbound only
Southbound: Exit to M1 Westbound only

A1(M) (Durham Section)

Junction 57
Northbound: No access,
    exit to A66(M) only
Southbound: No exit, access from A66(M) only
Junction 65
Northbound: Exit to A1 North-Westbound,
    and to A194(M) only
Southbound: Access from A1 South-Eastbound,
    and from A194(M) only

A3(M)

Junction 4
Northbound: No access, exit only
Southbound: No exit, access only

A38(M) Aston Expressway

Junction with Victoria Road, Aston
Northbound: No exit, access only
Southbound: No access, exit only

A48(M)

Junction with M4 (M4 Junc. 29)
South-Westbound: access from M4 Westbound
North-Eastbound: exit to M4 Eastbound only
Junction 29a
South-Westbound: Exit to A48 Westbound only
North-Eastbound:
    Access from A48 Eastbound only

A57(M) Mancunian Way

Junction with A34 Brook Street, Manchester
Eastbound: No access, exit to A34 Brook Street
    Southbound only
Westbound: No exit, access only

A58(M) Leeds Inner Ring Road

Junction with Park Lane/ Westgate
Southbound: No access, exit only

A64(M) Leeds Inner Ring Road (Continuation of A58(M))

Junction with A58 Clay Pit Lane
Eastbound: No Access
Westbound: No exit

A66(M)

Junction with A1(M) (A1(M) Junc. 57)
South-Westbound:
    Exit to A1(M) Southbound only
North-Eastbound:
    Access from A1(M) Northbound only

A74(M)

Junction 18
Northbound: No access
Southbound: No exit

A167(M) Newcastle Central Motorway

Junction with Camden Street
Northbound: No exit, access only
Southbound: No access or exit

A194(M)

Junction with A1(M) (A1(M) Junc. 65) and A1 Gateshead Western By-Pass
Southbound: Exit to A1(M) only
Northbound: Access from A1(M) only

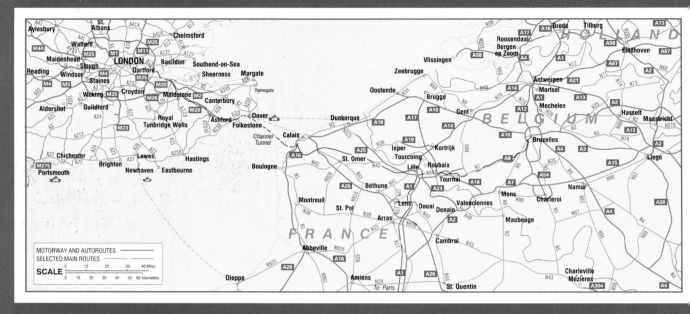

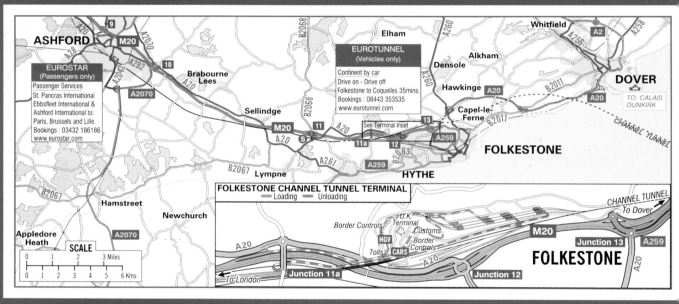

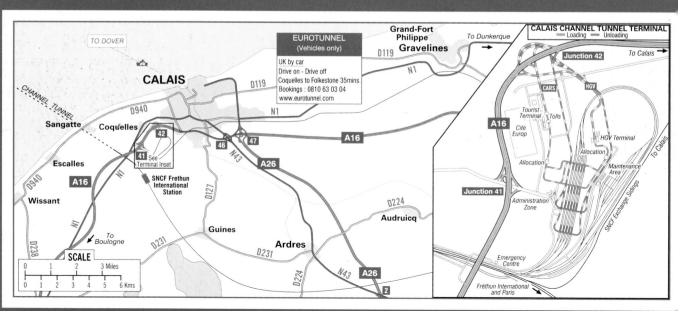